HENRY DAVID THOREAU

Henry David Thoreau

COLLECTED ESSAYS AND POEMS

THE LIBRARY OF AMERICA

Distributed to the trade
in the United States by Penguin Putnam Inc.
and in Canada by Penguin Books Canada Ltd.

Library of Congress Catalog Number: 00 046234
For cataloging information, see end of Index.
ISBN 1–883011–95–7

First Printing
The Library of America—124

Manufactured in the United States of America

ELIZABETH HALL WITHERELL
SELECTED THE CONTENTS FOR THIS VOLUME

Contents

ESSAYS

Aulus Persius Flaccus

I F YOU have imagined what a divine work is spread out for the poet, and approach this author too, in the hope of finding the field at length fairly entered on, you will hardly dissent from the words of the prologue,

> "Ipse semipaganus
> Ad sacra Vatum carmen affero nostrum."

Here is none of the interior dignity of Virgil, nor the elegance and fire of Horace, nor will any Sibyl be needed to remind you, that from those older Greek poets, there is a sad descent to Persius. Scarcely can you distinguish one harmonious sound, amid this unmusical bickering with the follies of men.

One sees how music has its place in thought, but hardly as yet in language. When the Muse arrives, we wait for her to remould language, and impart to it her own rhythm. Hitherto the verse groans and labors with its load, but goes not forward blithely, singing by the way. The best ode may be parodied, indeed is itself a parody, and has a poor and trivial sound, like a man stepping on the rounds of a ladder. Homer, and Shakspeare, and Milton, and Marvell, and Wordsworth, are but the rustling of leaves and crackling of twigs in the forest, and not yet the sound of any bird. The Muse has never lifted up her voice to sing. Most of all satire will not be sung. A Juvenal or Persius do not marry music to their verse, but are measured fault-finders at best; stand but just outside the faults they condemn, and so are concerned rather about the monster they have escaped, than the fair prospect before them. Let them live on an age, not a secular one, and they will have travelled out of his shadow and harm's way, and found other objects to ponder.

As long as there is satire, the poet is, as it were, *particeps criminis*. One sees not but he had best let bad take care of itself, and have to do only with what is beyond suspicion. If you light on the least vestige of truth, and it is the weight of the whole body still which stamps the faintest trace, an eter-

nity will not suffice to extol it, while no evil is so huge, but
you grudge to bestow on it a moment of hate. Truth never
turns to rebuke falsehood; her own straightforwardness is the
severest correction. Horace would not have written satire so
well, if he had not been inspired by it, as by a passion, and
fondly cherished his vein. In his odes, the love always exceeds
the hate, so that the severest satire still sings itself, and the
poet is satisfied, though the folly be not corrected.

A sort of necessary order in the development of Genius is,
first, Complaint; second, Plaint; third, Love. Complaint,
which is the condition of Persius, lies not in the province of
poetry. Ere long the enjoyment of a superior good would have
changed his disgust into regret. We can never have much sym-
pathy with the complainer; for after searching nature through,
we conclude he must be both plaintiff and defendant too, and
so had best come to a settlement without a hearing.

I know not but it would be truer to say, that the highest
strain of the muse is essentially plaintive. The saint's are still
tears of joy.

But the divinest poem, or the life of a great man, is the sever-
est satire; as impersonal as nature herself, and like the sighs of
her winds in the woods, which convey ever a slight reproof to
the hearer. The greater the genius, the keener the edge of the
satire.

Hence have we to do only with the rare and fragmentary
traits, which least belong to Persius, or, rather, are the prop-
erest utterance of his muse; since that which he says best at
any time is what he can best say at all times. The Spectators
and Ramblers have not failed to cull some quotable sentences
from this garden too, so pleasant is it to meet even the most
familiar truth in a new dress, when, if our neighbor had said
it, we should have passed it by as hackneyed. Out of these six
satires, you may perhaps select some twenty lines, which fit so
well as many thoughts, that they will recur to the scholar al-
most as readily as a natural image; though when translated
into familiar language, they lose that insular emphasis, which
fitted them for quotation. Such lines as the following no
translation can render commonplace. Contrasting the man of
true religion with those, that, with jealous privacy, would fain
carry on a secret commerce with the gods, he says,—

"Haud cuivis promptum est, murmurque humilesque
  susurros
Tollere de templis; et aperto vivere voto."

To the virtuous man, the universe is the only sanctum sanc-
torum, and the penetralia of the temple are the broad noon
of his existence. Why should he betake himself to a subter-
ranean crypt, as if it were the only holy ground in all the
world he had left unprofaned? The obedient soul would only
the more discover and familiarize things, and escape more and
more into light and air, as having henceforth done with se-
crecy, so that the universe shall not seem open enough for it.
At length, it is neglectful even of that silence which is consis-
tent with true modesty, but by its independence of all confi-
dence in its disclosures, makes that which it imparts so private
to the hearer, that it becomes the care of the whole world that
modesty be not infringed.

To the man who cherishes a secret in his breast, there is a
still greater secret unexplored. Our most indifferent acts may
be matter for secrecy, but whatever we do with the utmost
truthfulness and integrity, by virtue of its pureness, must be
transparent as light.

In the third satire he asks,

"Est aliquid quò tendis, et in quod dirigis arcum?
An passim sequeris corvos, testâve, lutove,
Securus quò pes ferat, atque ex tempore vivis?"

Language seems not to have justice done it, but is obviously
cramped and narrowed in its significance, when any meanness
is described. The truest construction is not put upon it. What
may readily be fashioned into a rule of wisdom, is here thrown
in the teeth of the sluggard, and constitutes the front of his
offence. Universally, the innocent man will come forth from
the sharpest inquisition and lecturings, the combined din of
reproof and commendation, with a faint sound of eulogy in
his ears. Our vices lie ever in the direction of our virtues, and
in their best estate are but plausible imitations of the latter.
Falsehood never attains to the dignity of entire falseness, but
is only an inferior sort of truth; if it were more thoroughly
false, it would incur danger of becoming true.

"Securus quò pes ferat, atque ex tempore *vivit*,"

is then the motto of a wise man. For first, as the subtle discernment of the language would have taught us, with all his negligence he is still secure; but the sluggard, notwithstanding his heedlessness, is insecure.

The life of a wise man is most of all extemporaneous, for he lives out of an eternity that includes all time. He is a child each moment, and reflects wisdom. The far darting thought of the child's mind tarries not for the development of manhood; it lightens itself, and needs not draw down lightning from the clouds. When we bask in a single ray from the mind of Zoroaster, we see how all subsequent time has been an idler, and has no apology for itself. But the cunning mind travels farther back than Zoroaster each instant, and comes quite down to the present with its revelation. All the thrift and industry of thinking give no man any stock in life; his credit with the inner world is no better, his capital no larger. He must try his fortune again to-day as yesterday. All questions rely on the present for their solution. Time measures nothing but itself. The word that is written may be postponed, but not that on the lip. If this is what the occasion says, let the occasion say it. From a real sympathy, all the world is forward to prompt him who gets up to live without his creed in his pocket.

In the fifth satire, which is the best, I find,

"Stat contrà ratio, et secretam garrit in aurem.
Ne liceat facere id, quod quis vitiabit agendo."

Only they who do not see how anything might be better done are forward to try their hand on it. Even the master workman must be encouraged by the reflection, that his awkwardness will be incompetent to do that harm, to which his skill may fail to do justice. Here is no apology for neglecting to do many things from a sense of our incapacity,—for what deed does not fall maimed and imperfect from our hands?— but only a warning to bungle less.

The satires of Persius are the farthest possible from inspired; evidently a chosen, not imposed subject. Perhaps I have given him credit for more earnestness than is apparent;

but certain it is, that that which alone we can call Persius, which is forever independent and consistent, was in earnest, and so sanctions the sober consideration of all. The artist and his work are not to be separated. The most wilfully foolish man cannot stand aloof from his folly, but the deed and the doer together make ever one sober fact. The buffoon may not bribe you to laugh always at his grimaces; they shall sculpture themselves in Egyptian granite, to stand heavy as the pyramids on the ground of his character.

The Service

Spes sibi quisque. Virgil
Each one his own hope.

THE brave man is the elder son of creation, who has stept boyantly into his inheritance, while the coward, who is the younger, waiteth patiently till he decease. He rides as wide of this earth's gravity as a star, and by yielding incessantly to all the impulses of the soul, is constantly drawn upward and becomes a fixed star. His bravery deals not so much in resolute action, as healthy and assured rest; its palmy state is a staying at home and compelling alliance in all directions. So stands his life to heaven, as some fair sunlit tree against the western horizon, and by sunrise is planted on some eastern hill, to glisten in the first rays of the dawn. The brave man braves nothing, nor knows he of his bravery. He is that sixth champion against Thebes, whom, when the proud devices of the rest have been recorded, the poet describes as "bearing a full orbed shield of solid brass,"

> "But there was no device upon its circle,
> For not to seem just but to be is his wish."

He does not present a gleaming edge to ward off harm, for that will oftenest attract the lightning, but rather is the all pervading ether, which the lightning does not strike but purify. So is the profanity of his companion as a flash across the face of his sky, which lights up and reveals its serene depths. Earth cannot shock the heavens, but its dull vapor and foul smoke make a bright cloud spot in the ether, and anon the sun, like a cunning artificer, will cut and paint it, and set it for a jewel in the breast of the sky.

His greatness is not measurable. His is not such a greatness as when we would erect a stupendous piece of art, and send far and near for materials, intending to lay the foundations deeper, and rear the structure higher, than ever, for hence results only a remarkable bulkiness without grandeur, lacking those true and simple proportions which are independent of size. He was not builded by that unwise generation, that would fain have reached the heavens by piling one brick upon another, but by a far wiser, that builded inward and not outward, having found out a shorter way, through the observance of a higher art. The pyramids some artisan may measure with his line; but if he give you the dimensions of the Parthenon in feet and inches, the figures will not embrace it like a cord, but dangle from its entablature like an elastic drapery.

His eye is the focus in which all the rays, from whatever side, are collected; for, itself being within and central, the entire circumference is revealed to it. Just as we scan the whole concave of the heavens at a glance, but can compass only one side of the pebble at our feet. So does his discretion give prevalence to his valor. "Discretion is the wise man's soul," saith the poet. His prudence may safely go many strides beyond the utmost rashness of the coward; for, while he observes strictly the golden mean, he seems to run through all extremes with impunity. Like the sun, which, to the poor worldling, now appears in the zenith, now in the horizon, and again is faintly reflected from the moon's disk, and has the credit of describing an entire great circle, crossing the equinoctial and solstitial colures, without detriment to his steadfastness or mediocrity. The golden mean, in ethics as in physics, is the center of the system, and that about which all revolve; and, though to a distant and plodding planet it be the uttermost extreme, yet one day, when that planet's year is complete, it will be found to be central. They who are alarmed lest Virtue should so far demean herself, as to be extremely good, have not yet wholly embraced her, but described only a slight arc of a few seconds about her, and from so small and ill defined a curvature, you can calculate no center whatever, but their mean is no better than meanness, nor their medium than mediocrity.

The coward wants resolution, which the brave man can do without. He recognizes no faith but a creed, thinking this straw, by which he is moored, does him good service, because his sheet anchor does not drag. "The house roof fights with the rain; he who is under shelter does not know it." In his religion, the ligature, which should be muscle and sinew, is rather like that thread which the accomplices of Cylon held in their hands, when they went abroad from the temple of Minerva, the other end being attached to the statue of the goddess. But frequently, as in their case, the thread breaks, being stretched, and he is left without an asylum.

The divinity in man is the true vestal fire of the temple, which is never permitted to go out, but burns as steadily, and with as pure a flame, on the obscure provincial altar, as in Numa's temple at Rome. In the meanest are all the materials of manhood, only they are not rightly disposed. We say justly that the weak person is flat, for like all flat substances, he does not stand in the direction of his strength, that is, on his edge, but affords a convenient surface to put upon. He slides all the way through life. Most things are strong in one direction; a straw longitudinally; a board in the direction of its edge; a knee transversely to its grain; but the brave man is a perfect sphere, which cannot fall on its flat side, and is equally strong every way. The coward is wretchedly spheroidal at best, too much educated or drawn out on one side, and depressed on the other; or may be likened to a hollow sphere, whose disposition of matter is best when the greatest bulk is intended.

We shall not attain to be spherical by lying on one or the other side for an eternity, but only by resigning ourselves implicitly to the law of gravity in us, shall we find our axis coincident with the celestial axis, and by revolving incessantly through all circles, acquire a perfect sphericity. Mankind, like the earth, revolve mainly from west to east, and so are flattened at the poles. But does not philosophy give hint of a movement commencing to be rotary at the poles too, which in a millennium will have acquired increased rapidity, and help restore an equilibrium? And when at length every star in the nebulae and milky way, has looked down with mild radiance for a season, exerting its whole influence as the pole star, the demands of science will in some degree be satisfied.

The grand and majestic have always somewhat of the undulatoriness of the sphere. It is the secret of majesty in the rolling gait of the elephant, and of all grace in action and in art. Always the line of beauty is a curve. When with pomp a huge sphere is drawn along the streets, by the efforts of a hundred men, I seem to discover each striving to imitate its gait, and keep step with it,—if possible to swell to its own diameter. But onward it moves, and conquers the multitude with its majesty. What shame then, that our lives, which might so well be the source of planetary motion, and sanction the order of the spheres, should be full of abruptness and angulosity, so as not to roll nor move majestically.

The Romans "made Fortune sirname to Fortitude," for fortitude is that alchemy that turns all things to good fortune. The man of fortitude, whom the Latins called *fortis*, is no other than that lucky person whom *fors* favors, or *vir summae fortis*. If we will, every bark may "carry Caesar and Caesar's fortune." For an impenetrable shield, stand inside yourself; he was no artist, but an artisan, who first made shields of brass. For armor of proof, *meâ virtute me involvo*, I wrap myself in my virtue;

> "Tumble me down; and I will sit
> Upon my ruins, smiling yet."

If you let a single ray of light through the shutter, it will go on diffusing itself without limit till it enlighten the world, but the shadow that was never so wide at first, as rapidly contracts till it comes to naught. The shadow of the moon, when it passes nearest the sun, is lost in space ere it can reach our earth to eclipse it. Always the system shines with uninterrupted light, for as the sun is so much larger than any planet, no shadow can travel far into space. We may bask always in the light of the system, always may step back out of the shade. No man's shadow is as large as his body, if the rays make a right angle with the reflecting surface. Let our lives be passed under the equator, with the sun in the meridian.

There is no ill which may not be dissipated like the dark, if you let in a stronger light upon it. Overcome evil with good. Practise no such narrow economy as they, whose bravery amounts to no more light than a farthing candle, before which most objects cast a shadow wider than themselves.

Nature refuses to sympathize with our sorrow, she has not provided for, but by a thousand contrivances against it; she has bevelled the margins of the eyelids, that the tears may not overflow on the cheeks. It was a conceit of Plutarch, ac-

counting for the preference given to signs observed on the
left hand, that men may have thought "things terrestrial and
mortal directly over against heavenly and divine things, and
do conjecture that the things which to us are on the left hand,
the gods send down from their right hand." If we are not
blind, we shall see how a right hand is stretched over all, as
well the unlucky as lucky, and that the ordering soul is only
right handed, distributing with one palm all our fates.

What first suggested that necessity was grim, and made fate
to be so fatal? The strongest is always the least violent.
Necessity is my eastern cushion on which I recline. My eye
revels in its prospect as in the summer haze. I ask no more
but to be left alone with it. It is the bosom of time and the
lap of eternity. To be necessary is to be needful, and necessity
is only another name for inflexibility of good. How I welcome
my grim fellow, and walk arm in arm with him. Let me too be
such a Necessity as he. I love him, he is so flexile, and yields
to me as the air to my body. I leap and dance in his midst, and
play with his beard till he smiles. I greet thee my elder
brother, who with thy touch ennoblest all things. Then is hol-
iday when naught intervenes betwixt me and thee. Must it be
so,—then is it good. The stars are thy interpreters to me.

Over Greece hangs the divine necessity ever a mellower
heaven of itself, whose light gilds the Acropolis and a thou-
sand fanes and groves.

WHAT MUSIC SHALL WE HAVE?

> Each more medodious note I hear
> Brings this reproach to me,
> That I alone afford the ear,
> Who would the music be.

THE brave man is the sole patron of music; he recognizes
it for his mother tongue; a more mellifluous and articu-
late language than words, in comparison with which, speech is
recent and temporary. It is his voice. His language must have
the same majestic movement and cadence, that philosophy as-
signs to the heavenly bodies. The steady flux of his thought
constitutes time in music. The universe falls in and keeps pace

with it, which before proceeded singly and discordant. Hence are poetry and song. When Bravery first grew afraid and went to war, it took music along with it. The soul delighted still to hear the echo of her own voice. Especially the soldier insists on agreement and harmony always. To secure these he falls out. Indeed, it is that friendship there is in war that makes it chivalrous and heroic. It was the dim sentiment of a noble friendship for the purest soul the world has seen, that gave to Europe a crusading era. War is but the compelling of peace. If the soldier marches to the sack of a town, he must be preceded by drum and trumpet, which shall identify his cause with the accordant universe. All things thus echo back his own spirit, and thus the hostile territory is preoccupied for him. He is no longer insulated, but infinitely related and familiar. The roll call musters for him all the forces of nature.

There is as much music in the world as virtue. In a world of peace and love music would be the universal language, and men greet each other in the fields in such accents, as a Beethoven now utters at rare intervals from a distance. All things obey music as they obey virtue. It is the herald of virtue. It is God's voice. In it are the centripetal and centrifugal forces. The universe needed only to hear a divine melody, that every star might fall into its proper place, and assume its true sphericity. It entails a surpassing affluence on the meanest thing; riding sublime over the heads of sages, and soothing the din of philosophy. When we listen to it we are so wise that we need not to know. All sounds, and more than all, silence, do fife and drum for us. The least creaking doth whet all our senses, and emit a tremulous light, like the aurora borealis, over things. As polishing expresses the vein in marble, and the grain in wood, so music brings out what of heroic lurks anywhere. It is either a sedative or a tonic to the soul. I read that "Plato thinks the gods never gave men music, the science of melody and harmony, for mere delectation or to tickle the ear; but that the discordant parts of the circulations, and beauteous fabric of the soul, and that of it that roves about the body, and many times for want of tune and air, breaks forth into many extravagances and excesses, might be sweetly recalled and artfully wound up to their former consent and agreement."

A sudden burst from a horn startles us, as if one had rashly provoked a wild beast. We admire his boldness, he dares wake the echoes which he cannot put to rest. The sound of a bugle in the stillness of the night, sends forth its voice to the farthest stars, and marshals them in new order and harmony. Instantly it finds a fit sounding board in the heavens. The notes flash out on the horizon like heat lightning, quickening the pulse of creation. The heavens say, Now is this my own earth.

To the sensitive soul the Universe has her own fixed measure and rhythm, which is its measure also and constitutes the regularity and health of its pulse. When the body marches to the measure of the soul then is true courage and invincible strength.

The coward would reduce this thrilling sphere music to a universal wail,—this melodious chant to a nasal cant. He thinks to conciliate all hostile influences by compelling his neighborhood into a partial concord with himself, but his music is no better than a jingle, which is akin to a jar,—jars regularly recurring. He blows a feeble blast of slender melody, because nature can have no more sympathy with such a soul, than it has of cheerful melody in itself. Hence hears he no accordant note in the universe, and is a coward, or consciously outcast and deserted man. But the brave man, without drum or trumpet, compels concord everywhere by the universality and tunefulness of his soul.

Let not the faithful sorrow that he has no ear for the more fickle and subtle harmonies of creation, if he be awake to the slower measure of virtue and truth. If his pulse does not beat in unison with the musician's quips and turns, it accords with the pulse beat of the ages.

A man's life should be a stately march to an unheard music, and when to his fellows it seems irregular and inharmonious, he will be stepping to a livelier measure, which only his nicer ear can detect. There will be no halt ever, but at most a marching on his post, or such a pause as is richer than any sound—when the deepened melody is no longer heard, but implicitly consented to with the whole life and being. He will take a false step never, even in the most arduous circumstances, for then the music will not fail to swell into corresponding volume and distinctness and rule the movement it accompanies.

NOT HOW MANY BUT WHERE THE ENEMY ARE

"What's brave, what's noble,
Let's do it after the high Roman fashion."
Shakspeare

WHEN my eye falls on the stupendous masses of the clouds, tossed into such irregular greatness across the cope of my sky, I feel that their grandeur is thrown away on the meanness of my employment. In vain the sun through morning and noon rolls defiance to man, and, as he sinks behind his cloudy fortress in the west, challenges him to equal greatness in his career; but from his humbleness he looks up to the domes, and minarets, and gilded battlements of the eternal city, and is content to be a suburban dweller outside the walls. We look in vain over earth for a Roman greatness, to take up the gauntlet which the heavens throw down. Idomeneus would not have demurred at the freshness of the last morning that rose to us, as unfit occasion to display his valor in; and of some such evening as this, methinks, that Greek fleet came to anchor in the bay of Aulis. Would that it were to us the eve of a more than ten years' war, a tithe of whose exploits, and Achillean withdrawals, and godly interferences, would stock a library of Iliads. Better that we have some of that testy spirit of knight errantry, and if we are so blind as to think the world is not rich enough nowadays to afford a real foe to combat, with our trusty swords and double handed maces, hew and mangle some unreal phantom of the brain. In the pale and shivering fogs of the morning, gathering them up betimes, and withdrawing sluggishly to their daylight haunts, I see Falsehood sneaking from the full blaze of truth, and with good relish could do execution on their rearward ranks with the first brand that came to hand. We too are such puny creatures as to be put to flight by the sun, and suffer our ardor to grow cool in proportion as his increases; our own short lived chivalry sounds a retreat with the fumes and vapors of the night, and we turn to meet mankind with its meek face preaching peace, and such nonresistance as the chaff that rides before the whirlwind. Let not our Peace be proclaimed by the rust on our swords, or our inability to draw them from their scabbards, but let her at least have so much work on her hands, as to keep those swords bright and sharp. The very dogs that bay the moon from farmyards o' these nights, do evince more heroism than is tamely barked forth in all the civil exhortations and war sermons of the age. And that day and night, which should be set down indelibly in men's hearts, must be learned from the pages of an almanack. One cannot wonder at the owlish habits of the race, which does not distinguish when its day ends and night begins, for as night is the season of rest, it would be hard to say when its toil ended and its rest began. Not to it

> —returns
> Day, or the sweet approach of even or morn,
> Or sight of vernal bloom, or summer's rose,
> Or flocks, or herds, or human face divine;
> But cloud instead, and ever-during dark
> Surrounds—

And so the time lapses without epoch or era, and we know some half score of mornings and evenings by tradition only. Almost the night is grieved and leaves her tears on the forelock of day, that men will not rush to her embrace, and fulfil, at length, the pledge so forwardly given in the youth of time. Men are a circumstance to themselves, instead of causing the universe to stand around the mute witness of their manhood, and the stars to forget their sphere music and chant an elegiac strain, that heroism should have departed out of their ranks and gone over to humanity.

It is not enough that our life is an easy one; we must live on the stretch, retiring to our rest like soldiers on the eve of a battle, looking forward with ardor to the strenuous sortie of the morrow. "Sit not down in the popular seats and common level of virtues, but endeavor to make them heroical. Offer not only peace offerings but holocausts unto God." To the brave soldier the rust and leisure of peace are harder than the fatigues of war. As our bodies court physical encounters, and languish in the mild and even climate of the tropics, so our souls thrive best on unrest and discontent. The soul is a sterner master than any King Frederick, for a true bravery would subject our bodies to rougher usage than even a grenadier could withstand. We too are dwellers within the purlieus of the camp. When the sun breaks through the morning mist, I seem to hear the din of war louder than when his chariot thundered on the plains of Troy. The thin fields of vapor spread like gauze over the woods, form extended lawns whereon high tournament is held

> before each van
> Prick forth the aery knights, and couch their spears,
> Till thickest legions close.

It behoves us to make life a steady progression, and not be defeated by its opportunities. The stream which first fell a drop from heaven, should be filtered by events till it burst out into springs of greater purity, and extract a diviner flavor from the accidents through which it passes. Shall man wear out sooner than the sun, and not rather dawn as freshly, and with such native dignity stalk down the hills of the east into the bustling vale of life, with as lofty and serene a countenance to roll onward through midday, to a yet fairer and more promising setting? In the crimson colors of the west I discern the budding hues of dawn. To my western brother it is rising pure and bright as it did to me, but only the evening exhibits in the still rear of day, the beauty which through morning and noon escaped me. Is not that which we call the gross atmosphere of evening the accumulated deed of the day, which absorbs the rays of beauty, and shows more richly than the naked promise of the dawn? Let us look to it, that by earnest toil in the heat of the noon, we get ready a rich western blaze against the evening.

Nor need we fear that the time will hang heavy when our toil is done, for our task is not such a piece of day labor, that a man must be thinking what he shall do next for a livelihood, but such, that as it began in endeavor, so will it end only when no more in heaven or on earth remains to be endeavored. Effort is the prerogative of virtue. Let not death be the sole task of life, the moment when we are rescued from death to life. And set to work,—if indeed that can be called a task

which all things do but alleviate. Nor will we suffer our hands
to lose one jot of their handiness by looking behind to a mean
recompense, knowing that our endeavor cannot be thwarted,
nor we be cheated of our earnings unless by not earning
them.

It concerns us rather to be somewhat here present than to
leave something behind us; for, if that were to be considered,
it is never the deed men praise, but some marble or canvass
which are only a staging to the real work. The hugest and
most effective deed may have no sensible result at all on
earth, but may paint itself in the heavens with new stars and
constellations. When in rare moments our whole being strives
with one consent, which we name a yearning, we may not
hope that our work will stand in any artist's gallery on earth.
The bravest deed, which for the most part is left quite out of
history, which alone wants the staleness of a deed done, and
the uncertainty of a deed doing, is the life of a great man. To
perform exploits is to be temporarily bold, as becomes a
courage that ebbs and flows, the soul quite vanquished by its
own deed subsiding into indifference and cowardice, but the
exploit of a brave life consists in its momentary completeness.

Every stroke of the chisel must enter our own flesh and
bone, he is a mere idolater and apprentice to art who suffers
it to grate dully on marble; for the true art is not merely a
sublime consolation, and holiday labor, which the gods have
given to sickly mortals, but such a masterpiece, as you may
imagine a dweller on the table lands of central Asia might
produce, with threescore and ten years for canvass, and the
faculties of a man for tools,—a human life,—wherein you
might hope to discover more than the freshness of Guido's
Aurora, or the mild light of Titian's landscapes;—no bald im-
itation nor even rival of nature, but rather the restored origi-
nal of which she is the reflection. For such a masterpiece as
this, whole galleries of Greece and Italy are a mere mixing of
colors and preparatory quarrying of marble.

Of such sort, then, be our crusade, which, while it inclines
chiefly to the hearty good will and activity of war, rather than
the insincerity and sloth of peace, will set an example to both
of calmness and energy;—as unconcerned for victory as care-
less of defeat, not seeking to lengthen our term of service, nor

to cut it short by a reprieve, but earnestly applying ourselves to the campaign before us. Nor let our warfare be a boorish and uncourteous one, but a higher courtesy attend its higher chivalry, though not to the slackening of its tougher duties and severer discipline; that so our camp may be a palaestra, wherein the dormant energies and affections of men may tug and wrestle, not to their discomfiture, but to their mutual exercise and development.

What were Godfrey and Gonzalo unless we breathed a life into them, and enacted their exploits as a prelude to our own? The past is the canvass on which our idea is painted,—the dim prospectus of our future field. We are dreaming of what we are to do. Methinks I hear the clarion sound, and clang of corselet and buckler, from many a silent hamlet of the soul. The signal gun has long since sounded and we are not yet on our posts. Let us make such haste as the morning, and such delay as the evening.

Natural History of Massachusetts

Reports—on the Fishes, Reptiles, and Birds; the Herbaceous Plants and Quadrupeds; the Insects Injurious to Vegetation; and the Invertebrate Animals—of Massachusetts. Published agreeably to an Order of the Legislature, by the Commissioners on the Zoological and Botanical Survey of the State.

PRELIMINARY NOTE.

We were thinking how we might best celebrate the good deed which the State of Massachusetts has done, in procuring the Scientific Survey of the Commonwealth, whose result is recorded in these volumes, when we found a near neighbor and friend of ours, dear also to the Muses, a native and an inhabitant of the town of Concord, who readily undertook to give us such comments as he had made on these books, and, better still, notes of his own conversation with nature in the woods and waters of this town. With all thankfulness we begged our friend to lay down the oar and fishing line, which none can handle better, and assume the pen, that Isaak Walton and White of Selborne might not want a successor, nor the fair meadows, to which we also have owed a home and the happiness of many years, their poet.

EDITOR OF THE DIAL.

Concord, Mass.

BOOKS of natural history make the most cheerful winter reading. I read in Audubon with a thrill of delight, when the snow covers the ground, of the magnolia, and the Florida keys, and their warm sea breezes; of the fence-rail, and the cotton-tree, and the migrations of the rice-bird; of the breaking up of winter in Labrador, and the melting of the snow on the forks of the Missouri; and owe an accession of health to these reminiscences of luxuriant nature.

> Within the circuit of this plodding life
> There enter moments of an azure hue,
> Untarnished fair as is the violet
> Or anemone, when the spring strews them

By some meandering rivulet, which make
The best philosophy untrue that aims
But to console man for his grievances.
I have remembered when the winter came,
High in my chamber in the frosty nights,
When in the still light of the cheerful moon,
On every twig and rail and jutting spout,
The icy spears were adding to their length
Against the arrows of the coming sun,
How in the shimmering noon of summer past
Some unrecorded beam slanted across
The upland pastures where the Johnswort grew;
Or heard, amid the verdure of my mind,
The bee's long smothered hum, on the blue flag
Loitering amidst the mead; or busy rill,
Which now through all its course stands still and dumb
Its own memorial,—purling at its play
Along the slopes, and through the meadows next,
Until its youthful sound was hushed at last
In the staid current of the lowland stream;
Or seen the furrows shine but late upturned,
And where the fieldfare followed in the rear,
When all the fields around lay bound and hoar
Beneath a thick integument of snow.
So by God's cheap economy made rich
To go upon my winter's task again.

I am singularly refreshed in winter when I hear of service
berries, poke-weed, juniper. Is not heaven made up of these
cheap summer glories? There is a singular health in those
words Labrador and East Main, which no desponding creed
recognises. How much more than federal are these states. If
there were no other vicissitudes than the seasons, our interest
would never tire. Much more is adoing than Congress wots
of. What journal do the persimmon and the buckeye keep,
and the sharp-shinned hawk? What is transpiring from sum-
mer to winter in the Carolinas, and the Great Pine Forest,
and the Valley of the Mohawk? The merely political aspect of
the land is never very cheering; men are degraded when con-
sidered as the members of a political organization. On this

side all lands present only the symptoms of decay. I see but Bunker Hill and Sing-Sing, the District of Columbia and Sullivan's Island, with a few avenues connecting them. But paltry are they all beside one blast of the east or the south wind which blows over them.

In society you will not find health, but in nature. Unless our feet at least stood in the midst of nature, all our faces would be pale and livid. Society is always diseased, and the best is the most so. There is no scent in it so wholesome as that of the pines, nor any fragrance so penetrating and restorative as the life-everlasting in high pastures. I would keep some book of natural history always by me as a sort of elixir, the reading of which should restore the tone of the system. To the sick, indeed, nature is sick, but to the well, a fountain of health. To him who contemplates a trait of natural beauty no harm nor disappointment can come. The doctrines of despair, of spiritual or political tyranny or servitude, were never taught by such as shared the serenity of nature. Surely good courage will not flag here on the Atlantic border, as long as we are flanked by the Fur Countries. There is enough in that sound to cheer one under any circumstances. The spruce, the hemlock, and the pine will not countenance despair. Methinks some creeds in vestries and churches do forget the hunter wrapped in furs by the Great Slave Lake, and that the Esquimaux sledges are drawn by dogs, and in the twilight of the northern night, the hunter does not give over to follow the seal and walrus on the ice. They are of sick and diseased imaginations who would toll the world's knell so soon. Cannot these sedentary sects do better than prepare the shrouds and write the epitaphs of those other busy living men? The practical faith of all men belies the preacher's consolation. What is any man's discourse to me, if I am not sensible of something in it as steady and cheery as the creak of crickets? In it the woods must be relieved against the sky. Men tire me when I am not constantly greeted and refreshed as by the flux of sparkling streams. Surely joy is the condition of life. Think of the young fry that leap in ponds, the myriads of insects ushered into being on a summer evening, the incessant note of the hyla with which the woods ring in the spring, the nonchalance of the butterfly carrying accident and change painted in a thousand hues upon its wings, or the brook minnow stoutly stemming the current, the lustre of whose scales worn bright by the attrition is reflected upon the bank.

We fancy that this din of religion, literature, and philosophy, which is heard in pulpits, lyceums, and parlors, vibrates through the universe, and is as catholic a sound as the creaking of the earth's axle; but if a man sleep soundly, he will forget it all between sunset and dawn. It is the three-inch swing of a pendulum in a cupboard, which the great pulse of nature vibrates by and through each instant. When we lift our eyelids and open our ears, it disappears with smoke and rattle like the cars on a railroad. When I detect a beauty in any of the recesses of nature, I am reminded, by the serene and retired spirit in which it requires to be contemplated, of the inexpressible privacy of a life,—how silent and unambitious it is. The beauty there is in mosses must be considered from the holiest, quietest nook. What an admirable training is science for the more active warfare of life. Indeed, the unchallenged bravery, which these studies imply, is far more impressive than the trumpeted valor of the warrior. I am pleased to learn that Thales was up and stirring by night not unfrequently, as his astronomical discoveries prove. Linnæus, setting out for Lapland, surveys his "comb" and "spare shirt," "leathern breeches" and "gauze cap to keep off gnats," with as much complacency as Bonaparte a park of artillery for the Russian campaign. The quiet bravery of the man is admirable. His eye is to take in fish, flower, and bird, quadruped and biped. Science is always brave, for to know, is to know good; doubt and danger quail before her eye. What the coward overlooks in his hurry, she calmly scrutinizes, breaking ground like a pioneer for the array of arts that follow in her train. But cowardice is unscientific; for there cannot be a science of ignorance. There may be a science of bravery, for that advances; but a retreat is rarely well conducted; if it is, then is it an orderly advance in the face of circumstances.

But to draw a little nearer to our promised topics. Entomology extends the limits of being in a new direction, so that I walk in nature with a sense of greater space and freedom. It suggests besides, that the universe is not rough-hewn, but perfect in its details. Nature will bear the closest inspection; she invites us to lay our eye level with the smallest leaf, and take an insect view of its plain. She has no interstices; every part is full of life. I explore, too, with pleasure, the sources of the myriad sounds which crowd the summer noon, and which seem the very grain and stuff of which eternity is made. Who does not remember the shrill roll-call of the harvest fly? There were ears for these sounds in Greece long ago, as Anacreon's ode will show.

> "We pronounce thee happy, Cicada,
> For on the tops of the trees,
> Drinking a little dew,
> Like any king thou singest.
> For thine are they all,
> Whatever thou seest in the fields,
> And whatever the woods bear.
> Thou art the friend of the husbandmen,
> In no respect injuring any one;
> And thou art honored among men,
> Sweet prophet of summer.
> The Muses love thee,
> And Phœbus himself loves thee,
> And has given thee a shrill song;
> Age does not wrack thee,
> Thou skilful, earthborn, song-loving,
> Unsuffering, bloodless one;
> Almost thou art like the gods."

In the autumn days, the creaking of crickets is heard at noon over all the land, and as in summer they are heard chiefly at night-fall, so then by their incessant chirp they usher in the evening of the year. Nor can all the vanities that vex the world alter one whit the measure that night has chosen. Every pulse-beat is in exact time with the cricket's chant and the tickings of the deathwatch in the wall. Alternate with these if you can.

About two hundred and eighty birds either reside permanently in the State, or spend the summer only, or make us a passing visit. Those which spend the winter with us have obtained our warmest sympathy. The nut-hatch and chicadee flitting in company through the dells of the wood, the one harshly scolding at the intruder, the other with a faint lisping note enticing him on, the jay screaming in the orchard, the crow cawing in unison with the storm, the partridge, like a russet link extended over from autumn to spring, preserving unbroken the chain of summers, the hawk with warrior-like firmness abiding the blasts of winter, the robin* and lark lurking by warm springs in the woods, the familiar snow-bird culling a few seeds in the garden, or a few crumbs in the yard, and occasionally the shrike, with heedless and unfrozen melody bringing back summer again;—

> His steady sails he never furls
> At any time o' year,
> And perching now on Winter's curls,
> He whistles in his ear.

As the spring advances and the ice is melting in the river, our earliest and straggling visitors make their appearance. Again does the old Teian poet sing as well for New England as for Greece, in the

RETURN OF SPRING.

> "Behold, how spring appearing,
> The Graces send forth roses;
> Behold, how the wave of the sea
> Is made smooth by the calm;
> Behold, how the duck dives;
> Behold, how the crane travels;
> And Titan shines constantly bright.
> The shadows of the clouds are moving;
> The works of man shine;
> The earth puts forth fruits;
> The fruit of the olive puts forth.

---

*A white robin and a white quail have occasionally been seen. It is mentioned in Audubon as remarkable that the nest of a robin should be found on the ground; but this bird seems to be less particular than most in the choice of a building spot. I have seen its nest placed under the thatched roof of a deserted barn, and in one instance, where the adjacent country was nearly destitute of trees, together with two of the phœbe, upon the end of a board in the loft of a sawmill, but a few feet from the saw, which vibrated several inches with the motion of the machinery.

The cup of Bacchus is crowned,
Along the leaves, along the branches,
The fruit, bending them down, flourishes."

The ducks alight at this season in the still water, in company with the gulls, which do not fail to improve an east wind to visit our meadows, and swim about by twos and threes, pluming themselves, and diving to peck at the root of the lily, and the cranberries which the frost has not loosened. The first flock of geese is seen beating to north, in long harrows and waving lines, the gingle of the song-sparrow salutes us from the shrubs and fences, the plaintive note of the lark comes clear and sweet from the meadow, and the bluebird, like an azure ray, glances past us in our walk. The fish-hawk, too, is occasionally seen at this season sailing majestically over the water, and he who has once observed it will not soon forget the majesty of its flight. It sails the air like a ship of the line, worthy to struggle with the elements, falling back from time to time like a ship on its beam ends, and holding its talons up as if ready for the arrows, in the attitude of the national bird. It is a great presence, as of the master of river and forest. Its eye would not quail before the owner of the soil, but make him feel like an intruder on its domains. And then its retreat, sailing so steadily away, is a kind of advance. I have by me one of a pair of ospreys, which have for some years fished in this vicinity, shot by a neighboring pond, measuring more than two feet in length, and six in the stretch of its wings. Nuttall mentions that "The ancients, particularly Aristotle, pretended that the ospreys taught their young to gaze at the sun, and those who were unable to do so were destroyed. Linnæus even believed, on ancient authority, that one of the feet of this bird had all the toes divided, while the other was partly webbed, so that it could swim with one foot, and grasp a fish with the other." But that educated eye is now dim, and those talons are nerveless. Its shrill scream seems yet to linger in its throat, and the roar of the sea in its wings. There is the tyranny of Jove in its claws, and his wrath in the erectile feathers of the head and neck. It reminds me of the Argonautic expedition, and would inspire the dullest to take flight over Parnassus.

The booming of the bittern, described by Goldsmith and Nuttall, is frequently heard in our fens, in the morning and evening, sounding like a pump, or the chopping of wood in a frosty morning in some distant farm-yard. The manner in which this sound is produced I have not seen anywhere described. On one occasion, the bird has been seen by one of my neighbors to thrust its bill into the water, and suck up as much as it could hold, then raising its head, it pumped it out again with four or five heaves of the neck, throwing it two or three feet, and making the sound each time.

At length the summer's eternity is ushered in by the cackle of the flicker among the oaks on the hill-side, and a new dynasty begins with calm security.

In May and June the woodland quire is in full tune, and given the immense spaces of hollow air, and this curious human ear, one does not see how the void could be better filled.

> Each summer sound
> Is a summer round.

As the season advances, and those birds which make us but a passing visit depart, the woods become silent again, and but few feathers ruffle the drowsy air. But the solitary rambler may still find a response and expression for every mood in the depths of the wood.

> Sometimes I hear the veery's* clarion,
> Or brazen trump of the impatient jay,
> And in secluded woods the chicadee
> Doles out her scanty notes, which sing the praise
> Of heroes, and set forth the loveliness
> Of virtue evermore.

The phœbe still sings in harmony with the sultry weather by the brink of the pond, nor are the desultory hours of noon in the midst of the village without their minstrel.

---

*This bird, which is so well described by Nuttall, but is apparently unknown by the author of the Report, is one of the most common in the woods in this vicinity, and in Cambridge I have heard the college yard ring with its trill. The boys call it "*yorrick*," from the sound of its querulous and chiding note, as it flits near the traveller through the underwood. The cowbird's egg is occasionally found in its nest, as mentioned by Audubon.

> Upon the lofty elm tree sprays
> The vireo rings the changes sweet,
> During the trivial summer days,
> Striving to lift our thoughts above the street.

With the autumn begins in some measure a new spring. The plover is heard whistling high in the air over the dry pastures, the finches flit from tree to tree, the bobolinks and flickers fly in flocks, and the goldfinch rides on the earliest blast, like a winged hyla peeping amid the rustle of the leaves. The crows, too, begin now to congregate; you may stand and count them as they fly low and straggling over the landscape, singly or by twos and threes, at intervals of half a mile, until a hundred have passed.

I have seen it suggested somewhere that the crow was brought to this country by the white man; but I shall as soon believe that the white man planted these pines and hemlocks. He is no spaniel to follow our steps; but rather flits about the clearings like the dusky spirit of the Indian, reminding me oftener of Philip and Powhatan, than of Winthrop and Smith. He is a relic of the dark ages. By just so slight, by just so lasting a tenure does superstition hold the world ever; there is the rook in England, and the crow in New England.

> Thou dusky spirit of the wood,
> Bird of an ancient brood,
> Flitting thy lonely way,
> A meteor in the summer's day,
> From wood to wood, from hill to hill,
> Low over forest, field, and rill,
> What wouldst thou say?
> Why shouldst thou haunt the day?
> What makes thy melancholy float?
> What bravery inspires thy throat,
> And bears thee up above the clouds,
> Over desponding human crowds,
> Which far below
> Lay thy haunts low?

The late walker or sailer, in the October evenings, may hear the murmuring of the snipe, circling over the meadows, the most spirit-like sound in nature; and still later in the autumn, when the frosts have tinged the leaves, a solitary loon pays a visit to our retired ponds, where he may lurk undisturbed till the season of moulting is passed, making the woods ring with his wild laughter. This bird, the Great Northern Diver, well deserves its name; for when pursued with a boat, it will dive, and swim like a fish under water, for sixty rods or more, as fast as a boat can be paddled, and its pursuer, if he would discover his game again, must put his ear to the surface to hear where it comes up. When it comes to the surface, it throws the water off with one shake of its wings, and calmly swims about until again disturbed.

These are the sights and sounds which reach our senses oftenest during the year. But sometimes one hears a quite new note, which has for back ground other Carolinas and Mexicos than the books describe, and learns that his ornithology has done him no service.

It appears from the Report that there are about forty quadrupeds belonging to the State, and among these one is glad to hear of a few bears, wolves, lynxes, and wildcats.

When our river overflows its banks in the spring, the wind from the meadows is laden with a strong scent of musk, and by its freshness advertises me of an unexplored wildness. Those backwoods are not far off then. I am affected by the sight of the cabins of the musk-rat, made of mud and grass, and raised three or four feet along the river, as when I read of the barrows of Asia. The musk-rat is the beaver of the settled States. Their number has even increased within a few years in this vicinity. Among the rivers which empty into the Merrimack, the Concord is known to the boatmen as a dead stream. The Indians are said to have called it Musketaquid, or Prairie river. Its current being much more sluggish, and its water more muddy than the rest, it abounds more in fish and game of every kind. According to the History of the town, "The fur trade here was once very important. As early as 1641, a company was formed in the colony, of which Major Willard of Concord was superintendent, and had the exclusive right to trade with the Indians in furs and other articles; and for this right they were obliged to pay into the public treasury one twentieth of all the furs they obtained." There are trappers in our midst still, as well as on the streams of the far west, who night and morning go the round of their traps, without fear of the Indian. One of these takes from one hundred and fifty to two hundred musk-rats in a year, and even thirty-six have been shot by one man in a day. Their fur, which is not nearly as valuable as formerly, is in good condition in the winter and spring only; and upon the breaking up of the ice, when they are driven out of their holes by the water, the greatest number is shot from boats, either swimming or resting on their stools, or slight supports of grass and reeds, by the side of the stream. Though they exhibit considerable cunning at other times, they are easily taken in a trap, which has only to be placed in their holes, or wherever they frequent, without any bait being used, though it is sometimes rubbed with their musk. In the winter the hunter cuts holes in the ice, and shoots them when they come to the surface. Their burrows are usually in the high banks of the river, with the entrance under water, and rising within to above the level of high water. Sometimes their nests, composed of dried meadow grass and flags, may be discovered where the bank is low and spongy, by the yielding of the ground under the feet. They have from three to seven or eight young in the spring.

Frequently, in the morning or evening, a long ripple is seen in the still water, where a musk-rat is crossing the stream, with only its nose above the surface, and sometimes a green bough in its mouth to build its house with. When it finds itself observed, it will dive and swim five or six rods under water, and at length conceal itself in its hole, or the weeds. It will remain under water for ten minutes at a time, and on one occasion has been seen, when undisturbed, to form an air bubble under the ice, which contracted and expanded as it breathed at leisure. When it suspects danger on shore, it will stand erect like a squirrel, and survey its neighborhood for several minutes, without moving.

In the fall, if a meadow intervene between their burrows and the stream, they erect cabins of mud and grass, three or four feet high, near its edge. These are not their breeding places, though young are sometimes found in them in late freshets, but rather their hunting lodges, to which they resort in the winter with their food, and for shelter. Their food consists chiefly of flags and fresh water muscles, the shells of the latter being left in large quantities around their lodges in the spring.

The Penobscot Indian wears the entire skin of a musk-rat, with the legs and tail dangling, and the head caught under his girdle, for a pouch, into which he puts his fishing tackle, and essences to scent his traps with.

The bear, wolf, lynx, wildcat, deer, beaver, and marten, have disappeared; the otter is rarely if ever seen at present; and the mink is less common than formerly.

Perhaps of all our untamed quadrupeds, the fox has obtained the widest and most familiar reputation, from the time of Pilpay and Æsop to the present day. His recent tracks still give variety to a winter's walk. I tread in the steps of the fox that has gone before me by some hours, or which perhaps I have started, with such a tiptoe of expectation, as if I were on the trail of the Spirit itself which resides in the wood, and expected soon to catch it in its lair. I am curious to know what has determined its graceful curvatures, and how surely they were coincident with the fluctuations of some mind. I know which way a mind wended, what horizon it faced, by the setting of these tracks, and whether it moved slowly or rapidly, by their greater or less intervals and distinctness; for the swiftest step leaves yet a lasting trace. Sometimes you will see the trails of many together, and where they have gambolled and gone through a hundred evolutions, which testify to a singular listlessness and leisure in nature.

When I see a fox run across the pond on the snow, with the carelessness of freedom, or at intervals trace his course in the sunshine along the ridge of a hill, I give up to him sun and earth as to their true proprietor. He does not go in the sun, but it seems to follow him, and there is a visible sympathy between him and it. Sometimes, when the snow lies light, and but five or six inches deep, you may give chase and come up with one on foot. In such a case he will show a remarkable presence of mind, choosing only the safest direction, though he may lose ground by it. Notwithstanding his fright, he will take no step which is not beautiful. His pace is a sort of leopard canter, as if he were in no wise impeded by the snow, but were husbanding his strength all the while. When the ground is uneven, the course is a series of graceful curves, conforming to the shape of the surface. He runs as though there were not a bone in his back, occasionally dropping his muzzle to the ground for a rod or two, and then tossing his head aloft, when satisfied of his course. When he comes to a declivity, he will put his fore feet together, and slide swiftly down it, shoving the snow before him. He treads so softly that you would hardly hear it from any nearness, and yet with such expression, that it would not be quite inaudible at any distance.

Of fishes, seventy-five genera and one hundred and seven species are described in the Report. The fisherman will be startled to learn that there are but about a dozen kinds in the ponds and streams of any inland town; and almost nothing is known of their habits. Only their names and residence make one love fishes. I would know even the number of their fin rays, and how many scales compose the lateral line. I am the wiser in respect to all knowledges, and the better qualified for all fortunes, for knowing that there is a minnow in the brook. Methinks I have need even of his sympathy and to be his fellow in a degree.

I have experienced such simple delight in the trivial matters of fishing and sporting, formerly, as might have inspired the muse of Homer or Shakspeare; and now when I turn the pages and ponder the plates of the Angler's Souvenir, I am fain to exclaim,—

> "Can these things be,
> And overcome us like a summer's cloud?"

Next to nature it seems as if man's actions were the most natural, they so gently accord with her. The small seines of flax stretched across the shallow and transparent parts of our river, are no more intrusion than the cobweb in the sun. I stay my boat in mid current, and look down in the sunny water to see the civil meshes of his nets, and wonder how the blustering people of the town could have done this elvish work. The twine looks like a new river weed, and is to the river as a beautiful memento of man's presence in nature, discovered as silently and delicately as a foot-print in the sand.

When the ice is covered with snow, I do not suspect the wealth under my feet; that there is as good as a mine under me wherever I go. How many pickerel are poised on easy fin fathoms below the loaded wain. The revolution of the seasons must be a curious phenomenon to them. At length the sun and wind brush aside their curtain, and they see the heavens again.

Early in the spring, after the ice has melted, is the time for spearing fish. Suddenly the wind shifts from north-east and east to west and south, and every icicle, which has tinkled on the meadow grass so long, trickles down its stem, and seeks its level unerringly with a million comrades. The steam curls up from every roof and fence.

> I see the civil sun drying earth's tears,
> Her tears of joy, which only faster flow.

In the brooks is heard the slight grating sound of small cakes of ice, floating with various speed, full of content and promise, and where the water gurgles under a natural bridge, you may hear these hasty rafts hold conversation in an under tone. Every rill is a channel for the juices of the meadow. In the ponds the ice cracks with a merry and inspiriting din, and down the larger streams is whirled grating hoarsely, and crashing its way along, which was so lately a highway for the woodman's team and the fox, sometimes with the tracks of the skaters still fresh upon it, and the holes cut for pickerel. Town committees anxiously inspect the bridges and causeways, as if by mere eye-force to intercede with the ice, and save the treasury.

> The river swelleth more and more,
> Like some sweet influence stealing o'er
> The passive town; and for a while
> Each tussuck makes a tiny isle,
> Where, on some friendly Ararat,
> Resteth the weary water-rat.
>
> No ripple shows Musketaquid,
> Her very current e'en is hid,
> As deepest souls do calmest rest,

When thoughts are swelling in the breast,
And she that in the summer's drought
Doth make a rippling and a rout,
Sleeps from Nahshawtuck to the Cliff,
Unruffled by a single skiff.
But by a thousand distant hills
The louder roar a thousand rills,
And many a spring which now is dumb,
And many a stream with smothered hum,
Doth swifter well and faster glide,
Though buried deep beneath the tide.

Our village shows a rural Venice,
Its broad lagoons where yonder fen is;
As lovely as the Bay of Naples
Yon placid cove amid the maples;
And in my neighbor's field of corn
I recognise the Golden Horn.

Here Nature taught from year to year,
When only red men came to hear,
Methinks 't was in this school of art
Venice and Naples learned their part,
But still their mistress, to my mind,
Her young disciples leaves behind.

The fisherman now repairs and launches his boat. The best time for spearing is at this season, before the weeds have begun to grow, and while the fishes lie in the shallow water, for in summer they prefer the cool depths, and in the autumn they are still more or less concealed by the grass. The first requisite is fuel for your crate; and for this purpose the roots of the pitch pine are commonly used, found under decayed stumps, where the trees have been felled eight or ten years.

With a crate, or jack, made of iron hoops, to contain your fire, and attached to the bow of your boat about three feet from the water, a fish-spear with seven tines, and fourteen feet long, a large basket, or barrow, to carry your fuel and bring back your fish, and a thick outer garment, you are equipped for a cruise. It should be a warm and still evening; and then with a fire crackling merrily at the prow, you may launch forth like a cucullo into the night. The dullest soul cannot go upon such an expedition without some of the spirit of adventure; as if he had stolen the boat of Charon and gone down the Styx on a midnight expedition into the realms of Pluto. And much speculation does this wandering star afford to the musing night-walker, leading him on and on, jack-o'lantern-like, over the meadows; or if he is wiser, he amuses himself with imagining what of human life, far in the silent night, is flitting moth-like round its candle. The silent navigator shoves his craft gently over the water, with a smothered pride and sense of benefaction, as if he were the phosphor, or light-bringer, to these dusky realms, or some sister moon, blessing the spaces with her light. The waters, for a rod or two on either hand and several feet in depth, are lit up with more than noon-day distinctness, and he enjoys the opportunity which so many have desired, for the roofs of a city are indeed raised, and he surveys the midnight economy of the fishes. There they lie in every variety of posture, some on their backs, with their white bellies uppermost, some suspended in mid water, some sculling gently along with a dreamy motion of the fins, and others quite active and wide awake,—a scene not unlike what the human city would present. Occasionally he will encounter a turtle selecting the choicest morsels, or a musk-rat resting on a tussuck. He may exercise his dexterity, if he sees fit, on the more distant and active fish, or fork the nearer into his boat, as potatoes out of a pot, or even take the sound sleepers with his hands. But these last accomplishments he will soon learn to dispense with, distinguishing the real object of his pursuit, and find compensation in the beauty and never ending novelty of his position. The pines growing down to the water's edge will show newly as in the glare of a conflagration, and as he floats under the willows with his light, the song-sparrow will often wake on her perch, and sing that strain at midnight, which she had meditated for the morning. And when he has done, he may have to steer his way home through the dark by the north star, and he will feel himself some degrees nearer to it for having lost his way on the earth.

The fishes commonly taken in this way are pickerel, suckers, perch, eels, pouts, breams, and shiners,—from thirty to sixty weight in a night. Some are hard to be recognised in the unnatural light, especially the perch, which, his dark bands being exaggerated, acquires a ferocious aspect. The number of these transverse bands, which the Report states to be seven, is, however, very variable, for in some of our ponds they have nine and ten even.

It appears that we have eight kinds of tortoises, twelve snakes,—but one of which is venomous,—nine frogs and toads, nine salamanders, and one lizard, for our neighbors.

I am particularly attracted by the motions of the serpent tribe. They make our hands and feet, the wings of the bird, and the fins of the fish seem very superfluous, as if nature had only indulged her fancy in making them. The black snake will dart into a bush when pursued, and circle round and round with an easy and graceful motion, amid the thin and bare twigs, five or six feet from the ground, as a bird flits from bough to bough, or hang in festoons between the forks. Elasticity and flexibleness in the simpler forms of animal life are equivalent to a complex system of limbs in the higher; and we have only to be as wise and wily as the serpent, to perform as difficult feats without the vulgar assistance of hands and feet.

In April, the snapping turtle, *Emysaurus serpentina*, is frequently taken on the meadows and in the river. The fisherman, taking sight over the calm surface, discovers its snout projecting above the water, at the distance of many rods, and easily secures his prey through its unwillingness to disturb the water by swimming hastily away, for, gradually drawing its head under, it remains resting on some limb or clump of grass. Its eggs, which are buried at a distance from the water, in some soft place, as a pigeon bed, are frequently devoured by the skunk. It will catch fish by day-light, as a toad catches flies, and is said to emit a transparent fluid from its mouth to attract them.

Nature has taken more care than the fondest parent for the education and refinement of her children. Consider the silent influence which flowers exert, no less upon the ditcher in the meadow than the lady in the bower. When I walk in the woods, I am reminded that a wise purveyor has been there before me; my most delicate experience is typified there. I am struck with the pleasing friendships and unanimities of nature, as when the moss on the trees takes the form of their leaves. In the most stupendous scenes you will see delicate and fragile features, as slight wreathes of vapor, dew-lines, feathery sprays, which suggest a high refinement, a noble blood and breeding, as it were. It is not hard to account for elves and fairies; they represent this light grace, this ethereal gentility. Bring a spray from the wood, or a crystal from the brook, and place it on your mantel, and your household ornaments will seem plebeian beside its nobler fashion and bearing. It will wave superior there, as if used to a more refined and polished circle. It has a salute and a response to all your enthusiasm and heroism.

In the winter, I stop short in the path to admire how the trees grow up without forethought, regardless of the time and circumstances. They do not wait as man does, but now is the golden age of the sapling. Earth, air, sun, and rain, are occasion enough; they were no better in primeval centuries. The "winter of *their* discontent" never comes. Witness the buds of the native poplar standing gaily out to the frost on the sides of its bare switches. They express a naked confidence. With cheerful heart one could be a sojourner in the wilderness, if he were sure to find there the catkins of the willow or the alder. When I read of them in the accounts of northern adventurers, by Baffin's Bay or Mackenzie's river, I see how even there too I could dwell. They are our little vegetable redeemers. Methinks our virtue will hold out till they come again. They are worthy to have had a greater than Minerva or Ceres for their inventor. Who was the benignant goddess that bestowed them on mankind?

Nature is mythical and mystical always, and works with the license and extravagance of genius. She has her luxurious and florid style as well as art. Having a pilgrim's cup to make, she gives to the whole, stem, bowl, handle, and nose, some fantastic shape, as if it were to be the car of some fabulous marine deity, a Nereus or Triton.

In the winter, the botanist needs not confine himself to his books and herbarium, and give over his out-door pursuits, but study a new department of vegetable physiology, what may be called crystalline botany, then. The winter of 1837 was unusually favorable for this. In December of that year the

Genius of vegetation seemed to hover by night over its summer haunts with unusual persistency. Such a hoar-frost, as is very uncommon here or anywhere, and whose full effects can never be witnessed after sunrise, occurred several times. As I went forth early on a still frosty morning, the trees looked like airy creatures of darkness caught napping, on this side huddled together with their grey hairs streaming in a secluded valley, which the sun had not penetrated, on that hurrying off in Indian file along some water-course, while the shrubs and grasses, like elves and fairies of the night, sought to hide their diminished heads in the snow. The river, viewed from the high bank, appeared of a yellowish green color, though all the landscape was white. Every tree, shrub, and spire of grass, that could raise its head above the snow, was covered with a dense ice-foliage, answering, as it were, leaf for leaf to its summer dress. Even the fences had put forth leaves in the night. The centre, diverging, and more minute fibres were perfectly distinct, and the edges regularly indented. These leaves were on the side of the twig or stubble opposite to the sun, meeting it for the most part at right angles, and there were others standing out at all possible angles upon these and upon one another, with no twig or stubble supporting them. When the first rays of the sun slanted over the scene, the grasses seemed hung with innumerable jewels, which jingled merrily as they were brushed by the foot of the traveller, and reflected all the hues of the rainbow as he moved from side to side. It struck me that these ghost leaves and the green ones whose forms they assume, were the creatures of but one law; that in obedience to the same law the vegetable juices swell gradually into the perfect leaf, on the one hand, and the crystalline particles troop to their standard in the same order, on the other. As if the material were indifferent, but the law one and invariable, and every plant in the spring but pushed up into and filled a permanent and eternal mould, which, summer and winter, forever is waiting to be filled.

This foliate structure is common to the coral and the plumage of birds, and to how large a part of animate and inanimate nature. The same independence of law on matter is observable in many other instances, as in the natural rhymes, when some animal form, color, or odor, has its counterpart in some vegetable. As, indeed, all rhymes imply an eternal melody, independent of any particular sense.

As confirmation of the fact, that vegetation is but a kind of crystallization, every one may observe how, upon the edge of the melting frost on the window, the needle-shaped particles are bundled together so as to resemble fields waving with grain, or shocks rising here and there from the stubble; on one side the vegetation of the torrid zone, high towering palms and wide-spread bannians, such as are seen in pictures of oriental scenery; on the other, arctic pines stiff frozen, with downcast branches.

Vegetation has been made the type of all growth; but as in crystals the law is more obvious, their material being more simple, and for the most part more transient and fleeting, would it not be as philosophical as convenient, to consider all growth, all filling up within the limits of nature, but a crystallization more or less rapid?

On this occasion, in the side of the high bank of the river, wherever the water or other cause had formed a cavity, its throat and outer edge, like the entrance to a citadel, bristled with a glistening ice-armor. In one place you might see minute ostrich feathers, which seemed the waving plumes of the warriors filing into the fortress; in another, the glancing, fan-shaped banners of the Lilliputian host; and in another, the needle-shaped particles collected into bundles, resembling the plumes of the pine, might pass for a phalanx of spears. From the under side of the ice in the brooks, where there was a thicker ice below, depended a mass of crystallization, four or five inches deep, in the form of prisms, with their lower ends open, which, when the ice was laid on its smooth side, resembled the roofs and steeples of a Gothic city, or the vessels of a crowded haven under a press of canvass. The very mud in the road, where the ice had melted, was crystallized with deep rectilinear fissures, and the crystalline masses in the sides of the ruts resembled exactly asbestos in the disposition of their needles. Around the roots of the stubble and flower-stalks, the frost was gathered into the form of irregular conical shells, or fairy rings. In some places the ice-crystals were lying upon granite rocks, directly over crystals of quartz, the frost-work of a longer night, crystals of a longer period, but to some eye unprejudiced by the short term of human life, melting as fast as the former.

In the Report on the Invertebrate Animals, this singular fact is recorded, which teaches us to put a new value on time and space. "The distribution of the marine shells is well worthy of notice as a geological fact. Cape Cod, the right arm of the Commonwealth, reaches out into the ocean, some fifty or sixty miles. It is nowhere many miles wide; but this narrow point of land has hitherto proved a barrier to the migrations of many species of Mollusca. Several genera and numerous species, which are separated by the intervention of only a few miles of land, are effectually prevented from mingling by the Cape, and do not pass from one side to the other. * * * * Of the one hundred and ninety-seven marine species, eighty-three do not pass to the south shore, and fifty are not found on the north shore of the Cape."

That common muscle, the *Unio complanatus*, or more properly *fluviatilis*, left in the spring by the musk-rat upon rocks and stumps, appears to have been an important article of food with the Indians. In one place, where they are said to have feasted, they are found in large quantities, at an elevation of thirty feet above the river, filling the soil to the depth of a foot, and mingled with ashes and Indian remains.

The works we have placed at the head of our chapter, with as much license as the preacher selects his text, are such as imply more labor than enthusiasm. The State wanted complete catalogues of its natural riches, with such additional facts merely as would be directly useful.

The Reports on Fishes, Reptiles, Insects, and Invertebrate Animals, however, indicate labor and research, and have a value independent of the object of the legislature.

Those on Herbaceous Plants and Birds cannot be of much value, as long as Bigelow and Nuttall are accessible. They serve but to indicate, with more or less exactness, what species are found in the State. We detect several errors ourselves, and a more practised eye would no doubt expand the list.

The Quadrupeds deserved a more final and instructive report than they have obtained.

These volumes deal much in measurements and minute descriptions, not interesting to the general reader, with only here and there a colored sentence to allure him, like those plants growing in dark forests, which bear only leaves without blossoms. But the ground was comparatively unbroken, and we will not complain of the pioneer, if he raises no flowers with his first crop. Let us not underrate the value of a fact; it will one day flower in a truth. It is astonishing how few facts of importance are added in a century to the natural history of any animal. The natural history of man himself is still being gradually written. Men are knowing enough after their fashion. Every countryman and dairymaid knows that the coats of the fourth stomach of the calf will curdle milk, and what particular mushroom is a safe and nutritious diet. You cannot go into any field or wood, but it will seem as if every stone had been turned, and the bark on every tree ripped up. But after all, it is much easier to discover than to see when the cover is off. It has been well said that "the attitude of inspection is prone." Wisdom does not inspect, but behold. We must look a long time before we can see. Slow are the beginnings of philosophy. He has something demoniacal in him, who can discern a law, or couple two facts. We can imagine a time when,—"Water runs down hill,"—may have been taught in the schools. The true man of science will know nature better by his finer organization; he will smell, taste, see, hear, feel, better than other men. His will be a deeper and finer experience. We do not learn by inference and deduction, and the application of mathematics to philosophy, but by direct intercourse and sympathy. It is with science as with ethics, we cannot know truth by contrivance and method; the Baconian is as false as any other, and with all the helps of machinery and the arts, the most scientific will still be the healthiest and friendliest man, and possess a more perfect Indian wisdom.

A Walk to Wachusett

The needles of the pine,
All to the west incline.

SUMMER and winter our eyes had rested on the dim outline of the mountains, to which distance and indistinctness lent a grandeur not their own, so that they served equally to interpret all the allusions of poets and travellers; whether with Homer, on a spring morning, we sat down on the many-peaked Olympus, or, with Virgil, and his compeers, roamed the Etrurian and Thessalian hills, or with Humboldt measured the more modern Andes and Teneriffe.

With frontier strength ye stand your ground,
With grand content ye circle round,
Tumultuous silence for all sound,
Ye distant nursery of rills,
Monadnock, and the Peterboro' hills;
Like some vast fleet,
Sailing through rain and sleet,
Through winter's cold and summer's heat;
Still holding on, upon your high emprise,
Until ye find a shore amid the skies;
Not skulking close to land,
With cargo contraband,
For they who sent a venture out by ye
Have set the sun to see
Their honesty.
Ships of the line, each one,
Ye to the westward run,
Always before the gale,
Under a press of sail,
With weight of metal all untold.
I seem to feel ye, in my firm seat here,
Immeasurable depth of hold,
And breadth of beam, and length of running gear.

Methinks ye take luxurious pleasure
In your novel western leisure;
So cool your brows, and freshly blue,
As Time had nought for ye to do;
For ye lie at your length,
An unappropriated strength,
Unhewn primeval timber,
For knees so stiff, for masts so limber;
The stock of which new earths are made,
One day to be our western trade,
Fit for the stanchions of a world
Which through the seas of space is hurled.

While we enjoy a lingering ray,
Ye still o'ertop the western day,
Reposing yonder, on God's croft,
Like solid stacks of hay.
Edged with silver, and with gold,
The clouds hang o'er in damask fold,
And with such depth of amber light
The west is dight,
Where still a few rays slant,
That even heaven seems extravagant.
On the earth's edge mountains and trees
Stand as they were on air graven,
Or as the vessels in a haven
Await the morning breeze.
I fancy even
Through your defiles windeth the way to heaven;
And yonder still, in spite of history's page,
Linger the golden and the silver age;
Upon the laboring gale
The news of future centuries is brought,
And of new dynasties of thought,
From your remotest vale.

But special I remember thee,
Wachusett, who like me
Standest alone without society.
Thy far blue eye,
A remnant of the sky,

Seen through the clearing or the gorge,
Or from the windows of the forge,
Doth leaven all it passes by.
Nothing is true,
But stands 'tween me and you,
Thou western pioneer,
Who knowst not shame nor fear,
By venturous spirit driven,
Under the eaves of heaven,
And can'st expand thee there,
And breathe enough of air?
Upholding heaven, holding down earth,
Thy pastime from they birth,
Not steadied by the one, nor leaning on the other;
May I approve myself thy worthy brother!

At length, like Rasselas, and other inhabitants of happy val-
leys, we resolved to scale the blue wall which bounds the
western horizon, though not without misgivings, that there-
after no visible fairy land would exist for us. But we will not
leap at once to our journey's end, though near, but imitate
Homer, who conducts his reader over the plain, and along the
resounding sea, though it be but to the tent of Achilles. In
the spaces of thought are the reaches of land and water, where
men go and come. The landscape lies far and fair within, and
the deepest thinker is the farthest travelled. Taking advantage
of the early hour, on a pleasant morning in July, my compan-
ion and I passed rapidly through Acton and Stow, stopping to
rest and refresh us on the bank of a small stream, a tributary
of the Assabet, in the latter town. As we traversed the cool
woods of Acton, with stout staves in our hands, we were
cheered by the song of the red-eye, the thrushes, the phœbe,
and the cuckoo; and as we passed through the open country,
we inhaled the fresh scent of every field, and all nature lay
passive, to be viewed and travelled. Every rail, every farm-
house, seen dimly in the twilight, every tinkling sound told of
peace and purity, and we moved happily along the dark roads,
enjoying not such privacy as the day leaves when it withdraws,
but such as it has not profaned. It was solitude with light,
which is better than darkness. But anon, the sound of the

mower's rifle was heard in the fields, and this, too, mingled
with the herd of days.

This part of our route lay through the country of hops.
Perhaps there is no plant which so well supplies the want of
the vine in American scenery, and reminds the traveller so of-
ten of Italy, and the South of France, as this, whether he tra-
verses the country when the hop-fields, as now, present solid
and regular masses of verdure, hanging in graceful festoons
from pole to pole, the cool coverts where fresh gales are born
to refresh the way-farer, or in September, when the women
and children, and the neighbors from far and near, are gath-
ered to pick the hops into long troughs, or later still, when
the poles stand piled in immense pyramids in the yards, or lie
in heaps by the roadside.

The culture of the hop, with the processes of picking, dry-
ing in the kiln, and packing for the market, as well as the uses
to which it is applied, so analogous to the culture and uses of
the grape, may afford a theme for future poets.

The mower in the adjacent meadow could not tell us the
name of the brook on whose banks we had rested, or whether
it had any, but his younger companion, perhaps his brother,
knew that it was Great Brook. Though they stood very near
together in the field, the things they knew were very far apart;
nor did they suspect each other's reserved knowledge, till the
stranger came by. In Bolton, while we rested on the rails of a
cottage fence, the strains of music which issued from within,
perhaps in compliment to us sojourners, reminded us that
thus far men were fed by the accustomed pleasures. So soon
did we begin to learn that man's life is rounded with the same
few facts, the same simple relations everywhere, and it is vain
to travel to find it new. The flowers grow more various ways
than he. But coming soon to higher land, which afforded a
prospect of the mountains, we thought we had not travelled
in vain, if it were only to hear a truer and wilder pronuncia-
tion of their names, from the lips of a farmer by the roadside;
not *Way*-tatic, *Way*-chusett, but *Wor*-tatic, *Wor*-chusett. It
made us ashamed of our tame and civil pronunciation, and
we looked upon him as born and bred farther west than we.
His tongue had a more generous accent than ours, as if
breath was cheaper when it wagged. A countryman, who

speaks but seldom, talks copiously, as it were, as his wife sets cream and cheese before you without stint. Before noon we had reached the highlands in the western part of Bolton, overlooking the valley of Lancaster, and affording the first fair and open prospect into the west, and here, on the top of a hill, in the shade of some oaks, near to where a spring bubbled out from a leaden pipe, we rested during the heat of the day, reading Virgil, and enjoying the scenery. It was such a place as one feels to be on the outside of the earth, for from it we could, in some measure, see the form and structure of the globe. There lay the object of our journey, coming upon us with unchanged proportions, though with a less ethereal aspect than had greeted our morning gaze, while further north, in successive order, slumbered the sister mountains along the horizon.

We could get no further into the Æneid than

—atque altæ mœnia Romæ,
—and the wall of high Rome,

before we were constrained to reflect by what myriad tests a work of genius has to be tried; that Virgil, away in Rome, two thousand years off, should have to unfold his meaning, the inspiration of Italian vales, to the pilgrim on the New England hills. This life so raw and modern, that so civil and ancient, and yet we read Virgil, mainly to be reminded of the identity of human nature in all ages, and by the poet's own account, we are both the children of a late age, and live equally under the reign of Jupiter.

"He shook honey from the leaves, and removed fire,
And stayed the wine, everywhere flowing in rivers,
That experience, by meditating, might invent various arts
By degrees, and seek the blade of corn in furrows,
And strike out hidden fire from the veins of the flint."

The old world stands severely behind the new, as one mountain yonder towers behind another, more dim and distant. Rome imposes her story still upon this late generation. The very children in the school we have this morning passed, have gone through her wars, and recited her alarms, ere they have heard of the wars of the neighboring Lancaster. The

roving eye still rests inevitably on her hills. She still holds up
the skirts of the sky, and makes the past remote.

The lay of the land hereabouts is well worthy the attention
of the traveller. The hill on which we were resting makes
part of an extensive range, running from south-west to north-
east, across the country, and separating the waters of the
Nashua from those of the Concord, whose banks we had left
in the morning, and by bearing in mind this fact, we could
easily determine whither each brook was bound that crossed
our path. Parallel to this, and fifteen miles further west, be-
yond the deep and broad valley in which lie Groton, Shirley,
Lancaster, and Boylston, runs the Wachusett range, in the
same general direction. The descent into the valley on the
Nashua side is, by far, the most sudden; and a couple of miles
brought us to the southern branch of that river, a shallow but
rapid stream, flowing between high and gravelly banks. But
we soon learned that there were no *gelidæ valles* into which we
had descended, and missing the coolness of the morning air,
feared it had become the sun's turn to try his power upon us.

> "The sultry sun had gained the middle sky,
>   And not a tree, and not an herb was nigh,"

and with melancholy pleasure we echoed the melodious plaint
of our fellow-traveller Hassan, in the desert,

> "Sad was the hour, and luckless was the day,
>   When first from Schiraz's walls I bent my way."

The air lay lifeless between the hills, as in a seething cal-
dron, with no leaf stirring, and instead of the fresh odor of
grass and clover, with which we had before been regaled, the
dry scent of every herb seemed merely medicinal. Yielding,
therefore, to the heat, we strolled into the woods, and along
the course of a rivulet, on whose banks we loitered, observing
at our leisure the products of these new fields. He who tra-
verses the woodland paths, at this season, will have occasion
to remember the small drooping bell-like flowers and slender
red stem of the dogs-bane, and the coarser stem and berry of
the poke, which are both common in remoter and wilder
scenes; and if "the sun casts such a reflecting heat from the
sweet fern," as makes him faint, when he is climbing the bare

hills, as they complained who first penetrated into these parts, the cool fragrance of the swamp pink restores him again, when traversing the valleys between.

On we went, and late in the afternoon refreshed ourselves by bathing our feet in every rill that crossed the road, and anon, as we were able to walk in the shadows of the hills, recovered our morning elasticity. Passing through Sterling, we reached the banks of the Stillwater, in the western part of the town, at evening, where is a small village collected. We fancied that there was already a certain western look about this place, a smell of pines and roar of water, recently confined by dams, belying its name, which were exceedingly grateful. When the first inroad has been made, a few acres levelled, and a few houses erected, the forest looks wilder than ever. Left to herself, nature is always more or less civilized, and delights in a certain refinement; but where the axe has encroached upon the edge of the forest, the dead and unsightly limbs of the pine, which she had concealed with green banks of verdure, are exposed to sight. This village had, as yet, no post-office, nor any settled name. As we entered upon its street, the villagers gazed after us, with a complacent, almost compassionate look, as if we were just making our debut in the world, at a late hour. "Nevertheless," did they seem to say, "come and study us, and learn men and manners." So is each one's world but a clearing in the forest, so much open and inclosed ground. The landlord had not yet returned from the field with his men, and the cows had yet to be milked. But though we met with no very hospitable reception here at first, we remembered the inscription on the wall of the Swedish inn, and were comforted, "You will find at Trolhate excellent bread, meat, and wine, provided you bring them with you." But I must confess it did somewhat disturb our pleasure, in this withdrawn spot, to have our own village newspaper handed us by our host, as if the greatest charm the country offered to the traveller was the facility of communication with the town. Let it recline on its own everlasting hills, and not be looking out from their summits for some petty Boston or New York in the horizon.

At intervals we heard the murmuring of water, and the slumberous breathing of crickets throughout the night, and

left the inn the next morning in the grey twilight, after it had
been hallowed by the night air, and when only the innocent
cows were stirring, with a kind of regret. It was only four
miles to the base of the mountain, and the scenery was al-
ready more picturesque. Our road lay along the course of the
Stillwater, which was breaking at the bottom of a deep ravine,
filled with pines and rocks, tumbling fresh from the moun-
tains, so soon, alas! to commence its career of usefulness. At
first a cloud hung between us and the summit, but it was
soon blown away. As we gathered the raspberries, which grew
abundantly by the roadside, that action seemed consistent
with a lofty prudence, as well as agreeable to the palate, as if
the traveller who ascends into a mountainous region should
fortify himself by eating of such light ambrosial fruits as grow
there, and drinking of the springs which gush out from the
mountain sides, as he gradually inhales the subtler and purer
atmosphere of those elevated places, thus propitiating the
mountain gods, by a sacrifice of their own fruits. The gross
products of the plains and valleys are for such as dwell therein;
but surely the juices of this berry have relation to the thin air
of the mountain tops.

In due time we began to ascend the mountain, passing,
first, through a maple wood, then a denser forest, which grad-
ually became dwarfed, till there were no trees whatever. We at
length pitched our tent on the summit. It is but nineteen
hundred feet above the village of Princeton, and three thou-
sand above the level of the sea; but by this slight elevation, it
is infinitely removed from the plain, and when we have
reached it, we feel a sense of remoteness, as if we had travelled
into distant regions, to Arabia Petrea, or the farthest east, so
withdrawn and solitary it seems. A robin upon a staff, was the
highest object in sight, thus easily triumphing over the height
of nature. Swallows were flying about us, and the chewink
and cuckoos were heard near at hand. The summit consists of
a few acres, destitute of trees, covered with bare rocks, inter-
spersed with blueberry bushes, raspberries, gooseberries,
strawberries, moss, and a fine wiry grass. The common yellow
lily, and dwarf cornel, grow abundantly in the crevices of the
rocks. This clear space, which is gently rounded, is bounded a
few feet lower by a thick shrubbery of oaks, with maples, as-

pens, beeches, cherries, and occasionally a mountain-ash intermingled, among which we found the bright blueberries of the Solomon's Seal, and the fruit of the pyrola. From the foundation of a wooden observatory, which was formerly erected on the highest point, forming a rude hollow structure of stone, a dozen feet in diameter, and five or six in height, we could dimly see Monadnock, rising in simple grandeur, in the north-west, nearly a thousand feet higher, still the "far blue mountain," though with an altered profile. But the first day the weather was so hazy that it was in vain we endeavored to unravel the obscurity. It was like looking into the sky again, and the patches of forest here and there seemed to flit like clouds over a lower heaven. As to voyagers of an aerial Polynesia, the earth seemed like an island in the ether; on every side, even as low as we, the sky shutting down, like an unfathomable deep, around it. A blue Pacific island, where who knows what islanders inhabit? and as we sail near its shores we see the waving of trees, and hear the lowing of kine.

We read Virgil and Wordsworth in our tent, with new pleasure there, while waiting for a clearer atmosphere, nor did the weather prevent our appreciating the simple truth and beauty of Peter Bell:

> "And he had lain beside his asses,
>   On lofty Cheviot hills."

> "And he had trudged through Yorkshire dales,
>   Among the rocks and winding *scars*,
>   Where deep and low the hamlets lie
>   Beneath their little patch of sky,
>   And little lot of stars."

Who knows but this hill may one day be a Helvellyn, or even a Parnassus, and the Muses haunt here, and other Homers frequent the neighboring plains,

> Not unconcerned Wachusett rears his head
>   Above the field, so late from nature won,
> With patient brow reserved, as one who read
>   New annals in the history of man.

The blueberries which the mountain afforded, added to the milk we had brought, made our frugal supper, while for entertainment, the even-song of the wood-thrush rung along the ridge. Our eyes rested on no painted ceiling, nor carpeted hall, but on skies of nature's painting, and hills and forests of her embroidery. Before sunset, we rambled along the ridge to the north, while a hawk soared still above us. It was a place where gods might wander, so solemn and solitary, and removed from all contagion with the plain. As the evening came on, the haze was condensed in vapor, and the landscape became more distinctly visible, and numerous sheets of water were brought to light,

> Et jam summa procul villarum culmina fumant,
> Majoresque cadunt altis de montibus umbræ.
>
> And now the tops of the villas smoke afar off,
> And the shadows fall longer from the high mountains.

As we stood on the stone tower while the sun was setting, we saw the shades of night creep gradually over the valleys of the east, and the inhabitants withdrew to their houses, and shut their doors, while the moon silently rose up, and took possession of that part. And then the same scene was repeated on the west side, as far as the Connecticut and the Green Mountains, and the sun's rays fell on us two alone, of all New England men.

It was the night but one before the full of the moon, so that we enjoyed uninterrupted light, so bright that we could see to read Wordsworth distinctly, and when in the evening we strolled on the summit, there was a fire blazing on Monadnock, which lighted up the whole western horizon, and by making us aware of a community of mountains, made our position seem less solitary. But at length the wind drove us to the shelter of our tent, and we closed its door for the night, and fell asleep.

It was a rich treat to hear the wind roar over the rocks, at intervals, when we waked, for it had grown quite cold and windy. The night was, in its elements, simple even to majesty in that bleak place—a bright moonlight and a piercing wind. It was at no time darker than twilight within the tent, and we could easily see the moon through its transparent roof as we lay; for there was the moon still above us, with Jupiter and Saturn on either hand, looking down on Wachusett, and it was a satisfaction to know that they were our fellow-travellers still, as high and out of our reach, as our own destiny. Truly the stars were given for a consolation to man. We should not know but our life were fated to be always grovelling, but it is permitted to behold them, and surely they are deserving of a fair destiny. We see laws which never fail, of whose failure we never conceived; and their lamps burn all the night, too, as well as all day, so rich and lavish is that nature, which can afford this superfluity of light.

The morning twilight began as soon as the moon had set, and we arose and kindled our fire, whose blaze might have been seen for thirty miles around. As the day-light increased, it was remarkable how rapidly the wind went down. There was no dew on the summit, but coldness supplied its place. When the dawn had reached its prime, we enjoyed the view of a distinct horizon line, and could fancy ourselves at sea, and the distant hills the waves in the horizon, as seen from the deck of a vessel. The cherry-birds flitted around us, the nesthatch and flicker were heard among the bushes, the tit-mouse perched within a few feet, and the song of the woodthrush again rung along the ridge. At length we saw the sun rise up out of the sea, and shine on Massachusetts, and from this moment the atmosphere grew more and more transparent till the time of our departure, and we began to re-alize the extent of the view, and how the earth, in some de-gree, answered to the heavens in breadth, the white villages to the constellations in the sky. There was little of the sublimity and grandeur which belong to mountain scenery, but an im-mense landscape to ponder on a summer's day. We could see how ample and roomy is nature. As far as the eye could reach, there was little life in the landscape; the few birds that flitted past did not crowd. The travellers on the remote highways, which intersect the country on every side, had no fellow-travellers for miles, before or behind. On every side, the eye ranged over successive circles of towns, rising one above an-other, like the terraces of a vineyard, till they were lost in the horizon. Wachusett is, in fact, the observatory of the state.

There lay Massachusetts, spread out before us in its length and breadth, like a map. There was the level horizon, which told of the sea on the east and south, the well-known hills of New Hampshire on the north, and the misty summit of the Hoosac and Green Mountains, first made visible to us the evening before, blue and unsubstantial, like some bank of clouds which the morning wind would dissipate, on the north-west and west. These last distant ranges, on which the eye rests unwearied, commence with an abrupt boulder in the north, beyond the Connecticut, and travel southward, with three or four peaks dimly seen. But Monadnock, rearing its masculine front in the north-west, is the grandest feature. As we beheld it we knew that it was the height of land between the two rivers, on this side the valley of the Merrimack, or that of the Connecticut, fluctuating with their blue seas of air. These rival vales, gradually extending their population and commerce along their respective streams, to what destiny who shall tell? Watatic, and the neighboring hills in this state and in New Hampshire, are a continuation of the same elevated range on which we were standing. But that New Hampshire bluff—that promontory of a state—causing day and night on this our state of Massachussets, will longest haunt our dreams.

We could, at length, realize the place mountains occupy on the land, and how they come into the general scheme of the universe. When first we climb their summits, and observe their lesser irregularities, we do not give credit to the comprehensive intelligence which shaped them; but when afterward we behold their outlines in the horizon, we confess that the hand which moulded their opposite slopes, making one to balance the other, worked round a deep centre, and was privy to the plan of the universe. So is the least part of nature in its bearings, referred to all space. These lesser mountain ranges, as well as the Alleghanies, run from north-east to south-west, and parallel with these mountain streams are the more fluent rivers, answering to the general direction of the coast, the bank of the great ocean stream itself. Even the clouds, with their thin bars, fall into the same direction by preference, and such is the course of the prevailing winds, and the migration of men and birds. A mountain chain determines many things for the statesman and philosopher. The improvements of civilization rather creep along its sides than cross its summit. How often is it a barrier to prejudice and fanaticism? In passing over these heights of land, through their thin atmosphere, the follies of the plain are refined and purified. As many species of plants do not scale their summits, so many species of folly do not cross the Alleghanies; it is only the hardy mountain plant that creeps quite over the ridge, and descends into the valley beyond.

It adds not a little grandeur to our conception of the flight of birds, especially of the duck tribe, and such as fly high in the air, to have ascended a mountain. We can now see what landmarks they are to their migrations; how the Catskills and Highlands have hardly sunk to them, when Wachusett and Monadnock open a passage to the north-east—how they are guided, too, in their course by the rivers and valleys, and who knows but by the stars, as well as the mountain ranges, and not by the petty landmarks which we use? The bird whose eye takes in the Green Mountains on the one side, and the ocean on the other, need not be at a loss to find its way.

At noon we descended the mountain, and having returned to the abodes of men, turned our faces to the east again; measuring our progress, from time to time, by the more ethereal hues, which the mountain assumed. Passing swiftly through Stillwater and Sterling, as with a downward impetus, (the reader will excuse the abruptness of the descent,) we found ourselves almost at home again in the green meadows of Lancaster, so like our own Concord, for both are watered by two streams which unite near their centres, and have many other features in common. There is an unexpected refinement about this scenery; level prairies of great extent, interspersed with elms, and hop-fields, and groves of trees, give it almost a classic appearance. This, it will be remembered, was the scene of Mrs. Rowlandson's capture, and of other events in the Indian wars, but from this July afternoon, and under that mild exterior, those times seemed as remote as the irruption of the Goths. They were the dark age of New England. On beholding a picture of a New England village as it then appeared, with a fair open prospect, and a light on trees and rivers, as if it were broad noon, we find we had not thought the sun shone in those days, or that men lived in broad daylight then. We do not imagine the sun shining on hill and valley during Philip's war, nor on the war-path of Paugus, or Standish, or Church, or Lovell, with serene summer weather, but a dim twilight or night did those events transpire in. They must have fought in the shade of their own dusky deeds.

At length, as we plodded along the dusty roads, our thoughts became as dusty as they; all thought indeed stopped, thinking broke down, or proceeded only passively in a sort of rhythmical cadence of the confused material of thought, and we found ourselves mechanically repeating some familiar measure which timed with our tread; some verse of the Robin Hood ballads, for instance, which one can recommend to travel by.

> "Swearers are swift, sayd lyttle John,
>   As the wind blows over the hill;
> For if it be never so loud this night,
>   To-morrow it may be still."

And so it went up hill and down till a stone interrupted the line, when a new verse was chosen.

> "His shoote it was but loosely shot,
>   Yet flewe not the arrowe in vaine,
> For it met one of the sheriffe's men,
>   And William-a-Trent was slaine."

There is, however, this consolation to the most way-worn traveller, upon the dustiest road, that the path his feet describe is so perfectly symbolical of human life—now climbing the hills, now descending into the vales. From the summits he beholds the heavens and the horizon, from the vales he looks up to the heights again. He is treading his old lessons still, and though he may be very weary and travel-worn, it is yet sincere experience.

Leaving the Nashua, we changed our route a little, and arrived at Stillriver village, in the western part of Harvard, just as the sun was setting. From this place, which lies to the northward, upon the western slope of the same range of hills, on which we had spent the noon before, in the adjacent town, the prospect is beautiful, and the grandeur of the mountain outlines unsurpassed. There was such a repose and quiet here at this hour, as if the very hill-sides were enjoying the scene, and as we passed slowly along, looking back over the country we had traversed, and listening to the evening song of the robin, we could not help contrasting the equanimity of nature with the bustle and impatience of man. His words and actions presume always a crisis near at hand, but she is forever silent and unpretending.

We rested that night at Harvard, and the next morning, while one bent his steps to the nearer village of Groton, the other took his separate and solitary way to the peaceful meadows of Concord; but let him not forget to record the brave hospitality of a farmer and his wife, who generously entertained him at their board, though the poor wayfarer could only congratulate the one on the continuance of hayweather, and silently accept the kindness of the other. Refreshed by this instance of generosity, no less than by the substantial viands set before him, he pushed forward with new vigor, and reached the banks of the Concord before the sun had climbed many degrees into the heavens.

And now that we have returned to the desert life of the plain, let us endeavor to impart a little of that mountain grandeur into it. We will remember within what walls we lie, and understand that this level life too has its summit, and why from the mountain top the deepest valleys have a tinge of blue; that there is elevation in every hour, as no part of the earth is so low that the heavens may not be seen from, and we have only to stand on the summit of our hour to command an uninterrupted horizon.

Sir Walter Raleigh

PERHAPS no one in English history better represents the heroic character than Sir Walter Raleigh; for Sidney has got to be almost as shadowy as Arthur himself. Raleigh's somewhat antique & Roman virtues appear in his numerous military and naval adventures, in his knightly conduct toward the Queen, in his poems and his employments in the tower, and not least in his death, but more than all in his constant soldier-like bearing and promise. He was the Bayard of peaceful as well as warlike enterprise, & few lives which are the subject of recent & trustworthy history are so agreeable to the imagination. Notwithstanding his temporary unpopularity, he especially possessed those prevalent and popular qualities which command the admiration of men. If an English Plutarch were to be written, Raleigh would be the best Greek or Roman among them all. He was one whose virtues if they were not distinctly great yet gave to virtue a current stamp and value as it were by the very grace and loftiness with which he carried them—one of nature's noblemen, who possessed the requisites to true nobility, without which no heraldry nor blood can avail. Among savages he would still have been the chief. He seems to have had, not a profounder or grander, but, so to speak, more, nature, than other men. The enthusiastic and often extravagant, but always hearty & emphatic tone in which he is spoken of by his contemporaries is not the least remarkable fact about him, and it does not matter much whether the current stories are true or not, since they at least prove his reputation.

It is not his praise to have been a saint and a seer in his generation, but "one of the gallantest worthies that ever England bred". The stories about him testify to a character rather than a virtue. As, for instance, that "he was damnably proud. Old Sir Robert Harley, of Brampton-Brian Castle, (who knew him), would say, 'twas a great question, who was the proudest, Sir Walter or Sir Thomas Overbury, but the difference that was, was judged on Sir Thomas' side;" that "In his youth his companions were boisterous blades, but generally those that had wit." A young contemporary says, "I have heard his enemies confess, that he was one of the weightiest and wisest men that this island ever bred". And another gives this character of him—"Who hath not known or read of this prodigy of wit and fortune, Sir Walter Raleigh, a man unfortunate in nothing else but in the greatness of his wit and advancement, whose eminent worth was such, both in domestic policy, foreign expeditions, and discoveries, in arts and literature, both practic and contemplative, that it might seem at once, to conquer example and imitation".

And what we are told of his personal appearance is accordant with the rest; that "he had in the outward man a good presence, in a handsome and well-compacted person", that "he was a tall, handsome, and bold man," and his "was thought a very good face", though "his countenance was somewhat spoiled by the unusual height of his forehead." "He was such a person (every way), that (as King Charles I. says of the Lord Strafford) a prince would rather be afraid of, than ashamed of—" and had an "awfulness and ascendency in his aspect over other mortals". And we are not disappointed to learn that he indulged in a splendid dress, and "notwithstanding his so great mastership in style, and his conversation with the learnedest and politest persons, yet he spake broad Devonshire to his dying day."

Such a character as this was well suited to the times in which he lived. His age was an unusually stirring one. The discovery of America and the successful progress of the Reformation opened a field for both the intellectual and physical energies of his generation. Its fathers were Calvin, and Knox, and Cranmer, and Pizarro, and Garcilaso; and its immediate forefathers Luther, and Raphael, and Bayard, and Angelo, and Ariosto, and Copernicus, and Machiavel, and Erasmus, and Cabot, and Ximenes, and Columbus. Its device might have been an anchor, a sword, and a quill. The Pizarro laid by his sword at intervals and took to his letters. The Columbus set sail for newer worlds still, by voyages which needed not the patronage of princes. The Bayard alighted from his steed to seek adventures no less arduous than heretofore, upon the ocean, and in the western world; and the Luther who had reformed religion, began now to reform politics and science.

In his youth, however it may have concerned him, Camoens was writing a heroic poem in Portugal, and the arts still had their representative in Paul Veronese of Italy. He may have been one to welcome the works of Tasso and Montaigne to England, and when he looked about him, have found such men as Cervantes & Sidney, men of like pursuits & not altogether dissimilar genius from himself, for his contemporaries, a Drake to rival him on the sea, and a Hudson in western adventure, a Halley, a Galileo, and a Kepler, for his astronomers, a Bacon, a Behmen, and a Burton, for his philosophers, and a Jonson—a Spenser, and a Shakspeare, his poets for refreshment and inspiration.

But that we may know how worthy he himself was to make one of this illustrious company, and appreciate this great activity and versatility of his genius, we will glance hastily at the various aspects of his life.

He was a proper knight, a born cavalier, and in the intervals of war betook himself still to the most vigorous arts of peace, though as if diverted from his proper aim. He makes us doubt if there is not some worthier apology for war than has been discovered, for its modes and manners were an instinct with him, and though in his writings he takes frequent occasion sincerely to condemn its folly, and show the better policy and advantage of peace, yet he speaks with the uncertain authority of a warrior still, to whom those juster wars are not simply the dire necessity implied. In whatever he is engaged we seem to see a plume waving over his head, and a sword dangling at his side. Born in 1552, the last year of the reign of Edward VI, we find that not long after, by such instinct as the young crab seeks the sea shore, he has already marched into France, as one of "a troop of a hundred gentlemen volunteers", who are described as "a gallant company, nobly mounted and accoutred, having on their colors the motto, *Finem det mihi virtus*"—Let valor be my end. And so in fact he marched on through life with this motto in his heart always.

All the peace of those days seems to have been but a truce, or casual interruption of the order of war. War with Spain especially was so much the rule rather than the exception, that the navigators and commanders of these two nations when abroad, acted on the presumption that their countries were at war at home, though they had left them at peace, and their respective colonies in America carried on war at their convenience with no infraction of the treaties between the mother countries. Raleigh especially seems to have regarded the Spaniards as his natural enemies, and he was not backward to develop this part of his nature.

When England was threatened with foreign invasion, the Queen looked to him especially for advice and assistance, and none was better able to give them than he. We cannot but admire the tone in which he speaks of his island, and how it is to be best defended, and the navy its chief strength maintained and improved. He speaks from England as his castle and his, as no other man's, is the voice of the state, for he does not assert the interests of an individual but of a commonwealth, and we see in him revived a Roman patriotism. His actions as they were public and for the public, were fit to be publicly rewarded, and we accordingly read with equanimity of gold chains and monopolies and other emoluments conferred on him from time to time for his various services—his military successes in Ireland "that commonwealth of common woe", as he even then described it,—his enterprise in the harbor of Cadiz,—his capture of Fayal from the Spaniards, and other exploits which perhaps more than anything else got him fame and a name during his life time.

If war was his earnest work, it was his pastime too, for in the peaceful intervals we hear of his participating heartily and bearing off the palm in the birth-day tournaments and tilting matches of the Queen, where the combatants vied with each other mainly who should come on to the ground in the most splendid dress and equipments—those tilts where it is said that his political rival Essex, whose wealth enabled him to lead the costliest train, but who ran very ill, and was thought the poorest knight of all, was wont to change his suit from orange to green, that it might be said that there was one in green who ran worse than one in orange.

None of the worthies of that age can be duly appreciated if we neglect to consider them in their relation to the new world. The stirring spirits stood with but one foot on the land. There were Drake, Hawkins, Hudson, Frobisher, and many others, and their worthy companion was Raleigh. As a navigator and naval commander he had few equals, and if the reader who has attended to his other actions inquires how he filled up the odd years, he will find that they were spent in numerous voyages to America, for the purposes of discovery and colonization, so that he would be more famous for these enterprises if they were not overshadowed by the number and variety of his pursuits.

His persevering care and oversight as the patron of Virginia, discovered and planted under his auspices in 1584 present him in an interesting light to the American reader. The work of colonization was well suited to his genius, and if the security of England herself had not required his attention and presence at this time he would possibly have realized some of his dreams in plantations and cities on our coast.

England has since felt the benefit of his experience in naval affairs. He was one of the first to assert their importance to her and exerted himself especially for the improvement of naval architecture on which he has left a treatise. And he also composed a discourse on the art of war at sea, a subject which at that time had never been treated.

We can least bear to consider Raleigh as a courtier, though the court of England at that time was a field not altogether unworthy of such a courtier. His competitors for fame and favor there, were Burleigh, Leicester, Sussex, Buckingham, and, be it remembered, Sir Philip Sidney, whose Arcadia was just finished when Raleigh came to court—his natural companion and other self, as it were, as if nature, in her anxiety to confer one specimen of a true knight and courtier on that age, had cast two in the same mould, lest one should miscarry. These two kindred spirits are said to have been mutually attracted toward each other. And there too was Queen Elizabeth herself, the centre of the court and of the kingdom, to whose service he consecrates himself, not so much as a subject to his sovereign, but as a knight to the service of his mistress. His intercourse with the Queen may well have begun with the incident of the cloak, for such continued to be its character afterwards. It has in the description an air of romance and might fitly have made a part of his friend Sidney's Arcadia. We are inclined to consider him as some knight, and a knight errant too, who had strayed into the precincts of the court, and practised there the arts which he had learned in bower and hall and in the lists.—Not that he knew not how to govern states as well as queens, but he brought to the task the gallantry and graces of chivalry as well as the judgment and experience of a practical modern Englishman. "The Queen", says one, "began to be taken with his elocution, and loved to hear his reasons to her demands, and the truth is she took him for a kind of oracle which nettled them all." He rose rapidly in her favor and became her indispensable counsellor in all matters which concerned the state, for he was minutely acquainted with the affairs of England, and none better understood her commercial interests. But though he made a good use of his influence for the most part when obtained, he could descend to the grossest flattery to obtain it, and we could wish him forever banished from the court, whose favors he so earnestly sought. But that he who was one while "the Queen of England's poor captive," could sometimes assume a manly and independent tone with her appears from his answer when she once exclaimed, on his asking a favor for a friend, "When, Sir Walter, will you cease to be a beggar?" "When your gracious majesty ceases to be a benefactor."

His court life exhibits him in mean and frivolous relations which make him lose that respect in our eyes which he had acquired elsewhere. The base use he made of his recovered influence, (after having been banished from the court and even suffered imprisonment in consequence of the Queen's displeasure,) to procure the disgrace and finally the execution of his rival Essex, who had been charged with treason, is the foulest stain upon his escutcheon, the one which it is hardest to reconcile with the nobleness and generosity which we are inclined to attribute to such a character. Revenge is most unheroic. Also his acceptance of bribes afterwards for using his influence in behalf of the Earl's adherents is not to be excused by the usage of the times. The times may change, but the laws of integrity and magnanimity are immutable. Nor are the terms on which he was the friend of Cecil, from motives of policy merely, more tolerable to consider. Yet we cannot but think that he frequently travelled a higher, though a parallel course with the mob, and though he had their suffrage, to some extent deserves the praise which Jonson applies to another—

"That to the vulgar canst thyself apply,
Treading a better path not contrary."

We gladly make haste to consider him in what the world calls his misfortune, after the death of Elizabeth and the accession of James 1st, when his essentially nobler nature was separated from the base company of the court, and the contaminations which his loyalty could not resist, though by imprisonment and the scaffold.

His enemies had already prejudiced the king against him before his accession to the throne, and when at length the English nobility were presented to his majesty, who, it will be remembered, was a Scotchman, and Raleigh's name was told, "Raleigh", exclaimed the king, "O my soule, mon, I have heard rawly of thee." His efforts to limit the king's power of introducing Scots into England, contributed to increase his jealousy and dislike, and he was shortly after accused by Lord Cobham of participating in a conspiracy to place the Lady Arabella Stuart on the throne, and owing mainly, it is thought, to the King's resentment, was tried and falsely convicted of high treason—though his accuser retracted in writing his whole accusation before the conclusion of the trial.

In connexion with his behavior to Essex, it should be remembered that by his conduct on his own trial he in a great measure removed the ill-will which existed against him on that account. At his trial, which is said to have been most unjustly and insolently conducted by Sir Edward Coke on the part of the Crown, "He answered" says one, "with that temper, wit, learning, courage, and judgment, that save that it went with the hazzard of his life, it was the happiest day that ever he spent. The two first that brought the news [of his condemnation] to the king were Roger Ashton, and a Scotsman, whereof one affirmed that never any man spake so well in times past, nor would do in the world to come: and the other said, that whereas when he saw him first, he was so led with the common hatred, that he would have gone a hundred miles to have seen him hanged, he would, ere he parted, have gone a thousand to have saved his life." Another says he "behaved himself so worthily, so wisely, and so temperately, that in half a day the mind of all the company was changed from the extremest hate to the extremest pity." And another "to the lords humble, but not prostrate; to the jury affable, but not fawning; to the king's counsel patient, but not yielding to the imputations laid upon him, or neglecting to repel them with the spirit which became an injured and honorable man." And finally he followed the sheriff out of court in the expressive words of Sir Thomas Overbury, "with admirable erection, but yet in such sort as became a man condemned."

Raleigh prepared himself for immediate execution, but after his pretended accomplices had gone through the ceremony of a mock execution and been pardoned by the King, it satisfied the policy of his enemies to retain him a prisoner in the tower for 13 years, with the sentence of death still unrevoked. In the meanwhile he solaced himself in his imprisonment with writing a history of the world and cultivating poetry and philosophy as the noblest deeds compatible with his confinement.

It is satisfactory to contrast with his mean personal relations while at court his connexion in the tower with the young prince Henry whose tastes and aspirations were of a stirring kind, as his friend and instructor. He addresses some of his shorter pieces to him, and in some instances they seem to have been written expressly for his use. He preaches to him as he was well able, from experience, a wiser philosophy than he had himself practised, and was particularly anxious to correct in him a love of popularity—which he had discovered, and gave him useful maxims for his conduct when he should take his father's place.

He lost neither health nor spirits by 13 years of captivity, but after having spent this the literary era of his life as in the retirement of his study, and having written the history of the old world, he began to dream of actions which would supply materials to the future historian of the new. It is interesting to consider him, a close prisoner as he was, preparing for voyages and adventures, which would require to roam more broadly than was consistent with the comfort or ambition of his freest contemporaries.

Already in 1595 8 years before his imprisonment, it will be remembered he had undertaken his first voyage to Guiana in person—mainly it is said to recover favor with the Queen—but doubtless it was much more to recover favor with himself and exercise his genius in fields more worthy of him than a corrupt court.

He continued to cherish this his favorite project, though a prisoner, and at length in the 13th year of his imprisonment, though the influence of his friends, and his confident assertions respecting the utility of the expedition to his country, he obtained his release and set sail for Guiana with twelve ships. But unfortunately he neglected to procure a formal pardon from the king, trusting to the opinion of Lord Bacon that this was unnecessary, since the sentence of death against him was virtually annulled, by the lives of others being committed to his hands. Acting on this presumption, and with the best intentions toward his country, and only his usual jealousy of Spain, he undertook to make good his engagements to himself and this world.

It is not easy for us at this day to realize what extravagant expectations Europe had formed respecting the wealth of the new world. We might suppose two whole continents with their adjacent seas & oceans, equal to the present known globe—stretching from pole to pole, and possessing every variety of soil, climate and productions, lying unexplored today—what would be the speculations of Broadway & State street?

The few travellers who had penetrated into the country of Guiana, whither Raleigh was bound, brought back accounts of noble streams flowing through majestic forests and a depth and luxuriance of soil which made England seem a barren waste in comparison. Its mineral wealth was reported to be as inexhaustible as the cupidity of its discoverers was unbounded. The very surface of the ground was said to be resplendent with gold, and men went covered with gold-dust, as Hottentots with grease. Raleigh was informed while at Trinidad by the Spanish governor who was his prisoner, that one John Martinez had at length penetrated into this country and the stories told by him of the wealth and extent of its cities, surpass the narratives of Marco Polo himself. He is said, in particular, to have reached the city of Manoa, to which he first gave the name of El Dorado, or The Gilded, the Indians conducting him blindfolded, "not removing the veil from his eyes till he was ready to enter the city. It was at noon that he passed the gates, and it took him all that day and the next, walking from sunrise to sunset, before he arrived at the Palace of Inga, where he resided for seven months, till he had made himself master of the language of the country". These, and even more fanciful accounts had Raleigh heard and pondered, both before and after his first visit to the country. No one was more familiar with the stories, both true and fabulous, respecting the discovery and resources of the new world, and none had a better right to know what great commanders and navigators had done there or anywhere than he. Such information would naturally flow to him of its own accord. That his ardor and faith were hardly cooled by actual observation may be gathered from the tone of his own description. He was the first Englishman who ascended the Orinoco, and he thus describes the adjacent country.

"On the banks were divers sorts of fruits good to eat, besides flowers and trees, of that variety as would be sufficient to make ten volumes of herbals. We relieved ourselves many times with the fruits of the country, and sometimes with fowl and fish; we saw also birds of all colors,—some carnation, some crimson, some tawny, purple, green, watched, and of all other sorts, both simple and mixed; as it was unto us a great good passing of the time to behold them."

The following is his description of the waterfalls and the province of Canuri, through which last the river runs.

"When we ascended to the tops of the first hills of the plains adjoining to the river, we beheld that wonderful breach of waters which was precipitated down Caroli, and might from that mountain see the river how it ran in three parts above twenty miles off; there appeared ten or twelve falls in sight, every one as high over the other as a church-tower, the water descending with that fury that the rebound made it seem as if it had been all covered over with a great shower of rain, and in some places we took it for a smoke that had risen over some great town. For mine own part I was well persuaded from thence to have returned, being a very ill footman; but the rest were all so desirous to go near the said strange thunder of waters, as they drew me on by little and little into the next valley. . . . . I never saw a more beautiful country nor more lively prospects: hills so raised here and there over the valleys; the river winding into divers branches; the plains adjoining, without bush or stubble, all fair green grass; the ground of hard sand, easy to march on either for horse or foot; the deer crossing in every path; the birds towards the evening singing on every tree with a thousand several tunes; cranes and herons, of white, crimson and carnation, perching on the river's side; the air fresh, with a gentle easterly wind; and every stone that we stopped to take up promising either gold or silver by his complexion."

In another place he says "To conclude, it is a country as yet untouched by the natives of the old world: never sacked, turned, or wrought; the face of the earth hath not been torn, nor the virtue and salt of the soil spent by manurance."

To the fabulous accounts of preceding adventurers Raleigh added many others equally absurd and poetical, as for instance, of a tribe "with eyes in their shoulders, and mouths in their breasts,"—but, it seems to us, with entire good faith, and no such flagrant intent to deceive as he has been accused of. "Weak policy it would be in me", says he, "to betray myself or my country with imaginations; neither am I so far in love with that watching, care, peril, disease, hard fare, and other mischiefs that accompany such voyages, as to woo myself again into any of them, were I not assured that the sun covereth not so much riches in any other part of the earth." It is easy to see that he was tempted not so much by the lustre of the gold, as by the splendor of the enterprise itself. It was the best move that peace allowed. The expeditions to Guiana and the ensuing golden dreams were not wholly unworthy of him, though he accomplished little more in the first voyage than to take formal possession of the country in the name of the Queen, and in the second, of the Spanish town of St. Thomas, as his enemies would say, in the name of himself. Perceiving that the Spaniards, who had been secretly informed of his designs through their ambassador in England, were prepared to thwart his endeavors, and resist his progress in the country, he procured the capture of this their principal town, which was also burnt against his orders.

But it seems to us that no *particular* exception is to be taken against these high-handed measures, though his enemies have made the greatest handle of them. His behavior on this occasion was part and parcel of his constant character. It would not be easy to say when he ceased to be an honorable soldier and became a freebooter, nor indeed is it of so much importance to inquire of a man what actions he performed at one and what at another period, as what manner of man he was at all periods. It was after all the same Raleigh who had won so much renown by land & sea, at home and abroad. It was his forte to deal vigorously with men, whether as a statesman, a courtier, a navigator, a planter of colonies, an accused person, a prisoner, an explorer of continents, or a military or naval commander, and it was a right hero's maxim of his that "good success admits of no examination", which in a liberal sense is true enough, for good success can only spring from good conduct; and that there was no cant in him on the subject of war, appears from his saying which indeed is very true, that "The necessity of war, which among human actions is most lawless, hath some kind of affinity and near resemblance with the necessity of law." It is to be remembered too that if the Spaniards found him a restless and uncompromising enemy—the Indians experienced in him a humane and gentle defender, and on his second visit to Guiana remembered his name and welcomed him with enthusiasm.

We are told that the Spanish Ambassador, on receiving intelligence of his doings in this country, rushed in to the presence of King James, exclaiming "Piratas—piratas"—pirates—pirates. And the king, to gratify his resentment, without bringing him to trial for this alledged new offence—with characteristic meanness and pusillanimity caused him to be executed upon the old sentence soon after his return to England.

The circumstances of his execution and how he bore himself on that memorable occasion when the sentence of death passed 15 years before was revived against him, after as a historian in his confinement he had visited the old world in his free imagination, and as an unrestrained adventurer the New, with his fleets and in person—are perhaps too well known to be repeated.—The reader will excuse our hasty rehearsal of the final scene.

We can pardon though not without hesitation his supposed attempt at suicide in the prospect of defeat and disgrace. No one can read his letter to his wife written while he was contemplating this act, without being reminded of the Roman Cato, and admiring while he condemns him. "I know", says he "that it is forbidden to destroy ourselves; but I trust it is forbidden in this sort—that we destroy not ourselves despairing of God's mercy."

Though his greatness seems to have forsaken him in his feigning himself sick and the base methods he took to avoid being brought to trial, yet he recovered himself at last, and happily withstood the trials which awaited him.

The night before his execution, besides writing letters of farewell to his wife, containing the most practical advice for the conduct of her life, he appears to have spent the time in writing verses on his condition, and among others this couplet "On the Snuff of a Candle".

> "Cowards fear to die; but courage stout,
>   Rather than live in snuff, will be put out."

And perhaps the following verses for an epitaph on himself,

> "Even such is time, that takes on trust
>   Our youth, our joys, our all we have,
>   And pays us but with age and dust;
>   Who in the dark and silent grave,
>   When we have wandered all our ways,
>   Shuts up the story of our days!
>   But from this earth, this grave, this dust,
>   The Lord shall raise me up, I trust."

His execution was appointed on Lord Mayor's day, that the pageants and shows might divert the attention of the people, but those pageants have long since been forgotten, while this tragedy is still remembered. He took a pipe of tobacco before he went to the scaffold, and appeared there with a serene countenance so that a stranger could not have told which was the condemned person. After exculpating himself in a speech to the people, and without ostentation having felt the edge of the axe, and disposed himself once as he wished to lie, he made a solemn prayer, and being directed to place himself so that his face should look to the east, his characteristic answer was "It mattered little how the head lay provided the heart was right."

The executioner being over-awed by his behavior was unable at first to perform his office—when Raleigh slowly raising his head exclaimed, "Strike away man, don't be afraid." "He was the most fearless of death," says the Bishop who attended him, "that ever was known, and the most resolute and confident, yet with reverence and conscience."

But we would not exaggerate the importance of these things—the death scenes of great men are agreeable to consider only when they make another and harmonious chapter of their lives, and we have accompanied our hero thus far, because he lived, so to speak, unto the end.

In his history of the world occurs this sentence:

"O eloquent, just, and mighty Death! Whom none could advise, thou hast persuaded, what none hath dared, thou hast done; and whom all the world hath flattered, thou only hast cast out of the world & despised; thou hast drawn together all the far-stretched greatness, all the pride, cruelty, and ambition of man, and covered it all over with these two narrow words,—Hic Iacet!"

Perhaps Raleigh was the man of the most general information and universal accomplishment of any in England. Though he excelled greatly in but few departments, yet he reached a more valuable mediocrity in many. "He seemed", said Fuller, "to be like Cato Uticensis, born to that only which he was about." He said he had been "a soldier, a sea-captain, and a courtier," but he had been much more than this. He embraced in his studies music, ornamental gardening, painting, history, antiquities, chemistry, and many arts beside. Especially he is said to have been "a great chemist," and "studied most in his sea-voyages, where he carried always a trunk of books along with him, and had nothing to divert him," and where also he carried his favorite pictures. In the tower, too, says one, "he doth spend all the day in distillations," and that this was more than a temporary recreation appears from the testimony of one who says he was operator to him for twelve years. Here also he conversed on poetry, philosophy, and literature with Hoskins, his fellow prisoner, whom Ben Jonson mentions as "the person who had polished him." He was a political economist far in advance of his age, and a sagacious and influential speaker in the House of

Commons. Science is indebted to him in more ways than one. In the midst of pressing public cares he interested himself to establish some means of universal communication between men of Science, for their mutual benefit, and actually set up what he termed, "an office of address", for this purpose. As a Mathematician he was the friend of Harriot, Dee, and the Earl of Northumberland. As an Antiquarian, he was a member of the first antiquarian society established in England, along with Spelman, Selden, Cotton, Camden, Savile, & Stow. He is said to have been the founder of the Mermaid Club, which met in Fleet Street, to which Shakspeare, Ben Jonson, Fletcher, Beaumont, Carew, Donne, &c., belonged. He has the fame of having first introduced the potato from Virginia, and the cherry from the Canaries into Ireland, where his garden was, and his manor of Sherborne "he beautified with gardens, and orchards, and groves of much variety and delight." And this fact evincing his attention to horticulture is related, that once, on occasion of the Queen's visiting him, he artificially retarded the ripening of some cherries, by stretching a wet canvass over the tree and removed it on a sunny day, so as to present the fruit ripe to the Queen a month later than usual. Not to omit a more doubtful, but not less celebrated benefit, it is said, that on the return of his first colonists from Virginia in 1586, tobacco was first effectually introduced into England, and its use encouraged by his influence and example.—And finally not to be outdone by the quacks, he invented a cordial which became very celebrated and bore his name, and was even administered to the Queen, and to the Prince in his last illness. One Febure writes that "Sir Walter, being a worthy successor of Mithridates, Matheolus, B. Valentine, Paracelsus, and others, has he affirms, selected all that is choicest in the animal, vegetable, and mineral world, and moreover manifested so much art and experience in the preparation of this great and admirable cordial as will of itself render him immortal."

We come at last to consider him as a literary man and a writer, concerning which aspect of his life we are least indebted to the historian for our facts.

As he was heroic with the sword, so was he with the pen. The History of the World, the task which he selected for his prison hours, was heroic in the undertaking and heroic in the achievement. The easy and cheerful heart with which he endured his confinement, turning his prison into a study, a parlor, and a laboratory, and his prison-yard into a garden, so that men did not so much pity as admire him—the steady purpose with which he set about fighting his battles, prosecuting his discoveries, and gathering his laurels, with the pen, if he might no longer do so with regiments & fleets—is itself an exploit. In writing the history of the world he was indeed at liberty; for he who contemplates truth and universal laws is free, whatever walls immure his body;—though to our brave prisoner thus employed mankind may have seemed but his poor fellow prisoners still.

Though this remarkable work interests us more, on the whole, as a part of the history of Raleigh, than as the history of the world, yet it was done like himself, and with no small success. The historian of Greece and Rome is usually unmanned by his subject as a peasant crouches before lords, but Raleigh, though he succumbs to the imposing fame of tradition and antediluvian story, and exhibits unnecessary reverence for a prophet or patriarch, from his habit of innate religious courtesy to the church, has done better than this whenever a hero offered. He stalks down through the aisles of the past, as through the avenues of a camp, with poets and historians for his heralds and guides, and from whatever side the faintest trump reaches his ear that way does he promptly turn, though to the neglect of many a gaudy pavilion.

From a work so little read in these days we will venture to quote as specimens the following criticisms on Alexander and the character of Epaminondas. They will at any rate teach our lips no bad habits. There is a natural emphasis in his style, like a man's tread, and a breathing space between the sentences, which the best of more modern writing does not furnish. His chapters are like English parks or rather like a Western forest, where the larger growth keeps down the underwood, and one may ride on horse back through the openings.

"Certainly the things that this king did, were marvellous, and would hardly have been undertaken by any man else; and though his father had determined to have invaded the lesser Asia, it is like enough that he would have contented himself with some part thereof, and not have discovered the river of Indus, as this man did. The swift course of victory, wherewith he ran over so large a portion of the world, in so short a space, may justly be imputed unto this, that he was never encountered by an equal spirit, concurring with equal power against him. Hereby it came to pass that his actions being limited by no greater opposition, than desart places, and the mere length of tedious journies could make, were like the Colossus of Rhodes, and not so much to be admired for the workmanship, though therein also praiseworthy, as for the huge bulk. For certainly the things performed by Xenophon, discover as brave a spirit as Alexander's, and working no less exquisitely, though the effects were less material, as were also the forces and power of command, by which it wrought. But he that would find the exact pattern of a noble commander, must look upon such as Epaminondas, that encountering worthy captains, and those better followed than themselves, have by their singular virtue overtopped their valiant enemies, and still prevailed over those, that would not have yielded one foot to any other. Such as these are, do seldom live to obtain great empires. For it is a work of more labor and longer time, to master the equal force of one hardy and well-ordered state, than to tread down and utterly subdue a multitude of servile nations, compounding the body of a gross unwieldly empire. Wherefore these *Parvo Potentes*, men that with little have done much upon enemies of like ability, are to be regarded as choice examples of worth; but great conquerors, to be rather admired for the substance of their actions, than the exquisite managing: exactness and greatness concurring so seldom, that I can find no instance of both in one, save only that brave Roman, Caesar."

Of Epaminondas he says, "So died Epaminondas, the worthiest man that ever was bred in that nation of Greece, and hardly to be matched in any age or country; for he equalled all others in the several virtues which in each of them were singular. His justice and sincerity, his temperance, wisdom, and high magnanimity, were no way inferior to his military virtues; in every part whereof he so excelled, that he could not but properly be called a wary, a valiant, a politic, a boun-

tiful, and a provident captain. Neither was his private conver-
sation unanswerable to those high parts which gave him
praise abroad; for he was grave, and yet very affable and cour-
teous; resolute in public business, but in his own particular,
easy and of much mildness; a lover of his people, bearing with
men's infirmities; witty and pleasant in speech—far from inso-
lence; master of his own affections, and furnished with all
qualities that might win and keep love. To these graces were
added great ability of body, and much eloquence, and very
deep knowledge in all parts of philosophy and learning;
wherewith his mind being enlightened, rested not in the
sweetness of contemplation, but broke forth into such effects
as gave unto Thebes, which had ever been an underling, a
dreadful reputation among all people adjoining, and the high-
est command in Greece".

For the most part an author only *writes* history, treating it as
a dead subject, but Raleigh *tells* it, like a fresh story. A man of
action himself, he knew when there was an action coming wor-
thy to be related, and does not disappoint the reader, as is too
commonly the case, by recording merely the traditionary ad-
miration or wonder. In commenting upon the military actions
of the ancients he easily and naturally digresses to some per-
haps equal action of his own, or within his experience, and tells
how they should have drawn up their fleets or men, with the
authority of an admiral or general. The alacrity with which he
adverts to some action within his experience, and slides down
from the dignified impersonality of the historian into the fa-
miliarity and interest of a party and eye-witness, is as attractive
as rare. He is often without reproach the Caesar of his own
story. He treats Scipio—Pompey—Hannibal, and the rest,
quite like equals, and he speaks like an eye-witness, and gives
life and reality to the narrative by his very lively understanding
and relating of it, especially in those parts in which the mere
scholar is most likely to fail. Every reader has observed what a
dust the historian commonly raises about the field of battle, to
serve as an apology for not making clear the disposition and
manoeuvring of the parties, so that the clearest idea one gets is
of a very vague counteraction, or standing over against one an-
other of two forces. In this history we, at least, have faith that
these things are right. Our author describes an ancient battle

with the vivacity and truth of an eye-witness, and perhaps in criticising the disposition of the forces, saying they should have stood thus or so, sometimes enforces his assertions in some such style, as "I remember being in the harbor of Cadiz &c.," so that, as in Herodotus and Thucydides, we associate the historian with the exploits he describes, but in this case not on account of his fame as a writer—but for the conspicuous part he acted on the world's stage—and his name is of equal mark to us with those of his heroes, so in the present instance, not only for his valor as a writer, but the part he acted in his generation, the life of the author seems fit to make the last chapter in the history he is writing. We expect that when his history is brought to a close it will include his own exploits. However, this is hardly a work to be consulted as authority now-a-days, but on the subject of its author's character. The natural breadth and grasp of the man is seen in the preface itself, which is a sermon with human life for its text. In the first books he discusses with childlike earnestness and an ingenuity which they little deserved the absurd and frivolous questions which engaged the theology and philosophy of his day. But even these are recommended by his sincerity and fine imagination, while the subsequent parts, or story itself, have the merit of being far more credible and lifelike than is common. He shows occasionally a poet's imagination and the innocence and purity of a child as it were under a knight's dress, such as were worthy of the friend of Spenser. The nobleness of his nature is everywhere apparent. The gentle and steady heart with which he cultivates philosophy and poetry in his prison, dissolving in the reader's imagination, the very walls and bars by his childlike confidence in truth and his own destiny, are affecting. Even Astrology, or, as he has elsewhere called it, "Star learning", comes recommended from his pen, and science will not refuse it.

"And certainly it cannot be doubted", says he, "but the stars are instruments of far greater use, than to give an obscure light, and for men to gaze on after sunset: it being manifest, that the diversity of seasons, the winters, & summers, more hot and cold, are not so uncertained by the sun and moon alone, who alway keep one and the same course; but that the stars have also their working therein.

And if we cannot deny but that God hath given virtues to springs & fountains, to cold earth, to plants and stones, minerals, and to the excremental parts of the basest living creatures, why should we rob the beautiful stars of their working powers? for seeing they are many in number, and of eminent beauty and magnitude, we may not think, that in the treasury of his wisdom, who is infinite, there can be wanting (even for every star) a peculiar virtue and operation; as every herb, plant, fruit, and flower adorning the face of the earth, hath the like. For as these were not created to beautifie the earth alone, and to cover and shadow her dusty face, but otherwise for the use of man and beast, to feed them and cure them; so were not those uncountable glorious bodies set in the firmament, to no other end, than to adorn it; but for instruments and organs of his divine Providence, so far as it hath pleased his just will to determine. Origen upon this place of *Genesis, Let there be light in the firmament, &c.,* affirmeth that the stars are not causes (meaning perchance binding causes;) but are as open books, wherein are contained and set down all things whatsoever to come; but not to be read by the eyes of human wisdom: which latter part I believe well, and this saying of Syracides withal; *That there are hid yet greater things than these be, and we have seen but a few of his works.* And though, for the capacity of men, we know somewhat, yet in the true and uttermost virtues of herbs and plants, which our selves sow and set, and which grow under our feet, we are in effect ignorant; much more in the powers and working of celestial bodies. . . . But in this question of fate, the middle course is to be followed, that as with the heathen we do not bind God to his creatures; so on the contrary, we do not rob those beautiful creatures of their powers and offices. . . . And that they wholly direct the reasonless mind, I am resolved; For all those which were created mortal, as birds beasts and the like, are left to their natural appetites; over all which, celestial bodies (as instruments and executioners of God's providence) have absolute dominion. . . . And S. Augustine: *Deus regit inferiora corpora per superiora,* God ruleth the bodies below by those above; . . . . It was therefore truly affirmed, *Sapiens adjuvabit opus astrorum, quemadmodum agricola terrae naturam;* A wise man assisteth the work of the stars, as the *husbandman helpeth the nature of the soil.* . . . . Lastly, we ought all to know, that God created the stars as he did the rest of the universal; whose influences may be called his reserved and unwritten laws. . . . But it was well said of *Plotinus* that the stars were significant, but not efficient, giving them yet something less than their due: and therefore as I do not consent with them who would make those glorious creatures of God virtueless: so I think that we derogate from his eternal and absolute power and providence, to ascribe to them the same dominion over our immortal souls, which they have over all bodily substances, and perishable natures: for the souls of men loving and fearing God, receive influence from that divine light it self, whereof the sun's clarity, and that of the stars, is by *Plato* called but a shadow. *Lumen est umbra Dei, Deus est lumen luminis;* Light is the shadow of God's brightness, who is the light of light."

We are reminded by this of Dubartas' poem on the "Probability of the Celestial Orbs being inhabited," translated by Sylvester.

> "I not believe that the great architect
> With all these fires the heavenly arches deck'd
> Only for shew, and with these glistering shields
> T'amaze poor shepherds, watching in the fields;
> I not believe that the least flow'r which pranks
> Our garden borders, or our common banks,
> And the least stone, that in her warming lap
> Our mother earth doth covetously wrap,
> Hath some peculiar virtue of its own,
> And that the glorious stars of heav'n have none."

Nor is the following brief review and exaltation of the subject of all history unworthy of a place in this History of the World.

"Man, thus compounded and formed by God, was an abstract or model, or brief story in the universal: . . . . for out of the earth and dust was formed the flesh of man, and therefore heavy and lumpish: the bones of his body we may compare to the hard rocks and stones, and therefore strong and durable; of which Ovid;

Inde genus durum sumus, experiensque laborum,
Et documenta damus qua simus origine nati:

From thence our kind hard-hearted is, enduring pain and
    care,
Approving, that our bodies of a stony nature are.

His bloud, which disperseth itself by the branches of veins
through all the body, may be resembled to those waters,
which are carried by brooks and rivers over all the earth; his
breath to the air, his natural heat to the inclosed warmth
which the earth hath in it self, which, stirred up by the heat
of the sun, assisteth nature in the speedier procreation of
those varieties, which the earth bringeth forth; our radical
moisture, oil or balsamum (whereon the natural heat feedeth
and is maintained) is resembled to the fat and fertility of the
earth; the hair of man's body, which adorns or overshadows
it, to the grass, which covereth the upper face and skin of the
earth; our generative power, to nature, which produceth all
things; our determinations to the light, wandering, and un-
stable clouds, carried everywhere with uncertain winds; our
eyes to the light of the sun and moon; and the beauty of our
youth, to the flowers of the spring, which either, in a very
short time, or with the sun's heat, dry up and wither away, or
the fierce puffs of wind blow them from the stalks; the
thoughts of our mind, to the motion of angels; and our pure
understanding (formerly called *mens* and that which always
looketh upwards) to those intellectual natures, which are al-
ways present with God; and lastly, our immortal souls (while
they are righteous) are by God himself beautified with the
title of his own image and similitude." But man is not in all
things like nature. "For this tide of man's life, after it once
turneth and declineth, ever runneth with a perpetual ebb and
falling stream, but never floweth again: our leaf once fallen,
springeth no more; neither doth the sun or the summer adorn
us again, with the garments of new leaves and flowers."

There is a flowing rhythm in some of these sentences like
the rippling of rivers—hardly to be matched in any prose or
verse. The following is his poem on the decay of oracles and
of pantheism.

"The fire which the Chaldeans worshipped for a god, is

crept into every man's chimney, which the lack of fuel starveth, water quencheth, and want of air suffocateth: Jupiter is no more vexed with Juno's jealousies; Death hath persuaded him to chastity, and her to patience; and that time which hath devoured it self, hath also eaten up both the bodies and images of him and his: yea their stately temples of stone and dureful marble. The houses and sumptuous buildings erected to Baal, can no where be found upon the earth, nor any monument of that glorious temple consecrated to Diana. There are none now in Phoenicia that lament the death of Adonis; nor any in Lybia, Creta, Thessalia, or elsewhere, that can ask counsel or help from Jupiter. The great god Pan hath broken his pipes, Apollo's priests are become speechless; and the trade of riddles in Oracles, with the Devil's telling men's fortunes therein, is taken up by counterfeit Egyptians and cozening Astrologers."

In his "Discourse of War in General" commencing with almost a heroic verse, "The ordinary theme and argument of history is war," are many things well thought and many more well said. He thus expands the maxim that corporations have no soul. "But no senate nor civil assembly can be under such natural impulses to honor and justice as single persons. For a majority is no-body when that majority is separated, and a collective body can have no synteresis, or divine ray, which is in the mind of every man, never assenting to evil, but upbraiding and tormenting him when he does it: but the honor and conscience that lies in the majority is too thin and diffusive to be efficacious; for a number can do a great wrong, and call it right, and not one of that majority blush for it." If his philosophy is for the most part poor, yet the conception and expression are rich and generous. His maxims are not true or impartial, but are conceived with a certain magnanimity which was natural to him, as if a selfish policy could easily afford to give place in him to a more universal and true.

As a fact evincing Raleigh's poetic culture and taste, it is said that in a visit to the poet Spenser, on the banks of the Mulla, which is described in "Colin Clout's come home again," he anticipated the judgment of posterity with respect to the Fairy Queen, and by his sympathy and advice encouraged the poet to go on with his work, which, by the advice of other friends, among whom was Sidney, he had laid aside. His own poems, though insignificant in respect to number and length, and not collected into a separate volume, or surely accredited to Raleigh, deserve the distinct attention of the lover of English poetry, and leave such an impression on the mind that this leaf of his laurels, for the time, well nigh overshadows all the rest. In these few rhymes, as in that country he describes, his life naturally culminates, and his secret aspirations appear. They are in some respects more trustworthy testimonials to his character than state papers or tradition; for poetry is a piece of very private history which unostentatiously lets us into the secret of a man's life, and is to the reader, what the eye is to the beholder, the characteristic feature, which cannot be distorted or made to deceive.

The pleasing poem entitled "A Description of the Country's Recreations", also printed among the poems of Sir Henry Wotton, is well known. The following, which bears evident marks of his pen, we will quote for its secure and continent rhythm.

"False Love and True Love."

"As you came from the holy land
    Of Walsingham,
Met you not with my true love
    By the way as you came?
How shall I know your true love,
    That have met many one
As I went to the holy land,
    That have come, that have gone.
She is neither white nor brown,
    But as the heavens fair;
There is none hath so divine a form
    In the earth or the air.
Such a one did I meet, good sir,
    Such an angelic face;
Who like a queen, like a nymph did appear,
    By her gait, by her grace:
She hath left me here all alone,
    All alone as unknown,

Who sometimes did me lead with herself,
 And me loved as her own:
What's the cause that she leaves you alone
 And a new way doth take:
Who loved you once as her own
 And her joy did you make?
I have loved her all my youth,
 But now, old as you see,
Love likes not the falling fruit
 From the withered tree:
Know that love is a careless child
 And forgets promise past,
He is blind, he is deaf, when he list,
 And in faith never fast:
His desire is a dureless content,
 And a trustless joy;
He is won with a world of despair,
 And is lost with a toy:
Of women-kind such indeed is the love,
 Or the word love abused;
Under which many childish desires
 And conceits are excused:
But true love is a durable fire
 In the mind ever burning;
Never sick, never old, never dead,
 From itself never turning."

The following will be new to many of our readers.

"The Shepherd's Praise of his sacred Diana"

"Prais'd be Diana's fair and harmless light;
 Prais'd be the dews wherewith she moists the ground;
Prais'd be her beams, the glory of the night;
 Prais'd be her power, by which all powers abound!

Prais'd be her nymphs, with whom she decks the woods;
 Prais'd be her knights, in whom true honor lives;
Prais'd be that force by which she moves the floods!
 Let that Diana shine, which all these gives!

In heaven, queen she is among the spheres;
    She mistress-like, makes all things to be pure;
Eternity in her oft-change she bears;
    She, Beauty is; by her, the fair endure.

Time wears her not; she doth his chariot guide;
    Mortality below her orb is placed;
By her the virtues of the stars down slide;
    In her is Virtue's perfect image cast!

A knowledge pure it is her worth to know:
With Circes let them dwell that think not so!"

Though we discover in his verses the vices of the courtier, and they are not equally sustained, as if his genius were warped by the frivolous society of the Court, he was capable of rising to unusual heights. His genius seems to have been fitted for short flights of unmatched sweetness and vigor, but by no means for the sustained loftiness of the epic poet. One who read his verses would say that he had not grown to be the man he promised. They have occasionally a strength of character and heroic tone rarely expressed or appreciated, and possess an excellence so peculiar, as to be almost unique specimens of their kind in the language. Those which have reference to his death have been oftenest quoted, and are the best. "The Soul's Errand" deserves to be remembered till her mission is accomplished in the world. We quote the following, not so well known—with some omissions, from the commencement of

"His Pilgrimage".

"Give me my scallop-shell of quiet,
    My staff of faith to walk upon;
My scrip of joy, immortal diet;
    My bottle of salvation;
My gown of glory, hope's true gage,
And thus I'll take my pilgrimage.

Blood must be my body's balmer,
    No other balm will here be given,
Whilst my soul like a quiet palmer,
    Travels to the land of heaven,
Over the silver mountains,

Where spring the nectar fountains;
> There will I kiss
> The bowl of bliss,
And drink mine everlasting fill
Upon every milken hill.
My soul will be adry before,
But after, it will thirst no more.

In that serene and blissful day,
> More peaceful pilgrims I shall see,
That have cast off their rags of clay,
> And walk apparell'd fresh like me."

But he wrote his poems, after all, rather with ships and fleets, and regiments of men and horse. At his bidding navies took their place in the channel, and even from prison he fitted out fleets with which to realize his golden dreams, and invited his companions to fresh adventures.

Raleigh might well be studied if only for the excellence of his style, for he is remarkable even in the midst of so many masters. All the distinguished writers of that period possess a greater vigor and naturalness than the more modern, and when we read a quotation from one of them in the midst of a modern author, we seem to have come suddenly upon a greener ground and greater depth and strength of soil. It is as if a green bough were laid across the page, and we are refreshed as by the sight of fresh grass in mid winter or early spring. You have constantly the warrant of life & experience in what you read. The little that is said is supplied by implication of the much that was done. The sentences are verdurous and blooming as evergreen and flowers, because they are rooted in fact and experience, but our false and florid sentences have only the tints of flowers without their sap or roots. Indeed where shall we look for standard English but to the words of a standard man? The word which is best said came very near not being spoken at all, for it is cousin to a deed which would have been better done. It must have taken the place of a deed by some urgent necessity, even by some misfortune, so that the truest writer will be some captive knight after all. And perhaps the fates had such a design, when having stored Raleigh so richly with the substance of life and experience, they made him a fast prisoner, and compelled him to make his words his deeds, and transfer to his expression the emphasis and sincerity of his action.

The necessity of labor, and conversation with many men and things, to the scholar, is rarely well remembered. Steady labor with the hands which engrosses the attention also, is the best method of removing palaver out of one's style both of talking and writing. If he has worked hard from morning till night, though he may have grieved that he could not be watching the train of his thoughts during that time, yet the few hasty lines which at evening record his day's experience will be more musical and true, than his freest but idle fancy could have furnished. He will not idly dance at his work who has wood to cut and cord before night-fall in the short days of winter, but every stroke will be husbanded and ring soberly through the wood; and so will the strokes of that scholar's pen, which at evening record the story of the day, ring soberly on the ear of the reader long after echoes of his axe have died away. The scholar may be sure he writes the tougher truth for the calluses on his palms. They give firmness to the sentence. We are often astonished by the force and precision of style to which hard working men, unpractised in writing, easily attain, when required to make the effort. As if sincerity and plainness, those ornaments of style, were better taught on the farm or in the workshop, than in the schools. The sentences written by such rude hands are nervous and tough, like hardened thongs, the sinews of the deer, or the roots of the pine. The scholar might frequently emulate the propriety and emphasis of the farmer's call to his team, and confess that if that were written it would surpass his labored sentences. Whose are the truly *labored* sentences? From the weak and flimsy periods of the politician and literary man we are glad to turn even to the description of work, the simple record of the month's labor in the farmer's almanack, to restore our tone and spirits. We like that a sentence should read as if its author, had he held a plough instead of a pen, could have drawn a furrow deep and straight to the end. The scholar requires hard labor to give an impetus to his thought; he will learn to grasp the pen firmly so, and wield it gracefully and effectually as an axe or sword. When we consider the weak and nerveless periods of some literary men, who perchance in feet and inches come up to the standard of their race, and are not deficient in girth also, we are amazed at the immense sacrifice of thews and sinews. What! these proportions, these bones, and this their work! Hands which could have felled an ox have hewed this fragile matter which would not have tasked a lady's fingers. Can this be a stalwart man's work, who has a marrow in his back, and a tendon Achilles in his heel? They who set up Stonehenge did somewhat, if they only laid out their strength for once, and stretched themselves.

Yet after all the truly efficient laborer will be found not to crowd his day with work, but saunter to his task surrounded by a wide halo of ease and leisure, and then do but what he likes best. He is anxious only about the kernels of time. Though the hen should set all day she could lay only one egg, and besides would not have picked up materials for another.

A perfectly healthy sentence is extremely rare. Sometimes we read one which was written while the world went round, while grass grew and water ran. But for the most part we miss the hue and fragrance of the thought. As if we could be satisfied with the dews of the morning or evening without their colors, or the heavens without their azure. The most attractive sentences are perhaps not the wisest but the surest and roundest. They are spoken firmly and conclusively as if the author had a right to know what he says; and if not wise, they have at least been well learned. At least he does not stand on a rolling stone, but is well assured of his footing—and if you dispute their doctrine you will yet allow that there is truth in their assurance. Raleigh's are of this sort, spoken with entire satisfaction and heartiness. They are not so much philosophy as poetry. With him it was always well done and nobly said. His learning was in his hand and he carried it by him and used it as adroitly as his sword. Aubrey says "He was no slug". He wields his pen as one who sits at his ease in his chair, and has a healthy and able body to back his wits, and not a torpid and diseased one to fetter them. In whichever hand is the pen we are sure there is a sword in the other. He sits with his armor on, and with one ear open to hear if the trumpet sound, as one who has stolen a little leisure from the duties of a camp; and we are confident that the whole man sat down to the writing of his books, as real and palpable as an Englishman can be; and not some curious brain only. Such a man's mere daily exercise in literature might well attract us, and Cecil has said, "He can toil terribly."

Raleigh seems to have been too genial and loyal a soul to resist the temptations of a court; but if to his genius and culture could have been added the temperament of Geo. Fox or Oliver Cromwell, perhaps the world would have had reason longer to remember him. He was however the most generous nature that could be drawn into the precincts of a court, and carried the courtier's life almost to the highest pitch of magnanimity and grace it was capable of. He was liberal and generous, as a prince,—that is, within bounds; heroic, as a knight in armor,—but not as a defenceless man. His was not the heroism of a Luther but of a Bayard, and had more of grace than of honest truth in it. He had more taste than appetite. There may be something petty in a refined taste,—it easily degenerates into effeminacy. It does not consider the broadest use, and is not content with simple good and bad, but is often fastidious, and curious, or nice only.

His faults, as we have hinted before, were those of a courtier and a soldier. In his counsels and aphorisms we see not unfrequently the haste and rashness of the soldier strangely mingled with the wisdom of the philosopher. Though his philosophy was not wide nor profound, it was continually giving way to the generosity of his nature, and he was not hard to be won to the right.

What he touches he adorns by a greater humanity and native nobleness, but he touches not the truest nor deepest. He does not in any sense unfold the new but embellishes the old, and with all his inclination to originality, he never was quite original, or steered his own course. He was of so fair and susceptible a nature rather than broad or deep that he delayed to slake his thirst at the nearest and most turbid wells of truth and beauty, and his homage to the least fair and noble, left no room for homage to the all fair. The misfortune and incongruity of the man appear in the fact that he was at once the author of the "Maxims of State", and "The Soul's Errand."

When we reconsider what we have said in the foregoing pages, we hesitate to apply any of their eulogy to the actual and historical Raleigh, or any of their condemnation to that ideal Raleigh which he suggests, for we must know the man of history as we know our contemporaries, not so much by his deeds, which often belie his real character, as by the expectation he begets in us—and there is a bloom and halo about the character of Raleigh which defies a close and literal scrutiny, and robs us of our critical acumen. With all his heroism, he was not heroic enough; with all his manliness, he was servile and dependent; with all his aspirations, he was ambitious. He was not upright nor constant, yet we would have trusted him; he could flatter and cringe, yet we should have respected him; and he could accept a bribe, yet we should confidently have appealed to his generosity.

Such a life is useful for us to contemplate as suggesting that a man is not to be measured by the virtue of his described actions or the wisdom of his expressed thoughts merely, but by that free character he is, and is felt to be, under all circumstances. Even talent is respectable only when it indicates a depth of character unfathomed. Surely, it is better that our wisdom appear in the constant success of our spirits, than in our business or the maxims which fall from our lips merely. We want not only a revelation but a nature behind to sustain it. Many silent, as well as famous, lives have been the result of no mean thought though it was never adequately expressed nor conceived; and perhaps the most illiterate and unphilosophical mind may yet be accustomed to think to the extent of the noblest action. We all know those in our own circle who do injustice to their entire character in their conversation and in writing, but who, if actually set over against us would not fail to make a wiser impression than many a wise thinker and speaker.

We are not a little profited by any life which teaches us not to despair of the race, and such effect has the steady and cheerful bravery of Raleigh. To march sturdily through life patiently and resolutely looking defiance at one's foes, that is one way, but we cannot help being more attracted by that kind of heroism which relaxes its brows in the presence of danger, and does not need to maintain itself strictly, but by a kind of sympathy with the universe, generously adorns the scene and the occasion, and loves valor so well that itself would be the defeated party only to behold it. When we consider the vast Xerxean army of reformers in these days, we cannot doubt that many a grim soul goes silent, the hero of some small intestine war; and it is somewhat to begin to live on corn bread solely for one who has before lived on bolted wheat;—but of this sort are not the deeds to be sung. These are not the Arthurs that inflame the imaginations of men. All fair action is the product of enthusiasm, and nature herself does nothing in the prose mood. We would fain witness a heroism which is literally illustrious, whose daily life is of the stuff of which our dreams are made—so that the world shall regard less what it does than how it does it, and its actions unsettle the common standards, and have a right to be done, however wrong they may be to the moralist.

Mere gross health and cheerfulness are no slight attraction, and some biographies have this charm mainly. For the most part the best man's spirit makes a fearful sprite to haunt his grave, and it adds not a little therefore to the credit of Little John, the celebrated follower of Robin Hood, reflecting favorably on the character of his life, that his grave was "long celebrous for the yielding of excellent whetstones".

A great cheerfulness indeed have all great wits and heroes possessed, almost a prophane levity to such as understood them not, but their religion had the broader basis of health and permanence. For the hero too has his religion, though it is the very opposite to that of the ascetic. It demands not a narrower cell but a wider world. He is perhaps the very best man of the world; the poet active, the saint enterprising; not the most godlike, but the most manlike. There have been souls of a heroic stamp, for whom this world seemed expressly made; as if creation had at last succeeded, for it seems to be thrown away on the saint; and their presence enhances the beauty and ampleness of nature herself, and where they walk, as Virgil says of the abodes of the blessed,

> *"Largior hic campos aether et lumine vestit*
> *Purpureo: Solemque suum, sua sidera norunt."*

Here a more copious air invests the fields, and clothes
With purple light: And they know their own sun and their
    own stars.

Dark Ages

WE should read history as little critically as we consider the landscape, and be more interested by the atmospheric tints, and various lights and shades which the intervening spaces create, than by its groundwork and composition. It is the morning now turned evening and seen in the west,—the same sun, but a new light and atmosphere. Its beauty is like the sunset; not a fresco painting on a wall, flat and bounded, but atmospheric and roving or free. In reality history fluctuates as the face of the landscape from morning to evening. What is of moment is its hue and color. Time hides no treasures; we want not its *then* but its *now*. We do not complain that the mountains in the horizon are blue and indistinct; they are the more like the heavens.

Of what moment are facts that can be lost,—which need to be commemorated? The monument of death will outlast the memory of the dead. The pyramids do not tell the tale that was confided to them; the living fact commemorates itself. Why look in the dark for light? Strictly speaking, the historical societies have not recovered one fact from oblivion, but are themselves instead of the fact that is lost. The researcher is more memorable than the researched. The crowd stood admiring the mist, and the dim outlines of the trees seen through it, when one of their number advanced to explore the phenomenon, and with fresh admiration, all eyes were turned on his dimly retreating figure. It is astonishing with how little coöperation of the societies, the past is remembered. Its story has indeed had a different muse than has been assigned it. There is a good instance of the manner in which all history began, in Alwákidi's Arabian Chronicle. "I was informed by *Ahmed Almatîn Aljorhami*, who had it from *Rephâa Ebn Kais Alámiri*, who had it from *Saiph Ebn Jabalah Alchátgami*, who had it from *Thabet Ebn Alkamah*, who said he was present at the action." These fathers of history were not anxious to preserve, but to learn the fact; and hence it was not forgotten. Critical acumen is exerted in vain to uncover the past; the *past* cannot be *presented*; we cannot know what we are not. But one veil hangs over past, present, and future, and it is the province of the historian to find out not what was, but what is. Where a battle has been fought, you will find nothing but the bones of men and beasts; where a battle is being fought there are hearts beating. We will sit on a mound and muse, and not try to make these skeletons stand on their legs again. Does nature remember, think you, that they *were* men, or not rather that they *are* bones?

Ancient history has an air of antiquity; it should be more modern. It is written as if the spectator should be thinking of the backside of the picture on the wall, or as if the author expected the dead would be his readers, and wished to detail to them their own experience. Men seem anxious to accomplish an orderly retreat through the centuries, earnestly rebuilding the works behind, as they are battered down by the encroachments of time; but while they loiter, they and their works both fall a prey to the arch enemy. It has neither the venerableness of antiquity, nor the freshness of the modern. It does as if it would go to the beginning of things, which natural history might with reason assume to do; but consider the Universal History, and then tell us—when did burdock and plantain sprout first? It has been so written for the most part, that the times it describes are with remarkable propriety called *dark ages.* They are dark, as one has observed, because we are so in the dark about them. The sun rarely shines in history, what with the dust and confusion; and when we meet with any cheering fact which implies the presence of this luminary, we excerpt and modernize it. As when we read in the history of the Saxons, that Edwin of Northumbria "caused stakes to be fixed in the highways where he had seen a clear spring," and "brazen dishes were chained to them, to refresh the weary sojourner, whose fatigues Edwin had himself experienced." This is worth all Arthur's twelve battles.

But it is fit the past should be dark; though the darkness is not so much a quality of the past, as of tradition. It is not a distance of time but a distance of relation, which makes thus dusky its memorials. What is near to the heart of this generation is fair and bright still. Greece lies outspread fair and sunshiny in floods of light, for there is the sun and day-light in her literature and art. Homer does not allow us to forget that the sun shone—nor Phidias, nor the Parthenon. Yet no era has been wholly dark, nor will we too hastily submit to the historian, and congratulate ourselves on a blaze of light. If we could pierce the obscurity of those remote years we should find it light enough; only there is not our day.—Some creatures are made to see in the dark.—There has always been the same amount of light in the world. The new and missing stars, the comets and eclipses do not affect the general illumination, for only our glasses appreciate them. The eyes of the oldest fossil remains, they tell us, indicate that the same laws of light prevailed then as now. Always the laws of light are the same, but the modes and degrees of seeing vary. The gods are partial to no era, but steadily shines their light in the heavens, while the eye of the beholder is turned to stone. There was but the eye and the sun from the first. The ages have not added a new ray to the one, nor altered a fibre of the other.

A Winter Walk

THE wind has gently murmured through the blinds, or puffed with feathery softness against the windows, and occasionally sighed like a summer zephyr lifting the leaves along, the livelong night. The meadow mouse has slept in his snug gallery in the sod, the owl has sat in a hollow tree in the depth of the swamp, the rabbit, the squirrel, and the fox have all been housed. The watch-dog has lain quiet on the hearth, and the cattle have stood silent in their stalls. The earth itself has slept, as it were its first, not its last sleep, save when some street-sign or wood-house door, has faintly creaked upon its hinge, cheering forlorn nature at her midnight work.—The only sound awake twixt Venus and Mars,—advertising us of a remote inward warmth, a divine cheer and fellowship, where gods are met together, but where it is very bleak for men to stand. But while the earth has slumbered, all the air has been alive with feathery flakes, descending, as if some northern Ceres reigned, showering her silvery grain over all the fields.

We sleep and at length awake to the still reality of a winter morning. The snow lies warm as cotton or down upon the window-sill; the broadened sash and frosted panes admit a dim and private light, which enhances the snug cheer within. The stillness of the morning is impressive. The floor creaks under our feet as we move toward the window to look abroad through some clear space over the fields. We see the roofs stand under their snow burden. From the eaves and fences hang stalactites of snow, and in the yard stand stalagmites covering some concealed core. The trees and shrubs rear white arms to the sky on every side, and where were walls and fences, we see fantastic forms stretching in frolic gambols across the dusky landscape, as if nature had strewn her fresh designs over the fields by night as models for man's art.

Silently we unlatch the door, letting the drift fall in, and step abroad to face the cutting air. Already the stars have lost some of their sparkle, and a dull leaden mist skirts the horizon. A lurid brazen light in the east proclaims the approach of day, while the western landscape is dim and spectral still, and

clothed in a sombre Tartarean light, like the shadowy realms.
They are Infernal sounds only that you hear,—the crowing of
cocks, the barking of dogs, the chopping of wood, the lowing
of kine, all seem to come from Pluto's barn-yard and beyond
the Styx;—not for any melancholy they suggest, but their twi-
light bustle is too solemn and mysterious for earth. The re-
cent tracks of the fox or otter, in the yard, remind us that
each hour of the night is crowded with events, and the
primeval nature is still working and making tracks in the snow.
Opening the gate, we tread briskly along the lone country
road, crunching the dry and crisped snow under our feet, or
aroused by the sharp clear creak of the wood-sled, just start-
ing for the distant market, from the early farmer's door,
where it has lain the summer long, dreaming amid the chips
and stubble. For through the drifts and powdered windows
we see the farmer's early candle, like a paled star, emitting a
lonely beam, as if some severe virtue were at its matins there.
And one by one the smokes begin to ascend from the chim-
neys amidst the trees and snows.

> The sluggish smoke curls up from some deep dell,
> The stiffened air exploring in the dawn,
> And making slow acquaintance with the day;
> Delaying now upon its heavenward course,
> In wreathed loiterings dallying with itself,
> With as uncertain purpose and slow deed,
> As its half-wakened master by the hearth,
> Whose mind still slumbering and sluggish thoughts
> Have not yet swept into the onward current
> Of the new day;—and now it streams afar,
> The while the chopper goes with step direct,
> And mind intent to swing the early axe.
> First in the dusky dawn he sends abroad
> His early scout, his emissary, smoke,
> The earliest, latest pilgrim from the roof,
> To feel the frosty air, inform the day;
> And while he crouches still beside the hearth,
> Nor musters courage to unbar the door,
> It has gone down the glen with the light wind,
> And o'er the plain unfurled its venturous wreath,

Draped the tree tops, loitered upon the hill,
And warmed the pinions of the early bird;
And now, perchance, high in the crispy air,
Has caught sight of the day o'er the earth's edge,
And greets its master's eye at his low door,
As some refulgent cloud in the upper sky.

We hear the sound of wood-chopping at the farmers' doors, far over the frozen earth, the baying of the house dog, and the distant clarion of the cock. The thin and frosty air conveys only the finer particles of sound to our ears, with short and sweet vibrations, as the waves subside soonest on the purest and lightest liquids, in which gross substances sink to the bottom. They come clear and bell-like, and from a greater distance in the horizon, as if there were fewer impediments than in summer to make them faint and ragged. The ground is sonorous, like seasoned wood, and even the ordinary rural sounds are melodious, and the jingling of the ice on the trees is sweet and liquid. There is the least possible moisture in the atmosphere, all being dried up, or congealed, and it is of such extreme tenuity and elasticity, that it becomes a source of delight. The withdrawn and tense sky seems groined like the aisles of a cathedral, and the polished air sparkles as if there were crystals of ice floating in it. Those who have resided in Greenland, tell us, that, when it freezes, "the sea smokes like burning turf land, and a fog or mist arises, called frost smoke," which "cutting smoke frequently raises blisters on the face and hands, and is very pernicious to the health." But this pure stinging cold is an elixir to the lungs, and not so much a frozen mist, as a crystallized midsummer haze, refined and purified by cold.

The sun at length rises through the distant woods, as if with the faint clashing swinging sound of cymbals, melting the air with his beams, and with such rapid steps the morning travels, that already his rays are gilding the distant western mountains. We step hastily along through the powdery snow, warmed by an inward heat, enjoying an Indian summer still, in the increased glow of thought and feeling. Probably if our lives were more conformed to nature, we should not need to defend ourselves against her heats and colds, but find her our constant nurse and friend, as do plants and quadrupeds. If our bodies were fed with pure and simple elements, and not with a stimulating and heating diet, they would afford no more pasture for cold than a leafless twig, but thrive like the trees, which find even winter genial to their expansion.

The wonderful purity of nature at this season is a most pleasing fact. Every decayed stump and moss-grown stone and rail, and the dead leaves of autumn, are concealed by a clean napkin of snow. In the bare fields and tinkling woods, see what virtue survives. In the coldest and bleakest places, the warmest charities still maintain a foot-hold. A cold and searching wind drives away all contagion, and nothing can withstand it but what has a virtue in it; and accordingly, whatever we meet with in cold and bleak places, as the tops of mountains, we respect for a sort of sturdy innocence, a Puritan toughness. All things beside seem to be called in for shelter, and what stays out must be part of the original frame of the universe, and of such valor as God himself. It is invigorating to breathe the cleansed air. Its greater fineness and purity are visible to the eye, and we would fain stay out long and late, that the gales may sigh through us too, as through the leafless trees, and fit us for the winter:—as if we hoped so to borrow some pure and steadfast virtue, which will stead us in all seasons.

At length we have reached the edge of the woods, and shut out the gadding town. We enter within their covert as we go under the roof of a cottage, and cross its threshold, all ceiled and banked up with snow. They are glad and warm still, and as genial and cheery in winter as in summer. As we stand in the midst of the pines, in the flickering and checkered light which straggles but little way into their maze, we wonder if the towns have ever heard their simple story. It seems to us that no traveller has ever explored them, and notwithstanding the wonders which science is elsewhere revealing every day, who would not like to hear their annals? Our humble villages in the plain, are their contribution. We borrow from the forest the boards which shelter, and the sticks which warm us. How important is their evergreen to the winter, that portion of the summer which does not fade, the permanent year, the unwithered grass. Thus simply, and with little expense of altitude, is the surface of the earth diversified. What would human life be without forests, those natural cities? From the tops of mountains they appear like smooth shaven lanes, yet whither shall we walk but in this taller grass?

There is a slumbering subterranean fire in nature which never goes out, and which no cold can chill. It finally melts the great snow, and in January or July is only buried under a thicker or thinner covering. In the coldest day it flows somewhere, and the snow melts around every tree. This field of winter rye, which sprouted late in the fall, and now speedily dissolves the snow, is where the fire is very thinly covered. We feel warmed by it. In the winter, warmth stands for all virtue, and we resort in thought to a trickling rill, with its bare stones shining in the sun, and to warm springs in the woods, with as much eagerness as rabbits and robins. The steam which rises from swamps and pools, is as dear and domestic as that of our own kettle. What fire could ever equal the sunshine of a winter's-day, when the meadow mice come out by the wallsides, and the chicadee lisps in the defiles of the wood? The warmth comes directly from the sun, and is not radiated from the earth, as in summer; and when we feel his beams on our back as we are treading some snowy dell, we are grateful as for a special kindness, and bless the sun which has followed us into that by-place.

This subterranean fire has its altar in each man's breast, for in the coldest day, and on the bleakest hill, the traveler cherishes a warmer fire within the folds of his cloak than is kindled on any hearth. A healthy man, indeed, is the complement of the seasons, and in winter, summer is in his heart. There is the south. Thither have all birds and insects migrated, and around the warm springs in his breast are gathered the robin and the lark.

In this glade covered with bushes of a year's growth, see how the silvery dust lies on every seared leaf and twig, deposited in such infinite and luxurious forms as by their very variety atone for the absence of color. Observe the tiny tracks of mice around every stem, and the triangular tracks of the rabbit. A pure elastic heaven hangs over all, as if the impurities of the summer sky, refined and shrunk by the chaste winter's cold, had been winnowed from the heavens upon the earth.

Nature confounds her summer distinction at this season. The heavens seem to be nearer the earth. The elements are less reserved and distinct. Water turns to ice, rain to snow. The day is but a Scandinavian night. The winter is an arctic summer.

How much more living is the life that is in nature, the furred life which still survives the stinging nights, and, from amidst fields and woods covered with frost and snow, sees the sun rise.

> "The foodless wilds
> Pour forth their brown inhabitants."

The grey-squirrel and rabbit are brisk and playful in the remote glens, even on the morning of the cold Friday. Here is our Lapland and Labrador, and for our Esquimaux and Knistenaux, Dog-ribbed Indians, Novazemblaites, and Spitzbergeners, are there not the ice-cutter and wood-chopper, the fox, muskrat, and mink?

Still, in the midst of the arctic day, we may trace the summer to its retreats, and sympathize with some contemporary life. Stretched over the brooks, in the midst of the frost-bound meadows, we may observe the submarine cottages of the caddice worms, the larvæ of the Plicipennes. Their small cylindrical caves built around themselves, composed of flags, sticks, grass, and withered leaves, shells and pebbles, in form and color like the wrecks which strew the bottom—now drifting along over the pebbly bottom, now whirling in tiny eddies and dashing down steep falls, or sweeping rapidly along with the current, or else swaying to and fro at the end of some grass blade or root. Anon they will leave their sunken habitations, and crawling up the stems of plants, or floating on the surface like gnats, or perfect insects, henceforth flutter over the surface of the water, or sacrifice their short lives in the flame of our candles at evening. Down yonder little glen the shrubs are drooping under their burden, and the red alder-berries contrast with the white ground. Here are the marks of a myriad feet which have already been abroad. The sun rises as proudly over such a glen, as over the valley of the Seine or the Tiber, and it seems the residence of a pure and self-subsistent valor, such as they never

witnessed; which never knew defeat nor fear. Here reign the
simplicity and purity of a primitive age, and a health and
hope far remote from towns and cities. Standing quite alone,
far in the forest, while the wind is shaking down snow from
the trees, and leaving the only human tracks behind us, we
find our reflections of a richer variety than the life of cities.
The chicadee and nut-hatch are more inspiring society than
the statesmen and philosophers, and we shall return to these
last, as to more vulgar companions. In this lonely glen, with its
brook draining the slopes, its creased ice and crystals of all
hues, where the spruces and hemlocks stand up on either side,
and the rush and sere wild oats in the rivulet itself, our lives are
more serene and worthy to contemplate.

As the day advances, the heat of the sun is reflected by the
hillsides, and we hear a faint but sweet music, where flows
the rill released from its fetters, and the icicles are melting
on the trees; and the nut-hatch and partridge are heard and
seen. The south wind melts the snow at noon, and the bare
ground appears with its withered grass and leaves, and we are
invigorated by the perfume which expands from it, as by the
scent of strong meats.

Let us go into this deserted woodman's hut, and see how
he has passed the long winter nights and the short and stormy
days. For here man has lived under this south hill-side, and it
seems a civilized and public spot. We have such associations as
when the traveller stands by the ruins of Palmyra or
Hecatompolis. Singing birds and flowers perchance have be-
gun to appear here, for flowers as well as weeds follow in the
footsteps of man. These hemlocks whispered over his head,
these hickory logs were his fuel, and these pitch-pine roots
kindled his fire; yonder foaming rill in the hollow, whose thin
and airy vapor still ascends as busily as ever, though he is far
off now, was his well. These hemlock boughs, and the straw
upon this raised platform, were his bed, and this broken dish
held his drink. But he has not been here this season, for the
phœbes built their nest upon this shelf last summer. I find
some embers left, as if he had but just gone out, where he
baked his pot of beans, and while at evening he smoked his
pipe, whose stemless bowl lies in the ashes, chatted with
his only companion, if perchance he had any, about the depth

of the snow on the morrow, already falling fast and thick without, or disputed whether the last sound was the screech of an owl, or the creak of a bough, or imagination only; and through this broad chimney-throat, in the late winter evening, ere he stretched himself upon the straw, he looked up to learn the progress of the storm, and seeing the bright stars of Cassiopeia's chair shining brightly down upon him, fell contentedly asleep.

See how many traces from which we may learn the chopper's history. From this stump we may guess the sharpness of his axe, and from the slope of the stroke, on which side he stood, and whether he cut down the tree without going round it or changing hands; and from the flexure of the splinters we may know which way it fell. This one chip contains inscribed on it the whole history of the wood-chopper and of the world. On this scrap of paper, which held his sugar or salt, perchance, or was the wadding of his gun, sitting on a log in the forest, with what interest we read the tattle of cities, of those larger huts, empty and to let, like this, in High-streets, and Broad-ways. The eaves are dripping on the south side of this simple roof, while the titmouse lisps in the pine, and the genial warmth of the sun around the door is somewhat kind and human.

After two seasons, this rude dwelling does not deform the scene. Already the birds resort to it, to build their nests, and you may track to its door the feet of many quadrupeds. Thus, for a long time, nature overlooks the encroachment and profanity of man. The wood still cheerfully and unsuspiciously echoes the strokes of the axe that fells it, and while they are few and seldom, they enhance its wildness, and all the elements strive to naturalize the sound.

Now our path begins to ascend gradually to the top of this high hill, from whose precipitous south side, we can look over the broad country, of forest, and field, and river, to the distant snowy mountains. See yonder thin column of smoke curling up through the woods from some invisible farmhouse; the standard raised over some rural homestead. There must be a warmer and more genial spot there below, as where we detect the vapor from a spring forming a cloud above the trees. What fine relations are established between the traveller who discovers this airy column from some eminence in the forest, and him who sits below. Up goes the smoke as silently and naturally as the vapor exhales from the leaves, and as busy disposing itself in wreathes as the housewife on the hearth below. It is a hieroglyphic of man's life, and suggests more intimate and important things than the boiling of a pot. Where its fine column rises above the forest, like an ensign, some human life has planted itself,—and such is the beginning of Rome, the establishment of the arts, and the foundation of empires, whether on the prairies of America, or the steppes of Asia.

And now we descend again to the brink of this woodland lake, which lies in a hollow of the hills, as if it were their expressed juice, and that of the leaves, which are annually steeped in it. Without outlet or inlet to the eye, it has still its history, in the lapse of its waves, in the rounded pebbles on its shore, and on the pines which grow down to its brink. It has not been idle, though sedentary, but, like Abu Musa, teaches that "sitting still at home is the heavenly way; the going out is the way of the world." Yet in its evaporation it travels as far as any. In summer it is the earth's liquid eye; a mirror in the breast of nature. The sins of the wood are washed out in it. See how the woods form an amphitheatre about it, and it is an arena for all the genialness of nature. All trees direct the traveller to its brink, all paths seek it out, birds fly to it, quadrupeds flee to it, and the very ground inclines toward it. It is nature's saloon, where she has sat down to her toilet. Consider her silent economy and tidiness; how the sun comes with his evaporation to sweep the dust from its surface each morning, and a fresh surface is constantly welling up; and annually, after whatever impurities have accumulated herein, its liquid transparency appears again in the spring. In summer a hushed music seems to sweep across its surface. But now a plain sheet of snow conceals it from our eyes, except when the wind has swept the ice bare, and the sere leaves are gliding from side to side, tacking and veering on their tiny voyages. Here is one just keeled up against a pebble on shore, a dry beach leaf, rocking still, as if it would soon start again. A skilful engineer, methinks, might project its course since it fell from the parent stem. Here are all the elements for such a calculation. Its present position, the direction of the wind, the level of the pond, and how much more is given. In its scarred edges and veins is its log rolled up.

We fancy ourselves in the interior of a larger house. The surface of the pond is our deal table or sanded floor, and the woods rise abruptly from its edge, like the walls of a cottage. The lines set to catch pickerel through the ice look like a larger culinary preparation, and the men stand about on the white ground like pieces of forest furniture. The actions of these men, at the distance of half a mile over the ice and snow, impress us as when we read the exploits of Alexander in history. They seem not unworthy of the scenery, and as momentous as the conquest of kingdoms.

Again we have wandered through the arches of the wood, until from its skirts we hear the distant booming of ice from yonder bay of the river, as if it were moved by some other and subtler tide than oceans know. To me it has a strange sound of home, thrilling as the voice of one's distant and noble kindred. A mild summer sun shines over forest and lake, and though there is but one green leaf for many rods, yet nature enjoys a serene health. Every sound is fraught with the same mysterious assurance of health, as well now the creaking of the boughs in January, as the soft sough of the wind in July.

> When Winter fringes every bough
>   With his fantastic wreath,
> And puts the seal of silence now
>   Upon the leaves beneath;
>
> When every stream in its pent-house
>   Goes gurgling on its way,
> And in his gallery the mouse
>   Nibbleth the meadow hay;
>
> Methinks the summer still is nigh,
>   And lurketh underneath,
> As that same meadow mouse doth lie
>   Snug in the last year's heath.

And if perchance the chicadee
    Lisp a faint note anon,
The snow is summer's canopy,
    Which she herself put on.

Fair blossoms deck the cheerful trees,
    And dazzling fruits depend,
The north wind sighs a summer breeze,
    The nipping frosts to fend,

Bringing glad tidings unto me,
    The while I stand all ear,
Of a serene eternity,
    Which need not winter fear.

Out on the silent pond straightway
    The restless ice doth crack,
And pond sprites merry gambols play
    Amid the deafening rack.

Eager I hasten to the vale,
    As if I heard brave news,
How nature held high festival,
    Which it were hard to lose.

I gambol with my neighbor ice,
    And sympathizing quake,
As each new crack darts in a trice
    Across the gladsome lake.

One with the cricket in the ground,
    And faggot on the hearth,
Resounds the rare domestic sound
    Along the forest path.

Before night we will take a journey on skates along the course of this meandering river, as full of novelty to one who sits by the cottage fire all the winter's day, as if it were over the polar ice, with captain Parry or Franklin; following the winding of the stream, now flowing amid hills, now spreading out into fair meadows, and forming a myriad coves and bays where the pine and hemlock overarch. The river flows in the rear of the towns, and we see all things from a new and wilder side. The fields and gardens come down to it with a frankness, and freedom from pretension, which they do not wear on the highway. It is the outside and edge of the earth. Our eyes are not offended by violent contrasts. The last rail of the farmer's fence is some swaying willow bough, which still preserves its freshness, and here at length all fences stop, and we no longer cross any road. We may go far up within the country now by the most retired and level road, never climbing a hill, but by broad levels ascending to the upland meadows. It is a beautiful illustration of the law of obedience, the flow of a river; the path for a sick man, a highway down which an acorn cup may float secure with its freight. Its slight occasional falls, whose precipices would not diversify the landscape, are celebrated by mist and spray, and attract the traveller from far and near. From the remote interior, its current conducts him by broad and easy steps, or by one gentle inclined plain, to the sea. Thus by an early and constant yielding to the inequalities of the ground, it secures itself the easiest passage.

No dominion of nature is quite closed to man at all times, and now we draw near to the empire of the fishes. Our feet glide swiftly over unfathomed depths, where in summer our line tempted the pout and perch, and where the stately pickerel lurked in the long corridors, formed by the bulrushes. The deep, impenetrable marsh, where the heron waded, and bittern squatted, is made pervious to our swift shoes, as if a thousand railroads had been made into it. With one impulse we are carried to the cabin of the muskrat, that earliest settler, and see him dart away under the transparent ice, like a furred fish, to his hole in the bank; and we glide rapidly over meadows where lately "the mower whet his scythe," through beds of frozen cranberries mixed with meadow grass. We skate near to where the blackbird, the pewee, and the kingbird hung their nests over the water, and the hornets builded from the maple on the swamp. How many gay warblers now following the sun, have radiated from this nest of silver birch and thistle down. On the swamp's outer edge was hung the supermarine village, where no foot penetrated. In this hollow tree the wood-duck reared her brood, and slid away each day to forage in yonder fen.

In winter, nature is a cabinet of curiosities, full of dried specimens, in their natural order and position. The meadows and forests are a *hortus siccus*. The leaves and grasses stand perfectly pressed by the air without screw or gum, and the bird's nests are not hung on an artificial twig, but where they builded them. We go about dry-shod to inspect the summer's work in the rank swamp, and see what a growth have got the alders, the willows, and the maples; testifying to how many warm suns, and fertilizing dews and showers. See what strides their boughs took in the luxuriant summer,—and anon these dormant buds will carry them onward and upward another span into the heavens.

Occasionally we wade through fields of snow, under whose depths the river is lost for many rods, to appear again to the right or left, where we least expected; still holding on its way underneath, with a faint, stertorous, rumbling sound, as if, like the bear and marmot, it too had hibernated, and we had followed its faint summer trail to where it earthed itself in snow and ice. At first we should have thought that rivers would be empty and dry in mid winter, or else frozen solid till the spring thawed them; but their volume is not diminished even, for only a superficial cold bridges their surface. The thousand springs which feed the lakes and streams are flowing still. The issues of a few surface springs only are closed, and they go to swell the deep reservoirs. Nature's wells are below the frost. The summer brooks are not filled with snow-water, nor does the mower quench his thirst with that alone. The streams are swollen when the snow melts in the spring, because nature's work has been delayed, the water being turned into ice and snow, whose particles are less smooth and round, and do not find their level so soon.

Far over the ice, between the hemlock woods and snow-clad hills, stands the pickerel fisher, his lines set in some retired cove, like a Finlander, with his arms thrust into the pouches of his dreadnought; with dull, snowy, fishy thoughts, himself a finless fish, separated a few inches from his race; dumb, erect, and made to be enveloped in clouds and snows, like the pines on shore. In these wild scenes, men stand about in the scenery, or move deliberately and heavily, having sacrificed the sprightliness and vivacity of towns to the dumb sobriety of nature. He does not make the scenery less wild, more than the jays and muskrats, but stands there as a part of it, as the natives are represented in the voyages of early navigators, at Nootka sound, and on the North-west coast, with their furs about them, before they were tempted to loquacity by a scrap of iron. He belongs to the natural family of man, and is planted deeper in nature and has more root than the inhabitants of towns. Go to him, ask what luck, and you will learn that he too is a worshipper of the unseen. Hear with what sincere deference and waving gesture in his tone, he speaks of the lake pickerel, which he has never seen, his primitive and ideal race of pickerel. He is connected with the shore still, as by a fish-line, and yet remembers the season when he took fish through the ice on the pond, while the peas were up in his garden at home.

But now, while we have loitered, the clouds have gathered again, and a few straggling snow-flakes are beginning to descend. Faster and faster they fall, shutting out the distant objects from sight. The snow falls on every wood and field, and no crevice is forgotten; by the river and the pond, on the hill and in the valley. Quadrupeds are confined to their coverts, and the birds sit upon their perches this peaceful hour. There is not so much sound as in fair weather, but silently and gradually every slope, and the grey walls and fences, and the polished ice, and the sere leaves, which were not buried before, are concealed, and the tracks of men and beasts are lost. With so little effort does nature reassert her rule, and blot out the traces of men. Hear how Homer has described the same. "The snow flakes fall thick and fast on a winter's day. The winds are lulled, and the snow falls incessant, covering the top of the mountains, and the hills, and the plains where the lotus tree grows, and the cultivated fields, and they are falling by the inlets and shores of the foaming sea, but are silently dissolved by the waves." The snow levels all things, and infolds them deeper on the bosom of nature, as, in the slow summer, vegetation creeps up to the entablature of the temple, and the turrets of the castle, and helps her to prevail over art.

The surly night-wind rustles through the wood, and warns

us to retrace our steps, while the sun goes down behind the thickening storm, and birds seek their roosts, and cattle their stalls.

> "Drooping the lab'rer ox
> Stands covered o'er with snow, and *now* demands
> The fruit of all his toil."

Though winter is represented in the almanac as an old man, facing the wind and sleet, and drawing his cloak about him, we rather think of him as a merry wood-chopper, and warm-blooded youth, as blithe as summer. The unexplored grandeur of the storm keeps up the spirits of the traveller. It does not trifle with us, but has a sweet earnestness. In winter we lead a more inward life. Our hearts are warm and merry, like cottages under drifts, whose windows and doors are half concealed, but from whose chimneys the smoke cheerfully ascends. The imprisoning drifts increase the sense of comfort which the house affords, and in the coldest days we are content to sit over the hearth and see the sky through the chimney top, enjoying the quiet and serene life that may be had in a warm corner by the chimney side, or feeling our pulse by listening to the low of cattle in the street, or the sound of the flail in distant barns all the long afternoon. No doubt a skilful physician could determine our health by observing how these simple and natural sounds affected us. We enjoy now, not an oriental, but a boreal leisure, around warm stoves and fireplaces, and watch the shadow of motes in the sunbeams.

Sometimes our fate grows too homely and familiarly serious ever to be cured. Consider how for three months the human destiny is wrapped in furs. The good Hebrew revelation takes no cognizance of all this cheerful snow. Is there no religion for the temperate and frigid zones? We know of no scripture which records the pure benignity of the gods on a New England winter night. Their praises have never been sung, only their wrath deprecated. The best scripture, after all, records but a meagre faith. Its saints live reserved and austere. Let a brave devout man spend the year in the woods of Maine or Labrador, and see if the Hebrew scriptures speak adequately of his condition and experience, from the setting in of winter to the breaking up of the ice.

Now commences, the long winter evening around the farmer's hearth, when the thoughts of the indwellers travel far abroad, and men are by nature and necessity charitable and liberal to all creatures. Now is the happy resistance to cold, when the farmer reaps his reward, and thinks of his preparedness for winter, and through the glittering panes, sees with equanimity "the mansion of the northern bear," for now the storm is over,

> "The full ethereal round,
> Infinite worlds disclosing to the view,
> Shines out intensely keen; and all one cope
> Of starry glitter glows from pole to pole."

The Landlord

U NDER the one word, house, are included the school
house, the alms house, the jail, the tavern, the dwelling
house; and the meanest shed or cave in which men live, con-
tains the elements of all these. But no where on the earth
stands the entire and perfect house. The Parthenon, St.
Peter's, the Gothic minster, the palace, the hovel, are but im-
perfect executions of an imperfect idea. Who would dwell in
them? Perhaps to the eye of the gods, the cottage is more
holy than the Parthenon, for they look down with no especial
favor upon the shrines formally dedicated to them, and that
should be the most sacred roof which shelters most of hu-
manity. Surely, then, the gods who are most interested in the
human race preside over the Tavern, where especially men
congregate. Methinks I see the thousand shrines erected to
Hospitality shining afar in all countries, as well Mahometan
and Jewish, as Christian, khans, and caravansaries, and inns,
whither all pilgrims without distinction resort.

Likewise we look in vain east or west over the earth to find
the perfect man; but each represents only some particular ex-
cellence. The Landlord is a man of more open and general
sympathies, who possesses a spirit of hospitality which is its
own reward, and feeds and shelters men from pure love of the
creatures. To be sure, this profession is as often filled by im-
perfect characters, and such as have sought it from unworthy
motives, as any other, but so much the more should we prize
the true and honest Landlord when we meet with him.

Who has not imagined to himself a country inn, where the
traveller shall really feel *in*, and at home, and at his public
house, who was before at his private house; whose host is in-
deed a *host*, and a *lord* of the *land*, a self-appointed brother of
his race; called to his place, beside, by all the winds of heaven
and his good genius, as truly as the preacher is called to
preach; a man of such universal sympathies, and so broad and
genial a human nature, that he would fain sacrifice the tender
but narrow ties of private friendship, to a broad, sunshiny,
fair-weather-and-foul friendship for his race; who loves men,

not as a philosopher, with philanthropy, nor as an overseer of the poor, with charity, but by a necessity of his nature, as he loves dogs and horses; and standing at his open door from morning till night, would fain see more and more of them come along the highway, and is never satiated. To him the sun and moon are but travellers, the one by day and the other by night; and they too patronise his house. To his imagination all things travel save his sign-post and himself; and though you may be his neighbor for years, he will show you only the civilities of the road. But on the other hand, while nations and individuals are alike selfish and exclusive, he loves all men equally; and if he treats his nearest neighbor as a stranger, since he has invited all nations to share his hospitality, the farthest travelled is in some measure kindred to him who takes him into the bosom of his family.

He keeps a house of entertainment at the sign of the Black Horse or the Spread Eagle, and is known far and wide, and his fame travels with increasing radius every year. All the neighborhood is in his interest, and if the traveller ask how far to a tavern, he receives some such answer as this: "Well, sir, there's a house about three miles from here, where they haven't taken down their sign yet; but it's only ten miles to Slocum's, and that's a capital house, both for man and beast." At three miles he passes a cheerless barrack, standing desolate behind its sign-post, neither public nor private, and has glimpses of a discontented couple who have mistaken their calling. At ten miles see where the Tavern stands,—really an *entertaining* prospect,—so public and inviting that only the rain and snow do not enter. It is no gay pavilion, made of bright stuffs, and furnished with nuts and gingerbread, but as plain and sincere as a caravansary; located in no Tarrytown, where you receive only the civilities of commerce, but far in the fields it exercises a primitive hospitality, amid the fresh scent of new hay and raspberries, if it be summer time, and the tinkling of cow-bells from invisible pastures; for it is a land flowing with milk and honey, and the newest milk courses in a broad deep stream across the premises.

In these retired places the tavern is first of all a house—elsewhere, last of all, or never—and warms and shelters its inhabitants. It is as simple and sincere in its essentials as the caves in which the first men dwelt, but it is also as open and public. The traveller steps across the threshold, and lo! he too is master, for he only can be called proprietor of the house here who behaves with most propriety in it. The Landlord stands clear back in nature, to my imagination, with his axe and spade felling trees and raising potatoes with the vigor of a pioneer; with Promethean energy making nature yield her increase to supply the wants of so many; and he is not so exhausted, nor of so short a stride, but that he comes forward even to the highway to this wide hospitality and publicity. Surely, he has solved some of the problems of life. He comes in at his back door, holding a log fresh cut for the hearth upon his shoulder with one hand, while he greets the newly arrived traveller with the other.

Here at length we have free range, as not in palaces, nor cottages, nor temples, and intrude no where. All the secrets of housekeeping are exhibited to the eyes of men, above and below, before and behind. This is the necessary way to live, men have confessed, in these days, and shall he skulk and hide? And why should we have any serious disgust at kitchens? Perhaps they are the holiest recess of the house. There is the hearth, after all,—and the settle, and the faggots, and the kettle, and the crickets. We have pleasant reminiscences of these. They are the heart, the left ventricle, the very vital part of the house. Here the real and sincere life which we meet in the streets was actually fed and sheltered. Here burns the taper that cheers the lonely traveller by night, and from this hearth ascend the smokes that populate the valley to his eyes by day. On the whole, a man may not be so little ashamed of any other part of his house, for here is his sincerity and earnest, at least. It may not be here that the besoms are plied most—it is not here that they need to be, for dust will not settle on the kitchen floor more than in nature.

Hence it will not do for the Landlord to possess too fine a nature. He must have health above the common accidents of life, subject to no modern fashionable diseases; but no taste, rather a vast relish or appetite. His sentiments on all subjects will be delivered as freely as the wind blows; there is nothing private or individual in them, though still original, but they are public, and of the hue of the heavens over his house,—a certain out-of-door obviousness and transparency not to be disputed. What he does, his manners are not to be complained of, though abstractly offensive, for it is what man does, and in him the race is exhibited. When he eats, he is liver and bowels, and the whole digestive apparatus to the company, and so all admit the thing is done. He must have no idiosyncracies, no particular bents or tendencies to this or that, but a general, uniform, and healthy development, such as his portly person indicates, offering himself equally on all sides to men. He is not one of your peaked and inhospitable men of genius, with particular tastes, but, as we said before, has one uniform relish, and taste which never aspires higher than a tavern sign, or the cut of a weather-cock. The man of genius, like a dog with a bone, or the slave who has swallowed a diamond, or a patient with the gravel, sits afar and retired, off the road, hangs out no sign of refreshment for man and beast, but says, by all possible hints and signs, I wish to be alone—good-bye—farewell. But the landlord can afford to live without privacy. He entertains no private thought, he cherishes no solitary hour, no sabbath day, but thinks—enough to assert the dignity of reason—and talks, and reads the newspaper. What he does not tell to one traveller, he tells to another. He never wants to be alone, but sleeps, wakes, eats, drinks, sociably, still remembering his race. He walks abroad through the thoughts of men, and the Iliad and Shakspeare are tame to him, who hears the rude but homely incidents of the road from every traveller. The mail might drive through his brain in the midst of his most lonely soliloquy, without disturbing his equanimity, provided it brought plenty of news and passengers. There can be no *pro*-fanity where there is no fane behind, and the whole world may see quite round him. Perchance his lines have fallen to him in dustier places, and he has heroically sat down where two roads meet, or at the Four Corners, or the Five Points, and his life is sublimely trivial for the good of men. The dust of travel blows ever in his eyes, and they preserve their clear, complacent look. The hourlies and half-hourlies, the dailies and weeklies, whirl on well worn tracks, round and round his house, as if it were the goal in the stadium, and still he sits within in unruffled serenity, with no show of retreat. His neighbor dwells timidly behind a screen of poplars and willows, and a fence with sheafs of spears at regular intervals, or defended against the tender palms of visitors by sharp spikes,—but the traveller's wheels rattle over the door-step of the tavern, and he cracks his whip in the entry. He is truly glad to see you, and sincere as the bull's-eye over his door. The traveller seeks to find, wherever he goes, some one who will stand in this broad and catholic relation to him, who will be an inhabitant of the land to him a stranger, and represent its human nature, as the rock stands for its inanimate nature; and this is he. As his crib furnishes provender for the traveller's horse, and his larder provisions for his appetite, so his conversation furnishes the necessary aliment to his spirits. He knows very well what a man wants, for he is a man himself, and as it were the farthest travelled, though he has never stirred from his door. He understands his needs and destiny. He would be well fed and lodged, there can be no doubt, and have the transient sympathy of a cheerful companion, and of a heart which always prophesies fair weather. And after all the greatest men, even, want much more the sympathy which every one can give, than that which the great only can impart. If he is not the most upright, let us allow him this praise, that he is the most downright of men. He has a hand to shake and to be shaken, and takes a sturdy and unquestionable interest in you, as if he had assumed the care of you, but if you will break his neck, he will even give you the best advice as to the method.

The great poets have not been ungrateful to their landlords. Mine host of the Tabard inn, in the Prologue to the Canterbury Tales, was an honor to his profession:

> "A semely man our Hoste was, with alle,
> For to han been an marshal in an halle.
> A large man he was, with eyen stepe;
> A fairer burgeis is ther non in Chepe:
> Bold of his speche, and wise, and well ytaught,
> And of manhood him lacked righte naught.
> Eke thereto, was he right a mery man,
> And after souper plaien he began,
> And spake of mirthe amonges other thinges,
> Whan that we hadden made our reckoninges."

He is the true house-band, and centre of the company—of greater fellowship and practical social talent than any. He it is, that proposes that each shall tell a tale to while away the time to Canterbury, and leads them himself, and concludes with his own tale:

> "Now, by my fader's soule that is ded,
> But ye be mery, smiteth of my hed:
> Hold up your hondes withouten more speche."

If we do not look up to the Landlord, we look round for him on all emergencies, for he is a man of infinite experience, who unites hands with wit. He is a more public character than a statesman—a publican, and not consequently a sinner; and surely, he, if any, should be exempted from taxation and military duty.

Talking with our host is next best and instructive to talking with one's self. It is a more conscious soliloquy; as it were, to speak generally, and try what we would say provided we had an audience. He has indulgent and open ears, and does not require petty and particular statements. "Heigho!" exclaims the traveller. Them's my sentiments, thinks mine host, and stands ready for what may come next, expressing the purest sympathy by his demeanor. "Hot as blazes!" says the other,—— "Hard weather, sir,—not much stirring now-a-days," says he. He is wiser than to contradict his guest in any case; he lets him go on, he lets him travel.

The latest sitter leaves him standing far in the night, prepared to live right on, while suns rise and set, and his "good-night" has as brisk a sound as his "good-morning," and the earliest riser finds him tasting his liquors in the bar ere flies begin to buzz, with a countenance fresh as the morning star over the sanded floor,—and not as one who had watched all night for travellers. And yet, if beds be the subject of conversation, it will appear that no man has been a sounder sleeper in his time.

Finally, as for his moral character, we do not hesitate to say, that he has no grain of vice or meanness in him, but represents just that degree of virtue which all men relish without being obliged to respect. He is a good man, as his bitters are good—an unquestionable goodness. Not what is called a good man,—good to be considered, as a work of art in galleries and museums,—but a good fellow, that is, good to be associated with. Who ever thought of the religion of an innkeeper—whether he was joined to the Church, partook of the sacrament, said his prayers, feared God, or the like? No doubt he has had his experiences, has felt a change, and is a firm believer in the perseverance of the saints. In this last, we suspect, does the peculiarity of his religion consist. But he keeps an inn, and not a conscience. How many fragrant charities, and sincere social virtues are implied in this daily offering of himself to the public. He cherishes good will to all, and gives the wayfarer as good and honest advice to direct him on his road, as the priest.

To conclude, the tavern will compare favorably with the church. The church is the place where prayers and sermons are delivered, but the tavern is where they are to take effect, and if the former are good, the latter cannot be bad.

Paradise (To Be) Regained*

W E LEARN that Mr. Etzler is a native of Germany, and originally published his book in Pennsylvania, ten or twelve years ago; and now a second English edition, from the original American one, is demanded by his readers across the water, owing, we suppose, to the recent spread of Fourier's doctrines. It is one of the signs of the times. We confess that we have risen from reading this book with enlarged ideas, and grander conceptions of our duties in this world. It did expand us a little. It is worth attending to, if only that it entertains large questions. Consider what Mr. Etzler proposes:

"Fellow Men! I promise to show the means of creating a paradise within ten years, where everything desirable for human life may be had by every man in superabundance, without labor, and without pay; where the whole face of nature shall be changed into the most beautiful forms, and man may live in the most magnificent palaces, in all imaginable refinements of luxury, and in the most delightful gardens; where he may accomplish, without labor, in one year, more than hitherto could be done in thousands of years; may level mountains, sink valleys, create lakes, drain lakes and swamps, and intersect the land everywhere with beautiful canals, and roads for transporting heavy loads of many thousand tons, and for travelling one thousand miles in twenty-four hours; may cover the ocean with floating islands movable in any desired direction with immense power and celerity, in perfect security, and with all comforts and luxuries, bearing gardens and palaces, with thousands of families, and provided with rivulets of sweet water; may explore the interior of the globe, and travel from pole to pole in a fortnight; provide himself with means, unheard of yet, for increasing his knowledge of the world, and so his intelligence; lead a life of continual happiness, of enjoyments yet unknown; free himself from almost all the evils that afflict mankind, except death, and even put death far beyond the common period of human life, and finally render it less afflicting. Mankind may thus live in and enjoy a new world, far superior to the present, and raise themselves far higher in the scale of being."

*The Paradise within the Reach of all Men, without Labor, by Powers of Nature and Machinery. An Address to all intelligent Men. In two parts. By J. A. Etzler. Part First. Second English Edition. pp. 55. London, 1842.

It would seem from this and various indications beside, that there is a transcendentalism in mechanics as well as in ethics. While the whole field of the one reformer lies beyond the boundaries of space, the other is pushing his schemes for the elevation of the race to its utmost limits. While one scours the heavens, the other sweeps the earth. One says he will reform himself, and then nature and circumstances will be right. Let us not obstruct ourselves, for that is the greatest friction. It is of little importance though a cloud obstruct the view of the astronomer compared with his own blindness. The other will reform nature and circumstances, and then man will be right. Talk no more vaguely, says he, of reforming the world—I will reform the globe itself. What matters it whether I remove this humor out of my flesh, or the pestilent humor from the fleshy part of the globe? Nay, is not the latter the more generous course? At present the globe goes with a shattered constitution in its orbit. Has it not asthma, and ague, and fever, and dropsy, and flatulence, and pleurisy, and is it not afflicted with vermin? Has it not its healthful laws counteracted, and its vital energy which will yet redeem it? No doubt the simple powers of nature properly directed by man would make it healthy and paradise; as the laws of man's own constitution but wait to be obeyed, to restore him to health and happiness. Our panaceas cure but few ails, our general hospitals are private and exclusive. We must set up another Hygeian than is now worshipped. Do not the quacks even direct small doses for children, larger for adults, and larger still for oxen and horses? Let us remember that we are to prescribe for the globe itself.

This fair homestead has fallen to us, and how little have we done to improve it, how little have we cleared and hedged and ditched! We are too inclined to go hence to a "better land," without lifting a finger, as our farmers are moving to the Ohio soil; but would it not be more heroic and faithful to till and redeem this New-England soil of the world? The still youthful energies of the globe have only to be directed in their proper channel. Every gazette brings accounts of the untutored freaks of the wind—shipwrecks and hurricanes which the mariner and planter accept as special or general providences; but they touch our consciences, they remind us of our sins. Another deluge would disgrace mankind. We confess we never had much respect for that antediluvian race. A thorough-bred business man cannot enter heartily upon the business of life without first looking into his accounts. How many things are now at loose ends. Who knows which way the wind will blow to-morrow? Let us not succumb to nature. We will marshal the clouds and restrain the tempests; we will bottle up pestilent exhalations, we will probe for earthquakes, grub them up; and give vent to the dangerous gases; we will disembowel the volcano, and extract its poison, take its seed out. We will wash water, and warm fire, and cool ice, and underprop the earth. We will teach birds to fly, and fishes to swim, and ruminants to chew the cud. It is time we had looked into these things.

And it becomes the moralist, too, to inquire what man might do to improve and beautify the system; what to make the stars shine more brightly, the sun more cheery and joyous, the moon more placid and content. Could he not heighten the tints of flowers and the melody of birds? Does he perform his duty to the inferior races? Should he not be a god to them? What is the part of magnanimity to the whale and the beaver? Should we not fear to exchange places with them for a day, lest by their behavior they should shame us? Might we not treat with magnanimity the shark and the tiger, not descend to meet them on their own level, with spears of sharks' teeth and bucklers of tiger's skin? We slander the hyena; man is the fiercest and cruelest animal. Ah! he is of little faith; even the erring comets and meteors would thank him, and return his kindness in their kind.

How meanly and grossly do we deal with nature! Could we not have a less gross labor? What else do these fine inventions suggest,—magnetism, the daguerreotype, electricity? Can we not do more than cut and trim the forest,—can we not assist in its interior economy, in the circulation of the sap? Now we work superficially and violently. We do not suspect how much might be done to improve our relation with animated nature; what kindness and refined courtesy there might be.

There are certain pursuits which, if not wholly poetic and true, do at least suggest a nobler and finer relation to nature than we know. The keeping of bees, for instance, is a very

slight interference. It is like directing the sunbeams. All na-
tions, from the remotest antiquity, have thus fingered nature.
There are Hymettus and Hybla, and how many bee-
renowned spots beside? There is nothing gross in the idea of
these little herds,—their hum like the faintest low of kine in
the meads. A pleasant reviewer has lately reminded us that
in some places they are led out to pasture where the flow-
ers are most abundant. "Columella tells us," says he, "that
the inhabitants of Arabia sent their hives into Attica to bene-
fit by the later-blowing flowers." Annually are the hives, in
immense pyramids, carried up the Nile in boats, and suffered
to float slowly down the stream by night, resting by day, as
the flowers put forth along the banks; and they determine the
richness of any locality, and so the profitableness of delay, by
the sinking of the boat in the water. We are told, by the same
reviewer, of a man in Germany, whose bees yielded more
honey than those of his neighbors, with no apparent advan-
tage; but at length he informed them that he had turned his
hives one degree more to the east, and so his bees, having
two hours the start in the morning, got the first sip of honey.
True, there is treachery and selfishness behind all this; but
these things suggest to the poetic mind what might be done.

Many examples there are of a grosser interference, yet not
without their apology. We saw last summer, on the side of a
mountain, a dog employed to churn for a farmer's family,
travelling upon a horizontal wheel, and though he had sore
eyes, an alarming cough, and withal a demure aspect, yet their
bread did get buttered for all that. Undoubtedly, in the most
brilliant successes, the first rank is always sacrificed. Much
useless travelling of horses, *in extenso*, has of late years been
improved for man's behoof, only two forces being taken
advantage of,—the gravity of the horse, which is the cen-
tripetal, and his centrifugal inclination to go a-head. Only
these two elements in the calculation. And is not the crea-
ture's whole economy better economized thus? Are not all fi-
nite beings better pleased with motions relative than absolute?
And what is the great globe itself but such a wheel,—a larger
tread-mill,—so that our horse's freest steps over prairies are
oftentimes balked and rendered of no avail by the earth's mo-
tion on its axis? But here he is the central agent and motive

power; and, for variety of scenery, being provided with a window in front, do not the ever-varying activity and fluctuating energy of the creature himself work the effect of the most varied scenery on a country road? It must be confessed that horses at present work too exclusively for men, rarely men for horses; and the brute degenerates in man's society.

It will be seen that we contemplate a time when man's will shall be law to the physical world, and he shall no longer be deterred by such abstractions as time and space, height and depth, weight and hardness, but shall indeed be the lord of creation. "Well," says the faithless reader, " 'life is short, but art is long;' where is the power that will effect all these changes?" This it is the very object of Mr. Etzler's volume to show. At present, he would merely remind us that there are innumerable and immeasurable powers already existing in nature, unimproved on a large scale, or for generous and universal ends, amply sufficient for these purposes. He would only indicate their existence, as a surveyor makes known the existence of a water-power on any stream; but for their application he refers us to a sequel to this book, called the "Mechanical System." A few of the most obvious and familiar of these powers are, the Wind, the Tide, the Waves, the Sunshine. Let us consider their value.

First, there is the power of the Wind, constantly exerted over the globe. It appears from observation of a sailing-vessel, and from scientific tables, that the average power of the wind is equal to that of one horse for every one hundred square feet. "We know," says our author—

"that ships of the first class carry sails two hundred feet high; we may, therefore, equally, on land, oppose to the wind surfaces of the same height. Imagine a line of such surfaces one mile, or about 5,000 feet, long; they would then contain 1,000,000 square feet. Let these surfaces intersect the direction of the wind at right angles, by some contrivance, and receive, consequently, its full power at all times. Its average power being equal to one horse for every 100 square feet, the total power would be equal to 1,000,000 divided by 100, or 10,000 horses' power. Allowing the power of one horse to equal that of ten men, the power of 10,000 horses is equal to 100,000 men. But as men cannot work uninterruptedly, but want about half the time for sleep and repose, the same power would be equal to 200,000 men. . . . We are not limited to the height of 200 feet; we might extend, if required, the application of this power to the height of the clouds, by means of kites."

But we will have one such fence for every square mile of the globe's surface, for, as the wind usually strikes the earth at an angle of more than two degrees, which is evident from observing its effect on the high sea, it admits of even a closer approach. As the surface of the globe contains about 200,000,000 square miles, the whole power of the wind on these surfaces would equal 40,000,000,000,000,000 men's power, and "would perform 80,000 times as much work as all the men on earth could effect with their nerves."

If it should be objected that this computation includes the surface of the ocean and uninhabitable regions of the earth, where this power could not be applied for our purposes, Mr. Etzler is quick with his reply—"But, you will recollect," says he, "that I have promised to show the means for rendering the ocean as inhabitable as the most fruitful dry land; and I do not exclude even the polar regions."

The reader will observe that our author uses the fence only as a convenient formula for expressing the power of the wind, and does not consider it a necessary method of its application. We do not attach much value to this statement of the comparative power of the wind and horse, for no common ground is mentioned on which they can be compared. Undoubtedly, each is incomparably excellent in its way, and every general comparison made for such practical purposes as are contemplated, which gives a preference to the one, must be made with some unfairness to the other. The scientific tables are, for the most part, true only in a tabular sense. We suspect that a loaded wagon, with a light sail, ten feet square, would not have been blown so far by the end of the year, under equal circumstances, as a common racer or dray horse would have drawn it. And how many crazy structures on our globe's surface, of the same dimensions, would wait for dry-rot if the traces of one horse were hitched to them, even to their windward side? Plainly, this is not the principle of comparison. But even the steady and constant force of the horse may be rated as equal to his weight at least. Yet we should prefer to let the zephyrs and gales bear, with all their weight, upon our fences, than that Dobbin, with feet braced, should lean ominously against them for a season.

Nevertheless, here is an almost incalculable power at our disposal, yet how trifling the use we make of it. It only serves to turn a few mills, blow a few vessels across the ocean, and a few trivial ends besides. What a poor compliment do we pay to our indefatigable and energetic servant!

"If you ask, perhaps, why this power is not used, if the statement be true, I have to ask in return, why is the power of steam so lately come to application? so many millions of men boiled water every day for many thousand years; they must have frequently seen that boiling water, in tightly closed pots or kettles, would lift the cover or burst the vessel with great violence. The power of steam was, therefore, as commonly known down to the least kitchen or wash-woman, as the power of wind; but close observation and reflection were bestowed neither on the one nor the other."

Men having discovered the power of falling water, which after all is comparatively slight, how eagerly do they seek out and improve these *privileges?* Let a difference of but a few feet in level be discovered on some stream near a populous town, some slight occasion for gravity to act, and the whole economy of the neighborhood is changed at once. Men do indeed speculate about and with this power as if it were the only privilege. But meanwhile this aerial stream is falling from far greater heights with more constant flow, never shrunk by drought, offering mill-sites wherever the wind blows; a Niagara in the air, with no Canada side;—only the application is hard.

There are the powers too of the Tide and Waves, constantly ebbing and flowing, lapsing and relapsing, but they serve man in but few ways. They turn a few tide mills, and perform a few other insignificant and accidental services only. We all perceive the effect of the tide; how imperceptibly it creeps up into our harbors and rivers, and raises the heaviest navies as easily as the lightest ship. Everything that floats must yield to it. But man, slow to take nature's constant hint of assistance, makes slight and irregular use of this power, in careening ships and getting them afloat when aground.

The following is Mr. Etzler's calculation on this head: To form a conception of the power which the tide affords, let us imagine a surface of 100 miles square, or 10,000 square miles, where the tide rises and sinks, on an average, 10 feet; how many men would it require to empty a basin of 10,000 square miles area, and 10 feet deep, filled with sea-water, in 6¼ hours and fill it again in the same time? As one man can raise 8 cubic feet of sea-water per minute, and in 6¼ hours 3,000, it would take 1,200,000,000 men, or as they could work only half the time, 2,400,000,000, to raise 3,000,000,000,000 cubic feet, or the whole quantity required in the given time.

This power may be applied in various ways. A large body, of the heaviest materials that will float, may first be raised by it, and being attached to the end of a balance reaching from the land, or from a stationary support, fastened to the bottom, when the tide falls, the whole weight will be brought to bear upon the end of the balance. Also when the tide rises it may be made to exert a nearly equal force in the opposite direction. It can be employed whenever a *point d'appui* can be obtained.

"However, the application of the tide being by establishments fixed on the ground, it is natural to begin with them near the shores in shallow water, and upon sands, which may be extended gradually further into the sea. The shores of the continent, islands, and sands, being generally surrounded by shallow water, not exceeding from 50 to 100 fathoms in depth, for 20, 50, or 100 miles and upward. The coasts of North America, with their extensive sand-banks, islands, and rocks, may easily afford, for this purpose, a ground about 3,000 miles long, and, on an average, 100 miles broad, or 300,000 square miles, which, with a power of 240,000 men per square mile, as stated, at 10 feet tide, will be equal to 72,000 millions of men, or for every mile of coast, a power of 24,000,000 men."

"Rafts, of any extent, fastened on the ground of the sea, along the shore, and stretching far into the sea, may be covered with fertile soil, bearing vegetables and trees, of every description, the finest gardens, equal to those the firm land may admit of, and buildings and machineries, which may operate, not only on the sea, where they are, but which also, by means of mechanical connections, may extend their operations for many miles into the continent. (Etzler's Mechanical System, page 24.) Thus this power may cultivate the artificial soil for many miles upon the surface of the sea, near the shores, and, for several miles, the dry land, along the shore, in the most superior manner imaginable; it may build cities along the shore, consisting of the most magnificent palaces, every one surrounded by gardens and the most delightful sceneries; it may level the hills and unevennesses, or raise eminences for enjoying open prospect into the country and upon the sea; it may cover the barren shore with fertile soil, and beautify the same in various ways; it may clear the sea of shallows, and make easy the approach to the land, not merely of vessels, but of large floating islands, which may come from, and go to distant parts of the world, islands that have every commodity and security for their inhabitants which the firm land affords."

"Thus may a power, derived from the gravity of the moon and the ocean, hitherto but the objects of idle curiosity to the studious man, be made eminently subservient for creating the most delightful abodes along the coasts, where men may enjoy at the same time all the advantages of sea and dry land; the coasts may hereafter be continuous paradisiacal skirts between land and sea, everywhere crowded with the densest population. The shores and the sea along them will be no more as raw nature presents them now, but everywhere of easy and charming access, not even molested by the roar of waves, shaped as it may suit the purposes of their inhabitants; the sea will be cleared of every obstruction to free passage every-where, and its productions in fishes, etc., will be gathered in large, appropriate receptacles, to present them to the inhabitants of the shores and of the sea."

Verily, the land would wear a busy aspect at the spring and neap tide, and these island ships—these *terræ infirmæ*—which realise the fables of antiquity, affect our imagination. We have often thought that the fittest locality for a human dwelling was on the edge of the land, that there the constant lesson and impression of the sea might sink deep into the life and character of the landsman, and perhaps impart a marine tint to his imagination. It is a noble word, that *mariner*—one who is conversant with the sea. There should be more of what it signifies in each of us. It is a worthy country to belong to—we look to see him not disgrace it. Perhaps we should be equally mariners and terreners, and even our Green Mountains need some of that sea-green to be mixed with them.

The computation of the power of the waves is less satisfactory. While only the average power of the wind, and the average height of the tide, were taken before now, the extreme height of the waves is used, for they are made to rise ten feet above the level of the sea, to which, adding ten more for depression, we have twenty feet, or the extreme height of a wave. Indeed, the power of the waves, which is produced by the wind blowing obliquely and at disadvantage upon the water, is made to be, not only three thousand times greater than that of the tide, but one hundred times greater than that of the wind itself, meeting its object at right angles. Moreover, this power is measured by the area of the vessel, and not by its length mainly, and it seems to be forgotten that the motion of the waves is chiefly undulatory, and exerts a power only within the limits of a vibration, else the very continents, with their extensive coasts, would soon be set adrift.

Finally, there is the power to be derived from sunshine, by the principle on which Archimedes contrived his burning mirrors, a multiplication of mirrors reflecting the rays of the sun upon the same spot, till the requisite degree of heat is obtained. The principal application of this power will be to the boiling of water and production of steam.

"How to create rivulets of sweet and wholesome water, on floating islands, in the midst of the ocean, will be no riddle now. Seawater changed into steam, will distil into sweet water, leaving the salt on the bottom. Thus the steam engines on floating islands, for their propulsion and other mechanical purposes, will serve, at the same time, for the distillery of sweet water, which, collected in basins, may be led through channels over the island, while, where required, it may be refrigerated by artificial means, and changed into cool water, surpassing, in salubrity, the best spring water, because nature hardly ever distils water so purely, and without admixture of less wholesome matter."

So much for these few and more obvious powers, already used to a trifling extent. But there are innumerable others in nature, not described nor discovered. These, however, will do for the present. This would be to make the sun and the moon equally our satellites. For, as the moon is the cause of the tides, and the sun the cause of the wind, which, in turn, is the cause of the waves, all the work of this planet would be performed by these far influences.

"But as these powers are very irregular and subject to interruptions; the next object is to show how they may be converted into powers that operate continually and uniformly for ever, until the machinery be worn out, or, in other words, into perpetual motions." . . . "Hitherto the power of the wind has been applied immediately upon the machinery for use, and we have had to wait the chances of the wind's blowing; while the operation was stopped as soon as the wind ceased to blow. But the manner, which I shall state hereafter, of applying this power, is to make it operate only for collecting or storing up power, and then to take out of this store, at any time, as much as may be wanted for final operation upon the machines. The power stored up is to react as required, and may do so long after the original power of the wind has ceased. And though the wind should cease for intervals of many months, we may have by the same power a uniform perpetual motion in a very simple way."

"The weight of a clock being wound up gives us an image of reaction. The sinking of this weight is the reaction of winding it up. It is not necessary to wait till it has run down before we wind up the weight, but it may be wound up at any time, partly or totally; and if done always before the weight reaches the bottom, the clock will be going perpetually. In a similar, though not in the same way, we may cause a reaction on a larger scale. We may raise, for instance, water by the immediate application of wind or steam to a pond upon some eminence, out of which, through an outlet, it may fall upon some wheel or other contrivance for setting machinery a going. Thus we may store up water in some eminent pond, and take out of this store, at any time, as much water through the outlet as we want to employ, by which means the original power may react for many days after it has ceased." . . . "Such reservoirs of moderate elevation or size need not be made artificially, but will be found made by nature very frequently, requiring but little aid for their completion. They require no regularity of form. Any valley with lower grounds in its vicinity, would answer the purpose. Small crevices may be filled up. Such places may be eligible for the beginning of enterprises of this kind."

The greater the height, of course the less water required. But suppose a level and dry country; then hill and valley, and "eminent pond," are to be constructed by main force; or if the springs are unusually low, then dirt and stones may be used, and the disadvantage arising from friction will be counterbalanced by their greater gravity. Nor shall a single rood of dry land be sunk in such artificial ponds as may be wasted, but their surfaces "may be covered with rafts decked with fertile earth, and all kinds of vegetables which may grow there as well as anywhere else."

And finally, by the use of thick envelopes retaining the heat, and other contrivances, "the power of steam caused by sunshine may react at will, and thus be rendered perpetual, no matter how often or how long the sunshine may be interrupted. (Etzler's Mechanical System)."

Here is power enough, one would think, to accomplish somewhat. These are the powers below. Oh ye millwrights, ye engineers, ye operatives and speculators of every class, never again complain of a want of power; it is the grossest form of infidelity. The question is not how we shall execute, but what. Let us not use in a niggardly manner what is thus generously offered.

Consider what revolutions are to be effected in agriculture. First, in the new country, a machine is to move along taking out trees and stones to any required depth, and piling them up in convenient heaps; then the same machine, "with a little alteration," is to plane the ground perfectly, till there shall be no hills nor valleys, making the requisite canals, ditches and roads, as it goes along. The same machine, "with some other little alterations," is then to sift the ground thoroughly, supply fertile soil from other places if wanted, and plant it; and finally, the same machine "with a little addition," is to reap and gather in the crop, thresh and grind it, or press it to oil, or prepare it any way for final use. For the description of these machines we are referred to "Etzler's Mechanical System, pages 11 to 27." We should be pleased to see that "Mechanical System," though we have not been able to ascertain whether it has been published, or only exists as yet in the design of the author. We have great faith in it. But we cannot stop for applications now.

"Any wilderness, even the most hideous and sterile, may be converted into the most fertile and delightful gardens. The most dismal swamps may be cleared of all their spontaneous growth, filled up and levelled, and intersected by canals, ditches and aqueducts, for draining them entirely. The soil, if required, may be meliorated, by covering or mixing it with rich soil taken from distant places, and the same be mouldered to fine dust, levelled, sifted from all roots, weeds and stones, and sowed and planted in the most beautiful order and symmetry, with fruit trees and vegetables of every kind that may stand the climate."

New facilities for transportation and locomotion are to be adopted:

"Large and commodious vehicles, for carrying many thousand tons, running over peculiarly adapted level roads, at the rate of forty miles per hour, or one thousand miles per day, may transport men and things, small houses, and whatever may serve for comfort and ease, by land. Floating islands, constructed of logs, or of wooden-stuff prepared in a similar manner, as is to be done with stone, and of live trees, which may be reared so as to interlace one another, and strengthen the whole, may be covered with gardens and palaces, and propelled by powerful engines, so as to run at an equal rate through seas and oceans. Thus, man may move, with the celerity of a bird's flight, in terrestrial paradises, from one climate to another, and see the world in all its variety, exchanging, with distant nations, the surplus of productions. The journey from one pole to another may be performed in a fortnight; the visit to a transmarine country in a week or two; or a journey round the world in one or two months by land and water. And why pass a dreary winter every year while there is yet room enough on the globe where nature is blessed with a perpetual summer, and with a far greater variety and luxuriance of vegetation? More than one-half the surface of the globe has no winter. Men will have it in their power to remove and prevent all bad influences of climate, and to enjoy, perpetually, only that temperature which suits their constitution and feeling best."

Who knows but by accumulating the power until the end of the present century, using meanwhile only the smallest allowance, reserving all that blows, all that shines, all that ebbs and flows, all that dashes, we may have got such a reserved accumulated power as to run the earth off its track into a new orbit, some summer, and so change the tedious vicissitude of the seasons? Or, perchance, coming generations will not abide the dissolution of the globe, but, availing themselves of future inventions in aerial locomotion, and the navigation of space, the entire race may migrate from the earth, to settle some vacant and more western planet, it may be still healthy, perchance unearthy, not composed of dirt and stones, whose primary strata only are strewn, and where no weeds are sown.

It took but little art, a simple application of natural laws, a canoe, a paddle, and a sail of matting, to people the isles of the Pacific, and a little more will people the shining isles of space. Do we not see in the firmament the lights carried along the shore by night, as Columbus did? Let us not despair nor mutiny.

"The dwellings also ought to be very different from what is known, if the full benefit of our means is to be enjoyed. They are to be of a structure for which we have no name yet. They are to be neither palaces, nor temples, nor cities, but a combination of all, superior to whatever is known. Earth may be baked into bricks, or even vitrified stone by heat,—we may bake large masses of any size and form into stone and vitrified substance of the greatest durability, lasting even thousands of years, out of clayey earth, or of stones ground to dust, by the application of burning mirrors. This is to be done in the open air, without other preparation than gathering the substance, grinding and mixing it with water and cement, moulding or casting it, and bringing the focus of the burning mirrors of proper size upon the same. The character of the architecture is to be quite different from what it ever has been hitherto; large solid masses are to be baked or cast in one piece, ready shaped in any form that may be desired. The building may, therefore, consist of columns two hundred feet high and upwards, of proportionate thickness, and of one entire piece of vitrified substance; huge pieces are to be moulded so as to join and hook on to each other firmly, by proper joints and folds, and not to yield in any way without breaking."

"Foundries, of any description, are to be heated by burning mirrors, and will require no labor, except the making of the first moulds and the superintendence for gathering the metal and taking the finished articles away."

Alas, in the present state of science, we must take the finished articles away; but think not that man will always be a victim of circumstances.

The countryman who visited the city and found the streets cluttered with bricks and lumber, reported that it was not yet finished, and one who considers the endless repairs and reforming of our houses, might well wonder when they will be done. But why may not the dwellings of men on this earth be built once for all of some durable material, some Roman or Etruscan masonry which will stand, so that time shall only adorn and beautify them? Why may we not finish the outward world for posterity, and leave them leisure to attend to the inner? Surely, all the gross necessities and economies might be cared for in a few years. All might be built and baked and stored up, during this, the term-time of the world, against the vacant eternity, and the globe go provisioned and furnished like our public vessels, for its voyage through space, as through some Pacific ocean, while we would "tie up the rudder and sleep before the wind," as those who sail from Lima to Manilla.

But, to go back a few years in imagination, think not that life in these crystal palaces is to bear any analogy to life in our present humble cottages. Far from it. Clothed, once for all, in some "flexible stuff," more durable than George Fox's suit of leather, composed of "fibres of vegetables," "glutinated" together by some "cohesive substances," and made into sheets, like paper, of any size or form, man will put far from him corroding care and the whole host of ills.

"The twenty-five halls in the inside of the square are to be each two hundred feet square and high; the forty corridors, each one hundred feet long and twenty wide; the eighty galleries, each from 1,000 to 1,250 feet long; about 7,000 private rooms, the whole surrounded and intersected by the grandest and most splendid colonnades imaginable; floors, ceilings, columns with their various beautiful and fanciful intervals, all shining, and reflecting to infinity all objects and persons, with splendid lustre of all beautiful colors, and fanciful shapes and pictures. All galleries, outside and within the halls, are to be provided with many thousand commodious and most elegant vehicles, in which persons may move up and down, like birds, in perfect security, and without exertion. Any member may procure himself all the common articles of his daily wants, by a short turn of some crank, without leaving his apartment; he may, at any time, bathe himself in cold or warm water, or in steam, or in some artificially prepared liquor for invigorating health. He may, at any time, give to the air in his apartment that temperature that suits his feeling best. He may cause, at any time, an agreeable scent of various kinds. He may, at any time, meliorate his breathing air,—that main vehicle of vital power. Thus, by a proper application of the physical knowledge of our days, man may be kept in a perpetual serenity of mind, and if there is no incurable disease or defect in his organism, in constant vigor of health, and his life be prolonged beyond any parallel which present times afford."

"One or two persons are sufficient to direct the kitchen business. They have nothing else to do but to superintend the cookery, and to watch the time of the victuals being done, and then to remove them, with the table and vessels, into the dining-hall, or to the respective private apartments, by a slight motion of the hand at some crank. Any extraordinary desire of any person may be satisfied by going to the place where the thing is to be had; and anything that requires a particular preparation in cooking or baking, may be done by the person who desires it."

This is one of those instances in which the individual genius is found to consent, as indeed it always does, at last, with the universal. These last sentences have a certain sad and sober truth, which reminds us of the scripture of all nations. All expression of truth does at length take the deep ethical form. Here is hint of a place the most eligible of any in space, and of a servitor, in comparison with whom, all other helps dwindle into insignificance. We hope to hear more of him anon, for even a crystal palace would be deficient without his invaluable services.

And as for the environs of the establishment,

"There will be afforded the most enrapturing views to be fancied, out of the private apartments, from the galleries, from the roof, from its turrets and cupolas,—gardens as far as the eye can see, full of fruits and flowers, arranged in the most beautiful order, with walks, colonnades, aqueducts, canals, ponds, plains, amphitheatres, terraces, fountains, sculptural works, pavilions, gondolas, places for public amusement, etc., to delight the eye and fancy, the taste and smell." . . . "The walks and roads are to be paved with hard vitrified, large plates, so as to be always clean from all dirt in any weather or season. . . . The channels being of vitrified substance, and the water perfectly clear, and filtrated or distilled if required, may afford the most beautiful scenes imaginable, while a variety of fishes is seen clear down to the bottom playing about, and the canals may afford at the same time, the means of gliding smoothly along between various sceneries of art and nature, in beautiful gondolas, while their surface and borders may be covered with fine land and aquatic birds. The walks may be covered with porticos adorned with magnificent columns, statues and sculptural works; all of vitrified substance, and lasting for ever, while the beauties of nature around heighten the magnificence and deliciousness."

"The night affords no less delight to fancy and feelings. An infinite variety of grand, beautiful and fanciful objects and sceneries, radiating with crystalline brilliancy, by the illumination of gas-light; the human figures themselves, arrayed in the most beautiful pomp fancy may suggest, or the eye desire, shining even with brilliancy of stuffs and diamonds, like stones of various colors, elegantly shaped and arranged around the body; all reflected a thousand-fold in huge mirrors and reflectors of various forms; theatrical scenes of a grandeur and magnificence, and enrapturing illusions, unknown yet, in which any person may be either a spectator or actor; the speech and the songs reverberating with increased sound, rendered more sonorous and harmonious than by nature, by vaultings that are moveable into any shape at any time; the sweetest and most impressive harmony of music, produced by song and instruments partly not known yet, may thrill through the nerves and vary with other amusements and delights."

"At night the roof, and the inside and outside of the whole square, are illuminated by gas-light, which in the mazes of many-colored crystal-like colonnades and vaultings, is reflected with a brilliancy that gives to the whole a lustre of precious stones, as far as the eye can see,—such are the future abodes of men." . . . "Such is the life reserved to true intelligence, but withheld from ignorance, prejudice, and stupid adherence to custom." . . . "Such is the domestic life to be enjoyed by every human individual that will partake of it. Love and affection may there be fostered and enjoyed without any of the obstructions that oppose, diminish, and destroy them in the present state of men." . . . "It would be as ridiculous, then, to dispute and quarrel about the means of life, as it would be now about water to drink along mighty rivers, or about the permission to breathe air in the atmosphere, or about sticks in our extensive woods."

Thus is Paradise to be Regained, and that old and stern decree at length reversed. Man shall no more earn his living by the sweat of his brow. All labor shall be reduced to "a short turn of some crank," and "taking the finished article away." But there is a crank,—oh, how hard to be turned! Could there not be a crank upon a crank,—an infinitely small crank?—we would fain inquire. No,—alas! not. But there is a certain divine energy in every man, but sparingly employed as yet, which may be called the crank within,—the crank after all,—the prime mover in all machinery,—quite indispensable to all work. Would that we might get our hands on its handle! In fact no work can be shirked. It may be postponed indefinitely, but not infinitely. Nor can any really important work be made easier by co-operation or machinery. Not one particle of labor now threatening any man can be routed without being performed. It cannot be hunted out of the vicinity like jackals and hyenas. It will not run. You may begin by sawing the little sticks, or you may saw the great sticks first, but sooner or later you must saw them both.

We will not be imposed upon by this vast application of forces. We believe that most things will have to be accomplished still by the application called Industry. We are rather pleased after all to consider the small private, but both constant and accumulated force, which stands behind every spade in the field. This it is that makes the valleys shine, and the deserts really bloom. Sometimes, we confess, we are so degenerate as to reflect with pleasure on the days when men were yoked like cattle, and drew a crooked stick for a plough. After all, the great interests and methods were the same.

It is a rather serious objection to Mr. Etzler's schemes, that they require time, men, and money, three very superfluous and inconvenient things for an honest and well-disposed man to deal with. "The whole world," he tells us, "might therefore be really changed into a paradise, within less than ten years, commencing from the first year of an association for the purpose of constructing and applying the machinery." We are sensible of a startling incongruity when time and money are mentioned in this connection. The ten years which are proposed would be a tedious while to wait, if every man were at his post and did his duty, but quite too short a period, if we are to take time for it. But this fault is by no means peculiar to Mr. Etzler's schemes. There is far too much hurry and bustle, and too little patience and privacy, in all our methods, as if something were to be accomplished in centuries. The true reformer does not want time, nor money, nor co-operation, nor advice. What is time but the stuff delay is made of? And depend upon it, our virtue will not live on the interest of our money. He expects no income but our outgoes; so soon as we begin to count the cost the cost begins. And as for advice, the information floating in the atmosphere of society is as evanescent and unserviceable to him as gossamer for clubs of Hercules. There is absolutely no common sense; it is common nonsense. If we are to risk a cent or a drop of our blood, who then shall advise us? For ourselves, we are too young for experience. Who is old enough? We are older by faith than by experience. In the unbending of the arm to do the deed there is experience worth all the maxims in the world.

"It will now be plainly seen that the execution of the proposals is not proper for individuals. Whether it be proper for government at this time, before the subject has become popular, is a question to be decided; all that is to be done, is to step forth, after mature reflection, to confess loudly one's conviction, and to constitute societies. Man is powerful but in union with many. Nothing great, for the improvement of his own condition, or that of his fellow men, can ever be effected by individual enterprise."

Alas! this is the crying sin of the age, this want of faith in the prevalence of a man. Nothing can be effected but by one man. He who wants help wants everything. True, this is the condition of our weakness, but it can never be the means of our recovery. We must first succeed alone, that we may enjoy our success together. We trust that the social movements which we witness indicate an aspiration not to be thus cheaply satisfied. In this matter of reforming the world, we have little faith in corporations; not thus was it first formed.

But our author is wise enough to say, that the raw materials for the accomplishment of his purposes, are "iron, copper, wood, earth chiefly, and a union of men whose eyes and understanding are not shut up by preconceptions." Aye, this last may be what we want mainly,—a company of "odd fellows" indeed.

"Small shares of twenty dollars will be sufficient,"—in all, from "200,000 to 300,000,"—"to create the first establishment for a whole community of from 3000 to 4000 individuals"—at the end of five years we shall have a principal of 200 millions of dollars, and so paradise will be wholly regained at the end of the tenth year. But, alas, the ten years have already elapsed, and there are no signs of Eden yet, for want of the requisite funds to begin the enterprise in a hopeful manner. Yet it seems a safe investment. Perchance they could be hired at a low rate, the property being mortgaged for security, and, if necessary, it could be given up in any stage of the enterprise, without loss, with the fixtures.

Mr. Etzler considers this "Address as a touchstone, to try whether our nation is in any way accessible to these great truths, for raising the human creature to a superior state of existence, in accordance with the knowledge and the spirit of the most cultivated minds of the present time." He has prepared a constitution, short and concise, consisting of twenty-one articles, so that wherever an association may spring up, it may go into operation without delay; and the editor informs us that "Communications on the subject of this book may be addressed to C. F. Stollmeyer, No. 6, Upper Charles street, Northampton square, London."

But we see two main difficulties in the way. First, the successful application of the powers by machinery, (we have not yet seen the "Mechanical System,") and, secondly, which is infinitely harder, the application of man to the work by faith. This it is, we fear, which will prolong the ten years to ten thousand at least. It will take a power more than "80,000 times greater than all the men on earth could effect with their nerves," to persuade men to use that which is already offered them. Even a greater than this physical power must be brought to bear upon that moral power. Faith, indeed, is all the reform that is needed; it is itself a reform. Doubtless, we are as slow to conceive of Paradise as of Heaven, of a perfect natural as of a perfect spiritual world. We see how past ages have loitered and erred; "Is perhaps our generation free from irrationality and error? Have we perhaps reached now the summit of human wisdom, and need no more to look out for mental or physical improvement?" Undoubtedly, we are never so visionary as to be prepared for what the next hour may bring forth.

Μέλλει· τὸ θεῖον δ᾽ἐστι τοιοῦτον φύσει.

The Divine is about to be, and such is its nature. In our wisest moments we are secreting a matter, which, like the lime of the shell fish, incrusts us quite over, and well for us, if, like it, we cast our shells from time to time, though they be pearl and of fairest tint. Let us consider under what disadvantages science has hitherto labored before we pronounce thus confidently on her progress.

"There was never any system in the productions of human labor; but they came into existence and fashion as chance directed men." "Only a few professional men of learning occupy themselves with teaching natural philosophy, chemistry, and the other branches of the sciences of nature, to a very limited extent, for very limited purposes, with very limited means." "The science of mechanics is but in a state of infancy. It is true, improvements are made upon improvements, instigated by patents of government; but they are made accidentally or at hap-hazard. There is no general system of this science, mathematical as it is, which developes its principles in their full extent, and the outlines of the application to which they lead. There is no idea of comparison between what is explored and what is yet to be explored in this science. The ancient Greeks placed mathematics at the head of their education. But we are glad to have filled our memory with notions, without troubling ourselves much with reasoning about them."

Mr. Etzler is not one of the enlightened practical men, the pioneers of the actual, who move with the slow deliberate tread of science, conserving the world; who execute the dreams of the last century, though they have no dreams of their own; yet he deals in the very raw but still solid material of all inventions. He has more of the practical than usually belongs to so bold a schemer, so resolute a dreamer. Yet his success is in theory, and not in practice, and he feeds our faith rather than contents our understanding. His book wants order, serenity, dignity, everything,—but it does not fail to impart what only man can impart to man of much importance, his own faith. It is true his dreams are not thrilling nor bright enough, and he leaves off to dream where he who dreams just before the dawn begins. His castles in the air fall to the ground, because they are not built lofty enough; they should be secured to heaven's roof. After all, the theories and speculations of men concern us more than their puny execution. It is with a certain coldness and languor that we loiter about the actual and so called practical. How little do the most wonderful inventions of modern times detain us. They insult nature. Every machine, or particular application, seems a slight outrage against universal laws. How many fine inventions are there which do not clutter the ground? We think that those only succeed which minister to our sensible and animal wants, which bake or brew, wash or warm, or the like. But are those of no account which are patented by fancy and imagination, and succeed so admirably in our dreams that they give the tone still to our waking thoughts? Already nature is serving all those uses which science slowly derives on a much higher and grander scale to him that will be served by her. When the sunshine falls on the path of the poet, he enjoys all those pure benefits and pleasures which the arts slowly and partially realize from age to age. The winds which fan his cheek waft him the sum of that profit and happiness which their lagging inventions supply.

The chief fault of this book is, that it aims to secure the greatest degree of gross comfort and pleasure merely. It paints a Mahometan's heaven, and stops short with singular abruptness when we think it is drawing near to the precincts of the Christian's,—and we trust we have not made here a distinction without a difference. Undoubtedly if we were to reform this outward life truly and thoroughly, we should find no duty of the inner omitted. It would be employment for our whole nature; and what we should do thereafter would be as vain a question as to ask the bird what it will do when its nest is built and its brood reared. But a moral reform must take place first, and then the necessity of the other will be superseded, and we shall sail and plough by its force alone. There is a speedier way than the Mechanical System can show to fill up marshes, to drown the roar of the waves, to tame hyenas, secure agreeable environs, diversify the land, and refresh it with "rivulets of sweet water," and that is by the power of rectitude and true behavior. It is only for a little while, only occasionally, methinks, that we want a garden. Surely a good man need not be at the labor to level a hill for the sake of a prospect, or raise fruits and flowers, and construct floating islands, for the sake of a paradise. He enjoys better prospects than lie behind any hill. Where an angel travels it will be paradise all the way, but where Satan travels it will be burning marl and cinders. What says Veeshnoo Sarma? "He whose mind is at ease is possessed of all riches. Is it not the same to one whose foot is enclosed in a shoe, as if the whole surface of the earth were covered with leather?"

He who is conversant with the supernal powers will not worship these inferior deities of the wind, the waves, tide, and sunshine. But we would not disparage the importance of such calculations as we have described. They are truths in physics, because they are true in ethics. The moral powers no one would presume to calculate. Suppose we could compare the moral with the physical, and say how many horse-power the force of love, for instance, blowing on every square foot of a man's soul, would equal. No doubt we are well aware of this force; figures would not increase our respect for it; the sunshine is equal to but one ray of its heat. The light of the sun is but the shadow of love. "The souls of men loving and fearing God," says Raleigh, "receive influence from that divine light itself, whereof the sun's clarity, and that of the stars, is by Plato called but a shadow. *Lumen est umbra Dei, Deus est Lumen Luminis.* Light is the shadow of God's brightness, who is the light of light," and, we may add, the heat of heat. Love is the wind, the tide, the waves, the sunshine. Its power is incalculable; it is many horse power. It never ceases, it never slacks; it can move the globe without a resting-place; it can warm without fire; it can feed without meat; it can clothe without garments; it can shelter without roof; it can make a paradise within which will dispense with a paradise without. But though the wisest men in all ages have labored to publish this force, and every human heart is, sooner or later, more or less, made to feel it, yet how little is actually applied to social ends. True, it is the motive power of all successful social machinery; but, as in physics, we have made the elements do only a little drudgery for us, steam to take the place of a few horses, wind of a few oars, water of a few cranks and hand-mills; as the mechanical forces have not yet been generously and largely applied to make the physical world answer to the ideal, so the power of love has been but meanly and sparingly applied, as yet. It has patented only such machines as the almshouses, the hospital, and the Bible Society, while its infinite wind is still blowing, and blowing down these very structures, too, from time to time. Still less are we accumulating its power, and preparing to act with greater energy at a future time. Shall we not contribute our shares to this enterprise, then?

Homer. Ossian. Chaucer.

EXTRACTS FROM A LECTURE ON POETRY,
READ BEFORE THE CONCORD LYCEUM,
NOVEMBER 29, 1843, BY HENRY D. THOREAU.

HOMER.

THE wisest definition of poetry the poet will instantly prove false by setting aside its requisitions. We can therefore publish only our advertisement of it.

There is no doubt that the loftiest written wisdom is rhymed or measured, is in form as well as substance poetry; and a volume, which should contain the condensed wisdom of mankind, need not have one rhythmless line. Yet poetry, though the last and finest result, is a natural fruit. As naturally as the oak bears an acorn, and the vine a gourd, man bears a poem, either spoken or done. It is the chief and most memorable success, for history is but a prose narrative of poetic deeds. What else have the Hindoos, the Persians, the Babylonians, the Egyptians, done, that can be told? It is the simplest relation of phenomena, and describes the commonest sensations with more truth than science does, and the latter at a distance slowly mimics its style and methods. The poet sings how the blood flows in his veins. He performs his functions, and is so well that he needs such stimulus to sing only as plants to put forth leaves and blossoms. He would strive in vain to modulate the remote and transient music which he sometimes hears, since his song is a vital function like breathing, and an integral result like weight. It is not the overflowing of life but its subsidence rather, and is drawn from under the feet of the poet. It is enough if Homer but say the sun sets. He is as serene as nature, and we can hardly detect the enthusiasm of the bard. It is as if nature spoke. He presents to us the simplest pictures of human life, so that childhood itself can understand them, and the man must not think twice to appreciate his naturalness. Each reader discovers for himself, that succeeding poets have done little else than copy his similes. His more memorable passages are as naturally bright, as gleams of sunlight in misty weather. Nature furnishes him not only with words, but with stereotyped lines and sentences from her mint.

> "As from the clouds appears the full moon,
>   All shining, and then again it goes behind the shadowy
>   clouds,
>   So Hector, at one time appeared among the foremost,
>   And at another in the rear, commanding; and all with brass
>   He shone, like to the lightning of ægis-bearing Zeus."

He conveys the least information, even the hour of the day, with such magnificence, and vast expense of natural imagery, as if it were a message from the gods.

> "While it was dawn, and sacred day was advancing,
>   For that space the weapons of both flew fast, and the people
>   fell;
>   But when now the woodcutter was preparing his morning
>   meal
>   In the recesses of the mountain, and had wearied his hands
>   With cutting lofty trees, and satiety came to his mind,
>   And the desire of sweet food took possession of his
>   thoughts;
>   Then the Danaans by their valor broke the phalanxes,
>   Shouting to their companions from rank to rank."

When the army of the Trojans passed the night under arms, keeping watch lest the enemy should re-embark under cover of the dark,

> "They, thinking great things, upon the neutral ground of war,
>   Sat all the night; and many fires burned for them.
>   As when in the heavens the stars round the bright moon
>   Appear beautiful, and the air is without wind;
>   And all the heights, and the extreme summits,
>   And the shady valleys appear; and the shepherd rejoices in
>   his heart;

So between the ships and the streams of Xanthus
Appeared the fires of the Trojans before Ilium."

The "white-armed goddess Juno," sent by the Father of
gods and men for Iris and Apollo,

"Went down the Idæan mountains to far Olympus,
As when the mind of a man, who has come over much earth,
Sallies forth, and he reflects with rapid thoughts,
There was I, and there, and remembers many things;
So swiftly the august Juno hastening flew through the air,
And came to high Olympus."

There are few books which are fit to be remembered in our
wisest hours, but the Iliad is brightest in the serenest days,
and imbodies still all the sunlight that fell on Asia Minor. No
modern joy or ecstasy of ours can lower its height or dim its
lustre; but there it lies in the east of literature, as it were the
earliest, latest production of the mind. The ruins of Egypt op-
press and stifle us with their dust, foulness preserved in cassia
and pitch, and swathed in linen; the death of that which never
lived. But the rays of Greek poetry struggle down to us, and
mingle with the sunbeams of the recent day. The statue of
Memnon is cast down, but the shaft of the Iliad still meets the
sun in his rising.

So too, no doubt, Homer had his Homer, and Orpheus his
Orpheus, in the dim antiquity which preceded them. The
mythological system of the ancients, and it is still the only
mythology of the moderns, the poem of mankind, interwoven
so wonderfully with their astronomy, and matching in
grandeur and harmony with the architecture of the Heavens
themselves, seems to point to a time when a mightier genius
inhabited the earth. But man is the great poet, and not
Homer nor Shakspeare; and our language itself, and the com-
mon arts of life are his work. Poetry is so universally true and
independent of experience, that it does not need any particu-
lar biography to illustrate it, but we refer it sooner or later to
some Orpheus or Linus, and after ages to the genius of hu-
manity, and the gods themselves.

OSSIAN.*

The genuine remains of Ossian, though of less fame and extent, are in many respects of the same stamp with the Iliad itself. He asserts the dignity of the bard no less than Homer, and in his era we hear of no other priest than he. It will not avail to call him a heathen because he personifies the sun and addresses it; and what if his heroes did "worship the ghosts of their fathers," their thin, airy, and unsubstantial forms? we but worship the ghosts of our fathers in more substantial forms. We cannot but respect the vigorous faith of those heathen, who sternly believed somewhat, and are inclined to say to the critics, who are offended by their superstitious rites, don't interrupt these men's prayers. As if we knew more about human life and a God, than the heathen and ancients. Does English theology contain the recent discoveries?

Ossian reminds us of the most refined and rudest eras, of Homer, Pindar, Isaiah, and the American Indian. In his poetry, as in Homer's, only the simplest and most enduring features of humanity are seen, such essential parts of a man as Stonehenge exhibits of a temple; we see the circles of stone, and the upright shaft alone. The phenomena of life acquire almost an unreal and gigantic size seen through his mists. Like all older and grander poetry, it is distinguished by the few elements in the lives of its heroes. They stand on the heath, between the stars and the earth, shrunk to the bones and sinews. The earth is a boundless plain for their deeds. They lead such a simple, dry, and everlasting life, as hardly needs depart with the flesh, but is transmitted entire from age to age. There are but few objects to distract their sight, and their life is as unencumbered as the course of the stars they gaze at.

---

*"The Genuine Remains of Ossian, Literally Translated, with a Preliminary Dissertation, by Patrick Macgregor. Published under the Patronage of the Highland Society of London. 1 vol. 12mo. London, 1841." We take pleasure in recommending this, the first literal English translation of the Gaelic originals of Ossian, which were left by Macpherson, and published agreeably to his intention, in 1807.

> "The wrathful kings, on cairns apart,
>   Look forward from behind their shields,
>   And mark the wandering stars,
>   That brilliant westward move."

It does not cost much for these heroes to live. They want not much furniture. They are such forms of men only as can be seen afar through the mist, and have no costume nor dialect, but for language there is the tongue itself, and for costume there are always the skins of beasts and the bark of trees to be had. They live out their years by the vigor of their constitutions. They survive storms and the spears of their foes, and perform a few heroic deeds, and then,

> "Mounds will answer questions of them,
>   For many future years."

Blind and infirm, they spend the remnant of their days listening to the lays of the bards, and feeling the weapons which laid their enemies low, and when at length they die, by a convulsion of nature, the bard allows us a short misty glance into futurity, yet as clear, perchance, as their lives had been. When Mac-Roine was slain,

> "His soul departed to his warlike sires,
>   To follow misty forms of boars,
>   In tempestuous islands bleak."

The hero's cairn is erected, and the bard sings a brief significant strain, which will suffice for epitaph and biography.

> "The weak will find his bow in the dwelling,
>   The feeble will attempt to bend it."

Compared with this simple, fibrous life, our civilized history appears the chronicle of debility, of fashion, and the arts of luxury. But the civilized man misses no real refinement in the poetry of the rudest era. It reminds him that civilization does but dress men. It makes shoes, but it does not toughen the soles of the feet. It makes cloth of finer texture, but it does not touch the skin. Inside the civilized man stands the savage still in the place of honor. We are those blue-eyed, yellow-haired Saxons, those slender, dark-haired Normans.

The profession of the bard attracted more respect in those days from the importance attached to fame. It was his province to record the deeds of heroes. When Ossian hears the traditions of inferior bards, he exclaims,

> "I straightway seize the unfutile tales,
>   And send them down in faithful verse."

His philosophy of life is expressed in the opening of the third Duan of Ca-Lodin.

> "Whence have sprung the things that are?
>   And whither roll the passing years?
>   Where does time conceal its two heads,
>   In dense impenetrable gloom,
>   Its surface marked with heroes' deeds alone?
>   I view the generations gone;
>   The past appears but dim;
>   As objects by the moon's faint beams,
>   Reflected from a distant lake.
>   I see, indeed, the thunder-bolts of war,
>   But there the unmighty joyless dwell,
>   All those who send not down their deeds
>   To far, succeeding times."

The ignoble warriors die and are forgotten;

> "Strangers come to build a tower,
>   And throw their ashes overhand;
>   Some rusted swords appear in dust;
>   One, bending forward, says,
>   'The arms belonged to heroes gone;
>   We never heard their praise in song.'"

The grandeur of the similes is another feature which characterizes great poetry. Ossian seems to speak a gigantic and universal language. The images and pictures occupy even much space in the landscape, as if they could be seen only from the sides of mountains, and plains with a wide horizon, or across arms of the sea. The machinery is so massive that it cannot be less than natural. Oivana says to the spirit of her father, "Grey-haired Torkil of Torne," seen in the skies,

"Thou glidest away like receding ships."

So when the hosts of Fingal and Starne approach to battle,

"With murmurs loud, like rivers far,
The race of Torne hither moved."

And when compelled to retire,

"dragging his spear behind,
Cudulin sank in the distant wood,
Like a fire unblazing ere it dies."

Nor did Fingal want a proper audience when he spoke;

"A thousand orators inclined
To hear the lay of Fingal."

The threats too would have deterred a man. Vengeance and terror were real. Trenmore threatens the young warrior, whom he meets on a foreign strand,

"Thy mother shall find thee pale on the shore,
While lessening on the waves she spies
The sails of him who slew her son."

If Ossian's heroes weep, it is from excess of strength, and not from weakness, a sacrifice or libation of fertile natures, like the perspiration of stone in summer's heat. We hardly know that tears have been shed, and it seems as if weeping were proper only for babes and heroes. Their joy and their sorrow are made of one stuff, like rain and snow, the rainbow and the mist. When Fillan was worsted in fight, and ashamed in the presence of Fingal,

"He strode away forthwith,
And bent in grief above a stream,
His cheeks bedewed with tears.
From time to time the thistles gray
He lopped with his inverted lance."

Crodar, blind and old, receives Ossian, son of Fingal, who comes to aid him in war,

" 'My eyes have failed,' says he, 'Crodar is blind,
  Is thy strength like that of thy fathers?
  Stretch, Ossian, thine arm to the hoary-haired.'
    I gave my arm to the king.
  The aged hero seized my hand;
  He heaved a heavy sigh;
  Tears flowed incessant down his cheek.
  'Strong art thou, son of the mighty,
  Though not so dreadful as Morven's prince. * * *
  Let my feast be spread in the hall,
  Let every sweet-voiced minstrel sing;
  Great is he who is within my wall,
  Sons of wave-echoing Croma.' "

Even Ossian himself, the hero-bard, pays tribute to the superior strength of his father Fingal.

"How beauteous, mighty man, was thy mind,
  Why succeeded Ossian without its strength?"

CHAUCER.

What a contrast between the stern and desolate poetry of Ossian, and that of Chaucer, and even of Shakspeare and Milton, much more of Dryden, and Pope, and Gray. Our summer of English poetry, like the Greek and Latin before it, seems well advanced toward its fall, and laden with the fruit and foliage of the season, with bright autumnal tints, but soon the winter will scatter its myriad clustering and shading leaves, and leave only a few desolate and fibrous boughs to sustain the snow and rime, and creak in the blasts of ages. We cannot escape the impression, that the Muse has stooped a little in her flight, when we come to the literature of civilized eras. Now first we hear of various ages and styles of poetry, but the poetry of runic monuments is for every age. The bard has lost the dignity and sacredness of his office. He has no more the bardic rage, and only conceives the deed, which he formerly stood ready to perform. Hosts of warriors, earnest for battle, could not mistake nor dispense with the ancient bard. His lays were heard in the pauses of the fight. There was no danger of his being overlooked by his contemporaries. But now the hero and the bard are of different professions. When we come to the pleasant English verse, it seems as if the storms had all cleared away, and it would never thunder and lighten more. The poet has come within doors, and exchanged the forest and crag for the fireside, the hut of the Gael, and Stonehenge with its circles of stones, for the house of the Englishman. No hero stands at the door prepared to break forth into song or heroic action, but we have instead a homely Englishman, who cultivates the art of poetry. We see the pleasant fireside, and hear the crackling fagots in all the verse. The towering and misty imagination of the bard has descended into the plain, and become a lowlander, and keeps flocks and herds. Poetry is one man's trade, and not all men's religion, and is split into many styles. It is pastoral, and lyric, and narrative, and didactic.

Notwithstanding the broad humanity of Chaucer, and the many social and domestic comforts which we meet with in his verse, we have to narrow our vision somewhat to consider him, as if he occupied less space in the landscape, and did not stretch over hill and valley as Ossian does. Yet, seen from the side of posterity, as the father of English poetry, preceded by a long silence or confusion in history, unenlivened by any strain of pure melody, we easily come to reverence him. Passing over the earlier continental poets, since we are bound to the pleasant archipelago of English poetry, Chaucer's is the first name after that misty weather in which Ossian lived, which can detain us long. Indeed, though he represents so different a culture and society, he may be regarded as in many respects the Homer of the English poets. Perhaps he is the youthfullest of them all. We return to him as to the purest well, the fountain furthest removed from the highway of desultory life. He is so natural and cheerful, compared with later poets, that we might almost regard him as a personification of spring. To the faithful reader his muse has even given an aspect to his times, and when he is fresh from perusing him, they seem related to the golden age. It is still the poetry of youth and life, rather than of thought; and though the moral vein is obvious and constant, it has not yet banished the sun and daylight from his verse. The loftiest strains of the muse are, for the most part, sublimely plaintive, and not a carol as free as nature's. The content which the sun shines to celebrate from morning to evening is unsung. The muse solaces herself, and is not ravished but consoled. There is a catastrophe implied, and a tragic element in all our verse, and less of the lark and morning dews, than of the nightingale and evening shades. But in Homer and Chaucer there is more of the innocence and serenity of youth, than in the more modern and moral poets. The Iliad is not sabbath but morning reading, and men cling to this old song, because they have still moments of unbaptized and uncommitted life, which give them an appetite for more. It represents no creed nor opinion, and we read it with a rare sense of freedom and irresponsibility, as if we trod on native ground, and were autochthones of the soil.

Chaucer had eminently the habits of a literary man and a scholar. We do not enough allow for the prevalence of this class. There were never any times so stirring, that there were not to be found some sedentary still. Through all those outwardly active ages, there were still monks in cloisters writing or copying folios. He was surrounded by the din of arms. The battles of Hallidon Hill and Neville's Cross, and the still more memorable battles of Crecy and Poictiers, were fought in his youth, but these did not concern our poet much, Wicliffe much more. He seems to have regarded himself always as one privileged to sit and converse with books. He helped to establish the literary class. His character, as one of the fathers of the English language, would alone make his works important, even those which have little poetical merit. A great philosophical and moral poet gives permanence to the language he uses, by making the best sound convey the best sense. He was as simple as Wordsworth in preferring his homely but vigorous Saxon tongue, when it was neglected by the court, and had not yet attained to the dignity of a literature, and rendered a similar service to his country to that which Dante rendered to Italy. If Greek sufficeth for Greek, and Arabic for Arabian, and Hebrew for Jew, and Latin for Latin, then English shall suffice for him, for any of these will serve to teach truth "right as divers pathes leaden divers folke the right waye to Rome." In the Testament of Love he writes, "Let then clerkes enditen in Latin, for they have the propertie

of science, and the knowinge in that facultie, and lette French-
men in their Frenche also enditen their queinte termes, for it
is kyndely to their mouthes, and let us shewe our fantasies
in soche wordes as we lerneden of our dames tonge."

He will know how to appreciate Chaucer best, who has
come down to him the natural way, through the meagre pas-
tures of Saxon and ante-Chaucerian poetry; and yet so human
and wise he seems after such diet, that he is liable to misjudge
him still. In the Saxon poetry extant, in the earliest English,
and the contemporary Scottish poetry, there is less to remind
the reader of the rudeness and vigor of youth, than of the fee-
bleness of a declining age. It is for the most part translation
or imitation merely, with only an occasional and slight tinge
of poetry, and oftentimes the falsehood and exaggeration of
fable, without its imagination to redeem it. It is astonishing to
how few thoughts so many sincere efforts give utterance. But
as they never sprang out of nature, so they will never root
themselves in nature. There are few traces of original genius,
and we look in vain to find antiquity restored, humanized,
and made blithe again, by the discovery of some natural sym-
pathy between it and the present. But when we come to
Chaucer we are relieved of many a load. He is fresh and mod-
ern still, and no dust settles on his true passages. It lightens
along the line, and we are reminded that flowers have
bloomed, and birds sung, and hearts beaten, in England.
Before the earnest gaze of the reader the rust and moss of
time gradually drop off, and the original green life is revealed.
He was a homely and domestic man, and did breathe quite as
modern men do. Only one trait, one little incident of human
biography needs to be truly recorded, that all the world may
think the author fit to wear the laurel crown. In the dearth we
have described, and at this distance of time, the bare processes
of living read like poetry, for all of human good or ill, heroic
or vulgar, lies very near to them. All that is truly great and in-
teresting to men, runs thus as level a course, and is as unaspir-
ing, as the plough in the furrow.

There is no wisdom which can take place of humanity, and
we find *that* in Chaucer. We can expand in his breadth
and think we could be that man's acquaintance. He was wor-
thy to be a citizen of England, while Petrarch and Boccaccio

lived in Italy, and Tell and Tamerlane in Switzerland and in Asia, and Bruce in Scotland, and Wickliffe, and Gower, and Edward the Third, and John of Gaunt, and the Black Prince, were his own countrymen; all stout and stirring names. The fame of Roger Bacon came down from the preceding century, and the name of Dante still exerted the influence of a living presence. On the whole, Chaucer impresses us, as greater than his reputation, and not a little like Homer and Shakspeare, for he would have held up his head in their company. Among early English poets he is the landlord and host, and has the authority of such. The affectionate mention, which succeeding early poets make of him, coupling him with Homer and Virgil, is to be taken into the account in estimating his character and influence. King James and Dunbar of Scotland speak with more love and reverence of him, than any modern author of his predecessors of the last century. The same childlike relation is without parallel now. We read him without criticism for the most part, for he pleads not his own cause, but speaks for his readers, and has that greatness of trust and reliance which compels popularity. He confides in the reader, and speaks privily with him, keeping nothing back. And in return his reader has great confidence in him, that he tells no lies, and reads his story with indulgence, as if it were the circumlocution of a child, but discovers afterwards that he has spoken with more directness and economy of words than a sage. He is never heartless,

> "For first the thing is thought within the hart,
> Er any word out from the mouth astart."

And so new as all his theme in those days, that he had not to invent, but only to tell.

We admire Chaucer for his sturdy English wit. The easy height he speaks from in his Prologue to the Canterbury Tales, as if he were equal to any of the company there assembled, is as good as any particular excellence in it. But though it is full of good sense and humanity, it is not transcendent poetry. For picturesque description of persons it is, perhaps, without a parallel in English poetry; yet it is essentially humorous, as the loftiest genius never is. Humor, however broad and genial, takes a narrower view than enthusiasm. The whole story of Chanticlere and Dame Partlett, in the Nonne's Preeste's tale, is genuine humanity. I know of nothing better in its kind, no more successful fabling of birds and beasts. If it is said of Shakspeare, that he is now Hamlet, and then Falstaff, it may be said of Chaucer that he sympathizes with brutes as well as men, and assumes their nature that he may speak from it. In this tale he puts on the very feathers and stature of the cock. To his own finer vein he added all the common wit and wisdom of his time, and every where in his works his remarkable knowledge of the world, and nice perception of character, his rare common sense and proverbial wisdom, are apparent. His genius does not soar like Milton's, but is genial and familiar. It shows great tenderness and delicacy, but not the heroic sentiment. It is only a greater portion of humanity with all its weakness. It is not heroic, as Raleigh's, nor pious, as Herbert's, nor philosophical, as Shakspeare's, but it is the child of the English muse, that child which is the father of the man. It is for the most part only an exceeding naturalness, perfect sincerity, with the behavior of a child rather than of a man.

Gentleness and delicacy of character are every where apparent in his verse. The simplest and humblest words come readily to his lips. No one can read the Prioress' tale, understanding the spirit in which it was written, and in which the child sings, *O alma redemptoris mater*, or the account of the departure of Custance with her child upon the sea, in the Man of Lawe's tale, without feeling the native innocence and refinement of the author. Nor can we be mistaken respecting the essential purity of his character, disregarding the apology of the manners of the age. His sincere sorrow in his later days for the grossness of his earlier works, and that he "cannot recall and annull" much that he had written, "but, alas, they are now continued from man to man, and I cannot do what I desire," is not to be forgotten. A simple pathos and feminine gentleness, which Wordsworth occasionally approaches, but does not equal, are peculiar to him. We are tempted to say, that his genius was feminine, not masculine. It was such a feminineness, however, as is rarest to find in woman, though not the appreciation of it. Perhaps it is not to be found at all in woman, but is only the feminine in man.

Such pure, childlike love of nature is not easily to be matched. Nor is it strange, that the poetry of so rude an age should contain such sweet and polished praise of nature, for her charms are not enhanced by civilization, as society's are, but by her own original and permanent refinement she at last subdues and educates man.

Chaucer's remarkably trustful and affectionate character appears in his familiar, yet innocent and reverent, manner of speaking of his God. He comes into his thought without any false reverence, and with no more parade than the zephyr to his ear. If nature is our mother, then God is our father. There is less love and simple practical trust in Shakspeare and Milton. How rarely in our English tongue do we find expressed any affection for God. There is no sentiment so rare as the love of God. Herbert almost alone expresses it, "Ah, my dear God!" Our poet uses similar words, and whenever he sees a beautiful person, or other object, prides himself on the "maistry" of his God. He reverently recommends Dido to be his bride,

> "if that God that heaven and yearth made,
> Would have a love for beauty and goodnesse,
> And womanhede, trouth, and semeliness."

He supplies the place to his imagination of the saints of the Catholic calendar, and has none of the attributes of a Scandinavian deity.

But, in justification of our praise, we must refer the hearer to his works themselves; to the Prologue to the Canterbury Tales, the account of Gentilesse, the Flower and the Leaf, the stories of Griselda, Virginia, Ariadne, and Blanche the Dutchesse, and much more of less distinguished merit. There are many poets of more taste and better manners, who knew how to leave out their dulness, but such negative genius cannot detain us long; we shall return to Chaucer still with love. Even the clown has taste, whose dictates, though he disregards them, are higher and purer than those which the artist obeys; and some natures, which are rude and ill developed, have yet a higher standard of perfection, than others which are refined and well balanced. Though the peasant's cot is dark, it has the evening star for taper, while the nobleman's saloon is meanly lighted. If we have to wander through many dull and prosaic passages in Chaucer, we have at least the satisfaction of knowing that it is not an artificial dulness, but too easily matched by many passages in life, and it is, perhaps, more pleasing, after all, to meet with a fine thought in its natural setting. We confess we feel a disposition commonly to concentrate sweets, and accumulate pleasures, but the poet may be presumed always to speak as a traveller, who leads us through a varied scenery, from one eminence to another, and, from time to time, a single casual thought rises naturally and inevitably, with such majesty and escort only as the first stars at evening. And surely fate has enshrined it in these circumstances for some end. Nature strews her nuts and flowers broadcast, and never collects them into heaps. This was the soil it grew in, and this the hour it bloomed in; if sun, wind, and rain, came here to cherish and expand the flower, shall not we come here to pluck it?

A true poem is distinguished, not so much by a felicitous expression, or any thought it suggests, as by the atmosphere which surrounds it. Most have beauty of outline merely, and are striking as the form and bearing of a stranger, but true verses come toward us indistinctly, as the very kernel of all friendliness, and envelope us in their spirit and fragrance. Much of our poetry has the very best manners, but no character. It is only an unusual precision and elasticity of speech, as if its author had taken, not an intoxicating draught, but an electuary. It has the distinct outline of sculpture, and chronicles an early hour. Under the influence of passion all men speak thus distinctly, but wrath is not always divine.

There are two classes of men called poets. The one cultivates life, the other art; one seeks food for nutriment, the other for flavor; one satisfies hunger, the other gratifies the palate. There are two kinds of writing, both great and rare; one that of genius, or the inspired, the other of intellect and taste, in the intervals of inspiration. The former is above criticism, always correct, giving the law to criticism. It vibrates and pulsates with life forever. It is sacred, and to be read with reverence, as the works of nature are studied. There are few instances of a sustained style of this kind; perhaps every man has spoken words, but the speaker is then careless of the record. Such a style removes us out of personal relations with its author, we do not take his words on our lips, but his sense into our hearts. It is the stream of inspiration, which bubbles out, now here, now there, now in this man, now in that. It matters not through what ice-crystals it is seen, now a fountain, now the ocean stream running under ground. It is in Shakspeare, Alpheus, in Burns, Arethuse; but ever the same. The other is self-possessed and wise. It is reverent of genius, and greedy of inspiration. It is conscious in the highest and the least degree. It consists with the most perfect command of the faculties. It dwells in a repose as of the desert, and objects are as distinct in it as oases or palms in the horizon of sand. The train of thought moves with subdued and measured step, like a caravan. But the pen is only an instrument in its hand, and not instinct with life, like a longer arm. It leaves a thin varnish or glaze over all its work. The works of Goethe furnish remarkable instances of the latter.

There is no just and serene criticism as yet. Our taste is too delicate and particular. It says nay to the poet's work, but never yea to his hope. It invites him to adorn his deformities, and not to cast them off by expansion, as the tree its bark. We are a people who live in a bright light, in houses of pearl and porcelain, and drink only light wines, whose teeth are easily set on edge by the least natural sour. If we had been consulted, the back bone of the earth would have been made, not of granite, but of Bristol spar. A modern author would have died in infancy in a ruder age. But the poet is something more than a scald, "a smoother and polisher of language"; he is a Cincinnatus in literature, and occupies no west end of the world, but, like the sun, indifferently selects his rhymes, and with a liberal taste weaves into his verse the planet and the stubble.

In these old books the stucco has long since crumbled away, and we read what was sculptured in the granite. They are rude and massive in their proportions, rather than smooth and delicate in their finish. The workers in stone polish only their chimney ornaments, but their pyramids are roughly done. There is a soberness in a rough aspect, as of unhewn granite, which addresses a depth in us, but a polished surface hits only the ball of the eye. The true finish is the work of time and the use to which a thing is put. The elements are still polishing the pyramids. Art may varnish and gild, but it can do no more. A work of genius is rough-hewn from the first, because it anticipates the lapse of time, and has an ingrained polish, which still appears when fragments are broken off, an essential quality of its substance. Its beauty is at the same time its strength, and it breaks with a lustre. The great poem must have the stamp of greatness as well as its essence. The reader easily goes within the shallowest contemporary poetry, and informs it with all the life and promise of the day, as the pilgrim goes within the temple, and hears the faintest strains of the worshippers; but it will have to speak to posterity, traversing these deserts, through the ruins of its outmost walls, by the grandeur and beauty of its proportions.

Herald of Freedom

WE HAVE occasionally, for several years, met with a number of this spirited journal, edited, as abolitionists need not be informed, by Nathaniel P. Rogers, once a counsellor at law in Plymouth, still further up the Merrimack, but now, in his riper years, come down the hills thus far, to be the Herald of Freedom to those parts. We have been refreshed not a little by the cheap cordial of his editorials, flowing like his own mountain-torrents, now clear and sparkling, now foaming and gritty, and always spiced with the essence of the fir and the Norway pine; but never dark nor muddy, nor threatening with smothered murmurs, like the rivers of the plain. The effect of one of his effusions reminds us of what the hydropathists say about the electricity in fresh spring-water, compared with that which has stood over night to suit weak nerves. We do not know of another notable and public instance of such pure, youthful, and hearty indignation at all wrong. The church itself must love it, if it have any heart, though he is said to have dealt rudely with its sanctity. His clean attachment to the right, however, sanctions the severest rebuke we have read.

We have neither room, nor inclination, to criticise this paper, or its cause, at length, but would speak of it in the free and uncalculating spirit of its author. Mr. Rogers seems to us to occupy an honorable and manly position in these days, and in this country, making the press a living and breathing organ to reach the hearts of men, and not merely "fine paper, and good type," with its civil pilot sitting aft, and magnanimously waiting for the news to arrive,—the vehicle of the earliest news, but the *latest intelligence*,—recording the indubitable and last results, the marriages and deaths, alone. The present editor is wide awake, and standing on the beak of his ship; not as a scientific explorer under government, but a yankee sealer, rather, who makes those unexplored continents his harbors in which to refit for more adventurous cruises. He is a fund of news and freshness in himself,—has the gift of speech, and the knack of writing, and if anything important takes place in the Granite State, we may be sure that we shall hear of it in good season. No other paper that we know keeps pace so well with one forward wave of the restless public thought and sentiment of New England, and asserts so faithfully and ingenuously the largest liberty in all things. There is, beside, more unpledged poetry in his prose, than in the verses of many an accepted rhymer; and we are occasionally advertised by a mellow hunter's note from his trumpet, that, unlike most reformers, his feet are still where they should be, on the turf, and that he looks out from a serener natural life into the turbid arena of politics. Nor is slavery always a sombre theme with him, but invested with the colors of his wit and fancy, and an evil to be abolished by other means than sorrow and bitterness of complaint. He will fight this fight with what cheer may be. But to speak of his composition. It is a genuine yankee style, without fiction,—real guessing and calculating to some purpose, and reminds us occasionally, as does all free, brave, and original writing, of its great master in these days, Thomas Carlyle. It has a life above grammar, and a meaning which need not be parsed to be understood. But like those same mountain-torrents, there is rather too much slope to his channel, and the rainbow sprays and evaporations go double-quick-time to heaven, while the body of his water falls headlong to the plain. We would have more pause and deliberation, occasionally, if only to bring his tide to a head,— more frequent expansions of the stream, still, bottomless mountain tarns, perchance island seas, and at length the deep ocean itself.

We cannot do better than enrich our pages with a few extracts from such articles as we have at hand. Who can help sympathizing with his righteous impatience, when invited to hold his peace or endeavor to convince the understandings of the people by well ordered arguments?

"Bandy *compliments* and *arguments* with the somnambulist, on 'table rock,' when all the waters of Lake Superior are thundering in the great horse-shoe, and deafening the very war of the elements! Would you not shout to him with a clap of thunder through a speaking-trumpet, if you could command it,—if possible to reach his senses in his appaling extremity! Did Jonah *argufy* with the city of Nineveh,—'yet forty days,' cried the vagabond prophet, 'and

Nineveh shall be overthrown!' That was his salutation. And did the 'Property and Standing' turn up their noses at him, and set the mob on to him? Did the clergy *discountenance* him, and call him extravagant, misguided, a divider of churches, a disturber of parishes? What would have become of that city, if they had done this? Did they 'approve his *principles*' but dislike his '*measures*' and his '*spirit*'!!

"Slavery must be cried down, denounced down, ridiculed down, and pro-slavery with it, or rather before it. Slavery will go when pro-slavery starts. The sheep will follow when the bell-wether leads. Down, then, with the bloody system, out of the land with it, and out of the world with it,—into the Red Sea with it. Men *sha'nt* be enslaved in this country any longer. Women and children *sha'nt* be flogged here any longer. If you undertake to hinder us, the worst is your own." . . . "But this is all fanaticism. *Wait and see.*"

He thus raises the anti-slavery 'war-whoop' in New Hampshire, when an important convention is to be held, sending the summons

"To none but the whole-hearted, fully-committed, cross-the-Rubicon spirits." . . . "From rich 'old Cheshire,' from Rockingham, with her horizon setting down away to the salt sea." . . . "From where the sun sets behind Kearsarge, even to where he rises gloriously over *Moses Norris's* own town of *Pittsfield*; and from Amoskeag to Ragged Mountains,—Coos—Upper Coos, home of the everlasting hills, send out your bold advocates of human rights,—wherever they lay, scattered by lonely lake, or Indian stream, or 'Grant,' or 'Location,'—from the trout-haunted brooks of the Amoriscoggin, and where the adventurous streamlet takes up its mountain march for the St. Lawrence.

"Scattered and insulated men, wherever the light of philanthropy and liberty has beamed in upon your solitary spirits, come down to us like your streams and clouds;—and our own Grafton, all about among your dear hills, and your mountain-flanked valleys—whether you *home* along the swift Ammonoosuck, the cold Pemigewassett, or the ox-bowed Connecticut." . . .

"We are slow, brethren, dishonorably slow, in a cause like ours. Our feet should be as 'hinds' feet.' 'Liberty lies bleeding.' The leaden-colored wing of slavery obscures the land with its baleful shadow. Let us come together, and inquire at the hand of the Lord, what is to be done."

And again; on occasion of the New England Convention, in the Second-Advent Tabernacle, in Boston, he desires to try one more blast, as it were, 'on Fabyan's White Mountain horn.'

"Ho, then, people of the Bay State,—men, women, and children; children, women, and men, scattered friends of the *friendless*, wheresoever ye inhabit,—if habitations ye have, as such friends have not *always*,—along the sea-beat border of Old Essex and the Puritan Landing, and up beyond sight of the sea-cloud, among the inland hills, where the sun rises and sets upon the dry land, in that vale of the Connecticut, too fair for human content, and too fertile for virtuous industry,—where deepens that haughtiest of earth's streams, on its seaward way, proud with the pride of old Massachusetts. Are there any friends of the friendless negro haunting such a valley as this? In God's name, I fear there are none, or few, for the very scene looks apathy and oblivion to the genius of humanity. I blow you the summons though. Come, if any of you are there.

"And gallant little Rhode Island; *transcendent* abolitionists of the tiny commonwealth. I need not call you. You are *called* the year round, and, instead of sleeping in your tents, stand harnessed, and with trumpets in your hands,—every one!

"Connecticut! yonder, the home of the Burleighs, the Monroes, and the Hudsons, and the native land of old George Benson! are you ready? 'All ready!'

"Maine here, off east, looking from my mountain post, like an everglade. Where is your Sam. Fessenden, who stood storm-proof 'gainst New Organization in '38? Has he too much name as a jurist and an orator, to be found at a New England Convention in '43? God forbid. Come one and all of you from 'Down East,' to Boston, on the 30th, and let the sails of your coasters whiten all the sea-road. Alas! there are scarce enough of you to man a fishing boat. Come up, mighty in your fewness.

"And green Vermont, what has become of your anti-slavery host,— thick as your mountain maples,—mastering your very politics,—not by balance of power, but by sturdy majority. Where are you now? Will you be at the *Advent* Meeting on the 30th of May? Has anti-slavery waxed too trying for your off-hand, how-are-ye, humanity? Have you heard the voice of Freedom of late? Next week will answer.

"Poor, cold, winter-ridden New-Hampshire,—winter-killed, I like to have said,—she will be there, bare-foot, and bare-legged, making tracks like her old bloody-footed volunteers at Trenton. She will be there, if she can work her passage. I guess her minstrelsy* will,—for birds can go independently of car, or tardy stage-coach." . . .

"Let them come as Macaulay says they did to the siege of Rome, when they did not leave old men and women enough to *begin* the harvests. Oh how few we should be, if every soul of us were there.

*The Hutchinsons.

How few, and yet it is the entire muster-roll of Freedom for all the land. We should have to beat up for recruits to complete the army of Gideon, or the *platoon* at the Spartan straits. The foe are like the grasshoppers for *multitude*, as for *moral power*. Thick grass mows the easier, as the Goth said of the enervated millions of falling Rome. They can't stand too thick, nor too tall for the anti-slavery scythe. Only be there at the mowing."

In noticing the doings of another Convention, he thus congratulates himself on the liberty of speech which anti-slavery concedes to all,—even to the Folsoms and Lamsons:—

"Denied a chance to speak elsewhere, because they are not mad after the fashion, they all flock to the anti-slavery boards as a kind of Asylum. And so the poor old enterprise has to father all the oddity of the times. It is a glory to anti-slavery, that she can allow the poor friends the right of speech. I hope she will always keep herself able to afford it. Let the constables wait on the State House, and Jail, and the *Meeting Houses.* Let the door-keeper at the Anti-Slavery Hall be that tall, celestial-faced Woman, that carries the flag on the National Standard, and says, 'without *concealment*,' as well as 'without compromise.' Let every body in, who has sanity enough to see the beauty of brotherly kindness, and let them say their fantasies, and magnanimously bear with them, seeing unkind pro-slavery drives them in upon *us.* We shall have *saner* and *sensibler* meetings then, than all others in the land put together."

More recently, speaking of the use which some of the clergy have made of Webster's plea in the Girard case, as a seasonable aid to the church, he proceeds:

"Webster is a great man, and the clergy run under his wing. They had better employ him as counsel against the Comeouters. He would'nt trust the defence on the Girard will plea though, if they did. He would not risk his fame on it, as a religious argument. He would go and consult William Bassett, of Lynn, on the principles of the 'Comeouters,' to learn their strength; and he would get him a testament, and go into it as he does into the Constitution, and after a year's study of it he would hardly come off in the argument as he did from the conflict with Carolina Hayne. On looking into the case, he would advise the clergy not to go to trial,—to settle,—or, if they could'nt to 'leave it out' to a reference of 'orthodox deacons.' "

We will quote from the same sheet his indignant and touching satire on the funeral of those public officers who were killed by the explosion on board the Princeton, together with the President's slave; an accident which reminds us how closely slavery is linked with the government of this nation. The President coming to preside over a nation of *free* men, and the man who stands *next to him a slave*!

"I saw account," says he, "of the burial of those slaughtered politicians. The hearses passed along, of Upshur, Gilmer, Kennon, Maxcy, and Gardner,—but the dead slave, who fell in company with them on the deck of the Princeton, was not there. He was held their equal by the impartial gun-burst, but not allowed by the *bereaved* nation a share in the funeral." . . . "Out upon their funeral, and upon the paltry procession that went in its train. Why did'nt they enquire for the body of the *other man* who fell on that deck! And why has'nt the nation inquired, and its press? I saw account of the scene in a barbarian print, called the Boston Atlas, and it was dumb on the absence of that body, as if no such man had fallen. Why, I demand in the name of human nature, was that sixth man of the game brought down by that great shot, left unburied and above ground,— for there is no account yet that his body has been allowed the rites of sepulture." . . . "They did'nt bury him even as a slave. They did'nt assign him a jim-crow place in that solemn procession, that he might follow to wait upon his enslavers in the land of spirits. They have gone there without slaves or waiters." . . . "The poor black man,—they enslaved and imbruted him all his life, and now he is dead, they have, for aught appears, left him to decay and waste above ground. Let the civilized world take note of the circumstance."

Such timely, pure, and unpremeditated expressions of a public sentiment, such publicity of genuine indignation and humanity, as abound every where in this journal, are the most generous gifts which a man can make.

But since our voyage Rogers has died, and now there is no one in New England to express the indignation or contempt which may still be felt at any cant or inhumanity.

When, on a certain occasion, one said to him, "Why do you go about as you do, agitating the community on the subject of abolition? Jesus Christ never preached abolitionism:" he replied, "Sir, I have two answers to your appeal to Jesus Christ. First, I deny your proposition, that he never preached abolition. That single precept of his—'Whatsoever ye would that men should do to you, do ye even so to them'—reduced to *practice*, would abolish slavery over the whole earth in twenty-four hours. That is my first answer. I deny your proposition. Secondly, granting your proposition to be true—and admitting what I deny—that Jesus Christ did not preach the abolition of slavery, then I say, *he did'nt do his duty.*"

His was not the wisdom of the head, but of the heart. If perhaps he had all the faults, he had more than the usual virtues of the radical. He loved his native soil, her hills and streams, like a Burns or Scott. As he rode to an antislavery convention, he viewed the country with a poet's eye, and some of his letters written back to his editorial substitute contain as true and pleasing pictures of New England life and scenery as are anywhere to be found.

Whoever heard of Swamscot before? "Swamscot is all fishermen. Their business is all on the deep. Their village is ranged along the ocean margin, where their brave little fleets lay drawn up, and which are out at day-break on the mighty blue—where you may see them brooding at anchor—still and intent at their *profound* trade, as so many flies on the back of a wincing horse, and for whose wincings they care as little as the Swamscot Fishers heed the restless heavings of the sea around their barks. Every thing about savors of fish. Nets hang out on every enclosure. Flakes, for curing the fish are attached to almost every dwelling. Every body has a boat—and you'll see a huge pair of sea boots lying before almost every door. The air too savors strongly of the common finny vocation. Beautiful little beaches slope out from the dwellings into the Bay, all along the village—where the fishing boats lie keeled up, at low water, with their useless anchors hooked deep into the sand. A stranded bark is a sad sight—especially if it is above high water mark, where the next tide can't relieve it and set it afloat again. The Swamscot boats though, all look cheery, and as if sure of the next sea-flow. The people are said to be the freest in the region—owing perhaps to their bold and adventurous life. The Priests can't ride them *out into the deep*, as they can the shore folks."

His style and vein though often exaggerated and affected were more native to New England than those of any of her sons, and unfinished as his pieces were, yet their literary merit has been overlooked.

Wendell Phillips Before Concord Lyceum

CONCORD, MASS. MARCH 12TH, 1845.

Mr. Editor:

We have now, for the third winter, had our spirits refreshed, and our faith in the destiny of the commonwealth strengthened, by the presence and the eloquence of Wendell Phillips; and we wish to tender to him our thanks and our sympathy. The admission of this gentleman into the Lyceum has been strenuously opposed by a respectable portion of our fellow citizens, who themselves, we trust, whose descendants, at least, we know, will be as faithful conservers of the true order, whenever that shall be the order of the day,—and in each instance, the people have voted that they *would hear him*, by coming themselves and bringing their friends to the lecture room, and being very silent that they *might* hear. We saw some men and women, who had long ago *come out, going in* once more through the free and hospitable portals of the Lyceum; and many of our neighbors confessed, that they had had a 'sound season' this once.

It was the speaker's aim to show what the state, and above all the church, had to do, and now, alas! have done, with Texas and slavery, and how much, on the other hand, the individual should have to do with church and state. These were fair themes, and not mistimed; and his words were addressed to 'fit audience, *and not* few.'

We must give Mr. Phillips the credit of being a clean, erect, and what was once called a consistent man. He at least is not responsible for slavery, nor for American Independence; for the hypocrisy and superstition of the church, nor the timidity and selfishness of the state; nor for the indifference and willing ignorance of any. He stands so distinctly, so firmly, and so effectively, alone, and one honest man is so much more than a host, that we cannot but feel that he does himself injustice when he reminds us of 'the American Society, which he represents.' It is rare that we have the pleasure of listening to so clear and orthodox a speaker, who obviously has so few cracks or flaws in his moral nature—who, having words at his command in a remarkable degree, has much more than words, if these should fail, in his unquestionable earnestness and integrity—and, aside from their admiration at his rhetoric, secures the genuine respect of his audience. He unconsciously tells his biography as he proceeds, and we see him early and earnestly deliberating on these subjects, and wisely and bravely, without counsel or consent of any, occupying a ground at first, from which the varying tides of public opinion cannot drive him.

No one could mistake the genuine modesty and truth with which he affirmed, when speaking of the framers of the Constitution,—'I am wiser than they,' which with him has improved these sixty years' experience of its working; or the uncompromising consistency and frankness of the prayer which concluded, not like the Thanksgiving proclamations, with—'God save the Commonwealth of Massachusetts,' but God dash it into a thousand pieces, till there shall not remain a fragment on which a man can stand, and dare not tell his name—referring to the case of Frederick _____. To our disgrace we know not what to call him, unless Scotland will lend us the spoils of one of her Douglasses, out of history or fiction, for a season, till we be hospitable and brave enough to hear his proper name,—a fugitive slave in one more sense than we; who has proved himself the possessor of a *fair* intellect, and has won a colorless reputation in these parts; and who, we trust, will be as superior to degradation from the sympathies of Freedom, as from the antipathies of slavery. When, said Mr. Phillips, he communicated to a New-Bedford audience, the other day, his purpose of writing his life, and telling his name, and the name of his master, and the place he ran from, the murmur ran round the room, and was anxiously whispered by the sons of the Pilgrims, 'He had better not!' and it was echoed under the shadow of Concord monument, 'He had better not!'

We would fain express our appreciation of the freedom and steady wisdom, so rare in the reformer, with which he declared that he was not born to abolish slavery, but to do right. We have heard a few, a very few, good political speakers, who afforded us the pleasure of great intellectual power and acuteness, of soldier-like steadiness, and of a graceful and natural oratory; but in this man the audience might detect a sort of moral principle and integrity, which was more stable than their firmness, more discriminating than his own intellect, and more graceful than his rhetoric, which was not working for temporary or trivial ends. It is so rare and encouraging to listen to an orator, who is content with another alliance than with the popular party, or even with the sympathising school of the martyrs, who can afford sometimes to be his own auditor if the mob stay away, and hears himself without reproof, that we feel ourselves in danger of slandering all mankind by affirming, that here is one, who is at the same time an eloquent speaker and a righteous man.

Perhaps, on the whole, the most interesting fact elicited by these addresses, is the readiness of the people at large, of whatever sect or party, to entertain, with good will and hospitality, the most revolutionary and heretical opinions, when frankly and adequately, and in some sort cheerfully, expressed. Such clear and candid declaration of opinion served like an electuary to whet and clarify the intellect of all parties, and furnished each one with an additional argument for that right he asserted.

We consider Mr. Phillips one of the most conspicuous and efficient champions of a true church and state now in the field, and would say to him, and such as are like him—'God speed you.' If you know of any champion in the ranks of his opponents, who has the valor and courtesy even of Paynim chivalry, if not the Christian graces and refinement of this knight, you will do us a service by directing him to these fields forthwith, where the lists are now open, and he shall be hospitably entertained. For as yet the Red-cross knight has shown us only the gallant device upon his shield, and his admirable command of his steed, prancing and curvetting in the empty lists; but we wait to see who, in the actual breaking of lances, will come tumbling upon the plain.

Thomas Carlyle and His Works

THOMAS CARLYLE is a Scotchman, born about fifty years ago, "at Ecclefechan, Annandale," according to one authority. "His parents 'good farmer people,' his father an elder in the Secession church there, and a man of strong native sense, whose words were said to 'nail a subject to the wall.'" We also hear of his "excellent mother," still alive, and of "her fine old covenanting accents, concerting with his transcendental tones." He seems to have gone to school at Annan, on the shore of the Solway Frith, and there, as he himself writes, "heard of famed professors, of high matters classical, mathematical, a whole Wonderland of Knowledge," from Edward Irving, then a young man "fresh from Edinburgh, with college prizes &c."—"come to see our schoolmaster, who had also been his." From this place, they say, you can look over into Wordsworth's country. Here first he may have become acquainted with Nature, with woods, such as are there, and rivers and brooks, some of whose names we have heard, and the last lapses of Atlantic billows. He got some of his education, too, more or less liberal, out of the University of Edinburgh, where, according to the same authority, he had to "support himself," partly by "private tuition, translations for the booksellers, &c.," and afterward, as we are glad to hear, "taught an academy in Dysart, at the same time that Irving was teaching in Kirkaldy," the usual middle passage of a literary life. He was destined for the church, but not by the powers that rule man's life; made his literary début in Fraser's Magazine, long ago; read here and there in English and French, with more or less profit, we may suppose, such of us at least as are not particularly informed, and at length found some words which spoke to his condition in the German language, and set himself earnestly to unravel that mystery—with what success many readers know.

After his marriage he "resided partly at Comely Bank, Edinburgh; and for a year or two at Craigenputtock, a wild and solitary farm-house in the upper part of Dumfriesshire," at which last place, amid barren heather hills, he was visited by our countryman Emerson. With Emerson he still corresponds. He was early intimate with Edward Irving, and continued to be his friend until the latter's death. Concerning this "freest, brotherliest, bravest human soul," and Carlyle's relation to him, those whom it concerns will do well to consult a notice of his death in Fraser's Magazine for 1835, reprinted in the Miscellanies. He also corresponded with Goethe. Laterly, we hear, the poet Sterling was his only intimate acquaintance in England.

He has spent the last quarter of his life in London, writing books; has the fame, as all readers know, of having made England acquainted with Germany, in late years, and done much else that is novel and remarkable in literature. He especially is the literary man of those parts. You may imagine him living in altogether a retired and simple way, with small family, in a quiet part of London, called Chelsea, a little out of the din of commerce, in "Cheyne Row," there, not far from the "Chelsea Hospital." "A little past this, and an old ivy-clad church, with its buried generations lying around it," writes one traveller, "you come to an antique street running at right angles with the Thames, and, a few steps from the river, you find Carlyle's name on the door."

"A Scotch lass ushers you into the second story front chamber, which is the spacious workshop of the world maker." Here he sits a long time together, with many books and papers about him; many new books, we have been told, on the upper shelves, uncut, with the "author's respects" in them; in late months, with many manuscripts in an old English hand, and innumerable pamphlets, from the public libraries, relating to the Cromwellian period; now, perhaps, looking out into the street on brick and pavement, for a change, and now upon some rod of grass ground in the rear; or, perchance, he steps over to the British Museum, and makes that his studio for the time. This is the fore part of the day; that is the way with literary men commonly; and then in the afternoon, we presume, he takes a short run of a mile or so through the suburbs out into the country; we think he would run that way, though so short a trip might not take him to very sylvan or rustic places. In the meanwhile, people are calling to *see* him, from various quarters, very few worthy of being *seen* by him, "distinguished travellers from America," not a few, to all and sundry of whom he gives freely of his yet unwritten rich and flashing soliloquy, in exchange for whatever they may have to offer; speaking his English, as they say, with a "broad Scotch accent," talking, to their astonishment and to ours, very much as he writes, a sort of Carlylese, his discourse "coming to its climaxes, ever and anon, in long, deep, chest-shaking bursts of laughter."

He goes to Scotland sometimes to visit his native heath-clad hills, having some interest still in the earth there; such names as Craigenputtock and Ecclefechan, which we have already quoted, stand for habitable places there to him; or he rides to the seacoast of England in his vacations, upon his horse Yankee, bought by the sale of his books here, as we have been told.

How, after all, he gets his living; what proportion of his daily bread he earns by day-labor or job-work with his pen, what he inherits, what steals—questions whose answers are so significant, and not to be omitted in his biography—we, alas! are unable to answer here. It may be worth the while to state that he is not a Reformer, in our sense of the term, eats, drinks, and sleeps, thinks and believes, professes and practices, not according to the New England standard, nor to the Old English wholly. Nevertheless, we are told that he is a sort of lion in certain quarters there, "an amicable centre for men of the most opposite opinions," and "listened to as an oracle," "smoking his perpetual pipe."

A rather tall, gaunt figure, with intent face, dark hair and complexion, and the air of a student; not altogether well in body, from sitting too long in his workhouse, he, born in the border country and descended from moss-troopers, it may be. We have seen several pictures of him here; one, a full length portrait, with hat and overall, if it did not tell us much, told the fewest lies; another, we remember, was well said to have "too combed a look;" one other also we have seen in which we discern some features of the man we are thinking of; but the only ones worth remembering, after all, are those which he has unconsciously drawn of himself.

•

When we remember how these volumes came over to us, with their encouragement and provocation from month to month, and what commotion they created in many private breasts, we wonder that the country did not ring, from shore to shore, from the Atlantic to the Pacific, with its greeting; and the Boones and Crocketts of the West make haste to hail him, whose wide humanity embraces them too. Of all that the packets have brought over to us, has there been any richer cargo than this? What else has been English news for so long a season? What else, of late years, has been England to us—to us who read books, we mean? Unless we remembered it as the scene where the age of Wordsworth was spending itself, and a few younger muses were trying their wings, and from time to time, as the residence of Landor; Carlyle alone, since the death of Coleridge, has kept the promise of England. It is the best apology for all the bustle and the sin of commerce, that it has made us acquainted with the thoughts of this man. Commerce would not concern us much if it were not for such results as this. New England owes him a debt which she will be slow to recognize. His earlier essays reached us at a time when Coleridge's were the only recent words which had made any notable impression so far, and they found a field unoccupied by him, before yet any words of moment had been uttered in our midst. He had this advantage, too, in a teacher, that he stood near to his pupils; and he has no doubt afforded reasonable encouragement and sympathy to many an independent but solitary thinker. Through him, as usher, we have been latterly, in a great measure, made acquainted with what philosophy and criticism the nineteenth century had to offer—admitted, so to speak, to the privileges of the century; and what he may yet have to say, is still expected here with more interest than any thing else from that quarter.

It is remarkable, but on the whole, perhaps, not to be lamented, that the world is so unkind to a new book. Any distinguished traveller who comes to our shores, is likely to get more dinners and speeches of welcome than he can well dispose of, but the best books, if noticed at all, meet with coldness and suspicion, or, what is worse, gratuitous, off-hand criticism. It is plain that the reviewers, both here and abroad, do not know how to dispose of this man. They approach him too easily, as if he were one of the men of letters about town, who grace Mr. Somebody's administration, merely; but he already belongs to literature, and depends neither on the favor of reviewers, nor the honesty of booksellers, nor the pleasure of readers for his success. He has more to impart than to receive from his generation. He is another such a strong and finished workman in his craft as Samuel Johnson was, and like him, makes the literary class respectable. As few are yet out of their apprenticeship, or even if they learn to be able writers, are at the same time able and valuable thinkers. The aged and critical eye, especially, is incapacitated to appreciate the works of this author. To such their meaning is impalpable and evanescent, and they seem to abound only in obstinate mannerisms, Germanisms, and whimsical ravings of all kinds, with now and then an unaccountably true and sensible remark. On the strength of this last, Carlyle is admitted to have what is called genius. We hardly know an old man to whom these volumes are not hopelessly sealed. The language, they say, is foolishness and a stumbling-block to them; but to many a clear-headed boy, they are plainest English, and despatched with such hasty relish as his bread and milk. The fathers wonder how it is that the children take to this diet so readily, and digest it with so little difficulty. They shake their heads with mistrust at their free and easy delight, and remark that "Mr. Carlyle is a very learned man;" for they, too, not to be out of fashion, have got grammar and dictionary, if the truth were known, and with the best faith cudgelled their brains to get a little way into the jungle, and they could not but confess, as often as they found the clue, that it was as intricate as Blackstone to follow, if you read it honestly. But merely reading, even with the best intentions, is not enough, you must almost have written these books yourself. Only he who has had the good fortune to read them in the nick of time, in the most perceptive and recipient season of life, can give any adequate account of them.

Many have tasted of this well with an odd suspicion, as if it were some fountain Arethuse which had flowed under the sea from Germany, as if the materials of his books had lain in some garret there, in danger of being appropriated for waste paper. Over what German ocean, from what Hercynian forest, he has been imported, piece-meal, into England, or whether he has now all arrived, we are not informed. This article is not invoiced in Hamburg, nor in London. Perhaps it was contraband. However, we suspect that this sort of goods cannot be imported in this way. No matter how skillful the stevedore, all things being got into sailing trim, wait for a Sunday, and aft wind, and then weigh anchor, and run up the main-sheet—straightway what of transcendent and permanent value is there resists the aft wind, and will doggedly stay behind that Sunday—it does not travel Sundays; while biscuit and pork make headway, and sailors cry heave-yo! it must part company, if it open a seam. It is not quite safe to send out a venture in this kind, unless yourself go supercargo. Where a man goes, there he is; but the slightest virtue is immovable—it is real estate, not personal; who would keep it, must consent to be bought and sold with it.

However, we need not dwell on this charge of a German extraction, it being generally admitted, by this time, that Carlyle is English, and an inhabitant of London. He has the English for his mother tongue, though with a Scotch accent, or never so many accents, and thoughts also, which are the legitimate growth of native soil, to utter therewith. His style is eminently colloquial—and no wonder it is strange to meet with in a book. It is not literary or classical; it has not the music of poetry, nor the pomp of philosophy, but the rhythms and cadences of conversation endlessly repeated. It resounds with emphatic, natural, lively, stirring tones, muttering, rattling, exploding, like shells and shot, and with like execution. So far as it is a merit in composition, that the written answer to the spoken word, and the spoken word to a fresh and pertinent thought in the mind, as well as to the half thoughts, the tumultuary misgivings and expectancies, this author is, perhaps, not to be matched in literature. In the streets men laugh and cry, but in books, never; they "whine, put finger i' the eye, and sob" only. One would think that all books of late, had adopted the falling inflexion. "A mother, if she wishes to sing her child to sleep," say the musical men, "will always adopt the falling inflexion." Would they but choose the rising inflexion, and wake the child up for once.

He is no mystic either, more than Newton or Arkwright, or Davy—and tolerates none. Not one obscure line, or half line, did he ever write. His meaning lies plain as the daylight, and he who runs may read; indeed, only he who runs *can* read, and keep up with the meaning. It has the distinctness of picture to his mind, and he tells us only what he sees printed in largest English type upon the face of things. He utters substantial English thoughts in plainest English dialects; for it must be confessed, he speaks more than one of these. All the shires of England, and all the shires of Europe, are laid under contribution to his genius; for to be English does not mean to be exclusive and narrow, and adapt one's self to the apprehension of his nearest neighbor only. And yet no writer is more thoroughly Saxon. In the translation of those fragments of Saxon poetry, we have met with the same rhythm that occurs so often in his poem on the French Revolution. And if you would know where many of those obnoxious Carlyleisms and Germanisms came from, read the best of Milton's prose, read those speeches of Cromwell which he has brought to light, or go and listen once more to your mother's tongue. So much for his German extraction.

Indeed, for fluency and skill in the use of the English tongue, he is a master unrivaled. His felicity and power of expression surpass even any of his special merits as a historian and critic. Therein his experience has not failed him, but furnished him with such a store of winged, aye, and legged words, as only a London life, perchance, could give account of; we had not understood the wealth of the language before. Nature is ransacked, and all the resorts and purlieus of humanity are taxed, to furnish the fittest symbol for his thought. He does not go to the dictionary, the word-book, but to the word-manufactory itself, and has made endless work for the lexicographers—yes, he has that same English for his mother-tongue, that you have, but with him it is no dumb, muttering, mumbling faculty, concealing the thoughts, but a keen, unwearied, resistless weapon. He has such command of it as neither you nor I have; and it would be well for any who have a lost horse to advertise, or a town-meeting warrant, or a sermon, or a letter to write, to study this universal letter-writer, for he knows more than the grammar or the dictionary.

The style is worth attending to, as one of the most important features of the man which we at this distance can discern. It is for once quite equal to the matter. It can carry all its load, and never breaks down nor staggers. His books are solid and workmanlike, as all that England does; and they are graceful and readable also. They tell of huge labor done, well done, and all the rubbish swept away, like the bright cutlery which glitters in shop-windows, while the coke and ashes, the turnings, filings, dust, and borings, lie far away at Birmingham, unheard of. He is a masterly clerk, scribe, reporter, and writer. He can reduce to writing most things— gestures, winks, nods, significant looks, patois, brogue, accent, pantomime, and how much that had passed for silence before, does he represent by written words. The countryman who puzzled the city lawyer, requiring him to write, among other things, his call to his horses, would hardly have puzzled him; he would have found a word for it, all right and classical, that would have started his team for him. Consider the ceaseless tide of speech forever flowing in countless cellars, garrets, *parlors*; that of the French, says Carlyle, "only ebbs toward the short hours of night," and what a drop in the bucket is the printed word. Feeling, thought, speech, writing, and we might add, poetry, inspiration—for so the circle is completed; how they gradually dwindle at length, passing through successive colanders, into your history and classics, from the roar of the ocean, the murmur of the forest, to the squeak of a mouse; so much only parsed and spelt out, and punctuated, at last. The few who can talk like a book, they only get reported commonly. But this writer reports a new "Lieferung."

One wonders how so much, after all, was expressed in the old way, so much here depends upon the emphasis, tone, pronunciation, style, and spirit of the reading. No writer uses so profusely all the aids to intelligibility which the printer's art affords. You wonder how others had contrived to write so many pages without emphatic or italicised words, they are so expressive, so natural, so indispensable here, as if none had ever used the demonstrative pronouns demonstratively before. In another's sentences the thought, though it may be immortal, is, as it were, embalmed, and does not *strike* you, but here it is so freshly living, even the body of it, not having passed through the ordeal of death, that it stirs in the very extremities, and the smallest particles and pronouns are all alive with it. It is not simple dictionary *it*, yours or mine, but IT. The words did not come at the command of grammar, but of a tyrannous, inexorable meaning; not like standing soldiers, by vote of parliament, but any able-bodied countryman pressed into the service, for "sire, it is not a revolt, it is a revolution."

We have never heard him speak, but we should say that Carlyle was a rare talker. He has broken the ice, and streams freely forth like a spring torrent. He does not trace back the stream of his thought, silently adventurous, up to its fountain-head, but is borne away with it, as it rushes through his brain like a torrent to overwhelm and fertilize. He holds a talk with you. His audience is such a tumultuous mob of thirty thousand, as assembled at the University of Paris, before printing was invented. Philosophy, on the other hand, does not talk, but write, or, when it comes personally before an audience, lecture or read; and therefore it must be read to-morrow, or a thousand years hence. But the talker must naturally be attended to at once; he does not talk on without an audience; the winds do not long bear the sound of his voice. Think of Carlyle reading his French Revolution to any audience. One might say it was never written, but spoken; and thereafter reported and printed, that those not within sound of his voice might know something about it. Some men read to you something which they have written, in a dead *language*, of course, but it may be in a living *letter*, in a Syriac, or Roman, or Runic character. Men must *speak* English who can *write* Sanscrit; and they must speak a modern language who write, perchance, an ancient and universal one. We do not live in those days when the learned used a learned language. There is no writing of Latin with Carlyle, but as Chaucer, with all reverence to Homer, and Virgil, and Messieurs the Normans, sung his poetry in the homely Saxon tongue,—and Locke has at least the merit of having done philosophy into English—so Carlyle has done a different philosophy still further into English, and thrown open the doors of literature and criticism to the populace.

Such a style—so diversified and variegated! It is like the face of a country; it is like a New England landscape, with farm-houses and villages, and cultivated spots, and belts of forests and blueberry-swamps round about it, with the fragrance of shad-blossoms and violets on certain winds. And as for the reading of it, it is novel enough to the reader who has used only the diligence, and old-line mail-coach. It is like travelling, sometimes on foot, sometimes in a gig tandem; sometimes in a full coach, over highways, mended and un-mended, for which you will prosecute the town; on level roads, through French departments, by Simplon roads over the Alps, and now and then he hauls up for a relay, and yokes in an unbroken colt of a Pegasus for a leader, driving off by cart-paths, and across lots, by corduroy roads and gridiron bridges; and where the bridges are gone, not even a string-piece left, and the reader has to set his breast and swim. You have got an expert driver this time, who has driven ten thousand miles, and was never known to upset; can drive six in hand on the edge of a precipice, and touch the leaders any-where with his snapper.

With wonderful art he grinds into paint for his picture all his moods and experiences, so that all his forces may be brought to the encounter. Apparently writing without a par-ticular design or responsibility, setting down his soliloquies from time to time, taking advantage of all his humors, when at length the hour comes to declare himself, he puts down in plain English, without quotation marks, what he, Thomas Carlyle, is ready to defend in the face of the world, and fathers the rest, often quite as defensible, only more modest, or plain spoken, or insinuating, upon "Sauerteig," or some other gen-tleman long employed on the subject. Rolling his subject how many ways in his mind, he meets it now face to face, wrestling with it at arm's length, and striving to get it down, or throws it over his head; and if that will not do, or whether it will do or not, tries the back-stitch and side-hug with it, and downs it again—scalps it, draws and quarters it, hangs it in chains, and leaves it to the winds and dogs. With his brows knit, his mind made up, his will resolved and resistless, he advances, crashing his way through the host of weak, half-formed, *dilet-tante* opinions, honest and dishonest ways of thinking, with their standards raised, sentimentalities and conjectures, and tramples them all into dust. See how he prevails; you don't even hear the groans of the wounded and dying. Certainly it is not so well worth the while to look through any man's eyes at history, for the time, as through his; and his way of looking at things is fastest getting adopted by his generation.

It is not in man to determine what his style shall be. He might as well determine what his thoughts shall be. We would not have had him write always as in the chapter on Burns, and the Life of Schiller, and elsewhere. No; his thoughts were ever irregular and impetuous. Perhaps as he grows older and writes more he acquires a truer expression; it is in some respects manlier, freer, struggling up to a level with its fountain-head. We think it is the richest prose style we know of.

Who cares what a man's style is, so it is intelligible—as intelligible as his thought. Literally and really, the style is no more than the *stylus*, the pen he writes with—and it is not worth scraping and polishing, and gilding, unless it will write his thoughts the better for it. It is something for use, and not to look at. The question for us is not whether Pope had a fine style, wrote with a peacock's feather, but whether he uttered useful thoughts. Translate a book a dozen times from one language to another, and what becomes of its style? Most books would be worn out and disappear in this ordeal. The pen which wrote it is soon destroyed, but the poem survives. We believe that Carlyle has, after all, more readers, and is better known to-day for this very originality of style, and that posterity will have reason to thank him for emancipating the language, in some measure, from the fetters which a merely conservative, aimless, and pedantic literary class had imposed upon it, and setting an example of greater freedom and naturalness. No man's thoughts are new, but the style of their expression is the never failing novelty which cheers and refreshes men. If we were to answer the question, whether the mass of men, as we know them, talk as the standard authors and reviewers write, or rather as this man writes, we should say that he alone begins to write their language at all, and that the former is, for the most part, the mere effigies of a language, not the best method of concealing one's thoughts even, but frequently a method of doing without thoughts at all.

In his graphic description of Richter's style, Carlyle describes his own pretty nearly; and no doubt he first got his own tongue loosened at that fountain, and was inspired by it to equal freedom and originality. "The language," as he says of Richter, "groans with indescribable metaphors and allusions to all things, human and divine, flowing onward, not like a river, but like an inundation; circling in complex eddies, chafing and gurgling, now this way, now that;" but in Carlyle, "the proper current" never "sinks out of sight amid the boundless uproar." Again: "His very language is Titanian— deep, strong, tumultuous, shining with a thousand hues, fused from a thousand elements, and winding in labyrinthic mazes."

In short, if it is desirable that a man be eloquent, that he talk much, and address himself to his own age mainly, then this is not a bad style of doing it. But if it is desired rather that he pioneer into unexplored regions of thought, and speak to silent centuries to come, then, indeed, we could wish that he had cultivated the style of Goethe more, that of Richter less; not that Goethe's is the kind of utterance most to be prized by mankind, but it will serve for a model of the best that can be successfully cultivated.

But for style, and fine writing, and Augustan ages—that is but a poor style, and vulgar writing, and a degenerate age, which allows us to remember these things. This man has something to communicate. Carlyle's are not, in the common sense, works of art in their origin and aim; and yet, perhaps, no living English writer evinces an equal literary talent. They are such works of art only as the plough, and corn-mill, and steam-engine—not as pictures and statues. Others speak with greater emphasis to scholars, as such, but none so earnestly and effectually to all who can read. Others give their advice, he gives his sympathy also. It is no small praise that he does not take upon himself the airs, has none of the whims, none of the pride, the nice vulgarities, the starched, impoverished isolation, and cold glitter of the spoiled children of genius. He does not need to husband his pearl, but excels by a greater humanity and sincerity.

He is singularly serious and untrivial. We are every where impressed by the rugged, unwearied, and rich sincerity of the man. We are sure that he never sacrificed one jot of his honest thought to art or whim, but to utter himself in the most direct and effectual way, that is the endeavor. These are merits which will wear well. When time has worn deeper into the substance of these books, this grain will appear. No such sermons have come to us here out of England, in late years, as those of this preacher; sermons to kings, and sermons to peasants, and sermons to all intermediate classes. It is in vain that John Bull, or any of his cousins, turns a deaf ear, and pretends not to hear them, nature will not soon be weary of repeating them. There are words less obviously true, more for the ages to hear, perhaps, but none so impossible for this age not to hear. What a cutting cimiter was that "Past and Present," going through heaps of silken stuffs, and glibly through the necks of men, too, without their knowing it, leaving no trace. He has the earnestness of a prophet. In an age of pedantry and dilettantism, he has no grain of these in his composition. There is no where else, surely, in recent readable English, or other books, such direct and effectual teaching, reproving, encouraging, stimulating, earnestly, vehemently, almost like Mahomet, like Luther; not looking behind him to see how his *Opera Omnia* will look, but forward to other work to be done. His writings are a gospel to the young of this generation; they will hear his manly, brotherly speech with responsive joy, and press forward to older or newer gospels.

We should omit a main attraction in these books, if we said nothing of their humor. Of this indispensable pledge of sanity, without some leaven of which the abstruse thinker may justly be suspected of mysticism, fanaticism, or insanity, there is a superabundance in Carlyle. Especially the transcendental philosophy needs the leaven of humor to render it light and digestible. In his later and longer works it is an unfailing accompaniment, reverberating through pages and chapters, long sustained without effort. The very punctuation, the italics, the quotation marks, the blank spaces and dashes, and the capitals, each and all are pressed into its service.

Every man, of course, has his fane, from which even the most innocent conscious humor is excluded; but in proportion as the writer's position is high above his fellows, the range of his humor is extended. To the thinker, all the institutions of men, as all imperfection, viewed from the point of equanimity, are legitimate subjects of humor. Whatever is not necessary, no matter how sad or personal, or universal a grievance, is, indeed, a jest more or less sublime.

Carlyle's humor is vigorous and Titanic, and has more sense in it than the sober philosophy of many another. It is not to be disposed of by laughter and smiles merely; it gets to be too serious for that—only they may laugh who are not hit by it. For those who love a merry jest, this is a strange kind of fun—rather too practical joking, if they understand it. The pleasant humor which the public loves, is but the innocent pranks of the ball-room, harmless flow of animal spirits, the light plushy pressure of dandy pumps, in comparison. But when an elephant takes to treading on your corns, why then you are lucky if you sit high, or wear cowhide. His humor is always subordinate to a serious purpose, though often the real charm for the reader, is not so much in the essential progress and final upshot of the chapter, as in this indirect side-light illustration of every hue. He sketches first with strong, practical English pencil, the essential features in outline, black on white, more faithfully than Dryasdust would have done, telling us wisely whom and what to mark, to save time, and then with brush of camel's hair, or sometimes with more expeditious swab, he lays on the bright and fast colors of his humor everywhere. One piece of solid work, be it known, we have determined to do, about which let there be no jesting, but all things else under the heavens, to the right and left of that, are for the time fair game. To us this humor is not wearisome, as almost every other is. Rabelais, for instance, is intolerable; one chapter is better than a volume—it may be sport to him, but it is death to us. A mere humorist, indeed, is a most unhappy man; and his readers are most unhappy also.

Humor is not so distinct a quality as for the purposes of criticism, it is commonly regarded, but allied to every, even the divinest faculty. The familiar and cheerful conversation about every hearth-side, if it be analyzed, will be found to be sweetened by this principle. There is not only a never-failing, pleasant, and earnest humor kept up there, embracing the domestic affairs, the dinner, and the scolding, but there is also a constant run upon the neighbors, and upon church and state, and to cherish and maintain this, in a great measure, the fire is kept burning, and the dinner provided. There will be neighbors, parties to a very genuine, even romantic friendship, whose whole audible salutation and intercourse, abstaining from the usual cordial expressions, grasping of hands, or affectionate farewells, consists in the mutual play and interchange of a genial and healthy humor, which excepts nothing, not even themselves, in its lawless range. The child plays continually, if you will let it, and all its life is a sort of practical humor of a very pure kind, often of so fine and ethereal a nature, that its parents, its uncles and cousins, can in no wise participate in it, but must stand aloof in silent admiration, and reverence even. The more quiet the more profound it is. Even nature is observed to have her playful moods or aspects, of which man seems sometimes to be the sport.

But, after all, we could sometimes dispense with the humor, though unquestionably incorporated in the blood, if it were replaced by this author's gravity. We should not apply to himself, without qualification, his remarks on the humor of Richter. With more repose in his inmost being, his humor would become more thoroughly genial and placid. Humor is apt to imply but a half satisfaction at best. In his pleasantest and most genial hour, man smiles but as the globe smiles, and the works of nature. The fruits *dry* ripe, and much as we relish some of them in their green and pulpy state, we lay up for our winter store, not out of these, but the rustling autumnal harvests. Though we never weary of this vivacious wit, while we are perusing its work, yet when we remember it from afar, we sometimes feel balked and disappointed, missing the security, the simplicity, and frankness, even the occasional magnanimity of acknowledged dullness and bungling. This never-failing success and brilliant talent become a reproach. To the most practical reader the humor is certainly too obvious and constant a quality. When we are to have dealings with a man, we prize the good faith and valor of soberness and gravity. There is always a more impressive statement than consists with these victorious comparisons. Besides, humor does not wear well. It is commonly enough said, that a joke will not bear repeating. The deepest humor will not keep.

Humors do not circulate but stagnate, or circulate partially. In the oldest literature, in the Hebrew, the Hindoo, the Persian, the Chinese, it is rarely humor, even the most divine, which still survives, but the most sober and private, painful or joyous thoughts, maxims of duty, to which the life of all men may be referred. After time has sifted the literature of a people, there is left only their SCRIPTURE, for that is WRITING, *par excellence*. This is as true of the poets, as of the philosophers and moralists by profession; for what subsides in any of these is the moral only, to re-appear as dry land at some remote epoch.

We confess that Carlyle's humor is rich, deep, and variegated, in direct communication with the back bone and risible muscles of the globe—and there is nothing like it; but much as we relish this jovial, this rapid and delugeous way of conveying one's views and impressions, when we would not converse but meditate, we pray for a man's diamond edition of his thought, without the colored illuminations in the margin—the fishes and dragons, and unicorns, the red or the blue ink, but its initial letter in distinct skeleton type, and the whole so clipped and condensed down to the very essence of it, that time will have little to do. We know not but we shall immigrate soon, and would fain take with us all the treasures of the east, and all kinds of *dry*, portable soups, in small tin canisters, which contain whole herds of English beeves, boiled down, will be acceptable.

The difference between this flashing, fitful writing and pure philosophy, is the difference between flame and light. The flame, indeed, yields light, but when we are so near as to observe the flame, we are apt to be incommoded by the heat and smoke. But the sun, that old Platonist, is set so far off in the heavens, that only a genial summer-heat and ineffable day-light can reach us. But many a time, we confess, in wintery weather, we have been glad to forsake the sun-light, and warm us by these Promethean flames.

Carlyle must undoubtedly plead guilty to the charge of mannerism. He not only has his vein, but his peculiar manner of working it. He has a style which can be imitated, and sometimes is an imitator of himself. Every man, though born and bred in the metropolis of the world, will still have some provincialism adhering to him; but in proportion as his aim is simple and earnest, he approaches at once the most ancient and the most modern men. There is no mannerism in the Scriptures. The style of proverbs, and indeed of all *maxims*, whether measured by sentences or by chapters, if they may be said to have any style, is one, and as the expression of one voice, merely an account of the matter by the latest witness. It is one advantage enjoyed by men of science, that they use only formulas which are universal. The common language and the common sense of mankind, it is most uncommon to meet with in the individual. Yet liberty of thought and speech is only liberty to think the universal thought, and speak the universal language of men, instead of being enslaved to a particular mode. Of this universal speech there is very little. It is equable and sure; from a depth within man which is beyond education and prejudice.

Certainly, no critic has anywhere said what is more to the purpose, than this which Carlyle's own writings furnish, which we quote, as well for its intrinsic merit as for its pertinence here. "It is true," says he, thinking of Richter, "the beaten paths of literature lead the safeliest to the goal; and the talent pleases us most, which submits to shine with new gracefulness through old forms. Nor is the noblest and most peculiar mind too noble or peculiar for working by prescribed laws; Sophocles, Shakspeare, Cervantes, and in Richter's own age, Goethe, how little did they innovate on the given forms of composition, how much in the spirit they breathed into them! All this is true; and Richter must lose of our esteem in proportion." And again, in the chapter on Goethe, "We read Goethe for years before we come to see wherein the distinguishing peculiarity of his understanding, of his disposition, even of his way of writing, consists! It seems quite a simple style, [that of his?] remarkable chiefly for its calmness, its perspicuity, in short, its commonness; and yet it is the most uncommon of all styles." And this, too, translated for us by the same pen from Schiller, which we will apply not merely to the outward form of his works, but to their inner form and substance. He is speaking of the artist. "Let some beneficent divinity snatch him, when a suckling, from the breast of his mother, and nurse him with the milk of a better time, that he may ripen to his full stature beneath a distant Grecian sky. And having grown to manhood, let him return, a foreign shape, into his century; not, however, to delight it by his presence, but, dreadful, like the son of Agamemnon, to purify it. The matter of his works he will take from the present, but their form he will derive from a nobler time; nay, from beyond all time, from the absolute unchanging unity of his own nature."

But enough of this. Our complaint is already out of all proportion to our discontent.

Carlyle's works, it is true, have not the stereotyped success which we call classic. They are a rich but inexpensive entertainment, at which we are not concerned lest the host has strained or impoverished himself to feed his guests. It is not the most lasting word, nor the loftiest wisdom, but rather the word which comes last. For his genius it was reserved to give expression to the thoughts which were throbbing in a million breasts. He has plucked the ripest fruit in the public garden; but this fruit already least concerned the tree that bore it, which was rather perfecting the bud at the foot of the leaf stalk. His works are not to be studied, but read with a swift satisfaction. Their flavor and gust is like what poets tell of the froth of wine, which can only be tasted once and hastily. On a review we can never find the pages we had read. The first impression is the truest and the deepest, and there is no reprint, no *double entendre*, so to speak, for the alert reader. Yet they are in some degree true natural products in this respect. All things are but once, and never repeated. The first faint blushes of the morning, gilding the mountain tops, the pale phosphor and saffron-colored clouds do verily transport us to the morning of creation; but what avails it to travel eastward, or look again there an hour hence? We should be as far in the day ourselves, mounting toward our meridian. These works were designed for such complete success that they serve but for a single occasion. It is the luxury of art, when its own instrument is manufactured for each particular and present use. The knife which slices the bread of Jove ceases to be a knife when this service is rendered.

But he is wilfully and pertinaciously unjust, even scurrilous, impolite, ungentlemanly; calls us "Imbeciles," "Dilettantes,"

"Philistines," implying sometimes what would not sound well expressed. If he would adopt the newspaper style, and take back these hard names—but where is the reader who does not derive some benefit from these epithets, applying them to himself? Think not that with each repetition of them there is a fresh overflowing of bile; oh no! Perhaps none at all after the first time, only a faithfulness, the right name being found, to apply it—"They are the same ones we meant before"—and ofttimes with a genuine sympathy and encouragement expressed. Indeed, there appears in all his writings a hearty and manly sympathy with all misfortune and wretchedness, and not a weak and sniveling one. They who suspect a Mephistophiles, or sneering, satirical devil, under all, have not learned the secret of true humor, which sympathizes with the gods themselves, in view of their grotesque, half-finished creatures.

He is, in fact, the best tempered, and not the least impartial of reviewers. He goes out of his way to do justice to profligates and quacks. There is somewhat even Christian, in the rarest and most peculiar sense, in his universal brotherliness, his simple, child-like endurance, and earnest, honest endeavor, with sympathy for the like. And this fact is not insignificant, that he is almost the only writer of biography, of the lives of men, in modern times. So kind and generous a tribute to the genius of Burns cannot be expected again, and is not needed. We honor him for his noble reverence for Luther, and his patient, almost reverent study of Goethe's genius, anxious that no shadow of his author's meaning escape him for want of trustful attention. There is nowhere else, surely, such determined and generous love of whatever is manly in history. His just appreciation of any, even inferior talent, especially of all sincerity, under whatever guise, and all true men of endeavor, must have impressed every reader. Witness the chapters on Werner, Heyne, even Cagliostro, and others. He is not likely to underrate his man. We are surprised to meet with such a discriminator of kingly qualities in these republican and democratic days, such genuine loyalty all thrown away upon the world.

Carlyle, to adopt his own classification, is himself the hero, as literary man. There is no more notable working-man in

England, in Manchester or Birmingham, or the mines round about. We know not how many hours a-day he toils, nor for what wages, exactly, we only know the results for us. We hear through the London fog and smoke the steady systole, diastole, and vibratory hum, from "Somebody's Works" there; the "Print Works," say some; the "Chemicals," say others; where something, at any rate, is manufactured which we remember to have seen in the market. This is the place, then. Literature has come to mean, to the ears of laboring men, something idle, something cunning and pretty merely, because the nine hundred and ninety-nine really write for fame or for amusement. But as the laborer works, and soberly by the sweat of his brow earns bread for his body, so this man *works* anxiously and *sadly*, to get bread of life, and dispense it. We cannot do better than quote his own estimate of labor from Sartor Resartus.

"Two men I honor, and no third. First; the toil-worn craftsman that with earth-made implement laboriously conquers the earth, and makes her man's. Venerable to me is the hard hand; crooked, coarse, wherein, notwithstanding, lies a cunning virtue, indefeasibly royal, as of the sceptre of this planet. Venerable, too, is the rugged face, all weather-tanned, besoiled, with its rude intelligence; for it is the face of a man living manlike. Oh, but the more venerable for thy rudeness, and even because we must pity as well as love thee. Hardly-entreated brother! For us was thy back so bent, for us were thy straight limbs and fingers so deformed; thou wert our conscript, on whom the lot fell, and fighting our battles wert so marred. For in thee, too, lay a god-created form, but it was not to be unfolded; encrusted must it stand with the thick adhesions and defacements of labor; and thy body, like thy soul, was not to know freedom. Yet toil on, toil on; *thou* art in thy duty, be out of it who may; thou toilest for the altogether indispensable, for daily bread."

"A second man I honor, and still more highly; him who is seen toiling for the spiritually indispensable; not daily bread, but the bread of life. Is not he, too, in his duty, endeavoring toward inward harmony, revealing this, by act or by word, through all his outward endeavors, be they high or low? Highest of all, when his outward and his inward endeavor are one; when we can name him Artist; not earthly craftsman only, but inspired thinker, that with heaven-made implement conquers heaven for us. If the poor and humble toil that we have food, must not the high and glorious toil for him in return, that he have light, have guidance, freedom, immortality? These two in all their degrees, I honor; all else is chaff and dust, which let the wind blow whither it listeth."

"Unspeakably touching is it, however, when I find both dignities united; and he that must toil outwardly for the lowest of man's wants, is also toiling inwardly for the highest. Sublimer in this world know I nothing than a peasant saint, could such now anywhere be met with. Such a one will take thee back to Nazareth itself; thou wilt see the splendor of heaven spring forth from the humblest depths of earth, like a light shining in great darkness."

Notwithstanding the very genuine, admirable, and loyal tributes to Burns, Schiller, Goethe, and others, Carlyle is not a critic of poetry. In the book of heroes, Shakspeare, the hero, as poet, comes off rather slimly. His sympathy, as we said, is with the men of endeavor; not using the life got, but still bravely getting their life. "In fact," as he says of Cromwell, "every where we have to notice the decisive, practical *eye* of this man; how he drives toward the practical and practicable; has a genuine insight into what *is* fact." You must have very stout legs to get noticed at all by him. He is thoroughly English in his love of practical men, and dislike for cant, and ardent enthusiastic heads that are not supported by any legs. He would kindly knock them down that they may regain some vigor by touching their mother earth. We have often wondered how he ever found out Burns, and must still refer a good share of his delight in him to neighborhood and early association. The Lycidas and Comus appearing in Blackwood's Magazine, would probably go unread by him, nor lead him to expect a Paradise Lost. The condition of England question is a practical one. The condition of England demands a hero, not a poet. Other things demand a poet; the poet answers other demands. Carlyle in London, with this question pressing on him so urgently, sees no occasion for minstrels and rhapsodists there. Kings may have their bards

when there are any kings. Homer would *certainly* go a beg-
ging there. He lives in Chelsea, not on the plains of Hindo-
stan, nor on the prairies of the West, where settlers are scarce,
and a man must at least go *whistling* to himself.

What he says of poetry is rapidly uttered, and suggestive of
a thought, rather than the deliberate development of any. He
answers your question, What is poetry? by writing a special
poem, as that Norse one, for instance, in the Book of Heroes,
altogether wild and original;—answers your question, What is
light? by kindling a blaze which dazzles you, and pales sun
and moon, and not as a peasant might, by opening a shutter.
And, certainly, you would say that this question never could
be answered but by the grandest of poems; yet he has not dull
breath and stupidity enough, perhaps, to give the most delib-
erate and universal answer, such as the fates wring from illit-
erate and unthinking men. He answers like Thor, with a
stroke of his hammer, whose dint makes a valley in the earth's
surface.

Carlyle is not a *seer*, but a brave looker-on and *reviewer*; not
the most free and catholic observer of men and events, for
they are likely to find him preoccupied, but unexpectedly free
and catholic when they fall within the focus of his lens. He
does not live in the present hour, and read men and books as
they occur for his theme, but having chosen this, he directs
his studies to this end.

But if he supplies us with arguments and illustrations
against himself, we will remember that we may perhaps be
convicted of error from the same source—stalking on these
lofty reviewer's stilts so far from the green pasturage around.
If we look again at his page, we are apt to retract somewhat
that we have said. Often a genuine poetic feeling dawns
through it, like the texture of the earth seen through the dead
grass and leaves in the spring. There is indeed more poetry in
this author than criticism on poetry. He often reminds us of
the ancient Scald, inspired by the grimmer features of life,
dwelling longer on Dante than on Shakspeare. We have not
recently met with a more solid and unquestionable piece of
poetic work than that episode of "The Ancient Monk," in
Past and Present, at once idyllic, narrative, heroic; a beautiful
restoration of a past age. There is nothing like it elsewhere

that we know of. The History of the French Revolution is a poem, at length got translated into prose; an Iliad, indeed, as he himself has it—"The destructive wrath of Sansculottism: this is what we speak, having unhappily no voice for singing."

One improvement we could suggest in this last, as indeed in most epics, that he should let in the sun oftener upon his picture. It does not often enough appear, but it is all revolution, the old way of human life turned simply bottom upward, so that when at length we are inadvertently reminded of the "Brest Shipping," a St. Domingo colony, and that anybody thinks of owning plantations, and simply turning up the soil there, and that now at length, after some years of this revolution, there is a falling off in the importation of sugar, we feel a queer surprise. Had they not sweetened their water with Revolution then? It would be well if there were several chapters headed "Work for the Month"—Revolution-work inclusive, of course—"Altitude of the Sun," "State of the Crops and Markets," "Meteorological Observations," "Attractive Industry," "Day Labor," &c., just to remind the reader that the French peasantry did something beside go without breeches, burn châteaus, get ready knotted cords, and embrace and throttle one another by turns. These things are sometimes hinted at, but they deserve a notice more in proportion to their importance. We want not only a background to the picture, but a ground under the feet also. We remark, too, occasionally, an unphilosophical habit, common enough elsewhere, in Alison's History of Modern Europe, for instance, of saying, undoubtedly with effect, that if a straw had not fallen this way or that, why then—but, of course, it is as easy in philosophy to make kingdoms rise and fall as straws. The old adage is as true for our purpose, which says that a miss is as good as a mile. Who shall say how near the man came to being killed who was not killed? If an apple had not fallen then we had never heard of Newton and the law of gravitation; as if they could not have contrived to let fall a pear as well.

The poet is blithe and cheery ever, and as well as nature. Carlyle has not the simple Homeric health of Wordsworth, nor the deliberate philosophic turn of Coleridge, nor the scholastic taste of Landor, but, though sick and under re-

straint, the constitutional vigor of one of his old Norse he-
roes, struggling in a lurid light, with Jötuns still, striving to
throw the old woman, and "she was Time"—striving to lift
the big cat—and that was "The Great World-Serpent, which,
tail in mouth, girds and keeps up the whole created world."
The smith, though so brawny and tough, I should not call the
healthiest man. There is too much shop-work, too great ex-
tremes of heat and cold, and incessant ten-pound-ten and
thrashing of the anvil, in his life. But the haymaker's is a true
sunny perspiration, produced by the extreme of summer heat
only, and conversant with the blast of the zephyr, not of the
forge-bellows. We know very well the nature of this man's
sadness, but we do not know the nature of his gladness.
There sits Bull in the court all the year round, with his hoarse
bark and discontented growl—not a cross dog, only a canine
habit, verging to madness some think—now separated from
the shuddering travellers only by the paling, now heard afar in
the horizon, even melodious there; baying the moon o'
nights, *baying the sun by day*, with his mastiff mouth. He
never goes after the cows, nor stretches in the sun, nor plays
with the children. Pray give him a longer rope, ye gods, or let
him go at large, and never taste raw meat more.

The poet will maintain serenity in spite of all disappoint-
ments. He is expected to preserve an unconcerned and
healthy outlook over the world while he lives. *Philosophia
practica est eruditionis meta*, philosophy practiced is the goal
of learning; and for that other, *Oratoris est celare artem*, we
might read, *Herois est celare pugnam*, the hero will conceal his
struggles. Poetry is the only life got, the only work done, the
only pure product and free labor of man, performed only
when he has put all the world under his feet, and conquered
the last of his foes.

Carlyle speaks of Nature with a certain unconscious pathos
for the most part. She is to him a receded but ever memo-
rable splendor, casting still a reflected light over all his
scenery. As we read his books here in New England, where
there are potatoes enough, and every man can get his living
peacefully and sportively as the birds and bees, and need think
no more of that, it seems to us as if by the world he often
meant London, at the head of the tide upon the Thames, the

sorest place on the face of the earth, the very citadel of con-
servatism. Possibly a South African village might have fur-
nished a more hopeful, and more exacting audience, or in the
silence of the wilderness and the desert, he might have ad-
dressed himself more entirely to his true audience posterity.

In his writings, we should say that he, as conspicuously as
any, though with little enough expressed or even conscious
sympathy, represents the Reformer class, and all the better for
not being the acknowledged leader of any. In him the univer-
sal plaint is most settled, unappeasable and serious. Until a
thousand named and nameless grievances are righted, there
will be no repose for him in the lap of nature, or the seclusion
of science and literature. By foreseeing it he hastens the crisis
in the affairs of England, and is as good as many years added
to her history.

As we said, we have no adequate word from him concern-
ing poets—Homer, Shakspeare; nor more, we might add, of
Saints—Jesus; nor philosophers—Socrates, Plato; nor mys-
tics—Swedenborg. He has no articulate sympathy at least
with such as these as yet. Odin, Mahomet, Cromwell, will
have justice at his hands, and we would leave him to write the
eulogies of all the giants of the will, but the kings of men,
whose kingdoms are wholly in the hearts of their subjects,
strictly transcendent and moral greatness, what is highest and
worthiest in character, he is not inclined to dwell upon or
point to. To do himself justice, and set some of his readers
right, he should give us some transcendent hero at length, to
rule his demigods and Titans; develop, perhaps, his reserved
and dumb reverence for Christ, not speaking to a London or
Church of England audience merely. Let *not* "sacred silence
meditate that sacred matter" forever, but let us have sacred
speech and sacred scripture thereon. True reverence is not
necessarily dumb, but ofttimes prattling and hilarious as chil-
dren in the spring.

Every man will include in his list of worthies those whom
he himself best represents. Carlyle, and our countryman
Emerson, whose place and influence must ere long obtain a
more distinct recognition, are, to a certain extent, the com-
plement of each other. The age could not do with one of
them, it cannot do with both. To make a broad and rude dis-

tinction, to suit our present purpose, the former, as critic, deals with the men of action—Mahomet, Luther, Cromwell; the latter with the thinkers—Plato, Shakspeare, Goethe, for though both have written upon Goethe, they do not meet in him. The one has more sympathy with the heroes, or practical reformers, the other with the observers, or philosophers. Put these worthies together, and you will have a pretty fair representation of mankind; yet with one or more memorable exceptions. To say nothing of Christ, who yet awaits a just appreciation from literature, the peacefully practical hero, whom Columbus may represent, is obviously slighted; but above and after all, the Man of the Age, come to be called working-man, it is obvious that none yet speaks to his condition, for the speaker is not yet in his condition. There is poetry and prophecy to cheer him, and advice of the head and heart to the hands; but no very memorable coöperation, it must be confessed, since the Christian era, or rather since Prometheus tried it. It is even a note-worthy fact, that a man addresses effectually in another only himself still, and what he himself does and is, alone can he prompt the other to do and to become. Like speaks to like only; labor to labor, philosophy to philosophy, criticism to criticism, poetry to poetry, &c. Literature speaks how much still to the past, how little to the future, how much to the east, how little to the west—

> In the East fames are won,
> In the West deeds are done.

One more merit in Carlyle, let the subject be what it may, is the freedom of prospect he allows, the entire absence of cant and dogma. He removes many cart-loads of rubbish, and leaves open a broad highway. His writings are all unfenced on the side of the future and the possible. He does not place himself across the passage out of his books, so that none may go freely out, but rather by the entrance, inviting all to come in and go through. No gins, no net-work, no pickets here, to restrain the free thinking reader. In many books called philosophical, we find ourselves running hither and thither, under and through, and sometimes quite unconsciously straddling some imaginary fence-work, which in our clairvoyance we had not noticed, but fortunately, not with such fatal consequences as happen to those birds which fly against a white-washed wall, mistaking it for fluid air. As we proceed the wreck of this dogmatic tissue collects about the organs of our perception, like cobwebs about the muzzles of hunting dogs in dewy mornings. If we look up with such eyes as these authors furnish, we see no heavens, but a low pent-roof of straw or tiles, as if we stood under a shed, with no sky-light through which to glimpse the blue.

Carlyle, though he does but inadvertently direct our eyes to the open heavens, nevertheless, lets us wander broadly underneath, and shows them to us reflected in innumerable pools and lakes. We have from him, occasionally, some hints of a possible science of astronomy even, and revelation of heavenly arcana, but nothing definite hitherto.

These volumes contain not the highest, but a very practicable wisdom, which startles and provokes, rather than informs us. Carlyle does not oblige us to think; we have thought enough for him already, but he compels us to act. We accompany him rapidly through an endless gallery of pictures, and glorious reminiscences of experiences unimproved. "Have you not had Moses and the prophets? Neither will ye be persuaded if one should rise from the dead." There is no calm philosophy of life here, such as you might put at the end of the Almanac, to hang over the farmer's hearth, how men shall live in these winter, in these summer days. No philosophy, properly speaking, of love, or friendship, or religion, or politics, or education, or nature, or spirit; perhaps a nearer approach to a philosophy of kingship, and of the place of the literary man, than of any thing else. A rare preacher, with prayer, and psalm, and sermon, and benediction, but no contemplation of man's life from serene oriental ground, nor yet from the stirring occidental. No thanksgiving sermon for the holydays, or the Easter vacations, when all men submit to float on the full currents of life. When we see with what spirits, though with little heroism enough, wood-choppers, drovers, and apprentices, take and spend life, playing all day long, sunning themselves, shading themselves, eating, drinking, sleeping, we think that the philosophy of their life written would be such a level natural history as the Gardener's

Calendar, and the works of the early botanists, inconceivably slow to come to practical conclusions; its premises away off before the first morning light, ere the heather was introduced into the British isles, and no inferences to be drawn during this noon of the day, not till after the remote evening shadows have begun to fall around.

There is no philosophy here for philosophers, only as every man is said to have his philosophy. No system but such as is the man himself; and, indeed, he stands compactly enough. No progress beyond the first assertion and challenge, as it were, with trumpet blast. One thing is certain, that we had best be doing something in good earnest, henceforth forever; that's an indispensable philosophy. The before impossible precept, *"know thyself,"* he translates into the partially possible one, *"know what thou canst work at."* Sartor Resartus is, perhaps, the sunniest and most philosophical, as it is the most autobiographical of his works, in which he drew most largely on the experience of his youth. But we miss everywhere a calm depth, like a lake, even stagnant, and must submit to rapidity and whirl, as on skates, with all kinds of skillful and antic motions, sculling, sliding, cutting punch-bowls and rings, forward and backward. The talent is very nearly equal to the genius. Sometimes it would be preferable to wade slowly through a Serbonian bog, and feel the juices of the meadow. We should say that he had not speculated far, but faithfully, living up to it. He lays all the stress still on the most elementary and initiatory maxims, introductory to philosophy. It is the experience of the religionist. He pauses at such a quotation as, "It is only with renunciation that life, properly speaking, can be said to begin;" or, "Doubt of any sort cannot be removed except by action;" or, "Do the duty which lies nearest thee." The chapters entitled, "The Everlasting No," and "The Everlasting Yea," contain what you might call the religious experience of his hero. In the latter, he assigns to him these words, brief, but as significant as any we remember in this author:—"One BIBLE I know, of whose plenary inspiration doubt is not so much as possible; nay, with my own eyes I saw the God's-hand writing it: thereof all other Bibles are but leaves." This belongs to "The Everlasting Yea;" yet he lingers unaccountably in "The Everlasting No," under the negative pole. "Truth!" he still cries with Teufelsdröckh, "though the heavens crush me for following her: no falsehood! though a whole celestial Lubberland were the price of apostacy." Again, "Living without God in the world, of God's light I was not utterly bereft; if my as yet sealed eyes, with their unspeakable longing, could nowhere see Him, nevertheless, in my heart He was present, and His heaven-written law still stood legible and sacred there." Again, "Ever from that time, [*the era of his Protest,*] the temper of my misery was changed: not fear or whining sorrow was it, but indignation and grim, fire-eyed defiance." And in the "Centre of Indifference," as editor, he observes, that "it was no longer a quite hopeless unrest," and then proceeds, not in his best style, "For the fire-baptized soul, long so scathed and thunder-riven, here feels its own freedom, which feeling is its Baphometic Baptism: the citadel of its whole kingdom it has thus gained by assault, and will keep inexpugnable; outward from which the remaining dominions, not, indeed, without hard battling, will doubtless by degrees be conquered and pacificated."

Beside some philosophers of larger vision, Carlyle stands like an honest, half-despairing boy, grasping at some details only of their world systems. Philosophy, certainly, is some account of truths, the fragments and very insignificant parts of which man will practice in this work-shop; truths infinite and in harmony with infinity; in respect to which the very objects and ends of the so-called practical philosopher, will be mere propositions, like the rest. It would be no reproach to a philosopher, that he knew the future better than the past, or even than the present. It is better worth knowing. He will prophesy, tell what is to be, or in other words, what alone is, under appearances, laying little stress on the boiling of the pot, or the Condition of England question. He has no more to do with the condition of England than with her national debt, which a vigorous generation would not inherit. The philosopher's conception of things will, above all, be truer than other men's, and his philosophy will subordinate all the circumstances of life. To live like a philosopher, is to live, not foolishly, like other men, but wisely, and according to universal laws. In this, which was the ancient sense, we think there has been no philosopher in modern times. The wisest and most practical men of recent history, to whom this epithet has been hastily applied, have lived comparatively meagre lives, of conformity and tradition, such as their fathers transmitted to them. But a man may live in what style he can. Between earth and heaven, there is room for all kinds. If he take counsel of fear and prudence, he has already failed. One who believed, by his very constitution, some truth which a few words express, would make a revolution never to be forgotten in this world; for it needs but a fraction of truth to found houses and empires on.

However, such distinctions as poet and philosopher, do not much assist our final estimate of a man; we do not lay much stress on them. "A man's a man for a' that." If Carlyle does not take two steps in philosophy, are there any who take three? Philosophy having crept clinging to the rocks, so far, puts out its feelers many ways in vain. It would be hard to surprise him by the relation of any important human experience, but in some nook or corner of his works, you will find that this, too, was sometimes dreamed of in his philosophy.

To sum up our most serious objections, in a few words, we should say that Carlyle indicates a depth,—and we mean not impliedly, but distinctly,—which he neglects to fathom. We want to know more about that which he wants to know as well. If any luminous star, or undissolvable nebula, is visible from his station, which is not visible from ours, the interests of science require that the fact be communicated to us. The universe expects every man to do his duty in his parallel of latitude. We want to hear more of his inmost life; his hymn and prayer, more; his elegy and eulogy, less; that he should speak more from his character, and less from his talent; communicate centrally with his readers, and not by a side; that he should say what he believes, without suspecting that men disbelieve it, out of his never-misunderstood nature. Homer and Shakspeare speak directly and confidently to us. The confidence implied in the unsuspicious tone of the world's worthies, is a great and encouraging fact. Dig up some of the earth you stand on, and show that. If he gave us religiously the meagre results of his experience, his style would be less picturesque and diversified, but more attractive and impressive. His genius can cover all the land with gorgeous palaces, but the reader does not abide in them, but pitches his tent rather in the desert and on the mountain peak.

When we look about for something to quote, as the fairest specimen of the man, we confess that we labor under an unusual difficulty; for his philosophy is so little of the proverbial or sentential kind, and opens so gradually, rising insensibly from the reviewer's level, and developing its thought completely and in detail, that we look in vain for the brilliant passages, for point and antithesis, and must end by quoting his works entire. What in a writer of less breadth would have been the proposition which would have bounded his discourse, his column of victory, his Pillar of Hercules, and *ne plus ultra*, is in Carlyle frequently the same thought unfolded; no Pillar of Hercules, but a considerable prospect, north and south, along the Atlantic coast. There are other pillars of Hercules, like beacons and light-houses, still further in the horizon, toward Atlantis, set up by a few ancient and modern travellers; but, so far as this traveller goes, he clears and colonizes, and all the surplus population of London is bound thither at once. What we would quote is, in fact, his vivacity, and not any particular wisdom or sense, which last is ever synonymous with sentence, [*sententia,*] as in his contemporaries, Coleridge, Landor and Wordsworth.

We have not attempted to discriminate between his works, but have rather regarded them all as one work, as is the man himself. We have not examined so much as remembered them. To do otherwise, would have required a more indifferent, and perhaps even less just review, than the present. The several chapters were thankfully received, as they came out, and now we find it impossible to say which was best; perhaps each was best in its turn. They do not require to be remembered by chapters—that is a merit—but are rather remembered as a well-known strain, reviving from time to time, when it had nearly died away, and always inspiring us to worthier and more persistent endeavors.

In his last work, "The Letters and Speeches of Oliver Cromwell," Carlyle has added a chapter to the history of England; has actually written a chapter of her history, and, in comparison with this, there seems to be no other,—this, and the thirty thousand or three hundred thousand pamphlets in the British Museum, and that is all. This book is a practical comment on Universal History. What if there were a British Museum in Athens and Babylon, and nameless cities! It throws light on the history of the Iliad and the labors of Pisistratus. History is, then, an account of memorable events that have sometime transpired, and not an incredible and confused fable, quarters for scholars merely, or a gymnasium for poets and orators. We may say that he has dug up a hero, who was buried alive in his battle-field, hauled him out of his cairn, on which every passer had cast a pamphlet. We had heard of their digging up Arthurs before to be sure they were there; and, to be sure they were there, their bones, seven feet of them; but they had to bury them again. Others have helped to make known Shakspeare, Milton, Herbert, to give a name to such treasures as we all possessed; but, in this instance, not only a lost character has been restored to our imaginations, but palpably a living body, as it were, to our senses, to wear and sustain the former. His Cromwell's restoration, if England will read it faithfully, and addressed to New England too. Every reader will make his own application.

To speak deliberately, we think that in this instance, vague rumor and a vague history have for the first time been subjected to a rigid scrutiny, and the wheat, with at least novel fidelity, sifted from the chaff; so that there remain for result,—First, Letters and Speeches of Oliver Cromwell, now for the first time read or readable, and well nigh as complete as the fates will permit; secondly, Deeds, making an imperfect and fragmentary life, which may, with probability, be fathered upon him; thirdly, this wreck of an ancient picture, the present editor has, to the best of his ability, restored, sedulously scraping away the daubings of successive bunglers, and endeavoring to catch the spirit of the artist himself. Not the worst, nor a barely possible, but for once the most favorable construction has been put upon this evidence of the life of a man, and the result is a picture of the ideal Cromwell, the perfection of the painter's art. Possibly this was the actual man. At any rate, this only can contain the actual hero. We confess that when we read these Letters and Speeches, unquestionably Cromwell's, with open and confident mind, we get glimpses occasionally of a grandeur and heroism, which even this editor has not proclaimed. His "Speeches" make us forget modern orators, and might go right into the next edition of the Old Testament, without alteration. Cromwell *was* another sort of man than *we* had taken him to be. These Letters and Speeches have supplied the lost key to his character. Verily another soldier than Bonaparte; rejoicing in the triumph of a psalm; to whom psalms were for Magna Charta and Heralds' Book, and whose victories were "crowning mercies." For stern, antique, and practical religion, a man unparalleled, since the Jewish dispensation, in the line of kings. An old Hebrew warrior, indeed, and last right-hand man of the Lord of Hosts, that has blown his ram's horn about Jericho. Yet, with a remarkable common sense and unexpected liberality, there was joined in him, too, such a divine madness, though with large and sublime features, as that of those dibblers of beans on St. George's Hill, whom Carlyle tells of. He still listened to ancient and decaying oracles. If his actions were not always what Christianity or the truest philosophy teaches, still they never fail to impress us as noble, and however violent, will always be pardoned to the great purpose and sincerity of the man. His unquestionable hardness, not to say willfulness, not prevailing by absolute truth and greatness of character, but honestly striving to bend things to his will, is yet grateful to consider in this or any age. As John Maidstone said, "He was a strong man in the dark perils of war; in the high places of the field, hope shone in him like a pillar of fire, when it had gone out in the others." And as Milton sang, whose least testimony cannot be spared—

> "Our chief of men,
> Guided by faith and matchless fortitude."

None ever spake to Cromwell before, sending a word of cheer across the centuries—not the "hear!" "hear!" of modern parliaments, but the congratulation and sympathy of a brother soul. The Letters and Speeches owe not a little to the "Intercalations" and "Annotations" of the "latest of the Commentators." The reader will not soon forget how like a happy merchant in the crowd, listening to his favorite speaker, he is all on the alert, and sympathetic, nudging his neighbors from time to time, and throwing in his responsive or inter-rogatory word. All is good, both that which he didn't hear, and that which he did. He not only makes him speak audibly, but he makes all parties listen to him, all England sitting round, and give in their comments, "groans," or "blushes," or "assent;" indulging sometimes in triumphant malicious applications to the present day, when there is a palpable hit; supplying the look and attitude of the speaker, and the tone of his voice, and even rescuing his unutterable, wrecked and submerged thought,—for this orator begins speaking any-where within sight of the beginning, and leaves off when the conclusion is visible. Our merchant listens, restless, mean-while, encouraging his fellow-auditors, when the speech grows dim and involved, and pleasantly congratulating them, when it runs smoothly; or, in touching soliloquy, he exclaims, "Poor Oliver, noble Oliver"—"Courage, my brave one!"

And all along, between the Letters and Speeches, as readers well remember, he has ready such a fresh top-of-the-morning salutation as conjures up the spirits of those days, and men go marching over English sward, not wired skeletons, but with firm, elastic muscles, and clang of armor on their thighs, if they wore swords, or the twang of psalms and canticles on their lips. His blunt, "Who are you?" put to the shadowy ghosts of history, they vanish into deeper obscurity than ever. Vivid phantasmagorian pictures of what is transpiring in England in the meanwhile, there are, not a few, better than if you had been there to see.

All of Carlyle's works might well enough be embraced under the title of one of them, a good specimen brick, "On Heroes, Hero-worship, and the Heroic in History." Of this department, he is the Chief Professor in the World's University, and even leaves Plutarch behind. Such intimate and living, such loyal and generous sympathy with the heroes of history, not one in one age only, but forty in forty ages, such an unparalleled reviewing and greeting of all past worth, with exceptions, to be sure,—but exceptions were the rule, before,—it was, indeed, to make this the age of review writ-ing, as if now one period of the human story were complet-ing itself, and getting its accounts settled. This soldier has told the stories with new emphasis, and will be a memorable

hander-down of fame to posterity. And with what wise dis-
crimination he has selected his men, with reference both to
his own genius and to theirs: Mahomet,—Dante,—Crom-
well,—Voltaire,—Johnson,—Burns,—Goethe,—Richter,—Schiller,
—Mirabeau; could any of these have been spared? These we
wanted to hear about. We have not as commonly the cold
and refined judgment of the scholar and critic merely, but
something more human and affecting. These eulogies have
the glow and warmth of friendship. There is sympathy not
with mere fames, and formless, incredible things, but with
kindred men,—not transiently, but life-long he has walked
with them.

The attitude of some, in relation to Carlyle's love of heroes,
and men of the sword, reminds us of the procedure at the
anti-slavery meetings, when some member, being warmed,
begins to speak with more latitude than usual of the Bible or
the Church, for a few prudent and devout ones to spring a
prayer upon him, as the saying is; that is, propose suddenly to
unite in prayer, and so solemnize the minds of the audience,
or dismiss them at once; which may oftener be to interrupt a
true prayer by most gratuitous profanity. But the spring of
this trap, we are glad to learn, has grown somewhat rusty, and
is not so sure of late.

No doubt, some of Carlyle's worthies, should they ever re-
turn to earth, would find themselves unpleasantly put upon
their good behavior, to sustain their characters; but if he can
return a man's life more perfect to our hands, than it was left
at his death, following out the design of its author, we shall
have no great cause to complain. We do not want a Da-
guerreotype likeness. All biography is the life of Adam,—a
much-experienced man,—and time withdraws something par-
tial from the story of every individual, that the historian may
supply something general. If these virtues were not in this
man, perhaps they are in his biographer,—no fatal mistake.
Really, in any other sense, we never do, nor desire to, come at
the historical man,—unless we rob his grave, that is the nearest
approach. Why did he die, then? *He* is with his bones, surely.

No doubt, Carlyle has a propensity to *exaggerate* the heroic
in history, that is, he creates you an ideal hero rather than an-
other thing, he has most of that material. This we allow in all

its senses, and in one narrower sense it is not so convenient. Yet what were history if he did not exaggerate it? How comes it that history never has to wait for facts, but for a man to write it? The ages may go on forgetting the facts never so long, he can remember two for every one forgotten. The musty records of history, like the catacombs, contain the perishable remains, but only in the breast of genius are embalmed the souls of heroes. There is very little of what is called criticism here; it is love and reverence, rather, which deal with qualities not relatively, but absolutely great; for whatever is admirable in a man is something infinite, to which we cannot set bounds. These sentiments allow the mortal to die, the immortal and divine to survive. There is something antique, even in his style of treating his subject, reminding us that Heroes and Demi-gods, Fates and Furies, still exist, the common man is nothing to him, but after death the hero is apotheosized and has a place in heaven, as in the religion of the Greeks.

Exaggeration! was ever any virtue attributed to a man without exaggeration? was ever any vice, without infinite exaggeration? Do we not exaggerate ourselves to ourselves, or do we recognize ourselves for the actual men we are? Are we not all great men? Yet what are we actually to speak of? We live by exaggeration, what else is it to anticipate more than we enjoy? The lightning is an exaggeration of the light. Exaggerated history is poetry, and truth referred to a new standard. To a small man every greater is an exaggeration. He who cannot exaggerate is not qualified to utter truth. No truth we think was ever expressed but with this sort of emphasis, so that for the time there seemed to be no other. Moreover, you must speak loud to those who are hard of hearing, and so you acquire a habit of shouting to those who are not. By an immense exaggeration we appreciate our Greek poetry and philosophy, and Egyptian ruins; our Shakspeares and Miltons, our Liberty and Christianity. We give importance to this hour over all other hours. We do not live by justice, but by grace. As the sort of justice which concerns us in our daily intercourse is not that administered by the judge, so the historical justice which we prize is not arrived at by nicely balancing the evidence. In order to appreciate any, even the humblest man, you must first, by some good fortune, have acquired a sentiment of admiration, even of reverence, for him, and there never were such exaggerators as these. Simple admiration for a hero renders a juster verdict than the wisest criticism, which necessarily degrades what is high to its own level. There is no danger in short of saying too much in praise of one man, provided you can say more in praise of a better man. If by exaggeration a man can create for us a hero, where there was nothing but dry bones before, we will thank him, and let Dryasdust administer historical justice. This is where a true history properly begins, when some genius arises, who can turn the dry and musty records into poetry. As we say, looking to the future, that what is best is truest, so, in one sense, we may say looking into the past, for the only past that we are to look at, must also be future to us. The great danger is not of excessive partiality or sympathy with one, but of a shallow justice to many, in which, after all, none gets his deserts. Who has not experienced that praise is truer than naked justice? As if man were to be the judge of his fellows, and should repress his rising sympathy with the prisoner at the bar, considering the many honest men abroad, whom he had never countenanced.

To try him by the German rule of referring an author to his own standard, we will quote the following from Carlyle's remarks on history, and leave the reader to consider how far his practice has been consistent with his theory. "Truly, if History is Philosophy teaching by experience, the writer fitted to compose history, is hitherto an unknown man. The experience itself would require all knowledge to record it, were the All-wisdom needful for such Philosophy as would interpret it, to be had for asking. Better were it that mere earthly historians should lower such pretensions, more suitable for omniscience than for human science; and aiming only at some picture of the things acted, which picture itself, will at best be a poor approximation, leave the inscrutable purport of them an acknowledged secret; or, at most, in reverent Faith, far different from that teaching of Philosophy, pause over the mysterious vestiges of Him, whose path is in the great deep of Time, whom history indeed reveals, but only all History and in Eternity, will clearly reveal."

•

Who lives in London to tell this generation who have been the great men of our race? We have read that on some exposed place in the city of Geneva, they have fixed a brazen indicater for the use of travellers, with the names of the mountain summits in the horizon marked upon it, "so that by taking sight across the index you can distinguish them at once. You will not mistake Mont Blanc, if you see him, but until you get accustomed to the panorama, you may easily mistake one of his court for the king." It stands there a piece of mute brass, that seems nevertheless to know in what vicinity it is: and there perchance it will stand, when the nation that placed it there has passed away, still in sympathy with the mountains, forever discriminating in the desert.

So, we may say, stands this man, pointing as long as he lives, in obedience to some spiritual magnetism, to the summits in the historical horizon, for the guidance of his fellows.

Truly, our greatest blessings are very cheap. To have our sunlight without paying for it, without any duty levied,—to have our poet there in England, to furnish us entertainment, and what is better, provocation, from year to year, all our lives long, to make the world seem richer for us, the age more respectable, and life better worth the living,—all without expense of acknowledgment even, but silently accepted out of the east, like morning light as a matter of course.

Civil Disobedience

I HEARTILY accept the motto,—"That government is best which governs least"; and I should like to see it acted up to more rapidly and systematically. Carried out, it finally amounts to this, which also I believe,—"That government is best which governs not at all"; and when men are prepared for it, that will be the kind of government which they will have. Government is at best but an expedient; but most governments are usually, and all governments are sometimes, inexpedient. The objections which have been brought against a standing army, and they are many and weighty, and deserve to prevail, may also at last be brought against a standing government. The standing army is only an arm of the standing government. The government itself, which is only the mode which the people have chosen to execute their will, is equally liable to be abused and perverted before the people can act through it. Witness the present Mexican war, the work of comparatively a few individuals using the standing government as their tool; for, in the outset, the people would not have consented to this measure.

This American government,—what is it but a tradition, though a recent one, endeavoring to transmit itself unimpaired to posterity, but each instant losing some of its integrity? It has not the vitality and force of a single living man; for a single man can bend it to his will. It is a sort of wooden gun to the people themselves. But it is not the less necessary for this; for the people must have some complicated machinery or other, and hear its din, to satisfy that idea of government which they have. Governments show thus how successfully men can be imposed on, even impose on themselves, for their own advantage. It is excellent, we must all allow. Yet this government never of itself furthered any enterprise, but by the alacrity with which it got out of its way. *It* does not keep the country free. *It* does not settle the West. *It* does not educate. The character inherent in the American people has done all that has been accomplished; and it would have done somewhat more, if the government had not sometimes got in its way. For government is an expedient by which men would fain succeed in letting one another alone; and, as has been said, when it is most expedient, the governed are most let alone by it. Trade and commerce, if they were not made of India-rubber, would never manage to bounce over the obstacles which legislators are continually putting in their way; and, if one were to judge these men wholly by the effects of their actions and not partly by their intentions, they would deserve to be classed and punished with those mischievous persons who put obstructions on the railroads.

But, to speak practically and as a citizen, unlike those who call themselves no-government men, I ask for, not at once no government, but *at once* a better government. Let every man make known what kind of government would command his respect, and that will be one step toward obtaining it.

After all, the practical reason why, when the power is once in the hands of the people, a majority are permitted, and for a long period continue, to rule, is not because they are most likely to be in the right, nor because this seems fairest to the minority, but because they are physically the strongest. But a government in which the majority rule in all cases cannot be based on justice, even as far as men understand it. Can there not be a government in which majorities do not virtually decide right and wrong, but conscience?—in which majorities decide only those questions to which the rule of expediency is applicable? Must the citizen ever for a moment, or in the least degree, resign his conscience to the legislator? Why has every man a conscience, then? I think that we should be men first, and subjects afterward. It is not desirable to cultivate a respect for the law, so much as for the right. The only obligation which I have a right to assume, is to do at any time what I think right. It is truly enough said, that a corporation has no conscience; but a corporation of conscientious men is a corporation *with* a conscience. Law never made men a whit more just; and, by means of their respect for it, even the well-disposed are daily made the agents of injustice. A common and natural result of an undue respect for law is, that you may see a file of soldiers, colonel, captain, corporal, privates, powder-monkeys, and all, marching in admirable order over hill and dale to the wars, against their wills, ay, against their common sense and consciences, which makes it very steep marching indeed, and produces a palpitation of the heart. They have no doubt that it is a damnable business in which they are concerned; they are all peaceably inclined. Now, what are they? Men at all? or small movable forts and magazines, at the service of some unscrupulous man in power? Visit the Navy-Yard, and behold a marine, such a man as an American government can make, or such as it can make a man with its black arts,—a mere shadow and reminiscence of humanity, a man laid out alive and standing, and already, as one may say, buried under arms with funeral accompaniments, though it may be,—

> "Not a drum was heard, not a funeral note,
>   As his corse to the rampart we hurried;
> Not a soldier discharged his farewell shot
>   O'er the grave where our hero we buried."

The mass of men serve the state thus, not as men mainly, but as machines, with their bodies. They are the standing army, and the militia, jailers, constables, posse comitatus, &c. In most cases there is no free exercise whatever of the judgment or of the moral sense; but they put themselves on a level with wood and earth and stones; and wooden men can perhaps be manufactured that will serve the purpose as well. Such command no more respect than men of straw or a lump of dirt. They have the same sort of worth only as horses and dogs. Yet such as these even are commonly esteemed good citizens. Others,—as most legislators, politicians, lawyers, ministers, and office-holders,—serve the state chiefly with their heads; and, as they rarely make any moral distinctions, they are as likely to serve the Devil, without *intending* it, as God. A very few, as heroes, patriots, martyrs, reformers in the great sense, and *men*, serve the state with their consciences also, and so necessarily resist it for the most part; and they are commonly treated as enemies by it. A wise man will only be useful as a man, and will not submit to be "clay," and "stop a hole to keep the wind away," but leave that office to his dust at least:—

> "I am too high-born to be propertied
> To be a secondary at control,
> Or useful serving-man and instrument
> To any sovereign state throughout the world."

He who gives himself entirely to his fellow-men appears to them useless and selfish; but he who gives himself partially to them is pronounced a benefactor and philanthropist.

How does it become a man to behave toward this American government to-day? I answer, that he cannot without disgrace be associated with it. I cannot for an instant recognize that political organization as *my* government which is the *slave's* government also.

All men recognize the right of revolution; that is, the right to refuse allegiance to, and to resist, the government, when its tyranny or its inefficiency are great and unendurable. But almost all say that such is not the case now. But such was the case, they think, in the Revolution of '75. If one were to tell me that this was a bad government because it taxed certain foreign commodities brought to its ports, it is most probable that I should not make an ado about it, for I can do without them. All machines have their friction; and possibly this does enough good to counterbalance the evil. At any rate, it is a great evil to make a stir about it. But when the friction comes to have its machine, and oppression and robbery are organized, I say, let us not have such a machine any longer. In other words, when a sixth of the population of a nation which has undertaken to be the refuge of liberty are slaves, and a whole country is unjustly overrun and conquered by a foreign army, and subjected to military law, I think that it is not too soon for honest men to rebel and revolutionize. What makes this duty the more urgent is the fact, that the country so overrun is not our own, but ours is the invading army.

Paley, a common authority with many on moral questions, in his chapter on the "Duty of Submission to Civil Government," resolves all civil obligation into expediency; and he proceeds to say, "that so long as the interest of the whole society requires it, that is, so long as the established government cannot be resisted or changed without public inconveniency, it is the will of God that the established government be obeyed, and no longer. . . . . This principle being admitted, the justice of every particular case of resistance is reduced to a computation of the quantity of the danger and grievance on the one side, and of the probability and expense of redressing it on the other." Of this, he says, every man shall judge for himself. But Paley appears never to have contemplated those cases to which the rule of expediency does not apply, in which a people, as well as an individual, must do justice, cost what it may. If I have unjustly wrested a plank from a drowning man, I must restore it to him though I drown myself. This, according to Paley, would be inconvenient. But he that would save his life, in such a case, shall lose it. This people must cease to hold slaves, and to make war on Mexico, though it cost them their existence as a people.

In their practice, nations agree with Paley; but does any one think that Massachusetts does exactly what is right at the present crisis?

> "A drab of state, a cloth-o'-silver slut,
>   To have her train borne up, and her soul trail in
>   the dirt."

Practically speaking, the opponents to a reform in Massachusetts are not a hundred thousand politicians at the South, but a hundred thousand merchants and farmers here, who are more interested in commerce and agriculture than they are in humanity, and are not prepared to do justice to the slave and to Mexico, *cost what it may.* I quarrel not with far-off foes, but with those who, near at home, co-operate with, and do the bidding of, those far away, and without whom the latter would be harmless. We are accustomed to say, that the mass of men are unprepared; but improvement is slow, because the few are not materially wiser or better than the many. It is not so important that many should be as good as you, as that there be some absolute goodness somewhere; for that will leaven the whole lump. There are thousands who are *in opinion* opposed to slavery and to the war, who yet in effect do nothing to put an end to them; who, esteeming themselves children of Washington and Franklin, sit down with their hands in their pockets, and say that they know not what to do, and do nothing; who even postpone the question of freedom to the question of free-trade, and quietly read the prices-current along with the latest advices from Mexico, after dinner, and, it may be, fall asleep over them both. What is the price-current of an honest man and patriot to-day? They hesitate, and they regret, and sometimes they petition; but they do nothing in earnest and with effect. They will wait, well disposed, for others to remedy the evil, that they may no longer have it to regret. At most, they give only a cheap vote, and a feeble countenance and God-speed, to the right, as it goes by them. There are nine hundred and ninety-nine patrons of virtue to one virtuous man. But it is easier to deal with the real possessor of a thing than with the temporary guardian of it.

All voting is a sort of gaming, like checkers or backgammon, with a slight moral tinge to it, a playing with right and wrong, with moral questions; and betting naturally accompanies it. The character of the voters is not staked. I cast my vote, perchance, as I think right; but I am not vitally concerned that that right should prevail. I am willing to leave it to the majority. Its obligation, therefore, never exceeds that of expediency. Even voting *for the right* is *doing* nothing for it. It is only expressing to men feebly your desire that it should prevail. A wise man will not leave the right to the mercy of chance, nor wish it to prevail through the power of the majority. There is but little virtue in the action of masses of men. When the majority shall at length vote for the abolition of slavery, it will be because they are indifferent to slavery, or because there is but little slavery left to be abolished by their vote. *They* will then be the only slaves. Only *his* vote can hasten the abolition of slavery who asserts his own freedom by his vote.

I hear of a convention to be held at Baltimore, or elsewhere, for the selection of a candidate for the Presidency, made up chiefly of editors, and men who are politicians by profession; but I think, what is it to any independent, intelligent, and respectable man what decision they may come to? Shall we not have the advantage of his wisdom and honesty, nevertheless? Can we not count upon some independent votes? Are there not many individuals in the country who do not attend conventions? But no: I find that the respectable man, so called, has immediately drifted from his position, and despairs of his country, when his country has more reason to despair of him. He forthwith adopts one of the candidates thus selected as the only *available* one, thus proving that he is himself *available* for any purposes of the demagogue. His vote is of no more worth than that of any unprincipled foreigner or hireling native, who may have been bought. O for a man who is a *man*, and, as my neighbor says, has a bone in his back which you cannot pass your hand through! Our statistics are at fault: the population has been returned too large. How many *men* are there to a square thousand miles in this country? Hardly one. Does not America offer any inducement for men to settle here? The American has dwindled into an Odd Fellow,—one who may be known by the development of his organ of gregariousness, and a manifest lack of intellect and cheerful self-reliance; whose first and chief concern, on coming into the world, is to see that the Almshouses are in good repair; and, before yet he has lawfully donned the virile garb, to collect a fund for the support of the widows and orphans that may be; who, in short, ventures to live only by the aid of the Mutual Insurance company, which has promised to bury him decently.

It is not a man's duty, as a matter of course, to devote himself to the eradication of any, even the most enormous wrong; he may still properly have other concerns to engage him; but it is his duty, at least, to wash his hands of it, and, if he gives it no thought longer, not to give it practically his support. If I devote myself to other pursuits and contemplations, I must first see, at least, that I do not pursue them sitting upon another man's shoulders. I must get off him first, that he may pursue his contemplations too. See what gross inconsistency is tolerated. I have heard some of my townsmen say, "I should like to have them order me out to help put down an insurrection of the slaves, or to march to Mexico;—see if I would go"; and yet these very men have each, directly by their allegiance, and so indirectly, at least, by their money, furnished a substitute. The soldier is applauded who refuses to serve in an unjust war by those who do not refuse to sustain the unjust government which makes the war; is applauded by those whose own act and authority he disregards and sets at naught;

as if the State were penitent to that degree that it hired one to scourge it while it sinned, but not to that degree that it left off sinning for a moment. Thus, under the name of Order and Civil Government, we are all made at last to pay homage to and support our own meanness. After the first blush of sin comes its indifference; and from immoral it becomes, as it were, *un*moral, and not quite unnecessary to that life which we have made.

The broadest and most prevalent error requires the most disinterested virtue to sustain it. The slight reproach to which the virtue of patriotism is commonly liable, the noble are most likely to incur. Those who, while they disapprove of the character and measures of a government, yield to it their allegiance and support, are undoubtedly its most conscientious supporters, and so frequently the most serious obstacles to reform. Some are petitioning the State to dissolve the Union, to disregard the requisitions of the President. Why do they not dissolve it themselves,—the union between themselves and the State,—and refuse to pay their quota into its treasury? Do not they stand in the same relation to the State, that the State does to the Union? And have not the same reasons prevented the State from resisting the Union, which have prevented them from resisting the State?

How can a man be satisfied to entertain an opinion merely, and enjoy *it*? Is there any enjoyment in it, if his opinion is that he is aggrieved? If you are cheated out of a single dollar by your neighbor, you do not rest satisfied with knowing that you are cheated, or with saying that you are cheated, or even with petitioning him to pay you your due; but you take effectual steps at once to obtain the full amount, and see that you are never cheated again. Action from principle, the perception and the performance of right, changes things and relations; it is essentially revolutionary, and does not consist wholly with anything which was. It not only divides states and churches, it divides families; ay, it divides the *individual*, separating the diabolical in him from the divine.

Unjust laws exist: shall we be content to obey them, or shall we endeavor to amend them, and obey them until we have succeeded, or shall we transgress them at once? Men generally, under such a government as this, think that they ought to wait until they have persuaded the majority to alter them. They think that, if they should resist, the remedy would be worse than the evil. But it is the fault of the government itself that the remedy *is* worse than the evil. *It* makes it worse. Why is it not more apt to anticipate and provide for reform? Why does it not cherish its wise minority? Why does it cry and resist before it is hurt? Why does it not encourage its citizens to be on the alert to point out its faults, and *do* better than it would have them? Why does it always crucify Christ, and excommunicate Copernicus and Luther, and pronounce Washington and Franklin rebels?

One would think, that a deliberate and practical denial of its authority was the only offence never contemplated by government; else, why has it not assigned its definite, its suitable and proportionate penalty? If a man who has no property refuses but once to earn nine shillings for the State, he is put in prison for a period unlimited by any law that I know, and determined only by the discretion of those who placed him there; but if he should steal ninety times nine shillings from the State, he is soon permitted to go at large again.

If the injustice is part of the necessary friction of the machine of government, let it go, let it go: perchance it will wear smooth,—certainly the machine will wear out. If the injustice has a spring, or a pulley, or a rope, or a crank, exclusively for itself, then perhaps you may consider whether the remedy will not be worse than the evil; but if it is of such a nature that it requires you to be the agent of injustice to another, then, I say, break the law. Let your life be a counter friction to stop the machine. What I have to do is to see, at any rate, that I do not lend myself to the wrong which I condemn.

As for adopting the ways which the State has provided for remedying the evil, I know not of such ways. They take too much time, and a man's life will be gone. I have other affairs to attend to. I came into this world, not chiefly to make this a good place to live in, but to live in it, be it good or bad. A man has not everything to do, but something; and because he cannot do *everything*, it is not necessary that he should do *something* wrong. It is not my business to be petitioning the Governor or the Legislature any more than it is theirs to petition me; and, if they should not hear my petition, what should I do then? But in this case the State has provided no way: its very Constitution is the evil. This may seem to be harsh and stubborn and unconciliatory; but it is to treat with the utmost kindness and consideration the only spirit that can appreciate or deserves it. So is all change for the better, like birth and death, which convulse the body.

I do not hesitate to say, that those who call themselves Abolitionists should at once effectually withdraw their support, both in person and property, from the government of Massachusetts, and not wait till they constitute a majority of one, before they suffer the right to prevail through them. I think that it is enough if they have God on their side, without waiting for that other one. Moreover, any man more right than his neighbors constitutes a majority of one already.

I meet this American government, or its representative, the State government, directly, and face to face, once a year—no more—in the person of its tax-gatherer; this is the only mode in which a man situated as I am necessarily meets it; and it then says distinctly, Recognize me; and the simplest, the most effectual, and, in the present posture of affairs, the indispensablest mode of treating with it on this head, of expressing your little satisfaction with and love for it, is to deny it then. My civil neighbor, the tax-gatherer, is the very man I have to deal with,—for it is, after all, with men and not with parchment that I quarrel,—and he has voluntarily chosen to be an agent of the government. How shall he ever know well what he is and does as an officer of the government, or as a man, until he is obliged to consider whether he shall treat me, his neighbor, for whom he has respect, as a neighbor and well-disposed man, or as a maniac and disturber of the peace, and see if he can get over this obstruction to his neighborliness without a ruder and more impetuous thought or speech corresponding with his action. I know this well, that if one thousand, if one hundred, if ten men whom I could name,—if ten *honest* men only,—ay, if *one* HONEST man, in this State of Massachusetts, *ceasing to hold slaves*, were actually to withdraw from this copartnership, and be locked up in the county jail therefor, it would be the abolition of slavery in America. For it matters not how small the beginning may seem to be: what is once well done is done forever. But we love better to talk about it: that we say is our mission. Reform keeps many scores of newspapers in its service, but not one man. If my esteemed neighbor, the State's ambassador, who will devote his days to the settlement of the question of human rights in the Council Chamber, instead of being threatened with the prisons of Carolina, were to sit down the prisoner of Massachusetts, that State which is so anxious to foist the sin of slavery upon her sister,—though at present she can discover only an act of inhospitality to be the ground of a quarrel with her,—the Legislature would not wholly waive the subject the following winter.

Under a government which imprisons any unjustly, the true place for a just man is also a prison. The proper place to-day, the only place which Massachusetts has provided for her freer and less desponding spirits, is in her prisons, to be put out and locked out of the State by her own act, as they have already put themselves out by their principles. It is there that the fugitive slave, and the Mexican prisoner on parole, and the Indian come to plead the wrongs of his race, should find them; on that separate, but more free and honorable ground, where the State places those who are not *with* her, but *against* her,—the only house in a slave State in which a free man can abide with honor. If any think that their influence would be lost there, and their voices no longer afflict the ear of the State, that they would not be as an enemy within its walls, they do not know by how much truth is stronger than error, nor how much more eloquently and effectively he can combat injustice who has experienced a little in his own person. Cast your whole vote, not a strip of paper merely, but your whole influence. A minority is powerless while it conforms to the majority; it is not even a minority then; but it is irresistible when it clogs by its whole weight. If the alternative is to keep all just men in prison, or give up war and slavery, the State will not hesitate which to choose. If a thousand men were not to pay their tax-bills this year, that would not be a violent and bloody measure, as it would be to pay them, and enable the State to commit violence and shed innocent blood. This is, in fact, the definition of a peaceable revolution, if any such is possible. If the tax-gatherer, or any other public officer, asks me, as one has done, "But what shall I do?" my answer is, "If you really wish to do anything, resign your office." When the subject has refused allegiance, and the officer has resigned his office, then the revolution is accomplished. But even suppose blood should flow. Is there not a sort of blood shed when the conscience is wounded? Through this wound a man's real manhood and immortality flow out, and he bleeds to an everlasting death. I see this blood flowing now.

I have contemplated the imprisonment of the offender, rather than the seizure of his goods,—though both will serve the same purpose,—because they who assert the purest right, and consequently are most dangerous to a corrupt State, commonly have not spent much time in accumulating property. To such the State renders comparatively small service, and a slight tax is wont to appear exorbitant, particularly if they are obliged to earn it by special labor with their hands. If there were one who lived wholly without the use of money, the State itself would hesitate to demand it of him. But the rich man,—not to make any invidious comparison,—is always sold to the institution which makes him rich. Absolutely speaking, the more money, the less virtue; for money comes between a man and his objects, and obtains them for him; and it was certainly no great virtue to obtain it. It puts to rest many questions which he would otherwise be taxed to answer; while the only new question which it puts is the hard but superfluous one, how to spend it. Thus his moral ground is taken from under his feet. The opportunities of living are diminished in proportion as what are called the "means" are increased. The best thing a man can do for his culture when he is rich is to endeavor to carry out those schemes which he entertained when he was poor. Christ answered the Herodians according to their condition. "Show me the tribute-money," said he;—and one took a penny out of his pocket;—if you use money which has the image of Cæsar on it, and which he has made current and valuable, that is, *if you are men of the State*, and gladly enjoy the advantages of Cæsar's government, then pay him back some of his own when he demands it; "Render therefore to Cæsar that which is Cæsar's, and to God those things which are God's,"—leaving them no wiser than before as to which was which; for they did not wish to know.

When I converse with the freest of my neighbors, I perceive that, whatever they may say about the magnitude and seriousness of the question, and their regard for the public tranquillity, the long and the short of the matter is, that they cannot spare the protection of the existing government, and they dread the consequences to their property and families of disobedience to it. For my own part, I should not like to think that I ever rely on the protection of the State. But, if I deny the authority of the State when it presents its tax-bill, it will soon take and waste all my property, and so harass me and my children without end. This is hard. This makes it impossible for a man to live honestly, and at the same time comfortably, in outward respects. It will not be worth the while to accumulate property; that would be sure to go again. You must hire or squat somewhere, and raise but a small crop, and eat that soon. You must live within yourself, and depend upon yourself always tucked up and ready for a start, and not have many affairs. A man may grow rich in Turkey even, if he will be in all respects a good subject of the Turkish government. Confucius said: "If a state is governed by the principles of reason, poverty and misery are subjects of shame; if a state is not governed by the principles of reason, riches and honors are the subjects of shame." No: until I want the protection of Massachusetts to be extended to me in some distant Southern port, where my liberty is endangered, or until I am bent solely on building up an estate at home by peaceful enterprise, I can afford to refuse allegiance to Massachusetts, and her right to my property and life. It costs me less in every sense to incur the penalty of disobedience to the State, than it would to obey. I should feel as if I were worth less in that case.

Some years ago, the State met me in behalf of the Church, and commanded me to pay a certain sum toward the support of a clergyman whose preaching my father attended, but never I myself. "Pay," it said, "or be locked up in the jail." I declined to pay. But, unfortunately, another man saw fit to pay it. I did not see why the schoolmaster should be taxed to support the priest, and not the priest the schoolmaster; for I was not the State's schoolmaster, but I supported myself by voluntary subscription. I did not see why the lyceum should not present its tax-bill, and have the State to back its demand, as well as the Church. However, at the request of the select-men, I condescended to make some such statement as this in writing:—"Know all men by these presents, that I, Henry Thoreau, do not wish to be regarded as a member of any in-corporated society which I have not joined." This I gave to the town clerk; and he has it. The State, having thus learned that I did not wish to be regarded as a member of that church, has never made a like demand on me since; though it said that it must adhere to its original presumption that time. If I had known how to name them, I should then have signed off in detail from all the societies which I never signed on to; but I did not know where to find a complete list.

I have paid no poll-tax for six years. I was put into a jail once on this account, for one night; and, as I stood consider-ing the walls of solid stone, two or three feet thick, the door of wood and iron, a foot thick, and the iron grating which strained the light, I could not help being struck with the fool-ishness of that institution which treated me as if I were mere flesh and blood and bones, to be locked up. I wondered that it should have concluded at length that this was the best use it could put me to, and had never thought to avail itself of my services in some way. I saw that, if there was a wall of stone between me and my townsmen, there was a still more difficult one to climb or break through, before they could get to be as free as I was. I did not for a moment feel confined, and the walls seemed a great waste of stone and mortar. I felt as if I alone of all my townsmen had paid my tax. They plainly did not know how to treat me, but behaved like persons who are underbred. In every threat and in every compliment there was a blunder; for they thought that my chief desire was to stand the other side of that stone wall. I could not but smile to see how industriously they locked the door on my meditations, which followed them out again without let or hindrance, and *they* were really all that was dangerous. As they could not reach me, they had resolved to punish my body; just as boys, if they cannot come at some person against whom they have a spite, will abuse his dog. I saw that the State was half-wit-ted, that it was timid as a lone woman with her silver spoons, and that it did not know its friends from its foes, and I lost all my remaining respect for it, and pitied it.

Thus the State never intentionally confronts a man's sense, intellectual or moral, but only his body, his senses. It is not armed with superior wit or honesty, but with superior physical strength. I was not born to be forced. I will breathe after my own fashion. Let us see who is the strongest. What force has a multitude? They only can force me who obey a higher law than I. They force me to become like themselves. I do not hear of *men* being *forced* to live this way or that by masses of men. What sort of life were that to live? When I meet a government which says to me, "Your money or your life," why should I be in haste to give it my money? It may be in a great strait, and not know what to do: I cannot help that. It must help itself; do as I do. It is not worth the while to snivel about it. I am not responsible for the successful working of the machinery of society. I am not the son of the engineer. I perceive that, when an acorn and a chestnut fall side by side, the one does not remain inert to make way for the other, but both obey their own laws, and spring and grow and flourish as best they can, till one, perchance, overshadows and destroys the other. If a plant cannot live according to its nature, it dies; and so a man.

The night in prison was novel and interesting enough. The prisoners in their shirt-sleeves were enjoying a chat and the evening air in the doorway, when I entered. But the jailer said, "Come, boys, it is time to lock up"; and so they dispersed, and I heard the sound of their steps returning into the hollow apartments. My room-mate was introduced to me by the jailer, as "a first-rate fellow and a clever man." When the door was locked, he showed me where to hang my hat, and how he managed matters there. The rooms were whitewashed once a month; and this one, at least, was the whitest, most simply furnished, and probably the neatest apartment in the town. He naturally wanted to know where I came from, and what brought me there; and, when I had told him, I asked him in my turn how he came there, presuming him to be an honest man, of course; and, as the world goes, I believe he was. "Why," said he, "they accuse me of burning a barn; but I never did it." As near as I could discover, he had probably gone to bed in a barn when drunk, and smoked his pipe there; and so a barn was burnt. He had the reputation of being a clever man, had been there some three months waiting for his trial to come on, and would have to wait as much longer; but he was quite domesticated and contented, since he got his board for nothing, and thought that he was well treated.

He occupied one window, and I the other; and I saw, that, if one stayed there long, his principal business would be to look out the window. I had soon read all the tracts that were left there, and examined where former prisoners had broken out, and where a grate had been sawed off, and heard the history of the various occupants of that room; for I found that even here there was a history and a gossip which never circulated beyond the walls of the jail. Probably this is the only house in the town where verses are composed, which are afterward printed in a circular form, but not published. I was shown quite a long list of verses which were composed by some young men who had been detected in an attempt to escape, who avenged themselves by singing them.

I pumped my fellow-prisoner as dry as I could, for fear I should never see him again; but at length he showed me which was my bed, and left me to blow out the lamp.

It was like travelling into a far country, such as I had never expected to behold, to lie there for one night. It seemed to me that I never had heard the town-clock strike before, nor the evening sounds of the village; for we slept with the windows open, which were inside the grating. It was to see my native village in the light of the Middle Ages, and our Concord was turned into a Rhine stream, and visions of knights and castles passed before me. They were the voices of old burghers that I heard in the streets. I was an involuntary spectator and auditor of whatever was done and said in the kitchen of the adjacent village-inn,—a wholly new and rare experience to me. It was a closer view of my native town. I was fairly inside of it. I never had seen its institutions before. This is one of its peculiar institutions; for it is a shire town. I began to comprehend what its inhabitants were about.

In the morning, our breakfasts were put through the hole in the door, in small oblong-square tin pans, made to fit, and holding a pint of chocolate, with brown bread, and an iron spoon. When they called for the vessels again, I was green enough to return what bread I had left; but my comrade seized it, and said that I should lay that up for lunch or dinner. Soon after he was let out to work at haying in a neighboring field, whither he went every day, and would not be back till noon; so he bade me good-day, saying that he doubted if he should see me again.

When I came out of prison,—for some one interfered, and paid that tax,—I did not perceive that great changes had taken place on the common, such as he observed who went in a youth, and emerged a tottering and gray-headed man; and yet a change had to my eyes come over the scene,—the town, and State, and country,—greater than any that mere time could effect. I saw yet more distinctly the State in which I lived. I saw to what extent the people among whom I lived could be trusted as good neighbors and friends; that their friendship was for summer weather only; that they did not greatly propose to do right; that they were a distinct race from me by their prejudices and superstitions, as the Chinamen and Malays are; that, in their sacrifices to humanity, they ran no risks, not even to their property; that, after all, they were not so noble but they treated the thief as he had treated them, and hoped, by a certain outward observance and a few prayers, and by walking in a particular straight though useless path from time to time, to save their souls. This may be to judge my neighbors harshly; for I believe that many of them are not aware that they have such an institution as the jail in their village.

It was formerly the custom in our village, when a poor debtor came out of jail, for his acquaintances to salute him, looking through their fingers, which were crossed to represent the grating of a jail window, "How do ye do?" My neighbors did not thus salute me, but first looked at me, and then at one another, as if I had returned from a long journey. I was put into jail as I was going to the shoemaker's to get a shoe which was mended. When I was let out the next morning, I proceeded to finish my errand, and having put on my mended shoe, joined a huckleberry party, who were impatient to put themselves under my conduct; and in half an hour,—for the horse was soon tackled,—was in the midst of a huckleberry field, on one of our highest hills, two miles off, and then the State was nowhere to be seen.

This is the whole history of "My Prisons."

I have never declined paying the highway tax, because I am as desirous of being a good neighbor as I am of being a bad subject; and, as for supporting schools, I am doing my part to educate my fellow-countrymen now. It is for no particular item in the tax-bill that I refuse to pay it. I simply wish to refuse allegiance to the State, to withdraw and stand aloof from it effectually. I do not care to trace the course of my dollar, if I could, till it buys a man or a musket to shoot one with,—the dollar is innocent,—but I am concerned to trace the effects of my allegiance. In fact, I quietly declare war with the State, after my fashion, though I will still make what use and get what advantage of her I can, as is usual in such cases.

If others pay the tax which is demanded of me, from a sympathy with the State, they do but what they have already done in their own case, or rather they abet injustice to a greater extent than the State requires. If they pay the tax from a mistaken interest in the individual taxed, to save his property, or prevent his going to jail, it is because they have not considered wisely how far they let their private feelings interfere with the public good.

This, then, is my position at present. But one cannot be too much on his guard in such a case, lest his action be biassed by obstinacy, or an undue regard for the opinions of men. Let him see that he does only what belongs to himself and to the hour.

I think sometimes, Why, this people mean well; they are only ignorant; they would do better if they knew how: why give your neighbors this pain to treat you as they are not inclined to? But I think again, this is no reason why I should do as they do, or permit others to suffer much greater pain of a different kind. Again, I sometimes say to myself, When many millions of men, without heat, without ill will, without personal feeling of any kind, demand of you a few shillings only, without the possibility, such is their constitution, of retracting or altering their present demand, and without the possibility, on your side, of appeal to any other millions, why expose yourself to this overwhelming brute force? You do not resist cold and hunger, the winds and the waves, thus obstinately; you quietly submit to a thousand similar necessities. You do not put your head into the fire. But just in proportion as I regard this as not wholly a brute force, but partly a human force, and consider that I have relations to those millions as to so many millions of men, and not of mere brute or inanimate things, I see that appeal is possible, first and instantaneously, from them to the Maker of them, and, secondly, from them to themselves. But, if I put my head deliberately into the fire, there is no appeal to fire or to the Maker of fire, and I have only myself to blame. If I could convince myself that I have any right to be satisfied with men as they are, and to treat them accordingly, and not according, in some respects, to my requisitions and expectations of what they and I ought to be, then, like a good Mussulman and fatalist, I should endeavor to be satisfied with things as they are, and say it is the will of God. And, above all, there is this difference between resisting this and a purely brute or natural force, that I can resist this with some effect; but I cannot expect, like Orpheus, to change the nature of the rocks and trees and beasts.

I do not wish to quarrel with any man or nation. I do not wish to split hairs, to make fine distinctions, or set myself up as better than my neighbors. I seek rather, I may say, even an excuse for conforming to the laws of the land. I am but too ready to conform to them. Indeed, I have reason to suspect myself on this head; and each year, as the tax-gatherer comes round, I find myself disposed to review the acts and position of the general and State governments, and the spirit of the people, to discover a pretext for conformity.

> "We must affect our country as our parents;
> And if at any time we alienate
> Our love or industry from doing it honor,
> We must respect effects and teach the soul
> Matter of conscience and religion,
> And not desire of rule or benefit."

I believe that the State will soon be able to take all my work of this sort out of my hands, and then I shall be no better a patriot than my fellow-countrymen. Seen from a lower point of view, the Constitution, with all its faults, is very good; the law and the courts are very respectable; even this State and this American government are, in many respects, very admirable and rare things, to be thankful for, such as a great many have described them; but seen from a point of view a little higher, they are what I have described them; seen from a higher still, and the highest, who shall say what they are, or that they are worth looking at or thinking of at all?

However, the government does not concern me much, and I shall bestow the fewest possible thoughts on it. It is not many moments that I live under a government, even in this world. If a man is thought-free, fancy-free, imagination-free, that which *is not* never for a long time appearing *to be* to him, unwise rulers or reformers cannot fatally interrupt him.

I know that most men think differently from myself; but those whose lives are by profession devoted to the study of

these or kindred subjects, content me as little as any. States-
men and legislators, standing so completely within the insti-
tution, never distinctly and nakedly behold it. They speak of
moving society, but have no resting-place without it. They
may be men of a certain experience and discrimination, and
have no doubt invented ingenious and even useful systems,
for which we sincerely thank them; but all their wit and use-
fulness lie within certain not very wide limits. They are wont
to forget that the world is not governed by policy and expe-
diency. Webster never goes behind government, and so can-
not speak with authority about it. His words are wisdom to
those legislators who contemplate no essential reform in the
existing government; but for thinkers, and those who legislate
for all time, he never once glances at the subject. I know of
those whose serene and wise speculations on this theme
would soon reveal the limits of his mind's range and hospital-
ity. Yet, compared with the cheap professions of most reform-
ers, and the still cheaper wisdom and eloquence of politicians
in general, his are almost the only sensible and valuable
words, and we thank Heaven for him. Comparatively, he is al-
ways strong, original, and, above all, practical. Still his quality
is not wisdom, but prudence. The lawyer's truth is not Truth,
but consistency, or a consistent expediency. Truth is always in
harmony with herself, and is not concerned chiefly to reveal
the justice that may consist with wrong-doing. He well de-
serves to be called, as he has been called, the Defender of
the Constitution. There are really no blows to be given by
him but defensive ones. He is not a leader, but a follower.
His leaders are the men of '87. "I have never made an ef-
fort," he says, "and never propose to make an effort; I have
never countenanced an effort, and never mean to counte-
nance an effort, to disturb the arrangement as originally
made, by which the various States came into the Union."
Still thinking of the sanction which the Constitution gives
to slavery, he says, "Because it was a part of the original
compact,—let it stand." Notwithstanding his special acute-
ness and ability, he is unable to take a fact out of its merely
political relations, and behold it as it lies absolutely to be dis-
posed of by the intellect,—what, for instance, it behooves a
man to do here in America to-day with regard to slavery,—

but ventures, or is driven, to make some such desperate an-
swer as the following, while professing to speak absolutely,
and as a private man,—from which what new and singular
code of social duties might be inferred? "The manner," says
he, "in which the governments of those States where slavery
exists are to regulate it, is for their own consideration, under
their responsibility to their constituents, to the general laws of
propriety, humanity, and justice, and to God. Associations
formed elsewhere, springing from a feeling of humanity, or
any other cause, have nothing whatever to do with it. They
have never received any encouragement from me, and they
never will."*

They who know of no purer sources of truth, who have
traced up its stream no higher, stand, and wisely stand, by the
Bible and the Constitution, and drink at it there with rever-
ence and humility; but they who behold where it comes trick-
ling into this lake or that pool, gird up their loins once more,
and continue their pilgrimage toward its fountain-head.

No man with a genius for legislation has appeared in
America. They are rare in the history of the world. There are
orators, politicians, and eloquent men, by the thousand; but
the speaker has not yet opened his mouth to speak, who is ca-
pable of settling the much-vexed questions of the day. We
love eloquence for its own sake, and not for any truth which
it may utter, or any heroism it may inspire. Our legislators
have not yet learned the comparative value of free-trade and
of freedom, of union, and of rectitude, to a nation. They have
no genius or talent for comparatively humble questions of
taxation and finance, commerce and manufactures and agri-
culture. If we were left solely to the wordy wit of legislators
in Congress for our guidance, uncorrected by the seasonable
experience and the effectual complaints of the people,
America would not long retain her rank among the nations.
For eighteen hundred years, though perchance I have no
right to say it, the New Testament has been written; yet
where is the legislator who has wisdom and practical talent
enough to avail himself of the light which it sheds on the sci-
ence of legislation?

*These extracts have been inserted since the Lecture was read.

The authority of government, even such as I am willing to submit to,—for I will cheerfully obey those who know and can do better than I, and in many things even those who neither know nor can do so well,—is still an impure one: to be strictly just, it must have the sanction and consent of the governed. It can have no pure right over my person and property but what I concede to it. The progress from an absolute to a limited monarchy, from a limited monarchy to a democracy, is a progress toward a true respect for the individual. Even the Chinese philosopher was wise enough to regard the individual as the basis of the empire. Is a democracy, such as we know it, the last improvement possible in government? Is it not possible to take a step further towards recognizing and organizing the rights of man? There will never be a really free and enlightened State, until the State comes to recognize the individual as a higher and independent power, from which all its own power and authority are derived, and treats him accordingly. I please myself with imagining a State at last which can afford to be just to all men, and to treat the individual with respect as a neighbor; which even would not think it inconsistent with its own repose, if a few were to live aloof from it, not meddling with it, nor embraced by it, who fulfilled all the duties of neighbors and fellow-men. A State which bore this kind of fruit, and suffered it to drop off as fast as it ripened, would prepare the way for a still more perfect and glorious State, which also I have imagined, but not yet anywhere seen.

Walking

I WISH to speak a word for Nature, for absolute freedom and wildness, as contrasted with a freedom and culture merely civil,—to regard man as an inhabitant, or a part and parcel of Nature, rather than a member of society. I wish to make an extreme statement, if so I may make an emphatic one, for there are enough champions of civilization: the minister, and the school-committee, and every one of you will take care of that.

I have met with but one or two persons in the course of my life who understood the art of Walking, that is, of taking walks,—who had a genius, so to speak, for *sauntering*: which word is beautifully derived "from idle people who roved about the country, in the Middle Ages, and asked charity, under pretence of going *à la Sainte Terre*," to the Holy Land, till the children exclaimed, "There goes a *Sainte-Terrer*," a Saunterer,—a Holy-Lander. They who never go to the Holy Land in their walks, as they pretend, are indeed mere idlers and vagabonds; but they who do go there are saunterers in the good sense, such as I mean. Some, however, would derive the word from *sans terre*, without land or a home, which, therefore, in the good sense, will mean, having no particular home, but equally at home everywhere. For this is the secret of successful sauntering. He who sits still in a house all the time may be the greatest vagrant of all; but the saunterer, in the good sense, is no more vagrant than the meandering river, which is all the while sedulously seeking the shortest course to the sea. But I prefer the first, which, indeed, is the most probable derivation. For every walk is a sort of crusade, preached by some Peter the Hermit in us, to go forth and reconquer this Holy Land from the hands of the Infidels.

It is true, we are but faint-hearted crusaders, even the walkers, nowadays, who undertake no persevering, never-ending enterprises. Our expeditions are but tours, and come round again at evening to the old hearth-side from which we set out. Half the walk is but retracing our steps. We should go forth on the shortest walk, perchance, in the spirit of undying adventure, never to return,—prepared to send back our embalmed hearts only as relics to our desolate kingdoms. If you are ready to leave father and mother, and brother and sister, and wife and child and friends, and never see them again,—if you have paid your debts, and made your will, and settled all your affairs, and are a free man, then you are ready for a walk.

To come down to my own experience, my companion and I, for I sometimes have a companion, take pleasure in fancying ourselves knights of a new, or rather an old, order,—not Equestrians or Chevaliers, not Ritters or Riders, but Walkers, a still more ancient and honorable class, I trust. The chivalric and heroic spirit which once belonged to the Rider seems now to reside in, or perchance to have subsided into, the Walker,—not the Knight, but Walker Errant. He is a sort of fourth estate, outside of Church and State and People.

We have felt that we almost alone hereabouts practised this noble art; though, to tell the truth, at least, if their own assertions are to be received, most of my townsmen would fain walk sometimes, as I do, but they cannot. No wealth can buy the requisite leisure, freedom, and independence, which are the capital in this profession. It comes only by the grace of God. It requires a direct dispensation from Heaven to become a walker. You must be born into the family of the Walkers. *Ambulator nascitur, non fit.* Some of my townsmen, it is true, can remember and have described to me some walks which they took ten years ago, in which they were so blessed as to lose themselves for half an hour in the woods; but I know very well that they have confined themselves to the highway ever since, whatever pretensions they may make to belong to this select class. No doubt they were elevated for a moment as by the reminiscence of a previous state of existence, when even they were foresters and outlaws.

> "When he came to grene wode,
>   In a mery mornynge,
>   There he herde the notes small
>   Of byrdes mery syngynge.

"It is ferre gone, sayd Robyn,
    That I was last here;
Me lyste a lytell for to shote
    At the donne dere."

I think that I cannot preserve my health and spirits, unless I spend four hours a day at least—and it is commonly more than that—sauntering through the woods and over the hills and fields, absolutely free from all worldly engagements. You may safely say, A penny for your thoughts, or a thousand pounds. When sometimes I am reminded that the mechanics and shopkeepers stay in their shops not only all the forenoon, but all the afternoon too, sitting with crossed legs, so many of them,—as if the legs were made to sit upon, and not to stand or walk upon,—I think that they deserve some credit for not having all committed suicide long ago.

I, who cannot stay in my chamber for a single day without acquiring some rust, and when sometimes I have stolen forth for a walk at the eleventh hour of four o'clock in the afternoon, too late to redeem the day, when the shades of night were already beginning to be mingled with the daylight, have felt as if I had committed some sin to be atoned for,—I confess that I am astonished at the power of endurance, to say nothing of the moral insensibility, of my neighbors who confine themselves to shops and offices the whole day for weeks and months, ay, and years almost together. I know not what manner of stuff they are of,—sitting there now at three o'clock in the afternoon, as if it were three o'clock in the morning. Bonaparte may talk of the three-o'clock-in-the-morning courage, but it is nothing to the courage which can sit down cheerfully at this hour in the afternoon over against one's self whom you have known all the morning, to starve out a garrison to whom you are bound by such strong ties of sympathy. I wonder that about this time, or say between four and five o'clock in the afternoon, too late for the morning papers and too early for the evening ones, there is not a general explosion heard up and down the street, scattering a legion of antiquated and housebred notions and whims to the four winds for an airing,—and so the evil cure itself.

How womankind, who are confined to the house still more than men, stand it I do not know; but I have ground to suspect that most of them do not *stand* it at all. When, early in a summer afternoon, we have been shaking the dust of the village from the skirts of our garments, making haste past those houses with purely Doric or Gothic fronts, which have such an air of repose about them, my companion whispers that probably about these times their occupants are all gone to bed. Then it is that I appreciate the beauty and the glory of architecture, which itself never turns in, but forever stands out and erect, keeping watch over the slumberers.

No doubt temperament, and, above all, age, have a good deal to do with it. As a man grows older, his ability to sit still and follow in-door occupations increases. He grows vespertinal in his habits as the evening of life approaches, till at last he comes forth only just before sundown, and gets all the walk that he requires in half an hour.

But the walking of which I speak has nothing in it akin to taking exercise, as it is called, as the sick take medicine at stated hours,—as the swinging of dumb-bells or chairs; but is itself the enterprise and adventure of the day. If you would get exercise, go in search of the springs of life. Think of a man's swinging dumb-bells for his health, when those springs are bubbling up in far-off pastures unsought by him!

Moreover, you must walk like a camel, which is said to be the only beast which ruminates when walking. When a traveller asked Wordsworth's servant to show him her master's study, she answered, "Here is his library, but his study is out of doors."

Living much out of doors, in the sun and wind, will no doubt produce a certain roughness of character,—will cause a thicker cuticle to grow over some of the finer qualities of our nature, as on the face and hands, or as severe manual labor robs the hands of some of their delicacy of touch. So staying in the house, on the other hand, may produce a softness and smoothness, not to say thinness of skin, accompanied by an increased sensibility to certain impressions. Perhaps we should be more susceptible to some influences important to our intellectual and moral growth, if the sun had shone and the wind blown on us a little less; and no doubt it is a nice matter to proportion rightly the thick and thin skin. But methinks that is a scurf that will fall off fast enough,—that the natural remedy is to be found in the proportion which the night bears to the day, the winter to the summer, thought to experience. There will be so much the more air and sunshine in our thoughts. The callous palms of the laborer are conversant with finer tissues of self-respect and heroism, whose touch thrills the heart, than the languid fingers of idleness. That is mere sentimentality that lies abed by day and thinks itself white, far from the tan and callus of experience.

When we walk, we naturally go to the fields and woods: what would become of us, if we walked only in a garden or a mall? Even some sects of philosophers have felt the necessity of importing the woods to themselves, since they did not go to the woods. "They planted groves and walks of Platanes," where they took *subdiales ambulationes* in porticos open to the air. Of course it is of no use to direct our steps to the woods, if they do not carry us thither. I am alarmed when it happens that I have walked a mile into the woods bodily, without getting there in spirit. In my afternoon walk I would fain forget all my morning occupations and my obligations to society. But it sometimes happens that I cannot easily shake off the village. The thought of some work will run in my head, and I am not where my body is,—I am out of my senses. In my walks I would fain return to my senses. What business have I in the woods, if I am thinking of something out of the woods? I suspect myself, and cannot help a shudder, when I find myself so implicated even in what are called good works,—for this may sometimes happen.

My vicinity affords many good walks; and though for so many years I have walked almost every day, and sometimes for several days together, I have not yet exhausted them. An absolutely new prospect is a great happiness, and I can still get this any afternoon. Two or three hours' walking will carry me to as strange a country as I expect ever to see. A single farmhouse which I had not seen before is sometimes as good as the dominions of the King of Dahomey. There is in fact a sort of harmony discoverable between the capabilities of the landscape within a circle of ten miles' radius, or the limits of an afternoon walk, and the threescore years and ten of human life. It will never become quite familiar to you.

Nowadays almost all man's improvements, so called, as the building of houses, and the cutting down of the forest and of all large trees, simply deform the landscape, and make it more and more tame and cheap. A people who would begin by burning the fences and let the forest stand! I saw the fences half consumed, their ends lost in the middle of the prairie, and some worldly miser with a surveyor looking after his bounds, while heaven had taken place around him, and he did not see the angels going to and fro, but was looking for an old posthole in the midst of paradise. I looked again, and saw him standing in the middle of a boggy, stygian fen, surrounded by devils, and he had found his bounds without a doubt, three little stones, where a stake had been driven, and looking nearer, I saw that the Prince of Darkness was his surveyor.

I can easily walk ten, fifteen, twenty, any number of miles, commencing at my own door, without going by any house, without crossing a road except where the fox and the mink do: first along by the river, and then the brook, and then the meadow and the wood-side. There are square miles in my vicinity which have no inhabitant. From many a hill I can see civilization and the abodes of man afar. The farmers and their works are scarcely more obvious than woodchucks and their burrows. Man and his affairs, church and state and school, trade and commerce, and manufactures and agriculture, even politics, the most alarming of them all,—I am pleased to see how little space they occupy in the landscape. Politics is but a narrow field, and that still narrower highway yonder leads to it. I sometimes direct the traveller thither. If you would go to the political world, follow the great road,—follow that market-man, keep his dust in your eyes, and it will lead you straight to it; for it, too, has its place merely, and does not occupy all space. I pass from it as from a bean-field into the forest, and it is forgotten. In one half-hour I can walk off to some portion of the earth's surface where a man does not stand from one year's end to another, and there, consequently, politics are not, for they are but as the cigar-smoke of a man.

The village is the place to which the roads tend, a sort of expansion of the highway, as a lake of a river. It is the body of which roads are the arms and legs,—a trivial or quadrivial place, the thoroughfare and ordinary of travellers. The word is from the Latin *villa*, which, together with *via*, a way, or more anciently *ved* and *vella*, Varro derives from *veho*, to carry, because the villa is the place to and from which things are carried. They who got their living by teaming were said *vellaturam facere*. Hence, too, apparently, the Latin word *vilis* and our vile; also *villain*. This suggests what kind of degeneracy villagers are liable to. They are wayworn by the travel that goes by and over them, without travelling themselves.

Some do not walk at all; others walk in the highways; a few walk across lots. Roads are made for horses and men of business. I do not travel in them much, comparatively, because I am not in a hurry to get to any tavern or grocery or livery-stable or depot to which they lead. I am a good horse to travel, but not from choice a roadster. The landscape-painter uses the figures of men to mark a road. He would not make that use of my figure. I walk out into a Nature such as the old prophets and poets, Menu, Moses, Homer, Chaucer, walked in. You may name it America, but it is not America: neither Americus Vespucius, nor Columbus, nor the rest were the discoverers of it. There is a truer account of it in mythology than in any history of America, so called, that I have seen.

However, there are a few old roads that may be trodden with profit, as if they led somewhere now that they are nearly discontinued. There is the Old Marlborough Road, which does not go to Marlborough now, methinks, unless that is Marlborough where it carries me. I am the bolder to speak of it here, because I presume that there are one or two such roads in every town.

THE OLD MARLBOROUGH ROAD.

> Where they once dug for money,
> But never found any;
> Where sometimes Martial Miles
> Singly files,
> And Elijah Wood,

I fear for no good:
No other man,
Save Elisha Dugan,—
O man of wild habits,
Partridges and rabbits,
Who hast no cares
Only to set snares,
Who liv'st all alone,
Close to the bone,
And where life is sweetest
Constantly eatest.
When the spring stirs my blood
With the instinct to travel,
I can get enough gravel
On the Old Marlborough Road.
Nobody repairs it,
For nobody wears it;
It is a living way,
As the Christians say.
Not many there be
Who enter therein,
Only the guests of the
Irishman Quin.
What is it, what is it,
But a direction out there,
And the bare possibility
Of going somewhere?
Great guide-boards of stone,
But travellers none;
Cenotaphs of the towns
Named on their crowns.
It is worth going to see
Where you *might* be.
What king
Did the thing,
I am still wondering;
Set up how or when,
By what selectmen,
Gourgas or Lee,
Clark or Darby?

They 're a great endeavor
To be something forever;
Blank tablets of stone,
Where a traveller might groan,
And in one sentence
Grave all that is known;
Which another might read,
In his extreme need.
I know one or two
Lines that would do,
Literature that might stand
All over the land,
Which a man could remember
Till next December,
And read again in the spring,
After the thawing.
  If with fancy unfurled
    You leave your abode,
You may go round the world
    By the Old Marlborough Road.

At present, in this vicinity, the best part of the land is not private property; the landscape is not owned, and the walker enjoys comparative freedom. But possibly the day will come when it will be partitioned off into so-called pleasure-grounds, in which a few will take a narrow and exclusive pleasure only,—when fences shall be multiplied, and man-traps and other engines invented to confine men to the *public* road, and walking over the surface of God's earth shall be construed to mean trespassing on some gentleman's grounds. To enjoy a thing exclusively is commonly to exclude yourself from the true enjoyment of it. Let us improve our opportunities, then, before the evil days come.

What is it that makes it so hard sometimes to determine whither we will walk? I believe that there is a subtile magnetism in Nature, which, if we unconsciously yield to it, will direct us aright. It is not indifferent to us which way we walk. There is a right way; but we are very liable from heedlessness and stupidity to take the wrong one. We would fain take that walk, never yet taken by us through this actual world, which is perfectly symbolical of the path which we love to travel in the interior and ideal world; and sometimes, no doubt, we find it difficult to choose our direction, because it does not yet exist distinctly in our idea.

When I go out of the house for a walk, uncertain as yet whither I will bend my steps, and submit myself to my instinct to decide for me, I find, strange and whimsical as it may seem, that I finally and inevitably settle southwest, toward some particular wood or meadow or deserted pasture or hill in that direction. My needle is slow to settle,—varies a few degrees, and does not always point due southwest, it is true, and it has good authority for this variation, but it always settles between west and south-southwest. The future lies that way to me, and the earth seems more unexhausted and richer on that side. The outline which would bound my walks would be, not a circle, but a parabola, or rather like one of those cometary orbits which have been thought to be non-returning curves, in this case opening westward, in which my house occupies the place of the sun. I turn round and round irresolute sometimes for a quarter of an hour, until I decide, for the thousandth time, that I will walk into the southwest or west. Eastward I go only by force; but westward I go free. Thither no business leads me. It is hard for me to believe that I shall find fair landscapes or sufficient wildness and freedom behind the eastern horizon. I am not excited by the prospect of a walk thither; but I believe that the forest which I see in the western horizon stretches uninterruptedly towards the setting sun, and that there are no towns nor cities in it of enough consequence to disturb me. Let me live where I will, on this side is the city, on that the wilderness, and ever I am leaving the city more and more, and withdrawing into the wilderness. I should not lay so much stress on this fact, if I did not believe that something like this is the prevailing tendency of my countrymen. I must walk toward Oregon, and not toward Europe. And that way the nation is moving, and I may say that mankind progress from east to west. Within a few years we have witnessed the phenomenon of a southeastward migration, in the settlement of Australia; but this affects us as a retrograde movement, and, judging from the moral and physical character of the first generation of Australians, has not yet proved a successful experiment. The eastern Tartars think that there is nothing west beyond Thibet. "The world ends there," say they; "beyond there is nothing but a shoreless sea." It is unmitigated East where they live.

We go eastward to realize history and study the works of art and literature, retracing the steps of the race; we go westward as into the future, with a spirit of enterprise and adventure. The Atlantic is a Lethean stream, in our passage over which we have had an opportunity to forget the Old World and its institutions. If we do not succeed this time, there is perhaps one more chance for the race left before it arrives on the banks of the Styx; and that is in the Lethe of the Pacific, which is three times as wide.

I know not how significant it is, or how far it is an evidence of singularity, that an individual should thus consent in his pettiest walk with the general movement of the race; but I know that something akin to the migratory instinct in birds and quadrupeds,—which, in some instances, is known to have affected the squirrel tribe, impelling them to a general and mysterious movement, in which they were seen, say some, crossing the broadest rivers, each on its particular chip, with its tail raised for a sail, and bridging narrower streams with their dead,—that something like the *furor* which affects the domestic cattle in the spring, and which is referred to a worm in their tails,—affects both nations and individuals, either perennially or from time to time. Not a flock of wild geese cackles over our town, but it to some extent unsettles the value of real estate here, and, if I were a broker, I should probably take that disturbance into account.

> "Than longen folk to gon on pilgrimages,
> And palmeres for to seken strange strondes."

Every sunset which I witness inspires me with the desire to go to a West as distant and as fair as that into which the sun goes down. He appears to migrate westward daily, and tempt us to follow him. He is the Great Western Pioneer whom the nations follow. We dream all night of those mountain-ridges in the horizon, though they may be of vapor only, which were last gilded by his rays. The island of Atlantis, and the islands and gardens of the Hesperides, a sort of terrestrial paradise, appear to have been the Great West of the ancients, enveloped in mystery and poetry. Who has not seen in imagination, when looking into the sunset sky, the gardens of the Hesperides, and the foundation of all those fables?

Columbus felt the westward tendency more strongly than any before. He obeyed it, and found a New World for Castile and Leon. The herd of men in those days scented fresh pastures from afar.

> "And now the sun had stretched out all the hills,
> And now was dropped into the western bay;
> At last *he* rose, and twitched his mantle blue;
> To-morrow to fresh woods and pastures new."

Where on the globe can there be found an area of equal extent with that occupied by the bulk of our States, so fertile and so rich and varied in its productions, and at the same time so habitable by the European, as this is? Michaux, who knew but part of them, says that "the species of large trees are much more numerous in North America than in Europe; in the United States there are more than one hundred and forty species that exceed thirty feet in height; in France there are but thirty that attain this size." Later botanists more than confirm his observations. Humboldt came to America to realize his youthful dreams of a tropical vegetation, and he beheld it in its greatest perfection in the primitive forests of the Amazon, the most gigantic wilderness on the earth, which he has so eloquently described. The geographer Guyot, himself a European, goes farther,—farther than I am ready to follow him; yet not when he says,—"As the plant is made for the animal, as the vegetable world is made for the animal world, America is made for the man of the Old World. . . . . The man of the Old World sets out upon his way. Leaving the highlands of Asia, he descends from station to station towards Europe. Each of his steps is marked by a new civilization superior to the preceding, by a greater power of development. Arrived at the Atlantic, he pauses on the shore of this unknown ocean, the bounds of which he knows not, and turns upon his footprints for an instant." When he has exhausted the rich soil of Europe, and reinvigorated himself, "then recommences his adventurous career westward as in the earliest ages." So far Guyot.

From this western impulse coming in contact with the barrier of the Atlantic sprang the commerce and enterprise of modern times. The younger Michaux, in his "Travels West of the Alleghanies in 1802," says that the common inquiry in the newly settled West was, " 'From what part of the world have you come?' As if these vast and fertile regions would naturally be the place of meeting and common country of all the inhabitants of the globe."

To use an obsolete Latin word, I might say, *Ex Oriente lux; ex Occidente* FRUX. From the East light; from the West fruit.

Sir Francis Head, an English traveller and a Governor-General of Canada, tells us that "in both the northern and southern hemispheres of the New World, Nature has not only outlined her works on a larger scale, but has painted the whole picture with brighter and more costly colors than she used in delineating and in beautifying the Old World. . . . . The heavens of America appear infinitely higher, the sky is bluer, the air is fresher, the cold is intenser, the moon looks larger, the stars are brighter, the thunder is louder, the lightning is vivider, the wind is stronger, the rain is heavier, the mountains are higher, the rivers longer, the forests bigger, the plains broader." This statement will do at least to set against Buffon's account of this part of the world and its productions.

Linnæus said long ago, "Nescio quæ facies *læta, glabra* plantis Americanis: I know not what there is of joyous and smooth in the aspect of American plants"; and I think that in this country there are no, or at most very few, *Africanæ bestiæ*, African beasts, as the Romans called them, and that in this respect also it is peculiarly fitted for the habitation of man. We are told that within three miles of the centre of the East-Indian city of Singapore, some of the inhabitants are annually carried off by tigers; but the traveller can lie down in the woods at night almost anywhere in North America without fear of wild beasts.

These are encouraging testimonies. If the moon looks larger here than in Europe, probably the sun looks larger also. If the heavens of America appear infinitely higher, and the stars brighter, I trust that these facts are symbolical of the height to which the philosophy and poetry and religion of her inhabitants may one day soar. At length, perchance, the immaterial heaven will appear as much higher to the American mind, and the intimations that star it as much brighter. For I believe that climate does thus react on man,—as there is something in the mountain-air that feeds the spirit and inspires. Will not man grow to greater perfection intellectually as well as physically under these influences? Or is it unimportant how many foggy days there are in his life? I trust that we shall be more imaginative, that our thoughts will be clearer, fresher, and more ethereal, as our sky,—our understanding more comprehensive and broader, like our plains,—our intellect generally on a grander scale, like our thunder and lightning, our rivers and mountains and forests,—and our hearts shall even correspond in breadth and depth and grandeur to our inland seas. Perchance there will appear to the traveller something, he knows not what, of *læta* and *glabra*, of joyous and serene, in our very faces. Else to what end does the world go on, and why was America discovered?

To Americans I hardly need to say,—

"Westward the star of empire takes its way."

As a true patriot, I should be ashamed to think that Adam in paradise was more favorably situated on the whole than the backwoodsman in this country.

Our sympathies in Massachusetts are not confined to New England; though we may be estranged from the South, we sympathize with the West. There is the home of the younger sons, as among the Scandinavians they took to the sea for their inheritance. It is too late to be studying Hebrew; it is more important to understand even the slang of to-day.

Some months ago I went to see a panorama of the Rhine. It was like a dream of the Middle Ages. I floated down its historic stream in something more than imagination, under bridges built by the Romans, and repaired by later heroes, past cities and castles whose very names were music to my ears, and each of which was the subject of a legend. There were Ehrenbreitstein and Rolandseck and Coblentz, which I knew only in history. They were ruins that interested me chiefly. There seemed to come up from its waters and its vine-

clad hills and valleys a hushed music as of Crusaders depart-
ing for the Holy Land. I floated along under the spell of en-
chantment, as if I had been transported to an heroic age, and
breathed an atmosphere of chivalry.

Soon after, I went to see a panorama of the Mississippi, and
as I worked my way up the river in the light of to-day, and
saw the steamboats wooding up, counted the rising cities,
gazed on the fresh ruins of Nauvoo, beheld the Indians mov-
ing west across the stream, and, as before I had looked up the
Moselle, now looked up the Ohio and the Missouri, and
heard the legends of Dubuque and of Wenona's Cliff,—still
thinking more of the future than of the past or present,—I
saw that this was a Rhine stream of a different kind; that the
foundations of castles were yet to be laid, and the famous
bridges were yet to be thrown over the river; and I felt that
this was the heroic age itself, though we know it not, for the
hero is commonly the simplest and obscurest of men.

The West of which I speak is but another name for the
Wild; and what I have been preparing to say is, that in
Wildness is the preservation of the world. Every tree sends its
fibres forth in search of the Wild. The cities import it at any
price. Men plough and sail for it. From the forest and wilder-
ness come the tonics and barks which brace mankind. Our an-
cestors were savages. The story of Romulus and Remus being
suckled by a wolf is not a meaningless fable. The founders of
every State which has risen to eminence have drawn their
nourishment and vigor from a similar wild source. It was be-
cause the children of the Empire were not suckled by the wolf
that they were conquered and displaced by the children of the
Northern forests who were.

I believe in the forest, and in the meadow, and in the night
in which the corn grows. We require an infusion of hemlock-
spruce or arbor-vitæ in our tea. There is a difference between
eating and drinking for strength and from mere gluttony. The
Hottentots eagerly devour the marrow of the koodoo and
other antelopes raw, as a matter of course. Some of our
Northern Indians eat raw the marrow of the Arctic reindeer,
as well as various other parts, including the summits of the
antlers, as long as they are soft. And herein, perchance, they

have stolen a march on the cooks of Paris. They get what usually goes to feed the fire. This is probably better than stall-fed beef and slaughter-house pork to make a man of. Give me a wildness whose glance no civilization can endure,—as if we lived on the marrow of koodoos devoured raw.

There are some intervals which border the strain of the wood-thrush, to which I would migrate,—wild lands where no settler has squatted it; to which, methinks, I am already acclimated.

The African hunter Cummings tells us that the skin of the eland, as well as that of most other antelopes just killed, emits the most delicious perfume of trees and grass. I would have every man so much like a wild antelope, so much a part and parcel of Nature, that his very person should thus sweetly advertise our senses of his presence, and remind us of those parts of Nature which he most haunts. I feel no disposition to be satirical, when the trapper's coat emits the odor of musquash even; it is a sweeter scent to me than that which commonly exhales from the merchant's or the scholar's garments. When I go into their wardrobes and handle their vestments, I am reminded of no grassy plains and flowery meads which they have frequented, but of dusty merchants' exchanges and libraries rather.

A tanned skin is something more than respectable, and perhaps olive is a fitter color than white for a man,—a denizen of the woods. "The pale white man!" I do not wonder that the African pitied him. Darwin the naturalist says, "A white man bathing by the side of a Tahitian was like a plant bleached by the gardener's art, compared with a fine, dark green one, growing vigorously in the open fields."

Ben Jonson exclaims,–

"How near to good is what is fair!"

So I would say,—

How near to good is what is *wild*!

Life consists with wildness. The most alive is the wildest. Not yet subdued to man, its presence refreshes him. One who pressed forward incessantly and never rested from his labors, who grew fast and made infinite demands on life, would always find himself in a new country or wilderness, and surrounded by the raw material of life. He would be climbing over the prostrate stems of primitive forest-trees.

Hope and the future for me are not in lawns and cultivated fields, not in towns and cities, but in the impervious and quaking swamps. When, formerly, I have analyzed my partiality for some farm which I had contemplated purchasing, I have frequently found that I was attracted solely by a few square rods of impermeable and unfathomable bog,—a natural sink in one corner of it. That was the jewel which dazzled me. I derive more of my subsistence from the swamps which surround my native town than from the cultivated gardens in the village. There are no richer parterres to my eyes than the dense beds of dwarf andromeda (*Cassandra calyculata*) which cover these tender places on the earth's surface. Botany cannot go farther than tell me the names of the shrubs which grow there,—the high-blueberry, panicled andromeda, lamb-kill, azalea, and rhodora,—all standing in the quaking sphagnum. I often think that I should like to have my house front on this mass of dull red bushes, omitting other flower plots and borders, transplanted spruce and trim box, even gravelled walks,—to have this fertile spot under my windows, not a few imported barrow-fulls of soil only to cover the sand which was thrown out in digging the cellar. Why not put my house, my parlor, behind this plot, instead of behind that meagre assemblage of curiosities, that poor apology for a Nature and Art, which I call my front-yard? It is an effort to clear up and make a decent appearance when the carpenter and mason have departed, though done as much for the passer-by as the dweller within. The most tasteful front-yard fence was never an agreeable object of study to me; the most elaborate ornaments, acorn-tops, or what not, soon wearied and disgusted me. Bring your sills up to the very edge of the swamp, then, (though it may not be the best place for a dry cellar,) so that there be no access on that side to citizens. Front-yards are not made to walk in, but, at most, through, and you could go in the back way.

Yes, though you may think me perverse, if it were proposed to me to dwell in the neighborhood of the most beautiful garden that ever human art contrived, or else of a dismal swamp, I should certainly decide for the swamp. How vain, then, have been all your labors, citizens, for me!

My spirits infallibly rise in proportion to the outward dreariness. Give me the ocean, the desert, or the wilderness! In the desert, pure air and solitude compensate for want of moisture and fertility. The traveller Burton says of it,—"Your *morale* improves; you become frank and cordial, hospitable and single-minded. . . . . In the desert, spirituous liquors excite only disgust. There is a keen enjoyment in a mere animal existence." They who have been travelling long on the steppes of Tartary say,—"On reëntering cultivated lands, the agitation, perplexity, and turmoil of civilization oppressed and suffocated us; the air seemed to fail us, and we felt every moment as if about to die of asphyxia." When I would recreate myself, I seek the darkest wood, the thickest and most interminable, and, to the citizen, most dismal swamp. I enter a swamp as a sacred place,—a *sanctum sanctorum*. There is the strength, the marrow of Nature. The wild-wood covers the virgin mould,—and the same soil is good for men and for trees. A man's health requires as many acres of meadow to his prospect as his farm does loads of muck. There are the strong meats on which he feeds. A town is saved, not more by the righteous men in it than by the woods and swamps that surround it. A township where one primitive forest waves above, while another primitive forest rots below,— such a town is fitted to raise not only corn and potatoes, but poets and philosophers for the coming ages. In such a soil grew Homer and Confucius and the rest, and out of such a wilderness comes the Reformer eating locusts and wild honey.

To preserve wild animals implies generally the creation of a forest for them to dwell in or resort to. So is it with man. A hundred years ago they sold bark in our streets peeled from our own woods. In the very aspect of those primitive and rugged trees, there was, methinks, a tanning principle which hardened and consolidated the fibres of men's thoughts. Ah! already I shudder for these comparatively degenerate days of my native village, when you cannot collect a load of bark of good thickness,—and we no longer produce tar and turpentine.

The civilized nations—Greece, Rome, England—have been sustained by the primitive forests which anciently rotted where they stand. They survive as long as the soil is not exhausted. Alas for human culture! little is to be expected of a nation, when the vegetable mould is exhausted, and it is compelled to make manure of the bones of its fathers. There the poet sustains himself merely by his own superfluous fat, and the philosopher comes down on his marrow-bones.

It is said to be the task of the American "to work the virgin soil," and that "agriculture here already assumes proportions unknown everywhere else." I think that the farmer displaces the Indian even because he redeems the meadow, and so makes himself stronger and in some respects more natural. I was surveying for a man the other day a single straight line one hundred and thirty-two rods long, through a swamp, at whose entrance might have been written the words which Dante read over the entrance to the infernal regions,—"Leave all hope, ye that enter,"—that is, of ever getting out again; where at one time I saw my employer actually up to his neck and swimming for his life in his property, though it was still winter. He had another similar swamp which I could not survey at all, because it was completely under water, and nevertheless, with regard to a third swamp, which I did *survey* from a distance, he remarked to me, true to his instincts, that he would not part with it for any consideration, on account of the mud which it contained. And that man intends to put a girdling ditch round the whole in the course of forty months, and so redeem it by the magic of his spade. I refer to him only as the type of a class.

The weapons with which we have gained our most important victories, which should be handed down as heirlooms from father to son, are not the sword and the lance, but the bush-whack, the turf-cutter, the spade, and the bog-hoe, rusted with the blood of many a meadow, and begrimed with the dust of many a hard-fought field. The very winds blew the Indian's cornfield into the meadow, and pointed out the way which he had not the skill to follow. He had no better implement with which to intrench himself in the land than a clam-shell. But the farmer is armed with plough and spade.

In Literature it is only the wild that attracts us. Dulness is but another name for tameness. It is the uncivilized free and wild thinking in "Hamlet" and the "Iliad," in all the Scriptures and Mythologies, not learned in the schools, that delights us. As the wild duck is more swift and beautiful than the tame, so is the wild—the mallard—thought, which 'mid falling dews wings its way above the fens. A truly good book is something as natural, and as unexpectedly and unaccountably fair and perfect, as a wild flower discovered on the prairies of the West or in the jungles of the East. Genius is a light which makes the darkness visible, like the lightning's flash, which perchance shatters the temple of knowledge itself,—and not a taper lighted at the hearth-stone of the race, which pales before the light of common day.

English literature, from the days of the minstrels to the Lake Poets,—Chaucer and Spenser and Milton, and even Shakspeare, included,—breathes no quite fresh and in this sense wild strain. It is an essentially tame and civilized literature, reflecting Greece and Rome. Her wilderness is a greenwood,—her wild man a Robin Hood. There is plenty of genial love of Nature, but not so much of Nature herself. Her chronicles inform us when her wild animals, but not when the wild man in her, became extinct.

The science of Humboldt is one thing, poetry is another thing. The poet to-day, notwithstanding all the discoveries of science, and the accumulated learning of mankind, enjoys no advantage over Homer.

Where is the literature which gives expression to Nature? He would be a poet who could impress the winds and streams into his service, to speak for him; who nailed words to their primitive senses, as farmers drive down stakes in the spring, which the frost has heaved; who derived his words as often as he used them,—transplanted them to his page with earth adhering to their roots; whose words were so true and fresh and natural that they would appear to expand like the buds at the approach of spring, though they lay half-smothered between two musty leaves in a library,—ay, to bloom and bear fruit there, after their kind, annually; for the faithful reader, in sympathy with surrounding Nature.

I do not know of any poetry to quote which adequately expresses this yearning for the Wild. Approached from this side, the best poetry is tame. I do not know where to find in any literature, ancient or modern, any account which contents me of that Nature with which even I am acquainted. You will perceive that I demand something which no Augustan nor Elizabethan age, which no *culture*, in short, can give. Mythology comes nearer to it than anything. How much more fertile a Nature, at least, has Grecian mythology its root in than English literature! Mythology is the crop which the Old World bore before its soil was exhausted, before the fancy and imagination were affected with blight; and which it still bears, wherever its pristine vigor is unabated. All other literatures endure only as the elms which overshadow our houses; but this is like the great dragon-tree of the Western Isles, as old as mankind, and, whether that does or not, will endure as long; for the decay of other literatures makes the soil in which it thrives.

The West is preparing to add its fables to those of the East. The valleys of the Ganges, the Nile, and the Rhine, having yielded their crop, it remains to be seen what the valleys of the Amazon, the Plate, the Orinoco, the St. Lawrence, and the Mississippi will produce. Perchance, when, in the course of ages, American liberty has become a fiction of the past,— as it is to some extent a fiction of the present,—the poets of the world will be inspired by American mythology.

The wildest dreams of wild men, even, are not the less true, though they may not recommend themselves to the sense which is most common among Englishmen and Americans to-day. It is not every truth that recommends itself to the common sense. Nature has a place for the wild clematis as well as for the cabbage. Some expressions of truth are reminiscent,—others merely *sensible*, as the phrase is,— others prophetic. Some forms of disease, even, may prophesy forms of health. The geologist has discovered that the figures of serpents, griffins, flying dragons, and other fanciful embellishments of heraldry, have their prototypes in the forms of fossil species which were extinct before man was created, and hence "indicate a faint and shadowy knowledge of a previous state of organic existence." The Hindoos dreamed that the earth rested on an elephant, and the elephant on a tortoise, and the tortoise on a serpent; and though it may be an unimportant coincidence, it will not be out of place here to state, that a fossil tortoise has lately been discovered in Asia large enough to support an elephant. I confess that I am partial to these wild fancies, which transcend the order of time and development. They are the sublimest recreation of the intellect. The partridge loves peas, but not those that go with her into the pot.

In short, all good things are wild and free. There is something in a strain of music, whether produced by an instrument or by the human voice,—take the sound of a bugle in a summer night, for instance,—which by its wildness, to speak without satire, reminds me of the cries emitted by wild beasts in their native forests. It is so much of their wildness as I can understand. Give me for my friends and neighbors wild men, not tame ones. The wildness of the savage is but a faint symbol of the awful ferity with which good men and lovers meet.

I love even to see the domestic animals reassert their native rights,—any evidence that they have not wholly lost their original wild habits and vigor; as when my neighbor's cow breaks out of her pasture early in the spring and boldly swims the river, a cold, gray tide, twenty-five or thirty rods wide, swollen by the melted snow. It is the buffalo crossing the Mississippi. This exploit confers some dignity on the herd in my eyes,—already dignified. The seeds of instinct are preserved under the thick hides of cattle and horses, like seeds in the bowels of the earth, an indefinite period.

Any sportiveness in cattle is unexpected. I saw one day a herd of a dozen bullocks and cows running about and frisking in unwieldy sport, like huge rats, even like kittens. They shook their heads, raised their tails, and rushed up and down a hill, and I perceived by their horns, as well as by their activity, their relation to the deer tribe. But, alas! a sudden loud *Whoa!* would have damped their ardor at once, reduced them from venison to beef, and stiffened their sides and sinews like the locomotive. Who but the Evil One has cried, "Whoa!" to mankind? Indeed, the life of cattle, like that of many men, is but a sort of locomotiveness; they move a side at a time, and man, by his machinery, is meeting the horse and ox half-way.

Whatever part the whip has touched is thenceforth palsied. Who would ever think of a *side* of any of the supple cat tribe, as we speak of a *side* of beef?

I rejoice that horses and steers have to be broken before they can be made the slaves of men, and that men themselves have some wild oats still left to sow before they become submissive members of society. Undoubtedly, all men are not equally fit subjects for civilization; and because the majority, like dogs and sheep, are tame by inherited disposition, this is no reason why the others should have their natures broken that they may be reduced to the same level. Men are in the main alike, but they were made several in order that they might be various. If a low use is to be served, one man will do nearly or quite as well as another; if a high one, individual excellence is to be regarded. Any man can stop a hole to keep the wind away, but no other man could serve so rare a use as the author of this illustration did. Confucius says,—"The skins of the tiger and the leopard, when they are tanned, are as the skins of the dog and the sheep tanned." But it is not the part of a true culture to tame tigers, any more than it is to make sheep ferocious; and tanning their skins for shoes is not the best use to which they can be put.

When looking over a list of men's names in a foreign language, as of military officers, or of authors who have written on a particular subject, I am reminded once more that there is nothing in a name. The name Menschikoff, for instance, has nothing in it to my ears more human than a whisker, and it may belong to a rat. As the names of the Poles and Russians are to us, so are ours to them. It is as if they had been named by the child's rigmarole,—*Iery wiery ichery van, tittle-tol-tan.* I see in my mind a herd of wild creatures swarming over the earth, and to each the herdsman has affixed some barbarous sound in his own dialect. The names of men are of course as cheap and meaningless as *Bose* and *Tray*, the names of dogs.

Methinks it would be some advantage to philosophy, if men were named merely in the gross, as they are known. It would be necessary only to know the genus, and perhaps the race or variety, to know the individual. We are not prepared to believe that every private soldier in a Roman army had a name of his own,—because we have not supposed that he had a character of his own. At present our only true names are nicknames. I knew a boy who, from his peculiar energy, was called "Buster" by his playmates, and this rightly supplanted his Christian name. Some travellers tell us that an Indian had no name given him at first, but earned it, and his name was his fame; and among some tribes he acquired a new name with every new exploit. It is pitiful when a man bears a name for convenience merely, who has earned neither name nor fame.

I will not allow mere names to make distinctions for me, but still see men in herds for all them. A familiar name cannot make a man less strange to me. It may be given to a savage who retains in secret his own wild title earned in the woods. We have a wild savage in us, and a savage name is perchance somewhere recorded as ours. I see that my neighbor, who bears the familiar epithet William, or Edwin, takes it off with his jacket. It does not adhere to him when asleep or in anger, or aroused by any passion or inspiration. I seem to hear pronounced by some of his kin at such a time his original wild name in some jaw-breaking or else melodious tongue.

Here is this vast, savage, howling mother of ours, Nature, lying all around, with such beauty, and such affection for her children, as the leopard; and yet we are so early weaned from her breast to society, to that culture which is exclusively an interaction of man on man,—a sort of breeding in and in, which produces at most a merely English nobility, a civilization destined to have a speedy limit.

In society, in the best institutions of men, it is easy to detect a certain precocity. When we should still be growing children, we are already little men. Give me a culture which imports much muck from the meadows, and deepens the soil,—not that which trusts to heating manures, and improved implements and modes of culture only!

Many a poor sore-eyed student that I have heard of would grow faster, both intellectually and physically, if, instead of sitting up so very late, he honestly slumbered a fool's allowance.

There may be an excess even of informing light. Niépce, a Frenchman, discovered "actinism," that power in the sun's rays which produces a chemical effect,—that granite rocks, and stone structures, and statues of metal, "are all alike destructively acted upon during the hours of sunshine, and, but for provisions of Nature no less wonderful, would soon perish under the delicate touch of the most subtile of the agencies of the universe." But he observed that "those bodies which underwent this change during the daylight possessed the power of restoring themselves to their original conditions during the hours of night, when this excitement was no longer influencing them." Hence it has been inferred that "the hours of darkness are as necessary to the inorganic creation as we know night and sleep are to the organic kingdom." Not even does the moon shine every night, but gives place to darkness.

I would not have every man nor every part of a man cultivated, any more than I would have every acre of earth cultivated: part will be tillage, but the greater part will be meadow and forest, not only serving an immediate use, but preparing a mould against a distant future, by the annual decay of the vegetation which it supports.

There are other letters for the child to learn than those which Cadmus invented. The Spaniards have a good term to express this wild and dusky knowledge,—*Gramática parda*, tawny grammar,—a kind of mother-wit derived from that same leopard to which I have referred.

We have heard of a Society for the Diffusion of Useful Knowledge. It is said that knowledge is power; and the like. Methinks there is equal need of a Society for the Diffusion of Useful Ignorance, what we will call Beautiful Knowledge, a knowledge useful in a higher sense: for what is most of our boasted so-called knowledge but a conceit that we know something, which robs us of the advantage of our actual ignorance? What we call knowledge is often our positive ignorance; ignorance our negative knowledge. By long years of patient industry and reading of the newspapers—for what are the libraries of science but files of newspapers?—a man accumulates a myriad facts, lays them up in his memory, and then when in some spring of his life he saunters abroad into the Great Fields of thought, he, as it were, goes to grass like a horse, and leaves all his harness behind in the stable. I would say to the Society for the Diffusion of Useful Knowledge, sometimes,—Go to grass. You have eaten hay long enough. The spring has come with its green crop. The very cows are driven to their country pastures before the end of May; though I have heard of one unnatural farmer who kept his cow in the barn and fed her on hay all the year round. So, frequently, the Society for the Diffusion of Useful Knowledge treats its cattle.

A man's ignorance sometimes is not only useful, but beautiful,—while his knowledge, so called, is oftentimes worse than useless, besides being ugly. Which is the best man to deal with,—he who knows nothing about a subject, and, what is extremely rare, knows that he knows nothing, or he who really knows something about it, but thinks that he knows all?

My desire for knowledge is intermittent; but my desire to bathe my head in atmospheres unknown to my feet is perennial and constant. The highest that we can attain to is not Knowledge, but Sympathy with Intelligence. I do not know that this higher knowledge amounts to anything more definite than a novel and grand surprise on a sudden revelation of the insufficiency of all that we called Knowledge before,—a discovery that there are more things in heaven and earth than are dreamed of in our philosophy. It is the lighting up of the mist by the sun. Man cannot *know* in any higher sense than this, any more than he can look serenely and with impunity in the face of the sun: Ὡς τὶ νοῶν, οὐ κεῖνον νοήσεις,—"You will not perceive that, as perceiving a particular thing," say the Chaldean Oracles.

There is something servile in the habit of seeking after a law which we may obey. We may study the laws of matter at and for our convenience, but a successful life knows no law. It is an unfortunate discovery certainly, that of a law which binds us where we did not know before that we were bound. Live free, child of the mist,—and with respect to knowledge we are all children of the mist. The man who takes the liberty to live is superior to all the laws, by virtue of his relation to the law-maker. "That is active duty," says the Vishnu Purana, "which is not for our bondage; that is knowledge which is for our liberation: all other duty is good only unto weariness; all other knowledge is only the cleverness of an artist."

•

It is remarkable how few events or crises there are in our histories; how little exercised we have been in our minds; how few experiences we have had. I would fain be assured that I am growing apace and rankly, though my very growth disturb this dull equanimity,—though it be with struggle through long, dark, muggy nights or seasons of gloom. It would be well, if all our lives were a divine tragedy even, instead of this trivial comedy or farce. Dante, Bunyan, and others, appear to have been exercised in their minds more than we: they were subjected to a kind of culture such as our district schools and colleges do not contemplate. Even Mahomet, though many may scream at his name, had a good deal more to live for, ay, and to die for, than they have commonly.

When, at rare intervals, some thought visits one, as perchance he is walking on a railroad, then indeed the cars go by without his hearing them. But soon, by some inexorable law, our life goes by and the cars return.

> "Gentle breeze, that wanderest unseen,
>   And bendest the thistles round Loira of storms,
>   Traveller of the windy glens,
>   Why hast thou left my ear so soon?"

While almost all men feel an attraction drawing them to society, few are attracted strongly to Nature. In their relation to Nature men appear to me for the most part, notwithstanding their arts, lower than the animals. It is not often a beautiful relation, as in the case of the animals. How little appreciation of the beauty of the landscape there is among us! We have to be told that the Greeks called the world Κόσμος, Beauty, or Order, but we do not see clearly why they did so, and we esteem it at best only a curious philological fact.

For my part, I feel that with regard to Nature I live a sort of border life, on the confines of a world into which I make occasional and transient forays only, and my patriotism and allegiance to the State into whose territories I seem to retreat are those of a moss-trooper. Unto a life which I call natural I would gladly follow even a will-o'-the-wisp through bogs and sloughs unimaginable, but no moon nor fire-fly has shown me the causeway to it. Nature is a personality so vast and universal that we have never seen one of her features. The walker in the familiar fields which stretch around my native town sometimes finds himself in another land than is described in their owners' deeds, as it were in some far-away field on the confines of the actual Concord, where her jurisdiction ceases, and the idea which the word Concord suggests ceases to be suggested. These farms which I have myself surveyed, these bounds which I have set up appear dimly still as through a mist; but they have no chemistry to fix them; they fade from the surface of the glass; and the picture which the painter painted stands out dimly from beneath. The world with which we are commonly acquainted leaves no trace, and it will have no anniversary.

I took a walk on Spaulding's Farm the other afternoon. I saw the setting sun lighting up the opposite side of a stately pine wood. Its golden rays straggled into the aisles of the wood as into some noble hall. I was impressed as if some ancient and altogether admirable and shining family had settled there in that part of the land called Concord, unknown to me,—to whom the sun was servant,—who had not gone into society in the village,—who had not been called on. I saw their park, their pleasure-ground, beyond through the wood, in Spaulding's cranberry-meadow. The pines furnished them with gables as they grew. Their house was not obvious to vision; the trees grew through it. I do not know whether I heard the sounds of a suppressed hilarity or not. They seemed to recline on the sunbeams. They have sons and daughters. They are quite well. The farmer's cart-path, which leads directly through their hall, does not in the least put them out,—as the muddy bottom of a pool is sometimes seen through the reflected skies. They never heard of Spaulding, and do not know that he is their neighbor,—notwithstanding I heard him whistle as he drove his team through the house. Nothing can equal the serenity of their lives. Their coat of arms is simply a lichen. I saw it painted on the pines and oaks. Their attics were in the tops of the trees. They are of no politics. There was no noise of labor. I did not perceive that they were weaving or spinning. Yet I did detect, when the wind lulled and hearing was done away, the finest imaginable sweet musical hum,—as of a distant hive in May, which perchance was the sound of their thinking. They had no idle thoughts, and no one without could see their work, for their industry was not as in knots and excrescences embayed.

But I find it difficult to remember them. They fade irrevocably out of my mind even now while I speak and endeavor to recall them, and recollect myself. It is only after a long and serious effort to recollect my best thoughts that I become again aware of their cohabitancy. If it were not for such families as this, I think I should move out of Concord.

We are accustomed to say in New England that few and fewer pigeons visit us every year. Our forests furnish no mast for them. So, it would seem, few and fewer thoughts visit each growing man from year to year, for the grove in our minds is laid waste,—sold to feed unnecessary fires of ambition, or sent to mill, and there is scarcely a twig left for them to perch on. They no longer build nor breed with us. In some more genial season, perchance, a faint shadow flits across the landscape of the mind, cast by the *wings* of some thought in its vernal or autumnal migration, but, looking up, we are unable to detect the substance of the thought itself. Our winged thoughts are turned to poultry. They no longer soar, and they attain only to a Shanghai and Cochin-China grandeur. Those *gra-a-ate thoughts*, those *gra-a-ate men* you hear of!

We hug the earth,—how rarely we mount! Methinks we might elevate ourselves a little more. We might climb a tree, at least. I found my account in climbing a tree once. It was a tall white pine, on the top of a hill; and though I got well pitched, I was well paid for it, for I discovered new mountains in the horizon which I had never seen before,—so much more of the earth and the heavens. I might have walked about the foot of the tree for threescore years and ten, and yet I certainly should never have seen them. But, above all, I discovered around me,—it was near the end of June,—on the ends of the topmost branches only, a few minute and delicate red cone-like blossoms, the fertile flower of the white pine looking heavenward. I carried straightway to the village the topmost spire, and showed it to stranger jurymen who walked the streets,—for it was court-week,—and to farmers and lumber-dealers and wood-choppers and hunters, and not one had ever seen the like before, but they wondered as at a star dropped down. Tell of ancient architects finishing their works on the tops of columns as perfectly as on the lower and more visible parts! Nature has from the first expanded the minute blossoms of the forest only toward the heavens, above men's heads and unobserved by them. We see only the flowers that are under our feet in the meadows. The pines have developed their delicate blossoms on the highest twigs of the wood every summer for ages, as well over the heads of Nature's red children as of her white ones; yet scarcely a farmer or hunter in the land has ever seen them.

Above all, we cannot afford not to live in the present. He is blessed over all mortals who loses no moment of the passing life in remembering the past. Unless our philosophy hears the cock crow in every barn-yard within our horizon, it is belated. That sound commonly reminds us that we are growing rusty and antique in our employments and habits of thought. His philosophy comes down to a more recent time than ours. There is something suggested by it that is a newer testament,—the gospel according to this moment. He has not fallen astern; he has got up early, and kept up early, and to be where he is is to be in season, in the foremost rank of time. It is an expression of the health and soundness of Nature, a brag for all the world,—healthiness as of a spring burst forth, a new fountain of the Muses, to celebrate this last instant of time. Where he lives no fugitive slave laws are passed. Who has not betrayed his master many times since last he heard that note?

The merit of this bird's strain is in its freedom from all plaintiveness. The singer can easily move us to tears or to laughter, but where is he who can excite in us a pure morning joy? When, in doleful dumps, breaking the awful stillness of our wooden sidewalk on a Sunday, or, perchance, a watcher in the house of mourning, I hear a cockerel crow far or near, I think to myself, "There is one of us well, at any rate,"—and with a sudden gush return to my senses.

We had a remarkable sunset one day last November. I was walking in a meadow, the source of a small brook, when the

sun at last, just before setting, after a cold gray day, reached a
clear stratum in the horizon, and the softest, brightest morn-
ing sunlight fell on the dry grass and on the stems of the trees
in the opposite horizon, and on the leaves of the shrub-oaks
on the hill-side, while our shadows stretched long over the
meadow eastward, as if we were the only motes in its beams.
It was such a light as we could not have imagined a moment
before, and the air also was so warm and serene that nothing
was wanting to make a paradise of that meadow. When we re-
flected that this was not a solitary phenomenon, never to hap-
pen again, but that it would happen forever and ever an
infinite number of evenings, and cheer and reassure the latest
child that walked there, it was more glorious still.

The sun sets on some retired meadow, where no house is
visible, with all the glory and splendor that it lavishes on
cities, and, perchance, as it has never set before,—where there
is but a solitary marsh-hawk to have his wings gilded by it, or
only a musquash looks out from his cabin, and there is some
little black-veined brook in the midst of the marsh, just be-
ginning to meander, winding slowly round a decaying stump.
We walked in so pure and bright a light, gilding the withered
grass and leaves, so softly and serenely bright, I thought I had
never bathed in such a golden flood, without a ripple or a
murmur to it. The west side of every wood and rising ground
gleamed like the boundary of Elysium, and the sun on our
backs seemed like a gentle herdsman driving us home at
evening.

So we saunter toward the Holy Land, till one day the sun
shall shine more brightly than ever he has done, shall per-
chance shine into our minds and hearts, and light up our
whole lives with a great awakening light, as warm and serene
and golden as on a bank-side in autumn.

A Yankee in Canada

"New England is by some affirmed to be an island, bounded on the north with the River Canada (so called from Monsieur Cane)."
—JOSSELYN'S RARETIES.

And still older, in Thomas Morton's "New English Canaan," published in 1632, it is said, on page 97, "From this Lake [Erocoise] Northwards is derived the famous River of Canada, so named, of Monsier de Cane, a French Lord, who first planted a Colony of French in America."

CHAPTER I.
CONCORD TO MONTREAL.

I FEAR that I have not got much to say about Canada, not having seen much; what I got by going to Canada was a cold. I left Concord, Massachusetts, Wednesday morning, September 25th, 1850, for Quebec. Fare, seven dollars there and back; distance from Boston, five hundred and ten miles; being obliged to leave Montreal on the return as soon as Friday, October 4th, or within ten days. I will not stop to tell the reader the names of my fellow-travellers; there were said to be fifteen hundred of them. I wished only to be set down in Canada, and take one honest walk there as I might in Concord woods of an afternoon.

The country was new to me beyond Fitchburg. In Ashburnham and afterward, as we were whirled rapidly along, I noticed the woodbine (*Ampelopsis quinquefolia*), its leaves now changed, for the most part on dead trees, draping them like a red scarf. It was a little exciting, suggesting bloodshed, or at least a military life, like an epaulet or sash, as if it were dyed with the blood of the trees whose wounds it was inadequate to stanch. For now the bloody autumn was come, and an Indian warfare was waged through the forest. These military trees appeared very numerous, for our rapid progress connected those that were even some miles apart. Does the woodbine prefer the elm? The first view of Monadnoc was obtained five or six miles this side of

Fitzwilliam, but nearest and best at Troy and beyond. Then there were the Troy cuts and embankments. Keene Street strikes the traveller favorably, it is so wide, level, straight, and long. I have heard one of my relatives, who was born and bred there, say that you could see a chicken run across it a mile off. I have also been told that when this town was settled they laid out a street four rods wide, but at a subsequent meeting of the proprietors one rose and remarked, "We have plenty of land, why not make the street eight rods wide?" and so they voted that it should be eight rods wide, and the town is known far and near for its handsome street. It was a cheap way of securing comfort, as well as fame, and I wish that all new towns would take pattern from this. It is best to lay our plans widely in youth, for then land is cheap, and it is but too easy to contract our views afterward. Youths so laid out, with broad avenues and parks, that they may make handsome and liberal old men! Show me a youth whose mind is like some Washington city of magnificent distances, prepared for the most remotely successful and glorious life after all, when those spaces shall be built over and the idea of the founder be realized. I trust that every New England boy will begin by laying out a Keene Street through his head, eight rods wide. I know one such Washington city of a man, whose lots as yet are only surveyed and staked out, and except a cluster of shanties here and there, only the Capitol stands there for all structures, and any day you may see from afar his princely idea borne coachwise along the spacious but yet empty avenues. Keene is built on a remarkably large and level interval, like the bed of a lake, and the surrounding hills, which are remote from its street, must afford some good walks. The scenery of mountain towns is commonly too much crowded. A town which is built on a plain of some extent, with an open horizon, and surrounded by hills at a distance, affords the best walks and views.

As we travel northwest up the country, sugar-maples, beeches, birches, hemlocks, spruce, butternuts, and ash trees prevail more and more. To the rapid traveller the number of elms in a town is the measure of its civility. One man in the cars has a bottle full of some liquor. The whole company smile whenever it is exhibited. I find no difficulty in con-

taining myself. The Westmoreland country looked attractive.
I heard a passenger giving the very obvious derivation of this
name, West-more-land, as if it were purely American, and he
had made a discovery; but I thought of "my cousin West-
moreland" in England. Every one will remember the ap-
proach to Bellows Falls, under a high cliff which rises from
the Connecticut. I was disappointed in the size of the river
here; it appeared shrunk to a mere mountain stream. The wa-
ter was evidently very low. The rivers which we had crossed
this forenoon possessed more of the character of mountain
streams than those in the vicinity of Concord, and I was sur-
prised to see everywhere traces of recent freshets, which had
carried away bridges and injured the railroad, though I had
heard nothing of it. In Ludlow, Mount Holly, and beyond,
there is interesting mountain scenery, not rugged and stupen-
dous, but such as you could easily ramble over,—long narrow
mountain vales through which to see the horizon. You are in
the midst of the Green Mountains. A few more elevated blue
peaks are seen from the neighborhood of Mount Holly, per-
haps Killington Peak is one. Sometimes, as on the Western
Railroad, you are whirled over mountainous embankments,
from which the scared horses in the valleys appear diminished
to hounds. All the hills blush; I think that autumn must be
the best season to journey over even the *Green* Mountains.
You frequently exclaim to yourself, what *red* maples! The
sugar-maple is not so red. You see some of the latter with rosy
spots or cheeks only, blushing on one side like fruit, while all
the rest of the tree is green, proving either some partiality in
the light or frosts, or some prematurity in particular branches.
Tall and slender ash-trees, whose foliage is turned to a dark
mulberry color, are frequent. The butternut, which is a re-
markably spreading tree, is turned completely yellow, thus
proving its relation to the hickories. I was also struck by the
bright yellow tints of the yellow-birch. The sugar-maple is re-
markable for its clean ankle. The groves of these trees looked
like vast forest sheds, their branches stopping short at a uni-
form height, four or five feet from the ground, like eaves, as
if they had been trimmed by art, so that you could look
under and through the whole grove with its leafy canopy, as
under a tent whose curtain is raised.

As you approach Lake Champlain you begin to see the New York mountains. The first view of the Lake at Vergennes is impressive, but rather from association than from any peculiarity in the scenery. It lies there so small (not appearing in that proportion to the width of the State that it does on the map), but beautifully quiet, like a picture of the Lake of Lucerne on a music-box, where you trace the name of Lucerne among the foliage; far more ideal than ever it looked on the map. It does not say, "Here I am, Lake Champlain," as the conductor might for it, but having studied the geography thirty years, you crossed over a hill one afternoon and beheld it. But it is only a glimpse that you get here. At Burlington you rush to a wharf and go on board a steamboat, two hundred and thirty-two miles from Boston. We left Concord at twenty minutes before eight in the morning, and were in Burlington about six at night, but too late to see the lake. We got our first fair view of the lake at dawn, just before reaching Plattsburg, and saw blue ranges of mountains on either hand, in New York and in Vermont, the former especially grand. A few white schooners, like gulls, were seen in the distance, for it is not waste and solitary like a lake in Tartary; but it was such a view as leaves not much to be said; indeed, I have postponed Lake Champlain to another day.

The oldest reference to these waters that I have yet seen is in the account of Cartier's discovery and exploration of the St. Lawrence in 1535. Samuel Champlain actually discovered and paddled up the Lake in July, 1609, eleven years before the settlement of Plymouth, accompanying a war-party of the Canadian Indians against the Iroquois. He describes the islands in it as not inhabited, although they are pleasant,—on account of the continual wars of the Indians, in consequence of which they withdraw from the rivers and lakes into the depths of the land, that they may not be surprised. "Continuing our course," says he, "in this lake, on the western side, viewing the country, I saw on the eastern side very high mountains, where there was snow on the summit. I inquired of the savages if those places were inhabited. They replied that they were, and that they were Iroquois, and that in those places there were beautiful valleys and plains fertile in corn, such as I have eaten in this country, with an infinity of other fruits." This is the earliest account of what is now Vermont.

The number of French Canadian gentlemen and ladies among the passengers, and the sound of the French language, advertised us by this time that we were being whirled towards some foreign vortex. And now we have left Rouse's Point, and entered the Sorel River, and passed the invisible barrier between the States and Canada. The shores of the Sorel, Richelieu, or St. John's River, are flat and reedy, where I had expected something more rough and mountainous for a natural boundary between two nations. Yet I saw a difference at once, in the few huts, in the pirogues on the shore, and as it were, in the shore itself. This was an interesting scenery to me, and the very reeds or rushes in the shallow water, and the tree-tops in the swamps, have left a pleasing impression. We had still a distant view behind us of two or three blue mountains in Vermont and New York. About nine o'clock in the forenoon we reached St. John's, an old frontier post three hundred and six miles from Boston and twenty-four from Montreal. We now discovered that we were in a foreign country, in a station-house of another nation. This building was a barn-like structure, looking as if it were the work of the villagers combined, like a log-house in a new settlement. My attention was caught by the double advertisements in French and English fastened to its posts, by the formality of the English, and the covert or open reference to their queen and the British lion. No gentlemanly conductor appeared, none whom you would know to be the conductor by his dress and demeanor; but erelong we began to see here and there a solid, red-faced, burly-looking Englishman, a little pursy perhaps, who made us ashamed of ourselves and our thin and nervous countrymen,—a grandfatherly personage, at home in his great-coat, who looked as if he might be a stage proprietor, certainly a railroad director, and knew, or had a right to know, when the cars did start. Then there were two or three pale-faced, black-eyed, loquacious Canadian French gentlemen there, shrugging their shoulders; pitted as if they had all had the small-pox. In the mean while some soldiers, red-coats, belonging to the barracks near by, were turned out to be drilled. At every important point in our route the soldiers showed themselves ready for us; though they were evidently rather raw recruits here, they manœuvred far better than our soldiers; yet, as usual, I heard some Yankees talk as if they were no great shakes, and they had seen the Acton Blues manœuvre as well. The officers spoke sharply to them, and appeared to be doing their part thoroughly. I heard one suddenly coming to the rear, exclaim, "Michael Donouy, take his name!" though I could not see what the latter did or omitted to do. It was whispered that Michael Donouy would have to suffer for that. I heard some of our party discussing the possibility of their driving these troops off the field with their umbrellas. I thought that the Yankee, though undisciplined, had this advantage at least, that he especially is a man who, everywhere and under all circumstances, is fully resolved to better his condition essentially, and therefore he could afford to be beaten at first; while the virtue of the Irishman, and to a great extent the Englishman, consists in merely maintaining his ground or condition. The Canadians here, a rather poor-looking race, clad in gray homespun, which gave them the appearance of being covered with dust, were riding about in caleches and small one-horse carts called charettes. The Yankees assumed that all the riders were racing, or at least exhibiting the paces of their horses, and saluted them accordingly. We saw but little of the village here, for nobody could tell us when the cars would start; that was kept a profound secret, perhaps for political reasons; and therefore we were tied to our seats. The inhabitants of St. John's and vicinity are described by an English traveller as "singularly unprepossessing," and before completing his period he adds, "besides, they are generally very much disaffected to the British crown." I suspect that that "besides" should have been a because.

At length, about noon, the cars began to roll towards La Prairie. The whole distance of fifteen miles was over a remarkably level country, resembling a Western prairie, with the mountains about Chambly visible in the northeast. This novel, but monotonous scenery, was exciting. At La Prairie we first took notice of the tinned roofs, but above all of the St. Lawrence, which looked like a lake; in fact it is considerably expanded here; it was nine miles across diagonally to

Montreal. Mount Royal in the rear of the city, and the island of St. Helen's opposite to it, were now conspicuous. We could also see the Sault St. Louis about five miles up the river, and the Sault Norman still farther eastward. The former are described as the most considerable rapids in the St. Lawrence; but we could see merely a gleam of light there as from a cobweb in the sun. Soon the city of Montreal was discovered with its tin roofs shining afar. Their reflections fell on the eye like a clash of cymbals on the ear. Above all the church of Notre Dame was conspicuous, and anon the Bonsecours market-house, occupying a commanding position on the quay, in the rear of the shipping. This city makes the more favorable impression from being approached by water, and also being built of stone, a gray limestone found on the island. Here, after travelling directly inland the whole breadth of New England, we had struck upon a city's harbor,—it made on me the impression of a seaport,—to which ships of six hundred tons can ascend, and where vessels drawing fifteen feet lie close to the wharf, five hundred and forty miles from the Gulf; the St. Lawrence being here two miles wide. There was a great crowd assembled on the ferry-boat wharf and on the quay to receive the Yankees, and flags of all colors were streaming from the vessels to celebrate their arrival. When the gun was fired, the gentry hurrahed again and again, and then the Canadian caleche-drivers, who were most interested in the matter, and who, I perceived, were separated from the former by a fence, hurrahed their welcome; first the broadcloth, then the homespun.

It was early in the afternoon when we stepped ashore. With a single companion, I soon found my way to the church of Notre Dame. I saw that it was of great size and signified something. It is said to be the largest ecclesiastical structure in North America, and can seat ten thousand. It is two hundred and fifty-five and a half feet long, and the groined ceiling is eighty feet above your head. The Catholic are the only churches which I have seen worth remembering, which are not almost wholly profane. I do not speak only of the rich and splendid like this, but of the humblest of them as well. Coming from the hurrahing mob and the rattling carriages, we pushed aside the listed door of this church, and found ourselves instantly in an atmosphere which might be sacred to thought and religion, if one had any. There sat one or two women who had stolen a moment from the concerns of the day, as they were passing; but, if there had been fifty people there, it would still have been the most solitary place imaginable. They did not look up at us, nor did one regard another. We walked softly down the broad-aisle with our hats in our hands. Presently came in a troop of Canadians, in their homespun, who had come to the city in the boat with us, and one and all kneeled down in the aisle before the high altar to their devotions, somewhat awkwardly, as cattle prepare to lie down, and there we left them. As if you were to catch some farmer's sons from Marlboro, come to cattle-show, silently kneeling in Concord meeting-house some Wednesday! Would there not soon be a mob peeping in at the windows? It is true, these Roman Catholics, priests and all, impress me as a people who have fallen far behind the significance of their symbols. It is as if an ox had strayed into a church and were trying to bethink himself. Nevertheless, they are capable of reverence; but we Yankees are a people in whom this sentiment has nearly died out, and in this respect we cannot bethink ourselves even as oxen. I did not mind the pictures nor the candles, whether tallow or tin. Those of the former which I looked at appeared tawdry. It matters little to me whether the pictures are by a neophyte of the Algonquin or the Italian tribe. But I was impressed by the quiet religious atmosphere of the place. It was a great cave in the midst of a city; and what were the altars and the tinsel but the sparkling stalactics, into which you entered in a moment, and where the still atmosphere and the sombre light disposed to serious and profitable thought? Such a cave at hand, which you can enter any day, is worth a thousand of our churches which are open only Sundays,—hardly long enough for an airing,—and then filled with a bustling congregation,—a church where the priest is the least part, where you do your own preaching, where the universe preaches to you and can be heard. I am not sure but this Catholic religion would be an admirable one if the priest were quite omitted. I think that I might go to church myself sometimes some Monday, if I lived in a city where there was such a one to go to. In Concord, to be sure, we do not need such.

Our forests are such a church, far grander and more sacred.
We dare not leave *our* meeting-houses open for fear they
would be profaned. Such a cave, such a shrine, in one of our
groves, for instance, how long would it be respected? for what
purposes would it be entered, by such baboons as we are? I
think of its value not only to religion, but to philosophy and
to poetry; besides a reading-room, to have a thinking-room in
every city! Perchance the time will come when every house
even will have not only its sleeping-rooms, and dining-room,
and talking-room or parlor, but its thinking-room also, and
the architects will put it into their plans. Let it be furnished
and ornamented with whatever conduces to serious and cre-
ative thought. I should not object to the holy water, or any
other simple symbol, if it were consecrated by the imagination
of the worshippers.

I heard that some Yankees bet that the candles were not
wax, but tin. A European assured them that they were wax;
but, inquiring of the sexton, he was surprised to learn that
they were tin filled with oil. The church was too poor to af-
ford wax. As for the Protestant churches, here or elsewhere,
they did not interest me, for it is only as caves that churches
interest me at all, and in that respect they were inferior.

Montreal makes the impression of a larger city than you
had expected to find, though you may have heard that it con-
tains nearly sixty thousand inhabitants. In the newer parts it
appeared to be growing fast like a small New York, and to be
considerably Americanized. The names of the squares re-
minded you of Paris,—the Champ de Mars, the Place
d'Armes, and others, and you felt as if a French revolution
might break out any moment. Glimpses of Mount Royal ris-
ing behind the town, and the names of some streets in that
direction, make one think of Edinburgh. That hill sets off this
city wonderfully. I inquired at a principal bookstore for books
published in Montreal. They said that there were none but
school-books and the like; they got their books from the
States. From time to time we met a priest in the streets, for
they are distinguished by their dress, like the *civil* police. Like
clergymen generally, with or without the gown, they made on
us the impression of effeminacy. We also met some Sisters of
Charity, dressed in black, with Shaker-shaped black bonnets

and crosses, and cadaverous faces, who looked as if they had almost cried their eyes out, their complexions parboiled with scalding tears; insulting the daylight by their presence, having taken an oath not to smile. By cadaverous I mean that their faces were like the faces of those who have been dead and buried for a year, and then untombed, with the life's grief upon them, and yet, for some unaccountable reason, the process of decay arrested.

> "Truth never fails her servant, sir, nor leaves him
> With the day's shame upon him."

They waited demurely on the sidewalk while a truck laden with raisins was driven in at the seminary of St. Sulpice, never once lifting their eyes from the ground.

The soldier here, as everywhere in Canada, appeared to be put forward, and by his best foot. They were in the proportion of the soldiers to the laborers in an African ant-hill. The inhabitants evidently rely on them in a great measure for music and entertainment. You would meet with them pacing back and forth before some guard-house or passage-way, guarding, regarding, and disregarding all kinds of law by turns, apparently for the sake of the discipline to themselves, and not because it was important to exclude anybody from entering that way. They reminded me of the men who are paid for piling up bricks and then throwing them down again. On every prominent ledge you could see England's hands holding the Canadas, and I judged by the redness of her knuckles that she would soon have to let go. In the rear of such a guard-house, in a large gravelled square or parade-ground, called the Champ de Mars, we saw a large body of soldiers being drilled, we being as yet the only spectators. But they did not appear to notice us any more than the devotees in the church, but were seemingly as indifferent to fewness of spectators as the phenomena of nature are, whatever they might have been thinking under their helmets of the Yankees that were to come. Each man wore white kid gloves. It was one of the most interesting sights which I saw in Canada. The problem appeared to be how to smooth down all individual protuberances or idiosyncrasies, and make a thousand men move as one man, animated by one central will; and there was some approach to success. They obeyed the signals of a commander who stood at a great distance, wand in hand; and the precision, and promptness, and harmony of their movements could not easily have been matched. The harmony was far more remarkable than that of any choir or band, and obtained, no doubt, at a greater cost. They made on me the impression, not of many individuals, but of one vast centipede of a man, good for all sorts of pulling down; and why not then for some kinds of building up? If men could combine thus earnestly, and patiently, and harmoniously to some really worthy end, what might they not accomplish? They now put their hands, and partially perchance their heads, together, and the result is that they are the imperfect tools of an imperfect and tyrannical government. But if they could put their hands and heads and hearts and all together, such a co-operation and harmony would be the very end and success for which government now exists in vain,—a government, as it were, not only with tools, but stock to trade with.

I was obliged to frame some sentences that sounded like French in order to deal with the market-women, who, for the most part, cannot speak English. According to the guidebook the relative population of this city stands nearly thus: two fifths are French Canadian; nearly one fifth British Canadian; one and a half fifth English, Irish, and Scotch; somewhat less than one half fifth Germans, United States people, and others. I saw nothing like pie for sale, and no good cake to put in my bundle, such as you can easily find in our towns, but plenty of fair-looking apples, for which Montreal Island is celebrated, and also pears, cheaper, and I thought better than ours, and peaches, which, though they were probably brought from the South, were as cheap as they commonly are with us. So imperative is the law of demand and supply that, as I have been told, the market of Montreal is sometimes supplied with green apples from the State of New York some weeks even before they are ripe in the latter place. I saw here the spruce wax which the Canadians chew, done up in little silvered papers, a penny a roll; also a small and shrivelled fruit which they called *cerises* mixed with many little stems somewhat like raisins, but I soon returned what I had bought, finding them rather insipid, only putting a sample in my pocket. Since my return, I find on comparison that it is the fruit of the sweet viburnum (*Viburnum Lentago*), which with us rarely holds on till it is ripe.

I stood on the deck of the steamer John Munn, late in the afternoon, when the second and third ferry-boats arrived from La Prairie, bringing the remainder of the Yankees. I never saw so many caleches, cabs, charettes, and similar vehicles collected before, and doubt if New York could easily furnish more. The handsome and substantial stone quay, which stretches a mile along the river-side, and protects the street from the ice, was thronged with the citizens who had turned out on foot and in carriages to welcome or to behold the Yankees. It was interesting to see the caleche drivers dash up and down the slope of the quay with their active little horses. They drive much faster than in our cities. I have been told that some of them come nine miles into the city every morning and return every night, without changing their horses during the day. In the midst of the crowd of carts, I observed one deep one loaded with sheep with their legs tied together, and their bodies piled one upon another, as if the driver had forgotten that they were sheep and not yet mutton. A sight, I trust, peculiar to Canada, though I fear that it is not.

CHAPTER II.
QUEBEC AND MONTMORENCI.

About six o'clock we started for Quebec, one hundred and eighty miles distant by the river; gliding past Longueil and Boucherville on the right, and *Pointe aux Trembles*, "so called from having been originally covered with aspens," and *Bout de l'Isle*, or the end of the island, on the left. I repeat these names not merely for want of more substantial facts to record, but because they sounded singularly poetic to my ears. There certainly was no lie in them. They suggested that some simple, and, perchance, heroic human life might have transpired there. There is all the poetry in the world in a name. It is a poem which the mass of men hear and read. What is poetry in the common sense, but a string of such jingling names? I want nothing better than a good word. The name of a thing may easily be more than the thing itself to me. Inexpressibly beautiful appears the recognition by man of the least natural fact, and the allying his life to it. All the world reiterating this slender truth, that aspens once grew there; and the swift inference is, that men were there to see them. And so it would be with the names of our native and neighboring villages, if we had not profaned them.

The daylight now failed us, and we went below; but I endeavored to console myself for being obliged to make this voyage by night, by thinking that I did not lose a great deal, the shores being low and rather unattractive, and that the river itself was much the more interesting object. I heard something in the night about the boat being at William Henry, Three Rivers, and in the Richelieu Rapids, but I was still where I had been when I lost sight of *Pointe aux Trembles.* To hear a man who has been waked up at midnight in the cabin of a steamboat, inquiring, "Waiter, where are we now?" is, as if at any moment of the earth's revolution round the sun, or of the system round its centre, one were to raise himself up and inquire of one of the deck hands, "Where are we now?"

I went on deck at daybreak, when we were thirty or forty miles above Quebec. The banks were now higher and more interesting. There was an "uninterrupted succession of white-washed cottages" on each side of the river. This is what every traveller tells. But it is not to be taken as an evidence of the populousness of the country in general, hardly even of the river banks. They have presented a similar appearance for a hundred years. The Swedish traveller and naturalist, Kalm, who descended this river in 1749, says: "It could really be called a village, beginning at Montreal and ending at Quebec, which is a distance of more than one hundred and eighty miles; for the farm-houses are never above five arpens, and sometimes but three asunder, a few places excepted." Even in 1684 Hontan said that the houses were not more than a gun-shot apart at most. Erelong we passed Cape Rouge, eight miles above Quebec, the mouth of the Chaudière on the opposite or south side, New Liverpool Cove with its lumber rafts and some shipping; then Sillery and Wolfe's Cove and the Heights of Abraham on the north, with now a view of Cape Diamond, and the citadel in front. The approach to

Quebec was very imposing. It was about six o'clock in the morning when we arrived. There is but a single street under the cliff on the south side of the cape, which was made by blasting the rocks and filling up the river. Three-story houses did not rise more than one fifth or one sixth the way up the nearly perpendicular rock, whose summit is three hundred and forty-five feet above the water. We saw, as we glided past, the sign on the side of the precipice, part way up, pointing to the spot where Montgomery was killed in 1775. Formerly it was the custom for those who went to Quebec for the first time to be ducked, or else pay a fine. Not even the Governor General escaped. But we were too many to be ducked, even if the custom-had not been abolished.*

Here we were, in the harbor of Quebec, still three hundred and sixty miles from the mouth of the St. Lawrence, in a basin two miles across, where the greatest depth is twenty-eight fathoms, and though the water is fresh, the tide rises seventeen to twenty-four feet,—a harbor "large and deep enough," says a British traveller, "to hold the English navy." I may as well state that, in 1844, the county of Quebec contained about forty-five thousand inhabitants (the city and suburbs having about forty-three thousand); about twenty-eight thousand being Canadians of French origin; eight thousand British; over seven thousand natives of Ireland; one thousand five hundred natives of England; the rest Scotch and others. Thirty-six thousand belong to the Church of Rome.

Separating ourselves from the crowd, we walked up a narrow street, thence ascended by some wooden steps, called the Break-neck Stairs, into another steep, narrow, and zigzag street, blasted through the rock, which last led through a low massive stone portal, called Prescott Gate, the principal thoroughfare into the Upper Town. This passage was defended by cannon, with a guard-house over it, a sentinel at his post, and other soldiers at hand ready to relieve him. I rubbed my eyes

---

*Hierosme Lalemant says in 1648, in his relation, he being Superior: "All those who come to New France know well enough the mountain of Notre Dame, because the pilots and sailors, being arrived at that part of the Great River which is opposite to those high mountains, baptize ordinarily for sport the new passengers, if they do not turn aside by some present the inundation of this baptism which one makes flow plentifully on their heads."

to be sure that I was in the nineteenth century, and was not entering one of those portals which sometimes adorn the frontispieces of new editions of old black-letter volumes. I thought it would be a good place to read Froissart's Chronicles. It was such a reminiscence of the Middle Ages as Scott's novels. Men apparently dwelt there for security. Peace be unto them! As if the inhabitants of New York were to go over to Castle William to live! What a place it must be to bring up children! Being safe through the gate we naturally took the street which was steepest, and after a few turns found ourselves on the Durham Terrace, a wooden platform on the site of the old castle of St. Louis, still one hundred and fifteen feet below the summit of the citadel, overlooking the Lower Town, the wharf where we had landed, the harbor, the Isle of Orleans, and the river and surrounding country to a great distance. It was literally a *splendid* view. We could see six or seven miles distant, in the northeast, an indentation in the lofty shore of the northern channel, apparently on one side of the harbor, which marked the mouth of the Montmorenci, whose celebrated fall was only a few rods in the rear.

At a shoe-shop, whither we were directed for this purpose, we got some of our American money changed into English. I found that American hard money would have answered as well, excepting cents, which fell very fast before their pennies, it taking two of the former to make one of the latter, and often the penny, which had cost us two cents, did us the service of one cent only. Moreover, our robust cents were compelled to meet on even terms a crew of vile half-penny tokens, and bungtown coppers, which had more brass in their composition, and so perchance made their way in the world. Wishing to get into the citadel, we were directed to the Jesuits' Barracks,—a good part of the public buildings here are barracks,—to get a pass of the Town Major. We did not heed the sentries at the gate, nor did they us, and what under the sun they were placed there for, unless to hinder a free circulation of the air, was not apparent. There we saw soldiers eating their breakfasts in their mess-room, from bare wooden tables in camp fashion. We were continually meeting with soldiers in the streets, carrying funny little tin pails of all shapes, even semicircular, as if made to pack conveniently. I supposed that they contained their dinners,—so many slices of bread and butter to each, perchance. Sometimes they were carrying some kind of military chest on a sort of bier or hand-barrow, with a springy, undulating, military step, all passengers giving way to them, even the charette-drivers stopping for them to pass,—as if the battle were being lost from an inadequate supply of powder. There was a regiment of Highlanders, and, as I understood, of Royal Irish, in the city; and by this time there was a regiment of Yankees also. I had already observed, looking up even from the water, the head and shoulders of some General Poniatowsky, with an enormous cocked hat and gun, peering over the roof of a house, away up where the chimney caps commonly are with us, as it were a caricature of war and military awfulness; but I had not gone far up St. Louis Street before my riddle was solved, by the apparition of a real live Highlander under a cocked hat, and with his knees out, standing and marching sentinel on the ramparts, between St. Louis and St. John's Gate. (It must be a holy war that is waged there.) We stood close by without fear and looked at him. His legs were somewhat tanned, and the hair had begun to grow on them, as some of our wise men predict that it will in such cases, but I did not think they were remarkable in any respect. Notwithstanding all his warlike gear, when I inquired of him the way to the Plains of Abraham, he could not answer me without betraying some bashfulness through his broad Scotch. Soon after, we passed another of these creatures standing sentry at the St. Louis Gate, who let us go by without shooting us, or even demanding the countersign. We then began to go through the gate, which was so thick and tunnel-like, as to remind me of those lines in Claudian's Old Man of Verona, about the getting out of the gate being the greater part of a journey;—as you might imagine yourself crawling through an architectural vignette *at the end* of a black-letter volume. We were then reminded that we had been in a fortress, from which we emerged by numerous zigzags in a ditch-like road, going a considerable distance to advance a few rods, where they could have shot us two or three times over, if their minds had been disposed as their guns were. The greatest, or rather the most prominent, part of this city was constructed with the design to offer the deadest resistance to leaden and iron missiles that might be cast against it. But it is a remarkable meteorological and psychological fact, that it is rarely known to rain lead with much violence, except on places so constructed. Keeping on about a mile we came to the Plains of Abraham,—for having got through with the Saints, we come next to the Patriarchs. Here the Highland regiment was being reviewed, while the band stood on one side and played,—methinks it was *La Claire Fontaine*, the national air of the Canadian French. This is the site where a real battle once took place, to commemorate which they have had a sham fight here almost every day since. The Highlanders manœuvred very well, and if the precision of their movements was less remarkable, they did not appear so stiffly erect as the English or Royal Irish, but had a more elastic and graceful gait, like a herd of their own red deer, or as if accustomed to stepping down the sides of mountains. But they made a sad impression on the whole, for it was obvious that all true manhood was in the process of being drilled out of them. I have no doubt that soldiers well drilled are, as a class, peculiarly destitute of originality and independence. The officers appeared like men dressed above their condition. It is impossible to give the soldier a good education, without making him a deserter. His natural foe is the government that drills him. What would any philanthropist, who felt an interest in these men's welfare, naturally do, but first of all teach them so to respect themselves, that they could not be hired for this work, whatever might be the consequences to this government or that;—not drill a few, but educate all. I observed one older man among them, gray as a wharf-rat, and supple as the Devil, marching lock-step with the rest who would have to pay for that elastic gait.

We returned to the citadel along the heights, plucking such flowers as grew there. There was an abundance of succory still in blossom, broad-leaved golden-rod, buttercups, thornbushes, Canada thistles, and ivy, on the very summit of Cape Diamond. I also found the bladder-campion in the neighborhood. We there enjoyed an extensive view, which I will describe in another place. Our pass, which stated that all the rules were "to be strictly enforced," as if they were determined to keep up the semblance of reality to the last gasp, opened to us the Dalhousie Gate, and we were conducted over the citadel by a bare-legged Highlander in cocked hat and full regimentals. He told us that he had been here about three years, and had formerly been stationed at Gibraltar. As if his regiment, having perchance been nestled amid the rocks of Edinburgh Castle, must flit from rock to rock thenceforth over the earth's surface, like a bald eagle, or other bird of prey, from eyrie to eyrie. As we were going out, we met the Yankees coming in, in a body, headed by a red-coated officer called the commandant, and escorted by many citizens, both English and French Canadian. I therefore immediately fell into the procession, and went round the citadel again with more intelligent guides, carrying, as before, all my effects with me. Seeing that nobody walked with the red-coated commandant, I attached myself to him, and though I was not what is called well-dressed, he did not know whether to repel me or not, for I talked like one who was not aware of any deficiency in that respect. Probably there was not one among all the Yankees who went to Canada this time, who was not more splendidly dressed than I was. It would have been a poor story if I had not enjoyed some distinction. I had on my "bad-weather clothes," like Olaf Trygesson the Northman, when he went to the Thing in England, where, by the way, he won his bride. As we stood by the thirty-two-pounder on the summit of Cape Diamond, which is fired three times a day, the commandant told me that it would carry to the Isle of Orleans, four miles distant, and that no hostile vessel could come round the island. I now saw the subterranean or, rather, "casemated barracks" of the soldiers, which I had not noticed before, though I might have walked over them. They had very narrow windows, serving as loop-holes for musketry, and small iron chimneys rising above the ground. There we saw the soldiers at home and in an undress, splitting wood,—I looked to see whether with swords or axes,—and in various ways endeavoring to realize that their nation was now at peace with this part of the world. A part of each regiment, chiefly officers, are allowed to marry. A grandfatherly, would-be witty Englishman could give a Yankee whom he was patronizing no reason for the bare knees of the Highlanders, other than oddity. The rock within the citadel is a little convex, so that shells falling on it would roll toward the circumference, where the barracks of the soldiers and officers are; it has been proposed, therefore, to make it slightly concave, so that they may roll into the centre, where they would be comparatively harmless; and it is estimated that to do this would cost twenty thousand pounds sterling. It may be well to remember this when I build my next house, and have the roof "all correct" for bombshells.

At mid-afternoon we made haste down *Sault-au-Matelot* street, towards the Falls of Montmorenci, about eight miles down the St. Lawrence, on the north side, leaving the further examination of Quebec till our return. On our way, we saw men in the streets sawing logs pit-fashion, and afterward, with a common wood-saw and horse, cutting the planks into squares for paving the streets. This looked very shiftless, especially in a country abounding in water-power, and reminded me that I was no longer in Yankee land. I found, on inquiry, that the excuse for this was, that labor was so cheap; and I thought, with some pain, how cheap men are here! I have since learned that the English traveller, Warburton, remarked, soon after landing at Quebec, that everything was cheap there but men. That must be the difference between going thither from New and from Old England. I had already observed the dogs harnessed to their little milk-carts, which contain a single large can, lying asleep in the gutters regardless of the horses, while they rested from their labors, at different stages of the ascent in the Upper Town. I was surprised at the regular and extensive use made of these animals for drawing, not only milk, but groceries, wood, &c. It reminded me that the dog commonly is not put to any use. Cats catch mice; but dogs only worry the cats. Kalm, a hundred years ago, saw sledges here for ladies to ride in, drawn by a pair of dogs. He says, "A middle-sized dog is sufficient to draw a single person, when the roads are good"; and he was told by old people, that horses were very scarce in their youth, and almost all the land-carriage was then effected by dogs. They made me think of the Esquimaux, who, in fact, are the next people on the north. Charlevoix says, that the first horses were introduced in 1665.

We crossed Dorchester Bridge, over the St. Charles, the little river in which Cartier, the discoverer of the St. Lawrence, put his ships, and spent the winter of 1535, and found ourselves on an excellent macadamized road, called *Le Chemin de Beauport*. We had left Concord Wednesday morning, and we endeavored to realize that now, Friday morning, we were taking a walk in Canada, in the Seigniory of Beauport, a foreign country, which a few days before had seemed almost as far off as England and France. Instead of rambling to Flint's Pond or the Sudbury Meadows, we found ourselves, after being a little detained in cars and steamboats,—after spending half a night at Burlington, and half a day at Montreal,—taking a walk down the bank of the St. Lawrence to the Falls of Montmorenci and elsewhere. Well, I thought to myself, here I am in a foreign country; let me have my eyes about me, and take it all in. It already looked and felt a good deal colder than it had in New England, as we might have expected it would. I realized fully that I was four degrees nearer the pole, and shuddered at the thought; and I wondered if it were possible that the peaches might not be all gone when I returned. It was an atmosphere that made me think of the fur-trade, which is so interesting a department in Canada, for I had for all head-covering a thin palm-leaf hat without lining, that cost twenty-five cents, and over my coat one of those unspeakably cheap, as well as thin, brown linen sacks of the Oak Hall pattern, which every summer appear all over New England, thick as the leaves upon the trees. It was a thoroughly Yankee costume, which some of my fellow-travellers wore in the cars to save their coats a dusting. I wore mine, at first, because it looked better than the coat it covered, and last, because two coats were warmer than one, though one was thin and dirty. I never wear my best coat on a journey, though perchance I could show a certificate to prove that I have a more costly one, at least, at home, if that were all that a gentleman required. It is not wise for a traveller to go dressed. I should no more think of it than of putting on a clean dicky and blacking my shoes to go a-fishing; as if you were going out to dine, when, in fact, the genuine traveller is going out to work hard, and fare harder,—to eat a crust by the wayside whenever he can get it. Honest travelling is about as dirty work as you can do, and a man needs a pair of overalls for it. As for blacking my shoes in such a case, I should as soon think of blacking my face. I carry a piece of tallow to preserve the leather, and keep out the water; that's all; and many an officious shoe-black, who carried off my shoes when I was slumbering, mistaking me for a gentleman, has had occasion to repent it before he produced a gloss on them.

My pack, in fact, was soon made, for I keep a short list of those articles which, from frequent experience, I have found indispensable to the foot-traveller; and, when I am about to start, I have only to consult that, to be sure that nothing is omitted, and, what is more important, nothing superfluous inserted. Most of my fellow-travellers carried carpet-bags, or valises. Sometimes one had two or three ponderous yellow valises in his clutch, at each hitch of the cars, as if we were going to have another rush for seats; and when there was a rush in earnest, and there were not a few, I would see my man in the crowd, with two or three affectionate lusty fellows along each side of his arm, between his shoulder and his valises, which last held them tight to his back, like the nut on the end of a screw. I could not help asking in my mind, What so great cause for showing Canada to those valises, when perhaps your very nieces had to stay at home for want of an escort? I should have liked to be present when the custom-house officer came aboard of him, and asked him to declare upon his honor if he had anything but wearing apparel in them. Even the elephant carries but a small trunk on his journeys. The perfection of travelling is to travel without baggage. After considerable reflection and experience, I have concluded that the best bag for the foot-traveller is made with a handkerchief, or, if he study appearances, a piece of stiff brown paper, well tied up, with a fresh piece within to put outside when the first is torn. That is good for both town and country, and none will know but you are carrying home the silk for a new gown for your wife, when it may be a dirty shirt. A bundle which you can carry literally under your arm, and which will shrink and swell with its contents. I never found the carpet-bag of equal capacity, which was not a bundle of itself. We styled ourselves the Knights of the Umbrella and the Bundle; for wherever we went, whether to Notre Dame or Mount

Royal, or the Champ-de-Mars, to the Town Major's or the Bishop's Palace, to the Citadel, with a bare-legged Highlander for our escort, or to the Plains of Abraham, to dinner or to bed, the umbrella and the bundle went with us; for we wished to be ready to digress at any moment. We made it our home nowhere in particular, but everywhere where our umbrella and bundle were. It would have been an amusing circumstance, if the Mayor of one of those cities had politely asked us where we were staying. We could only have answered, that we were staying with his Honor for the time being. I was amused when, after our return, some green ones inquired if we found it easy to get accommodated; as if we went abroad to get accommodated, when we can get that at home.

We met with many charettes, bringing wood and stone to the city. The most ordinary looking horses travelled faster than ours, or, perhaps they were ordinary looking, because, as I am told, the Canadians do not use the curry-comb. Moreover, it is said, that on the approach of winter their horses acquire an increased quantity of hair, to protect them from the cold. If this be true, some of our horses would make you think winter were approaching, even in midsummer. We soon began to see women and girls at work in the fields, digging potatoes alone, or bundling up the grain which the men cut. They appeared in rude health, with a great deal of color in their cheeks, and, if their occupation had made them coarse, it impressed me as better in its effects than making shirts at fourpence apiece, or doing nothing at all; unless it be chewing slate pencils, with still smaller results. They were much more agreeable objects, with their great broad-brimmed hats and flowing dresses, than the men and boys. We afterwards saw them doing various other kinds of work; indeed, I thought that we saw more women at work out of doors than men. On our return, we observed in this town a girl with Indian boots, nearly two feet high, taking the harness off a dog. The purity and transparency of the atmosphere were wonderful. When we had been walking an hour, we were surprised, on turning round, to see how near the city, with its glittering tin roofs, still looked. A village ten miles off did not appear to be more than three or four. I was convinced that you could see objects distinctly there much farther than here. It is true the villages are of a dazzling white, but the dazzle is to be referred, perhaps, to the transparency of the atmosphere as much as to the whitewash.

We were now fairly in the village of Beauport, though there was still but one road. The houses stood close upon this, without any front-yards, and at any angle with it, as if they had dropped down, being set with more reference to the road which the sun travels. It being about sundown, and the Falls not far off, we began to look round for a lodging, for we preferred to put up at a private house, that we might see more of the inhabitants. We inquired first at the most promising looking houses, if, indeed, any were promising. When we knocked, they shouted some French word for come in, perhaps *entrez*, and we asked for a lodging in English; but we found, unexpectedly, that they spoke French only. Then we went along and tried another house, being generally saluted by a rush of two or three little curs, which readily distinguished a foreigner, and which we were prepared now to hear bark in French. Our first question would be, *Parlez-vous Anglais?* but the invariable answer was, *Non, monsieur*; and we soon found that the inhabitants were exclusively French Canadians, and nobody spoke English at all, any more than in France; that, in fact, we were in a foreign country, where the inhabitants uttered not one familiar sound to us. Then we tried by turns to talk French with them, in which we succeeded sometimes pretty well, but for the most part, pretty ill. *Pouvez-vous nous donner un lit cette nuit?* we would ask, and then they would answer with French volubility, so that we could catch only a word here and there. We could understand the women and children generally better than the men, and they us; and thus, after a while, we would learn that they had no more beds than they used.

So we were compelled to inquire: *Y a-t-il une maison publique ici?* (*auberge* we should have said, perhaps, for they seemed never to have heard of the other), and they answered at length that there was no tavern, unless we could get lodgings at the mill, *le moulin*, which we had passed; or they would direct us to a grocery, and almost every house had a small grocery at one end of it. We called on the public notary or village lawyer, but he had no more beds nor English than the rest. At one house there was so good a misunderstanding at once established through the politeness of all parties, that we were encouraged to walk in and sit down, and ask for a glass of water; and having drank their water, we thought it was as good as to have tasted their salt. When our host and his wife spoke of their poor accommodations, meaning for themselves, we assured them that they were good enough, for we thought that they were only apologizing for the poorness of the accommodations they were about to offer us, and we did not discover our mistake till they took us up a ladder into a loft, and showed to our eyes what they had been laboring in vain to communicate to our brains through our ears, that they had but that one apartment with its few beds for the whole family. We made our *a-dieus* forthwith, and with gravity, perceiving the literal signification of that word. We were finally taken in at a sort of public-house, whose master worked for Patterson, the proprietor of the extensive sawmills driven by a portion of the Montmorenci stolen from the fall, whose roar we now heard. We here talked, or murdered French all the evening, with the master of the house and his family, and probably had a more amusing time than if we had completely understood one another. At length they showed us to a bed in their best chamber, very high to get into, with a low wooden rail to it. It had no cotton sheets, but coarse, home-made, dark colored, linen ones. Afterward, we had to do with sheets still coarser than these, and nearly the color of our blankets. There was a large open buffet loaded with crockery, in one corner of the room, as if to display their wealth to travellers, and pictures of Scripture scenes, French, Italian, and Spanish, hung around. Our hostess came back directly to inquire if we would have brandy for breakfast. The next morning, when I asked their names, she took down the temperance pledges of herself and husband, and children, which were hanging against the wall. They were Jean Baptiste Binet, and his wife, Geneviève Binet. Jean Baptiste is the sobriquet of the French Canadians.

After breakfast we proceeded to the fall, which was within half a mile, and at this distance its rustling sound, like the wind among the leaves, filled all the air. We were disappointed to find that we were in some measure shut out from the west side of the fall by the private grounds and fences of Patterson, who appropriates not only a part of the water for his mill, but a still larger part of the prospect, so that we were obliged to trespass. This gentleman's mansion-house and grounds were formerly occupied by the Duke of Kent, father to Queen Victoria. It appeared to me in bad taste for an individual, though he were the father of Queen Victoria, to obtrude himself with his land titles, or at least his fences, on so remarkable a natural phenomenon, which should, in every sense, belong to mankind. Some falls should even be kept sacred from the intrusion of mills and factories, as water privileges in another than the millwright's sense. This small river falls perpendicularly nearly two hundred and fifty feet at one pitch. The St. Lawrence falls only one hundred and sixty-four feet at Niagara. It is a very simple and noble fall, and leaves nothing to be desired; but the most that I could say of it would only have the force of one other testimony to assure the reader that it is there. We looked directly down on it from the point of a projecting rock, and saw far below us, on a low promontory, the grass kept fresh and green by the perpetual drizzle, looking like moss. The rock is a kind of slate, in the crevices of which grew ferns and golden-rods. The prevailing trees on the shores were spruce and arbor-vitæ,—the latter very large and now full of fruit,—also aspens, alders, and the mountain-ash with its berries. Every emigrant who arrives in this country by way of the St. Lawrence, as he opens a point of the Isle of Orleans, sees the Montmorenci tumbling into the Great River thus magnificently in a vast white sheet, making its contribution with emphasis. Roberval's pilot, Jean Alphonse, saw this fall thus, and described it, in 1542. It is a splendid introduction to the scenery of Quebec. Instead of an artificial fountain in its square, Quebec has this magnificent natural waterfall to adorn one side of its harbor. Within the mouth of the chasm below, which can be entered only at ebb tide, we had a grand view at once of Quebec and of the fall. Kalm says that the noise of the fall is sometimes heard at Quebec, about eight miles distant, and is a sign of a northeast wind. The side of this chasm, of soft and crumbling slate too steep to climb, was among the memorable features of the scene. In the winter of 1829 the frozen spray of the fall, descending on the ice of the St. Lawrence, made a hill one hundred and twenty-six feet high. It is an annual phenomenon which some think may help explain the formation of glaciers.

In the vicinity of the fall we began to notice what looked like our red-fruited thorn bushes, grown to the size of ordinary apple-trees, very common, and full of large red or yellow fruit, which the inhabitants called *pommettes*, but I did not learn that they were put to any use.

CHAPTER III.
ST. ANNE.

By the middle of the forenoon, though it was a rainy day, we were once more on our way down the north bank of the St. Lawrence, in a northeasterly direction, toward the Falls of St. Anne, which are about thirty miles from Quebec. The settled, more level, and fertile portion of Canada East may be described rudely as a triangle, with its apex slanting toward the northeast, about one hundred miles wide at its base, and from two to three, or even four hundred miles long, if you reckon its narrow northeastern extremity; it being the immediate valley of the St. Lawrence and its tributaries, rising by a single or by successive terraces toward the mountains on either hand. Though the words Canada East on the map stretch over many rivers and lakes and unexplored wildernesses, the actual Canada, which might be the colored portion of the map, is but a little clearing on the banks of the river, which one of those syllables would more than cover. The banks of the St. Lawrence are rather low from Montreal to the Richelieu Rapids, about forty miles above Quebec. Thence they rise gradually to Cape Diamond, or Quebec. Where we now were, eight miles northeast of Quebec, the mountains which form the northern side of this triangle were only five or six miles distant from the river, gradually departing farther and farther from it, on the west, till they reach the Ottawa, and making haste to meet it on the east, at Cape Tourmente, now in plain sight about twenty miles distant. So that we were travelling in a very narrow and sharp triangle between the mountains and the river, tilted up toward

the mountains on the north, never losing sight of our great
fellow-traveller on our right. According to Bouchette's
Topographical Description of the Canadas, we were in the
Seigniory of the Côte de Beaupré, in the county of Mont-
morenci, and the district of Quebec; in that part of Canada
which was the first to be settled, and where the face of the
country and the population have undergone the least change
from the beginning, where the influence of the States and of
Europe is least felt, and the inhabitants see little or nothing of
the world over the walls of Quebec. This Seigniory was
granted in 1636, and is now the property of the Seminary of
Quebec. It is the most mountainous one in the province.
There are some half a dozen parishes in it, each containing a
church, parsonage-house, grist-mill, and several saw-mills. We
were now in the most westerly parish called Ange Gardien, or
the Guardian Angel, which is bounded on the west by the
Montmorenci. The north bank of the St. Lawrence here is
formed on a grand scale. It slopes gently, either directly from
the shore, or from the edge of an interval, till, at the distance
of about a mile, it attains the height of four or five hundred
feet. The single road runs along the side of the slope two or
three hundred feet above the river at first, and from a quarter
of a mile to a mile distant from it, and affords fine views of
the north channel, which is about a mile wide, and of the
beautiful Isle of Orleans, about twenty miles long by five
wide, where grow the best apples and plums in the Quebec
District.

Though there was but this single road, it was a continuous
village for as far as we walked this day and the next, or about
thirty miles down the river, the houses being as near together
all the way as in the middle of one of our smallest straggling
country villages, and we could never tell by their number
when we were on the skirts of a parish, for the road never ran
through the fields or woods. We were told that it was just six
miles from one parish church to another. I thought that we
saw every house in Ange Gardien. Therefore, as it was a
muddy day, we never got out of the mud, nor out of the vil-
lage, unless we got over the fence; then indeed, if it was on
the north side, we were out of the civilized world. There were
sometimes a few more houses near the church, it is true, but

we had only to go a quarter of a mile from the road to the top of the bank to find ourselves on the verge of the uninhabited, and, for the most part, unexplored wilderness stretching toward Hudson's Bay. The farms accordingly were extremely long and narrow, each having a frontage on the river. Bouchette accounts for this peculiar manner of laying out a village by referring to "the social character of the Canadian peasant, who is singularly fond of neighborhood," also to the advantage arising from a concentration of strength in Indian times. Each farm, called *terre*, he says, is, in nine cases out of ten, three arpents wide by thirty deep, that is, very nearly thirty-five by three hundred and forty-nine of our rods; sometimes one half arpent by thirty, or one to sixty; sometimes, in fact, a few yards by half a mile. Of course it costs more for fences. A remarkable difference between the Canadian and the New England character appears from the fact that in 1745, the French government were obliged to pass a law forbidding the farmers or *censitaires* building on land less than one and a half arpents front by thirty or forty deep, under a certain penalty, in order to compel emigration, and bring the seigneur's estates all under cultivation; and it is thought that they have now less reluctance to leave the paternal roof than formerly, "removing beyond the sight of the parish spire, or the sound of the parish bell." But I find that in the previous or seventeenth century, the complaint, often renewed, was of a totally opposite character, namely, that the inhabitants dispersed and exposed themselves to the Iroquois. Accordingly, about 1664, the king was obliged to order that "they should make no more clearings except one next to another, and that they should reduce their parishes to the form of the parishes in France as much as possible." The Canadians of those days, at least, possessed a roving spirit of adventure which carried them further, in exposure to hardship and danger, than ever the New England colonist went, and led them, though not to clear and colonize the wilderness, yet to range over it as *coureurs de bois*, or runners of the woods, or as Hontan prefers to call them *coureurs de risques*, runners of risks; to say nothing of their enterprising priesthood; and Charlevoix thinks that if the authorities had taken the right steps to prevent the youth from ranging the woods (*de courir les bois*) they would have had an excellent militia to fight the Indians and English.

The road, in this clayey looking soil, was exceedingly muddy in consequence of the night's rain. We met an old woman directing her dog, which was harnessed to a little cart, to the least muddy part of it. It was a beggarly sight. But harnessed to the cart as he was, we heard him barking after we had passed, though we looked anywhere but to the cart to see where the dog was that barked. The houses commonly fronted the south, whatever angle they might make with the road; and frequently they had no door nor cheerful window on the roadside. Half the time they stood fifteen to forty rods from the road, and there was no very obvious passage to them, so that you would suppose that there must be another road running by them. They were of stone, rather coarsely mortared, but neatly whitewashed, almost invariably one story high and long in proportion to their height, with a shingled roof, the shingles being pointed, for ornament, at the eaves, like the pickets of a fence, and also one row half-way up the roof. The gables sometimes projected a foot or two at the ridge-pole only. Yet they were very humble and unpretending dwellings. They commonly had the date of their erection on them. The windows opened in the middle, like blinds, and were frequently provided with solid shutters. Sometimes, when we walked along the back side of a house which stood near the road, we observed stout stakes leaning against it, by which the shutters, now pushed half open, were fastened at night; within, the houses were neatly ceiled with wood not painted. The oven was commonly out of doors, built of stone and mortar, frequently on a raised platform of planks. The cellar was often on the opposite side of the road, in front of or behind the houses, looking like an ice-house with us with a lattice door for summer. The very few mechanics whom we met had an old-Bettyish look, in their aprons and *bonnets rouges*, like fools' caps. The men wore commonly the same *bonnet rouge*, or red woollen or worsted cap, or sometimes blue or gray, looking to us as if they had got up with their night-caps on, and, in fact, I afterwards found that they had. Their clothes were of the cloth of the country, *étoffe du pays*, gray or some other plain color. The women looked stout, with gowns that stood out stiffly, also, for the most part, apparently of some home-made stuff. We also saw some specimens of the more characteristic winter dress of the Canadian, and I have since frequently detected him in New England by his coarse gray homespun capote and picturesque red sash, and his well-furred cap, made to protect his ears against the severity of his climate.

It drizzled all day, so that the roads did not improve. We began now to meet with wooden crosses frequently, by the roadside, about a dozen feet high, often old and toppling down, sometimes standing in a square wooden platform, sometimes in a pile of stones, with a little niche containing a picture of the Virgin and Child, or of Christ alone, sometimes with a string of beads, and covered with a piece of glass to keep out the rain, with the words, *pour la vierge*, or *Iniri*, on them. Frequently, on the cross-bar, there would be quite a collection of symbolical knickknacks, looking like an Italian's board; the representation in wood of a hand, a hammer, spikes, pincers, a flask of vinegar, a ladder, &c., the whole, perchance, surmounted by a weathercock; but I could not look at an honest weathercock in this walk without mistrusting that there was some covert reference in it to St. Peter. From time to time we passed a little one-story chapel-like building, with a tin-roofed spire, a shrine, perhaps it would be called, close to the pathside, with a lattice door, through which we could see an altar, and pictures about the walls; equally open, through rain and shine, though there was no getting into it. At these places the inhabitants kneeled and perhaps breathed a short prayer. We saw one school-house in our walk, and listened to the sounds which issued from it; but it appeared like a place where the process, not of enlightening, but of obfuscating the mind was going on, and the pupils received only so much light as could penetrate the shadow of the Catholic Church. The churches were very picturesque, and their interior much more showy than the dwelling-houses promised. They were of stone, for it was ordered, in 1699, that that should be their material. They had tinned spires, and quaint ornaments. That of l'Ange Gardien had a dial on it, with the Middle Age Roman numerals on its face, and some images in niches on the outside. Probably its counterpart has

existed in Normandy for a thousand years. At the church of
Chateau Richer, which is the next parish to l'Ange Gardien,
we read, looking over the wall, the inscriptions in the adjacent
churchyard, which began with, "*Ici git*" or "*Repose*," and one
over a boy contained, "*Priez pour lui.*" This answered as well
as Père la Chaise. We knocked at the door of the curé's house
here, when a sleek friar-like personage, in his sacerdotal robe,
appeared. To our *Parlez-vous Anglais?* even he answered,
"*Non, monsieur*"; but at last we made him understand what
we wanted. It was to find the ruins of the old *chateau*. "*Ah!
oui! oui!*" he exclaimed, and, donning his coat, hastened
forth, and conducted us to a small heap of rubbish which we
had already examined. He said that fifteen years before, it was
plus considérable. Seeing at that moment three little red birds
fly out of a crevice in the ruins, up into an arbor-vitæ tree,
which grew out of them, I asked him their names, in such
French as I could muster, but he neither understood me nor
ornithology; he only inquired where we had *appris à parler
Français*; we told him, *dans les États-Unis*; and so we bowed
him into his house again. I was surprised to find a man wear-
ing a black coat, and with apparently no work to do, even in
that part of the world.

The universal salutation from the inhabitants whom we met
was *bon jour*, at the same time touching the hat; with *bon
jour*, and touching your hat, you may go smoothly through
all Canada East. A little boy, meeting us, would remark, "*Bon
jour, Monsieur; le chemin est mauvais*," Good morning, sir; it
is bad walking. Sir Francis Head says that the immigrant is
forward to "appreciate the happiness of living in a land in
which the old country's servile custom of touching the hat
does not exist," but he was thinking of Canada West, of
course. It would, indeed, be a serious bore to be obliged to
touch your hat several times a day. A Yankee has not leisure
for it.

We saw peas, and even beans, collected into heaps in the
fields. The former are an important crop here, and, I suppose,
are not so much infested by the weevil as with us. There were
plenty of apples, very fair and sound, by the roadside, but
they were so small as to suggest the origin of the apple in the
crab. There was also a small red fruit which they called *snells*,

and another, also red and very acid, whose name a little boy wrote for me "*pinbéna.*" It is probably the same with, or similar to, the *pembina* of the voyageurs, a species of viburnum, which, according to Richardson, has given its name to many of the rivers of Rupert's Land. The forest trees were spruce, arbor-vitæ, firs, birches, beeches, two or three kinds of maple, bass-wood, wild-cherry, aspens, &c., but no pitch pines (*Pinus rigida*). I saw very few, if any, trees which had been set out for shade or ornament. The water was commonly running streams or springs in the bank by the roadside, and was excellent. The parishes are commonly separated by a stream, and frequently the farms. I noticed that the fields were furrowed or thrown into beds seven or eight feet wide to dry the soil.

At the *Rivière du Sault à la Puce*, which, I suppose, means the River of the Fall of the Flea, was advertised in English, as the sportsmen are English, "The best Snipe-shooting grounds," over the door of a small public-house. These words being English affected me as if I had been absent now ten years from my country, and for so long had not heard the sound of my native language, and every one of them was as interesting to me as if I had been a snipe-shooter, and they had been snipes. The prunella or self-heal, in the grass here, was an old acquaintance. We frequently saw the inhabitants washing, or cooking for their pigs, and in one place hackling flax by the roadside. It was pleasant to see these usually domestic operations carried on out of doors, even in that cold country.

At twilight we reached a bridge over a little river, the boundary between Chateau Richer and St. Anne, *le premier pont de St. Anne,* and at dark the church of *La Bonne St. Anne.* Formerly vessels from France, when they came in sight of this church, gave "a general discharge of their artillery," as a sign of joy that they had escaped all the dangers of the river. Though all the while we had grand views of the adjacent country far up and down the river, and, for the most part, when we turned about, of Quebec in the horizon behind us, and we never beheld it without new surprise and admiration; yet, throughout our walk, the Great River of Canada on our right hand was the main feature in the landscape, and this expands so rapidly below the Isle of Orleans, and creates such a breadth of level horizon above its waters in that direction, that, looking down the river as we approached the extremity of that island, the St. Lawrence seemed to be opening into the ocean, though we were still about three hundred and twenty-five miles from what can be called its mouth.*

When we inquired here for a *maison publique* we were directed apparently to that private house where we were most likely to find entertainment. There were no guideboards where we walked, because there was but one road; there were no shops nor signs, because there were no artisans to speak of, and the people raised their own provisions; and there were no taverns, because there were no travellers. We here bespoke lodging and breakfast. They had, as usual, a large old-fashioned, two-storied box-stove in the middle of the room, out of which, in due time, there was sure to be forthcoming a supper, breakfast, or dinner. The lower half held the fire, the upper the hot air, and as it was a cool Canadian evening, this was a comforting sight to us. Being four or five feet high it warmed the whole person as you stood by it. The stove was plainly a very important article of furniture in Canada, and was not set aside during the summer. Its size, and the respect which was paid to it, told of the severe winters which it had seen and prevailed over. The master of the house, in his long-pointed, red woollen cap, had a thoroughly antique physiognomy of the old Norman stamp. He might have come over with Jacques Cartier. His was the hardest French to understand of any we had heard yet, for there was a great difference between one speaker and another, and this man talked with a pipe in his mouth beside, a kind of tobacco French. I asked him what he called his dog. He shouted *Brock!* (the name of the breed). We like to hear the cat called *min*,—min! min! min! I inquired if we could cross the river here to the Isle of Orleans, thinking to return that way when we had been to the

---

*From McCulloch's Geographical Dictionary we learn that "immediately beyond the Island of Orleans it is a mile broad; where the Saguenay joins it, eighteen miles; at Point Peter, upwards of thirty; at the Bay of Seven Islands, seventy miles; and at the Island of Anticosti (about three hundred and fifty miles from Quebec) it rolls a flood into the ocean nearly one hundred miles across."

Falls. He answered, "*S'il ne fait pas un trop grand vent,*" If there is not too much wind. They use small boats, or pirogues, and the waves are often too high for them. He wore, as usual, something between a moccasin and a boot, which he called *bottes Indiennes,* Indian boots, and had made himself. The tops were of calf or sheep-skin, and the soles of cowhide turned up like a mocassin. They were yellow or reddish, the leather never having been tanned nor colored. The women wore the same. He told us that he had travelled ten leagues due north into the bush. He had been to the Falls of St. Anne, and said that they were more beautiful, but not greater, than Montmorenci, *plus beau, mais non plus grand que Montmorenci.* As soon as we had retired, the family commenced their devotions. A little boy officiated, and for a long time we heard him muttering over his prayers.

In the morning, after a breakfast of tea, maple-sugar, bread and butter, and what I suppose is called *potage* (potatoes and meat boiled with flour), the universal dish as we found, perhaps the national one, I ran over to the Church of La Bonne St. Anne, whose matin bell we had heard, it being Sunday morning. Our book said that this church had "long been an object of interest, from the miraculous cures said to have been wrought on visitors to the shrine." There was a profusion of gilding, and I counted more than twenty-five crutches suspended on the walls, some for grown persons, some for children, which it was to be inferred so many sick had been able to dispense with; but they looked as if they had been made to order by the carpenter who made the church. There were one or two villagers at their devotions at that early hour, who did not look up, but when they had sat a long time with their little book before the picture of one saint, went to another. Our whole walk was through a thoroughly Catholic country, and there was no trace of any other religion. I doubt if there are any more simple and unsophisticated Catholics anywhere. Emery de Caen, Champlain's contemporary, told the Huguenot sailors that "Monseigneur, the Duke de Ventadour (Viceroy), did not wish that they should sing psalms in the Great River."

On our way to the Falls, we met the habitans coming to the Church of La Bonne St. Anne, walking or riding in charettes

by families. I remarked that they were universally of small
stature. The toll-man at the bridge over the St. Anne was the
first man we had chanced to meet, since we left Quebec, who
could speak a word of English. How good French the inhab-
itants of this part of Canada speak, I am not competent to
say; I only know that it is not made impure by being mixed
with English. I do not know why it should not be as good as
is spoken in Normandy. Charlevoix, who was here a hundred
years ago, observes, "The French language is nowhere spoken
with greater purity, there being no accent perceptible"; and
Potherie said "they had no dialect, which, indeed, is generally
lost in a colony."

The falls, which we were in search of, are three miles up the
St. Anne. We followed for a short distance a foot-path up the
east bank of this river, through handsome sugar-maple and
arbor-vitæ groves. Having lost the path which led to a house
where we were to get further directions, we dashed at once
into the woods, steering by guess and by compass, climbing
directly through woods, a steep hill, or mountain, five or six
hundred feet high, which was, in fact, only the bank of the St.
Lawrence. Beyond this we by good luck fell into another
path, and following this or a branch of it, at our discretion,
through a forest consisting of large white pines,—the first we
had seen in our walk,—we at length heard the roar of falling
water, and came out at the head of the Falls of St. Anne. We
had descended into a ravine or cleft in the mountain, whose
walls rose still a hundred feet above us, though we were near
its top, and we now stood on a very rocky shore, where the
water had lately flowed a dozen feet higher, as appeared by
the stones and drift-wood, and large birches twisted and
splintered as a farmer twists a withe. Here the river, one or
two hundred feet wide, came flowing rapidly over a rocky bed
out of that interesting wilderness which stretches toward
Hudson's Bay and Davis's Straits. Ha-ha Bay, on the
Saguenay, was about one hundred miles north of where we
stood. Looking on the map, I find that the first country on
the north which bears a name is that part of Rupert's Land
called East Main. This river, called after the holy Anne, flow-
ing from such a direction, here tumbled over a precipice, at
present by three channels, how far down I do not know, but

far enough for all our purposes, and to as good a distance as if twice as far. It matters little whether you call it one, or two, or three hundred feet; at any rate, it was a sufficient Water-privilege for us. I crossed the principal channel directly over the verge of the fall, where it was contracted to about fifteen feet in width by a dead tree, which had been dropped across and secured in a cleft of the opposite rock, and a smaller one a few feet higher, which served for a hand-rail. This bridge was rotten as well as small and slippery, being stripped of bark, and I was obliged to seize a moment to pass when the falling water did not surge over it, and mid-way, though at the expense of wet feet, I looked down probably more than a hundred feet, into the mist and foam below. This gave me the freedom of an island of precipitous rock, by which I descended as by giant steps, the rock being composed of large cubical masses, clothed with delicate close-hugging lichens of various colors, kept fresh and bright by the moisture, till I viewed the first fall from the front, and looked down still deeper to where the second and third channels fell into a remarkably large circular basin worn in the stone. The falling water seemed to jar the very rocks, and the noise to be ever increasing. The vista down stream was through a narrow and deep cleft in the mountain, all white suds at the bottom; but a sudden angle in this gorge prevented my seeing through to the bottom of the fall. Returning to the shore, I made my way down stream through the forest to see how far the fall extended, and how the river came out of that adventure. It was to clamber along the side of a precipitous mountain of loose mossy rocks, covered with a damp primitive forest, and terminating at the bottom in an abrupt precipice over the stream. This was the east side of the fall. At length, after a quarter of a mile, I got down to still water, and, on looking up through the winding gorge, I could just see to the foot of the fall which I had before examined; while from the opposite side of the stream, here much contracted, rose a perpendicular wall, I will not venture to say how many hundred feet, but only that it was the highest perpendicular wall of bare rock that I ever saw. In front of me tumbled in from the summit of the cliff a tributary stream, making a beautiful cascade, which was a remarkable fall in itself, and there was a cleft in this

precipice, apparently four or five feet wide, perfectly straight
up and down from top to bottom, which, from its cavernous
depth and darkness, appeared merely as *a black streak*. This
precipice is not sloped, nor is the material soft and crumbling
slate as at Montmorenci, but it rises perfectly perpendicular,
like the side of a mountain fortress, and is cracked into vast
cubical masses of gray and black rock shining with moisture,
as if it were the ruin of an ancient wall built by Titans.
Birches, spruces, mountain-ashes with their bright red berries,
arbor-vitæs, white pines, alders, &c., overhung this chasm on
the very verge of the cliff and in the crevices, and here and
there were buttresses of rock supporting trees part way down,
yet so as to enhance, not injure, the effect of the bare rock.
Take it altogether, it was a most wild and rugged and stupen-
dous chasm, so deep and narrow where a river had worn itself
a passage through a mountain of rock, and all around was the
comparatively untrodden wilderness.

This was the limit of our walk down the St. Lawrence.
Early in the afternoon we began to retrace our steps, not be-
ing able to cross the north channel and return by the Isle of
Orleans, on account of the *trop grand vent*, or too great wind.
Though the waves did run pretty high, it was evident that the
inhabitants of Montmorenci County were no sailors, and
made but little use of the river. When we reached the bridge,
between St. Anne and Chateau Richer, I ran back a little way
to ask a man in the field the name of the river which we were
crossing, but for a long time I could not make out what he
said, for he was one of the more unintelligible Jacques Cartier
men. At last it flashed upon me that it was *La Rivière au
Chien*, or the Dog River, which my eyes beheld, which
brought to my mind the life of the Canadian voyageur and
coureur de bois, a more western and wilder Arcadia, methinks,
than the world has ever seen; for the Greeks, with all their
wood and river gods, were not so qualified to name the nat-
ural features of a country, as the ancestors of these French
Canadians; and if any people had a right to substitute their
own for the Indian names, it was they. They have preceded
the pioneer on our own frontiers, and named the *prairie* for
us. *La Rivière au Chien* cannot, by any license of language, be
translated into Dog River, for that is not such a giving it to

the dogs, and recognizing their place in creation as the French implies. One of the tributaries of the St. Anne is named *La Rivière de la Rose*; and farther east are, *La Rivière de la Blondelle*, and *La Rivière de la Friponne*. Their very *rivière* meanders more than our *river*.

Yet the impression which this country made on me was commonly different from this. To a traveller from the Old World, Canada East may appear like a new country, and its inhabitants like colonists, but to me, coming from New England, and being a very green traveller withal,—notwithstanding what I have said about Hudson's Bay,—it appeared as old as Normandy itself, and realized much that I had heard of Europe and the Middle Ages. Even the names of humble Canadian villages affected me as if they had been those of the renowned cities of antiquity. To be told by a habitan, when I asked the name of a village in sight, that it is *St. Fereole* or *St. Anne*, the *Guardian Angel* or the *Holy Joseph's*; or of a mountain, that it was *Bélange* or *St. Hyacinthe*! As soon as you leave the States, these saintly names begin. *St. John* is the first town you stop at (fortunately we did not see it), and thenceforward, the names of the mountains, and streams, and villages reel, if I may so speak, with the intoxication of poetry;— *Chambly, Longueil, Pointe aux Trembles, Bartholomy*, &c., &c.; as if it needed only a little foreign accent, a few more liquids and vowels perchance in the language, to make us locate our ideals at once. I began to dream of Provence and the Troubadours, and of places and things which have no existence on the earth. They veiled the Indian and the primitive forest, and the woods toward Hudson's Bay, were only as the forests of France and Germany. I could not at once bring myself to believe that the inhabitants who pronounced daily those beautiful and, to me, significant names, lead as prosaic lives as we of New England. In short, the Canada which I saw was not merely a place for railroads to terminate in and for criminals to run to.

When I asked the man to whom I have referred, if there were any falls on the Rivière au Chien,—for I saw that it came over the same high bank with the Montmorenci and St. Anne,—he answered that there were. How far? I inquired. *Trois quatres lieue*. How high? *Je pense, quatre-vingt-dix pieds;*

that is, ninety feet. We turned aside to look at the falls of the *Rivière du Sault à la Puce*, half a mile from the road, which before we had passed in our haste and ignorance, and we pronounced them as beautiful as any that we saw; yet they seemed to make no account of them there, and, when first we inquired the way to the Falls, directed us to Montmorenci, seven miles distant. It was evident that this was the country for waterfalls; that every stream that empties into the St. Lawrence, for some hundreds of miles, must have a great fall or cascade on it, and in its passage through the mountains was, for a short distance, a small Saguenay, with its upright walls. This fall of La Puce, the least remarkable of the four which we visited in this vicinity, we had never heard of till we came to Canada, and yet, so far as I know, there is nothing of the kind in New England to be compared with it. Most travellers in Canada would not hear of it, though they might go so near as to hear it. Since my return I find that in the topographical description of the country mention is made of "two or three romantic falls" on this stream, though we saw and heard of but this one. Ask the inhabitants respecting any stream, if there is a fall on it, and they will perchance tell you of something as interesting as Bashpish or the Catskill, which no traveller has ever seen, or if they have not found it, you may possibly trace up the stream and discover it yourself. Falls there are a drug; and we became quite dissipated in respect to them. We had drank too much of them. Beside these which I have referred to, there are a thousand other falls on the St. Lawrence and its tributaries which I have not seen nor heard of; and above all there is one which I have heard of, called Niagara, so that I think that this river must be the most remarkable for its falls of any in the world.

At a house near the western boundary of Chateau Richer, whose master was said to speak a very little English, having recently lived at Quebec, we got lodging for the night. As usual, we had to go down a lane to get round to the south side of the house where the door was, away from the road. For these Canadian houses have no front door, properly speaking. Every part is for the use of the occupant exclusively, and no part has reference to the traveller or to travel. Every New England house, on the contrary, has a front and principal door opening to the great world, though it may be on the cold side, for it stands on the highway of nations, and the road which runs by it comes from the Old World and goes to the far West; but the Canadian's door opens into his back-yard and farm alone, and the road which runs behind his house leads only from the church of one saint to that of another. We found a large family, hired men, wife and children, just eating their supper. They prepared some for us afterwards. The hired men were a merry crew of short, black-eyed fellows, and the wife a thin-faced, sharp-featured French Canadian woman. Our host's English staggered us rather more than any French we had heard yet; indeed, we found that even we spoke better French than he did English, and we concluded that a less crime would be committed on the whole if we spoke French with him, and in no respect aided or abetted his attempts to speak English. We had a long and merry chat with the family this Sunday evening in their spacious kitchen. While my companion smoked a pipe and parlez-vous'd with one party, I parleyed and gesticulated to another. The whole family was enlisted, and I kept a little girl writing what was otherwise unintelligible. The geography getting obscure, we called for chalk, and the greasy oiled table-cloth having been wiped,—for it needed no French, but only a sentence from the universal language of looks on my part, to indicate that it needed it,—we drew the St. Lawrence, with its parishes, thereon, and thenceforward went on swimmingly, by turns handling the chalk and committing to the table-cloth what would otherwise have been left in a limbo of unintelligibility. This was greatly to the entertainment of all parties. I was amused to hear how much use they made of the word *oui* in conversation with one another. After repeated single insertions of it, one would suddenly throw back his head at the same time with his chair, and exclaim rapidly, "*oui! oui! oui! oui!*" like a Yankee driving pigs. Our host told us that the farms thereabouts were generally two acres, or three hundred and sixty French feet wide, by one and a half leagues, (?) or a little more than four and a half of our miles deep. This use of the word *acre* as long measure arises from the fact that the French acre or arpent, the arpent of Paris, makes a square of ten perches, of eighteen feet each on a side,

a Paris foot being equal to 1.06575 English feet. He said that
the wood was cut off about one mile from the river. The rest
was "bush," and beyond that the "Queen's bush." Old as the
country is, each landholder bounds on the primitive forest,
and fuel bears no price. As I had forgotten the French for
sickle, they went out in the evening to the barn and got one,
and so clenched the certainty of our understanding one an-
other. Then, wishing to learn if they used the cradle, and not
knowing any French word for this instrument, I set up the
knives and forks on the blade of the sickle to represent one; at
which they all exclaimed that they knew and had used it.
When *snells* were mentioned they went out in the dark and
plucked some. They were pretty good. They said they had
three kinds of plums growing wild,—blue, white, and red, the
two former much alike and the best. Also they asked me if I
would have *des pommes*, some apples, and got me some. They
were exceedingly fair and glossy, and it was evident that there
was no worm in them; but they were as hard almost as a
stone, as if the season was too short to mellow them. We had
seen no soft and yellow apples by the roadside. I declined eat-
ing one, much as I admired it, observing that it would be
good *dans le printemps*, in the spring. In the morning when
the mistress had set the eggs a-frying she nodded to a thick-
set, jolly-looking fellow, who rolled up his sleeves, seized the
long-handled griddle, and commenced a series of revolutions
and evolutions with it, ever and anon tossing its contents into
the air, where they turned completely topsy-turvy and came
down t' other side up; and this he repeated till they were
done. That appeared to be his duty when eggs were con-
cerned. I did not chance to witness this performance, but my
companion did, and he pronounced it a master-piece in its
way. This man's farm, with the buildings, cost seven hundred
pounds; some smaller ones, two hundred.

In 1827, Montmorenci County, to which the Isle of Orleans
has since been added, was nearly as large as Massachusetts,
being the eighth county out of forty (in Lower Canada) in ex-
tent; but by far the greater part still must continue to be
waste land, lying, as it were, under the walls of Quebec.

I quote these old statistics, not merely because of the diffi-
culty of obtaining more recent ones, but also because I saw

there so little evidence of any recent growth. There were in this county, at the same date, five Roman Catholic churches, and no others, five curés and five presbyteries, two schools, two corn-mills, four saw-mills, one carding-mill,—no medical man, or notary or lawyer,—five shopkeepers, four taverns (we saw no sign of any, though, after a little hesitation, we were sometimes directed to some undistinguished hut as such), thirty artisans, and five river crafts, whose tonnage amounted to sixty-nine tons! This, notwithstanding that it has a frontage of more than thirty miles on the river, and the population is almost wholly confined to its banks. This describes nearly enough what we saw. But double some of these figures, which, however, its growth will not warrant, and you have described a poverty which not even its severity of climate and ruggedness of soil will suffice to account for. The principal productions were wheat, potatoes, oats, hay, peas, flax, maple-sugar, &c., &c.; linen, cloth, or *étoffe du pays*, flannel, and homespun, or *petite étoffe*.

In Lower Canada, according to Bouchette, there are two tenures,—the feudal and the socage. Tenanciers, censitaires, or holders of land *en roture*, pay a small annual rent to the seigneurs, to which "is added some article of provision, such as a couple of fowls, or a goose, or a bushel of wheat." "They are also bound to grind their corn at the *moulin banal*, or the lord's mill, where one fourteenth part of it is taken for his use" as toll. He says that the toll is one twelfth in the United States, where competition exists. It is not permitted to exceed one sixteenth in Massachusetts. But worse than this monopolizing of mill rents is what are called *lods et ventes*, or mutation fines. According to which the seigneur has "a right to a twelfth part of the purchase-money of every estate within his seigniory that changes its owner by sale." This is over and above the sum paid to the seller. In such cases, moreover, "the lord possesses the *droit de retrait*, which is the privilege of pre-emption at the highest bidden price within forty days after the sale has taken place,"—a right which, however, is said to be seldom exercised. "Lands held by Roman Catholics are further subject to the payment to their curates of one twenty-sixth part of all the grain produced upon them, and to occasional assessments for building and repairing churches,"

&c.,—a tax to which they are not subject if the proprietors change their faith; but they are not the less attached to their church in consequence. There are, however, various modifications of the feudal tenure. Under the socage tenure, which is that of the townships or more recent settlements, English, Irish, Scotch, and others, and generally of Canada West, the landholder is wholly unshackled by such conditions as I have quoted, and "is bound to no other obligations than those of allegiance to the king and obedience to the laws." Throughout Canada "a freehold of forty shillings yearly value, or the payment of ten pounds rent annually, is the qualification for voters." In 1846 more than one sixth of the whole population of Canada East were qualified to vote for members of Parliament,—a greater proportion than enjoy a similar privilege in the United States.

The population which we had seen the last two days,—I mean the habitans of Montmorenci County,—appeared very inferior, intellectually and even physically, to that of New England. In some respects they were incredibly filthy. It was evident that they had not advanced since the settlement of the country, that they were quite behind the age, and fairly represented their ancestors in Normandy a thousand years ago. Even in respect to the common arts of life, they are not so far advanced as a frontier town in the West three years old. They have no money invested in railroad stock, and probably never will have. If they have got a French phrase for a railroad, it is as much as you can expect of them. They are very far from a revolution; have no quarrel with Church or State, but their vice and their virtue is content. As for annexation, they have never dreamed of it; indeed, they have not a clear idea what or where the States are. The English government has been remarkably liberal to its Catholic subjects in Canada, permitting them to wear their own fetters, both political and religious, as far as was possible for subjects. Their government is even too good for them. Parliament passed "an act [in 1825] to provide for the extinction of feudal and seigniorial rights and burdens on lands in Lower Canada, and for the gradual conversion of those tenures into the tenure of free and common socage," &c. But as late as 1831, at least, the design of the act was likely to be frustrated, owing to the reluctance of the seigniors and peasants. It has been observed by another that the French Canadians do not extend nor perpetuate their influence. The British, Irish, and other immigrants, who have settled the townships, are found to have imitated the American settlers, and not the French. They reminded me in this of the Indians, whom they were slow to displace and to whose habits of life they themselves more readily conformed than the Indians to theirs. The Governor-General Denouville remarked, in 1685, that some had long thought that it was necessary to bring the Indians near them in order to Frenchify (*franciser*) them, but that they had every reason to think themselves in an error; for those who had come near them and were even collected in villages in the midst of the colony had not become French, but the French, who had haunted them, had become savages. Kalm said: "Though many nations imitate the French customs, yet I observed, on the contrary, that the French in Canada, in many respects, follow the customs of the Indians, with whom they converse every day. They make use of the tobacco-pipes, shoes, garters, and girdles of the Indians. They follow the Indian way of making war with exactness; they mix the same things with tobacco (he might have said that both French and English learned the use itself of this weed of the Indian); they make use of the Indian bark-boats, and row them in the Indian way; they wrap square pieces of cloth round their feet instead of stockings; and have adopted many other Indian fashions." Thus, while the descendants of the Pilgrims are teaching the English to make pegged boots, the descendants of the French in Canada are wearing the Indian moccasin still. The French, to their credit be it said, to a certain extent respected the Indians as a separate and independent people, and spoke of them and contrasted themselves with them as the English have never done. They not only went to war with them as allies, but they lived at home with them as neighbors. In 1627 the French king declared "that the descendants of the French, settled in" New France, "and the savages who should be brought to the knowledge of the faith, and should make profession of it, should be counted and reputed French born (*Naturels François*); and as such could emigrate to France, when it seemed good to them, and there acquire, will, inherit, &c., &c., without obtaining letters of naturalization." When the English had possession of Quebec, in 1630, the Indians, attempting to practise the same familiarity with them that they had with the French, were driven out of their houses with blows; which accident taught them a difference between the two races, and attached them yet more to the French. The impression made on me was, that the French Canadians were even sharing the fate of the Indians, or at least gradually disappearing in what is called the Saxon current.

The English did not come to America from a mere love of adventure, nor to truck with or convert the savages, nor to hold offices under the crown, as the French to a great extent did, but to live in earnest and with freedom. The latter overran a great extent of country, selling strong water, and collecting its furs, and converting its inhabitants,—or at least baptizing its dying infants (*enfans moribonds*),—without *improving* it. First, went the *coureur de bois* with the *eau de vie*; then followed, if he did not precede, the heroic missionary with the *eau d'immortalité*. It was freedom to hunt, and fish, and convert, not to work, that they sought. Hontan says that the *coureurs de bois* lived like sailors ashore. In no part of the seventeenth century could the French be said to have had a foothold in Canada; they held only by the fur of the wild animals which they were exterminating. To enable the poor seigneurs to get their living, it was permitted by a decree passed in the reign of Louis the Fourteenth, in 1685, "to all nobles and gentlemen settled in Canada, to engage in commerce, without being called to account or reputed to have done anything derogatory." The reader can infer to what extent they had engaged in agriculture, and how their farms must have shone by this time. The New England youth, on the other hand, were never *coureurs de bois* nor *voyageurs*, but backwoodsmen and sailors rather. Of all nations the English undoubtedly have proved hitherto that they had the most business here.

Yet I am not sure but I have most sympathy with that spirit of adventure which distinguished the French and Spaniards of those days, and made them especially the explorers of the American Continent,—which so early carried the former to the Great Lakes and the Mississippi on the north, and the latter to the same river on the south. It was long before our frontiers reached their settlements in the West. So far as inland discovery was concerned, the adventurous spirit of the English was that of sailors who land but for a day, and their enterprise the enterprise of traders.

There was apparently a greater equality of condition among the habitans of Montmorenci County than in New England. They are an almost exclusively agricultural, and so far independent, population, each family producing nearly all the necessaries of life for itself. If the Canadian wants energy, perchance he possesses those virtues, social and others, which the Yankee lacks, in which case he cannot be regarded as a poor man.

CHAPTER IV.

THE WALLS OF QUEBEC.

After spending the night at a farm-house in Chateau-Richer, about a dozen miles northeast of Quebec, we set out on our return to the city. We stopped at the next house, a picturesque old stone mill, over the *Chipré*,—for so the name sounded,—such as you will nowhere see in the States, and asked the millers the age of the mill. They went up stairs to call the master; but the crabbed old miser asked why we wanted to know, and would tell us only for some compensation. I wanted French to give him a piece of my mind. I had got enough to talk on a pinch, but not to quarrel; so I had to come away, looking all I would have said. This was the utmost incivility we met with in Canada. In Beauport, within a few miles of Quebec, we turned aside to look at a church which was just being completed,—a very large and handsome edifice of stone, with a green bough stuck in its gable, of some significance to Catholics. The comparative wealth of the Church in this country was apparent; for in this village we did not see one good house besides. They were all humble cottages; and yet this appeared to me a more imposing structure than any church in Boston. But I am no judge of these things.

Re-entering Quebec through St. John's Gate, we took a caleche in Market Square for the Falls of the Chaudière, about nine miles southwest of the city, for which we were to pay so much, beside forty sous for tolls. The driver, as usual, spoke French only. The number of these vehicles is very great for so small a town. They are like one of our chaises that has lost its top, only stouter and longer in the body, with a seat for the driver where the dasher is with us, and broad leather ears on each side to protect the riders from the wheel and keep children from falling out. They had an easy jaunting look, which, as our hours were numbered, persuaded us to be riders. We met with them on every road near Quebec these days, each with its complement of two inquisitive-looking foreigners and a Canadian driver, the former evidently enjoying their novel experience, for commonly it is only the horse whose language you do not understand; but they were one remove further from him by the intervention of an equally unintelligible driver. We crossed the St. Lawrence to Point Levi in a French-Canadian ferry-boat, which was inconvenient and dirty, and managed with great noise and bustle. The current was very strong and tumultuous, and the boat tossed enough to make some sick, though it was only a mile across; yet the wind was not to be compared with that of the day before, and we saw that the Canadians had a good excuse for not taking us over to the Isle of Orleans in a pirogue, however shiftless they may be for not having provided any other conveyance. The route which we took to the Chaudière did not afford us those views of Quebec which we had expected, and the country and inhabitants appeared less interesting to a traveller than those we had seen. The Falls of the Chaudière are three miles from its mouth on the south side of the St. Lawrence. Though they were the largest which I saw in Canada, I was not proportionately interested by them, probably from satiety. I did not see any *peculiar* propriety in the name *Chaudière*, or caldron. I saw here the most brilliant rainbow that I ever imagined. It was just across the stream below the precipice, formed on the mist which this tremendous fall produced; and I stood on a level with the key-stone of its arch. It was not a few faint prismatic colors merely, but a full semi-circle, only four or five rods in diameter, though as wide as usual, so intensely bright as to pain the eye, and apparently as substantial as an arch of stone. It changed its position and colors as we moved, and was the brighter because the sun shone so clearly and the mist was so thick. Evidently a picture painted on mist for the men and animals that came to the falls to look at; but for what special purpose beyond this, I know not. At the farthest point in this ride, and when most inland, unexpectedly at a turn in the road we descried the frowning citadel of Quebec in the horizon, like the beak of a bird of prey. We returned by the river-road under the bank, which is very high, abrupt, and rocky. When we were opposite to Quebec, I was surprised to see that in the Lower Town, under the shadow of the rock, the lamps were lit, twinkling not unlike crystals in a cavern, while the citadel high above, and we, too, on the south shore, were in broad daylight. As we were too late for the ferry-boat that night, we put up at a *maison de pension* at Point Levi. The usual two-story stove was here placed against an opening in the partition shaped like a fireplace, and so warmed several rooms. We could not understand their French here very well, but the *potage* was just like what we had had before. There were many small chambers with doorways but no doors. The walls of our chamber, all around and overhead, were neatly ceiled, and the timbers cased with wood unpainted. The pillows were checkered and tasselled, and the usual long-pointed red woollen or worsted night-cap was placed on each. I pulled mine out to see how it was made. It was in the form of a double cone, one end tucked into the other; just such, it appeared, as I saw men wearing all day in the streets. Probably I should have put it on if the cold had been then, as it is sometimes there, thirty or forty degrees below zero.

When we landed at Quebec the next morning, a man lay on his back on the wharf, apparently dying, in the midst of a crowd and directly in the path of the horses, groaning, *"O ma conscience!"* I thought that he pronounced his French more distinctly than any I heard, as if the dying had already acquired the accents of a universal language. Having secured the only unengaged berths in the Lord Sydenham steamer, which was to leave Quebec before sundown, and being resolved, now that I had seen somewhat of the country, to get an idea of the city, I proceeded to walk round the Upper Town, or fortified portion, which is two miles and three quarters in circuit, alone, as near as I could get to the cliff and the walls, like a rat looking for a hole; going round by the south-

west, where there is but a single street between the cliff and
the water, and up the long, wooden stairs, through the sub-
urbs northward to the King's Woodyard, which I thought
must have been a long way from his fireplace, and under the
cliffs of the St. Charles, where the drains issue under the
walls, and the walls are loop-holed for musketry; so returning
by Mountain Street and Prescott Gate to the Upper Town.
Having found my way by an obscure passage near the St.
Louis Gate to the glacis on the north of the citadel proper,—
I believe that I was the only visitor then in the city who got
in there,—I enjoyed a prospect nearly as good as from within
the citadel itself, which I had explored some days before. As I
walked on the glacis I heard the sound of a bagpipe from the
soldiers' dwellings in the rock, and was further soothed and
affected by the sight of a soldier's cat walking up a cleeted
plank into a high loop-hole, designed for *mus-catry*, as serene
as Wisdom herself, and with a gracefully waving motion of
her tail, as if her ways were ways of pleasantness and all her
paths were peace. Scaling a slat fence, where a small force
might have checked me, I got out of the esplanade into the
Governor's Garden, and read the well-known inscription on
Wolfe and Montcalm's monument, which for saying much in
little, and that to the purpose, undoubtedly deserved the
prize medal which it received:

MORTEM . VIRTUS . COMMUNEM .
FAMAM . HISTORIA .
MONUMENTUM . POSTERITAS .
DEDIT.

Valor gave them one death, history one fame, posterity one
monument. The Government Garden has for nosegays, amid
kitchen vegetables, beside the common garden flowers, the
usual complement of cannon directed toward some future
and possible enemy. I then returned up St. Louis Street to the
esplanade and ramparts there, and went round the Upper
Town once more, though I was very tired, this time on the
inside of the wall; for I knew that the wall was the main thing
in Quebec, and had cost a great deal of money, and therefore
I must make the most of it. In fact, these are the only re-
markable walls we have in North America, though we have a

good deal of Virginia fence, it is true. Moreover, I cannot say but I yielded in some measure to the soldier instinct, and, having but a short time to spare, thought it best to examine the wall thoroughly, that I might be the better prepared if I should ever be called that way again in the service of my country. I committed all the gates to memory in their order, which did not cost me so much trouble as it would have done at the hundred-gated city, there being only five; nor were they so hard to remember as those seven of Bœotian Thebes; and, moreover, I thought that, if seven champions were enough against the latter, one would be enough against Quebec, though he bore for all armor and device only an umbrella and a bundle. I took the nunneries as I went, for I had learned to distinguish them by the blinds; and I observed also the foundling hospitals and the convents, and whatever was attached to, or in the vicinity of the walls. All the rest I omitted, as naturally as one would the inside of an inedible shellfish. These were the only pearls, and the wall the only mother-of-pearl for me. Quebec is chiefly famous for the thickness of its parietal bones. The technical terms of its conchology may stagger a beginner a little at first, such as *banlieue, esplanade, glacis, ravelin, cavalier,* &c., &c., but with the aid of a comprehensive dictionary you soon learn the nature of your ground. I was surprised at the extent of the artillery barracks, built so long ago,—*Casernes Nouvelles,* they used to be called,—nearly six hundred feet in length by forty in depth, where the sentries, like peripatetic philosophers, were so absorbed in thought, as not to notice me when I passed in and out at the gates. Within, are "small arms of every description, sufficient for the equipment of twenty thousand men," so arranged as to give a startling *coup d'œil* to strangers. I did not enter, not wishing to get a black eye; for they are said to be "in a state of complete repair and readiness for immediate use." Here, for a short time, I lost sight of the wall, but I recovered it again on emerging from the barrack yard. There I met with a Scotchman who appeared to have business with the wall, like myself; and, being thus mutually drawn together by a similarity of tastes, we had a little conversation *sub mœnibus,* that is, by an angle of the wall which sheltered us. He lived about thirty miles northwest of

Quebec; had been nineteen years in the country; said he was disappointed that he was not brought to America after all, but found himself still under British rule and where his own language was not spoken; that many Scotch, Irish, and English were disappointed in like manner, and either went to the States, or pushed up the river to Canada West, nearer to the States, and where their language was spoken. He talked of visiting the States some time; and, as he seemed ignorant of geography, I warned him that it was one thing to visit the State of Massachusetts, and another to visit the State of California. He said it was colder there than usual at that season, and he was lucky to have brought his thick togue, or frock-coat, with him; thought it would snow, and then be pleasant and warm. That is the way we are always thinking. However, his words were music to me in my thin hat and sack.

At the ramparts on the cliff near the old Parliament House I counted twenty-four thirty-two-pounders in a row, pointed over the harbor, with their balls piled pyramid-wise between them,—there are said to be in all about one hundred and eighty guns mounted at Quebec,—all which were faithfully kept dusted by officials, in accordance with the motto, "In time of peace prepare for war"; but I saw no preparations for peace: she was plainly an uninvited guest.

Having thus completed the circuit of this fortress, both within and without, I went no farther by the wall for fear that I should become wall-eyed. However, I think that I deserve to be made a member of the Royal Sappers and Miners.

In short, I observed everywhere the most perfect arrangements for keeping a wall in order, not even permitting the lichens to grow on it, which some think an ornament; but then I saw no cultivation nor pasturing within it to pay for the outlay, and cattle were strictly forbidden to feed on the glacis under the severest penalties. Where the dogs get their milk I don't know, and I fear it is bloody at best.

The citadel of Quebec says, "I *will* live here, and you sha'n't prevent me." To which you return, that you have not the slightest objection; live and let live. The Martello towers looked, for all the world, exactly like abandoned wind-mills which had not had a grist to grind these hundred years. Indeed, the whole castle here was a "folly,"—England's folly,—and, in more senses than one, a castle in the air. The inhabitants and the government are gradually waking up to a sense of this truth; for I heard something said about their abandoning the wall around the Upper Town, and confining the fortifications to the citadel of forty acres. Of course they will finally reduce their intrenchments to the circumference of their own brave hearts.

The most modern fortifications have an air of antiquity about them; they have the aspect of ruins in better or worse repair from the day they are built, because they are not really the work of this age. The very place where the soldier resides has a peculiar tendency to become old and dilapidated, as the word *barrack* implies. I couple all fortifications in my mind with the dismantled Spanish forts to be found in so many parts of the world; and if in any place they are not actually dismantled, it is because that there the intellect of the inhabitants is dismantled. The commanding officer of an old fort near Valdivia in South America, when a traveller remarked to him that, with one discharge, his gun-carriages would certainly fall to pieces, gravely replied, "No, I am sure, sir, they would stand two." Perhaps the guns of Quebec would stand three. Such structures carry us back to the Middle Ages, the siege of Jerusalem, and St. Jean d'Acre, and the days of the Bucaniers. In the armory of the citadel they showed me a clumsy implement, long since useless, which they called a Lombard gun. I thought that their whole citadel was such a Lombard gun, fit object for the museums of the curious. Such works do not consist with the development of the intellect. Huge stone structures of all kinds, both in their erection and by their influence when erected, rather oppress than liberate the mind. They are tombs for the souls of men, as frequently for their bodies also. The sentinel with his musket beside a man with his umbrella is spectral. There is not sufficient reason for his existence. Does my friend there, with a bullet resting on half an ounce of powder, think that he needs that argument in conversing with me? The fort was the first institution that was founded here, and it is amusing to read in Champlain how assiduously they worked at it almost from the first day of the settlement. The founders of the colony thought this an excellent site for a wall,—and no doubt it was a better site, in some respects, for a wall than for a city,—but it chanced that a city got behind it. It chanced, too, that a Lower Town got before it, and clung like an oyster to the outside of the crags, as you may see at low tide. It is as if you were to come to a country village surrounded by palisades in the old Indian fashion,—interesting only as a relic of antiquity and barbarism. A fortified town is like a man cased in the heavy armor of antiquity, with a horse-load of broadswords and small arms slung to him, endeavoring to go about his business. Or is this an indispensable machinery for the good government of the country? The inhabitants of California succeed pretty well, and are doing better and better every day, without any such institution. What use has this fortress served, to look at it even from the soldiers' point of view? At first the French took care of it; yet Wolfe sailed by it with impunity, and took the town of Quebec without experiencing any hinderance at last from its fortifications. They were only the bone for which the parties fought. Then the English began to take care of it. So of any fort in the world,—that in Boston harbor, for instance. We shall at length hear that an enemy sailed by it in the night, for it cannot sail itself, and both it and its inhabitants are always benighted. How often we read that the enemy occupied a position which commanded the old, and so the fort was evacuated. Have not the school-house and the printing-press occupied a position which commands such a fort as this?

However, this is a ruin kept in remarkably good repair. There are some eight hundred or thousand men there to exhibit it. One regiment goes bare-legged to increase the attraction. If you wish to study the muscles of the leg about the knee, repair to Quebec. This universal exhibition in Canada of the tools and sinews of war reminded me of the keeper of a menagerie showing his animals' claws. It was the English leopard showing his claws. Always the *royal* something or other; as, at the menagerie, the Royal Bengal Tiger. Silliman states that "the cold is so intense in the winter nights, particularly on Cape Diamond, that the sentinels cannot stand it more than one hour, and are relieved at the expiration of that time"; "and even, as it is said, at much shorter intervals, in case of the most extreme cold." What a natural or unnatural

fool must that soldier be,—to say nothing of his govern-
ment,—who, when quicksilver is freezing and blood is ceasing
to be quick, will stand to have his face frozen, watching the
walls of Quebec, though, so far as they are concerned, both
honest and dishonest men all the world over have been in
their beds nearly half a century,—or at least for that space
travellers have visited Quebec only as they would read history.
I shall never again wake up in a colder night than usual, but I
shall think how rapidly the sentinels are relieving one another
on the walls of Quebec, their quicksilver being all frozen, as
if apprehensive that some hostile Wolfe may even then be
scaling the Heights of Abraham, or some persevering Arnold
about to issue from the wilderness; some Malay or Japanese,
perchance, coming round by the northwest coast, have cho-
sen that moment to assault the citadel! Why I should as
soon expect to find the sentinels still relieving one another
on the walls of Nineveh, which have so long been buried to
the world! What a troublesome thing a wall is! I thought it
was to defend me, and not I it. Of course, if they had no wall
they would not need to have any sentinels.

You might venture to advertise this farm as well fenced
with substantial stone walls (saying nothing about the eight
hundred Highlanders and Royal Irish who are required to
keep them from toppling down); stock and tools to go with
the land if desired. But it would not be wise for the seller to
exhibit his farm-book.

Why should Canada, wild and unsettled as it is, impress us
as an older country than the States, unless because her insti-
tutions are old? All things appeared to contend there, as I
have implied, with a certain rust of antiquity,—such as forms
on old armor and iron guns,—the rust of conventions and
formalities. It is said that the metallic roofs of Montreal and
Quebec keep sound and bright for forty years in some cases.
But if the rust was not on the tinned roofs and spires, it was
on the inhabitants and their institutions. Yet the work of bur-
nishing goes briskly forward. I imagined that the government
vessels at the wharves were laden with rotten-stone and oxalic
acid,—that is what the first ship from England in the spring
comes freighted with,—and the hands of the colonial legisla-
ture are cased in wash-leather. The principal exports must be

*gun*ny bags, verdigrease, and iron rust. Those who first built
this fort, coming from Old France with the memory and tra-
dition of feudal days and customs weighing on them, were
unquestionably behind their age; and those who now inhabit
and repair it are behind their ancestors or predecessors. Those
old chevaliers thought that they could transplant the feudal
system to America. It has been set out, but it has not thriven.
Notwithstanding that Canada was settled first, and, unlike
New England, for a long series of years enjoyed the fostering
care of the mother country,—notwithstanding that, as Char-
levoix tells us, it had more of the ancient *noblesse* among its
early settlers than any other of the French colonies, and per-
haps than all the others together,—there are in both the
Canadas but 600,000 of French descent to-day,—about half
so many as the population of Massachusetts. The whole pop-
ulation of both Canadas is but about 1,700,000 Canadians,
English, Irish, Scotch, Indians, and all, put together! Samuel
Laing, in his essay on the Northmen, to whom especially,
rather than the Saxons, he refers the energy and indeed the
excellence of the English character, observes that, when they
occupied Scandinavia, "each man possessed his lot of land
without reference to, or acknowledgment of, any other
man,—without any local chief to whom his military service or
other quit-rent for his land was due,—without tenure from,
or duty or obligation to, any superior, real or fictitious, except
the general sovereign. The individual settler held his land, as
his descendants in Norway still express it, by the same right as
the king held his crown,—by udal right, or adel,—that is, no-
ble right." The French have occupied Canada, not *udally*, or
by noble right, but *feudally*, or by ignoble right. They are a
nation of peasants.

It was evident that, both on account of the feudal system
and the aristocratic government, a private man was not worth
so much in Canada as in the United States; and, if your
wealth in any measure consists in manliness, in originality, and
independence, you had better stay here. How could a peace-
able, freethinking man live neighbor to the Forty-ninth
Regiment? A New-Englander would naturally be a bad citi-
zen, probably a rebel, there,—certainly if he were already a
rebel at home. I suspect that a poor man who is not servile is

a much rarer phenomenon there and in England than in the
Northern United States. An Englishman, methinks,—not to
speak of other European nations,—habitually regards himself
merely as a constituent part of the English nation; he is a
member of the royal regiment of Englishmen, and is proud of
his company, as he has reason to be proud of it. But an
American,—one who has made a tolerable use of his oppor-
tunities,—cares, comparatively, little about such things, and is
advantageously nearer to the primitive and the ultimate con-
dition of man in these respects. It is a government, that
English one,—like most other European ones,—that cannot
afford to be forgotten, as you would naturally forget it; under
which one cannot be wholesomely neglected, and grow up a
man and not an Englishman merely,—cannot be a poet even
without danger of being made poet-laureate! Give me a coun-
try where it is the most natural thing in the world for a gov-
ernment that does not understand you to let you alone. One
would say that a true Englishman could speculate only within
bounds. (It is true the Americans have proved that they, in
more than one sense, can *speculate* without bounds.) He has
to pay his respects to so many things, that, before he knows
it, he *may* have paid away all he is worth. What makes the
United States government, on the whole, more tolerable,—I
mean for us lucky white men,—is the fact that there is so
much less of government with us. Here it is only once in a
month or a year that a man *needs* remember that institution;
and those who go to Congress can play the game of the
Kilkenny cats there without fatal consequences to those who
stay at home,—their term is so short: but in Canada you are
reminded of the government every day. It parades itself be-
fore you. It is not content to be the servant, but will be the
master; and every day it goes out to the Plains of Abraham or
to the Champ de Mars and exhibits itself and its tools.
Everywhere there appeared an attempt to make and to pre-
serve trivial and otherwise transient distinctions. In the streets
of Montreal and Quebec you met not only with soldiers in
red, and shuffling priests in unmistakable black and white,
with Sisters of Charity gone into mourning for their deceased
relative,—not to mention the nuns of various orders depend-
ing on the fashion of a tear, of whom you heard,—but youths

belonging to some seminary or other, wearing coats edged with white, who looked as if their expanding hearts were already repressed with a piece of tape. In short, the inhabitants of Canada appeared to be suffering between two fires,—the soldiery and the priesthood.

CHAPTER V.
THE SCENERY OF QUEBEC; AND THE RIVER ST. LAWRENCE.

About twelve o'clock this day, being in the Lower Town, I looked up at the signal-gun by the flag-staff on Cape Diamond, and saw a soldier up in the heavens there making preparations to fire it,—both he and the gun in bold relief against the sky. Soon after, being warned by the boom of the gun to look up again, there was only the cannon in the sky, the smoke just blowing away from it, as if the soldier, having touched it off, had concealed himself for effect, leaving the sound to echo grandly from shore to shore, and far up and down the river. This answered the purpose of a dinner-horn.

There are no such restaurateurs in Quebec or Montreal as there are in Boston. I hunted an hour or two in vain in this town to find one, till I lost my appetite. In one house, called a restaurateur, where lunches were advertised, I found only tables covered with bottles and glasses innumerable, containing apparently a sample of every liquid that has been known since the earth dried up after the flood, but no scent of solid food did I perceive gross enough to excite a hungry mouse. In short, I saw nothing to tempt me there, but a large map of Canada against the wall. In another place I once more got as far as the bottles, and then asked for a bill of fare; was told to walk up stairs; had no bill of fare, nothing but fare. "Have you any pies or puddings?" I inquired, for I am obliged to keep my savageness in check by a low diet. "No, sir; we've nice mutton-chop, roast beef, beef-steak, cutlets," and so on. A burly Englishman, who was in the midst of the siege of a piece of roast beef, and of whom I have never had a front view to this day, turned half round, with his mouth half full, and remarked, "You'll find no pies nor puddings in Quebec, sir; they don't make any here." I found that it was even so, and therefore bought some musty cake and some fruit in the open market-place. This market-place by the water-side, where the old women sat by their tables in the open air, amid a dense crowd jabbering all languages, was the best place in Quebec to observe the people; and the ferry-boats, continually coming and going with their motley crews and cargoes, added much to the entertainment. I also saw them getting water from the river, for Quebec is supplied with water by cart and barrel. This city impressed me as wholly foreign and French, for I scarcely heard the sound of the English language in the streets. More than three fifths of the inhabitants are of French origin; and if the traveller did not visit the fortifications particularly, he might not be reminded that the English have any foothold here; and, in any case, if he looked no farther than Quebec, they would appear to have planted themselves in Canada only as they have in Spain at Gibraltar; and he who plants upon a rock cannot expect much increase. The novel sights and sounds by the water-side made me think of such ports as Boulogne, Dieppe, Rouen, and Havre de Grace, which I have never seen; but I have no doubt that they present similar scenes. I was much amused from first to last with the sounds made by the charette and caleche drivers. It was that part of their foreign language that you heard the most of,—the French they talked to their horses,—and which they talked the loudest. It was a more novel sound to me than the French of conversation. The streets resounded with the cries, "*Qui donc!*" "*March tôt!*" I suspect that many of our horses which came from Canada would prick up their ears at these sounds. Of the shops, I was most attracted by those where furs and Indian works were sold, as containing articles of genuine Canadian manufacture. I have been told that two townsmen of mine, who were interested in horticulture, travelling once in Canada, and being in Quebec, thought it would be a good opportunity to obtain seeds of the real Canada crook-neck squash. So they went into a shop where such things were advertised, and inquired for the same. The shopkeeper had the very thing they wanted. "But are you sure," they asked, "that these are the genuine Canada crook-neck?" "O yes, gentlemen," answered he, "they are a lot which I have received directly from Boston." I resolved that my Canada crook-neck seeds should be such as had grown in Canada.

Too much has not been said about the scenery of Quebec. The fortifications of Cape Diamond are omnipresent. They preside, they frown over the river and surrounding country. You travel ten, twenty, thirty miles up or down the river's banks, you ramble fifteen miles amid the hills on either side, and then, when you have long since forgotten them, perchance slept on them by the way, at a turn of the road or of your body, there they are still, with their geometry against the sky. The child that is born and brought up thirty miles distant, and has never travelled to the city, reads his country's history, sees the level lines of the citadel amid the cloud-built citadels in the western horizon, and is told that that is Quebec. No wonder if Jacques Cartier's pilot exclaimed in Norman French, *Que bec!*—"What a beak!"—when he saw this cape, as some suppose. Every modern traveller involuntarily uses a similar expression. Particularly it is said that its sudden apparition on turning Point Levi makes a memorable impression on him who arrives by water. The view from Cape Diamond has been compared by European travellers with the most remarkable views of a similar kind in Europe, such as from Edinburgh Castle, Gibraltar, Cintra, and others, and preferred by many. A main peculiarity in this, compared with other views which I have beheld, is that it is from the ramparts of a fortified city, and not from a solitary and majestic river cape alone that this view is obtained. I associate the beauty of Quebec with the steel-like and flashing air, which may be peculiar to that season of the year, in which the blue flowers of the succory and some late golden-rods and buttercups on the summit of Cape Diamond were almost my only companions,—the former bluer than the heavens they faced. Yet even I yielded in some degree to the influence of historical associations, and found it hard to attend to the geology of Cape Diamond or the botany of the Plains of Abraham. I still remember the harbor far beneath me, sparkling like silver in the sun,—the answering highlands of Point Levi on the southeast,—the frowning Cap Tourmente abruptly bounding the seaward view far in the northeast,—the villages of Lorette and Charlesbourg on the north,—and further west the distant

Val Cartier, sparkling with white cottages, hardly removed by distance through the clear air,—not to mention a few blue mountains along the horizon in that direction. You look out from the ramparts of the citadel beyond the frontiers of civilization. Yonder small group of hills, according to the guidebook, forms "the portal of the wilds which are trodden only by the feet of the Indian hunters as far as Hudson's Bay." It is but a few years since Bouchette declared that the country ten leagues north of the British capital of North America was as little known as the middle of Africa. Thus the citadel under my feet, and all historical associations, were swept away again by an influence from the wilds and from nature, as if the beholder had read her history,—an influence which, like the Great River itself, flowed from the Arctic fastnesses and Western forests with irresistible tide over all.

The most interesting object in Canada to me was the River St. Lawrence, known far and wide, and for centuries, as the Great River. Cartier, its discoverer, sailed up it as far as Montreal in 1535,—nearly a century before the coming of the Pilgrims; and I have seen a pretty accurate map of it so far, containing the city of "Hochelaga" and the river "Saguenay," in Ortelius's *Theatrum Orbis Terrarum*, printed at Antwerp in 1575,—the first edition having appeared in 1570,—in which the famous cities of "Norumbega" and "Orsinora" stand on the rough-blocked continent where New England is to-day, and the fabulous but unfortunate Isle of Demons, and Frislant, and others, lie off and on in the unfrequented sea, some of them prowling near what is now the course of the Cunard steamers. In this ponderous folio of the "Ptolemy of his age," said to be the first general atlas published after the revival of the sciences in Europe, only one page of which is devoted to the topography of the *Novus Orbis*, the St. Lawrence is the only large river, whether drawn from fancy or from observation, on the east side of North America. It was famous in Europe before the other rivers of North America were heard of, notwithstanding that the mouth of the Mississippi is said to have been discovered first, and its stream was reached by Soto not long after; but the St. Lawrence had attracted settlers to its cold shores long before the Mississippi, or even the Hudson, was known to the world. Schoolcraft was misled by

Gallatin into saying that Narvaez discovered the Mississippi. De Vega does *not* say so. The first explorers declared that the summer in that country was as warm as France, and they named one of the bays in the Gulf of St. Lawrence the Bay of Chaleur, or of warmth; but they said nothing about the winter being as cold as Greenland. In the manuscript account of Cartier's second voyage, attributed by some to that navigator himself, it is called "the greatest river, without comparison, that is known to have ever been seen." The savages told him that it was the "*chemin du Canada*,"—the highway to Canada,—"which goes so far that no man had ever been to the end that they had heard." The Saguenay, one of its tributaries, which the panorama has made known to New England within three years, is described by Cartier, in 1535, and still more particularly by Jean Alphonse, in 1542, who adds, "I think that this river comes from the sea of Cathay, for in this place there issues a strong current, and there runs there a terrible tide." The early explorers saw many whales and other sea-monsters far up the St. Lawrence. Champlain, in his map, represents a whale spouting in the harbor of Quebec, three hundred and sixty miles from what is called the mouth of the river; and Charlevoix takes his reader to the summit of Cape Diamond to see the "porpoises, white as snow," sporting on the surface of the harbor of Quebec. And Boucher says in 1664, "from there (Tadoussac) to Montreal is found a great quantity of *Marsouins blancs*." Several whales have been taken pretty high up the river since I was there. P. H. Gosse, in his "Canadian Naturalist," p. 171 (London, 1840), speaks of "the white dolphin of the St. Lawrence (*Delphinus Canadensis*)," as considered different from those of the sea. "The Natural History Society of Montreal offered a prize, a few years ago, for an essay on the *Cetacea* of the St. Lawrence, which was, I believe, handed in." In Champlain's day it was commonly called "the Great River of Canada." More than one nation has claimed it. In Ogilby's "America of 1670," in the map *Novi Belgii*, it is called "De Groote Rivier van Niew Nederlandt." It bears different names in different parts of its course, as it flows through what were formerly the territories of different nations. From the Gulf to Lake Ontario it is called at present the St. Lawrence; from Montreal to the same place it is frequently called the Cateraqui; and higher up it is known successively as the Niagara, Detroit, St. Clair, St. Mary's, and St. Louis rivers. Humboldt, speaking of the Orinoco, says that this name is unknown in the interior of the country; so likewise the tribes that dwell about the sources of the St. Lawrence have never heard the name which it bears in the lower part of its course. It rises near another father of waters,—the Mississippi,—issuing from a remarkable spring far up in the woods, called Lake Superior, fifteen hundred miles in circumference; and several other springs there are thereabouts which feed it. It makes such a noise in its tumbling down at one place as is heard all round the world. Bouchette, the Surveyor-General of the Canadas, calls it "the most splendid river on the globe"; says that it is two thousand statute miles long (more recent geographers make it four or five hundred miles longer); that at the Rivière du Sud it is eleven miles wide; at the Traverse, thirteen; at the Paps of Matane, twenty-five; at the Seven Islands, seventy-three; and at its mouth, from Cape Rosier to the Mingan Settlements in Labrador, near one hundred and five (?) miles wide. According to Captain Bayfield's recent chart it is about *ninety-six* geographical miles wide at the latter place, measuring at right angles with the stream. It has much the largest estuary, regarding both length and breadth, of any river on the globe. Humboldt says that the river Plate, which has the broadest estuary of the South American rivers, is ninety-two geographical miles wide at its mouth; also he found the Orinoco to be more than three miles wide at five hundred and sixty miles from its mouth; but he does not tell us that ships of six hundred tons can sail up it so far, as they can up the St. Lawrence to Montreal,—an equal distance. If he had described a fleet of such ships at anchor in a city's port so far inland, we should have got a very different idea of the Orinoco. Perhaps Charlevoix describes the St. Lawrence truly as the most *navigable* river in the world. Between Montreal and Quebec it averages about two miles wide. The tide is felt as far up as Three Rivers, four hundred and thirty-two miles, which is as far as from Boston to Washington. As far up as Cap aux Oyes, sixty or seventy miles below Quebec, Kalm found a great part of the plants near the shore to be marine, as glass-wort (*Salicornia*), seaside pease (*Pisum maritimum*), sea-milkwort (*Glaux*), beach-grass (*Psamma arenarium*), seaside plantain (*Plantago maritima*), the sea-rocket (*Bunias cakile*), &c.

The geographer Guyot observes that the Maranon is three thousand miles long, and gathers its waters from a surface of a million and a half square miles; that the Mississippi is also three thousand miles long, but its basin covers only from eight to nine hundred thousand square miles; that the St. Lawrence is eighteen hundred miles long, and its basin covers more than a million square miles (Darby says five hundred thousand); and speaking of the lakes, he adds, "These vast fresh-water seas, together with the St. Lawrence, cover a surface of nearly one hundred thousand square miles, and it has been calculated that they contain about one half of all the fresh water on the surface of our planet." But all these calculations are necessarily very rude and inaccurate. Its tributaries, the Ottawa, St. Maurice, and Saguenay, are great rivers themselves. The latter is said to be more than one thousand (?) feet deep at its mouth, while its cliffs rise perpendicularly an equal distance above its surface. Pilots say there are no soundings till one hundred and fifty miles up the St. Lawrence. The greatest sounding in the river, given on Bayfield's chart of the gulf and river, is two hundred and twenty-eight fathoms. McTaggart, an engineer, observes that "the Ottawa is larger than all the rivers in Great Britain, were they running in one." The traveller Grey writes: "A dozen Danubes, Rhines, Taguses, and Thameses would be nothing to twenty miles of fresh water in breadth (as where he happened to be), from ten to forty fathoms in depth." And again: "There is not perhaps in the whole extent of this immense continent so fine an approach to it as by the river St. Lawrence. In the Southern States you have, in general, a level country for many miles inland; here you are introduced at once into a majestic scenery, where everything is on a grand scale,—mountains, woods, lakes, rivers, precipices, waterfalls."

We have not yet the data for a minute comparison of the St. Lawrence with the South American rivers; but it is obvious that, taking it in connection with its lakes, its estuary, and its falls, it easily bears off the palm from all the rivers on the globe; for though, as Bouchette observes, it may not carry to the ocean a greater volume of water than the Amazon and Mississippi, its surface and cubic mass are far greater than theirs. But, unfortunately, this noble river is closed by ice from the beginning of December to the middle of April. The arrival of the first vessel from England when the ice breaks up is, therefore, a great event, as when the salmon, shad, and alewives come up a river in the spring to relieve the famishing inhabitants on its banks. Who can say what would have been the history of this continent if, as has been suggested, this river had emptied into the sea where New York stands!

After visiting the Museum and taking one more look at the wall, I made haste to the Lord Sydenham steamer, which at five o'clock was to leave for Montreal. I had already taken a seat on deck, but finding that I had still an hour and a half to spare, and remembering that large map of Canada which I had seen in the parlor of the restaurateur in my search after pudding, and realizing that I might never see the like out of the country, I returned thither, asked liberty to look at the map, rolled up the mahogany table, put my handkerchief on it, stood on it, and copied all I wanted before the maid came in and said to me standing on the table, "Some gentlemen want the room, sir"; and I retreated without having broken the neck of a single bottle, or my own, very thankful and willing to pay for all the solid food I had got. We were soon abreast of Cap Rouge, eight miles above Quebec, after we got underway. It was in this place, then called "*Fort du France Roy*," that the Sieur de Roberval with his company, having sent home two of his three ships, spent the winter of 1542–43. It appears that they fared in the following manner (I translate from the original): "Each mess had only two loaves, weighing each a pound, and half a pound of beef. They ate pork for dinner, with half a pound of butter, and beef for supper, with about two handfuls of beans, without butter. Wednesdays, Fridays, and Saturdays they ate salted cod, and sometimes green, for dinner, with butter; and porpoise and beans for supper. Monsieur Roberval administered good justice, and punished each according to his offence. One, named Michel Gaillon, was hung for theft; John of Nantes was put in irons and imprisoned for his fault; and others were likewise put in irons; and many were whipped, both men and women; by which means they lived in peace and tranquillity." In an account of a voyage up this river, printed in the Jesuit Relations in the year 1664, it is said: "It was an interesting navigation for us in ascending the river from Cap Tourment to Quebec, to see on this side and on that, for the space of eight leagues, the farms and the houses of the company, built by our French, all along these shores. On the right, the seigniories of Beauport, of Notre Dames des Anges; and on the left, this beautiful Isle of Orleans." The same traveller names among the fruits of the country observed at the Isles of Richelieu, at the head of Lake St. Peter, "kinds (*des espèces*) of little apples or haws (*semelles*), and of pears, which only ripen with the frost."

Night came on before we had passed the high banks. We had come from Montreal to Quebec in one night. The return voyage, against the stream, takes but an hour longer. Jacques Cartier, the first white man who is known to have ascended this river, thus speaks of his voyage from what is now Quebec to the foot of Lake St. Peter, or about half-way to Montreal: "From the said day, the 19th, even to the 28th of the said month, [September, 1535] we had been navigating up the said river without losing hour or day, during which time we had seen and found as much country and lands as level as we could desire, full of the most beautiful trees in the world," which he goes on to describe. But we merely slept and woke again to find that we had passed through all that country which he was eight days in sailing through. He must have had a troubled sleep. We were not long enough on the river to realize that it had length; we got only the impression of its breadth, as if we had passed over a lake a mile or two in breadth and several miles long, though we might thus have slept through a European kingdom. Being at the head of Lake St. Peter, on the above-mentioned 28th of September, dealing with the natives, Cartier says: "We inquired of them by signs if this was the route to Hochelaga [Montreal]; and they answered that it was, and that there were yet three days' journeys to go there." He finally arrived at Hochelaga on the 2d of October.

When I went on deck at dawn we had already passed through Lake St. Peter, and saw islands ahead of us. Our boat advancing with a strong and steady pulse over the calm surface, we felt as if we were permitted to be awake in the scenery of a dream. Many vivacious Lombardy poplars along the distant shores gave them a novel and lively, though artificial, look, and contrasted strangely with the slender and graceful elms on both shores and islands. The church of Varennes, fifteen miles from Montreal, was conspicuous at a great distance before us, appearing to belong to, and rise out of, the river; and now, and before, Mount Royal indicated where the city was. We arrived about seven o'clock, and set forth immediately to ascend the mountain, two miles distant, going across lots in spite of numerous signs threatening the severest penalties to trespassers, past an old building known as the Mac Tavish property,—Simon Mac Tavish, I suppose, whom Silliman refers to as "in a sense the founder of the Northwestern Company." His tomb was behind in the woods, with a remarkably high wall and higher monument. The family returned to Europe. He could not have imagined how dead he would be in a few years, and all the more dead and forgotten for being buried under such a mass of gloomy stone, where not even memory could get at him without a crowbar. Ah! poor man, with that last end of his! However, he may have been the worthiest of mortals for aught that I know. From the mountain-top we got a view of the whole city; the flat, fertile, extensive island; the noble sea of the St. Lawrence swelling into lakes; the mountains about St. Hyacinth, and in Vermont and New York; and the mouth of the Ottawa in the west, overlooking that St. Ann's where the voyageur sings his "parting hymn," and bids adieu to civilization,—a name, thanks to Moore's verses, the most suggestive of poetic associations of any in Canada. We, too, climbed the hill which Cartier, first of white men, ascended, and named Mont-real, (the 3d of October, O. S., 1535,) and, like him, "we saw the said river as far as we could see, *grand, large, et spacieux*, going to the southwest," toward that land whither Donnacona had told the discoverer that he had been a month's journey from Canada, where there grew "*force Canelle et Girofle*," much cinnamon and cloves, and where also, as the natives told him, were three great lakes and afterward *une mer douce*,—a sweet sea,—*de laquelle n'est mention avoir vu le bout*, of which there is no mention to have seen the end. But instead of an Indian town far in the interior of a new world, with guides to show us where the river came from, we found a splendid and bustling stone-built city of white men, and only a few squalid Indians offered to sell us baskets at the Lachine Railroad Depot, and Hochelaga is, perchance, but the fancy name of an engine company or an eating-house.

We left Montreal Wednesday, the 2d of October, late in the afternoon. In the La Prairie cars the Yankees made themselves merry, imitating the cries of the charette-drivers to perfection, greatly to the amusement of some French-Canadian travellers, and they kept it up all the way to Boston. I saw one person on board the boat at St. John's, and one or two more elsewhere in Canada, wearing homespun gray great-coats, or capotes, with conical and comical hoods, which fell back between their shoulders like small bags, ready to be turned up over the head when occasion required, though a hat usurped that place now. They looked as if they would be convenient and proper enough as long as the coats were new and tidy, but would soon come to have a beggarly and unsightly look, akin to rags and dust-holes. We reached Burlington early in the morning, where the Yankees tried to pass off their Canada coppers, but the news-boys knew better. Returning through the Green Mountains, I was reminded that I had not seen in Canada such brilliant autumnal tints as I had previously seen in Vermont. Perhaps there was not yet so great and sudden a contrast with the summer heats in the former country as in these mountain valleys. As we were passing through Ashburnham, by a new white house which stood at some distance in a field, one passenger exclaimed, so that all in the car could hear him, "There, there's not so good a house as that in all Canada!" I did not much wonder at his remark, for there is a neatness, as well as evident prosperity, a certain elastic easiness of circumstances, so to speak, when not rich, about a New England house, as if the proprietor could at least afford to make repairs in the spring, which the Canadian houses do not suggest. Though of stone, they are not better constructed than a stone barn would be with us; the only building, except the chateau, on which money and taste are expended, being the church. In Canada an ordinary New

England house would be mistaken for the chateau, and while every village here contains at least several gentlemen or "squires," *there* there is but one to a seigniory.

I got home this Thursday evening, having spent just one week in Canada and travelled eleven hundred miles. The whole expense of this journey, including two guide-books and a map, which cost one dollar twelve and a half cents, was twelve dollars seventy-five cents. I do not suppose that I have seen all British America; that could not be done by a cheap excursion, unless it were a cheap excursion to the Icy Sea, as seen by Hearne or McKenzie, and then, no doubt, some interesting features would be omitted. I wished to go a little way behind that word *Canadense*, of which naturalists make such frequent use; and I should like still right well to make a longer excursion on foot through the wilder parts of Canada, which perhaps might be called *Iter Canadense*.

Love

WHAT the essential difference between man and woman is that they should be thus attracted to one another, no one has satisfactorily answered. Perhaps we must acknowledge the justness of the distinction which assigns to man the sphere of wisdom, and to woman that of love, though neither belongs exclusively to either. Man is continually saying to woman, Why will you not be more wise? Woman is continually saying to man, Why will you not be more loving? It is not in their wills to be wise or to be loving; but, unless each is both wise and loving, there can be neither wisdom nor love.

All transcendent goodness is one, though appreciated in different ways, or by different senses. In beauty we see it, in music we hear it, in fragrance we scent it, in the palatable the pure palate tastes it, and in rare health the whole body feels it. The variety is in the surface or manifestation; but the radical identity we fail to express. The lover sees in the glance of his beloved the same beauty that in the sunset paints the western skies. It is the same daimon, here lurking under a human eyelid, and there under the closing eyelids of the day. Here, in small compass, is the ancient and natural beauty of evening and morning. What loving astronomer has ever fathomed the ethereal depths of the eye?

The maiden conceals a fairer flower and sweeter fruit than any calyx in the field; and, if she goes with averted face, confiding in her purity and high resolves, she will make the heavens retrospective, and all nature humbly confess its queen.

Under the influence of this sentiment, man is a string of an Æolian harp, which vibrates with the zephyrs of the eternal morning.

There is at first thought something trivial in the commonness of love. So many Indian youths and maidens along these banks have in ages past yielded to the influence of this great civilizer. Nevertheless, this generation is not disgusted nor discouraged, for love is no individual's experience; and though we are imperfect mediums, it does not partake of our imperfection; though we are finite, it is infinite and eternal;

and the same divine influence broods over these banks, whatever race may inhabit them, and perchance still would, even if the human race did not dwell here.

Perhaps an instinct survives through the intensest actual love, which prevents entire abandonment and devotion, and makes the most ardent lover a little reserved. It is the anticipation of change. For the most ardent lover is not the less practically wise, and seeks a love which will last forever.

Considering how few poetical friendships there are, it is remarkable that so many are married. It would seem as if men yielded too easy an obedience to nature without consulting their genius. One may be drunk with love without being any nearer to finding his mate. There is more of good nature than of good sense at the bottom of most marriages. But the good nature must have the counsel of the good spirit or Intelligence. If common sense had been consulted, how many marriages would never have taken place; if uncommon or divine sense, how few marriages such as we witness would ever have taken place!

Our love may be ascending or descending. What is its character, if it may be said of it,—

> "We must *respect* the souls above,
> But only *those below* we *love*."

Love is a severe critic. Hate can pardon more than love. They who aspire to love worthily, subject themselves to an ordeal more rigid than any other.

Is your friend such a one that an increase of worth on your part will surely make her more your friend? Is she retained,— is she attracted,—by more nobleness in you,—by more of that virtue which is peculiarly yours; or is she indifferent and blind to that? Is she to be flattered and won by your meeting her on any other than the ascending path? Then duty requires that you separate from her.

Love must be as much a light as a flame.

Where there is not discernment, the behavior even of the purest soul may in effect amount to coarseness.

A man of fine perceptions is more truly feminine than a merely sentimental woman. The heart is blind, but Love is not blind. None of the gods is so discriminating.

In Love & Friendship the imagination is as much exercised as the heart, and if either is outraged, the other will be estranged. It is commonly the imagination which is wounded first, rather than the heart, it is so much the more sensitive.

Comparatively, we can excuse any offence against the heart, but not against the imagination. The imagination knows— nothing escapes its glance from out its eyry—and it controls the breast. My heart may still yearn toward the valley, but my imagination will not permit me to jump off the precipice that debars me from it, for it is wounded, its wings are clipt, and it cannot fly, even descendingly. Our "blundering hearts"! some poet says. The imagination never forgets, it is a re-membering. It is not foundationless, but most reasonable, and it alone uses all the knowledge of the intellect.

Love is the profoundest of secrets. Divulged, even to the beloved, it is no longer Love. As if it were merely I that loved you. When love ceases, then it is divulged.

In our intercourse with one we love, we wish to have answered those questions at the end of which we do not raise our voice; against which we put no interrogation mark, answered with the same unfailing, universal aim toward every point of the compass.

I require that thou knowest everything without being told anything. I parted from my beloved because there was one thing which I had to tell her. She *questioned* me. She should have known all by sympathy. That I had to tell it her was the difference between us,—the misunderstanding.

A lover never hears anything that is *told*, for that is commonly either false or stale; but he hears things taking place, as the sentinels heard Trenck mining in the ground, and thought it was moles.

The relation may be profaned in many ways. The parties may not regard it with equal sacredness. What if the lover should learn that his beloved dealt in incantations and philters! What if he should hear that she consulted a clairvoyant! The spell would be instantly broken.

If to chaffer and higgle are bad in trade, they are much worse in Love. It demands directness as of an arrow.

There is danger that we lose sight of what our friend is absolutely, while considering what she is to us alone.

The lover wants no partiality. He says, Be so kind as to be just.

> Canst thou love with thy mind,
>   And reason with thy heart?
> Canst thou be kind,
>   And from thy darling part?
>
> Canst thou range earth, sea, and air,
>   And so meet me everywhere?
> Through all events I will pursue thee,
>   Through all persons I will woo thee.

I need thy hate as much as thy love. Thou wilt not repel me entirely when thou repellest what is evil in me.

> Indeed, indeed, I cannot tell,
> Though I ponder on it well,
> Which were easier to state,
> All my love or all my hate.
> Surely, surely, thou wilt trust me
> When I say thou dost disgust me.
> O I hate thee with a hate
> That would fain annihilate;
> Yet, sometimes, against my will,
> My dear Friend, I love thee still.
> It were treason to our love,
> And a sin to God above,
> One iota to abate
> Of a pure, impartial hate.

It is not enough that we are truthful; we must cherish and carry out high purposes to be truthful about.

It must be rare, indeed, that we meet with one to whom we are prepared to be quite ideally related, as she to us. We should have no reserve; we should give the whole of ourselves to that society; we should have no duty aside from that. One who could bear to be so wonderfully and beautifully exaggerated every day. I would take my friend out of her low self and set her higher, infinitely higher, and *there* know her. But, commonly, men are as much afraid of love as of hate. They have lower engagements. They have near ends to serve. They have not imagination enough to be thus employed about a human being, but must be coopering a barrel, forsooth.

What a difference, whether, in all your walks, you meet only strangers, or in one house is one who knows you, and whom you know. To have a brother or a sister! To have a gold mine on your farm! To find diamonds in the gravel heaps before your door! How rare these things are! To share the day with you,—to people the earth. Whether to have a god or a goddess for companion in your walks, or to walk alone with hinds and villains and carles. Would not a friend enhance the beauty of the landscape as much as a deer or hare? Everything would acknowledge and serve such a relation; the corn in the field, and the cranberries in the meadow. The flowers would bloom, and the birds sing, with a new impulse. There would be more fair days in the year.

The object of love expands and grows before us to eternity, until it includes all that is lovely, and we become all that can love.

Chastity & Sensuality

THE SUBJECT of Sex is a remarkable one, since, though its phenomena concern us so much both directly and indirectly, and, sooner or later it occupies the thoughts of all, yet, all mankind, as it were, agree to be silent about it, at least the sexes commonly one to another. One of the most interesting of all human facts is veiled more completely than any mystery. It is treated with such secrecy and awe, as surely do not go to any religion. I believe that it is unusual even for the most intimate friends to communicate the pleasures and anxieties connected with this fact,—much as the external affairs of love, its comings & goings, are bruited. The Shakers do not exaggerate it so much by their manner of speaking of it, as all mankind by their manner of keeping silence about it. Not that men should speak on this or any subject without having any thing worthy to say; but it is plain that the education of man has hardly commenced, there is so little genuine intercommunication.

In a pure society, the subject of copulation would not be so often avoided from shame and not from reverence, winked out of sight, and hinted at only, but treated naturally and simply,—perhaps simply avoided, like the kindred mysteries. If it cannot be spoken of for shame, how can it be acted of? But doubtless there is far more purity as well as more impurity, than is apparent.

Men commonly couple with their idea of marriage a slight degree at least of sensuality, but every lover, the world over, believes in its inconceivable purity.

If it is the result of a pure love, there can be nothing sensual in marriage. Chastity is something positive, not negative. It is the virtue of the married especially. All lusts or base pleasures must give place to loftier delights. They who meet as superior beings cannot perform the deeds of inferior ones. The deeds of love are less questionable than any action of an individual can be, for, it being founded on the rarest mutual respect, the parties incessantly stimulate each other to a loftier and purer life, and the act in which they are associated must be pure and noble indeed, for innocence and purity can have no equal. In this relation we deal with one whom we respect more religiously even than we respect our better selves, and we shall necessarily conduct as in the presence of God. What presence can be more awful to the lover than that of his beloved?

If you seek the warmth even of affection from a similar motive to that from which cats and dogs and slothful persons hug the fire, because your temperature is low through sloth, you are on the downward road, and it is but to plunge yet deeper into sloth. Better the cold affection of the sun reflected from fields of ice and snow, or his warmth in some still wintry dell. The warmth of celestial love does not relax, but nerves and braces its enjoyer. Warm your body by healthful exercise, not by cowering over a stove. Warm your spirit by performing independently noble deeds, not by ignobly seeking the sympathy of your fellows who are no better than yourself. A man's social and spiritual discipline must answer to his corporeal. He must lean on a friend who has a hard breast, as he would lie on a hard bed. He must drink cold water for his only beverage. So he must not hear sweetened and colored words, but pure and refreshing truths. He must daily bathe in truth cold as spring water, not warmed by the sympathy of friends.

Can love be in aught allied to dissipation? Let us love by refusing not accepting one another. Love and lust are far asunder. The one is good, the other bad. When the affectionate sympathize by their higher natures, there is love; but there is danger that they will sympathize by their lower natures, and then there is lust. It is not necessary that this be deliberate, hardly even conscious, but in the close contact of affection there is danger that we may stain and pollute one another, for we cannot embrace but with an entire embrace.

We must love our friend so much that she shall be associated with our purest and holiest thoughts alone. When there is impurity, we have "descended to meet," though we knew it not.

The *luxury* of affection,—there's the danger. There must be some nerve and heroism in our love, as of a winter morning. In the religion of all nations a purity is hinted at, which,

I fear, men never attain to. We may love and not elevate one another. The love that takes us as it finds us, degrades us. What watch we must keep over the fairest and purest of our affections, lest there be some taint about them. May we so love as never to have occasion to repent of our love.

There is to be attributed to sensuality the loss to language of how many pregnant symbols.

Flowers, which, by their infinite hues and fragrance celebrate the marriage of the plants are intended for a symbol of the open and unsuspected beauty of all true marriage, when man's flowering season arrives.

Virginity too is a budding flower, and by an impure marriage the virgin is deflowered. Whoever loves flowers, loves virgins and chastity. Love and lust are as far asunder as a flower garden is from a brothel.

J. Biberg, in the "Amoenitates Botanicae", edited by Linnaeus, observes, (I translate from the Latin) "the organs of generation which in the animal kingdom are for the most part concealed by nature as if they were to be ashamed of, in the vegetable kingdom are exposed to the eyes of all; and when the nuptials of plants are celebrated, it is wonderful what delight they afford to the beholder, refreshing the senses with the most agreeable color and the sweetest odor, and at the same time bees and other insects, not to mention the humming bird, extract honey from their nectaries, and gather wax from their effete pollen." Linnaeus himself calls the calyx the *thalamus*, or bridal chamber, and the corolla the *aulaeum* or tapestry of it, and proceeds to explain thus every part of the flower.

Who knows but evil spirits might corrupt the flowers themselves, rob them of their fragrance and their fair hues, and turn their marriage into a secret shame & defilement? Already they are of various qualities, and there is one whose nuptials fill the lowlands in June with the odor of carrion.

The intercourse of the sexes, I have dreamed, is incredibly beautiful, too fair to be remembered. I have had thoughts about it, but they are among the most fleeting and irrecoverable in my experience. It is strange that men will talk of miracles, revelation, inspiration, and the like, as things past, while love remains.

A true marriage will differ in no wise from illumination. In all perception of the truth there is a divine ecstasy, an inexpressible delirium of joy, as when a youth embraces his betrothed virgin. The ultimate delights of a true marriage are one with this.

No wonder that out of such a union, not as end, but as accompaniment, comes the undying race of man. The womb is a most fertile soil.

Some have asked if the stock of men could not be improved,—if they could not be bred as cattle. Let Love be purified and all the rest will follow. A pure love is thus indeed the panacea for all the ills of the world.

The only excuse for reproduction is improvement. Nature abhors repetition. Beasts merely propagate their kind, but the offspring of noble men & women will be superior to themselves, as their aspirations are. By their fruits ye shall know them.

Slavery in Massachusetts

I LATELY attended a meeting of the citizens of Concord, expecting, as one among many, to speak on the subject of slavery in Massachusetts; but I was surprised and disappointed to find that what had called my townsmen together was the destiny of Nebraska, and not of Massachusetts, and that what I had to say would be entirely out of order. I had thought that the house was on fire, and not the prairie; but though several of the citizens of Massachusetts are now in prison for attempting to rescue a slave from her own clutches, not one of the speakers at that meeting expressed regret for it, not one even referred to it. It was only the disposition of some wild lands a thousand miles off, which appeared to concern them. The inhabitants of Concord are not prepared to stand by one of their own bridges, but talk only of taking up a position on the highlands beyond the Yellowstone river. Our Buttricks, and Davises, and Hosmers are retreating thither, and I fear that they will have no Lexington Common between them and the enemy. There is not one slave in Nebraska; there are perhaps a million slaves in Massachusetts.

They who have been bred in the school of politics fail now and always to face the facts. Their measures are half measures and make-shifts, merely. They put off the day of settlement indefinitely, and meanwhile, the debt accumulates. Though the Fugitive Slave Law had not been the subject of discussion on that occasion, it was at length faintly resolved by my townsmen, at an adjourned meeting, as I learn, that the compromise compact of 1820 having been repudiated by one of the parties, 'Therefore, . . . the Fugitive Slave Law must be repealed.' But this is not the reason why an iniquitous law should be repealed. The fact which the politician faces is merely, that there is less honor among thieves than was supposed, and not the fact that they are thieves.

As I had no opportunity to express my thoughts at that meeting, will you allow me to do so here?

Again it happens that the Boston Court House is full of armed men, holding prisoner and trying a MAN, to find out if he is not really a SLAVE. Does any one think that Justice or God awaits Mr. Loring's decision? For him to sit there deciding still, when this question is already decided from eternity to eternity, and the unlettered slave himself, and the multitude around, have long since heard and assented to the decision, is simply to make himself ridiculous. We may be tempted to ask from whom he received his commission, and who he is that received it; what novel statutes he obeys, and what precedents are to him of authority. Such an arbiter's very existence is an impertinence. We do not ask him to make up his mind, but to make up his pack.

I listen to hear the voice of a Governor, Commander-in-Chief of the forces of Massachusetts. I hear only the creaking of crickets and the hum of insects which now fill the summer air. The Governor's exploit is to review the troops on muster days. I have seen him on horseback, with his hat off, listening to a chaplain's prayer. It chances that is all I have ever seen of a Governor. I think that I could manage to get along without one. If *he* is not of the least use to prevent my being kidnapped, pray of what important use is he likely to be to me? When freedom is most endangered, he dwells in the deepest obscurity. A distinguished clergyman told me that he chose the profession of a clergyman, because it afforded the most leisure for literary pursuits. I would recommend to him the profession of a Governor.

Three years ago, also, when the Simm's tragedy was acted, I said to myself, there is such an officer, if not such a man, as the Governor of Massachusetts,—what has he been about the last fortnight? Has he had as much as he could do to keep on the fence during this moral earthquake? It seemed to me that no keener satire could have been aimed at, no more cutting insult have been offered to that man, than just what happened—the absence of all inquiry after him in that crisis. The worst and the most I chance to know of him is, that he did not improve that opportunity to make himself known, and worthily known. He could at least have *resigned* himself into fame. It appeared to be forgotten that there was such a man, or such an office. Yet no doubt he was endeavoring to fill the gubernatorial chair all the while. He was no Governor of mine. He did not govern me.

But at last, in the present case, the Governor was heard from. After he and the United States Government had perfectly succeeded in robbing a poor innocent black man of his liberty for life, and, as far as they could, of his Creator's likeness in his breast, he made a speech to his accomplices, at a congratulatory supper!

I have read a recent law of this State, making it penal for 'any officer of the Commonwealth' to 'detain, or aid in the . . . detention,' any where within its limits, 'of any person, for the reason that he is claimed as a fugitive slave.' Also, it was a matter of notoriety that a writ of replevin to take the fugitive out of the custody of the United States Marshal could not be served, for want of sufficient force to aid the officer.

I had thought that the Governor was in some sense the executive officer of the State; that it was his business, as a Governor, to see that the laws of the State were executed; while, as a man, he took care that he did not, by so doing, break the laws of humanity; but when there is any special important use for him, he is useless, or worse than useless, and permits the laws of the State to go unexecuted. Perhaps I do not know what are the duties of a Governor; but if to be a Governor requires to subject one's self to so much ignominy without remedy, if it is to put a restraint upon my manhood, I shall take care never to be Governor of Massachusetts. I have not read far in the statutes of this Commonwealth. It is not profitable reading. They do not always say what is true; and they do not always mean what they say. What I am concerned to know is, that that man's influence and authority were on the side of the slaveholder, and not of the slave—of the guilty, and not of the innocent —of injustice, and not of justice. I never saw him of whom I speak; indeed, I did not know that he was Governor until this event occurred. I heard of him and Anthony Burns at the same time, and thus, undoubtedly, most will hear of him. So far am I from being governed by him. I do not mean that it was any thing to his discredit that I had not heard of him, only that I heard what I did. The worst I shall say of him is, that he proved no better than the majority of his constituents would be likely to prove. In my opinion, he was not equal to the occasion.

The whole military force of the State is at the service of a
Mr. Suttle, a slaveholder from Virginia, to enable him to catch
a man whom he calls his property; but not a soldier is offered
to save a citizen of Massachusetts from being kidnapped! Is
this what all these soldiers, all this *training* has been for these
seventy-nine years past? Have they been trained merely to rob
Mexico, and carry back fugitive slaves to their masters?

These very nights, I heard the sound of a drum in our
streets. There were men *training* still; and for what? I could
with an effort pardon the cockerels of Concord for crowing
still, for they, perchance, had not been beaten that morning;
but I could not excuse this rub-a-dub of the 'trainers.' The
slave was carried back by exactly such as these, i.e., by the sol-
dier, of whom the best you can say in this connection is, that
he is a fool made conspicuous by a painted coat.

Three years ago, also, just a week after the authorities of
Boston assembled to carry back a perfectly innocent man, and
one whom they knew to be innocent, into slavery, the inhab-
itants of Concord caused the bells to be rung and the can-
nons to be fired, to celebrate their liberty—and the courage
and love of liberty of their ancestors who fought at the
bridge. As if *those* three millions had fought for the right to be
free themselves, but to hold in slavery three million others.
Now-a-days, men wear a fool's cap, and call it a liberty cap. I
do not know but there are some, who, if they were tied to a
whipping-post, and could but get one hand free, would use it
to ring the bells and fire the cannons, to celebrate *their* lib-
erty. So some of my townsmen took the liberty to ring and
fire; that was the extent of their freedom; and when the sound
of the bells died away, their liberty died away also; when the
powder was all expended, their liberty went off with the
smoke.

The joke could be no broader, if the inmates of the prisons
were to subscribe for all the powder to be used in such
salutes, and hire the jailers to do the firing and ringing for
them, while they enjoyed it through the grating.

This is what I thought about my neighbors.

Every humane and intelligent inhabitant of Concord, when
he or she heard those bells and those cannons, thought not
with pride of the events of the 19th of April, 1775, but with

shame of the events of the 12th of April, 1851. But now we have half buried that old shame under a new one.

Massachusetts sat waiting Mr. Loring's decision, as if it could in any way affect her own criminality. Her crime, the most conspicuous and fatal crime of all, was permitting him to be the umpire in such a case. It was really the trial of Massachusetts. Every moment that she hesitated to set this man free—every moment that she now hesitates to atone for her crime, she is convicted. The Commissioner on her case is God; not Edward G. God, but simple God.

I wish my countrymen to consider, that whatever the human law may be, neither an individual nor a nation can ever commit the least act of injustice against the obscurest individual, without having to pay the penalty for it. A government which deliberately enacts injustice, and persists in it, will at length ever become the laughing-stock of the world.

Much has been said about American slavery, but I think that we do not even yet realize what slavery is. If I were seriously to propose to Congress to make mankind into sausages, I have no doubt that most of the members would smile at my proposition, and if any believed me to be in earnest, they would think that I proposed something much worse than Congress had ever done. But if any of them will tell me that to make a man into a sausage would be much worse,—would be any worse, than to make him into a slave,—than it was to enact the Fugitive Slave Law, I will accuse him of foolishness, of intellectual incapacity, of making a distinction without a difference. The one is just as sensible a proposition as the other.

I hear a good deal said about trampling this law under foot. Why, one need not go out of his way to do that. This law rises not to the level of the head or the reason; its natural habitat is in the dirt. It was born and bred, and has its life only in the dust and mire, on a level with the feet, and he who walks with freedom, and does not with Hindoo mercy avoid treading on every venomous reptile, will inevitably tread on it, and so trample it under foot,—and Webster, its maker, with it, like the dirt-bug and its ball.

Recent events will be valuable as a criticism on the administration of justice in our midst, or, rather, as showing what are the true resources of justice in any community. It has come to this, that the friends of liberty, the friends of the slave, have shuddered when they have understood that his fate was left to the legal tribunals of the country to be decided. Free men have no faith that justice will be awarded in such a case; the judge may decide this way or that; it is a kind of accident, at best. It is evident that he is not a competent authority in so important a case. It is no time, then, to be judging according to his precedents, but to establish a precedent for the future. I would much rather trust to the sentiment of the people. In their vote, you would get something of some value, at least, however small; but, in the other case, only the trammelled judgment of an individual, of no significance, be it which way it might.

It is to some extent fatal to the courts, when the people are compelled to go behind them. I do not wish to believe that the courts were made for fair weather, and for very civil cases merely,—but think of leaving it to any court in the land to decide whether more than three millions of people, in this case, a sixth part of a nation, have a right to be freemen or not! But it has been left to the courts of *justice*, so-called—to the Supreme Court of the land—and, as you all know, recognizing no authority but the Constitution, it has decided that the three millions are, and shall continue to be, slaves. Such judges as these are merely the inspectors of a pick-lock and murderer's tools, to tell him whether they are in working order or not, and there they think that their responsibility ends. There was a prior case on the docket, which they, as judges appointed by God, had no right to skip; which having been justly settled, they would have been saved from this humiliation. It was the case of the murderer himself.

The law will never make men free; it is men who have got to make the law free. They are the lovers of law and order, who observe the law when the government breaks it.

Among human beings, the judge whose words seal the fate of a man furthest into eternity, is not he who merely pronounces the verdict of the law, but he, whoever he may be, who, from a love of truth, and unprejudiced by any custom or enactment of men, utters a true opinion or *sentence* concerning him. He it is that *sentences* him. Whoever has discerned truth, has received his commission from a higher source than the chiefest justice in the world, who can discern only law. He finds himself constituted judge of the judge.—Strange that it should be necessary to state such simple truths.

I am more and more convinced that, with reference to any public question, it is more important to know what the country thinks of it, than what the city thinks. The city does not *think* much. On any moral question, I would rather have the opinion of Boxboro than of Boston and New York put together. When the former speaks, I feel as if somebody *had* spoken, as if *humanity* was yet, and a reasonable being had asserted its rights,—as if some unprejudiced men among the country's hills had at length turned their attention to the subject, and by a few sensible words redeemed the reputation of the race. When, in some obscure country town, the farmers come together to a special town meeting, to express their opinion on some subject which is vexing the land, that, I think, is the true Congress, and the most respectable one that is ever assembled in the United States.

It is evident that there are, in this Commonwealth, at least, two parties, becoming more and more distinct—the party of the city, and the party of the country. I know that the country is mean enough, but I am glad to believe that there is a slight difference in her favor. But as yet, she has few, if any organs, through which to express herself. The editorials which she reads, like the news, come from the sea-board. Let us, the inhabitants of the country, cultivate self-respect. Let us not send to the city for aught more essential than our broadcloths and groceries, or, if we read the opinions of the city, let us entertain opinions of our own.

Among measures to be adopted, I would suggest to make as earnest and vigorous an assault on the Press as has already been made, and with effect, on the Church. The Church has much improved within a few years; but the Press is almost, without exception, corrupt. I believe that, in this country, the press exerts a greater and a more pernicious influence than the Church did in its worst period. We are not a religious people, but we are a nation of politicians. We do not care for the Bible, but we do care for the newspaper. At any meeting of politicians,—like that at Concord the other evening, for

instance,—how impertinent it would be to quote from the
Bible! how pertinent to quote from a newspaper or from the
Constitution! The newspaper is a Bible which we read every
morning and every afternoon, standing and sitting, riding and
walking. It is a Bible which every man carries in his pocket,
which lies on every table and counter, and which the mail,
and thousands of missionaries, are continually dispensing. It
is, in short, the only book which America has printed, and
which America reads. So wide is its influence. The editor is a
preacher whom you voluntarily support. Your tax is com-
monly one cent daily, and it costs nothing for pew hire. But
how many of these preachers preach the truth? I repeat the
testimony of many an intelligent foreigner, as well as my own
convictions, when I say, that probably no country was ever
ruled by so mean a class of tyrants as, with a few noble ex-
ceptions, are the editors of the periodical press in *this* country.
And as they live and rule only by their servility, and appealing
to the worst, and not the better nature of man, the people
who read them are in the condition of the dog that returns to
his vomit.

The *Liberator* and the *Commonwealth* were the only papers
in Boston, as far as I know, which made themselves heard in
condemnation of the cowardice and meanness of the author-
ities of that city, as exhibited in '51. The other journals, almost
without exception, by their manner of referring to and speak-
ing of the Fugitive Slave Law, and the carrying back of the
slave Simms, insulted the common sense of the country, at
least. And, for the most part, they did this, one would say, be-
cause they thought so to secure the approbation of their pa-
trons, not being aware that a sounder sentiment prevailed to
any extent in the heart of the Commonwealth. I am told that
some of them have improved of late; but they are still emi-
nently time-serving. Such is the character they have won.

But, thank fortune, this preacher can be even more easily
reached by the weapons of the reformer than could the recre-
ant priest. The free men of New England have only to refrain
from purchasing and reading these sheets, have only to with-
hold their cents, to kill a score of them at once. One whom I
respect told me that he purchased Mitchell's *Citizen* in the
cars, and then threw it out the window. But would not his

contempt have been more fatally expressed, if he had not bought it?

Are they Americans? are they New Englanders? are they inhabitants of Lexington, and Concord, and Framingham, who read and support the Boston *Post, Mail, Journal, Advertiser, Courier,* and *Times?* Are these the Flags of our Union? I am not a newspaper reader, and may omit to name the worst.

Could slavery suggest a more complete servility than some of these journals exhibit? Is there any dust which their conduct does not lick, and make fouler still with its slime? I do not know whether the Boston *Herald* is still in existence, but I remember to have seen it about the streets when Simms was carried off. Did it not act its part well—serve its master faithfully? How could it have gone lower on its belly? How can a man stoop lower than he is low? do more than put his extremities in the place of the head he has? than make his head his lower extremity? When I have taken up this paper with my cuffs turned up, I have heard the gurgling of the sewer through every column. I have felt that I was handling a paper picked out of the public gutters, a leaf from the gospel of the gambling-house, the groggery and the brothel, harmonizing with the gospel of the Merchants' Exchange.

The majority of the men of the North, and of the South, and East, and West, are not men of principle. If they vote, they do not send men to Congress on errands of humanity, but while their brothers and sisters are being scourged and hung for loving liberty, while——I might here insert all that slavery implies and is,——it is the mismanagement of wood and iron and stone and gold which concerns them. Do what you will, O Government! with my wife and children, my mother and brother, my father and sister, I will obey your commands to the letter. It will indeed grieve me if you hurt them, if you deliver them to overseers to be hunted by hounds or to be whipped to death; but nevertheless, I will peaceably pursue my chosen calling on this fair earth, until perchance, one day, when I have put on mourning for them dead, I shall have persuaded you to relent. Such is the attitude, such are the words of Massachusetts.

Rather than do thus, I need not say what match I would touch, what system endeavor to blow up,—but as I love my life, I would side with the light, and let the dark earth roll from under me, calling my mother and my brother to follow.

I would remind my countrymen, that they are to be men first, and Americans only at a late and convenient hour. No matter how valuable law may be to protect your property, even to keep soul and body together, if it do not keep you and humanity together.

I am sorry to say, that I doubt if there is a judge in Massachusetts who is prepared to resign his office, and get his living innocently, whenever it is required of him to pass sentence under a law which is merely contrary to the law of God. I am compelled to see that they put themselves, or rather, are by character, in this respect, exactly on a level with the marine who discharges his musket in any direction he is ordered to. They are just as much tools and as little men. Certainly, they are not the more to be respected, because their master enslaves their understandings and consciences, instead of their bodies.

The judges and lawyers,—simply as such, I mean,—and all men of expediency, try this case by a very low and incompetent standard. They consider, not whether the Fugitive Slave Law is right, but whether it is what they call *constitutional*. Is virtue constitutional, or vice? Is equity constitutional, or iniquity? In important moral and vital questions like this, it is just as impertinent to ask whether a law is constitutional or not, as to ask whether it is profitable or not. They persist in being the servants of the worst of men, and not the servants of humanity. The question is not whether you or your grandfather, seventy years ago, did not enter into an agreement to serve the devil, and that service is not accordingly now due; but whether you will not now, for once and at last, serve God,—in spite of your own past recreancy, or that of your ancestor,—by obeying that eternal and only just CONSTITUTION, which He, and not any Jefferson or Adams, has written in your being.

The amount of it is, if the majority vote the devil to be God, the minority will live and behave accordingly, and obey the successful candidate, trusting that some time or other, by some Speaker's casting vote, perhaps, they may reinstate God. This is the highest principle I can get out of or invent for my neighbors. These men act as if they believed that they could safely slide down hill a little way—or a good way—and would surely come to a place, by and by, where they could begin to slide up again. This is expediency, or choosing that course which offers the slightest obstacles to the feet, that is, a down-hill one. But there is no such thing as accomplishing a righteous reform by the use of 'expediency.' There is no such thing as sliding up hill. In morals, the only sliders are back-sliders.

Thus we steadily worship Mammon, both School, and State, and Church, and the Seventh Day curse God with a tintamar from one end of the Union to the other.

Will mankind never learn that policy is not morality—that it never secures any moral right, but considers merely what is expedient? chooses the available candidate, who is invariably the devil,—and what right have his constituents to be surprised, because the devil does not behave like an angel of light? What is wanted is men, not of policy, but of probity—who recognize a higher law than the Constitution, or the decision of the majority. The fate of the country does not depend on how you vote at the polls—the worst man is as strong as the best at that game; it does not depend on what kind of paper you drop into the ballot-box once a year, but on what kind of man you drop from your chamber into the street every morning.

What should concern Massachusetts is not the Nebraska Bill, nor the Fugitive Slave Bill, but her own slaveholding and servility. Let the State dissolve her union with the slaveholder. She may wriggle and hesitate, and ask leave to read the Constitution once more; but she can find no respectable law or precedent which sanctions the continuance of such a Union for an instant.

Let each inhabitant of the State dissolve his union with her, as long as she delays to do her duty.

The events of the past month teach me to distrust Fame. I see that she does not finely discriminate, but coarsely hurrahs. She considers not the simple heroism of an action, but only as it is connected with its apparent consequences. She praises till she is hoarse the easy exploit of the Boston tea party, but will be comparatively silent about the braver and more disinterestedly heroic attack on the Boston Court-House, simply because it was unsuccessful!

Covered with disgrace, the State has sat down coolly to try for their lives and liberties the men who attempted to do its duty for it. And this is called *justice*! They who have shown that they can behave particularly well may perchance be put under bonds for *their good behavior*. They whom truth requires at present to plead guilty, are of all the inhabitants of the State, pre-eminently innocent. While the Governor, and the Mayor, and countless officers of the Commonwealth, are at large, the champions of liberty are imprisoned.

Only they are guiltless, who commit the crime of contempt of such a Court. It behoves every man to see that his influence is on the side of justice, and let the courts make their own characters. My sympathies in this case are wholly with the accused, and wholly against the accusers and their judges. Justice is sweet and musical; but injustice is harsh and discordant. The judge still sits grinding at his organ, but it yields no music, and we hear only the sound of the handle. He believes that all the music resides in the handle, and the crowd toss him their coppers the same as before.

Do you suppose that that Massachusetts which is now doing these things,—which hesitates to crown these men, some of whose lawyers, and even judges, perchance, may be driven to take refuge in some poor quibble, that they may not wholly outrage their instinctive sense of justice,—do you suppose that she is any thing but base and servile? that she is the champion of liberty?

Show me a free State, and a court truly of justice, and I will fight for them, if need be; but show me Massachusetts, and I refuse her my allegiance, and express contempt for her courts.

The effect of a good government is to make life more valuable,—of a bad one, to make it less valuable. We can afford that railroad, and all merely material stock, should lose some of its value, for that only compels us to live more simply and economically; but suppose that the value of life itself should be diminished! How can we make a less demand on man and nature, how live more economically in respect to virtue and all noble qualities, than we do? I have lived for the last month,—and I think that every man in Massachusetts capable of the sentiment of patriotism must have had a similar experience,—with the sense of having suffered a vast and indefinite loss. I did not know at first what ailed me. At last it occurred to me that what I had lost was a country. I had never respected the Government near to which I had lived, but I had foolishly thought that I might manage to live here, minding my private affairs, and forget it. For my part, my old and worthiest pursuits have lost I cannot say how much of their attraction, and I feel that my investment in life here is worth many per cent. less since Massachusetts last deliberately sent back an innocent man, Anthony Burns, to slavery. I dwelt before, perhaps, in the illusion that my life passed somewhere only *between* heaven and hell, but now I cannot persuade myself that I do not dwell *wholly within* hell. The site of that political organization called Massachusetts is to me morally covered with volcanic scoriæ and cinders, such as Milton describes in the infernal regions. If there is any hell more unprincipled than our rulers, and we, the ruled, I feel curious to see it. Life itself being worth less, all things with it, which minister to it, are worth less. Suppose you have a small library, with pictures to adorn the walls—a garden laid out around— and contemplate scientific and literary pursuits, &c., and discover all at once that your villa, with all its contents, is located in hell, and that the justice of the peace has a cloven foot and forked tail—do not these things suddenly lose their value in your eyes?

I feel that, to some extent, the State has fatally interfered with my lawful business. It has not only interrupted me in my passage through Court street on errands of trade, but it has interrupted me and every man on his onward and upward path, on which he had trusted soon to leave Court street far behind. What right had it to remind me of Court street? I have found that hollow which even I had relied on for solid.

I am surprised to see men going about their business as if nothing had happened. I say to myself—Unfortunates! they have not heard the news. I am surprised that the man whom I just met on horseback should be so earnest to overtake his newly-bought cows running away—since all property is insecure—and if they do not run away again, they may be taken away from him when he gets them. Fool! does he not know that his seed-corn is worth less this year—that all beneficent harvests fail as you approach the empire of hell? No prudent man will build a stone house under these circumstances, or engage in any peaceful enterprise which it requires a long time to accomplish. Art is as long as ever, but life is more interrupted and less available for a man's proper pursuits. It is not an era of repose. We have used up all our inherited freedom. If we would save our lives, we must fight for them.

I walk toward one of our ponds, but what signifies the beauty of nature when men are base? We walk to lakes to see our serenity reflected in them; when we are not serene, we go not to them. Who can be serene in a country where both the rulers and the ruled are without principle? The remembrance of my country spoils my walk. My thoughts are murder to the State, and involuntarily go plotting against her.

But it chanced the other day that I scented a white water-lily, and a season I had waited for had arrived. It is the emblem of purity. It bursts up so pure and fair to the eye, and so sweet to the scent, as if to show us what purity and sweetness reside in, and can be extracted from, the slime and muck of earth. I think I have plucked the first one that has opened for a mile. What confirmation of our hopes is in the fragrance of this flower! I shall not so soon despair of the world for it, notwithstanding slavery, and the cowardice and want of principle of Northern men. It suggests what kind of laws have prevailed longest and widest, and still prevail, and that the time may come when man's deeds will smell as sweet. Such is the odor which the plant emits. If Nature can compound this fragrance still annually, I shall believe her still young and full of vigor, her integrity and genius unimpaired, and that there is virtue even in man, too, who is fitted to perceive and love it. It reminds me that Nature has been partner to no Missouri Compromise. I scent no compromise in the fragrance of the water-lily. It is not a *Nymphœa Douglassii*. In it, the sweet, and pure, and innocent, are wholly sundered from the obscene and baleful. I do not scent in this the time-serving irresolution of a Massachusetts Governor, nor of a Boston Mayor. So behave that the odor of your actions may enhance the general sweetness of the atmosphere, that when we behold or scent a flower, we may not be reminded how inconsistent your deeds are with it; for all odor is but one form of advertisement of a moral quality, and if fair actions had not been performed, the lily would not smell sweet. The foul slime stands for the sloth and vice of man, the decay of humanity; the fragrant flower that springs from it, for the purity and courage which are immortal.

Slavery and servility have produced no sweet-scented flower annually, to charm the senses of men, for they have no real life: they are merely a decaying and a death, offensive to all healthy nostrils. We do not complain that they *live*, but that they do not *get buried*. Let the living bury them; even they are good for manure.

Life Without Principle

At a lyceum, not long since, I felt that the lecturer had chosen a theme too foreign to himself, and so failed to interest me as much as he might have done. He described things not in or near to his heart, but toward his extremities and superficies. There was, in this sense, no truly central or centralizing thought in the lecture. I would have had him deal with his privatest experience, as the poet does. The greatest compliment that was ever paid me was when one asked me what I *thought*, and attended to my answer. I am surprised, as well as delighted, when this happens, it is such a rare use he would make of me, as if he were acquainted with the tool. Commonly, if men want anything of me, it is only to know how many acres I make of their land,—since I am a surveyor,—or, at most, what trivial news I have burdened myself with. They never will go to law for my meat; they prefer the shell. A man once came a considerable distance to ask me to lecture on Slavery; but on conversing with him, I found that he and his clique expected seven-eighths of the lecture to be theirs, and only one-eighth mine; so I declined. I take it for granted, when I am invited to lecture anywhere,—for I have had a little experience in that business,—that there is a desire to hear what I *think* on some subject, though I may be the greatest fool in the country,—and not that I should say pleasant things merely, or such as the audience will assent to; and I resolve, accordingly, that I will give them a strong dose of myself. They have sent for me, and engaged to pay for me, and I am determined that they shall have me, though I bore them beyond all precedent.

So now I would say something similar to you, my readers. Since *you* are my readers, and I have not been much of a traveller, I will not talk about people a thousand miles off, but come as near home as I can. As the time is short, I will leave out all the flattery, and retain all the criticism.

Let us consider the way in which we spend our lives.

This world is a place of business. What an infinite bustle! I am awaked almost every night by the panting of the locomotive. It interrupts my dreams. There is no sabbath. It would be glorious to see mankind at leisure for once. It is nothing but work, work, work. I cannot easily buy a blank-book to write thoughts in; they are commonly ruled for dollars and cents. An Irishman, seeing me making a minute in the fields, took it for granted that I was calculating my wages. If a man was tossed out of a window when an infant, and so made a cripple for life, or scared out of his wits by the Indians, it is regretted chiefly because he was thus incapacitated for—business! I think that there is nothing, not even crime, more opposed to poetry, to philosophy, ay, to life itself, than this incessant business.

There is a coarse and boisterous money-making fellow in the outskirts of our town, who is going to build a bank-wall under the hill along the edge of his meadow. The powers have put this into his head to keep him out of mischief, and he wishes me to spend three weeks digging there with him. The result will be that he will perhaps get some more money to hoard, and leave for his heirs to spend foolishly. If I do this, most will commend me as an industrious and hard-working man; but if I choose to devote myself to certain labors which yield more real profit, though but little money, they may be inclined to look on me as an idler. Nevertheless, as I do not need the police of meaningless labor to regulate me, and do not see anything absolutely praiseworthy in this fellow's undertaking, any more than in many an enterprise of our own or foreign governments, however amusing it may be to him or them, I prefer to finish my education at a different school.

If a man walk in the woods for love of them half of each day, he is in danger of being regarded as a loafer; but if he spends his whole day as a speculator, shearing off those woods and making earth bald before her time, he is esteemed an industrious and enterprising citizen. As if a town had no interest in its forests but to cut them down!

Most men would feel insulted, if it were proposed to employ them in throwing stones over a wall, and then in throwing them back, merely that they might earn their wages. But many are no more worthily employed now. For instance: just after sunrise, one summer morning, I noticed one of my neighbors walking beside his team, which was slowly drawing a heavy hewn stone swung under the axle, surrounded by an atmosphere of industry,—his day's work begun,—his brow commenced to sweat,—a reproach to all sluggards and idlers,—pausing abreast the shoulders of his oxen, and half turning round with a flourish of his merciful whip, while they gained their length on him. And I thought, Such is the labor which the American Congress exists to protect,—honest, manly toil,—honest as the day is long,—that makes his bread taste sweet, and keeps society sweet,—which all men respect and have consecrated: one of the sacred band, doing the needful, but irksome drudgery. Indeed, I felt a slight reproach, because I observed this from the window, and was not abroad and stirring about a similar business. The day went by, and at evening I passed the yard of another neighbor, who keeps many servants, and spends much money foolishly, while he adds nothing to the common stock, and there I saw the stone of the morning lying beside a whimsical structure intended to adorn this Lord Timothy Dexter's premises, and the dignity forthwith departed from the teamster's labor, in my eyes. In my opinion, the sun was made to light worthier toil than this. I may add, that his employer has since run off, in debt to a good part of the town, and, after passing through Chancery, has settled somewhere else, there to become once more a patron of the arts.

The ways by which you may get money almost without exception lead downward. To have done anything by which you earned money *merely* is to have been truly idle or worse. If the laborer gets no more than the wages which his employer pays him, he is cheated, he cheats himself. If you would get money as a writer or lecturer, you must be popular, which is to go down perpendicularly. Those services which the community will most readily pay for it is most disagreeable to render. You are paid for being something less than a man. The State does not commonly reward a genius any more wisely. Even the poet-laureate would rather not have to celebrate the accidents of royalty. He must be bribed with a pipe of wine; and perhaps another poet is called away from his muse to gauge that very pipe. As for my own business, even that kind of surveying which I could do with most satisfaction my employers do not want. They would prefer that I should do my work coarsely and not too well, ay, not well enough. When I observe that there are different ways of surveying, my employer commonly asks which will give him the most land, not which is most correct. I once invented a rule for measuring cord-wood, and tried to introduce it in Boston; but the measurer there told me that the sellers did not wish to have their wood measured correctly,—that he was already too accurate for them, and therefore they commonly got their wood measured in Charlestown before crossing the bridge.

The aim of the laborer should be, not to get his living, to get "a good job," but to perform well a certain work; and, even in a pecuniary sense, it would be economy for a town to pay its laborers so well that they would not feel that they were working for low ends, as for a livelihood merely, but for scientific, or even moral ends. Do not hire a man who does your work for money, but him who does it for love of it.

It is remarkable that there are few men so well employed, so much to their minds, but that a little money or fame would commonly buy them off from their present pursuit. I see advertisements for *active* young men, as if activity were the whole of a young man's capital. Yet I have been surprised when one has with confidence proposed to me, a grown man, to embark in some enterprise of his, as if I had absolutely nothing to do, my life having been a complete failure hitherto. What a doubtful compliment this is to pay me! As if he had met me half-way across the ocean beating up against the wind, but bound nowhere, and proposed to me to go along with him! If I did, what do you think the underwriters would say? No, no! I am not without employment at this stage of the voyage. To tell the truth, I saw an advertisement for able-bodied seamen, when I was a boy, sauntering in my native port, and as soon as I came of age I embarked.

The community has no bribe that will tempt a wise man. You may raise money enough to tunnel a mountain, but you cannot raise money enough to hire a man who is minding *his own* business. An efficient and valuable man does what he can, whether the community pay him for it or not. The inefficient offer their inefficiency to the highest bidder, and are forever expecting to be put into office. One would suppose that they were rarely disappointed.

Perhaps I am more than usually jealous with respect to my freedom. I feel that my connection with and obligation to society are still very slight and transient. Those slight labors which afford me a livelihood, and by which it is allowed that I am to some extent serviceable to my contemporaries, are as yet commonly a pleasure to me, and I am not often reminded that they are a necessity. So far I am successful. But I foresee, that, if my wants should be much increased, the labor required to supply them would become a drudgery. If I should sell both my forenoons and afternoons to society, as most appear to do, I am sure, that, for me, there would be nothing left worth living for. I trust that I shall never thus sell my birthright for a mess of pottage. I wish to suggest that a man may be very industrious, and yet not spend his time well. There is no more fatal blunderer than he who consumes the greater part of his life getting his living. All great enterprises are self-supporting. The poet, for instance, must sustain his body by his poetry, as a steam planing-mill feeds its boilers with the shavings it makes. You must get your living by loving. But as it is said of the merchants that ninety-seven in a hundred fail, so the life of men generally, tried by this standard, is a failure, and bankruptcy may be surely prophesied.

Merely to come into the world the heir of a fortune is not to be born, but to be still-born, rather. To be supported by the charity of friends, or a government-pension,—provided you continue to breathe,—by whatever fine synonymes you describe these relations, is to go into the almshouse. On Sundays the poor debtor goes to church to take an account of stock, and finds, of course, that his outgoes have been greater than his income. In the Catholic Church, especially, they go into Chancery, make a clean confession, give up all, and think to start again. Thus men will lie on their backs, talking about the fall of man, and never make an effort to get up.

As for the comparative demand which men make on life, it is an important difference between two, that the one is satisfied with a level success, that his marks can all be hit by point-blank shots, but the other, however low and unsuccessful his life may be, constantly elevates his aim, though at a very slight angle to the horizon. I should much rather be the last man,—though, as the Orientals say, "Greatness doth not approach him who is forever looking down; and all those who are looking high are growing poor."

It is remarkable that there is little or nothing to be remembered written on the subject of getting a living: how to make getting a living not merely honest and honorable, but altogether inviting and glorious; for if *getting* a living is not so, then living is not. One would think, from looking at literature, that this question had never disturbed a solitary individual's musings. Is it that men are too much disgusted with their experience to speak of it? The lesson of value which money teaches, which the Author of the Universe has taken so much pains to teach us, we are inclined to skip altogether. As for the means of living, it is wonderful how indifferent men of all classes are about it, even reformers, so called,—whether they inherit, or earn, or steal it. I think that society has done nothing for us in this respect, or at least has undone what she has done. Cold and hunger seem more friendly to my nature than those methods which men have adopted and advise to ward them off.

The title *wise* is, for the most part, falsely applied. How can one be a wise man, if he does not know any better how to live than other men?—if he is only more cunning and intellectually subtle? Does Wisdom work in a tread-mill? or does she teach how to succeed *by her example*? Is there any such thing as wisdom not applied to life? Is she merely the miller who grinds the finest logic? It is pertinent to ask if Plato got his *living* in a better way or more successfully than his contemporaries,—or did he succumb to the difficulties of life like other men? Did he seem to prevail over some of them merely by indifference, or by assuming grand airs? or find it easier to live, because his aunt remembered him in her will? The ways in which most men get their living, that is, live, are mere make-shifts, and a shirking of the real business of life,—chiefly because they do not know, but partly because they do not mean, any better.

The rush to California, for instance, and the attitude, not merely of merchants, but of philosophers and prophets, so called, in relation to it, reflect the greatest disgrace on mankind. That so many are ready to live by luck, and so get the means of commanding the labor of others less lucky, with-

out contributing any value to society! And that is called en-
terprise! I know of no more startling development of the im-
morality of trade, and all the common modes of getting a
living. The philosophy and poetry and religion of such a man-
kind are not worth the dust of a puff-ball. The hog that gets
his living by rooting, stirring up the soil so, would be
ashamed of such company. If I could command the wealth of
all the worlds by lifting my finger, I would not pay *such* a
price for it. Even Mahomet knew that God did not make this
world in jest. It makes God to be a moneyed gentleman who
scatters a handful of pennies in order to see mankind scram-
ble for them. The world's raffle! A subsistence in the domains
of Nature a thing to be raffled for! What a comment, what a
satire on our institutions! The conclusion will be, that
mankind will hang itself upon a tree. And have all the pre-
cepts in all the Bibles taught men only this? and is the last and
most admirable invention of the human race only an im-
proved muck-rake? Is this the ground on which Orientals and
Occidentals meet? Did God direct us so to get our living, dig-
ging where we never planted,—and He would, perchance, re-
ward us with lumps of gold?

God gave the righteous man a certificate entitling him to
food and raiment, but the unrighteous man found a *facsimile*
of the same in God's coffers, and appropriated it, and ob-
tained food and raiment like the former. It is one of the most
extensive systems of counterfeiting that the world has seen. I
did not know that mankind were suffering for want of gold.
I have seen a little of it. I know that it is very malleable, but
not so malleable as wit. A grain of gold will gild a great sur-
face, but not so much as a grain of wisdom.

The gold-digger in the ravines of the mountains is as much
a gambler as his fellow in the saloons of San Francisco. What
difference does it make, whether you shake dirt or shake dice?
If you win, society is the loser. The gold-digger is the enemy
of the honest laborer, whatever checks and compensations
there may be. It is not enough to tell me that you worked
hard to get your gold. So does the Devil work hard. The way
of transgressors may be hard in many respects. The humblest
observer who goes to the mines sees and says that gold-dig-
ging is of the character of a lottery; the gold thus obtained is

not the same thing with the wages of honest toil. But, practically, he forgets what he has seen, for he has seen only the fact, not the principle, and goes into trade there, that is, buys a ticket in what commonly proves another lottery, where the fact is not so obvious.

After reading Howitt's account of the Australian gold-diggings one evening, I had in my mind's eye, all night, the numerous valleys, with their streams, all cut up with foul pits, from ten to one hundred feet deep, and half a dozen feet across, as close as they can be dug, and partly filled with water,—the locality to which men furiously rush to probe for their fortunes,—uncertain where they shall break ground,—not knowing but the gold is under their camp itself,—sometimes digging one hundred and sixty feet before they strike the vein, or then missing it by a foot,—turned into demons, and regardless of each other's rights, in their thirst for riches,—whole valleys, for thirty miles, suddenly honeycombed by the pits of the miners, so that even hundreds are drowned in them,—standing in water, and covered with mud and clay, they work night and day, dying of exposure and disease. Having read this, and partly forgotten it, I was thinking, accidentally, of my own unsatisfactory life, doing as others do; and with that vision of the diggings still before me, I asked myself, why I might not be washing some gold daily, though it were only the finest particles,—why I might not sink a shaft down to the gold within me, and work that mine. *There* is a Ballarat, a Bendigo for you,—what though it were a Sulky Gully? At any rate, I might pursue some path, however solitary and narrow and crooked, in which I could walk with love and reverence. Wherever a man separates from the multitude, and goes his own way in this mood, there indeed is a fork in the road, though ordinary travellers may see only a gap in the paling. His solitary path across-lots will turn out the *higher way* of the two.

Men rush to California and Australia as if the true gold were to be found in that direction; but that is to go to the very opposite extreme to where it lies. They go prospecting farther and farther away from the true lead, and are most unfortunate when they think themselves most successful. Is not our *native* soil auriferous? Does not a stream from the golden

mountains flow through our native valley? and has not this for
more than geologic ages been bringing down the shining par-
ticles and forming the nuggets for us? Yet, strange to tell, if a
digger steal away, prospecting for this true gold, into the un-
explored solitudes around us, there is no danger that any will
dog his steps, and endeavor to supplant him. He may claim
and undermine the whole valley even, both the cultivated and
the uncultivated portions, his whole life long in peace, for no
one will ever dispute his claim. They will not mind his cradles
or his toms. He is not confined to a claim twelve feet square,
as at Ballarat, but may mine anywhere, and wash the whole
wide world in his tom.

Howitt says of the man who found the great nugget which
weighed twenty-eight pounds, at the Bendigo diggings in
Australia:—"He soon began to drink; got a horse and rode all
about, generally at full gallop, and when he met people, called
out to inquire if they knew who he was, and then kindly in-
formed them that he was 'the bloody wretch that had found
the nugget.' At last he rode full speed against a tree, and
nearly knocked his brains out." I think, however, there was no
danger of that, for he had already knocked his brains out
against the nugget. Howitt adds, "He is a hopelessly ruined
man." But he is a type of the class. They are all fast men. Hear
some of the names of the places where they dig:—"Jackass
Flat,"—"Sheep's-Head Gully,"—"Murderer's Bar," etc. Is
there no satire in these names? Let them carry their ill-gotten
wealth where they will, I am thinking it will still be "Jackass
Flat," if not "Murderer's Bar," where they live.

The last resource of our energy has been the robbing of
graveyards on the Isthmus of Darien, an enterprise which ap-
pears to be but in its infancy; for, according to late accounts,
an act has passed its second reading in the legislature of New
Granada, regulating this kind of mining; and a correspondent
of the *Tribune* writes:—"In the dry season, when the weather
will permit of the country being properly prospected, no
doubt other rich '*guacas*' [that is, graveyards] will be found."
To emigrants he says:—"Do not come before December; take
the Isthmus route in preference to the Boca del Toro one;
bring no useless baggage, and do not cumber yourself with a
tent; but a good pair of blankets will be necessary; a pick,

shovel, and axe of good material will be almost all that is required": advice which might have been taken from the "Burker's Guide." And he concludes with this line in Italics and small capitals: "*If you are doing well at home,* STAY THERE," which may fairly be interpreted to mean, "If you are getting a good living by robbing graveyards at home, stay there."

But why go to California for a text? She is the child of New England, bred at her own school and church.

It is remarkable that among all the preachers there are so few moral teachers. The prophets are employed in excusing the ways of men. Most reverend seniors, the *illuminati* of the age, tell me, with a gracious, reminiscent smile, betwixt an aspiration and a shudder, not to be too tender about these things,—to lump all that, that is, make a lump of gold of it. The highest advice I have heard on these subjects was grovelling. The burden of it was,—It is not worth your while to undertake to reform the world in this particular. Do not ask how your bread is buttered; it will make you sick, if you do,—and the like. A man had better starve at once than lose his innocence in the process of getting his bread. If within the sophisticated man there is not an unsophisticated one, then he is but one of the Devil's angels. As we grow old, we live more coarsely, we relax a little in our disciplines, and, to some extent, cease to obey our finest instincts. But we should be fastidious to the extreme of sanity, disregarding the gibes of those who are more unfortunate than ourselves.

In our science and philosophy, even, there is commonly no true and absolute account of things. The spirit of sect and bigotry has planted its hoof amid the stars. You have only to discuss the problem, whether the stars are inhabited or not, in order to discover it. Why must we daub the heavens as well as the earth? It was an unfortunate discovery that Dr. Kane was a Mason, and that Sir John Franklin was another. But it was a more cruel suggestion that possibly that was the reason why the former went in search of the latter. There is not a popular magazine in this country that would dare to print a child's thought on important subjects without comment. It must be submitted to the D. D.s. I would it were the chicka-dee-dees.

You come from attending the funeral of mankind to attend

to a natural phenomenon. A little thought is sexton to all the world.

I hardly know an *intellectual* man, even, who is so broad and truly liberal that you can think aloud in his society. Most with whom you endeavor to talk soon come to a stand against some institution in which they appear to hold stock,—that is, some particular, not universal, way of viewing things. They will continually thrust their own low roof, with its narrow skylight, between you and the sky, when it is the unobstructed heavens you would view. Get out of the way with your cobwebs, wash your windows, I say! In some lyceums they tell me that they have voted to exclude the subject of religion. But how do I know what their religion is, and when I am near to or far from it? I have walked into such an arena and done my best to make a clean breast of what religion I have experienced, and the audience never suspected what I was about. The lecture was as harmless as moonshine to them. Whereas, if I had read to them the biography of the greatest scamps in history, they might have thought that I had written the lives of the deacons of their church. Ordinarily, the inquiry is, Where did you come from? or, Where are you going? That was a more pertinent question which I overheard one of my auditors put to another once,—"What does he lecture for?" It made me quake in my shoes.

To speak impartially, the best men that I know are not serene, a world in themselves. For the most part, they dwell in forms, and flatter and study effect only more finely than the rest. We select granite for the underpinning of our houses and barns; we build fences of stone; but we do not ourselves rest on an underpinning of granitic truth, the lowest primitive rock. Our sills are rotten. What stuff is the man made of who is not coexistent in our thought with the purest and subtilest truth? I often accuse my finest acquaintances of an immense frivolity; for, while there are manners and compliments we do not meet, we do not teach one another the lessons of honesty and sincerity that the brutes do, or of steadiness and solidity that the rocks do. The fault is commonly mutual, however; for we do not habitually demand any more of each other.

That excitement about Kossuth, consider how characteristic, but superficial, it was!—only another kind of politics or dancing. Men were making speeches to him all over the country, but each expressed only the thought, or the want of thought, of the multitude. No man stood on truth. They were merely banded together, as usual, one leaning on another, and all together on nothing; as the Hindoos made the world rest on an elephant, the elephant on a tortoise, and the tortoise on a serpent, and had nothing to put under the serpent. For all fruit of that stir we have the Kossuth hat.

Just so hollow and ineffectual, for the most part, is our ordinary conversation. Surface meets surface. When our life ceases to be inward and private, conversation degenerates into mere gossip. We rarely meet a man who can tell us any news which he has not read in a newspaper, or been told by his neighbor; and, for the most part, the only difference between us and our fellow is, that he has seen the newspaper, or been out to tea, and we have not. In proportion as our inward life fails, we go more constantly and desperately to the post-office. You may depend on it, that the poor fellow who walks away with the greatest number of letters, proud of his extensive correspondence, has not heard from himself this long while.

I do not know but it is too much to read one newspaper a week. I have tried it recently, and for so long it seems to me that I have not dwelt in my native region. The sun, the clouds, the snow, the trees say not so much to me. You cannot serve two masters. It requires more than a day's devotion to know and to possess the wealth of a day.

We may well be ashamed to tell what things we have read or heard in our day. I do not know why my news should be so trivial,—considering what one's dreams and expectations are, why the developments should be so paltry. The news we hear, for the most part, is not news to our genius. It is the stalest repetition. You are often tempted to ask, why such stress is laid on a particular experience which you have had,—that, after twenty-five years, you should meet Hobbins, Registrar of Deeds, again on the sidewalk. Have you not budged an inch, then? Such is the daily news. Its facts appear to float in the atmosphere, insignificant as the sporules of

fungi, and impinge on some neglected *thallus*, or surface
of our minds, which affords a basis for them, and hence a para-
sitic growth. We should wash ourselves clean of such news. Of
what consequence, though our planet explode, if there is no
character involved in the explosion? In health we have not the
least curiosity about such events. We do not live for idle
amusement. I would not run round a corner to see the world
blow up.

All summer, and far into the autumn, perchance, you un-
consciously went by the newspapers and the news, and now
you find it was because the morning and the evening were full
of news to you. Your walks were full of incidents. You at-
tended, not to the affairs of Europe, but to your own affairs
in Massachusetts fields. If you chance to live and move and
have your being in that thin stratum in which the events that
make the news transpire,—thinner than the paper on which it
is printed,—then these things will fill the world for you; but if
you soar above or dive below that plane, you cannot remem-
ber nor be reminded of them. Really to see the sun rise or go
down every day, so to relate ourselves to a universal fact,
would preserve us sane forever. Nations! What are nations?
Tartars, and Huns, and Chinamen! Like insects, they swarm.
The historian strives in vain to make them memorable. It is
for want of a man that there are so many men. It is individu-
als that populate the world. Any man thinking may say with
the Spirit of Lodin,—

> "I look down from my height on nations,
> And they become ashes before me;—
> Calm is my dwelling in the clouds;
> Pleasant are the great fields of my rest."

Pray, let us live without being drawn by dogs, Esquimaux-
fashion, tearing over hill and dale, and biting each other's ears.

Not without a slight shudder at the danger, I often per-
ceive how near I had come to admitting into my mind the de-
tails of some trivial affair,—the news of the street; and I am
astonished to observe how willing men are to lumber their
minds with such rubbish,—to permit idle rumors and inci-
dents of the most insignificant kind to intrude on ground
which should be sacred to thought. Shall the mind be a

public arena, where the affairs of the street and the gossip of the tea-table chiefly are discussed? Or shall it be a quarter of heaven itself,—an hypæthral temple, consecrated to the service of the gods? I find it so difficult to dispose of the few facts which to me are significant, that I hesitate to burden my attention with those which are insignificant, which only a divine mind could illustrate. Such is, for the most part, the news in newspapers and conversation. It is important to preserve the mind's chastity in this respect. Think of admitting the details of a single case of the criminal court into our thoughts, to stalk profanely through their very *sanctum sanctorum* for an hour, ay, for many hours! to make a very barroom of the mind's inmost apartment, as if for so long the dust of the street had occupied us,—the very street itself, with all its travel, its bustle, and filth had passed through our thoughts' shrine! Would it not be an intellectual and moral suicide? When I have been compelled to sit spectator and auditor in a court-room for some hours, and have seen my neighbors, who were not compelled, stealing in from time to time, and tiptoeing about with washed hands and faces, it has appeared to my mind's eye, that, when they took off their hats, their ears suddenly expanded into vast hoppers for sound, between which even their narrow heads were crowded. Like the vanes of windmills, they caught the broad, but shallow stream of sound, which, after a few titillating gyrations in their coggy brains, passed out the other side. I wondered if, when they got home, they were as careful to wash their ears as before their hands and faces. It has seemed to me, at such a time, that the auditors and the witnesses, the jury and the counsel, the judge and the criminal at the bar,— if I may presume him guilty before he is convicted,—were all equally criminal, and a thunderbolt might be expected to descend and consume them all together.

By all kinds of traps and sign-boards, threatening the extreme penalty of the divine law, exclude such trespassers from the only ground which can be sacred to you. It is so hard to forget what it is worse than useless to remember! If I am to be a thoroughfare, I prefer that it be of the mountain-brooks, the Parnassian streams, and not the town-sewers. There is inspiration, that gossip which comes to the ear of the attentive mind from the courts of heaven. There is the profane and stale revelation of the bar-room and the police court. The same ear is fitted to receive both communications. Only the character of the hearer determines to which it shall be open, and to which closed. I believe that the mind can be permanently profaned by the habit of attending to trivial things, so that all our thoughts shall be tinged with triviality. Our very intellect shall be macadamized, as it were,—its foundation broken into fragments for the wheels of travel to roll over; and if you would know what will make the most durable pavement, surpassing rolled stones, spruce blocks, and asphaltum, you have only to look into some of our minds which have been subjected to this treatment so long.

If we have thus desecrated ourselves,—as who has not?—the remedy will be by wariness and devotion to reconsecrate ourselves, and make once more a fane of the mind. We should treat our minds, that is, ourselves, as innocent and ingenuous children, whose guardians we are, and be careful what objects and what subjects we thrust on their attention. Read not the Times. Read the Eternities. Conventionalities are at length as bad as impurities. Even the facts of science may dust the mind by their dryness, unless they are in a sense effaced each morning, or rather rendered fertile by the dews of fresh and living truth. Knowledge does not come to us by details, but in flashes of light from heaven. Yes, every thought that passes through the mind helps to wear and tear it, and to deepen the ruts, which, as in the streets of Pompeii, evince how much it has been used. How many things there are concerning which we might well deliberate, whether we had better know them,—had better let their peddling-carts be driven, even at the slowest trot or walk, over that bridge of glorious span by which we trust to pass at last from the farthest brink of time to the nearest shore of eternity! Have we no culture, no refinement,—but skill only to live coarsely and serve the Devil?—to acquire a little worldly wealth, or fame, or liberty, and make a false show with it, as if we were all husk and shell, with no tender and living kernel to us? Shall our institutions be like those chestnut-burs which contain abortive nuts, perfect only to prick the fingers?

America is said to be the arena on which the battle of freedom is to be fought; but surely it cannot be freedom in a merely political sense that is meant. Even if we grant that the American has freed himself from a political tyrant, he is still the slave of an economical and moral tyrant. Now that the republic—the *res-publica*—has been settled, it is time to look after the *res-privata*,—the private state,—to see, as the Roman senate charged its consuls, *"ne quid res-*PRIVATA *detrimenti caperet,"* that the *private* state receive no detriment.

Do we call this the land of the free? What is it to be free from King George and continue the slaves of King Prejudice? What is it to be born free and not to live free? What is the value of any political freedom, but as a means to moral freedom? Is it a freedom to be slaves, or a freedom to be free, of which we boast? We are a nation of politicians, concerned about the outmost defences only of freedom. It is our children's children who may perchance be really free. We tax ourselves unjustly. There is a part of us which is not represented. It is taxation without representation. We quarter troops, we quarter fools and cattle of all sorts upon ourselves. We quarter our gross bodies on our poor souls, till the former eat up all the latter's substance.

With respect to a true culture and manhood, we are essentially provincial still, not metropolitan,—mere Jonathans. We are provincial, because we do not find at home our standards,—because we do not worship truth, but the reflection of truth,—because we are warped and narrowed by an exclusive devotion to trade and commerce and manufactures and agriculture and the like, which are but means, and not the end.

So is the English Parliament provincial. Mere country-bumpkins, they betray themselves, when any more important question arises for them to settle, the Irish question, for instance,—the English question why did I not say? Their natures are subdued to what they work in. Their "good breeding" respects only secondary objects. The finest manners in the world are awkwardness and fatuity, when contrasted with a finer intelligence. They appear but as the fashions of past days,—mere courtliness, knee-buckles and small-clothes, out of date. It is the vice, but not the excellence of manners, that they are continually being deserted by the character; they are cast-off clothes or shells, claiming the re-

spect which belonged to the living creature. You are pre-
sented with the shells instead of the meat, and it is no excuse
generally, that, in the case of some fishes, the shells are of
more worth than the meat. The man who thrusts his manners
upon me does as if he were to insist on introducing me to his
cabinet of curiosities, when I wished to see himself. It was not
in this sense that the poet Decker called Christ "the first true
gentleman that ever breathed." I repeat that in this sense the
most splendid court in Christendom is provincial, having au-
thority to consult about Transalpine interests only, and not
the affairs of Rome. A praetor or proconsul would suffice to
settle the questions which absorb the attention of the English
Parliament and the American Congress.

Government and legislation! these I thought were re-
spectable professions. We have heard of heaven-born Numas,
Lycurguses, and Solons, in the history of the world, whose
names at least may stand for ideal legislators; but think of leg-
islating to *regulate* the breeding of slaves, or the exportation
of tobacco! What have divine legislators to do with the ex-
portation or the importation of tobacco? What humane ones
with the breeding of slaves? Suppose you were to submit the
question to any son of God,—and has He no children in
the nineteenth century? is it a family which is extinct?—
in what condition would you get it again? What shall a
State like Virginia say for itself at the last day, in which these
have been the principal, the staple productions? What ground
is there for patriotism in such a State? I derive my facts from
statistical tables which the States themselves have published.

A commerce that whitens every sea in quest of nuts and
raisins, and makes slaves of its sailors for this purpose! I saw,
the other day, a vessel which had been wrecked, and many
lives lost, and her cargo of rags, juniper-berries, and bitter al-
monds were strewn along the shore. It seemed hardly worth
the while to tempt the dangers of the sea between Leghorn
and New York for the sake of a cargo of juniper-berries and
bitter almonds. America sending to the Old World for her bit-
ters! Is not the sea-brine, is not shipwreck, bitter enough to
make the cup of life go down here? Yet such, to a great ex-
tent, is our boasted commerce; and there are those who style
themselves statesmen and philosophers who are so blind as to

think that progress and civilization depend on precisely this kind of interchange and activity,—the activity of flies about a molasses-hogshead. Very well, observes one, if men were oysters. And very well, answer I, if men were mosquitoes.

Lieutenant Herndon, whom our Government sent to explore the Amazon, and, it is said, to extend the area of Slavery, observed that there was wanting there "an industrious and active population, who know what the comforts of life are, and who have artificial wants to draw out the great resources of the country." But what are the "artificial wants" to be encouraged? Not the love of luxuries, like the tobacco and slaves of, I believe, his native Virginia, nor the ice and granite and other material wealth of our native New England; nor are "the great resources of a country" that fertility or barrenness of soil which produces these. The chief want, in every State that I have been into, was a high and earnest purpose in its inhabitants. This alone draws out "the great resources" of Nature, and at last taxes her beyond her resources; for man naturally dies out of her. When we want culture more than potatoes, and illumination more than sugar-plums, then the great resources of a world are taxed and drawn out, and the result, or staple production, is, not slaves, nor operatives, but men,—those rare fruits called heroes, saints, poets, philosophers, and redeemers.

In short, as a snow-drift is formed where there is a lull in the wind, so, one would say, where there is a lull of truth, an institution springs up. But the truth blows right on over it, nevertheless, and at length blows it down.

What is called politics is comparatively something so superficial and inhuman, that, practically, I have never fairly recognized that it concerns me at all. The newspapers, I perceive, devote some of their columns specially to politics or government without charge; and this, one would say, is all that saves it; but, as I love literature, and, to some extent, the truth also, I never read those columns at any rate. I do not wish to blunt my sense of right so much. I have not got to answer for having read a single President's Message. A strange age of the world this, when empires, kingdoms, and republics come a-begging to a private man's door, and utter their complaints at his elbow! I cannot take up a newspaper but I find that some wretched government or other, hard pushed, and on its last legs, is interceding with me, the reader, to vote for it,—more importunate than an Italian beggar; and if I have a mind to look at its certificate, made, perchance, by some benevolent merchant's clerk, or the skipper that brought it over, for it cannot speak a word of English itself, I shall probably read of the eruption of some Vesuvius, or the overflowing of some Po, true or forged, which brought it into this condition. I do not hesitate, in such a case, to suggest work, or the almshouse; or why not keep its castle in silence, as I do commonly? The poor President, what with preserving his popularity and doing his duty, is completely bewildered. The newspapers are the ruling power. Any other government is reduced to a few marines at Fort Independence. If a man neglects to read the Daily Times, Government will go down on its knees to him, for this is the only treason in these days.

Those things which now most engage the attention of men, as politics and the daily routine, are, it is true, vital functions of human society, but should be unconsciously performed, like the corresponding functions of the physical body. They are *infra*-human, a kind of vegetation. I sometimes awake to a half-consciousness of them going on about me, as a man may become conscious of some of the processes of digestion in a morbid state, and so have the dyspepsia, as it is called. It is as if a thinker submitted himself to be rasped by the great gizzard of creation. Politics is, as it were, the gizzard of society, full of grit and gravel, and the two political parties are its two opposite halves,—sometimes split into quarters, it may be, which grind on each other. Not only individuals, but States, have thus a confirmed dyspepsia, which expresses itself, you can imagine by what sort of eloquence. Thus our life is not altogether a forgetting, but also, alas! to a great extent, a remembering of that which we should never have been conscious of, certainly not in our waking hours. Why should we not meet, not always as dyspeptics, to tell our bad dreams, but sometimes as *eu*peptics, to congratulate each other on the ever glorious morning? I do not make an exorbitant demand, surely.

Autumnal Tints

EUROPEANS coming to America are surprised by the brilliancy of our autumnal foliage. There is no account of such a phenomenon in English poetry, because the trees acquire but few bright colors there. The most that Thomson says on this subject in his "Autumn" is contained in the lines,—

> "But see the fading many-colored woods,
>   Shade deepening over shade, the country round
>   Imbrown; a crowded umbrage, dusk and dun,
>   Of every hue, from wan declining green to sooty dark":—

and in the line in which he speaks of

> "Autumn beaming o'er the yellow woods."

The autumnal change of our woods has not made a deep impression on our own literature yet. October has hardly tinged our poetry.

A great many, who have spent their lives in cities, and have never chanced to come into the country at this season, have never seen this, the flower, or rather the ripe fruit, of the year. I remember riding with one such citizen, who, though a fortnight too late for the most brilliant tints, was taken by surprise, and would not believe that there had been any brighter. He had never heard of this phenomenon before. Not only many in our towns have never witnessed it, but it is scarcely remembered by the majority from year to year.

Most appear to confound changed leaves with withered ones, as if they were to confound ripe apples with rotten ones. I think that the change to some higher color in a leaf is an evidence that it has arrived at a late and perfect maturity, answering to the maturity of fruits. It is generally the lowest and oldest leaves which change first. But as the perfect winged and usually bright-colored insect is short-lived, so the leaves ripen but to fall.

Generally, every fruit, on ripening, and just before it falls, when it commences a more independent and individual existence, requiring less nourishment from any source, and that not so much from the earth through its stem as from the sun and air, acquires a bright tint. So do leaves. The physiologist says it is "due to an increased absorption of oxygen." That is the scientific account of the matter,—only a reassertion of the fact. But I am more interested in the rosy cheek than I am to know what particular diet the maiden fed on. The very forest and herbage, the pellicle of the earth, must acquire a bright color, an evidence of its ripeness,—as if the globe itself were a fruit on its stem, with ever a cheek toward the sun.

Flowers are but colored leaves, fruits but ripe ones. The edible part of most fruits is, as the physiologist says, "the parenchyma or fleshy tissue of the leaf" of which they are formed.

Our appetites have commonly confined our views of ripeness and its phenomena, color, mellowness, and perfectness, to the fruits which we eat, and we are wont to forget that an immense harvest which we do not eat, hardly use at all, is annually ripened by Nature. At our annual Cattle Shows and Horticultural Exhibitions, we make, as we think, a great show of fair fruits, destined, however, to a rather ignoble end, fruits not valued for their beauty chiefly. But round about and within our towns there is annually another show of fruits, on an infinitely grander scale, fruits which address our taste for beauty alone.

October is the month of painted leaves. Their rich glow now flashes round the world. As fruits and leaves and the day itself acquire a bright tint just before they fall, so the year near its setting. October is its sunset sky; November the later twilight.

I formerly thought that it would be worth the while to get a specimen leaf from each changing tree, shrub, and herbaceous plant, when it had acquired its brightest characteristic color, in its transition from the green to the brown state, outline it, and copy its color exactly, with paint, in a book, which should be entitled, *"October, or Autumnal Tints"*;—beginning with the earliest reddening,—Woodbine and the lake of radical leaves, and coming down through the Maples, Hickories, and Sumachs, and many beautifully freckled leaves less generally known, to the latest Oaks and Aspens. What a memento such a book would be! You would need only to turn over its

leaves to take a ramble through the autumn woods whenever
you pleased. Or if I could preserve the leaves themselves, un-
faded, it would be better still. I have made but little progress
toward such a book, but I have endeavored, instead, to de-
scribe all these bright tints in the order in which they present
themselves. The following are some extracts from my notes.

THE PURPLE GRASSES.

By the twentieth of August, everywhere in woods and
swamps, we are reminded of the fall, both by the richly spot-
ted Sarsaparilla-leaves and Brakes, and the withering and
blackened Skunk-Cabbage and Hellebore, and, by the river-
side, the already blackening Pontederia.

The Purple Grass (*Eragrostis pectinacea*) is now in the
height of its beauty. I remember still when I first noticed this
grass particularly. Standing on a hill-side near our river, I saw,
thirty or forty rods off, a stripe of purple half a dozen rods
long, under the edge of a wood, where the ground sloped to-
ward a meadow. It was as high-colored and interesting,
though not quite so bright, as the patches of Rhexia, being a
darker purple, like a berry's stain laid on close and thick. On
going to and examining it, I found it to be a kind of grass in
bloom, hardly a foot high, with but few green blades, and a
fine spreading panicle of purple flowers, a shallow, purplish
mist trembling around me. Close at hand it appeared but a
dull purple, and made little impression on the eye; it was even
difficult to detect; and if you plucked a single plant, you were
surprised to find how thin it was, and how little color it had.
But viewed at a distance in a favorable light, it was of a fine
lively purple, flower-like, enriching the earth. Such puny
causes combine to produce these decided effects. I was the
more surprised and charmed because grass is commonly of a
sober and humble color.

With its beautiful purple blush it reminds me, and supplies
the place, of the Rhexia, which is now leaving off, and it is
one of the most interesting phenomena of August. The finest
patches of it grow on waste strips or selvages of land at the
base of dry hills, just above the edge of the meadows, where
the greedy mower does not deign to swing his scythe; for this

is a thin and poor grass, beneath his notice. Or, it may be, because it is so beautiful he does not know that it exists; for the same eye does not see this and Timothy. He carefully gets the meadow hay and the more nutritious grasses which grow next to that, but he leaves this fine purple mist for the walker's harvest,—fodder for his fancy stock. Higher up the hill, perchance, grow also Blackberries, John's-Wort, and neglected, withered, and wiry June-Grass. How fortunate that it grows in such places, and not in the midst of the rank grasses which are annually cut! Nature thus keeps use and beauty distinct. I know many such localities, where it does not fail to present itself annually, and paint the earth with its blush. It grows on the gentle slopes, either in a continuous patch or in scattered and rounded tufts a foot in diameter, and it lasts till it is killed by the first smart frosts.

In most plants the corolla or calyx is the part which attains the highest color, and is the most attractive; in many it is the seed-vessel or fruit; in others, as the Red Maple, the leaves; and in others still it is the very culm itself which is the principal flower or blooming part.

The last is especially the case with the Poke or Garget (*Phytolacca decandra*). Some which stand under our cliffs quite dazzle me with their purple stems now and early in September. They are as interesting to me as most flowers, and one of the most important fruits of our autumn. Every part is flower, (or fruit,) such is its superfluity of color,—stem, branch, peduncle, pedicel, petiole, and even the at length yellowish purple-veined leaves. Its cylindrical racemes of berries of various hues, from green to dark purple, six or seven inches long, are gracefully drooping on all sides, offering repasts to the birds; and even the sepals from which the birds have picked the berries are a brilliant lake-red, with crimson flame-like reflections, equal to anything of the kind,—all on fire with ripeness. Hence the *lacca*, from *lac*, lake. There are at the same time flower-buds, flowers, green berries, dark purple or ripe ones, and these flower-like sepals, all on the same plant.

We love to see any redness in the vegetation of the temperate zone. It is the color of colors. This plant speaks to our blood. It asks a bright sun on it to make it show to best advantage, and it must be seen at this season of the year. On warm hill-sides its stems are ripe by the twenty-third of August. At that date I walked through a beautiful grove of them, six or seven feet high, on the side of one of our cliffs, where they ripen early. Quite to the ground they were a deep brilliant purple with a bloom, contrasting with the still clear green leaves. It appears a rare triumph of Nature to have produced and perfected such a plant, as if this were enough for a summer. What a perfect maturity it arrives at! It is the emblem of a successful life concluded by a death not premature, which is an ornament to Nature. What if we were to mature as perfectly, root and branch, glowing in the midst of our decay, like the Poke! I confess that it excites me to behold them. I cut one for a cane, for I would fain handle and lean on it. I love to press the berries between my fingers, and see their juice staining my hand. To walk amid these upright, branching casks of purple wine, which retain and diffuse a sunset glow, tasting each one with your eye, instead of counting the pipes on a London dock, what a privilege! For Nature's vintage is not confined to the vine. Our poets have sung of wine, the product of a foreign plant which commonly they never saw, as if our own plants had no juice in them more than the singers. Indeed, this has been called by some the American Grape, and, though a native of America, its juices are used in some foreign countries to improve the color of the wine; so that the poetaster may be celebrating the virtues of the Poke without knowing it. Here are berries enough to paint afresh the western sky, and play the bacchanal with, if you will. And what flutes its ensanguined stems would make, to be used in such a dance! It is truly a royal plant. I could spend the evening of the year musing amid the Poke-stems. And perchance amid these groves might arise at last a new school of philosophy or poetry. It lasts all through September.

At the same time with this, or near the end of August, a to me very interesting genus of grasses, Andropogons, or Beard-Grasses, is in its prime. *Andropogon furcatus*, Forked Beard-Grass, or call it Purple-Fingered Grass; *Andropogon scoparius*, Purple Wood-Grass; and *Andropogon* (now called *Sorghum*) *nutans*, Indian-Grass. The first is a very tall and slender-culmed grass, three to seven feet high, with four or five purple finger-like spikes raying upward from the top. The second is also quite slender, growing in tufts two feet high by one wide, with culms often somewhat curving, which, as the spikes go out of bloom, have a whitish fuzzy look. These two are prevailing grasses at this season on dry and sandy fields and hill-sides. The culms of both, not to mention their pretty flowers, reflect a purple tinge, and help to declare the ripeness of the year. Perhaps I have the more sympathy with them because they are despised by the farmer, and occupy sterile and neglected soil. They are high-colored, like ripe grapes, and express a maturity which the spring did not suggest. Only the August sun could have thus burnished these culms and leaves. The farmer has long since done his upland haying, and he will not condescend to bring his scythe to where these slender wild grasses have at length flowered thinly; you often see spaces of bare sand amid them. But I walk encouraged between the tufts of Purple Wood-Grass, over the sandy fields, and along the edge of the Shrub-Oaks, glad to recognize these simple contemporaries. With thoughts cutting a broad swathe I "get" them, with horse-raking thoughts I gather them into windrows. The fine-eared poet may hear the whetting of my scythe. These two were almost the first grasses that I learned to distinguish, for I had not known by how many friends I was surrounded,—I had seen them simply as grasses standing. The purple of their culms also excites me like that of the Poke-Weed stems.

Think what refuge there is for one, before August is over, from college commencements and society that isolates! I can skulk amid the tufts of Purple Wood-Grass on the borders of the "Great Fields." Wherever I walk these afternoons, the Purple-Fingered Grass also stands like a guide-board, and points my thoughts to more poetic paths than they have lately travelled.

A man shall perhaps rush by and trample down plants as high as his head, and cannot be said to know that they exist, though he may have cut many tons of them, littered his stables with them, and fed them to his cattle for years. Yet, if he ever favorably attends to them, he may be overcome by their beauty. Each humblest plant, or weed, as we call it, stands there to express some thought or mood of ours; and yet how long it stands in vain! I had walked over those Great Fields so

many Augusts, and never yet distinctly recognized these pur-
ple companions that I had there. I had brushed against them
and trodden on them, forsooth; and now, at last, they, as it
were, rose up and blessed me. Beauty and true wealth are al-
ways thus cheap and despised. Heaven might be defined as
the place which men avoid. Who can doubt that these grasses,
which the farmer says are of no account to him, find some
compensation in your appreciation of them? I may say that I
never saw them before,—though, when I came to look them
face to face, there did come down to me a purple gleam from
previous years; and now, wherever I go, I see hardly anything
else. It is the reign and presidency of the Andropogons.

Almost the very sands confess the ripening influence of the
August sun, and methinks, together with the slender grasses
waving over them, reflect a purple tinge. The impurpled
sands! Such is the consequence of all this sunshine absorbed
into the pores of plants and of the earth. All sap or blood is
now wine-colored. At last we have not only the purple sea,
but the purple land.

The Chestnut Beard-Grass, Indian-Grass, or Wood-Grass,
growing here and there in waste places, but more rare than
the former, (from two to four or five feet high,) is still hand-
somer and of more vivid colors than its congeners, and might
well have caught the Indian's eye. It has a long, narrow, one-
sided, and slightly nodding panicle of bright purple and yel-
low flowers, like a banner raised above its reedy leaves. These
bright standards are now advanced on the distant hill-sides,
not in large armies, but in scattered troops or single file, like
the red men. They stand thus fair and bright, representative
of the race which they are named after, but for the most part
unobserved as they. The expression of this grass haunted me
for a week, after I first passed and noticed it, like the glance
of an eye. It stands like an Indian chief taking a last look at his
favorite hunting-grounds.

THE RED MAPLE.

By the twenty-fifth of September, the Red Maples generally
are beginning to be ripe. Some large ones have been conspic-
uously changing for a week, and some single trees are now

very brilliant. I notice a small one, half a mile off across a meadow, against the green wood-side there, a far brighter red than the blossoms of any tree in summer, and more conspicuous. I have observed this tree for several autumns invariably changing earlier than its fellows, just as one tree ripens its fruit earlier than another. It might serve to mark the season, perhaps. I should be sorry, if it were cut down. I know of two or three such trees in different parts of our town, which might, perhaps, be propagated from, as early ripeners or September trees, and their seed be advertised in the market, as well as that of radishes, if we cared as much about them.

At present, these burning bushes stand chiefly along the edge of the meadows, or I distinguish them afar on the hillsides here and there. Sometimes you will see many small ones in a swamp turned quite crimson when all other trees around are still perfectly green, and the former appear so much the brighter for it. They take you by surprise, as you are going by on one side, across the fields, thus early in the season, as if it were some gay encampment of the red men, or other foresters, of whose arrival you had not heard.

Some single trees, wholly bright scarlet, seen against others of their kind still freshly green, or against evergreens, are more memorable than whole groves will be by-and-by. How beautiful, when a whole tree is like one great scarlet fruit full of ripe juices, every leaf, from lowest limb to topmost spire, all aglow, especially if you look toward the sun! What more remarkable object can there be in the landscape? Visible for miles, too fair to be believed. If such a phenomenon occurred but once, it would be handed down by tradition to posterity, and get into the mythology at last.

The whole tree thus ripening in advance of its fellows attains a singular preëminence, and sometimes maintains it for a week or two. I am thrilled at the sight of it, bearing aloft its scarlet standard for the regiment of green-clad foresters around and I go half a mile out of my way to examine it. A single tree becomes thus the crowning beauty of some meadowy vale, and the expression of the whole surrounding forest is at once more spirited for it.

A small Red Maple has grown, perchance, far away at

the head of some retired valley, a mile from any road, un-
observed. It has faithfully discharged the duties of a Maple
there, all winter and summer, neglected none of its econo-
mies, but added to its stature in the virtue which belongs
to a Maple, by a steady growth for so many months, never
having gone gadding abroad, and is nearer heaven than
it was in the spring. It has faithfully husbanded its sap,
and afforded a shelter to the wandering bird, has long since
ripened its seeds and committed them to the winds, and has
the satisfaction of knowing, perhaps, that a thousand little
well-behaved Maples are already settled in life somewhere.
It deserves well of Mapledom. Its leaves have been asking it
from time to time, in a whisper, "When shall we redden?"
And now, in this month of September, this month of travel-
ling, when men are hastening to the sea-side, or the moun-
tains, or the lakes, this modest Maple, still without budging
an inch, travels in its reputation,—runs up its scarlet flag on
that hill-side, which shows that it has finished its summer's
work before all other trees, and withdraws from the contest.
At the eleventh hour of the year, the tree which no scrutiny
could have detected here when it was most industrious is
thus, by the tint of its maturity, by its very blushes, revealed
at last to the careless and distant traveller, and leads his
thoughts away from the dusty road into those brave soli-
tudes which it inhabits. It flashes out conspicuous with all
the virtue and beauty of a Maple,—*Acer rubrum*. We may
now read its title, or *rubric*, clear. Its *virtues*, not its sins, are
as scarlet.

Notwithstanding the Red Maple is the most intense scarlet
of any of our trees, the Sugar-Maple has been the most cele-
brated, and Michaux in his "Sylva" does not speak of the au-
tumnal color of the former. About the second of October,
these trees, both large and small, are most brilliant, though
many are still green. In "sprout-lands" they seem to vie with
one another, and ever some particular one in the midst of the
crowd will be of a peculiarly pure scarlet, and by its more in-
tense color attract our eye even at a distance, and carry off
the palm. A large Red-Maple swamp, when at the height of
its change, is the most obviously brilliant of all tangible

things, where I dwell, so abundant is this tree with us. It varies much both in form and color. A great many are merely yellow, more scarlet, others scarlet deepening into crimson, more red than common. Look at yonder swamp of Maples mixed with Pines, at the base of a Pine-clad hill, a quarter of a mile off, so that you get the full effect of the bright colors, without detecting the imperfections of the leaves, and see their yellow, scarlet, and crimson fires, of all tints, mingled and contrasted with the green. Some Maples are yet green, only yellow or crimson-tipped on the edges of their flakes, like the edges of a Hazel-Nut burr; some are wholly brilliant scarlet, raying out regularly and finely every way, bilaterally, like the veins of a leaf; others, of more irregular form, when I turn my head slightly, emptying out some of its earthiness and concealing the trunk of the tree, seem to rest heavily flake on flake, like yellow and scarlet clouds, wreath upon wreath, or like snow-drifts driving through the air, stratified by the wind. It adds greatly to the beauty of such a swamp at this season, that, even though there may be no other trees interspersed, it is not seen as a simple mass of color, but, different trees being of different colors and hues, the outline of each crescent tree-top is distinct, and where one laps on to another. Yet a painter would hardly venture to make them thus distinct a quarter of a mile off.

As I go across a meadow directly toward a low rising ground this bright afternoon, I see, some fifty rods off toward the sun, the top of a Maple swamp just appearing over the sheeny russet edge of the hill, a stripe apparently twenty rods long by ten feet deep, of the most intensely brilliant scarlet, orange, and yellow, equal to any flowers or fruits, or any tints ever painted. As I advance, lowering the edge of the hill which makes the firm foreground or lower frame of the picture, the depth of the brilliant grove revealed steadily increases, suggesting that the whole of the inclosed valley is filled with such color. One wonders that the tithing-men and fathers of the town are not out to see what the trees mean by their high colors and exuberance of spirits, fearing that some mischief is brewing. I do not see what the Puritans did at this season, when the Maples blaze out in scarlet. They certainly could not have worshipped in groves then. Perhaps that is what they built meeting-houses and fenced them round with horse-sheds for.

THE ELM.

Now, too, the first of October, or later, the Elms are at the height of their autumnal beauty, great brownish-yellow masses, warm from their September oven, hanging over the highway. Their leaves are perfectly ripe. I wonder if there is any answering ripeness in the lives of the men who live beneath them. As I look down our street, which is lined with them, they remind me both by their form and color of yellowing sheaves of grain, as if the harvest had indeed come to the village itself, and we might expect to find some maturity and *flavor* in the thoughts of the villagers at last. Under those bright rustling yellow piles just ready to fall on the heads of the walkers, how can any crudity or greenness of thought or act prevail? When I stand where half a dozen large Elms droop over a house, it is as if I stood within a ripe pumpkin-rind, and I feel as mellow as if I were the pulp, though I may be somewhat stringy and seedy withal. What is the late greenness of the English Elm, like a cucumber out of season, which does not know when to have done, compared with the early and golden maturity of the American tree? The street is the scene of a great harvest-home. It would be worth the while to set out these trees, if only for their autumnal value. Think of these great yellow canopies or parasols held over our heads and houses by the mile together, making the village all one and compact,—an *ulmarium*, which is at the same time a nursery of men! And then how gently and unobserved they drop their burden and let in the sun when it is wanted, their leaves not heard when they fall on our roofs and in our streets; and thus the village parasol is shut up and put away! I see the market-man driving into the village, and disappearing under its canopy of Elm-tops, with *his* crop, as into a great granary or barnyard. I am tempted to go thither as to a husking of thoughts, now dry and ripe, and ready to be separated from their integuments; but, alas! I foresee that it will be chiefly husks and little thought, blasted pig-corn, fit only for cob-meal,—for, as you sow, so shall you reap.

FALLEN LEAVES.

By the sixth of October the leaves generally begin to fall, in successive showers, after frost or rain; but the principal leaf-harvest, the acme of the *Fall*, is commonly about the sixteenth. Some morning at that date there is perhaps a harder frost than we have seen, and ice formed under the pump, and now, when the morning wind rises, the leaves come down in denser showers than ever. They suddenly form thick beds or carpets on the ground, in this gentle air, or even without wind, just the size and form of the tree above. Some trees, as small Hickories, appear to have dropped their leaves instantaneously, as a soldier grounds arms at a signal; and those of the Hickory, being bright yellow still, though withered, reflect a blaze of light from the ground where they lie. Down they have come on all sides, at the first earnest touch of autumn's wand, making a sound like rain.

Or else it is after moist and rainy weather that we notice how great a fall of leaves there has been in the night, though it may not yet be the touch that loosens the Rock-Maple leaf. The streets are thickly strewn with the trophies, and fallen Elm-leaves make a dark brown pavement under our feet. After some remarkably warm Indian-summer day or days, I perceive that it is the unusual heat which, more than anything, causes the leaves to fall, there having been, perhaps, no frost nor rain for some time. The intense heat suddenly ripens and wilts them, just as it softens and ripens peaches and other fruits, and causes them to drop.

The leaves of late Red Maples, still bright, strew the earth, often crimson-spotted on a yellow ground, like some wild apples,—though they preserve these bright colors on the ground but a day or two, especially if it rains. On causeways I go by trees here and there all bare and smoke-like, having lost their brilliant clothing; but there it lies, nearly as bright as ever, on the ground on one side, and making nearly as regular a figure as lately on the tree. I would rather say that I first observe the trees thus flat on the ground like a permanent colored shadow, and they suggest to look for the boughs that bore them. A queen might be proud to walk where these gallant trees have spread their bright cloaks in the mud. I see wagons roll over them as a shadow or a reflection, and the drivers heed them just as little as they did their shadows before.

Birds'-nests, in the Huckleberry and other shrubs, and in trees, are already being filled with the withered leaves. So many have fallen in the woods, that a squirrel cannot run after a falling nut without being heard. Boys are raking them in the streets, if only for the pleasure of dealing with such clean crisp substances. Some sweep the paths scrupulously neat, and then stand to see the next breath strew them with new trophies. The swamp-floor is thickly covered, and the *Lycopodium lucidulum* looks suddenly greener amid them. In dense woods they half-cover pools that are three or four rods long. The other day I could hardly find a well-known spring, and even suspected that it had dried up, for it was completely concealed by freshly fallen leaves; and when I swept them aside and revealed it, it was like striking the earth, with Aaron's rod, for a new spring. Wet grounds about the edges of swamps look dry with them. At one swamp, where I was surveying, thinking to step on a leafy shore from a rail, I got into the water more than a foot deep.

When I go to the river the day after the principal fall of leaves, the sixteenth, I find my boat all covered, bottom and seats, with the leaves of the Golden Willow under which it is moored, and I set sail with a cargo of them rustling under my feet. If I empty it, it will be full again to-morrow. I do not regard them as litter, to be swept out, but accept them as suitable straw or matting for the bottom of my carriage. When I turn up into the mouth of the Assabet, which is wooded, large fleets of leaves are floating on its surface, as it were getting out to sea, with room to tack; but next the shore, a little farther up, they are thicker than foam, quite concealing the water for a rod in width, under and amid the Alders, Button-Bushes, and Maples, still perfectly light and dry, with fibre unrelaxed; and at a rocky bend where they are met and stopped by the morning wind, they sometimes form a broad and dense crescent quite across the river. When I turn my prow that way, and the wave which it makes strikes them, list what a pleasant rustling from these dry substances grating on one another! Often it is their undulation only which reveals the water beneath them. Also every motion of the wood-turtle on the shore is betrayed by their rustling there. Or even in mid-channel, when the wind rises, I hear them blown with a rustling sound. Higher up they are slowly moving round and round in some great eddy which the river makes, as that at the "Leaning Hemlocks," where the water is deep, and the current is wearing into the bank.

Perchance, in the afternoon of such a day, when the water is perfectly calm and full of reflections, I paddle gently down the main stream, and, turning up the Assabet, reach a quiet cove, where I unexpectedly find myself surrounded by myriads of leaves, like fellow-voyagers, which seem to have the same purpose, or want of purpose with myself. See this great fleet of scattered leaf-boats which we paddle amid, in this smooth river-bay, each one curled up on every side by the sun's skill, each nerve a stiff spruce-knee,—like boats of hide, and of all patterns, Charon's boat probably among the rest, and some with lofty prows and poops, like the stately vessels of the ancients, scarcely moving in the sluggish current,—like the great fleets, the dense Chinese cities of boats, with which you mingle on entering some great mart, some New York or Canton, which we are all steadily approaching together. How gently each has been deposited on the water! No violence has been used towards them yet, though, perchance, palpitating hearts were present at the launching. And painted ducks, too, the splendid wood-duck among the rest, often come to sail and float amid the painted leaves,—barks of a nobler model still!

What wholesome herb-drinks are to be had in the swamps now! What strong medicinal, but rich, scents from the decaying leaves! The rain falling on the freshly dried herbs and leaves, and filling the pools and ditches into which they have dropped thus clean and rigid, will soon convert them into tea,—green, black, brown, and yellow teas, of all degrees of strength, enough to set all Nature a-gossiping. Whether we drink them or not, as yet, before their strength is drawn, these leaves, dried on great Nature's coppers, are of such various pure and delicate tints as might make the fame of Oriental teas.

How they are mixed up, of all species, Oak and Maple and Chestnut and Birch! But Nature is not cluttered with them; she is a perfect husbandman; she stores them all. Consider what a vast crop is thus annually shed on the earth! This, more than any mere grain or seed, is the great harvest of the year. The trees are now repaying the earth with interest what they have taken from it. They are discounting. They are about to add a leaf's thickness to the depth of the soil. This is the beautiful way in which Nature gets her muck, while I chaffer with this man and that, who talks to me about sulphur and the cost of carting. We are all the richer for their decay. I am more interested in this crop than in the English grass alone or in the corn. It prepares the virgin mould for future cornfields and forests, on which the earth fattens. It keeps our homestead in good heart.

For beautiful variety no crop can be compared with this. Here is not merely the plain yellow of the grains, but nearly all the colors that we know, the brightest blue not excepted: the early blushing Maple, the Poison-Sumach blazing its sins as scarlet, the mulberry Ash, the rich chrome-yellow of the Poplars, the brilliant red Huckleberry, with which the hills' backs are painted, like those of sheep. The frost touches them, and, with the slightest breath of returning day or jarring of earth's axle, see in what showers they come floating down! The ground is all party-colored with them. But they still live in the soil, whose fertility and bulk they increase, and in the forests that spring from it. They stoop to rise, to mount higher in coming years, by subtle chemistry, climbing by the sap in the trees, and the sapling's first fruits thus shed, transmuted at last, may adorn its crown, when, in after-years, it has become the monarch of the forest.

It is pleasant to walk over the beds of these fresh, crisp, and rustling leaves. How beautifully they go to their graves! how gently lay themselves down and turn to mould!—painted of a thousand hues, and fit to make the beds of us living. So they troop to their last resting-place, light and frisky. They put on no weeds, but merrily they go scampering over the earth, selecting the spot, choosing a lot, ordering no iron fence, whispering all through the woods about it,—some choosing the spot where the bodies of men are mouldering beneath, and meeting them half-way. How many flutterings before they rest quietly in their graves! They that soared so loftily, how contentedly they return to dust again, and are laid low, resigned to lie and decay at the foot of the tree, and afford nourishment to new generations of their kind, as well as to flutter on high! They teach us how to die. One wonders if the time will ever come when men, with their boasted faith in immortality, will lie down as gracefully and as ripe,—with such an Indian-summer serenity will shed their bodies, as they do their hair and nails.

When the leaves fall, the whole earth is a cemetery pleasant to walk in. I love to wander and muse over them in their graves. Here are no lying nor vain epitaphs. What though you own no lot at Mount Auburn? Your lot is surely cast somewhere in this vast cemetery, which has been consecrated from of old. You need attend no auction to secure a place. There is room enough here. The Loose-strife shall bloom and the Huckleberry-bird sing over your bones. The woodman and hunter shall be your sextons, and the children shall tread upon the borders as much as they will. Let us walk in the cemetery of the leaves,—this is your true Greenwood Cemetery.

THE SUGAR-MAPLE.

But think not that the splendor of the year is over; for as one leaf does not make a summer, neither does one fallen leaf make an autumn. The smallest Sugar-Maples in our streets make a great show as early as the fifth of October, more than any other trees there. As I look up the Main Street, they appear like painted screens standing before the houses; yet many are green. But now, or generally by the seventeenth of October, when almost all Red Maples, and some White Maples, are bare, the large Sugar-Maples also are in their glory, glowing with yellow and red, and show unexpectedly bright and delicate tints. They are remarkable for the contrast they often afford of deep blushing red on one half and green on the other. They become at length dense masses of rich yellow with a deep scarlet blush, or more than blush, on the exposed surfaces. They are the brightest trees now in the street.

The large ones on our Common are particularly beautiful. A delicate, but warmer than golden yellow is now the prevailing color, with scarlet cheeks. Yet, standing on the east side of the Common just before sundown, when the western light is transmitted through them, I see that their yellow even, compared with the pale lemon yellow of an Elm close by, amounts to a scarlet, without noticing the bright scarlet portions. Generally, they are great regular oval masses of yellow and scarlet. All the sunny warmth of the season, the Indian summer, seems to be absorbed in their leaves. The lowest and inmost leaves next the bole are, as usual, of the most delicate yellow and green, like the complexion of young men brought up in the house. There is an auction on the Common to-day, but its red flag is hard to be discerned amid this blaze of color.

Little did the fathers of the town anticipate this brilliant success, when they caused to be imported from farther in the country some straight poles with their tops cut off, which they called Sugar-Maples; and, as I remember, after they were set out, a neighboring merchant's clerk, by way of jest, planted beans about them. Those which were then jestingly called bean-poles are to-day far the most beautiful objects noticeable in our streets. They are worth all and more than they have cost,—though one of the selectmen, while setting them out, took the cold which occasioned his death,—if only because they have filled the open eyes of children with their rich color unstintedly so many Octobers. We will not ask them to yield us sugar in the spring, while they afford us so fair a prospect in the autumn. Wealth in-doors may be the inheritance of few, but it is equally distributed on the Common. All children alike can revel in this golden harvest.

Surely trees should be set in our streets with a view to their October splendor; though I doubt whether this is ever considered by the "Tree Society." Do you not think it will make some odds to these children that they were brought up under the Maples? Hundreds of eyes are steadily drinking in this color, and by these teachers even the truants are caught and educated the moment they step abroad. Indeed, neither the truant nor the studious is at present taught color in the schools. These are instead of the bright colors in apothecaries' shops and city windows. It is a pity that we have no more *Red* Maples, and some Hickories, in our streets as well. Our paint-box is very imperfectly filled. Instead of, or beside, supplying such paint-boxes as we do, we might supply these natural colors to the young. Where else will they study color under greater advantages? What School of Design can vie with this? Think how much the eyes of painters of all kinds, and of manufacturers of cloth and paper, and paper-stainers, and countless others, are to be educated by these autumnal colors. The stationer's envelopes may be of very various tints, yet not so various as those of the leaves of a single tree. If you want a different shade or tint of a particular color, you have only to look farther within or without the tree or the wood. These leaves are not many dipped in one dye, as at the dye-house, but they are dyed in light of infinitely various degrees of strength, and left to set and dry there.

Shall the names of so many of our colors continue to be derived from those of obscure foreign localities, as Naples yellow, Prussian blue, raw Sienna, burnt Umber, Gamboge?—(surely the Tyrian purple must have faded by this time)—or from comparatively trivial articles of commerce,—chocolate, lemon, coffee, cinnamon, claret?—(shall we compare our Hickory to a lemon, or a lemon to a Hickory?)—or from ores and oxides which few ever see? Shall we so often, when describing to our neighbors the color of something we have seen, refer them, not to some natural object in our neighborhood, but perchance to a bit of earth fetched from the other side of the planet, which possibly they may find at the apothecary's, but which probably neither they nor we ever saw? Have we not an *earth* under our feet,—ay, and a sky over our heads? Or is the last *all* ultramarine? What do we know of sapphire, amethyst, emerald, ruby, amber, and the like,—most of us who take these names in vain? Leave these precious words to cabinet-keepers, virtuosos, and maids-of-honor,—to the Nabobs, Begums, and Chobdars of Hindostan, or wherever else. I do not see why, since America and her autumn woods have been discovered, our leaves should not compete with the precious stones in giving names to colors; and, indeed, I believe that in course of time the names of some of our trees and shrubs, as well as flowers, will get into our popular chromatic nomenclature.

But of much more importance than a knowledge of the names and distinctions of color is the joy and exhilaration which these colored leaves excite. Already these brilliant trees throughout the street, without any more variety, are at least equal to an annual festival and holiday, or a week of such. These are cheap and innocent gala-days, celebrated by one and all without the aid of committees or marshals, such a show as may safely be licensed, not attracting gamblers or rum-sellers, nor requiring any special police to keep the peace. And poor indeed must be that New-England village's October which has not the Maple in its streets. This October festival costs no powder, nor ringing of bells, but every tree is a living liberty-pole on which a thousand bright flags are waving.

No wonder that we must have our annual Cattle-Show, and Fall Training, and perhaps Cornwallis, our September Courts, and the like. Nature herself holds her annual fair in October, not only in the streets, but in every hollow and on every hill-side. When lately we looked into that Red-Maple swamp all a-blaze, where the trees were clothed in their vestures of most dazzling tints, did it not suggest a thousand gypsies be-neath,—a race capable of wild delight,—or even the fabled fawns, satyrs, and wood-nymphs come back to earth? Or was it only a congregation of wearied wood-choppers, or of pro-prietors come to inspect their lots, that we thought of? Or, earlier still, when we paddled on the river through that fine-grained September air, did there not appear to be something new going on under the sparkling surface of the stream, a shaking of props, at least, so that we made haste in order to be up in time? Did not the rows of yellowing Willows and Button-Bushes on each side seem like rows of booths, under which, perhaps, some fluviatile egg-pop equally yellow was ef-fervescing? Did not all these suggest that man's spirits should rise as high as Nature's,—should hang out their flag, and the routine of his life be interrupted by an analogous expression of joy and hilarity?

No annual training or muster of soldiery, no celebration with its scarfs and banners, could import into the town a hun-dredth part of the annual splendor of our October. We have only to set the trees, or let them stand, and Nature will find the colored drapery,—flags of all her nations, some of whose private signals hardly the botanist can read,—while we walk under the triumphal arches of the Elms. Leave it to Nature to appoint the days, whether the same as in neighboring States or not, and let the clergy read her proclamations, if they can understand them. Behold what a brilliant drapery is her Woodbine flag! What public-spirited merchant, think you, has contributed this part of the show? There is no handsomer shingling and paint than this vine, at present covering a whole side of some houses. I do not believe that the Ivy *never sear* is comparable to it. No wonder it has been extensively introduced into London. Let us have a good many Maples and Hickories and Scarlet Oaks, then, I say. Blaze away! Shall that dirty roll of bunting in the gun-house be all the colors a village can display? A village is not complete, unless it have these trees to mark the season in it. They are important, like the town-clock. A village that has them not will not be found to work well. It has a screw loose, an essential part is wanting. Let us have Willows for spring, Elms for summer, Maples and Walnuts and Tupeloes for autumn, Evergreens for winter, and Oaks for all seasons. What is a gallery in a house to a gallery in the streets, which every market-man rides through, whether he will or not? Of course, there is not a picture-gallery in the country which would be worth so much to us as is the western view at sunset under the Elms of our main street. They are the frame to a picture which is daily painted behind them. An avenue of Elms as large as our largest and three miles long would seem to lead to some admirable place, though only C—— were at the end of it.

A village needs these innocent stimulants of bright and cheering prospects to keep off melancholy and superstition. Show me two villages, one embowered in trees and blazing with all the glories of October, the other a merely trivial and treeless waste, or with only a single tree or two for suicides, and I shall be sure that in the latter will be found the most starved and bigoted religionists and the most desperate drinkers. Every wash-tub and milk-can and gravestone will be exposed. The inhabitants will disappear abruptly behind their barns and houses, like desert Arabs amid their rocks, and I shall look to see spears in their hands. They will be ready to accept the most barren and forlorn doctrine,—as that the world is speedily coming to an end, or has already got to it, or that they themselves are turned wrong side outward. They will perchance crack their dry joints at one another and call it a spiritual communication.

But to confine ourselves to the Maples. What if we were to take half as much pains in protecting them as we do in setting them out,—not stupidly tie our horses to our dahlia-stems?

What meant the fathers by establishing this *perfectly living* institution before the church,—this institution which needs no repairing nor repainting, which is continually enlarged and repaired by its growth? Surely they

> "Wrought in a sad sincerity;
>   Themselves from God they could not free;
>   They *planted* better than they knew;—
>   The conscious *trees* to beauty grew."

Verily these Maples are cheap preachers, permanently settled, which preach their half-century, and century, ay, and century-and-a-half sermons, with constantly increasing unction and influence, ministering to many generations of men; and the least we can do is to supply them with suitable colleagues as they grow infirm.

THE SCARLET OAK.

Belonging to a genus which is remarkable for the beautiful form of its leaves, I suspect that some Scarlet-Oak leaves surpass those of all other Oaks in the rich and wild beauty of their outlines. I judge from an acquaintance with twelve species, and from drawings which I have seen of many others.

Stand under this tree and see how finely its leaves are cut against the sky,—as it were, only a few sharp points extending from a midrib. They look like double, treble, or quadruple crosses. They are far more ethereal than the less deeply scolloped Oak-leaves. They have so little leafy *terra firma* that they appear melting away in the light, and scarcely obstruct our view. The leaves of very young plants are, like those of full-grown Oaks of other species, more entire, simple, and lumpish in their outlines; but these, raised high on old trees, have solved the leafy problem. Lifted higher and higher, and sublimated more and more, putting off some earthiness

and cultivating more intimacy with the light each year, they
have at length the least possible amount of earthy matter, and
the greatest spread and grasp of skyey influences. There they
dance, arm in arm with the light,—tripping it on fantastic
points, fit partners in those aërial halls. So intimately mingled
are they with it, that, what with their slenderness and their
glossy surfaces, you can hardly tell at last what in the dance is
leaf and what is light. And when no zephyr stirs, they are at
most but a rich tracery to the forest-windows.

I am again struck with their beauty, when, a month later,
they thickly strew the ground in the woods, piled one upon
another under my feet. They are then brown above, but pur-
ple beneath. With their narrow lobes and their bold deep
scollops reaching almost to the middle, they suggest that the
material must be cheap, or else there has been a lavish expense
in their creation, as if so much had been cut out. Or else they
seem to us the remnants of the stuff out of which leaves have
been cut with a die. Indeed, when they lie thus one upon an-
other, they remind me of a pile of scrap-tin.*

Or bring one home, and study it closely at your leisure,
by the fireside. It is a type, not from any Oxford font, not
in the Basque nor the arrow-headed character, not found on
the Rosetta Stone, but destined to be copied in sculpture
one day, if they ever get to whittling stone here. What a wild
and pleasing outline, a combination of graceful curves and
angles! The eye rests with equal delight on what is not leaf
and on what is leaf,—on the broad, free, open sinuses, and
on the long, sharp, bristle-pointed lobes. A simple oval out-
line would include it all, if you connected the points of the
leaf; but how much richer is it than that, with its half-dozen
deep scollops, in which the eye and thought of the beholder
are embayed! If I were a drawing-master, I would set my
pupils to copying these leaves, that they might learn to draw
firmly and gracefully.

Regarded as water, it is like a pond with half a dozen broad
rounded promontories extending nearly to its middle, half
from each side, while its watery bays extend far inland, like

*The original of the leaf copied on the next page was picked from such a
pile.

sharp friths, at each of whose heads several fine streams empty
in,—almost a leafy archipelago.

But it oftener suggests land, and, as Dionysius and Pliny
compared the form of the Morea to that of the leaf of the
Oriental Plane-tree, so this leaf reminds me of some fair wild
island in the ocean, whose extensive coast, alternate rounded
bays with smooth strands, and sharp-pointed rocky capes,
mark it as fitted for the habitation of man, and destined to be-

come a centre of civilization at last. To the sailor's eye, it is a
much-indented shore. Is it not, in fact, a shore to the aërial
ocean, on which the windy surf beats? At sight of this leaf we
are all mariners,—if not vikings, buccaneers, and filibusters.
Both our love of repose and our spirit of adventure are ad-
dressed. In our most casual glance, perchance, we think, that,
if we succeed in doubling those sharp capes, we shall find
deep, smooth, and secure havens in the ample bays. How dif-

ferent from the White-Oak leaf, with its rounded headlands, on which no light-house need be placed! That is an England, with its long civil history, that may be read. This is some still unsettled New-found Island or Celebes. Shall we go and be rajahs there?

By the twenty-sixth of October the large Scarlet Oaks are in their prime, when other Oaks are usually withered. They have been kindling their fires for a week past, and now generally burst into a blaze. This alone of *our* indigenous deciduous trees (excepting the Dogwood, of which I do not know half a dozen, and they are but large bushes) is now in its glory. The two Aspens and the Sugar-Maple come nearest to it in date, but they have lost the greater part of their leaves. Of evergreens, only the Pitch-Pine is still commonly bright.

But it requires a particular alertness, if not devotion to these phenomena, to appreciate the wide-spread, but late and unexpected glory of the Scarlet Oaks. I do not speak here of the small trees and shrubs, which are commonly observed, and which are now withered, but of the large trees. Most go in and shut their doors, thinking that bleak and colorless November has already come, when some of the most brilliant and memorable colors are not yet lit.

This very perfect and vigorous one, about forty feet high, standing in an open pasture, which was quite glossy green on the twelfth, is now, the twenty-sixth, completely changed to bright dark scarlet,—every leaf, between you and the sun, as if it had been dipped into a scarlet dye. The whole tree is much like a heart in form, as well as color. Was not this worth waiting for? Little did you think, ten days ago, that that cold green tree would assume such color as this. Its leaves are still firmly attached, while those of other trees are falling around it. It seems to say,—"I am the last to blush, but I blush deeper than any of ye. I bring up the rear in my red coat. We Scarlet ones, alone of Oaks, have not given up the fight."

The sap is now, and even far into November, frequently flowing fast in these trees, as in Maples in the spring; and apparently their bright tints, now that most other Oaks are withered, are connected with this phenomenon. They are full of life. It has a pleasantly astringent, acorn-like taste, this strong Oak-wine, as I find on tapping them with my knife.

Looking across this woodland valley, a quarter of a mile wide, how rich those Scarlet Oaks, embosomed in Pines, their bright red branches intimately intermingled with them! They have their full effect there. The Pine-boughs are the green calyx to their red petals. Or, as we go along a road in the woods, the sun striking endwise through it, and lighting up the red tents of the Oaks, which on each side are mingled with the liquid green of the Pines, makes a very gorgeous scene. Indeed, without the evergreens for contrast, the autumnal tints would lose much of their effect.

The Scarlet Oak asks a clear sky and the brightness of late October days. These bring out its colors. If the sun goes into a cloud, they become comparatively indistinct. As I sit on a cliff in the southwest part of our town, the sun is now getting low, and the woods in Lincoln, south and east of me, are lit up by its more level rays; and in the Scarlet Oaks, scattered so equally over the forest, there is brought out a more brilliant redness than I had believed was in them. Every tree of this species which is visible in those directions, even to the horizon, now stands out distinctly red. Some great ones lift their red backs high above the woods, in the next town, like huge roses with a myriad of fine petals; and some more slender ones, in a small grove of White Pines on Pine Hill in the east, on the very verge of the horizon, alternating with the Pines on the edge of the grove, and shouldering them with their red coats, look like soldiers in red amid hunters in green. This time it is Lincoln green, too. Till the sun got low, I did not believe that there were so many redcoats in the forest army. Theirs is an intense burning red, which would lose some of its strength, methinks, with every step you might take toward them; for the shade that lurks amid their foliage does not report itself at this distance, and they are unanimously red. The focus of their reflected color is in the atmosphere far on this side. Every such tree becomes a nucleus of red, as it were, where, with the declining sun, that color grows and glows. It is partly borrowed fire, gathering strength from the sun on its way to your eye. It has only some comparatively dull red leaves for a rallying-point, or kindling-stuff, to start it, and it becomes an intense scarlet or red mist, or fire, which finds fuel for itself in the very atmosphere. So vivacious is redness. The very rails reflect a rosy light at this hour and season. You see a redder tree than exists.

If you wish to count the Scarlet Oaks, do it now. In a clear day stand thus on a hill-top in the woods, when the sun is an hour high, and every one within range of your vision, excepting in the west, will be revealed. You might live to the age of Methuselah and never find a tithe of them, otherwise. Yet sometimes even in a dark day I have thought them as bright as I ever saw them. Looking westward, their colors are lost in a blaze of light; but in other directions the whole forest is a flower-garden, in which these late roses burn, alternating with green, while the so-called "gardeners," walking here and there, perchance, beneath, with spade and water-pot, see only a few little asters amid withered leaves.

These are *my* China-asters, *my* late garden-flowers. It costs me nothing for a gardener. The falling leaves, all over the forest, are protecting the roots of my plants. Only look at what is to be seen, and you will have garden enough, without deepening the soil in your yard. We have only to elevate our view a little, to see the whole forest as a garden. The blossoming of the Scarlet Oak,—the forest-flower, surpassing all in splendor (at least since the Maple)! I do not know but they interest me more than the Maples, they are so widely and equally dispersed throughout the forest; they are so hardy, a nobler tree on the whole;—our chief November flower, abiding the approach of winter with us, imparting warmth to early November prospects. It is remarkable that the latest bright color that is general should be this deep, dark scarlet and red, the intensest of colors. The ripest fruit of the year; like the cheek of a hard, glossy, red apple from the cold Isle of Orleans, which will not be mellow for eating till next spring! When I rise to a hill-top, a thousand of these great Oak roses, distributed on every side, as far as the horizon! I admire them four or five miles off! This my unfailing prospect for a fortnight past! This late forest-flower surpasses all that spring or summer could do. Their colors were but rare and dainty specks comparatively, (created for the near-sighted, who walk amid the humblest herbs and underwoods,) and made no impression on a distant eye. Now it is an extended forest or a mountain-side, through or along which we journey from day to day, that bursts into bloom. Comparatively, our gardening is on a petty scale,—the gardener still nursing a few asters amid dead weeds, ignorant of the gigantic asters and roses, which, as it were, overshadow him, and ask for none of his care. It is like a little red paint ground on a saucer, and held up against the sunset sky. Why not take more elevated and broader views, walk in the great garden, not skulk in a little "debauched" nook of it? consider the beauty of the forest, and not merely of a few impounded herbs?

Let your walks now be a little more adventurous; ascend the hills. If about the last of October, you ascend any hill in the outskirts of our town, and probably of yours, and look over the forest, you may see——well, what I have endeavored to describe. All this you surely *will* see, and much more, if you are prepared to see it,—if you *look* for it. Otherwise, regular and universal as this phenomenon is, whether you stand on the hill-top or in the hollow, you will think for threescore years and ten that all the wood is, at this season, sear and brown. Objects are concealed from our view, not so much because they are out of the course of our visual ray as because we do not bring our minds and eyes to bear on them; for there is no power to see in the eye itself, any more than in any other jelly. We do not realize how far and widely, or how near and narrowly, we are to look. The greater part of the phenomena of Nature are for this reason concealed from us all our lives. The gardener sees only the gardener's garden. Here, too, as in political economy, the supply answers to the demand. Nature does not cast pearls before swine. There is just as much beauty visible to us in the landscape as we are prepared to appreciate,—not a grain more. The actual objects which one man will see from a particular hill-top are just as different from those which another will see as the beholders are different. The Scarlet Oak must, in a sense, be in your eye when you go forth. We cannot see anything until we are possessed with the idea of it, take it into our heads,—and then we can hardly see anything else. In my botanical rambles, I find, that, first, the idea, or image, of a plant occupies my thoughts, though it may seem very foreign to this locality,— no nearer than Hudson's Bay,—and for some weeks or months I go thinking of it, and expecting it, unconsciously,

and at length I surely see it. This is the history of my finding
a score or more of rare plants, which I could name. A man
sees only what concerns him. A botanist absorbed in the study
of grasses does not distinguish the grandest Pasture Oaks. He,
as it were, tramples down Oaks unwittingly in his walk, or at
most sees only their shadows. I have found that it required a
different intention of the eye, in the same locality, to see dif-
ferent plants, even when they were closely allied, as *Juncaceæ*
and *Gramineæ*: when I was looking for the former, I did not
see the latter in the midst of them. How much more, then, it
requires different intentions of the eye and of the mind to at-
tend to different departments of knowledge! How differently
the poet and the naturalist look at objects!

Take a New-England selectman, and set him on the high-
est of our hills, and tell him to look,—sharpening his sight to
the utmost, and putting on the glasses that suit him best, (ay,
using a spy-glass, if he likes,)—and make a full report. What,
probably, will he *spy*?—what will he *select* to look at? Of
course, he will see a Brocken spectre of himself. He will see
several meeting-houses, at least, and, perhaps, that somebody
ought to be assessed higher than he is, since he has so hand-
some a wood-lot. Now take Julius Cæsar, or Immanuel
Swedenborg, or a Fegee-Islander, and set him up there. Or
suppose all together, and let them compare notes afterward.
Will it appear that they have enjoyed the same prospect? What
they will see will be as different as Rome was from Heaven or
Hell, or the last from the Fegee Islands. For aught we know,
as strange a man as any of these is always at our elbow.

Why, it takes a sharp-shooter to bring down even such triv-
ial game as snipes and woodcocks; he must take very particu-
lar aim, and know what he is aiming at. He would stand a
very small chance, if he fired at random into the sky, being
told that snipes were flying there. And so is it with him that
shoots at beauty; though he wait till the sky falls, he will not
bag any if he does not already know its seasons and haunts,
and the color of its wing,—if he has not dreamed of it, so that
he can *anticipate* it; then, indeed, he flushes it at every step,
shoots double and on the wing, with both barrels, even in
cornfields. The sportsman trains himself, dresses and watches
unweariedly, and loads and primes for his particular game. He

prays for it, and offers sacrifices, and so he gets it. After due
and long preparation, schooling his eye and hand, dreaming
awake and asleep, with gun and paddle and boat he goes out
after meadow-hens, which most of his townsmen never saw
nor dreamed of, and paddles for miles against a head-wind,
and wades in water up to his knees, being out all day without
his dinner, and *therefore* he gets them. He had them half-way
into his bag when he started, and has only to shove them
down. The true sportsman can shoot you almost any of his
game from his windows: what else has he windows or eyes
for? It comes and perches at last on the barrel of his gun; but
the rest of the world never see it *with the feathers on.* The
geese fly exactly under his zenith, and honk when they get
there, and he will keep himself supplied by firing up his chim-
ney; twenty musquash have the refusal of each one of his traps
before it is empty. If he lives, and his game-spirit increases,
heaven and earth shall fail him sooner than game; and when
he dies, he will go to more extensive, and, perchance, happier
hunting-grounds. The fisherman, too, dreams of fish, sees a
bobbing cork in his dreams, till he can almost catch them in
his sink-spout. I knew a girl who, being sent to pick huckle-
berries, picked wild gooseberries by the quart, where no one
else knew that there were any, because she was accustomed to
pick them up country where she came from. The astronomer
knows where to go star-gathering, and sees one clearly in his
mind before any have seen it with a glass. The hen scratches
and finds her food right under where she stands; but such is
not the way with the hawk.

These bright leaves which I have mentioned are not the ex-
ception, but the rule; for I believe that all leaves, even grasses
and mosses, acquire brighter colors just before their fall.
When you come to observe faithfully the changes of each
humblest plant, you find that each has, sooner or later, its pe-
culiar autumnal tint; and if you undertake to make a complete
list of the bright tints, it will be nearly as long as a catalogue
of the plants in your vicinity.

A Plea for Captain John Brown

I TRUST that you will pardon me for being here. I do not wish to force my thoughts upon you, but I feel forced myself. Little as I know of Captain Brown, I would fain do my part to correct the tone and the statements of the newspapers, and of my countrymen generally, respecting his character and actions. It costs us nothing to be just. We can at least express our sympathy with, and admiration of, him and his companions, and that is what I now propose to do.

First, as to his history.

I will endeavor to omit, as much as possible, what you have already read. I need not describe his person to you, for probably most of you have seen and will not soon forget him. I am told that his grandfather, John Brown, was an officer in the Revolution; that he himself was born in Connecticut about the beginning of this century, but early went with his father to Ohio. I heard him say that his father was a contractor who furnished beef to the army there, in the war of 1812; that he accompanied him to the camp, and assisted him in that employment, seeing a good deal of military life, more, perhaps, than if he had been a soldier, for he was often present at the councils of the officers. Especially, he learned by experience how armies are supplied and maintained in the field—a work which, he observed, requires at least as much experience and skill as to lead them in battle. He said that few persons had any conception of the cost, even the pecuniary cost, of firing a single bullet in war. He saw enough, at any rate, to disgust him with a military life, indeed to excite in him a great abhorrence of it; so much so, that though he was tempted by the offer of some petty office in the army, when he was about eighteen, he not only declined that, but he also refused to train when warned, and was fined for it. He then resolved that he would never have anything to do with any war, unless it were a war for liberty.

When the troubles in Kansas began, he sent several of his sons thither to strengthen the party of the Free State men, fitting them out with such weapons as he had; telling them that if the troubles should increase, and there should be need of him, he would follow to assist them with his hand and counsel. This, as you all know, he soon after did; and it was through his agency, far more than any other's, that Kansas was made free.

For a part of his life he was a surveyor, and at one time he was engaged in wool-growing, and he went to Europe as an agent about that business. There, as every where, he had his eyes about him, and made many original observations. He said, for instance, that he saw why the soil of England was so rich, and that of Germany (I think it was) so poor, and he thought of writing to some of the crowned heads about it. It was because in England the peasantry live on the soil which they cultivate, but in Germany they are gathered into villages, at night. It is a pity that he did not make a book of his observations.

I should say that he was an old-fashioned man in his respect for the Constitution, and his faith in the permanence of this Union. Slavery he deemed to be wholly opposed to these, and he was its determined foe.

He was by descent and birth a New England farmer, a man of great common sense, deliberate and practical as that class is, and tenfold more so. He was like the best of those who stood at Concord Bridge once, on Lexington Common, and on Bunker Hill, only he was firmer and higher principled than any that I have chanced to hear of as there. It was no abolition lecturer that converted him. Ethan Allen and Stark, with whom he may in some respects be compared, were rangers in a lower and less important field. They could bravely face their country's foes, but he had the courage to face his country herself, when she was in the wrong. A Western writer says, to account for his escape from so many perils, that he was concealed under a "rural exterior;" as if, in that prairie land, a hero should, by good rights, wear a citizen's dress only.

He did not go to the college called Harvard, good old Alma Mater as she is. He was not fed on the pap that is there furnished. As he phrased it, "I know no more of grammar than one of your calves." But he went to the great university of the West, where he sedulously pursued the study of Liberty, for which he had early betrayed a fondness, and having taken many degrees, he finally commenced the public practice of Humanity in Kansas, as you all know. Such were *his humanities*, and not any study of grammar. He would have left a Greek accent slanting the wrong way, and righted up a falling man.

He was one of that class of whom we hear a great deal, but, for the most part, see nothing at all—the Puritans. It would be in vain to kill him. He died lately in the time of Cromwell, but he reappeared here. Why should he not? Some of the Puritan stock are said to have come over and settled in New England. They were a class that did something else than celebrate their forefathers' day, and eat parched corn in remembrance of that time. They were neither Democrats nor Republicans, but men of simple habits, straightforward, prayerful; not thinking much of rulers who did not fear God, not making many compromises, nor seeking after available candidates.

"In his camp," as one has recently written, and as I have myself heard him state, "he permitted no profanity; no man of loose morals was suffered to remain there, unless, indeed, as a prisoner of war. 'I would rather,' said he, 'have the small-pox, yellow fever, and cholera, all together in my camp, than a man without principle. . . . It is a mistake, sir, that our people make, when they think that bullies are the best fighters, or that they are the fit men to oppose these Southerners. Give me men of good principles,—God-fearing men,—men who respect themselves, and with a dozen of them I will oppose any hundred such men as these Buford ruffians.' " He said that if one offered himself to be a soldier under him, who was forward to tell what he could or would do, if he could only get sight of the enemy, he had but little confidence in him.

He was never able to find more than a score or so of recruits whom he would accept, and only about a dozen, among them his sons, in whom he had perfect faith. When he was here, some years ago, he showed to a few a little manuscript book,—his "orderly book" I think he called it,—containing the names of his company in Kansas, and the rules by which they bound themselves; and he stated that several of them had already sealed the contract with their blood. When some one remarked that, with the addition of a chaplain, it would have been a perfect Cromwellian troop, he observed that he would have been glad to add a chaplain to the list, if he could have found one who could fill that office worthily. It is easy enough to find one for the United States army. I believe that he had prayers in his camp morning and evening, nevertheless.

He was a man of Spartan habits, and at sixty was scrupulous about his diet at your table, excusing himself by saying that he must eat sparingly and fare hard, as became a soldier or one who was fitting himself for difficult enterprises, a life of exposure.

A man of rare common sense and directness of speech, as of action; a transcendentalist above all, a man of ideas and principles,—that was what distinguished him. Not yielding to a whim or transient impulse, but carrying out the purpose of a life. I noticed that he did not overstate any thing, but spoke within bounds. I remember, particularly, how, in his speech here, he referred to what his family had suffered in Kansas, without ever giving the least vent to his pent-up fire. It was a volcano with an ordinary chimney-flue. Also referring to the deeds of certain Border Ruffians, he said, rapidly paring away his speech, like an experienced soldier, keeping a reserve of force and meaning, "They had a perfect right to be hung." He was not in the least a rhetorician, was not talking to Buncombe or his constituents any where, had no need to invent any thing, but to tell the simple truth, and communicate his own resolution; therefore he appeared incomparably strong, and eloquence in Congress and elsewhere seemed to me at a discount. It was like the speeches of Cromwell compared with those of an ordinary king.

As for his tact and prudence, I will merely say, that at a time when scarcely a man from the Free States was able to reach Kansas by any direct route, at least without having his arms taken from him, he, carrying what imperfect guns and other weapons he could collect, openly and slowly drove an ox-cart through Missouri, apparently in the capacity of a surveyor, with his surveying compass exposed in it, and so passed unsuspected, and had ample opportunity to learn the designs of the enemy. For some time after his arrival he still followed the same profession. When, for instance, he saw a knot of the ruffians on the prairie, discussing, of course, the single topic which then occupied their minds, he would, perhaps, take his compass and one of his sons, and proceed to run an imaginary line right through the very spot on which that conclave had assembled, and when he came up to them, he would naturally pause and have some talk with them, learning their news, and, at last, all their plans perfectly; and having thus completed his real survey, he would resume his imaginary one, and run on his line till he was out of sight.

When I expressed surprise that he could live in Kansas at all, with a price set upon his head, and so large a number, including the authorities, exasperated against him, he accounted for it by saying, "It is perfectly well understood that I will not be taken." Much of the time for some years he has had to skulk in swamps, suffering from poverty and from sickness, which was the consequence of exposure, befriended only by Indians and a few whites. But though it might be known that he was lurking in a particular swamp, his foes commonly did not care to go in after him. He could even come out into a town where there were more Border Ruffians than Free State men, and transact some business, without delaying long, and yet not be molested; for said he, "No little handful of men were willing to undertake it, and a large body could not be got together in season."

As for his recent failure, we do not know the facts about it. It was evidently far from being a wild and desperate attempt. His enemy, Mr. Vallandigham, is compelled to say, that "it was among the best planned and executed conspiracies that ever failed."

Not to mention his other successes, was it a failure, or did it show a want of good management, to deliver from bondage a dozen human beings, and walk off with them by broad daylight, for weeks if not months, at a leisurely pace, through one State after another, for half the length of the North, conspicuous to all parties, with a price set upon his head, going into a court room on his way and telling what he had done, thus convincing Missouri that it was not profitable to try to hold slaves in his neighborhood?—and this, not because the government menials were lenient, but because they were afraid of him.

Yet he did not attribute his success, foolishly, to "his star," or to any magic. He said, truly, that the reason why such greatly superior numbers quailed before him, was, as one of his prisoners confessed, because they *lacked a cause*—a kind of armor which he and his party never lacked. When the time came, few men were found willing to lay down their lives in defence of what they knew to be wrong; they did not like that this should be their last act in this world.

But to make haste to *his* last act, and its effects.

The newspapers seem to ignore, or perhaps are really ignorant of the fact, that there are at least as many as two or three individuals to a town throughout the North, who think much as the present speaker does about him and his enterprise. I do not hesitate to say that they are an important and growing party. We aspire to be something more than stupid and timid chattels, pretending to read history and our bibles, but desecrating every house and every day we breathe in. Perhaps anxious politicians may prove that only seventeen white men and five negroes were concerned in the late enterprise, but their very anxiety to prove this might suggest to themselves that all is not told. Why do they still dodge the truth? They are so anxious because of a dim consciousness of the fact, which they do not distinctly face, that at least a million of the free inhabitants of the United States would have rejoiced if it had succeeded. They at most only criticise the tactics. Though we wear no crape, the thought of that man's position and probable fate is spoiling many a man's day here at the North for other thinking. If any one who has seen him here can pursue successfully any other train of thought, I do not know what he is made of. If there is any such who gets his usual allowance of sleep, I will warrant him to fatten easily under any circumstances which do not touch his body or purse. I put a piece of paper and a pencil under my pillow, and when I could not sleep, I wrote in the dark.

On the whole, my respect for my fellow-men, except as one may outweigh a million, is not being increased these days. I have noticed the cold-blooded way in which newspaper writers and men generally speak of this event, as if an ordinary malefactor, though one of unusual "pluck,"—as the Governor of Virginia is reported to have said, using the language of the cock-pit, "the gamest man he ever saw,"—had been caught, and were about to be hung. He was not dreaming of his foes when the governor thought he looked so brave. It turns what sweetness I have to gall, to hear, or hear of, the remarks of some of my neighbors. When we heard at first that he was dead, one of my townsmen observed that "he died as the fool dieth;" which, pardon me, for an instant suggested a likeness in him dying to my neighbor living. Others, craven-hearted, said disparagingly, that "he threw his life away," because he resisted the government. Which way have they thrown *their* lives, pray?—Such as would praise a man for attacking singly an ordinary band of thieves or murderers. I hear another ask, Yankee-like, "What will he gain by it?" as if he expected to fill his pockets by this enterprise. Such a one has no idea of gain but in this worldly sense. If it does not lead to a "surprise" party, if he does not get a new pair of boots, or a vote of thanks, it must be a failure. "But he won't gain any thing by it." Well, no, I don't suppose he could get four-and-six-pence a day for being hung, take the year round; but then he stands a chance to save a considerable part of his soul—and *such* a soul!—when *you* do not. No doubt you can get more in your market for a quart of milk than for a quart of blood, but that is not the market that heroes carry their blood to.

Such do not know that like the seed is the fruit, and that, in the moral world, when good seed is planted, good fruit is inevitable, and does not depend on our watering and cultivating; that when you plant, or bury, a hero in his field, a crop of heroes is sure to spring up. This is a seed of such force and vitality, that it does not ask our leave to germinate.

The momentary charge at Balaclava, in obedience to a blundering command, proving what a perfect machine the soldier is, has, properly enough, been celebrated by a poet laureate; but the steady, and for the most part successful charge of this man, for some years, against the legions of Slavery, in obedience to an infinitely higher command, is as much more memorable than that, as an intelligent and con-scientious man is superior to a machine. Do you think that that will go unsung?

"Served him right"—"A dangerous man"—"He is un-doubtedly insane." So they proceed to live their sane, and wise, and altogether admirable lives, reading their Plutarch a little, but chiefly pausing at that feat of Putnam, who was let down into a wolf's den; and in this wise they nourish themselves for brave and patriotic deeds some time or other. The Tract Society could afford to print that story of Putnam. You might open the district schools with the reading of it, for there is nothing about Slavery or the Church in it; unless it occurs to the reader that some pastors are *wolves* in sheep's clothing. "The American Board of Commissioners for Foreign Missions" even, might dare to protest against *that* wolf. I have heard of boards, and of American boards, but it chances that I never heard of this particular lumber till lately. And yet I hear of Northern men, women, and children, by families, buying a "life membership" in such societies as these;—a life-membership in the grave! You can get buried cheaper than that.

Our foes are in our midst and all about us. There is hardly a house but is divided against itself, for our foe is the all but universal woodenness of both head and heart, the want of vitality in man, which is the effect of our vice; and hence are begotten fear, superstition, bigotry, persecution, and slavery of all kinds. We are mere figure-heads upon a hulk, with livers in the place of hearts. The curse is the worship of idols, which at length changes the worshipper into a stone image himself; and the New Englander is just as much an idolater as the Hindoo. This man was an exception, for he did not set up even a political graven image between him and his God.

A church that can never have done with excommunicating Christ while it exists! Away with your broad and flat churches, and your narrow and tall churches! Take a step forward, and invent a new style of out-houses. Invent a salt that will save you, and defend our nostrils.

The modern Christian is a man who has consented to say all the prayers in the liturgy, provided you will let him go straight to bed and sleep quietly afterward. All his prayers begin with "Now I lay me down to sleep," and he is forever looking forward to the time when he shall go to his "*long* rest." He has consented to perform certain old established charities, too, after a fashion, but he does not wish to hear of any new-fangled ones; he doesn't wish to have any supplementary articles added to the contract, to fit it to the present time. He shows the whites of his eyes on the Sabbath, and the blacks all the rest of the week. The evil is not merely a stagnation of blood, but a stagnation of spirit. Many, no doubt, are well disposed, but sluggish by constitution and by habit, and they cannot conceive of a man who is actuated by higher motives than they are. Accordingly they pronounce this man insane, for they know that *they* could never act as he does, as long as they are themselves.

We dream of foreign countries, of other times and races of men, placing them at a distance in history or space; but let some significant event like the present occur in our midst, and we discover, often, this distance and this strangeness between us and our nearest neighbors. *They* are our Austrias, and Chinas, and South Sea Islands. Our crowded society becomes well spaced all at once, clean and handsome to the eye, a city of magnificent distances. We discover why it was that we never got beyond compliments and surfaces with them before; we become aware of as many versts between us and them as there are between a wandering Tartar and a Chinese town. The thoughtful man becomes a hermit in the thoroughfares of the market-place. Impassable seas suddenly find their level between us, or dumb steppes stretch themselves out there. It is the difference of constitution, of intelligence, and faith, and not streams and mountains, that make the true and impassable boundaries between individuals and between states. None but the like-minded can come plenipotentiary to our court.

I read all the newspapers I could get within a week after this event, and I do not remember in them a single expression of sympathy for these men. I have since seen one noble statement, in a Boston paper, not editorial. Some voluminous sheets decided not to print the full report of Brown's words to the exclusion of other matter. It was as if a publisher should reject the manuscript of the New Testament, and print Wilson's last speech. The same journal which contained this pregnant news, was chiefly filled, in parallel columns, with the reports of the political conventions that were being held. But the descent to them was too steep. They should have been spared this contrast, been printed in an extra at least. To turn from the voices and deeds of earnest men to the *cackling* of political conventions! Office seekers and speech-makers, who do not so much as lay an honest egg, but wear their breasts bare upon an egg of chalk! Their great game is the game of straws, or rather that universal aboriginal game of the platter, at which the Indians cried *hub, hub!* Exclude the reports of religious and political conventions, and publish the words of a living man.

But I object not so much to what they have omitted as to what they have inserted. Even the *Liberator* called it "a misguided, wild, and apparently insane . . . effort." As for the herd of newspapers and magazines, I do not chance to know an editor in the country who will deliberately print anything which he knows will ultimately and permanently reduce the number of his subscribers. They do not believe that it would be expedient. How then can they print truth? If we do not say pleasant things, they argue, nobody will attend to us. And so they do like some travelling auctioneers, who sing an obscene song in order to draw a crowd around them. Republican editors, obliged to get their sentences ready for the morning edition, and accustomed to look at every thing by the twilight of politics, express no admiration, nor true sorrow even, but call these men "deluded fanatics"—"mistaken men"—"insane," or "crazed." It suggests what a *sane* set of editors we are blessed with, *not* "mistaken men"; who know very well on which side their bread is buttered, at least.

A man does a brave and humane deed, and at once, on all sides, we hear people and parties declaring, "I didn't do it, nor countenance *him* to do it, in any conceivable way. It can't be fairly inferred from my past career." I, for one, am not interested to hear you define your position. I don't know that I ever was, or ever shall be. I think it is mere egotism, or impertinent at this time. Ye needn't take so much pains to wash your skirts of him. No intelligent man will ever be convinced that he was any creature of yours. He went and came, as he himself informs us, "under the auspices of John Brown and nobody else." The Republican party does not perceive how many his *failure* will make to vote more correctly than they would have them. They have counted the votes of Pennsylvania & Co., but they have not correctly counted Captain Brown's vote. He has taken the wind out of their sails, the little wind they had, and they may as well lie to and repair.

What though he did not belong to your clique! Though you may not approve of his method or his principles, recognize his magnanimity. Would you not like to claim kindredship with him in that, though in no other thing he is like, or likely, to you? Do you think that you would lose your reputation so? What you lost at the spile, you would gain at the bung.

If they do not mean all this, then they do not speak the truth, and say what they mean. They are simply at their old tricks still.

"It was always conceded to him," *says one who calls him crazy,* "that he was a conscientious man, very modest in his demeanor, apparently inoffensive, until the subject of Slavery was introduced, when he would exhibit a feeling of indignation unparalleled."

The slave-ship is on her way, crowded with its dying victims; new cargoes are being added in mid ocean; a small crew of slaveholders, countenanced by a large body of passengers, is smothering four millions under the hatches, and yet the politician asserts that the only proper way by which deliverance is to be obtained, is by "the quiet diffusion of the sentiments of humanity," without any "outbreak." As if the sentiments of humanity were ever found unaccompanied by its deeds, and you could disperse them, all finished to order, the pure article, as easily as water with a watering-pot, and so lay the dust. What is that that I hear cast overboard? The bodies of the dead that have found deliverance. That is the way we are "diffusing" humanity, and its sentiments with it.

Prominent and influential editors, accustomed to deal with politicians, men of an infinitely lower grade, say, in their ignorance, that he acted "on the principle of revenge." They do not know the man. They must enlarge themselves to conceive of him. I have no doubt that the time will come when they will begin to see him as he was. They have got to conceive of a man of faith and of religious principle, and not a politician or an Indian; of a man who did not wait till he was personally interfered with, or thwarted in some harmless business, before he gave his life to the cause of the oppressed.

If Walker may be considered the representative of the South, I wish I could say that Brown was the representative of the North. He was a superior man. He did not value his bodily life in comparison with ideal things. He did not recognize unjust human laws, but resisted them as he was bid. For once we are lifted out of the trivialness and dust of politics into the region of truth and manhood. No man in America has ever stood up so persistently and effectively for the dignity of human nature, knowing himself for a man, and the equal of any and all governments. In that sense he was the most American of us all. He needed no babbling lawyer, making false issues, to defend him. He was more than a match for all the judges that American voters, or office-holders of whatever grade, can create. He could not have been tried by a jury of his peers, because his peers did not exist. When a man stands up serenely against the condemnation and vengeance of mankind, rising above them literally *by a whole body*,—even though he were of late the vilest murderer, who has settled that matter with himself,—the spectacle is a sublime one,—didn't ye know it, ye Liberators, ye Tribunes, ye Republicans?—and we become criminal in comparison. Do yourselves the honor to recognize him. He needs none of your respect.

As for the Democratic journals, they are not human enough to affect me at all. I do not feel indignation at any thing they may say.

I am aware that I anticipate a little, that he was still, at the last accounts, alive in the hands of his foes; but that being the case, I have all along found myself thinking and speaking of him as physically dead.

I do not believe in erecting statues to those who still live in our hearts, whose bones have not yet crumbled in the earth around us, but I would rather see the statue of Captain Brown in the Massachusetts State-House yard, than that of any other man whom I know. I rejoice that I live in this age—that I am his contemporary.

What a contrast, when we turn to that political party which is so anxiously shuffling him and his plot out of its way, and looking around for some available slaveholder, perhaps, to be its candidate, at least for one who will execute the Fugitive Slave Law, and all those other unjust laws which he took up arms to annul!

Insane! A father and six sons, and one son-in-law, and several more men besides,—as many at least as twelve disciples,—all struck with insanity at once; while the sane tyrant holds with a firmer gripe than ever his four millions of slaves, and a thousand sane editors, his abettors, are saving their country and their bacon! Just as insane were his efforts in Kansas. Ask the tyrant who is his most dangerous foe, the sane man or the insane. Do the thousands who know him best, who have rejoiced at his deeds in Kansas, and have afforded him material aid there, think him insane? Such a use of this word is a mere trope with most who persist in using it, and I have no doubt that many of the rest have already in silence retracted their words.

Read his admirable answers to Mason and others. How they are dwarfed and defeated by the contrast! On the one side, half brutish, half timid questioning; on the other, truth, clear as lightning, crashing into their obscene temples. They are made to stand with Pilate, and Gessler, and the Inquisition. How ineffectual their speech and action! and what a void their silence! They are but helpless tools in this great work. It was no human power that gathered them about this preacher.

What have Massachusetts and the North sent a few *sane* representatives to Congress for, of late years?—to declare with effect what kind of sentiments? All their speeches put together and boiled down,—and probably they themselves will confess it,—do not match for manly directness and force, and for simple truth, the few casual remarks of crazy John Brown, on the floor of the Harper's Ferry engine house;—that man whom you are about to hang, to send to the other world, though not to represent *you* there. No, he was not our representative in any sense. He was too fair a specimen of a man to represent the like of us. Who, then, *were* his constituents? If you read his words understandingly you will find out. In his case there is no idle eloquence, no made, nor maiden speech, no compliments to the oppressor. Truth is his inspirer, and earnestness the polisher of his sentences. He could afford to lose his Sharps' rifles, while he retained his faculty of speech, a Sharps' rifle of infinitely surer and longer range.

And the *New York Herald* reports the conversation "*verbatim*"! It does not know of what undying words it is made the vehicle.

I have no respect for the penetration of any man who can read the report of that conversation, and still call the principal in it insane. It has the ring of a saner sanity than an ordinary discipline and habits of life, than an ordinary organization, secure. Take any sentence of it—"Any questions that I can honorably answer, I will; not otherwise. So far as I am myself concerned, I have told every thing truthfully. I value my word, sir." The few who talk about his vindictive spirit, while they really admire his heroism, have no test by which to detect a noble man, no amalgam to combine with his pure gold. They mix their own dross with it.

It is a relief to turn from these slanders to the testimony of his more truthful, but frightened, jailers and hangmen. Governor Wise speaks far more justly and appreciatingly of him than any Northern editor, or politician, or public personage, that I chance to have heard from. I know that you can afford to hear him again on this subject. He says: "They are themselves mistaken who take him to be a madman. . . . He is cool, collected, and indomitable, and it is but just to him to say, that he was humane to his prisoners. . . . And he inspired me with great trust in his integrity as a man of truth. He is a fanatic, vain and garrulous," (I leave that part to Mr. Wise) "but firm, truthful, and intelligent. His men, too, who survive, are like him. . . . Colonel Washington says that he was the coolest and firmest man he ever saw in defying danger and death. With one son dead by his side, and another shot through, he felt the pulse of his dying son with one hand, and held his rifle with the other, and commanded his men with the utmost composure, encouraging them to be firm, and to sell their lives as dear as they could. Of the three white prisoners, Brown, Stevens, and Coppoc, it was hard to say which was most firm. . . ."

Almost the first Northern men whom the slaveholder has learned to respect!

The testimony of Mr. Vallandigham, though less valuable,

is of the same purport, that "it is vain to underrate either the man or his conspiracy. . . . He is the farthest possible remove from the ordinary ruffian, fanatic, or madman."

"All is quiet at Harper's Ferry," say the journals. What is the character of that calm which follows when the law and the slaveholder prevail? I regard this event as a touchstone designed to bring out, with glaring distinctness, the character of this government. We needed to be thus assisted to see it by the light of history. It needed to see itself. When a government puts forth its strength on the side of injustice, as ours to maintain Slavery and kill the liberators of the slave, it reveals itself a merely brute force, or worse, a demoniacal force. It is the head of the Plug Uglies. It is more manifest than ever that tyranny rules. I see this government to be effectually allied with France and Austria in oppressing mankind. There sits a tyrant holding fettered four millions of slaves; here comes their heroic liberator. This most hypocritical and diabolical government looks up from its seat on the gasping four millions, and inquires with an assumption of innocence, "What do you assault me for? Am I not an honest man? Cease agitation on this subject, or I will make a slave of you, too, or else hang you."

We talk about a *representative* government; but what a monster of a government is that where the noblest faculties of the mind, and the *whole* heart, are not *represented*. A semi-human tiger or ox, stalking over the earth, with its heart taken out and the top of its brain shot away. Heroes have fought well on their stumps when their legs were shot off, but I never heard of any good done by such a government as that.

The only government that I recognize,—and it matters not how few are at the head of it, or how small its army,—is that power that establishes justice in the land, never that which establishes injustice. What shall we think of a government to which all the truly brave and just men in the land are enemies, standing between it and those whom it oppresses? A government that pretends to be Christian and crucifies a million Christs every day!

Treason! Where does such treason take its rise? I cannot help thinking of you as you deserve, ye governments. Can you dry up the fountains of thought? High treason, when it is resistance to tyranny here below, has its origin in, and is first committed by the power that makes and forever recreates man. When you have caught and hung all these human rebels, you have accomplished nothing but your own guilt, for you have not struck at the fountain head. You presume to contend with a foe against whom West Point cadets and rifled cannon *point* not. Can all the art of the cannon-founder tempt matter to turn against its maker? Is the form in which the founder thinks he casts it more essential than the constitution of it and of himself?

The United States have a coffle of four millions of slaves. They are determined to keep them in this condition; and Massachusetts is one of the confederated overseers to prevent their escape. Such are not all the inhabitants of Massachusetts, but such are they who rule and are obeyed here. It was Massachusetts, as well as Virginia, that put down this insurrection at Harper's Ferry. She sent the marines there, and she will have to pay the penalty of her sin.

Suppose that there is a society in this State that out of its own purse and magnanimity saves all the fugitive slaves that run to us, and protects our colored fellow-citizens, and leaves the other work to the Government, so-called. Is not that government fast losing its occupation, and becoming contemptible to mankind? If private men are obliged to perform the offices of government, to protect the weak and dispense justice, then the government becomes only a hired man, or clerk, to perform menial or indifferent services. Of course, that is but the shadow of a government whose existence necessitates a Vigilant Committee. What should we think of the oriental Cadi even, behind whom worked in secret a Vigilant Committee? But such is the character of our Northern States generally; each has its Vigilant Committee. And, to a certain extent, these crazy governments recognize and accept this relation. They say, virtually, "We'll be glad to work for you on these terms, only don't make a noise about it." And thus the government, its salary being insured, withdraws into the back shop, taking the constitution with it, and bestows most of its labor on repairing that. When I hear it at work sometimes, as I go by, it reminds me, at best, of those farmers who in winter contrive to turn a penny by following the coopering business. And what kind of spirit is their barrel made to hold? They speculate in stocks, and bore holes in mountains, but they are not competent to lay out even a decent highway. The only *free* road, the Underground Railroad, is owned and managed by the Vigilant Committee. *They* have tunnelled under the whole breadth of the land. Such a government is losing its power and respectability as surely as water runs out of a leaky vessel, and is held by one that can contain it.

I hear many condemn these men because they were so few. When were the good and the brave ever in a majority? Would you have had him wait till that time came?—till you and I came over to him? The very fact that he had no rabble or troop of hirelings about him would alone distinguish him from ordinary heroes. His company was small indeed, because few could be found worthy to pass muster. Each one who there laid down his life for the poor and oppressed, was a picked man, called out of many thousands, if not millions; apparently a man of principle, of rare courage and devoted humanity, ready to sacrifice his life at any moment for the benefit of his fellow man. It may be doubted if there were as many more their equals in these respects in all the country—I speak of his followers only—for their leader, no doubt, scoured the land far and wide, seeking to swell his troop. These alone were ready to step between the oppressor and the oppressed. Surely, they were the very best men you could select to be hung. That was the greatest compliment which this country could pay them. They were ripe for her gallows. She has tried a long time, she has hung a good many, but never found the right one before.

When I think of him, and his six sons, and his son in law,— not to enumerate the others,—enlisted for this fight; proceeding coolly, reverently, humanely to work, for months if not years, sleeping and waking upon it, summering and wintering the thought, without expecting any reward but a good conscience, while almost all America stood ranked on the other side, I say again that it affects me as a sublime spectacle. If he had had any journal advocating *"his cause,"* any organ as the phrase is, monotonously and wearisomely playing the same old tune, and then passing round the hat, it would have been fatal to his efficiency. If he had acted in any way so as to be let alone by the government, he might have been suspected. It was the fact that the tyrant must give place to him, or he to the tyrant, that distinguished him from all the reformers of the day that I know.

It was his peculiar doctrine that a man has a perfect right to interfere by force with the slaveholder, in order to rescue the slave. I agree with him. They who are continually shocked by slavery have some right to be shocked by the violent death of the slaveholder, but no others. Such will be more shocked by his life than by his death. I shall not be forward to think him mistaken in his method who quickest succeeds to liberate the slave. I speak for the slave when I say, that I prefer the philanthropy of Captain Brown to that philanthropy which neither shoots me nor liberates me. At any rate, I do not think it is quite sane for one to spend his whole life in talking or writing about this matter, unless he is continuously inspired, and I have not done so. A man may have other affairs to attend to. I do not wish to kill nor to be killed, but I can foresee circumstances in which both these things would be by me unavoidable. We preserve the so-called "peace" of our community by deeds of petty violence every day. Look at the policeman's billy and hand cuffs! Look at the jail! Look at the gallows! Look at the chaplain of the regiment! We are hoping only to live safely on the outskirts of *this* provisional army. So we defend ourselves and our hen roosts, and maintain slavery. I know that the mass of my countrymen think that the only righteous use that can be made of Sharps' rifles and revolvers is to fight duels with them, when we are insulted by other nations, or to hunt Indians, or shoot fugitive slaves with them, or the like. I think that for once the Sharps' rifles and the revolvers were employed in a righteous cause. The tools were in the hands of one who could use them.

The same indignation that is said to have cleared the temple once will clear it again. The question is not about the weapon, but the spirit in which you use it. No man has appeared in America as yet who loved his fellow man so well, and treated him so tenderly. He lived for him. He took up his life and he laid it down for him. What sort of violence is that which is encouraged, not by soldiers but by peaceable citizens, not so much by lay-men as by ministers of the gospel, not so much by the fighting sects as by the Quakers, and not so much by Quaker men as by Quaker women?

This event advertises me that there is such a fact as death— the possibility of a man's dying. It seems as if no man had ever died in America before, for in order to die you must first have lived. I don't believe in the hearses and palls and funerals that they have had. There was no death in the case, because there had been no life; they merely rotted or sloughed off, pretty much as they had rotted or sloughed along. No temple's vail was rent, only a hole dug somewhere. Let the dead bury their dead. The best of them fairly ran down like a clock. Franklin—Washington—they were let off without dying; they were merely missing one day. I hear a good many pretend that they are going to die;—or that they have died for aught that I know. Nonsense! I'll defy them to do it. They haven't got life enough in them. They'll deliquesce like fungi, and keep a hundred eulogists mopping the spot where they left off. Only half a dozen or so have died since the world began. Do you think that you are going to die, sir? No! there's no hope of you. You haven't got your lesson yet. You've got to stay after school. We make a needless ado about capital punishment—taking lives, when there is no life to take. *Memento mori!* We don't understand that sublime sentence which some worthy got sculptured on his gravestone once. We've interpreted it in a grovelling and snivelling sense; we've wholly forgotten how to die.

But be sure you do die, nevertheless. Do your work, and finish it. If you know how to begin, you will know when to end.

These men, in teaching us how to die, have at the same time taught us how to live. If this man's acts and words do not create a revival, it will be the severest possible satire on the acts and words that do. It is the best news that America has ever heard. It has already quickened the feeble pulse of the North, and infused more and more generous blood into her veins and heart, than any number of years of what is called commercial and political prosperity could. How many a man who was lately contemplating suicide has now something to live for!

One writer says that Brown's peculiar monomania made him to be "dreaded by the Missourians as a supernatural being." Sure enough, a hero in the midst of us cowards is always so dreaded. He is just that thing. He shows himself superior to nature. He has a spark of divinity in him.

> "Unless above himself he can
> Erect himself, how poor a thing is man!"

Newspaper editors argue also that it is a proof of his *insanity* that he thought he was appointed to do this work which he did—that he did not suspect himself for a moment! They talk as if it were impossible that a man could be "divinely appointed" in these days to do any work whatever; as if vows and religion were out of date as connected with any man's daily work,—as if the agent to abolish Slavery could only be somebody appointed by the President, or by some political party. They talk as if a man's death were a failure, and his continued life, be it of whatever character, were a success.

When I reflect to what a cause this man devoted himself, and how religiously, and then reflect to what cause his judges and all who condemn him so angrily and fluently devote themselves, I see that they are as far apart as the heavens and earth are asunder.

The amount of it is, our *"leading men"* are a harmless kind of folk, and they know *well enough* that *they* were not divinely appointed, but elected by the votes of their party.

Who is it whose safety requires that Captain Brown be hung? Is it indispensable to any Northern man? Is there no resource but to cast these men also to the Minotaur? If you do not wish it say so distinctly. While these things are being done, beauty stands veiled and music is a screeching lie. Think of him—of his rare qualities! such a man as it takes ages to make, and ages to understand; no mock hero, nor the representative of any party. A man such as the sun may not rise upon again in this benighted land. To whose making went the costliest material, the finest adamant; sent to be the redeemer of those in captivity. And the only use to which you can put him is to hang him at the end of a rope! You who pretend to care for Christ crucified, consider what you are about to do to him who offered himself to be the savior of four millions of men.

Any man knows when he is justified, and all the wits in the world cannot enlighten him on that point. The murderer always knows that he is justly punished; but when a government takes the life of a man without the consent of his conscience, it is an audacious government, and is taking a step towards its own dissolution. Is it not possible that an individual may be right and a government wrong? Are laws to be enforced simply because they were made? or declared by any number of men to be good, if they are *not* good? Is there any necessity for a man's being a tool to perform a deed of which his better nature disapproves? Is it the intention of lawmakers that *good* men shall be hung ever? Are judges to interpret the law according to the letter, and not the spirit? What right have *you* to enter into a compact with yourself that you *will* do thus or so, against the light within you? Is it for *you* to *make up* your mind—to form any resolution whatever—and not accept the convictions that are forced upon you, and which ever pass your understanding? I do not believe in lawyers, in that mode of attacking or defending a man, because you descend to meet the judge on his own ground, and, in cases of the highest importance, it is of no consequence whether a man breaks a human law or not. Let lawyers decide trivial cases. Business men may arrange that among themselves. If they were the interpreters of the everlasting laws which rightfully bind man, that would be another thing. A counterfeiting law-factory, standing half in a slave land and half in a free! What kind of laws for free men can you expect from that?

I am here to plead his cause with you. I plead not for his life, but for his character—his immortal life; and so it becomes your cause wholly, and is not his in the least. Some eighteen hundred years ago Christ was crucified; this morning, perchance, Captain Brown was hung. These are the two ends of a chain which is not without its links. He is not Old Brown any longer; he is an Angel of Light.

I see now that it was necessary that the bravest and humanest man in all the country should be hung. Perhaps he saw it himself. I *almost fear* that I may yet hear of his deliverance, doubting if a prolonged life, if *any* life, can do as much good as his death.

"Misguided"! "Garrulous"! "Insane"! "Vindictive"! So ye write in your easy chairs, and thus he wounded responds from the floor of the Armory, clear as a cloudless sky, true as the voice of nature is: "No man sent me here; it was my own prompting and that of my Maker. I acknowledge no master in human form."

And in what a sweet and noble strain he proceeds, addressing his captors, who stand over him: "I think, my friends, you are guilty of a great wrong against God and humanity, and it would be perfectly right for any one to interfere with you so far as to free those you wilfully and wickedly hold in bondage."

And referring to his movement: "It is, in my opinion, the greatest service a man can render to God."

"I pity the poor in bondage that have none to help them; that is why I am here; not to gratify any personal animosity, revenge, or vindictive spirit. It is my sympathy with the oppressed and the wronged, that are as good as you, and as precious in the sight of God."

You don't know your testament when you see it.

"I want you to understand that I respect the rights of the poorest and weakest of colored people, oppressed by the slave power, just as much as I do those of the most wealthy and powerful."

"I wish to say, furthermore, that you had better, all you people at the South, prepare yourselves for a settlement of that question, that must come up for settlement sooner than you are prepared for it. The sooner you are prepared the better. You may dispose of me very easily. I am nearly disposed of now; but this question is still to be settled—this negro question, I mean; the end of that is not yet."

I foresee the time when the painter will paint that scene, no longer going to Rome for a subject; the poet will sing it; the historian record it; and, with the Landing of the Pilgrims and the Declaration of Independence, it will be the ornament of some future national gallery, when at least the present form of Slavery shall be no more here. We shall then be at liberty to weep for Captain Brown. Then, and not till then, we will take our revenge.

Martyrdom of John Brown

So universal and widely related is any transcendent moral greatness—so nearly identical with greatness every where and in every age, as a pyramid contracts the nearer you approach its apex—that, when I now look over my commonplace book of poetry, I find that the best of it is oftenest applicable, in part or wholly, to the case of Captain Brown. Only what is true, and strong, and solemnly earnest will recommend itself to our mood at this time. Almost any noble verse may be read, either as his elegy, or eulogy, or be made the text of an oration on him. Indeed, such are now discerned to be the parts of a universal liturgy, applicable to those rare cases of heroes and martyrs, for which the ritual of no church has provided. This is the formula established on high,—their burial service—to which every great genius has contributed its stanza or line. As Marvell wrote,

"When the sword glitters o'er the judge's head,
And fear has coward churchmen silenced,
Then is the poet's time; 'tis then he draws,
And single fights forsaken virtue's cause.
He when the wheel of empire whirleth back,
And though the world's disjointed axel crack,
Sings still of ancient rights and better times,
Seeks suff'ring good, arraigns successful crimes."

The sense of grand poetry, read by the light of this event, is brought out distinctly, like an invisible writing held to the fire.

"All heads must come
To the cold tomb,
Only the actions of the just
Smell sweet and blossom in the dust."

We have heard that the Boston lady who recently visited our hero in prison found him wearing still the clothes all cut and torn by sabres and by bayonet thrusts, in which he had been taken prisoner; and thus he had gone to his trial, and without a hat. She spent her time in the prison mending those clothes, and, for a memento, brought home a pin covered with blood.—What are the clothes that endure?

> "The garments lasting evermore
> Are works of mercy to the poor;
> And neither tetter, time, nor moth
> Shall fray that silk, or fret this cloth."

The well known verses called "The Soul's Errand," supposed, by some, to have been written by Sir Walter Raleigh, when he was expecting to be executed the following day, are at least worthy of such an origin, and are equally applicable to the present case. Hear them.

> Go, Soul, the body's guest,
> Upon a thankless arrant;
> Fear not to touch the best,
> The truth shall be thy warrant:
> Go, since I needs must die,
> And give the world the lie.
>
> Go, tell the court it glows
> And shines like rotten wood;
> Go, tell the church it shows
> What's good, and doth no good;
> If church and court reply,
> Then give them both the lie.
>
> Tell potentates they live
> Acting by others' actions;
> Not loved unless they give,
> Not strong but by their factions:
> If potentates reply,
> Give potentates the lie.
>
> Tell men of high condition,
> That rule affairs of state,
> Their purpose is ambition,
> Their practice only hate;
> And if they once reply,
> Then give them all the lie.

Tell zeal, it lacks devotion;
   Tell love, it is but lust;
Tell time, it is but motion;
   Tell flesh, it is but dust;
      And wish them not reply,
      For thou must give the lie.

Tell age, it daily wasteth;
   Tell honor, how it alters;
Tell beauty, how she blasteth;
   Tell favor, how she falters;
      And as they shall reply,
      Give each of them the lie.

Tell fortune of her blindness;
   Tell nature of decay;
Tell friendship of unkindness;
   Tell justice of delay;
      And if they dare reply,
      Then give them all the lie.

And when thou hast, as I
   Commanded thee, done blabbing,
Although to give the lie
   Deserves no less than stabbing,
      Yet stab at thee who will,
      No stab the soul can kill.

"When I am dead,
   Let not the day be writ—"
Nor bell be tolled—*
   "Love will remember it"
When hate is cold.

You, Agricola, are fortunate, not only because your life was glorious, but because your death was timely. As they tell us who heard your last words, unchanged and willing you

---

*The selectmen of the town refused to allow the bell to be tolled on this occasion.

accepted your fate; as if, as far as in your power, you would make the emperor appear innocent. But, besides the bitterness of having lost a parent, it adds to our grief, that it was not permitted us to minister to your health, . . . to gaze on your countenance, and receive your last embrace; surely, we might have caught some words and commands which we could have treasured in the inmost part of our souls. This is our pain, this our wound. . . . You were buried with the fewer tears, and in your last earthly light, your eyes looked around for something which they did not see.

If there is any abode for the spirits of the pious; if, as wise men suppose, great souls are not extinguished with the body, may you rest placidly, and call your family from weak regrets, and womanly laments, to the contemplation of your virtues, which must not be lamented, either silently or aloud. Let us honor you by our admiration, rather than by short-lived praises, and, if nature aid us, by our emulation of you. That is true honor, that the piety of whoever is most akin to you. This also I would teach your family, so to venerate your memory, as to call to mind all your actions and words, and embrace your character and the form of your soul, rather than of your body; not because I think that statues which are made of marble or brass are to be condemned, but as the features of men, so images of the features, are frail and perishable. The form of the soul is eternal; and this we can retain and express, not by a foreign material and art, but by our own lives. Whatever of Agricola we have loved, whatever we have admired, remains, and will remain, in the minds of men, and the records of history, through the eternity of ages. For oblivion will overtake many of the ancients, as if they were inglorious and ignoble: Agricola, described and transmitted to posterity, will survive.

The Last Days of John Brown

JOHN BROWN'S career for the last six weeks of his life was meteor-like, flashing through the darkness in which we live. I know of nothing so miraculous in our history.

If any person, in a lecture or conversation at that time, cited any ancient example of heroism, such as Cato or Tell or Winkelried, passing over the recent deeds and words of Brown, it was felt by any intelligent audience of Northern men to be tame and inexcusably far-fetched.

For my own part, I commonly attend more to nature than to man, but any affecting human event may blind our eyes to natural objects. I was so absorbed in him as to be surprised whenever I detected the routine of the natural world surviving still, or met persons going about their affairs indifferent. It appeared strange to me that the 'little dipper' should be still diving quietly in the river, as of yore; and it suggested that this bird might continue to dive here when Concord should be no more.

I felt that he, a prisoner in the midst of his enemies, and under sentence of death, if consulted as to his next step or resource, could answer more wisely than all his countrymen beside. He best understood his position; he contemplated it most calmly. Comparatively, all other men, North and South, were beside themselves. Our thoughts could not revert to any greater or wiser or better man with whom to contrast him, for he, then and there, was above them all. The man this country was about to hang appeared the greatest and best in it.

Years were not required for a revolution of public opinion; days, nay, hours, produced marked changes in this case. Fifty who were ready to say on going into our meeting in honor of him in Concord, that he ought to be hung, would not say it when they came out. They heard his words read, they saw the earnest faces of the congregation; and perhaps they joined at last in singing the hymn in his praise.

The order of instructors was reversed. I heard that one preacher, who at first was shocked and stood aloof, felt obliged at last, after he was hung, to make him the subject of a sermon, in which, to some extent, he eulogized the man, but said that his act was a failure. An influential class-teacher thought it necessary, after the services, to tell his grown-up pupils, that at first he thought as the preacher did then, but now he thought that John Brown was right. But it was understood that his pupils were as much ahead of the teacher, as he was ahead of the priest; and I know for a certainty, that very little boys at home had already asked their parents, in a tone of surprise, why God did not interfere to save him. In each case, the constituted teachers were only half conscious that they were not *leading*, but being *dragged*, with some loss of time and power.

The more conscientious preachers, the Bible men, they who talk about principle, and doing to others as you would that they should do unto you,—how could they fail to recognize him, by far the greatest preacher of them all, with the Bible in his life and in his acts, the embodiment of principle, who actually carried out the golden rule? All whose moral sense had been aroused, who had a calling from on high to preach, sided with him. What confessions he extracted from the cold and conservative! It is remarkable, but on the whole it is well, that it did not prove the occasion for a new sect of *Brownites* being formed in our midst.

They, whether within the Church or out of it, who adhere to the spirit and let go the letter, and are accordingly called infidel, were as usual foremost to recognize him. Men have been hung in the South before for attempting to rescue slaves, and the North was not much stirred by it. Whence, then, this wonderful difference? We were not so sure of *their* devotion to principle. We made a subtle distinction, forgot human laws, and did homage to an idea. The North, I mean the *living* North, was suddenly all transcendental. It went behind the human law, it went behind the apparent failure, and recognized eternal justice and glory. Commonly, men live according to a formula, and are satisfied if the order of law is observed, but in this instance they, to some extent, returned to original perceptions, and there was a slight revival of old religion. They saw that what was called order was confusion, what was called justice, injustice, and that the best was deemed the worst. This attitude suggested a more intelligent

and generous spirit than that which actuated our fore-
fathers, and the possibility, in the course of ages, of a revolu-
tion in behalf of another and an oppressed people.

Most Northern men, and a few Southern ones, were won-
derfully stirred by Brown's behavior and words. They saw and
felt that they were heroic and noble, and that there had been
nothing quite equal to them in their kind in this country, or
in the recent history of the world. But the minority were un-
moved by them. They were only surprised and provoked by
the attitude of their neighbors. They saw that Brown was
Brave, and that he believed that he had done right, but they
did not detect any further peculiarity in him. Not being ac-
customed to make fine distinctions, or to appreciate magna-
nimity, they read his letters and speeches as if they read them
not. They were not aware when they approached a heroic
statement—they did not know when they *burned*. They did
not feel that he spoke with authority, and hence they only re-
membered that the *law* must be executed. They remembered
the old formula, but did not hear the new revelation. The
man who does not recognize in Brown's words a wisdom and
nobleness, and therefore an authority, superior to our laws, is
a modern Democrat. This is the test by which to discover
him. He is not wilfully but constitutionally blind on this side,
and he is consistent with himself. Such has been his past life;
no doubt of it. In like manner he has read history and his
Bible, and he accepts, or seems to accept, the last only as an
established formula, and not because he has been convicted
by it. You will not find kindred sentiments in his common-
place book, if he has one.

When a noble deed is done, who is likely to appreciate it?
They who are noble themselves. I was not surprised that cer-
tain of my neighbors spoke of John Brown as an ordinary
felon, for who are they? They have either much flesh, or much
office, or much coarseness of some kind. They are not ether-
ial natures in any sense. The dark qualities predominate in
them. Several of them are decidedly pachydermatous. I say it
in sorrow, not in anger. How can a man behold the light, who
has no answering inward light? They are true to their *right*,
but when they look this way they *see* nothing, they are blind.
For the children of the light to contend with them is as if

there should be a contest between eagles and owls. Show me a man who feels bitterly toward John Brown, and let me hear what noble verse he can repeat. He'll be as dumb as if his lips were stone.

It is not every man who can be a Christian, even in a very moderate sense, whatever education you give him. It is a matter of constitution and temperament, after all. He may have to be born again many times. I have known many a man who pretended to be a Christian, in whom it was ridiculous, for he had no genius for it. It is not every man who can be a freeman, even.

Editors persevered for a good while in saying that Brown was crazy: but at last they said only that it was 'a crazy scheme,' and the only evidence brought to prove it was that it cost him his life. I have no doubt that if he had gone with five thousand men, liberated a thousand slaves, killed a hundred or two slaveholders, and had as many more killed on his own side, but not lost his own life, these same editors would have called it by a more respectable name. Yet he has been far more successful than that. He has liberated many thousands of slaves, both North and South. They seem to have known nothing about living or dying for a principle. They all called him crazy then; who calls him crazy now?

All through the excitement occasioned by his remarkable attempt and subsequent behavior, the Massachusetts Legislature, not taking any steps for the defence of her citizens who were likely to be carried to Virginia as witnesses and exposed to the violence of a slaveholding mob, was wholly absorbed in a liquor-agency question, and indulging in poor jokes on the word 'extension.' Bad spirits occupied their thoughts. I am sure that no statesman up to the occasion could have attended to that question at all at that time,—a very vulgar question to attend to at any time.

When I looked into a liturgy of the Church of England, printed near the end of the last century, in order to find a service applicable to the case of Brown, I found that the only martyr recognized and provided for by it was King Charles the First, an eminent scamp. Of all the inhabitants of England and of the world, he was the only one according to this authority, whom that church had made a martyr and saint of;

and for more than a century it had celebrated his martyrdom,
so called, by an annual service. What a satire on the Church is
that!

Look not to legislatures and churches for your guidance,
nor to any soulless, *incorporated* bodies, but to *inspirited* or
inspired ones.

What avail all your scholarly accomplishments and learning,
compared with wisdom and manhood? To omit his other be-
havior, see what a work this comparatively unread and unlet-
tered man wrote within six weeks. Where is our professor of
belles lettres or of logic and rhetoric, who can write so well?
He wrote in prison, not a history of the world, like Raleigh,
but an American book which I think will live longer than that.
I do not know of such words, uttered under such circum-
stances, and so copiously withal, in Roman or English or any
history. What a variety of themes he touched on in that short
space! There are words in that letter to his wife, respecting
the education of his daughters, which deserve to be framed
and hung over every mantlepiece in the land. Compare this
earnest wisdom with that of Poor Richard.

The death of Irving, which at any other time would have
attracted universal attention, having occurred while these
things were transpiring, went almost unobserved. I shall have
to read of it in the biography of authors.

Literary gentlemen, editors and critics, think that they
know how to write, because they have studied grammar and
rhetoric; but they are egregiously mistaken. The *art* of com-
position is as simple as the discharge of a bullet from a rifle,
and its master-pieces imply an infinitely greater force behind
them. This unlettered man's speaking and writing are stan-
dard English. Some words and phrases deemed vulgarisms
and Americanisms before, he has made standard American;
such as '*It will pay.*' It suggests that the one great rule of
composition—and if I were a professor of rhetoric, I should
insist on this—is to *speak the truth*. This first, this second, this
third; pebbles in your mouth or not. This demands earnest-
ness and manhood chiefly.

We seem to have forgotten that the expression, a *liberal*
education, originally meant among the Romans one worthy
of *free* men; while the learning of trades and professions by

which to get your livelihood merely, was considered worthy of *slaves* only. But taking a hint from the word, I would go a step further and say, that it is not the man of wealth and leisure simply, though devoted to art, or science, or literature, who, in a true sense, is *liberally* educated, but only the earnest and *free* man. In a slaveholding country like this, there can be no such thing as a *liberal* education tolerated by the State; and those scholars of Austria and France who, however learned they may be, are contented under their tyrannies, have received only a *servile* education.

Nothing could his enemies do, but it redounded to his infinite advantage—that is, to the advantage of his cause. They did not hang him at once, but reserved him to preach to them. And then there was another great blunder. They did not hang his four followers with him; that scene was still postponed; and so his victory was prolonged and completed. No theatrical manager could have arranged things so wisely to give effect to his behavior and words. And who, think you, *was* the manager? Who placed the slave woman and her child, whom he stooped to kiss for a symbol, between his prison and the gallows?

We soon saw, as he saw, that he was not to be pardoned or rescued by men. That would have been to disarm him, to restore to him a material weapon, a Sharps' rifle, when he had taken up the sword of the spirit—the sword with which he has really won his greatest and most memorable victories. Now he has not laid aside the sword of the spirit, for he is pure spirit himself, and his sword is pure spirit also.

> 'He nothing common did or mean
> Upon that memorable scene,
> Nor called the gods with vulgar spite,
> To vindicate his helpless right;
> But bowed his comely head
> Down as upon a bed.'

What a transit was that of his horizontal body alone, but just cut down from the gallows-tree! We read, that at such a time it passed through Philadelphia, and by Saturday night had reached New York. Thus, like a meteor it shot through the Union from the southern regions toward the north! No such freight had the cars borne since they carried him southward alive.

On the day of his translation, I heard, to be sure, that he was *hung*, but I did not know what that meant; I felt no sorrow on that account; but not for a day or two did I even *hear* that he was *dead*, and not after any number of days shall I believe it. Of all the men who were said to be my contemporaries, it seemed to me that John Brown was the only one who *had not died*. I never hear of a man named Brown now,—and I hear of them pretty often,—I never hear of any particularly brave and earnest man, but my first thought is of John Brown, and what relation he may be to him. I meet him at every turn. He is more alive than ever he was. He has earned immortality. He is not confined to North Elba nor to Kansas. He is no longer working in secret. He works in public, and in the clearest light that shines on this land.

The Succession of Forest Trees

EVERY man is entitled to come to Cattle-shows, even a transcendentalist; and for my part I am more interested in the men than in the cattle. I wish to see once more those old familiar faces, whose names I do not know, which for me represent the Middlesex country, and come as near being indigenous to the soil as a white man can; the men who are not above their business, whose coats are not too black, whose shoes do not shine very much, who never wear gloves to conceal their hands. It is true there are some queer specimens of humanity attracted to our festival, but all are welcome. I am pretty sure to meet once more that weak-minded and whimsical fellow, generally weak-bodied too, who prefers a crooked stick for a cane; perfectly useless, you would say, only bizarre, fit for a cabinet, like a petrified snake. A ram's horn would be as convenient, and is yet more curiously twisted. He brings that much indulged bit of the country with him, from some town's end or other, and introduces it to Concord groves as if he had promised it so much sometime.

So some, it seems to me, elect their rulers for their crookedness. But I think that a straight stick makes the best cane, and an upright man the best ruler. Or why choose a man to do plain work who is distinguished for his "oddity?" However, I do not know but you will think that they have committed this mistake who invited me to speak to you to-day.

In my capacity of surveyor, I have often talked with some of you, my employers, at your dinner-tables, after having gone round and round and behind your farming, and ascertained exactly what its limits were. Moreover, taking a surveyor's and a naturalist's liberty, I have been in the habit of going across your lots much oftener than is usual as many of you, perhaps to your sorrow, are aware. Yet many of you, to my relief, have seemed not to be aware of it; and when I came across you in some out-of-the-way nook of your farms, have inquired, with an air of surprise, if I were not lost, since you had never seen me in that part of the town or county before; when, if the truth were known, and it had not been for betraying my secret, I might with more propriety have inquired if *you* were not lost, since I had never seen *you* there before. I have several times shown the proprietor the shortest way out of his wood-lot.

Therefore, it would seem that I have some title to speak to you to-day; and, considering what that title is, and the occasion that has called us together, I need offer no apology if I invite your attention for the few moments that are allotted me, to a purely scientific subject.

At those dinner tables referred to, I have often been asked as many of you have been, if I could tell how it happened that when a pine wood was cut down an oak one sprang up, and *vice versa*. To which I have answered, and now answer, that I can tell—that it is no mystery to me. As I am not aware that this has been clearly shown by any one, I shall lay the more stress on this point. Let me lead you back into your wood-lots again.

When a single tree or a forest springs up naturally where none of its kind grew before, I do not hesitate to say, though in some quarters still it may sound paradoxical, that it came from a seed. Of the various ways by which trees are *known* to be propagated—by transplanting, cuttings, and the like—this is the only supposable one under these circumstances. No such tree has ever been known to spring from any thing else. If any one asserts that it sprang from something else, or from nothing the burden of proof lies with him.

It remains then only to show how the seed is transported from where it grows, to where it is planted. This is done chiefly by the agency of the wind, water and animals. The lighter seeds, as those of pines and maples, are transported chiefly by wind and water; the heavier, as acorns and nuts, by animals.

In all the pines, a very thin membrane, in appearance much like an insect's wing, grows over and around the seed, and independent of it, while the latter is being developed within its base. Indeed, this is often perfectly developed though the seed is abortive, nature being, you would say, more sure to provide the means of transporting the seed, than to provide the seed to be transported. In other words, a beautiful thin sack is woven around the seed, with a handle to it such as the wind can take hold of, and it is then committed to the wind, expressly that it may transport the seed and extend the range of the species; and this it does as effectually as when seeds are sent by mail in a different kind of sack from the patent office. There is a patent office at the seat of government of the universe, whose managers are as much interested in the dispersion of seeds as any body at Washington can be, and their operations are infinitely more extensive and regular.

There is then no necessity for supposing that the pines have sprung up from nothing, and I am aware that I am not at all peculiar in asserting that they come from seeds, though the mode of their propagation *by nature* has been but little attended to. They are very extensively raised from the seed in Europe, and are beginning to be here.

When you cut down an oak wood, a pine wood will not *at once* spring up there unless there are, or have been, quite recently, seed-bearing pines near enough for the seeds to be blown from them. But, adjacent to a forest of pines, if you prevent other crops from growing there, you will surely have an extension of your pine forest, provided the soil is suitable.

As for the heavy seeds and nuts which are not furnished with wings, the notion is still a very common one that, when the trees which bear these spring up where none of their kind were noticed before, they have come from seeds or other principles spontaneously generated there in an unusual manner, or which have lain dormant in the soil for centuries, or perhaps been called into activity by the heat of a burning. I do not believe these assertions and I will state some of the ways in which, according to my observation, such forests are planted and raised.

Every one of these seeds, too, will be found to be winged or legged in another fashion. Surely it is not wonderful that cherry trees of all kinds are widely dispersed, since their fruit is well known to be the favorite feed of various birds. Many kinds are called bird-cherries and they appropriate many more kinds, which are not so called. Eating cherries is a bird-like employment, and unless we disperse the seeds occasionally as they do I shall think that the birds have the best right to them. See how artfully the seed of a cherry is placed in order that a bird may be compelled to transport it—in the very midst of a tempting pericarp, so that the creature that would devour this must commonly take the stone also into its mouth or bill. If you ever ate a cherry, and did not make two bites of it, you must have perceived it—right in the center of the luscious morsel, a large earthly residuum left on the tongue. We thus take into our mouths cherry stones as big as peas, a dozen at once, for Nature can persuade us to do almost anything when she would compass her ends. Some wild men and children instinctively swallow these, like the birds when in a hurry, as the shortest way to get rid of them. Thus, though these seeds are not provided with vegetable wings, Nature has impelled the thrush tribe to take them into their bills and fly away with them, and they are winged in another sense, and more effectually than the seeds of pines, for these are carried even against the wind. The consequence is, that cherry trees grow not only here but there. The same is true of a great many other seeds.

But to come to the observation which suggested these remarks. As I have said, I suspect that I can throw some light on the fact, that when hereabouts a dense pine wood is cut down, oaks and other hard woods may at once take its place. I have got only to show that the acorns and nuts, provided they are grown in the neighborhood, are regularly planted in such woods; for I assert that if an oak tree has not grown within ten miles, and man has not carried acorns thither, then the oak wood will not spring up at once when a pine wood is cut down.

Apparently, there were only pines there before. They are cut off, and after a year or two you see oaks and other hard woods springing up there, with scarcely a pine amid them, and the wonder commonly is how the seed could have been lying in the ground so long without decaying. But the truth is, that it has not been lying in the ground so long, but is regularly planted each year by various quadrupeds and birds.

In this neighborhood, where oaks and pines are about equally dispersed, if you look through the thickest pine wood, even the seemingly exclusive pitch-pine ones, you will commonly detect many little oaks, birches, and other hard woods sprung from seeds carried into the thicket by squirrels and other animals, and also blown thither, but which are over-shadowed and choaked by the pines. The denser the ever-green wood, the more likely it is to be well planted with these seeds, because the planters incline to resort with their forage to the closest covert. They also carry it into birch and other woods. This planting is carried on annually, and the plants annually die; but when the pines are cleared off, the oaks having got just the start they want, and now secured favorable conditions, immediately spring up to trees.

Apparently, the shade of a dense pine wood is more unfavorable to the springing up of pines than of oaks within it, though the former may come up abundantly when the pines are cut, if there chance to be sound seed in the ground.

But when you cut off a lot of hard wood, very often the little pines mixed with it, have a similar start, for the squirrels have carried off the nuts to the pines and not to the more open wood, and they commonly make pretty clean work of it—to say nothing about the soil being, in a measure, exhausted for the same kind of crop.

If a pine wood is surrounded by a white oak one chiefly, white oak may be expected to succeed when the pines are cut. If it is surrounded instead by an edging of shrub oaks, then you will probably have a dense shrub-oak thicket.

I have no time to go into details, but will say, in a word, that while the wind is conveying the seeds of pines into hard woods and open lands, the squirrels and other animals are conveying the seeds of oaks and walnuts into the pine woods, and thus a rotation of crops is kept up.

I affirmed this confidently many years ago, and an occasional examination of dense pine woods confirmed me in my opinion. It has long been known to observers that squirrels bury nuts in the ground, but I am not aware that any one has thus accounted for the regular succession of forests.

On the 24th of September, in '57, as I was paddling down the Assabet, in this town, I saw a red squirrel run along the bank under some herbage, with something large in its mouth. It stopped near the foot of a hemlock, within a couple of rods of me, and, hastily pawing a hole with its fore feet, dropped its booty into it and covered it up and retreated part way up the trunk of the tree. As I approached the shore to examine the deposit, the squirrel, descending part way, betrayed no little anxiety about its treasure, and made two or three motions to recover it before it finally retreated. Digging there, I found two green pig nuts joined together, with the thick husks on, buried about an inch and a half under the reddish soil of decayed hemlock leaves, just the right depth to plant it. In short, this squirrel was then engaged in accomplishing two objects, to wit, laying up a store of Winter food for itself, and planting a hickory wood for all creation. If the squirrel was killed, or neglected its deposit, a hickory would spring up. The nearest hickory tree was twenty rods distant. These nuts were there still just fourteen days later, but were gone when I looked again, Nov. 21, or six weeks later still.

I have since examined more carefully several dense woods, which are said to be, and are apparently exclusively pine, and always with the same result. For instance, I walked the same day to a small, but very dense and handsome white-pine grove, about fifteen rods square, in the east part of this town. The trees are large for Concord, being from ten to twenty inches in diameter, and as exclusively pine as any wood that I know. Indeed, I selected this wood because I thought it the least likely to contain anything else. It stands on an open plain or pasture, except that it adjoins another small pine wood, which has a few little oaks in it, on the south-east side. On every other side, it was at least thirty rods from the nearest woods. Standing on the edge of this grove and looking through it, for it is quite level and free from underwood, for the most part bare, red carpeted ground, you would have said that there was not a hard wood tree on it, young or old. But on looking carefully along over its floor I discovered, though it was not till my eye had got used to the search, that, alternating with their ferns, and small blueberry bushes, there was not merely here and there, but as often as every five feet, and with a degree of regularity, a little oak, from three to twelve inches high, and in one place I found a green acorn dropped by the base of a pine.

I confess I was surprised to find my theory so perfectly proved in this case. One of the principal agents in this planting, the red squirrels, were all the while curiously inspecting me, while I was inspecting their plantation. Some of the little oaks had been browsed by cows, which resorted to this wood for shade.

After some years the hard woods, as I have said, evidently find such a locality unfavorable to their growth, the pines being allowed to stand. As an evidence of this, I observed a red maple, twenty-five feet long, which had been recently prostrated, as if by the wind, though it was still covered with green leaves, the only maple in any position in the wood.

But although these oaks almost invariably die if the pines are not cut down, it is probable that they do better for a few years under their shelter than they would anywhere else.

The very extensive and thorough experiments of the English have at length led them to adopt a method of raising oaks almost precisely like this, which somewhat earlier had been adopted by nature and her squirrels here; they have simply rediscovered the value of pines as nurses for oaks. The English experimenters seem early and generally to have found out the importance of using trees of some kind as nurse plants for the young oaks. I quote from Loudon what he describes as "the ultimatum on the subject of planting and sheltering oaks"—an "abstract of the practice adopted by the Government officers in the national forests" of England, prepared by Alexander Milne.

At first some oaks had been planted by themselves, and others mixed with Scotch pines; "but in all cases," says Mr. Milne, "where oaks were planted actually among the pines, and surrounded by them [though the soil be inferior], the oaks were bound to be much the best." . . . "For several years past, the plan pursued has been to plant the inclosures with Scotch pines only [a tree very similar to our pitch pine]. . . And when the pines have got to the hight of five or six feet, then to put in good strong oak plants of about four or five years' growth among the pines—not cutting away any pines at first, unless they happen to be so strong and thick as to overshadow the oaks. In about two years, it becomes necessary to shred the branches of the pines, to give light and air to the oaks, and in about two or three more years to begin gradually to remove the pines altogether, taking out a certain number each year, so that, at the end of twenty or twenty-five years, not a single Scotch pine shall be left; although, for the first ten or twelve years, the plantation may have appeared to contain nothing else but pine. The advantage of this mode of planting has been found to be that the pines dry and ameliorate the soil, destroying the coarse grass and brambles which frequently choke and injure oaks; and that no mending over is necessary, as scarcely an oak so planted is found to fail."

Thus much the English planters have discovered by patient experiment, and, for aught I know, they have taken out a patent for it; but they appear not to have discovered that it was discovered before, and that they are merely adopting the method of Nature, which she long ago made patent to all. She is all the while planting the oaks amid the pines without our knowledge, and at last, instead of Government officers, we send a party of wood-choppers to cut down the pines, and so rescue an oak forest, at which we wonder as if it had dropped from the skies.

As I walk amid hickories even in August, I hear the sound of green pig-nuts falling from time to time, cut off by the chickaree over my head. In the Fall, I notice on the ground, either within or in the neighborhood of oak woods, on all sides of the town, stout oak twigs three or four inches long, bearing half-a-dozen empty acorn-cups, which have been gnawed off by squirrels, on both sides of the nuts, in order to make them more portable.

The jays scream and the red squirrels scold while you are clubbing and shaking the chestnut trees, for they are there on the same errand, and two of a trade never agree. I frequently see a red or gray squirrel cast down a green chestnut bur, as I am going through the woods, and I used to think, sometimes, that they were cast at me. In fact, they are so busy about it in the midst of the chestnut season, that you cannot stand long in the woods without hearing one fall.

A sportsman told me that he had, the day before—that was in the middle of October—seen a green chestnut bur dropt on our great river meadow, fifty rods from the nearest wood, and much further from the nearest chestnut tree, and he could not tell how it came there.

Occasionally, when chestnuting in midwinter, I find thirty or forty nuts in a pile, left in its gallery, just under the leaves, by the common wood-mouse (*mus leucopus*).

But especially in the Winter the extent to which this transportation and planting of nuts is carried on is made apparent by the snow. In almost every wood, you will see where the red or gray squirrels have pawed down through the snow in a hundred places, sometimes two feet deep, and almost always directly to a nut or a pine-cone, as directly as if they had started from it and bored upward—which you and I could not have done. It would be difficult for us to find one before the snow falls. Commonly, no doubt, they had deposited them there in the Fall. You wonder if they remember the localities, or discover them by the scent. The red squirrel commonly has its Winter abode in the earth under a thicket of evergreens, frequently under a small clump of evergreens in the midst of a deciduous wood. If there are any nut-trees, which still retain their nuts, standing at a distance without the wood, their paths often lead directly to and from them. We, therefore, need not suppose an oak standing here and there *in* the wood in order to seed it, but if a few stand within twenty or thirty rods of it, it is sufficient.

I think that I may venture to say that every white-pine cone that falls to the earth naturally in this town, before opening and losing its seeds and almost every pitch-pine one that falls at all, is cut off by a squirrel, and they begin to pluck them long before they are ripe, so that when the crop of white-pine cones is a small one, as it commonly is, they cut off thus almost every one of those before it fairly ripens. I think, moreover, that their design, if I may so speak, in cutting them off green, is partly to prevent their opening and losing their seeds, and these are the ones for which they dig through the snow, and the only white-pine cones which contain anything then. I have counted in one heap, within a diameter of four feet, the cores of 239 pitch-pine cones which had been cut off and stripped by the red squirrel the previous Winter.

The nuts thus left on the surface, or buried just beneath it, are placed in the most favorable circumstances for germinating. I have sometimes wondered how those which merely fell on the surface of the earth got planted; but, by the end of December, I find the chestnuts of the same year partially mixed with the mold, as it were, under the decaying and moldy leaves, where there is all the moisture and manure they want, for the nuts fall first. In a plentiful year, a large proportion of the nuts are thus covered loosely an inch deep, and are, of course, somewhat concealed from squirrels. One Winter, when the crop had been abundant, I got, with the aid of a rake, many quarts of these nuts as late as the 10th of January, and though some bought at the store the same day were more than half of them moldy, I did not find a single moldy one among these which I picked from under the wet and moldy leaves, where they had been snowed on once or twice. Nature knows how to pick them best. They were still plump and tender. Apparently, they do not heat there, though wet. In the Spring, they were all sprouting.

Loudon says that "when the nut [of the common walnut of Europe] is to be preserved through the Winter for the purpose of planting in the following Spring, it should be laid in a rot heap, as soon as gathered, with the husk on; and the heap should be turned over frequently in the course of the Winter."

Here, again, he is stealing Nature's "thunder." How can a poor mortal do otherwise? for it is she that finds fingers to steal with, and the treasure to be stolen. In the planting of the seeds of most trees, the best gardeners do no more than follow nature, though they may not know it. Generally, both large and small ones are most sure to germinate, and succeed best, when only beaten into the earth with the back of a spade and then covered with leaves or straw. These results to which planters have arrived, remind us of the experience of Kane and his companions at the North, who, when learning to live in that climate, were surprised to find themselves steadily adopting the customs of the natives, simply becoming Esquimaux. So, when we experiment in planting forests, we find ourselves at last doing as Nature does. Would it not be well to consult with Nature in the outset? for she is the most extensive and experienced planter of us all, not excepting the Dukes of Athol.

In short, they who have not attended particularly to this subject, are but little aware to what an extent quadrupeds and birds are employed, especially in the Fall, in collecting, and so disseminating and planting the seeds of trees. It is the most constant employment of the squirrels at that season, and you rarely meet with one that has not a nut in its mouth, or is not just going to get one. One squirrel-hunter of this town told me that he knew of a walnut tree which bore particularly good nuts, but that on going to gather them one Fall, he found that he had been anticipated by a family of a dozen red squirrels. He took out of the tree, which was hollow, one bushel and three pecks by measurement without the husks, and they supplied him and his family for the Winter. It would be easy to multiply instances of this kind. How commonly in the Fall you see the cheek-pouches of the striped squirrel distended by a quantity of nuts! This species gets its scientific name *Tamias*, or the steward, from its habit of storing up nuts and other seeds. Look under a nut-tree a month after the nuts have fallen and see what proportion of sound nuts to the abortive ones and shells, you will find ordinarily. They have been already eaten, or dispersed far and wide. The ground looks like a platform before a grocery, where the gossips of the village sit and crack nuts and less savory jokes. You have come, you would say, after the feast was over, and are presented with the shells only.

Occasionally, when threading the woods in the Fall, you will hear a sound as if some one had broken a twig, and, looking up, see a jay pecking at an acorn, or you will see a flock of them at once about it, in the top of an oak, and hear them break them off. They then fly to a suitable limb, and, placing the acorn under one foot, hammer away at it busily, making a sound like a wood pecker's tapping, looking round from time to time to see if any foe is approaching, and soon reach the meat, and nibble at it, holding up their heads to swallow, while they hold the remainder very firmly with their claws. Nevertheless, it often drops to the ground before the bird has done with it. I can confirm what Wm. Bartram wrote to Wilson, the Ornithologist, that "The jay is one of the most useful agents in the economy of nature, for disseminating forest trees and other nuciferous and hard-seeded vegetables on which they feed. Their chief employment during the Autumnal season is foraging to supply their Winter stores. In performing this necessary duty they drop abundance of seed in their flight over fields, hedges, and by fences where they alight to deposit them in the post-holes, &c. It is remarkable what numbers of young trees rise up in fields and pastures after a wet Winter and Spring. These birds alone are capable, in a few years time, to replant all the cleared lands."

I have noticed that squirrels also frequently drop their nuts in open land, which will still further account for the oaks and walnuts which spring up in pastures, for, depend on it, every new tree comes from a seed. When I examine the little oaks, one or two years old, in such places, I invariably find the empty acorn from which they sprung.

So far from the seed having lain dormant in the soil since oaks grew there before, as many believe, it is well known that it is difficult to preserve the vitality of acorns long enough to transport them to Europe; and it is recommended in Loudon's Arboretum, as the safest course, to sprout them in pots on the voyage. The same authority states that "very few acorns of any species will germinate after having been kept a year," that beach mast "only retains its vital properties one year," and the black walnut "seldom more than six months after it has ripened." I have frequently found that in November almost every acorn left on the ground had sprouted. What with frost, drouth, moisture, and worms, the greater part are soon destroyed. Yet it is stated by one botanical writer that "Acorns that have lain for centuries, on being plowed up, have soon vegetated."

Mr. George B. Emerson, in his valuable Report on the Trees and Shrubs of this State, says of the pines: "The tenacity of life of the seeds is remarkable. They will remain for many years unchanged in the ground, protected by the coolness and deep shade of the forest above them. But when the forest is removed, and the warmth of the sun admitted, they immediately vegetate." Since he does not tell us on what observations his remark is founded, I must doubt its truth. Besides, the experience of nursery men makes it the more questionable.

The stories of wheat raised from seed buried with an ancient Egyptian, and of raspberries raised from seed found in the stomach of a man in England, who is supposed to have died sixteen or seventeen hundred years ago, are generally discredited, simply because the evidence is not conclusive.

Several men of science, Dr. Carpenter among them, have used the statement that beach-plums sprang up in sand which was dug up forty miles inland in Maine, to prove that the seed had lain there a very long time, and some have inferred that the coast has receded so far. But it seems to me necessary to their argument to show, first, that beach-plums grow only on a beach. They are not uncommon here, which is about half that distance from the shore, and I remember a dense patch a few miles north of us twenty five miles inland, from which the fruit was annually carried to market. How much further inland they grow, I know not. Dr. Chas. T. Jackson speaks of finding beach-plums (perhaps they were this kind), more than 100 miles inland in Maine.

It chances that similar objections lie against all the more notorious instances of the kind on record.

Yet I am prepared to believe that some seeds, especially small ones, may retain their vitality for centuries under favorable circumstances. In the Spring of 1859, the old Hunt House, so called, in this town, whose chimney bore the date 1703, was taken down. This stood on land which belonged to John Winthrop the first Governor of Massachusetts, and a part of the house was evidently much older than the above date, and belonged to the Winthrop family. For many years, I have ransacked this neighborhood for plants, and consider myself familiar with its productions. Thinking of the seed which are said to be sometimes dug up at an unusual depth in the earth, and thus to reproduce long extinct plants, it occurred to me last Fall that some new or rare plants might have sprung up in the cellar of this house, which had been covered from the light so long. Searching there on the 22d of September I found, among other rank weeds, a species of nettle (Urtica urens) which I had not found before; dill, which I had not seen growing spontaneously; the Jerusalem oak (Chenopodium botrys) which I had seen wild in but one place; black nightshade (Solanium nigrum), which is quite rare hereabouts, and common tobacco, which, though it was often cultivated here in the last century, has for fifty years been an unknown plant in this town, and a few months before this not even I had heard that one man in the north part of the town was cultivating a few plants for his own use. I have no doubt that some or all of these plants sprang from seeds which had long been buried under or about that house, and that that tobacco is an additional evidence that the plant was formerly cultivated here. The cellar has been filled up this year, and four of those plants, including the tobacco, are now again extinct in that locality.

It is true, I have shown that the animals consume a great part of the seeds of trees, and so, at least, effectually prevent their becoming trees; but in all these cases, as I have said, the consumer is compelled to be at the same time the disperser and planter, and this is the tax which he pays to nature. I think it is Linnæus, who says that while the swine is rooting for acorns he is planting acorns.

Though I do not believe that a plant will spring up where no seed has been, I have great faith in a seed—a, to me, equally mysterious origin for it. Convince me that you have a seed there, and I am prepared to expect wonders. I shall even believe that the millennium is at hand, and that the reign of justice is about to commence, when the Patent Office, or Government, begins to distribute, and the people to plant the seeds of these things.

In the Spring of '57, I planted six seeds sent to me from the Patent Office and labeled, I think, *"Poitrine jaune grosse,"* large yellow squash, two came up, and one bore a squash which weighed 123½ pounds, the other bore four, weighing together 186¼ pounds. Who would have believed that there were 310 pounds of *Poitrine jaune grosse* in that corner of my garden? These seeds were the bait I used to catch it, my ferrets which I sent into its burrow, my brace of terriers which unearthed it. A little mysterious hoeing and manuring was all the *abra cadabra presto-change*, that I used, and lo! true to the label, they found for me 310 pounds of *poitrine jaune grosse* there, where it was never known to be, nor was before. These talismen had perchance sprung from America at first, and returned to it with unabated force. The big squash took a premium at your fair that Fall, and I understood that the man who bought it intended to sell the seeds for 10 cents a piece—(were they not cheap at that)? But I have more hounds of the same breed. I learn that one which I dispatched to a distant town, true to its instinct, points the large yellow squash there too, where no hound ever found it before, as its ancestors did here and in France.

Other seeds I have which will find other things in that corner of my garden, in like fashion, almost any fruit you wish, every year for ages, until the crop more than fills the whole garden. You have but little more to do than throw up your cap for entertainment these American days. Perfect alchemists I keep, who can transmute substances without end; and thus the corner of my garden is an inexhaustible treasure chest. Here you can dig, not gold, but the value which gold merely represents; and there is no Signor Blitz about it. Yet farmers' sons will stare by the hour to see a juggler draw ribbons from his throat, though he tells them it is all deception. Surely, men love darkness rather than light.

Wild Apples

THE HISTORY OF THE APPLE-TREE.

IT IS remarkable how closely the history of the Apple-tree is connected with that of man. The geologist tells us that the order of the *Rosaceæ*, which includes the Apple, also the true Grasses, and the *Labiatæ*, or Mints, were introduced only a short time previous to the appearance of man on the globe.

It appears that apples made a part of the food of that unknown primitive people whose traces have lately been found at the bottom of the Swiss lakes, supposed to be older than the foundation of Rome, so old that they had no metallic implements. An entire black and shrivelled Crab-Apple has been recovered from their stores.

Tacitus says of the ancient Germans, that they satisfied their hunger with wild apples (*agrestia poma*) among other things.

Niebuhr observes that "the words for a house, a field, a plough, ploughing, wine, oil, milk, sheep, apples, and others relating to agriculture and the gentler way of life, agree in Latin and Greek, while the Latin words for all objects pertaining to war or the chase are utterly alien from the Greek." Thus the apple-tree may be considered a symbol of peace no less than the olive.

The apple was early so important, and generally distributed, that its name traced to its root in many languages signifies fruit in general. Μῆλον, in Greek, means an apple, also the fruit of other trees, also a sheep and any cattle, and finally riches in general.

The apple-tree has been celebrated by the Hebrews, Greeks, Romans, and Scandinavians. Some have thought that the first human pair were tempted by its fruit. Goddesses are fabled to have contended for it, dragons were set to watch it, and heroes were employed to pluck it.

The tree is mentioned in at least three places in the Old Testament, and its fruit in two or three more. Solomon sings,—"As the apple-tree among the trees of the wood, so is my beloved among the sons." And again,—"Stay me with

444

flagons, comfort me with apples." The noblest part of man's noblest feature is named from this fruit, "the apple of the eye."

The apple-tree is also mentioned by Homer and Herodotus. Ulysses saw in the glorious garden of Alcinoüs "pears and pomegranates, and apple-trees bearing beautiful fruit" (καὶ μηλέαι ἀγλαόκαρποι). And according to Homer, apples were among the fruits which Tantalus could not pluck, the wind ever blowing their boughs away from him. Theophrastus knew and described the apple-tree as a botanist.

According to the Prose Edda, "Iduna keeps in a box the apples which the gods, when they feel old age approaching, have only to taste of to become young again. It is in this manner that they will be kept in renovated youth until Ragnarök" (or the destruction of the gods).

I learn from Loudon that "the ancient Welsh bards were rewarded for excelling in song by the token of the apple-spray"; and "in the Highlands of Scotland the apple-tree is the badge of the clan Lamont."

The apple-tree (*Pyrus malus*) belongs chiefly to the northern temperate zone. Loudon says, that "it grows spontaneously in every part of Europe except the frigid zone, and throughout Western Asia, China, and Japan." We have also two or three varieties of the apple indigenous in North America. The cultivated apple-tree was first introduced into this country by the earliest settlers, and it is thought to do as well or better here than anywhere else. Probably some of the varieties which are now cultivated were first introduced into Britain by the Romans.

Pliny, adopting the distinction of Theophrastus, says,—"Of trees there are some which are altogether wild (*sylvestres*), some more civilized (*urbaniores*)." Theophrastus includes the apple among the last; and, indeed, it is in this sense the most civilized of all trees. It is as harmless as a dove, as beautiful as a rose, and as valuable as flocks and herds. It has been longer cultivated than any other, and so is more humanized; and who knows but, like the dog, it will at length be no longer traceable to its wild original? It migrates with man, like the dog and horse and cow: first, perchance, from Greece to Italy, thence to England, thence to America; and our Western emigrant is still marching steadily toward the setting sun with the seeds of the apple in his pocket, or perhaps a few young trees strapped to his load. At least a million apple-trees are thus set farther westward this year than any cultivated ones grew last year. Consider how the Blossom-Week, like the Sabbath, is thus annually spreading over the prairies; for when man migrates, he carries with him not only his birds, quadrupeds, insects, vegetables, and his very sward, but his orchard also.

The leaves and tender twigs are an agreeable food to many domestic animals, as the cow, horse, sheep, and goat; and the fruit is sought after by the first, as well as by the hog. Thus there appears to have existed a natural alliance between these animals and this tree from the first. "The fruit of the Crab in the forests of France" is said to be "a great resource for the wild-boar."

Not only the Indian, but many indigenous insects, birds, and quadrupeds, welcomed the apple-tree to these shores. The tent-caterpillar saddled her eggs on the very first twig that was formed, and it has since shared her affections with the wild cherry; and the canker-worm also in a measure abandoned the elm to feed on it. As it grew apace, the blue-bird, robin, cherry-bird, king-bird, and many more, came with haste and built their nests and warbled in its boughs, and so became orchard-birds, and multiplied more than ever. It was an era in the history of their race. The downy woodpecker found such a savory morsel under its bark, that he perforated it in a ring quite round the tree, before he left it,—a thing which he had never done before, to my knowledge. It did not take the partridge long to find out how sweet its buds were, and every winter eve she flew, and still flies, from the wood, to pluck them, much to the farmer's sorrow. The rabbit, too, was not slow to learn the taste of its twigs and bark; and when the fruit was ripe, the squirrel half-rolled, half-carried it to his hole; and even the musquash crept up the bank from the brook at evening, and greedily devoured it, until he had worn a path in the grass there; and when it was frozen and thawed, the crow and the jay were glad to taste it occasionally. The owl crept into the first apple-tree that became hollow, and fairly hooted with delight, finding it just the place for him; so, settling down into it, he has remained there ever since.

My theme being the Wild Apple, I will merely glance at some of the seasons in the annual growth of the cultivated apple, and pass on to my special province.

The flowers of the apple are perhaps the most beautiful of any tree's, so copious and so delicious to both sight and scent. The walker is frequently tempted to turn and linger near some more than usually handsome one, whose blossoms are two-thirds expanded. How superior it is in these respects to the pear, whose blossoms are neither colored nor fragrant!

By the middle of July, green apples are so large as to remind us of coddling, and of the autumn. The sward is commonly strewed with little ones which fall still-born, as it were,—Nature thus thinning them for us. The Roman writer Palladius said,—"If apples are inclined to fall before their time, a stone placed in a split root will retain them." Some such notion, still surviving, may account for some of the stones which we see placed to be overgrown in the forks of trees. They have a saying in Suffolk, England,—

> "At Michaelmas time, or a little before,
> Half an apple goes to the core."

Early apples begin to be ripe about the first of August; but I think that none of them are so good to eat as some to smell. One is worth more to scent your handkerchief with than any perfume which they sell in the shops. The fragrance of some fruits is not to be forgotten, along with that of flowers. Some gnarly apple which I pick up in the road reminds me by its fragrance of all the wealth of Pomona,—carrying me forward to those days when they will be collected in golden and ruddy heaps in the orchards and about the cider-mills.

A week or two later, as you are going by orchards or gardens, especially in the evenings, you pass through a little region possessed by the fragrance of ripe apples, and thus enjoy them without price, and without robbing anybody.

There is thus about all natural products a certain volatile and ethereal quality which represents their highest value, and which cannot be vulgarized, or bought and sold. No mortal has ever enjoyed the perfect flavor of any fruit, and only the godlike among men begin to taste its ambrosial qualities. For nectar and ambrosia are only those fine flavors of every earthly fruit which our coarse palates fail to perceive,—just as we occupy the heaven of the gods without knowing it. When I see a particularly mean man carrying a load of fair and fragrant early apples to market, I seem to see a contest going on between him and his horse, on the one side, and the apples on the other, and, to my mind, the apples always gain it. Pliny says that apples are the heaviest of all things, and that the oxen begin to sweat at the mere sight of a load of them. Our driver begins to lose his load the moment he tries to transport them to where they do not belong, that is, to any but the most beautiful. Though he gets out from time to time, and feels of them, and thinks they are all there, I see the stream of their evanescent and celestial qualities going to heaven from his cart, while the pulp and skin and core only are going to market. They are not apples, but pomace. Are not these still Iduna's apples, the taste of which keeps the gods forever young? and think you that they will let Loki or Thjassi carry them off to Jötunheim, while they grow wrinkled and gray? No, for Ragnarök, or the destruction of the gods, is not yet.

There is another thinning of the fruit, commonly near the end of August or in September, when the ground is strewn with windfalls; and this happens especially when high winds occur after rain. In some orchards you may see fully three-quarters of the whole crop on the ground, lying in a circular form beneath the trees, yet hard and green,—or, if it is a hillside, rolled far down the hill. However, it is an ill wind that blows nobody any good. All the country over, people are busy picking up the windfalls, and this will make them cheap for early apple-pies.

In October, the leaves falling, the apples are more distinct on the trees. I saw one year in a neighboring town some trees fuller of fruit than I remembered to have ever seen before, small yellow apples hanging over the road. The branches were gracefully drooping with their weight, like a barberry-bush, so that the whole tree acquired a new character. Even the topmost branches, instead of standing erect, spread and drooped in all directions; and there were so many poles supporting the lower ones, that they looked like pictures of banian-trees. As an old English manuscript says, "The mo appelen the tree bereth, the more sche boweth to the folk."

Surely the apple is the noblest of fruits. Let the most beautiful or the swiftest have it. That should be the "going" price of apples.

Between the fifth and twentieth of October I see the barrels lie under the trees. And perhaps I talk with one who is selecting some choice barrels to fulfil an order. He turns a specked one over many times before he leaves it out. If I were to tell what is passing in my mind, I should say that every one was specked which he had handled; for he rubs off all the bloom, and those fugacious ethereal qualities leave it. Cool evenings prompt the farmers to make haste, and at length I see only the ladders here and there left leaning against the trees.

It would be well, if we accepted these gifts with more joy and gratitude, and did not think it enough simply to put a fresh load of compost about the tree. Some old English customs are suggestive at least. I find them described chiefly in Brand's "Popular Antiquities." It appears that "on Christmas eve the farmer and their men in Devonshire take a large bowl of cider, with a toast in it, and carrying it in state to the orchard, they salute the apple-trees with much ceremony, in order to make them bear well the next season." This salutation consists in "throwing some of the cider about the roots of the tree, placing bits of the toast on the branches," and then, "encircling one of the best bearing trees in the orchard, they drink the following toast three several times:—

> 'Here 's to thee, old apple-tree,
> Whence thou mayst bud, and whence thou mayst blow,
> And whence thou mayst bear apples enow!
>   Hats-full! caps-full!
>   Bushel, bushel, sacks-full!
>   And my pockets full, too! Hurra!' "

Also what was called "apple-howling" used to be practised in various counties of England on New-Year's eve. A troop of boys visited the different orchards, and, encircling the apple-trees, repeated the following words:—

> "Stand fast, root! bear well, top!
> Pray God send us a good howling crop:
>   Every twig, apples big;
>   Every bough, apples enow!"

"They then shout in chorus, one of the boys accompanying them on a cow's horn. During this ceremony they rap the trees with their sticks." This is called "wassailing" the trees, and is thought by some to be "a relic of the heathen sacrifice to Pomona."

Herrick sings,—

> "Wassaile the trees that they may beare
> You many a plum and many a peare;
> For more or less fruits they will bring
> As you so give them wassailing."

Our poets have as yet a better right to sing of cider than of wine; but it behooves them to sing better than English Phillips did, else they will do no credit to their Muse.

THE WILD APPLE.

So much for the more civilized apple-trees (*ubaniores*, as Pliny calls them). I love better to go through the old orchards of ungrafted apple-trees, at whatever season of the year,—so irregularly planted: sometimes two trees standing close together; and the rows so devious that you would think that they not only had grown while the owner was sleeping, but had been set out by him in a somnambulic state. The rows of grafted fruit will never tempt me to wander amid them like these. But I now, alas, speak rather from memory than from any recent experience, such ravages have been made!

Some soils, like a rocky tract called the Easterbrooks Country in my neighborhood, are so suited to the apple, that it will grow faster in them without any care, or if only the ground is broken up once a year, than it will in many places with any amount of care. The owners of this tract allow that the soil is excellent for fruit, but they say that it is so rocky that they have not patience to plough it, and that, together with the distance, is the reason why it is not cultivated. There are, or were recently, extensive orchards there standing without order. Nay, they spring up wild and bear well there in the midst of pines, birches, maples, and oaks. I am often surprised to see rising amid these trees the rounded tops of apple-trees glowing with red or yellow fruit, in harmony with the autumnal tints of the forest.

Going up the side of a cliff about the first of November, I saw a vigorous young apple-tree, which, planted by birds or cows, had shot up amid the rocks and open woods there, and had now much fruit on it, uninjured by the frosts, when all cultivated apples were gathered. It was a rank wild growth, with many green leaves on it still, and made an impression of thorniness. The fruit was hard and green, but looked as if it would be palatable in the winter. Some was dangling on the twigs, but more half-buried in the wet leaves under the tree, or rolled far down the hill amid the rocks. The owner knows nothing of it. The day was not observed when it first blossomed, nor when it first bore fruit, unless by the chickadee. There was no dancing on the green beneath it in its honor, and now there is no hand to pluck its fruit,—which is only gnawed by squirrels, as I perceive. It has done double duty,— not only borne this crop, but each twig has grown a foot into the air. And this is *such* fruit! bigger than many berries, we must admit, and carried home will be sound and palatable next spring. What care I for Iduna's apples so long as I can get these?

When I go by this shrub thus late and hardy, and see its dangling fruit, I respect the tree, and I am grateful for Nature's bounty, even though I cannot eat it. Here on this rugged and woody hill-side has grown an apple-tree, not planted by man, no relic of a former orchard, but a natural growth, like the pines and oaks. Most fruits which we prize and use depend entirely on our care. Corn and grain, potatoes, peaches, melons, etc., depend altogether on our planting; but the apple emulates man's independence and enterprise. It is not simply carried, as I have said, but, like him, to some extent, it has migrated to this New World, and is even, here and there, making its way amid the aboriginal trees; just as the ox and dog and horse sometimes run wild and maintain themselves.

Even the sourest and crabbedest apple, growing in the most unfavorable position, suggests such thoughts as these, it is so noble a fruit.

THE CRAB.

Nevertheless, *our* wild apple is wild only like myself, perchance, who belong not to the aboriginal race here, but have strayed into the woods from the cultivated stock. Wilder still, as I have said, there grows elsewhere in this country a native and aboriginal Crab-Apple, *Malus coronaria*, "whose nature has not yet been modified by cultivation." It is found from Western New-York to Minnesota, and southward. Michaux says that its ordinary height "is fifteen or eighteen feet, but it is sometimes found twenty-five or thirty feet high," and that the large ones "exactly resemble the common apple-tree." "The flowers are white mingled with rose-color, and are collected in corymbs." They are remarkable for their delicious odor. The fruit, according to him, is about an inch and a half in diameter, and is intensely acid. Yet they make fine sweetmeats, and also cider of them. He concludes, that, "if, on being cultivated, it does not yield new and palatable varieties, it will at least be celebrated for the beauty of its flowers, and for the sweetness of its perfume."

I never saw the Crab-Apple till May, 1861. I had heard of it through Michaux, but more modern botanists, so far as I know, have not treated it as of any peculiar importance. Thus it was a half-fabulous tree to me. I contemplated a pilgrimage to the "Glades," a portion of Pennsylvania where it was said to grow to perfection. I thought of sending to a nursery for it, but doubted if they had it, or would distinguish it from European varieties. At last I had occasion to go to Minnesota, and on entering Michigan I began to notice from the cars a tree with handsome rose-colored flowers. At first I thought it some variety of thorn; but it was not long before the truth flashed on me, that this was my long-sought Crab-Apple. It was the prevailing flowering shrub or tree to be seen from the cars at that season of the year—about the middle of May. But the cars never stopped before one, and so I was launched on the bosom of the Mississippi without having touched one, experiencing the fate of Tantalus. On arriving at St. Anthony's Falls, I was sorry to be told that I was too far north for the Crab-Apple. Nevertheless I succeeded in finding it about eight miles west of the Falls; touched it and smelled it, and secured a lingering corymb of flowers for my herbarium. This must have been near its northern limit.

HOW THE WILD APPLE GROWS.

But though these are indigenous, like the Indians, I doubt whether they are any hardier than those backwoodsmen among the apple-trees, which, though descended from cultivated stocks, plant themselves in distant fields and forests, where the soil is favorable to them. I know of no trees which have more difficulties to contend with, and which more sturdily resist their foes. These are the ones whose story we have to tell. It oftentimes reads thus:—

Near the beginning of May, we notice little thickets of apple-trees just springing up in the pastures where cattle have been,—as the rocky ones of our Easterbrooks Country, or the top of Nobscot Hill, in Sudbury. One or two of these perhaps survive the drought and other accidents,—their very birth-place defending them against the encroaching grass and some other dangers, at first.

> In two years' time 't had thus
>   Reached the level of the rocks,
> Admired the stretching world,
>   Nor feared the wandering flocks.
>
> But at this tender age
>   Its sufferings began:
> There came a browsing ox
>   And cut it down a span.

This time, perhaps, the ox does not notice it amid the grass; but the next year, when it has grown more stout, he recognizes it for a fellow-emigrant from the old country, the flavor of whose leaves and twigs he well knows; and though at first he pauses to welcome it, and express his surprise, and gets for answer, "The same cause that brought you here brought me," he nevertheless browses it again, reflecting, it may be, that he has some title to it.

Thus cut down annually, it does not despair; but, putting forth two short twigs for every one cut off, it spreads out low along the ground in the hollows or between the rocks, growing more stout and scrubby, until it forms, not a tree as yet, but a little pyramidal, stiff, twiggy mass, almost as solid and impenetrable as a rock. Some of the densest and most impenetrable clumps of bushes that I have ever seen, as well on account of the closeness and stubbornness of their branches as of their thorns, have been these wild-apple scrubs. They are more like the scrubby fir and black spruce on which you stand, and sometimes walk, on the tops of mountains, where cold is the demon they contend with, than anything else. No wonder they are prompted to grow thorns at last, to defend themselves against such foes. In their thorniness, however, there is no malice, only some malic acid.

The rocky pastures of the tract I have referred to—for they maintain their ground best in a rocky field—are thickly sprinkled with these little tufts, reminding you often of some rigid gray mosses or lichens, and you see thousands of little trees just springing up between them, with the seed still attached to them.

Being regularly clipped all around each year by the cows, as a hedge with shears, they are often of a perfect conical or pyramidal form, from one to four feet high, and more or less sharp, as if trimmed by the gardener's art. In the pastures on Nobscot Hill and its spurs, they make fine dark shadows when the sun is low. They are also an excellent covert from hawks for many small birds that roost and build in them. Whole flocks perch in them at night, and I have seen three robins' nests in one which was six feet in diameter.

No doubt many of these are already old trees, if you reckon from the day they were planted, but infants still when you consider their development and the long life before them. I counted the annual rings of some which were just one foot high, and as wide as high, and found that they were about twelve years old, but quite sound and thrifty! They were so low that they were unnoticed by the walker, while many of their contemporaries from the nurseries were already bearing considerable crops. But what you gain in time is perhaps in this case, too, lost in power,—that is, in the vigor of the tree. This is their pyramidal state.

The cows continue to browse them thus for twenty years or more, keeping them down and compelling them to spread, until at last they are so broad that they become their own fence, when some interior shoot, which their foes cannot reach, darts upward with joy: for it has not forgotten its high calling, and bears its own peculiar fruit in triumph.

Such are the tactics by which it finally defeats its bovine foes. Now, if you have watched the progress of a particular shrub, you will see that it is no longer a simple pyramid or cone, but that out of its apex there rises a sprig or two, growing more lustily perchance than an orchard-tree, since the plant now devotes the whole of its repressed energy to these upright parts. In a short time these become a small tree, an inverted pyramid resting on the apex of the other, so that the whole has now the form of a vast hour-glass. The spreading bottom, having served its purpose, finally disappears, and the generous tree permits the now harmless cows to come in and stand in its shade, and rub against and redden its trunk,which has grown in spite of them, and even to taste a part of its fruit, and so disperse the seed.

Thus the cows create their own shade and food; and the tree, its hour-glass being inverted, lives a second life, as it were.

It is an important question with some nowadays, whether you should trim young apple-trees as high as your nose or as high as your eyes. The ox trims them up as high as he can reach, and that is about the right height, I think.

In spite of wandering kine, and other adverse circumstances, that despised shrub, valued only by small birds as a covert and shelter from hawks, has its blossom-week at last, and in course of time its harvest, sincere, though small.

By the end of some October, when its leaves have fallen, I frequently see such a central sprig, whose progress I have watched, when I thought it had forgotten its destiny, as I had, bearing its first crop of small green or yellow or rosy fruit, which the cows cannot get at over the bushy and thorny

hedge which surrounds it, and I make haste to taste the new
and undescribed variety. We have all heard of the numerous
varieties of fruit invented by Van Mons and Knight. This is
the system of Van Cow, and she has invented far more and
more memorable varieties than both of them.

Through what hardships it may attain to bear a sweet fruit!
Though somewhat small, it may prove equal, if not superior,
in flavor to that which has grown in a garden,—will perchance
be all the sweeter and more palatable for the very difficulties
it has had to contend with. Who knows but this chance wild
fruit, planted by a cow or a bird on some remote and rocky
hill-side, where it is as yet unobserved by man, may be the
choicest of all its kind, and foreign potentates shall hear of it,
and royal societies seek to propagate it, though the virtues of
the perhaps truly crabbed owner of the soil may never be
heard of,—at least, beyond the limits of his village? It was
thus the Porter and the Baldwin grew.

Every wild-apple shrub excites our expectation thus,
somewhat as every wild child. It is, perhaps, a prince in dis-
guise. What a lesson to man! So are human beings, referred
to the highest standard, the celestial fruit which they suggest
and aspire to bear, browsed on by fate; and only the most per-
sistent and strongest genius defends itself and prevails, sends
a tender scion upward at last, and drops its perfect fruit on
the ungrateful earth. Poets and philosophers and statesmen
thus spring up in the country pastures, and outlast the hosts
of unoriginal men.

Such is always the pursuit of knowledge. The celestial
fruits, the golden apples of the Hesperides, are ever guarded
by a hundred-headed dragon which never sleeps, so that it is
an Herculean labor to pluck them.

This is one, and the most remarkable way, in which the wild
apple is propagated; but commonly it springs up at wide in-
tervals in woods and swamps, and by the sides of roads, as the
soil may suit it, and grows with comparative rapidity. Those
which grow in dense woods are very tall and slender. I fre-
quently pluck from these trees a perfectly mild and tamed
fruit. As Palladius says, *"Et injussu consternitur ubere mali"*:
And the ground is strewn with the fruit of an unbidden
apple-tree.

It is an old notion, that, if these wild trees do not bear a valuable fruit of their own, they are the best stocks by which to transmit to posterity the most highly prized qualities of others. However, I am not in search of stocks, but the wild fruit itself, whose fierce gust has suffered no "inteneration." It is not my

> "highest plot
> To plant the Bergamot."

THE FRUIT, AND ITS FLAVOR.

The time for wild apples is the last of October and the first of November. They then get to be palatable, for they ripen late, and they are still perhaps as beautiful as ever. I make a great account of these fruits, which the farmers do not think it worth the while to gather,—wild flavors of the Muse, vivacious and inspiriting. The farmer thinks that he has better in his barrels, but he is mistaken, unless he has a walker's appetite and imagination, neither of which can he have.

Such as grow quite wild, and are left out till the first of November, I presume that the owner does not mean to gather. They belong to children as wild as themselves,—to certain active boys that I know,—to the wild-eyed woman of the fields, to whom nothing comes amiss, who gleans after all the world,—and, moreover, to us walkers. We have met with them, and they are ours. These rights, long enough insisted upon, have come to be an institution in some old countries, where they have learned how to live. I hear that "the custom of grippling, which may be called apple-gleaning, is, or was formerly, practised in Herefordshire. It consists in leaving a few apples, which are called the gripples, on every tree, after the general gathering, for the boys, who go with climbing-poles and bags to collect them."

As for those I speak of, I pluck them as a wild fruit, native to this quarter of the earth,—fruit of old trees that have been dying ever since I was a boy and are not yet dead, frequented only by the woodpecker and the squirrel, deserted now by the owner, who has not faith enough to look under their boughs.

From the appearance of the tree-top, at a little distance, you would expect nothing but lichens to drop from it, but your faith is rewarded by finding the ground strewn with spirited fruit,—some of it, perhaps, collected at squirrel-holes, with the marks of their teeth by which they carried them,—some containing a cricket or two silently feeding within, and some, especially in damp days, a shelless snail. The very sticks and stones lodged in the tree-top might have convinced you of the savoriness of the fruit which has been so eagerly sought after in past years.

I have seen no account of these among the "Fruits and Fruit-Trees of America," though they are more memorable to my taste than the grafted kinds; more racy and wild American flavors do they possess, when October and November, when December and January, and perhaps February and March even, have assuaged them somewhat. An old farmer in my neighborhood, who always selects the right word, says that "they have a kind of bow-arrow tang."

Apples for grafting appear to have been selected commonly, not so much for their spirited flavor, as for their mildness, their size, and bearing qualities,—not so much for their beauty, as for their fairness and soundness. Indeed, I have no faith in the selected lists of pomological gentlemen. Their "Favorites" and "None-suches" and "Seek-no-farthers," when I have fruited them, commonly turn out very tame and forgetable. They are eaten with comparatively little zest and have no real *tang* nor *smack* to them.

What if some of these wildings are acrid and puckery, genuine *verjuice*, do they not still belong to the *Pomaceæ*, which are uniformly innocent and kind to our race? I still begrudge them to the cider-mill. Perhaps they are not fairly ripe yet.

No wonder that these small and high-colored apples are thought to make the best cider. Loudon quotes from the "Herefordshire Report," that "apples of a small size are always, if equal in quality, to be preferred to those of a larger size, in order that the rind and kernel may bear the greatest proportion to the pulp, which affords the weakest and most watery juice." And he says, that, "to prove this, Dr. Symonds, of Hereford, about the year 1800, made one hogshead of cider entirely from the rinds and cores of apples, and another from the pulp only, when the first was found of extraordinary strength and flavor, while the latter was sweet and insipid."

Evelyn says that the "Red-strake" was the favorite cider-apple in his day; and he quotes one Dr. Newburg as saying, "In Jersey 't is a general observation, as I hear, that the more of red any apple has in its rind, the more proper it is for this use. Pale-faced apples they exclude as much as may be from their cider-vat." This opinion still prevails.

All apples are good in November. Those which the farmer leaves out as unsalable, and unpalatable to those who frequent the markets, are choicest fruit to the walker. But it is remarkable that the wild apple, which I praise as so spirited and racy when eaten in the fields or woods, being brought into the house, has frequently a harsh and crabbed taste. The Saunterer's Apple not even the saunterer can eat in the house. The palate rejects it there, as it does haws and acorns, and demands a tamed one; for there you miss the November air, which is the sauce it is to be eaten with. Accordingly, when Tityrus, seeing the lengthening shadows, invites Meliboeus to go home and pass the night with him, he promises him *mild* apples and soft chestnuts,—*mitia poma, astaneæ molles.* I frequently pluck wild apples of so rich and spicy a flavor that I wonder all orchardists do not get a scion from that tree, and I fail not to bring home my pockets full. But perchance, when I take one out of my desk and taste it in my chamber, I find it unexpectedly crude,—sour enough to set a squirrel's teeth on edge and make a jay scream.

These apples have hung in the wind and frost and rain till they have absorbed the qualities of the weather or season, and thus are highly *seasoned*, and they *pierce* and *sting* and *permeate* us with their spirit. They must be eaten in *season*, accordingly,—that is, out-of-doors.

To appreciate the wild and sharp flavors of these October fruits, it is necessary that you be breathing the sharp October or November air. The out-door air and exercise which the walker gets give a different tone to his palate, and he craves a fruit which the sedentary would call harsh and crabbed. They must be eaten in the fields, when your system is all aglow with exercise, when the frosty weather nips your fingers, the wind rattles the bare boughs or rustles the few remaining leaves, and the jay is heard screaming around. What is sour in the house a bracing walk makes sweet. Some of these apples might be labelled, "To be eaten in the wind."

Of course no flavors are thrown away; they are intended for the taste that is up to them. Some apples have two distinct flavors, and perhaps one-half of them must be eaten in the house, the other out-doors. One Peter Whitney wrote from Northborough in 1782, for the Proceedings of the Boston Academy, describing an apple-tree in that town "producing fruit of opposite qualities, part of the same apple being frequently sour and the other sweet"; also some all sour, and others all sweet, and this diversity on all parts of the tree.

There is a wild apple on Nawshawtuct Hill in my town which has to me a peculiarly pleasant bitter tang, not perceived till it is three-quarters tasted. It remains on the tongue. As you eat it, it smells exactly like a squash-bug. It is a sort of triumph to eat and relish it.

I hear that the fruit of a kind of plum-tree in Provence is "called *Prunes sibarelles*, because it is impossible to whistle after having eaten them, from their sourness." But perhaps they were only eaten in the house and in summer, and if tried out-of-doors in a stinging atmosphere, who knows but you could whistle an octave higher and clearer?

In the fields only are the sours and bitters of Nature appreciated; just as the wood-chopper eats his meal in a sunny glade, in the middle of a winter day, with content, basks in a sunny ray there and dreams of summer in a degree of cold which, experienced in a chamber, would make a student miserable. They who are at work abroad are not cold, but rather it is they who sit shivering in houses. As with temperatures, so with flavors; as with cold and heat, so with sour and sweet. This natural raciness, the sours and bitters which the diseased palate refuses, are the true condiments.

Let your condiments be in the condition of your senses. To appreciate the flavor of these wild apples requires vigorous and healthy senses, *papillæ* firm and erect on the tongue and palate, not easily flattened and tamed.

From my experience with wild apples, I can understand that there may be reason for a savage's preferring many kinds of food which the civilized man rejects. The former has the palate of an out-door man. It takes a savage or wild taste to appreciate a wild fruit.

What a healthy out-of-door appetite it takes to relish the apple of life, the apple of the world, then!

> "Nor is it every apple I desire,
>   Nor that which pleases every palate best;
> 'T is not the lasting Deuxan I require,
>   Nor yet the red-cheeked Greening I request,
> Nor that which first beshrewed the name of wife,
> Nor that whose beauty caused the golden strife:
> No, no! bring me an apple from the tree of life!"

So there is one *thought* for the field, another for the house. I would have my thoughts, like wild apples, to be food for walkers, and will not warrant them to be palatable, if tasted in the house.

THEIR BEAUTY.

Almost all wild apples are handsome. They cannot be too gnarly and crabbed and rusty to look at. The gnarliest will have some redeeming traits even to the eye. You will discover some evening redness dashed or sprinkled on some protuberance or in some cavity. It is rare that the summer lets an apple go without streaking or spotting it on some part of its sphere. It will have some red stains, commemorating the mornings and evenings it has witnessed; some dark and rusty blotches, in memory of the clouds and foggy, mildewy days that have passed over it; and a spacious field of green reflecting the general face of Nature,—green even as the fields; or a yellow ground, which implies a milder flavor,—yellow as the harvest, or russet as the hills.

Apples, these I mean, unspeakably fair,—apples not of Discord, but of Concord! Yet not so rare but that the homeliest may have a share. Painted by the frosts, some a uniform clear bright yellow, or red, or crimson, as if their spheres had regularly revolved, and enjoyed the influence of the sun on all sides alike,—some with the faintest pink blush imaginable,—some brindled with deep red streaks like a cow, or with hundreds of fine blood-red rays running regularly from the

stem-dimple to the blossom-end, like meridional lines, on a
straw-colored ground,—some touched with a greenish rust,
like a fine lichen, here and there, with crimson blotches or
eyes more or less confluent and fiery when wet,—and others
gnarly, and freckled or peppered all over on the stem side with
fine crimson spots on a white ground, as if accidentally sprin-
kled from the brush of Him who paints the autumn leaves.
Others, again, are sometimes red inside, perfused with a beau-
tiful blush, fairy food, too beautiful to eat,—apple of the
Hesperides, apple of the evening sky! But like shells and peb-
bles on the sea-shore, they must be seen as they sparkle amid
the withering leaves in some dell in the woods, in the autum-
nal air, or as they lie in the wet grass, and not when they have
wilted and faded in the house.

THE NAMING OF THEM.

It would be a pleasant pastime to find suitable names for
the hundred varieties which go to a single heap at the cider-
mill. Would it not tax a man's invention,—no one to be
named after a man, and all in the *lingua vernacula*? Who shall
stand godfather at the christening of the wild apples? It would
exhaust the Latin and Greek languages, if they were used, and
make the *lingua vernacula* flag. We should have to call in the
sunrise and the sunset, the rainbow and the autumn woods
and the wild flowers, and the woodpecker and the purple
finch and the squirrel and the jay and the butterfly, the
November traveller and the truant boy, to our aid.

In 1836 there were in the garden of the London
Horticultural Society more than fourteen hundred distinct
sorts. But here are species which they have not in their cata-
logue, not to mention the varieties which our Crab might
yield to cultivation.

Let us enumerate a few of these. I find myself compelled,
after all, to give the Latin names of some for the benefit of
those who live where English is not spoken,—for they are
likely to have a world-wide reputation.

There is, first of all, the Wood-Apple (*Malus sylvatica*);
the Blue-Jay Apple; the Apple which grows in Dells in the
Woods, (*sylvestrivallis*,) also in Hollows in Pastures (*campe-*

strivallis); the Apple that grows in an old Cellar-Hole (*Malus cellaris*); the Meadow-Apple; the Partridge-Apple; the Truant's Apple, (*Cessatoris,*) which no boy will ever go by without knocking off some, however *late* it may be; the Saunterer's Apple,—you must lose yourself before you can find the way to that; the Beauty of the Air (*Decus Aëris*); December-Eating; the Frozen-Thawed, (*gelato-soluta,*) good only in that state; the Concord Apple, possibly the same with the *Musketaquidensis*; the Assabet Apple; the Brindled Apple; Wine of New England; the Chickaree Apple; the Green Apple (*Malus viridis*);—this has many synonymes; in an imperfect state, it is the *Cholera morbifera aut dysenterifera, puerulis dilectissima*;—the Apple which Atalanta stopped to pick up; the Hedge-Apple (*Malus Sepium*); the Slug-Apple (*limacea*); the Railroad-Apple, which perhaps came from a core thrown out of the cars; the Apple whose Fruit we tasted in our Youth; our Particular Apple, not to be found in any catalogue,— *Pedestrium Solatium*; also the Apple where hangs the Forgotten Scythe; Iduna's Apples, and the Apples which Loki found in the Wood; and a great many more I have on my list, too numerous to mention,—all of them good. As Bodæus exclaims, referring to the cultivated kinds, and adapting Virgil to his case, so I, adapting Bodæus,—

> "Not if I had a hundred tongues, a hundred mouths,
> An iron voice, could I describe all the forms
> And reckon up all the names of these *wild apples*."

THE LAST GLEANING.

By the middle of November the wild apples have lost some of their brilliancy, and have chiefly fallen. A great part are decayed on the ground, and the sound ones are more palatable than before. The note of the chickadee sounds now more distinct, as you wander amid the old trees, and the autumnal dandelion is half-closed and tearful. But still, if you are a skilful gleaner, you may get many a pocket-full even of grafted fruit, long after apples are supposed to be gone out-of-doors. I know a Blue-Pearmain tree, growing within the edge of a swamp, almost as good as wild. You would not suppose that there was any fruit left there, on the first survey, but you must look according to system. Those which lie exposed are quite brown and rotten now, or perchance a few still show one blooming cheek here and there amid the wet leaves. Nevertheless, with experienced eyes, I explore amid the bare alders and the huckleberry-bushes and the withered sedge, and in the crevices of the rocks, which are full of leaves, and pry under the fallen and decaying ferns, which, with apple and alder leaves, thickly strew the ground. For I know that they lie concealed, fallen into hollows long since and covered up by the leaves of the tree itself,—a proper kind of packing. From these lurking-places, anywhere within the circumference of the tree, I draw forth the fruit, all wet and glossy, maybe nibbled by rabbits and hollowed out by crickets and perhaps with a leaf or two cemented to it, (as Curzon an old manuscript from a monastery's mouldy cellar,) but still with a rich bloom on it, and at least as ripe and well kept, if not better than those in barrels, more crisp and lively than they. If these resources fail to yield anything, I have learned to look between the bases of the suckers which spring thickly from some horizontal limb, for now and then one lodges there, or in the very midst of an alder-clump, where they are covered by leaves, safe from cows which may have smelled them out. If I am sharp-set, for I do not refuse the Blue-Pearmain, I fill my pockets on each side; and as I retrace my steps in the frosty eve, being perhaps four or five miles from home, I eat one first from this side, and then from that, to keep my balance.

I learn from Topsell's Gesner, whose authority appears to be Albertus, that the following is the way in which the hedge-hog collects and carries home his apples. He says,—"His meat is apples, worms, or grapes: when he findeth apples or grapes on the earth, he rolleth himself upon them, until he have filled all his prickles, and then carrieth them home to his den, never bearing above one in his mouth; and if it fortune that one of them fall off by the way, he likewise shaketh off all the residue, and walloweth upon them afresh, until they be all settled upon his back again. So, forth he goeth, making a noise like a cart-wheel; and if he have any young ones in his nest, they pull off his load wherewithal he is loaded, eating thereof what they please, and laying up the residue for the time to come."

THE "FROZEN-THAWED" APPLE.

Toward the end of November, though some of the sound ones are yet more mellow and perhaps more edible, they have generally, like the leaves, lost their beauty, and are beginning to freeze. It is finger-cold, and prudent farmers get in their barrelled apples, and bring you the apples and cider which they have engaged; for it is time to put them into the cellar. Perhaps a few on the ground show their red cheeks above the early snow, and occasionally some even preserve their color and soundness under the snow throughout the winter. But generally at the beginning of the winter they freeze hard, and soon, though undecayed, acquire the color of a baked apple.

Before the end of December, generally, they experience their first thawing. Those which a month ago were sour, crabbed, and quite unpalatable to the civilized taste, such at least as were frozen while sound, let a warmer sun come to thaw them, for they are extremely sensitive to its rays, are found to be filled with a rich sweet cider, better than any bottled cider that I know of, and with which I am better acquainted than with wine. All apples are good in this state, and your jaws are the cider-press. Others, which have more substance, are a sweet and luscious food,—in my opinion of more worth than the pine-apples which are imported from the West Indies. Those which lately even I tasted only to repent of it,— for I am semi-civilized,—which the farmer willingly left on the tree, I am now glad to find have the property of hanging on like the leaves of the young oaks. It is a way to keep cider sweet without boiling. Let the frost come to freeze them first, solid as stones, and then the rain or a warm winter day to thaw them, and they will seem to have borrowed a flavor from heaven through the medium of the air in which they hang. Or perchance you find, when you get home, that those which rattled in your pocket have thawed, and the ice is turned to cider. But after the third or fourth freezing and thawing they will not be found so good.

What are the imported half-ripe fruits of the torrid South, to this fruit matured by the cold of the frigid North? These are those crabbed apples with which I cheated my companion, and kept a smooth face that I might tempt him to eat. Now we both greedily fill our pockets with them,—bending to drink the cup and save our lappets from the overflowing juice,—and grow more social with their wine. Was there one that hung so high and sheltered by the tangled branches that our sticks could not dislodge it?

It is a fruit never carried to market, that I am aware of,— quite distinct from the apple of the markets, as from dried apple and cider,—and it is not every winter that produces it in perfection.

The era of the Wild Apple will soon be past. It is a fruit which will probably become extinct in New England. You may still wander through old orchards of native fruit of great extent, which for the most part went to the cider-mill, now all gone to decay. I have heard of an orchard in a distant town, on the side of a hill, where the apples rolled down and lay four feet deep against a wall on the lower side, and this the owner cut down for fear they should be made into cider. Since the temperance reform and the general introduction of grafted fruit, no native apple-trees, such as I see everywhere in deserted pastures, and where the woods have grown up around them, are set out. I fear that he who walks over these fields a century hence will not know the pleasure of knocking off wild apples. Ah, poor man, there are many pleasures which he will not know! Notwithstanding the prevalence of the Baldwin and the Porter, I doubt if so extensive orchards are set out to-day in my town as there were a century ago, when those vast straggling cider-orchards were planted, when men both ate and drank apples, when the pomace-heap was the only nursery, and trees cost nothing but the trouble of setting them out. Men could afford then to stick a tree by every wall-side and let it take its chance. I see nobody planting trees to-day in such out-of-the-way places, along the lonely roads and lanes, and at the bottom of dells in the wood. Now that they have grafted trees, and pay a price for them, they collect them into a plat by their houses, and fence them in,—and the end of it all will be that we shall be compelled to look for our apples in a barrel.

This is "The word of the Lord that came to Joel the son of Pethuel.

"Hear this, ye old men, and give ear, all ye inhabitants of the land! Hath this been in your days, or even in the days of your fathers? . . . .

"That which the palmer-worm hath left hath the locust eaten; and that which the locust hath left hath the canker-worm eaten; and that which the canker-worm hath left hath the caterpillar eaten.

"Awake, ye drunkards, and weep! and howl, all ye drinkers of wine, because of the new wine! for it is cut off from your mouth.

"For a nation is come up upon my land, strong, and without number, whose teeth are the teeth of a lion, and he hath the cheek-teeth of a great lion.

"He hath laid my vine waste, and barked my fig-tree; he hath made it clean bare, and cast it away; the branches thereof are made white. . . . .

"Be ye ashamed, O ye husbandmen! howl, O ye vine-dressers! . . . .

"The vine is dried up, and the fig-tree languisheth; the pomegranate-tree, the palm-tree also, and the apple-tree, even all the trees of the field, are withered: because joy is withered away from the sons of men."

Huckleberries

Agrestem tenui meditabor arundine musam
I am going to play a rustic strain on my slender reed—
non injussa cano—
but I trust that I do not sing unbidden things.

MANY public speakers are accustomed, as I think foolishly, to talk about what they call *little things* in a patronising way sometimes, advising, perhaps, that they be not wholly neglected; but in making this distinction they really use no juster measure than a ten-foot pole, and their own ignorance. According to this rule a small potatoe is a little thing, a big one a great thing. A hogshead-full of anything—the big cheese which it took so many oxen to draw—a national salute—a state-muster—a fat ox—the horse Columbus—or Mr. Blank—the Ossian Boy—there is no danger that any body will call these *little things*. A cartwheel is a great thing—a snow flake a little thing. The *Wellingtonia gigantea*—the famous California tree, is a great thing—the seed from which it sprang a little thing—scarcely one traveller has noticed the seed at all—and so with all the seeds or origins of things. But Pliny said—*In minimis Natura praestat*—Nature excels in the least things.

In this country a political speech, whether by Mr. Seward or Caleb Cushing, is a great thing, a ray of light a little thing. It would be felt to be a greater national calamity if you should take six inches from the corporeal bulk of one or two gentlemen in Congress, than if you should take a yard from their wisdom and manhood.

I have noticed that whatever is thought to be covered by the word *education*—whether reading, writing or 'rithmetick—is a great thing, but almost all that constitutes education is a little thing in the estimation of such speakers as I refer to. In short, whatever they know and care but *little* about is a little thing, and accordingly almost everything good or great is little in their sense, and is very slow to grow any bigger.

When the husk gets separated from the kernel, almost all men run after the husk and pay their respects to that. It is only the husk of Christianity that is so bruited and wide spread in this world, the kernel is still the very least and rarest of all things. There is not a single church founded on it. To obey the higher law is generally considered the last manifestation of littleness.

I have observed that many English naturalists have a pitiful habit of speaking of their proper pursuit as a sort of trifling or waste of time—a mere interruption to more important employments and 'severer studies'—for which they must ask pardon of the reader. As if they would have you believe that all the rest of their lives was consecrated to some truly great and serious enterprise. But it happens that we never hear more of this, as we certainly should, if it were only some great public or philanthropic service, and therefore conclude that they have been engaged in the heroic and magnanimous enterprise of feeding, clothing, housing and warming themselves and their dependents, the chief value of all which was that it enabled them to pursue just these studies of which they speak so slightingly. The 'severer study' they refer to was keeping their accounts. Comparatively speaking—what they call their graver pursuits and severer studies was the real trifling and misspense of life—and were they such fools as not to know it? It is, in effect at least, mere cant. All mankind have depended on them for this intellectual food.

I presume that every one of my audience knows what a huckleberry is—has seen a huckleberry—gathered a huckleberry—nay tasted a huckleberry—and that being the case, that you will not be averse to revisiting the huckleberry field in imagination this evening, though the pleasure of this excursion may fall as far short of the reality, as the flavor of a dried huckleberry is inferior to that of a fresh one.

Huckleberries begin to be ripe July third (or generally the thirteenth), are thick enough to pick about the twenty-second, at their height about the fifth of August, and last fresh till after the middle of that month.

This, as you know, is an upright shrub more or less stout depending on the exposure, with a spreading bushy top—a dark brown bark—red recent shoots and thick leaves. The flowers are smaller and much more red than those of the other species.

It is said to range from the Saskatchewan to the mountains of Georgia, and from the Atlantic to the Mississippi in this latitude—but it abounds over but a small part of this area, and there are large tracts where it is not found at all.

By botanists it is called of late, but I think without good reason, *Gaylussacia resinosa*, after the celebrated French chemist. If he had been the first to distil its juices and put them in this globular bag, he would deserve this honor, or if he had been a celebrated picker of huckleberries, perchance paid for his schooling so, or only notoriously a lover of them, we should not so much object. But it does not appear that he ever saw one. What if a committee of Parisian naturalists had been appointed to break this important news to an Indian maiden who had just filled her basket on the shore of Lake Huron! It is as if we should hear that the Daguerreotype had been *finally* named after the distinguished Chippeway conjurer, The-Wind-that-Blows. By another it has been called *Andromeda baccata*, the berry bearing andromeda—but he evidently lived far away from huckleberries and milk.

I observe green huckleberries by the nineteenth of June, and perhaps three weeks later, when I have forgotten them, I first notice on some hill side exposed to the light, some black or blue ones amid the green ones and the leaves, always sooner than I had expected, and though they may be manifestly premature, I make it a point to taste them, and so inaugurate the huckleberry season.

In a day or two the black are so thick among the green ones that they no longer incur the suspicion of being worm-eaten, and perhaps a day later I pluck a handful from one bush, and I do not fail to make report of it when I get home, though it is rarely believed, most people are so behind hand in their year's accounts.

Early in August, in a favorable year, the hills are black with them. At Nagog Pond I have seen a hundred bushels in one field—the bushes drooping over the rocks with the weight of them—and a very handsome sight they are, though you should not pluck one of them. They are of various forms, colors and flavors—some round—some pear-shaped—some glossy black—some dull black, some blue with a tough and thick skin (though they are never of the peculiar light blue of blueberries with a bloom)—some sweeter, some more insipid—etc., etc., more varieties than botanists take notice of.

To-day perhaps you gather some of those large, often pear-shaped, sweet blue ones which grow tall and thinly amid the rubbish where woods have been cut. They have not borne there before for a century—being over-shadowed and stinted by the forest—but they have the more concentrated their juices—and profited by the new recipes which nature has given them—and now they offer to you fruit of the very finest flavor, like wine of the oldest vintage.

And tomorrow you come to a strong moist soil where the black ones shine with such a gloss—every one its eye on you, and the blue are so large and firm, that you can hardly believe them to be huckleberries at all, or edible; but you seem to have travelled into a foreign country, or else are dreaming.

They are a firmer berry than most of the whortleberry family—and hence are the most marketable.

If you look closely at a huckleberry you will see that it is dotted, as if sprinkled over with a yellow dust or meal, which looks as if it could be rubbed off. Through a microscope, it looks like a resin which has exuded, and on the small green fruit is of a conspicuous light orange or lemon color, like small specks of yellow lichens. It is apparently the same with that shining resinous matter which so conspicously covers the leaves when they are unfolding, making them sticky to the touch—whence this species is called *resinosa* or resinous.

There is a variety growing in swamps—a very tall and slender bush drooping or bent like grass to one side—commonly three or four feet high, but often seven feet—the berries, which are later than the former, are round and glossy black— with resinous dots as usual—and grow in flattish topped racemes—sometimes ten or twelve together, though generally more scattered. I call it the swamp-huckleberry.

But the most marked variety is the *red*-huckleberry—the *white* of some, (for the less ripe are whitish)—which ripens at the same time with the black. It is red with a white cheek, often slightly pear-shaped, semitransparent with a luster, very finely and indistinctly white dotted. It is as easily distinguished from the common in the green state as when ripe. I know of but three or four places in the town where they grow. It might be called *Gaylussacia resinosa var. erythrocarpa*.

I once did some surveying for a man, who remarked, but not till the job was nearly done, that he did not know when he should pay me. I did not at first pay much heed to this observation, though it was unusual, supposing that he meant to pay me within a reasonable time. Nevertheless it occurred to me that if he did not know when he should pay me still less did I know when I should be paid. He added, however, that I was perfectly secure, for there were the pigs in the stye (and as nice pigs as ever were seen) and there was his farm itself which I had surveyed, and knew was there as much as he. All this had its due influence in increasing my sense of security, as you may suppose. After many months he sent me a quart of red huckleberries, for they grew on his farm, and this I thought was ominous; he distinguished me altogether too much by this gift, since I was not his particular friend. I saw that it was the first installment of my dues—and that it would go a great way toward being the last. In the course of years he paid a part of the debt in money, and that is the last that I have heard of it. I shall beware of red huckleberry gifts in the future.

Then there is the Late Whortleberry—Dangleberry or Blue Tangles—whose fruit does not begin to be ripe until about a month after huckleberries begin, when these and blueberries are commonly shrivelled and spoiling—on about August seventh, and is in its prime near the end of August.

This is a tall and handsome bush about twice as high as a huckleberry bush, with altogether a glaucous aspect, growing in shady copses where it is rather moist, and to produce much fruit it seems to require wet weather.

The fruit is one of the handsomest of berries, smooth, round and blue, larger than most huckleberries and more transparent, on long stems dangling two or three inches, and more or less tangled. By the inexperienced it is suspected to be poisonous, and so avoided, and perhaps is the more fair and memorable to them on that account. Though quite good to eat, it has a peculiar, slightly astringent, and compared with most huckleberries, not altogether pleasant flavor, and a tough skin.

At the end of the first week of September, they are commonly the only edible Whortleberries which are quite fresh. They are rare hereabouts however, and it is only in certain years that you can find enough for a pudding.

There is still another kind of Huckleberry growing in this town, called the *Hairy Huckleberry*, which ripens about the same time with the last. It is quite rare, growing only in the wildest and most neglected places, such as cold sphagnous swamps where the *Andromeda polifolia* and *Kalmia glauca* are found, and in some almost equally neglected but firmer low ground. The berries are oblong and black, and, with us, roughened with short hairs. It is the only species of *Vaccinieae* that I know of in this town whose fruit is inedible; though I have seen another kind of Whortleberry, the *Deerberry* or Squaw Huckleberry, growing in another part of the state, whose fruit is said to be equally inedible. The former is merely insipid however. Some which grow on firmer ground have a little more flavor, but the thick and shaggy-feeling coats of the berries left in the mouth are far from agreeable to the palate.

Both these and Dangleberries are placed in the same genus (or section) with the common huckleberry.

Huckleberries are very apt to dry up and not attain their proper size—unless rain comes to save them before the end of July. They will be dried quite hard and black by drought even before they have ripened. On the other hand they frequently burst open and are so spoiled in consequence of copious rains when they are fully ripe.

They *begin* to be soft and wormy as early as the middle of August, and generally about the twentieth the children cease to carry them round to sell, as they are suspected by the purchasers.

How late when the huckleberries begin to be wormy and the pickers are deserting the fields! The walker feels very solitary now.

But in woods and other cool places they commonly last quite fresh a week or more longer, depending on the season. In some years when there are far more berries than pickers or even worms, and the birds appear to pass them by, I have found them plump, fresh, and quite thick, though with a

somewhat dried taste, the fourteenth of October, when the
bushes were mostly leafless, and the leaves that were left, were
all red, and they continued to hold on after the leaves had all
fallen, till they were softened and spoiled by rain.

Sometimes they begin to dry up generally by the middle of
August—after they are ripe, but before spoiling, and by the
end of that month I have seen the bushes so withered and
brown owing to the drought, that they appeared dead like
those which you see broken off by the pickers, or as if burnt.

I have seen the hills still black with them, though hard and
shrivelled as if dried in a pan, late in September. And one year
I saw an abundance of them still holding on the eleventh of
December, they having dried ripe prematurely, but these had
no sweetness left. The sight of them thus dried by nature may
have originally suggested to the Indians to dry them artifi-
cially.

High-blueberries, the second kind of low-blueberries,
huckleberries and low-blackberries are all at their height gen-
erally during the first week of August. In the dog-days (or the
first ten of them) they abound and attain their full size.

Huckleberries are classed by botanists with the cranberries
(both bog and mountain)—snowberry, bearberry—mayflower,
checkerberry—the andromedas, clethra, laurels, azaleas, rho-
dora, ledum, pyrolas, prince's pine, Indian pipes, and many
other plants, and they are called all together the Heath Family,
they being in many respects similar to and occupying similar
ground with the heaths of the Old World, which we have not.
If the first botanists had been American this might have been
called the Huckleberry Family including the heaths. Plants of
this order (*Ericaceae*) are said to be among the earliest ones
found in a fossil state, and one would say that they promised to
last as long as any on this globe. George B. Emerson says that
the whortleberry differs from the heath proper, 'essentially
only in its juicy fruit surrounded by the calyx segments.'

The genus to which the whortleberries belong, is called by
most botanists *Vaccinium*, which I am inclined to think is
properly derived from *bacca*, a berry, as if these were the chief
of all berries, though the etymology of this word is in dispute.

Whortle- or Hurtleberry, Bilberry, and Blae or Blea, that is
blue berry are the names given in England originally to the

fruit of the *Vaccinium myrtillus* which we have not in New England and also to the more scarce and local *Vaccinium uliginosum* which we have.

The word whortleberry is said to be derived from the Saxon *heort-berg* (or *heorot-berg*), the hart's berry.

Hurts is an old English word used in heraldry, where, according to Bailey, it is 'certain balls resembling hurtleberries.'

The Germans say *Heidel-beere*, that is *heath berry*.

Huckleberry—this word is used by Lawson in 1709—appears to be an American word derived from Whortleberry—and applied to fruits of the same family, but for the most part of different species from the English whortleberries. According to the Dictionary the word berry is from the Saxon *beria*—a grape or cluster of grapes. A French name of whortleberry is 'raisin des bois'—grape of the woods. It is evident that the word berry has a new significance in America.

We do not realize how rich our country is in berries. The ancient Greeks and Romans appear not to have made much account of strawberries, huckleberries, melons etc. because they had not got them.

The Englishman Lindley, in his *Natural System of Botany*, says that the *Vaccinieae* are 'Natives of North America, where they are found in great abundance as far as high northern latitudes; sparingly in Europe; and not uncommonly on high land in the Sandwich Islands.'

Or as George B. Emerson states it, they 'are found chiefly in the temperate, or on mountains in the warmer regions of America. Some are found in Europe; some on the continent and islands of Asia, and on islands in the Atlantic, Pacific and Indian Oceans.' 'The whortleberries and cranberries,' says he, 'take the place, throughout the northern part of this continent, of the heaths of the corresponding climates of Europe; and fill it with no less of beauty, and incomparably more of use.'

According to the last arrangement of our plants, we have fourteen species of the Whortleberry Family (*Vaccinieae*) in New England, eleven of which bear edible berries, eight, berries which are eaten raw, and five of the last kind are abundant—to wit—the huckleberry—the bluet or Pennsylvania blueberry—the Canada blueberry (in the northern part of New England)—the second or common low blueberry—and the high or swamp-blueberry (not to mention the Dangle-berry, which is common in some seasons and localities).

On the other hand I gather from Loudon and others that there are only two species growing in England, which are eaten raw, answering to our eight—to wit, the Bilberry (*V. myrtillus*) and the Blea-berry or Bog Whortleberry (*V. uliginosum*), both of which are found in North America, and the last is the common one on the summit of the White Mountains, but in Great Britain it is found only in the northern part of England and in Scotland. This leaves only one in England to our five which are abundant.

In short, it chances that of the thirty-two species of *Vaccinium* which Loudon describes, all except the above two and four more are referred to North America alone, and only three or possibly four are found in Europe.

Yet the few Englishmen with whom I have spoken on this subject love to think and to say that they have as many huckleberries as we. I will therefore quote the most which their own authorities say not already quoted, about the abundance and value of their only two kinds which are eaten raw.

Loudon says of the bog whortleberry (*V. uliginosum*), 'The berries are agreeable but inferior in flavor to those of *Vaccinium myrtillus* [the bilberry]; eaten in large quantities, they occasion giddiness, and a slight headache.'

And of their only common whortleberry (*V. myrtillus*), he says, 'It is found in every country in Britain, from Cornwall to Caithness, least frequently in the south-eastern countries, and increases in quantity as we advance northward.' It 'is an elegant and also a fruit-bearing plant.' The berries 'are eaten in tarts or with cream, or made into a jelly, in the northern and western counties of England; and, in other parts of the country they are made into pies and puddings.' They 'are very acceptable to children either eaten by themselves, or with milk' or otherwise. They 'have an astringent quality.'

Coleman in his "Woodlands, Heaths, and Hedges," says 'The traveller in our upland and mountain districts can hardly have failed to notice, as his almost constant companion, this cheerful little shrub, . . . it flourishes best in a high airy situation, only the summits of the very loftiest mountains of which this country can boast being too elevated for this hardy little mountaineer.' 'In Yorkshire, and many parts of the north, large quantities of bilberries are brought into the market, being extensively used as an ingredient in pies and puddings, or preserved in the form of jam. . . . Much, however, of the relish of these wilding fruits must be set down to the exhilarating air, and those charms of scenery that form the accessories of a mountain feast; . . . One of the prettiest sights that greet one's eye in the districts where it abounds, is that of a party of rustic children "a-bilberrying" (for the greater portion of those that come to market are collected by children); there they may be seen, knee deep in the "wires," or clambering over the broken gray rocks to some rich nest of berries, their tanned faces glowing with health, and their picturesque dress (or undress)—with here and there bits of bright red, blue, or white—to the painter's eye contrasting beautifully with the purple, gray and brown of the moorland, and forming altogether rich pictorial subjects.'

These authorities tell us that children and others eat the fruit, just as they tell us that the birds do. It is evident from all this that whortleberries do not make an important part of the regular food of the Old English people in their season, as they do of the New Englanders. What should we think of a summer in which we did not taste a huckleberry pudding? That is to Jonathan what his plum pudding is to John Bull.

Yet Dr. Manassah Cutler, one of the earliest New England botanists, speaks of the huckleberry lightly as being merely a fruit which children love to eat with their milk. What ingratitude thus to shield himself behind the children! I should not wonder if it turned out that Dr. Manassah Cutler ate his huckleberry pudding or pie regularly through the season, as many his equals do. I should have pardoned him had he frankly put in his thumb and pulled out a plum, and cried 'What a Great Doctor am I?' But probably he was lead astray by reading English books or it may be that the Whites did not make so much use of them in his time.

Widely dispersed as their bilberry may still be in England, it was undoubtedly far more abundant there once. One botanist says that 'This is one of the species, that if allowed, would overrun Britain, and form, with *Culluna vulgaris* (heather) and *Empetrum nigrum* (crowberry, which grows on our

White Mountains), much of the natural physiognomical char-
acter of its vegetation.'

The genus *Gaylussacia*, to which our huckleberry belongs,
has no representative in Great Britain, nor does our species
extend very far northward in this country.

So I might say of edible berries generally, that there are far
fewer kinds in Old than in New England.

Take the *rubuses* or what you might call bramble berries,
for instance, to which genus our raspberries, blackberries and
thimbleberries belong. According to Loudon there are five
kinds indigenous in Britain to our eight. But of these five only
two appear to be at all common, while we have four kinds
both very common and very good. The Englishman Coleman
says of their best, the English raspberry, which species we also
cultivate, that 'the wilding is not sufficiently abundant to have
much importance.'

And the same is true of wild fruits generally. Hips and haws
are much more important comparatively there than here,
where they have hardly got any popular name.

I state this to show how contented and thankful we ought
to be.

It is to be remembered that the vegetation of Great Britain
is that of a much more northern latitude than where we live,
that some of our alpine shrubs are found on the plain there
and their two whortleberries are alpine or extreme northern
plants with us.

If you look closely you will find blueberry and huckleberry
bushes under your feet, though they may be feeble and bar-
ren, throughout all our woods, the most persevering Native
Americans, ready to shoot up into place and power at the next
election among the plants, ready to reclothe the hills when
man has laid them bare and feed all kinds of pensioners. What
though the woods be cut down; it appears that this emergency
was long ago anticipated and provided for by Nature, and the
interregnum is not allowed to be a barren one. She not only
begins instantly to heal that scar, but she compensates us for
the loss and refreshes us with fruits such as the forest did not
produce. As the sandal wood is said to diffuse a perfume
around the woodman who cuts it—so in this case Nature re-
wards with unexpected fruits the hand that lays her waste.

I have only to remember each year where the woods have been cut just long enough to know where to look for them. It is to refresh us thus once in a century that they bide their time on the forest floor. If the farmer mows and burns over his overgrown pasture for the benefit of the grass, or to keep the children out, the huckleberries spring up there more vigorous than ever, and the fresh blueberry shoots tinge the earth crimson. All our hills are, or have been, huckleberry hills, the three hills of Boston and no doubt Bunker Hill among the rest. My mother remembers a woman who went a-whortleberrying where Dr. Lowell's church now stands.

In short the whortleberry bushes in the Northern States and British America are a sort of miniature forest surviving under the great forest, and reappearing when the latter is cut, and also extending northward beyond it. The small berry-bearing shrubs of this family, as the crowberry, bilberry, and cranberry, are called by the Esquimaux in Greenland, 'berry grass,' and Crantz says that the Greenlanders cover their winter houses with 'bilberry bushes,' together with turf and earth. They also burn them; and I hear that some body in this neighborhood has invented a machine for cutting up huckleberry bushes for fuel.

It is remarkable how universally, as it respects soil and exposure, the whortleberry family is distributed with us, almost we may say a new species for every thousand feet of elevation. One kind or another, of those of which I am speaking, flourishing in every soil and locality.

There is the high blueberry in swamps—the second low blueberry, with the huckleberry, on almost all fields and hills—the Pennsylvanian and Canada blueberries especially in cool and airy places in openings in the woods and on hills and mountains, while we have two kinds confined to the alpine tops of our highest mountains—the family thus ranging from the lowest valleys to the highest mountain tops, and forming the prevailing small shrubbery of a great part of New England.

The same is true *hereabouts* of a single species of this family, the huckleberry proper. I do not know of a spot where any shrub grows in this neighborhood, but one or another variety of the huckleberry may also grow there. It is stated in

Loudon that all the plants of this order 'require a peat soil, or a soil of a close cohesive nature,' but this is not the case with the huckleberry. It grows on the tops of our highest hills—no pasture is too rocky or barren for it—it grows in such deserts as we have, standing in pure sand—and at the same time it flourishes in the strongest and most fertile soil. One variety is peculiar to quaking bogs where there can hardly be said to be any soil beneath, to say nothing of another but unpalatable species, the hairy huckleberry, which is found there. It also extends through all our woods more or less thinly, and a distinct species, the dangleberry, belongs especially to moist woods and thickets.

Such care has Nature taken to furnish to birds and quadrupeds, and to men, a palatable berry of this kind, slightly modified by soil and climate, wherever the consumer may chance to be. Corn and potatoes, apples and pears, have comparatively a narrow range, but we can fill our basket with whortleberries on the summit of Mount Washington, above almost all other shrubs with which we are familiar, the same kind which they have in Greenland, and again when we get home, with another species in our lowest swamps, such as the Greenlanders never dreamed of.

The berries *which I celebrate*, appear to have a range, most of them, very nearly coterminous with what has been called the Algonquin Family of Indians, whose territories embraced what are now the Eastern, Middle and Northwestern States—and the Canadas—and surrounded those of the Iroquois in what is now New York. These were the small fruits of the Algonquin and Iroquois Families.

Of course the Indians naturally made a much greater account of wild fruits than we do, and among the most important of these were huckleberries.

They taught us not only the use of corn and how to plant it, but also of whortleberries and how to dry them for winter. We should have hesitated long before we tasted some kinds if they had not set us the example, knowing by old experience that they were not only harmless but salutary. I have added a few to my number of edible berries, by walking behind an Indian in Maine, and observing that he ate some which I never thought of tasting before.

To convince you of the extensive use which the Indians made of huckleberries, I will quote at length the testimony of the most observing travellers, on this subject, as nearly as possible in the order in which it was given us; for it is only after listening patiently to such reiterated and concurring testimony, of various dates—and respecting widely distant localities—that we come to realize the truth.

But little is said by the discoverers of the use which the Indians made of the fresh berries in their season—the hand to mouth use of them—because there was little to be said—though in this form they may have been much the most important to them. We have volumes of recipes, called cookbooks—but when a fruit or a tart is ready for the table, nothing remains but to eat it without any more words. We therefore have few or no accounts of Indians going a-huckleberrying—though they had more than a six weeks' vacation for that purpose, and probably camped on the huckleberry field.

I will go far enough back for my authorities to show that they did not learn the use of these berries from us whites.

In the year 1615, Champlain, the founder of Quebec, being far up the Ottawa spying out the land and taking notes among the Algonquins, on his way to the Fresh Water Sea since called Lake Huron—observed that the natives made a business of collecting and drying for winter use, a small berry which he calls blues, and also raspberries—the former is the common blueberry of those regions, by some considered a variety of our early low blueberry (*Vaccinium Pennsylvanicum*); and again when near the lake he observes that the natives make a kind of bread of pounded corn sifted and mixed with mashed beans which have been boiled—and sometimes they put dried blueberries and raspberries into it.

This was five years before the Pilgrims crossed the Atlantic, and is the first account of huckleberry cake that I know of.

Gabriel Sagard, a Franciscan Friar, in the account of his visit to the Huron Country in 1624, says, 'There is so great a quantity of blues, which the Hurons call *Ohentaque*, and other little fruits which they call by a general name *Hahique*, that the savages regularly dry them for the winter, as we do prunes in the sun, and that serves them for comfits for the sick, and to give taste to their *sagamite* [or gruel, making a kind of plum porridge], and also to put into the little loaves (or cakes, *pains*) which they cook under the ashes.'

According to him they put not only blueberries and raspberries into their bread but strawberries, 'wild mulberries (*meures champestres*) and other little fruits dry and green.'

Indeed the gathering of blueberries by the savages is spoken of by the early French explorers as a regular and important harvest with them.

Le Jeune, the Superior of the Jesuits in Canada—residing at Quebec—in his Relation for 1639—says of the savages that 'Some figure to themselves a paradise full of *bluets*.'

Roger Williams, who knew the Indians well, in his account of those in his neighborhood—published in 1643—tells us that '*Sautaash* are those currants (grapes and whortleberries) dried by the natives, and so preserved all the year, which they beat to powder and mingle it with their parched meal, and make a delicate dish which they call *Sautauthig*, which is as sweet to them as plum or spice cake to the English.'

But Nathaniel Morton, in his *New England's Memorial*, printed in 1669—speaking of white men going to treat with Canonicus, a Narraghanset Indian, about Mr. Oldham's death in 1636—says 'Boiled chestnuts is their white bread, and because they would be extraordinary in their feasting, they strove for variety after the English manner, boiling puddings made of beaten corn, putting therein great store of black berries, somewhat like currants'—no doubt whortleberries. This *seems* to *imply* that the Indians imitated the English—or set before their guests dishes to which they themselves were not accustomed—or which were extra-ordinary. But we have seen that these dishes were not new or unusual to them and it was the whites who imitated the Indians rather.

John Josselyn—in his *New England's Rarities*, published in 1672—says under the fruits of New England, 'Bill-berries, two kinds, black and sky colored, which is more frequent. . . . The Indians dry them in the sun and sell them to the English by the bushel, who make use of them instead of currence, putting of them into puddens, both boyled and baked, and into water gruel.'

The largest Indian huckleberry party that I have heard of is mentioned in the life of Captain Church who, it is said, when in pursuit of King Phillip in the summer of 1676, came across a large body of Indians, chiefly squaws, gathering whortleberries on a plain near where New Bedford now is, and killed and took prisoner sixty-six of them—some throwing away their baskets and their berries in their flight. They told him that their husbands and brothers, a hundred of them, who with others had their rendezvous in a great cedar swamp nearby, had recently left them to gather whortleberries there, while they went to Sconticut Neck to kill cattle and horses for further and more substantial provisions.

La Hontan in 1689, writing from the Great Lakes, repeats what so many French travellers had said about the Indians drying and preserving blueberries—saying, 'The savages of the north make a great harvest of them in summer, which is a great resource especially when the chase fails them.' They were herein more provident than we commonly suppose.

Father Rasles—who was making a Dictionary of the Abenaki Language in 1691 (at Norridgewock?)—says that their word for blueberries was fresh *Satar*, dry *Sakisatar*—and the words in their name for July meant when the blueberries are ripe. This shows how important they were to them.

Father Hennepin—who writes in 1697—says that his captors, Naudowessi (the Sioux!), near the falls of St. Anthony, feasted on wild-rice seasoned with blueberries, 'which they dry in the sun during the summer, and which are as good as raisins of Corinth'—[that is, the imported currants].

The Englishman John Lawson, who published an account of the Carolinas in 1709, says of North Carolina, 'The hurts, huckleberries or blues of this country are four sorts. . . . The first sort is the same blue or bilberry that grows plentifully in the North of England.' 'The second sort grows on a small bush,' the fruit being larger than the last. The third grows three or four feet high in low land. 'The fourth sort grows upon trees, some ten and twelve foot high, and the thickness of a man's arm; these are found in the runs and low grounds. . . . The Indians get many bushels, and dry them on mats, whereof they make plum bread, and many other eatables.' He is the first author that I remember who uses the word 'huckleberry.'

The well known natural botanist John Bartram, when re-
turning to Philadelphia in 1743 from a Journey through what
was then the wilderness of Pennsylvania and New York, to the
Iroquois and Lake Ontario, says that he 'found [when in
Pennsylvania] an Indian squaw drying huckleberries. This is
done by setting four forked sticks in the ground, about three
or four feet high, then others across, over them the stalks of
our common *Jacea* or *Saratula*, on these lie the berries, as malt
is spread on the hair cloth over the kiln. Underneath she had
kindled a smoke fire, which one of her children was tending.'

Kalm, in his travels in this country in 1748–9, writes, 'On
my travels through the country of the Iroquois, they offered
me, whenever they designed to treat me well, fresh maize
bread, baked in an oblong shape, mixed with dried huckle-
berries, which lay as close in it as the raisins in a plumb
pudding.'

The Moravian missionary Heckewelder, who spent a great
part of his life among the Delawares toward the end of the
last century, states that they mixed with their bread, which
was six inches in diameter by one inch thick—'whortleberries
green or dry, but not boiled.'

Lewis and Clarke in 1805 found the Indians west of the
Rocky Mountains using dried berries extensively.

And finally in Owen's Geological Survey of *Wisconsin, Iowa
and Minnesota*—published in 1852—occurs the following.
'*Vaccinium Pennsylvanicum* (*Lam.*) [that is, our early low
blueberry]—Barrens on the upper St. Croix. This is the com-
mon Huckleberry, associated with the characteristic growth of
the *Pinus Banksiana*, covering its sandy ridges with a verdant
undergrowth, and an unsurpassed luxuriance of fruit. By the
Indians these are collected and smoke dried in great quanti-
ties, and in this form constitute an agreeable article of food.'

Hence you see that the Indians from time immemorial,
down to the present day, all over the northern part of
America—have made far more extensive use of the whortle-
berry—at all seasons and in various ways—than we—and that
they were far more important to them than to us.

It appears from the above evidence that the Indians used
their dried berries commonly in the form of a cake, and also
of huckleberry porridge or pudding.

What we call huckleberry cake made of Indian meal and huckleberries was evidently the principal cake of the aborigines—though they also used other berries and fruits in a similar manner and often put things into their cake which would not have been agreeable to our palates—though I do not hear that they ever put any soda or pearl ash or alum into it. We have no national cake so universal and well known as this was in all parts of the country where corn and huckleberries grew.

They enjoyed it all alone ages before our ancestors heard of their Indian corn—or their huckleberries—and probably if you had travelled here a thousand years ago it would have been offered you alike on the Connecticut, the Potomac, the Niagara, the Ottawa and the Mississippi.

The last Indian of Nantucket, who died a few years ago, was very properly represented in a painting which I saw there, with a basket full of huckleberries in his hand, as if to hint at the employment of his last days. I trust that I may not outlive the last of the huckleberries.

Tanner, who was taken captive by the Indians in 1789, and spent a good part of his life as an Indian, gives the Chippeway names of at least five kinds of whortleberries. He gives 'meen—blue berry, meen-un—blue berries,' and says that 'this is a word that enters into the composition of almost all words which are used as the names of fruits,' that is as a terminal syllable. Hence this would appear to have been the typical berry—or berry of berries—among the Chippeway as it is among us.

I think that it would be well if the Indian names, were as far as possible restored and applied to the numerous species of huckleberries, by our botanists—instead of the very inadequate—Greek and Latin or English ones at present used. They might serve both a scientific and popular use. Certainly it is not the best point of view to look at this peculiarly American family as it were from the other side of the Atlantic. It is still in doubt whether the Latin word for the genus *Vaccinium* means a berry or a flower.

Botanists, on the look out for what they thought a respectable descent, have long been inclined to trace this family backward to Mount Ida. Tourneforte does not hesitate to give it the ancient name of *Vine of Mount Ida*. The common English Raspberry also is called *Rubus Idaea* or the Mount

Ida bramble—from the old Greek name. The truth of it seems to be that blueberries and raspberries flourish best in cool and airy situations, on hills and mountains, and I can easily believe that something *like* these at least grows on Mount Ida. But Mount Monadnoc is as good as Mount Ida, and probably better for blueberries, though its name is said to mean *Bad Rock*. But the worst rocks are the best for poets' uses. Let us then exchange that oriental uncertainty for this western certainty.

We have in the northern states a few wild plums and inedible crab apples—a few palatable grapes—and many tolerable nuts—but I think that the various species of berries are our *wild fruits* which are to be compared with the more celebrated ones of the tropics, and for my part I would not exchange fruits with them—for the object is not merely to get a ship-load of something which you can eat or sell, but the pleasure of gathering it is to be taken into the account.

What is the pear crop as yet to the huckleberry crop? Horticulturists make a great ado about their pears, but how many families raise or buy a barrel of pears in a year all told? They are comparatively insignificant. I do not taste more than half a dozen pears annually, and I suspect that the majority fare worse even than I. (This was written before my neighbor's pear-orchard began to bear. Now he frequently fills my own and others' pockets with the fruit.) But Nature heaps the table with berries for six weeks or more. Indeed the apple crop is not so important as the huckleberry crop. Probably the apples consumed in this town annually do not amount to more than one barrel per family. But what is this to a month or more of huckleberrying to every man, woman and child, and the birds into the bargain. Even the crop of oranges, lemons, nuts, raisins, figs, quinces, etc. is of little importance to us compared with these.

They are not unprofitable in a pecuniary sense; I hear that some of the inhabitants of Ashby sold $2000 worth of huckleberries in '56.

In May and June all our hills and fields are adorned with a profusion of the pretty little more or less bell-shaped flowers of this family, commonly turned toward the earth and more or less tinged with red or pink, and resounding with the hum

of insects, each one the forerunner of a berry the most nat-
ural, wholesome and palatable that the soil can produce. I
think to myself, these are the blossoms of the *Vaccinieae* or
Whortleberry family, which affords so large a portion of our
berries; the berry-promising flower of the *Vaccinieae*! This
crop grows wild all over the country—wholesome, bountiful
and free, a real ambrosia. And yet men, the foolish demons
that they are, devote themselves to the culture of tobacco, in-
venting slavery and a thousand other curses for that pur-
pose—with infinite pains and inhumanity go raise tobacco all
their lives, and that is the staple instead of huckleberries.
Wreathes of tobacco smoke go up from this land, the only in-
cense which its inhabitants burn in honor of their gods. With
what authority can such as we distinguish between Christians
and Mahometans? Almost every interest, as the codfish and
mackerel interest, gets represented at the General Court—but
not the huckleberry interest. The first discoverers and explor-
ers of the land make report of this fruit—but the last make
comparatively little account of them.

Blueberries and huckleberries are such simple, wholesome
and universal fruits that they concern our race much. It is
hard to imagine any country without this kind of berry, on
which men live like birds. Still covering our hills as when the
red men lived here. Are they not the the principal wild fruit?

What means this profusion of berries at this season only?
Nature does her best to feed her children, and the broods of
birds just matured find plenty to eat now. Every bush and
vine does its part and offers a wholesome and palatable diet to
the way-farer. He need not go out of the road to get as many
berries as he wants—of various kinds and qualities according
as his road leads him over high or low, wooded or open
ground—huckleberries of different colors and flavors almost
everywhere—the second kind of low blueberry largest in the
moist ground—high blueberries with their agreeable acid
when his way lies through a swamp, and low blackberries of
two or more varieties on almost every sandy plain and bank
and stone heap.

Man at length stands in such a relation to Nature as the an-
imals which pluck and eat as they go. The fields and hills are a
table constantly spread. Diet-drinks, cordials, wines of all kinds

and qualities, are bottled up in the skins of countless berries for their refreshment, and they quaff them at every turn. They seem offered to us not so much for food as for sociality, inviting us to a pic-nic with Nature. We pluck and eat in remembrance of her. It is a sort of sacrament—a communion—the *not* forbidden fruits, which no serpent tempts us to eat. Slight and innocent savors which relate us to Nature, make us her guests, and entitle us to her regard and protection.

When I see, as now, in climbing one of our hills, huckleberry and blueberry bushes bent to the ground with fruit, I think of them as fruits fit to grow on the most Olympian or heaven-pointing hills.

It does not occur to you at first that where such thoughts are suggested is Mount Olympus, and that you who taste these berries are a god. Why in his only royal moments should man abdicate his throne?

You eat these berries in the dry pastures where they grow not to gratify an appetite, but as simply and naturally as thoughts come into your mind, as if they were the food of thought, dry as itself, and surely they nourish the brain there.

Occasionally there is an unusual profusion of these fruits to compensate for the scarcity of a previous year. I remember some seasons when favorable moist weather had expanded the berries to their full size, so that the hill-sides were literally black with them. There were infinitely more of all kinds than any and all creatures could use.

One such year, on the side of Conantum Hill, they were literally five or six species deep. First, if you searched low down in the shade under all, you found still fresh the great light blue earliest blueberries, bluets, in heavy clusters—that most Olympian fruit of all—delicate flavored, thin-skinned and cool—then, next above, the still denser masses or clusters of the second low blueberry of various varieties, firm and sweet food—and rising above these large blue and black huckleberries of various qualities—and over these ran rampant the low blackberry weighing down the thicket with its wreathes of black fruit, and binding it together in a trembling mass— while here and there the high blackberry, just beginning to be ripe, towered over all the rest. Thus, as it were, the berries hung up lightly in masses or heaps, separated by their leaves and twigs so that the air could circulate through and preserve them; and you went daintily wading through this thicket, picking perhaps only the finest of the high blackberries, as big as the end of your thumb, however big that may be, or clutching here and there a handful of huckleberries for variety, but never suspecting the delicious, cool blue-bloomed ones, which you were crushing with your feet under all. I have in such a case spread aside the bushes and revealed the last kind to those who had never in all their lives seen or heard of it before.

Each such patch, each bush—seems fuller and blacker than the last, as you proceed, and the huckleberries at length swell so big, as if aping the blackberries, that you mark the spot for future years.

There is all this profusion and yet you see neither birds nor beasts eating them—only ants and the huckleberry-bug. It seems fortunate for us that those cows in their pasture do not love them, but pass them by. We do not perceive that birds and quadrupeds make any use of them because they are so abundant we do not miss them, and they are not compelled to come when we are for them. Yet they are far more important to them than to us. We do not notice the robin when it plucks a huckleberry as we do when it visits our favorite cherry tree—and the fox pays his visits to the fields when we are not there.

I once carried my arms full of these bushes to my boat, and while I was rowing homeward two ladies, who were my companions, picked three pints from these alone, casting the bare bushes into the stream from time to time.

Even in ordinary years, when berries are comparatively scarce, I sometimes unexpectedly find so many in some distant and unfrequented part of the town, between and about the careless farmers' houses and walls, that the soil seems more fertile than where I live. Every bush and bramble bears its fruit. The very sides of the road are a fruit garden. The earth there teems with blackberries, huckleberries, thimbleberries, fresh and abundant—no signs of drought nor of pickers. Great shining black berries peep out at me from under the leaves upon the rocks. Do the rocks hold moisture? or are there no fingers to pluck these fruits? I seem to have wan-

dered into a land of greater fertility—some up country Eden.
These are the Delectable Hills. It is a land flowing with milk
and huckleberries, only they have not yet put the berries into
the milk. *There* the herbage never withers, *there* are abundant
dews. I ask myself, What are the virtues of the inhabitants that
they are thus blessed?

> *O fortunatos nimium, sua si bona norint Agricolas*—
> O too fortunate husbandmen if they knew their own
>   happiness.

These berries are further important as introducing children
to the fields and woods. The season of berrying is so far re-
spected that the school children have a vacation then—and
many little fingers are busy picking these small fruits. It is
even a pastime, not a drudgery—though it often pays well be-
side. The First of August is to them the anniversary of Eman-
cipation in New England.

Women and children who never visit distant hills, fields and
swamps on any other errand are seen making haste thither
now with half their domestic utensils in their hands. The
wood-chopper goes into the swamp for fuel in the winter; his
wife and children for berries in the summer.

Now you will see who is the thorough countrywoman who
does not go to the beach—conversant with berries and nuts—
a masculine wild-eyed woman of the fields.

Now for a ride in the hay-rigging to that far off Elysium
that Zachariah See-all alighted on—but has not mentioned
to every person—in the hay-rigging without springs—trying
to sensitive nerves and to full pails, for all alike sit on the
bottom—such a ride is favorable to conversation for the in-
cessant rumble hides all defects and fills the otherwise awe-
ful pauses—to be introduced to new scenes more memorable
than the berries—but to the old walker the straggling party
itself half concealed amid the bushes is the most novel and
interesting feature. If hot the boys break up the bushes and
carry them to some shady place where the girls can pick
them at their ease. But this is a lazy and improvident way—
and gives an unsightly look to the hill. There are many
events not in the program. If you have an ear for music—
perhaps one is the sound of a cow bell—never heard before—

or a sudden thunder shower putting you to flight—or a breakdown.

I served my apprenticeship and have since done considerable journeywork in the huckleberry field. Though I never paid for my schooling and clothing in that way, it was some of the best schooling that I got and paid for itself. Theodore Parker is not the only New England boy who has got his education by picking huckleberries, though he may not have gone to Harvard thereafter, nor to any school more distant than the huckleberry field. *There* was the university itself where you could learn the everlasting Laws, and Medicine and Theology, not under Story, and Warren, and Ware, but far wiser professors than they. Why such haste to go from the huckleberry field to the College yard?

As in old times they who dwelt on the heath, remote from towns, being backward to adopt the doctrines which prevailed in towns, were called heathen in a bad sense, so I trust that we dwellers in the huckleberry pastures, which are our heathlands, shall be slow to adopt the notions of large towns and cities, though perchance we may be nicknamed huckleberry people. But the worst of it is that the emissaries of the towns come more for our berries than they do for our salvation.

Occasionally, in still summer forenoons, when perhaps a mantua-maker was to be dined, and a huckleberry pudding had been decided on (by the authorities), I a lad of ten was despatched to a neighboring hill alone. My scholastic education could be thus far tampered with, and an excuse might be found. No matter how scarce the berries on the near hills, the exact number necessary for a pudding could surely be collected by eleven o'clock—and all ripe ones too though I turned some round three times to be sure they were not premature. My rule in such cases was never to eat one till my dish was full; for going a-berrying implies more things than eating the berries. They at home got nothing but the pudding, a comparatively heavy affair—but I got the forenoon out of doors—to say nothing about the appetite for the pudding. They got only the plums that were in the pudding, but I got the far sweeter plums that never go into it.

At other times, when I had companions, some of them used to bring such remarkably shaped dishes, that I was often curious to see how the berries disposed of themselves in them. Some brought a coffee-pot to the huckleberry field, and such a vessel possessed this advantage at least, that if a greedy boy had skimmed off a handful or two on his way home, he had only to close the lid and give his vessel a shake to have it full again. I have seen this done all round when the party got as far homeward as the Dutch House. It can probably be done with any vessel that has much side to it.

There was a Young America then, which has become Old America, but its principles and motives are still the same, only applied to other things. Sometimes, just before reaching the spot—every boy rushed to the hill side and hastily selecting a spot—shouted 'I speak for this place,' indicating its bounds, and another 'I speak for that,' and so on—and this was sometimes considered good law for the huckleberry field. At any rate it is a law similar to this by which we have taken possession of the territory of Indians and Mexicans.

I once met with a whole family, father, mother, and children, ravaging a huckleberry field in this wise. They cut up the bushes as they went and beat them over the edge of a bushel basket, till they had it full of berries, ripe and green, leaves, sticks etc., and so they passed along out of my sight like wild men.

I well remember with what a sense of freedom and spirit of adventure I used to take my way across the fields with my pail, some years later, toward some distant hill or swamp, when dismissed for all day, and I would not now exchange such an expansion of all my being for all the learning in the world. Liberation and enlargement—such is the fruit which all culture aims to secure. I suddenly knew more about my books than if I had never ceased studying them. I found myself in a schoolroom where I could not fail to see and hear things worth seeing and hearing—where I could not help getting my lesson—for my lesson came to me. Such experience often repeated, was the chief encouragement to go to the Academy and study a book at last.

But ah we have fallen on evil days! I hear of pickers ordered out of the huckleberry fields, and I see stakes set up with written notices forbidding any to pick them. Some let their fields or allow so much for the picking. *Sic transit gloria ruris.* I do not mean to blame any, but all—to bewail our fates generally. We are not grateful enough that we have lived a part of our lives before these things occurred. What becomes of the true value of country life—what, if you must go to market for it? It has come to this, that the butcher now brings round our huckleberries in his cart. Why, it is as if the hangman were to perform the marriage ceremony. Such is the inevitable tendency of our civilization, to reduce huckleberries to a level with beef-steaks—that is to blot out four fifths of it, or the going a-huckleberrying, and leave only a pudding, that part which is the fittest accompaniment to a beef-steak. You all know what it is to go a-beef-steaking. It is to knock your old fellow laborer Bright on the head to begin with—or possibly to cut a steak from him running in the Abyssinian fashion and wait for another to grow there. The butcher's item in chalk on the door is now 'Calf's head and huckleberries.'

I suspect that the inhabitants of England and the continent of Europe have thus lost in a measure their natural rights, with the increase of population and monopolies. The wild fruits of the earth disappear before civilization, or only the husks of them are to be found in large markets. The whole country becomes, as it were, a town or beaten common, and almost the only fruits left are a few hips and haws.

What sort of a country is that where the huckleberry fields are private property? When I pass such fields on the highway, my heart sinks within me. I see a blight on the land. Nature is under a veil there. I make haste away from the accursed spot. Nothing could deform her fair face more. I cannot think of it ever after but as the place where fair and palatable berries, are converted into money, where the huckleberry is desecrated.

It is true, we have as good a right to make berries private property, as to make wild grass and trees such—it is not worse than a thousand other practices which custom has sanctioned—but that is the worst of it, for it suggests how bad the rest are, and to what result our civilization and division of labor naturally tend, to make all things venal.

A., a professional huckleberry picker, has hired B.'s field, and, we will suppose, is now gathering the crop, with a patent huckleberry horse rake.

C., a professed cook, is superintending the boiling of a pudding made of some of the berries.

While Professor D.—for whom the pudding is intended, sits in his library writing a book—a work on the *Vaccinieae* of course.

And now the result of this downward course will be seen in that work—which should be the ultimate fruit of the huckleberry field. It will be worthless. It will have none of the spirit of the huckleberry in it, and the reading of it will be a weariness of the flesh.

I believe in a different kind of division of labor—that Professor D. should be encouraged to divide himself freely between his library and the huckleberry field.

What I chiefly regret in this case, is the in effect dog-in-the-manger result; for at the same time that we exclude mankind from gathering berries in our field, we exclude them from gathering health and happiness and inspiration, and a hundred other far finer and nobler fruits than berries, which are found there, but which we have no notion of gathering and shall not gather ourselves, nor ever carry to market, for there is no market for them, but let them rot on the bushes.

We thus strike only one more blow at a simple and wholesome relation to nature. I do not know but this is the excuse of those who have lately taken to swinging bags of beans and ringing dumb bells. As long as the berries are free to all comers they are beautiful, though they may be few and small, but tell me that this is a blueberry swamp which somebody has hired, and I shall not want even to look at it. We so commit the berries to the wrong hands, that is to the hands of those who cannot appreciate them. This is proved by the fact that if we do not pay them some money, these parties will at once cease to pick them. They have no other interest in berries but a pecuniary one. Such is the constitution of our society that we make a compromise and permit the berries to be degraded, to be enslaved, as it were.

Accordingly in laying claim for the first time to the spontaneous fruit of our pastures, we are inevitably aware of a little meanness, and the merry berry party which we turn away naturally looks down on and despises us. If it were left to the berries to say who should have them, is it not likely that they would prefer to be gathered by the party of children in the hay-rigging, who have come to have a good time merely?

This is one of the taxes which we pay for having a rail-road. All our improvements, so called, tend to convert the country into the town. But I do not see clearly that these successive losses are ever quite made up to us. This suggests, as I have said, what origin and foundation many of our institutions have. I do not say this by way of complaining of this custom in particular, which is beginning to prevail—not that I love Caesar less but Rome more. It is my own way of living that I complain of as well as yours—and therefore I trust that my remarks will come home to you. I hope that I am not so poor a shot, like most clergymen, as to fire into a crowd of a thousand men without hitting somebody—though I do not aim at any one.

Thus we behave like oxen in a flower garden. The true fruit of Nature can only be plucked with a fluttering heart and a delicate hand, not bribed by any earthly reward. No hired man can help us to gather that crop.

Among the Indians, the earth and its productions generally were common and free to all the tribe, like the air and water—but among us who have supplanted the Indians, the public retain only a small yard or common in the middle of the village, with perhaps a grave-yard beside it, and the right of way, by sufferance, by a particular narrow route, which is annually becoming narrower, from one such yard to another. I doubt if you can ride out five miles in any direction without coming to where some individual is tolling in the road—and he expects the time when it will all revert to him or his heirs. This is the way we civilized men have arranged it.

I am not overflowing with respect and gratitude to the fathers who thus laid out our New England villages, whatever precedent they were influenced by, for I think that a 'prentice hand liberated from Old English prejudices could have done much better in this new world. If they were in earnest seeking thus far away 'freedom to worship God,' as some assure us—why did they not secure a little more of it, when it was so cheap and they were about it? At the same time that they built meeting-houses why did they not preserve from desecration and destruction far grander temples not made with hands?

What are the natural features which make a township handsome—and worth going far to dwell in? A river with its waterfalls—meadows, lakes—hills, cliffs or individual rocks, a forest and single ancient trees—such things are beautiful. They have a high use which dollars and cents never represent. If the inhabitants of a town were wise they would seek to preserve these things though at a considerable expense. For such things educate far more than any hired teachers or preachers, or any at present recognized system of school education.

I do not think him fit to be the founder of a state or even of a town who does not foresee the use of these things, but legislates as it were, for oxen chiefly.

It would be worth the while if in each town there were a committee appointed, to see that the beauty of the town received no detriment. If here is the largest boulder in the country, then it should not belong to an individual nor be made into door-steps. In some countries precious metals belong to the crown—so here more precious objects of great natural beauty should belong to the public.

Let us try to keep the new world new, and while we make a wary use of the city, preserve as far as possible the advantages of living in the country.

I think of no natural feature which is a greater ornament and treasure to this town than the river. It is one of the things which determine whether a man will live here or in another place, and it is one of the first objects which we show to a stranger. In this respect we enjoy a great advantage over those neighboring towns which have no river. Yet the town, as a corporation, has never turned any but the most purely utilitarian eyes upon it—and has done nothing to preserve its natural beauty.

They who laid out the town should have made the river available as a common possession forever. The town collectively should at least have done as much as an individual of taste who owns an equal area commonly does in England. Indeed I think that not only the channel but one or both banks of every river should be a public highway—for a river is not useful merely to float on. In this case, one bank might have been reserved as a public walk and the trees that adorned it have been protected, and frequent avenues have been provided leading to it from the main street. This would have cost but few acres of land and but little wood, and we should all have been gainers by it. Now it is accessible only at the bridges at points comparatively distant from the town, and there there is not a foot of shore to stand on unless you trespass on somebody's lot—and if you attempt a quiet stroll down the bank—you soon meet with fences built at right angles with the stream and projecting far over the water—where individuals, naturally enough, under the present arrangement—seek to monopolize the shore. At last we shall get our only view of the stream from the meeting house belfry.

As for the trees which fringed the shore within my remembrance—where are they? and where will the remnant of them be after ten years more?

So if there is any central and commanding hill-top, it should be reserved for the public use. Think of a mountain top in the township—even to the Indians a sacred place—only accessible through private grounds. A temple as it were which you cannot enter without trespassing—nay the temple itself private property and standing in a man's cow yard—for such is commonly the case. New Hampshire courts have lately been deciding, as if it was for them to decide, whether the top of Mount Washington belonged to A or B—and it being decided in favor of B, I hear that he went up one winter with the proper officers and took formal possession. That area should be left unappropriated for modesty and reverence's sake—if only to suggest that the traveller who climbs thither in a degree rises above himself, as well as his native valley, and leaves some of his grovelling habits behind.

I know it is a mere figure of speech to talk about temples nowadays, when men recognize none, and associate the word with heathenism. Most men, it appears to me, do not care for Nature, and would sell their share in all her beauty, for as long as they may live, for a stated and not very large sum. Thank God they cannot yet fly and lay waste the sky as well as the earth. We are safe on that side for the present. It is for the very reason that some do not care for these things that we need to combine to protect all from the vandalism of a few.

It is true, we as yet take liberties and go across lots in most directions but we naturally take fewer and fewer liberties every year, as we meet with more resistance, and we shall soon be reduced to the same straights they are in England, where going across lots is out of the question—and we must ask leave to walk in some lady's park.

There are a few hopeful signs. There is the growing *library*—and then the town does set trees along the highways. But does not the broad landscape itself deserve attention?

We cut down the few old oaks which witnessed the transfer of the township from the Indian to the white man, and perchance commence our museum with a cartridge box taken from a British soldier in 1775. How little we insist on truly grand and beautiful natural features. There may be the most beautiful landscapes in the world within a dozen miles of us, for aught we know—for their inhabitants do not value nor perceive them—and so have not made them known to others—but if a grain of gold were picked up there, or a pearl found in a fresh-water clam, the whole state would resound with the news.

Thousands annually seek the White Mountains to be refreshed by their wild and primitive beauty—but when the country was discovered a similar kind of beauty prevailed all over it—and much of this might have been preserved for our present refreshment if a little foresight and taste had been used.

I do not believe that there is a town in this country which realizes in what its true wealth consists.

I visited the town of Boxboro only eight miles west of us last fall—and far the handsomest and most memorable thing which I saw there, was its noble oak wood. I doubt if there is a finer one in Massachusetts. Let it stand fifty years longer and men will make pilgrimages to it from all parts of the country, and for a worthier object than to shoot squirrels in it—and yet I said to myself, Boxboro would be very like the rest of New England, if she were ashamed of that wood-land. Probably, if the history of this town is written, the historian will have omitted to say a word about this forest—the most interesting thing in it—and lay all the stress on the history of the parish.

It turned out that I was not far from right—for not long after I came across a very brief historical notice of Stow—which then included Boxboro—written by the Reverend John Gardiner in the *Massachusetts Historical Collections*, nearly a hundred years ago. In which Mr. Gardiner, after telling us who was his predecessor in the ministry, and when he himself was settled, goes on to say, 'As for any remarkables, I am of mind there have been the fewest of any town of our standing in the Province. . . . I can't call to mind above one thing worthy of public notice, and that is the grave of Mr. John Green' who, it appears, when in England, 'was made clerk of the exchequer' by Cromwell. 'Whether he was excluded the act of oblivion or not I cannot tell,' says Mr. Gardiner. At any rate he returned to New England and as Gardiner tells us 'lived and died, and lies buried in this place.'

I can assure Mr. Gardiner that he was not excluded from the act of oblivion.

It is true Boxboro was less peculiar for its woods at that date—but they were not less interesting absolutely.

I remember talking a few years ago with a young man who had undertaken to write the history of his native town—a wild and mountainous town far up country, whose very name suggested a hundred things to me, and I almost wished I had the task to do myself—so few of the original settlers had been driven out—and not a single clerk of the exchequer buried in it. But to my chagrin I found that the author was complaining of want of materials, and that the crowning fact of his story was that the town had been the residence of General C— and the family mansion was still standing.

I have since heard, however, that Boxboro is content to have that forest stand, instead of the houses and farms that might supplant it—not because of its beauty—but because the land pays a much larger tax now than it would then.

Nevertheless it is likely to be cut off within a few years for ship-timber and the like. It is too precious to be thus disposed of. I think that it would be wise for the state to purchase and preserve a few such forests.

If the people of Massachusetts are ready to found a professorship of Natural History—so they must see the importance of preserving some portions of nature herself unimpaired.

I find that the rising generation in this town do not know what an oak or a pine is, having seen only inferior specimens. Shall we hire a man to lecture on botany, on oaks for instance, our noblest plants—while we permit others to cut down the few best specimens of these trees that are left? It is like teaching children Latin and Greek while we burn the books printed in those languages.

I think that each town should have a park, or rather a primitive forest, of five hundred or a thousand acres, either in one body or several—where a stick should never be cut for fuel— nor for the navy, nor to make wagons, but stand and decay for higher uses—a common possession forever, for instruction and recreation.

All Walden wood might have been reserved, with Walden in the midst of it, and the Easterbrooks country, an uncultivated area of some four square miles in the north of the town, might have been our huckleberry field. If any owners of these tracts are about to leave the world without natural heirs who need or deserve to be specially remembered, they will do wisely to abandon the possession to all mankind, and not will them to some individual who perhaps has enough already—and so correct the error that was made when the town was laid out. As some give to Harvard College or another Institution, so one might give a forest or a huckleberry field to Concord. This town surely is an institution which deserves to be remembered. Forget the heathen in foreign parts, and remember the pagans and savages here.

We hear of cow commons and ministerial lots, but we want *men* commons and *lay* lots as well. There is meadow and pasture and woodlot for the town's poor, why not a forest and huckleberry field for the town's rich?

We boast of our system of education, but why stop at schoolmasters and schoolhouses? We are all schoolmasters and our schoolhouse is the universe. To attend chiefly to the desk or schoolhouse, while we neglect the scenery in which it is placed, is absurd. If we do not look out we shall find our fine schoolhouse standing in a cow yard at last.

It frequently happens that what the city prides itself on most is its park—those acres which require to be the least altered from their original condition.

Live in each season as it passes; breathe the air, drink the drink, taste the fruit, and resign yourself to the influences of each. Let these be your only diet-drink and botanical medicines.

In August live on berries, not dried meats and pemmican as if you were on shipboard making your way through a waste ocean, or in the Darien Grounds, and so die of ship-fever and scurvy. Some will die of ship-fever and scurvy in an Illinois prairie, they lead such stifled and scurvy lives.

Be blown on by all the winds. Open all your pores and bathe in all the tides of nature, in all her streams and oceans, at all seasons. Miasma and infection are from within, not without. The invalid brought to the brink of the grave by an unnatural life, instead of imbibing the great influence that nature is—drinks only of the tea made of a particular herb— while he still continues his unnatural life—saves at the spile and wastes at the bung. He does not love nature or his life and so sickens and dies and no doctor can save him.

Grow green with spring—yellow and ripe with autumn. Drink of each season's influence as a vial, a true panacea of all remedies mixed for your especial use. The vials of summer never made a man sick, only those which he had stored in his cellar. Drink the wines not of your own but of nature's bottling—not kept in a goat- or pig-skin, but in the skins of a myriad fair berries.

Let Nature do your bottling, as also your pickling and preserving.

For all nature is doing her best each moment to make us well. She exists for no other end. Do not resist her. With the least inclination to be well we should not be sick. Men have discovered, or think that they have discovered the salutariness of a few wild things only, and not of all nature. Why nature is but another name for health. Some men think that they are not well in Spring or Summer or Autumn or Winter, (if you will excuse the pun) it is only because they are not indeed *well*, that is fairly *in* those seasons.

POEMS

POEMS

In days of yore, tis said, the swimming alder
Fashioned rude, with branches lopt, and stripped of its
    smooth coat,
Where fallen tree was none, and rippling streams vast breadth
Forbade adventurous leap, the brawny swain did bear
Secure to farthest shore.
The book has passed away, and with the book the lay
Which in my youthful days I loved to ponder.
Of curious things it told, how wise men 3 of Gotham
In a bowl did venture out to sea,
And darkly hints their awful fate
If men have dared the main to tempt in such frail barks,
Why may not wash tub round, or bread-troughs square
    oblong
Suffice to cross the purling wave and gain the destin'd port.

Fair Haven

When little hills like lambs did skip,
And Joshua ruled in heaven,
Unmindful rolled Musketuquid,
  Nor budged an inch Fair Haven.

When principle is like to yield,
To selfish fear, or craven,
And fickle mortals round me fall,
  I'll not forget Fair Haven.

If there's a cliff in this wide world,
'S, a stepping stone to heaven,
A pleasant, craggy, short hand cut,
  It sure must be Fair Haven.

Oft have I climbed thy craggy steep,
Where ceaseless wheels the raven,
And whiled away an hour at e'en,
 For love of thee, Fair Haven.

If e'er my bark be tempest-tossed,
And every hope the wave in,
And this frail hulk shall spring a leak,
 I'll steer for thee, Fair Haven.

When cares press heavy on my soul,
And devils blue are craven,
Or e'er I lay me down to rest,
 I'll think of thee, Fair Haven.

And when I take my last long rest,
And quiet sleep my grave in,
What kindlier covering for my breast,
 Than thy warm turf Fair Haven.

Voyagers Song

Gentle river, gentle river
Swift as glides thy stream along,
Many a bold Canadian voyageur,
Bravely swelled the gay chanson

Thus of old our valiant fathers,
Many a lagging year agone
Gliding oer the rippling waters,
Taught to banish care in song.

Now the sun's behind the willows,
Now he gleams along the lake,
Hark across the bounding billows
Liquid songs the echoes wake.

Rise Apollo up before us,
E'ne the lark's begun her lay
Let us all in deafning chorus
Praise the glorious king of day.

Thus we lead a life of pleasure,
Thus we while the hours away,
Thus we revel beyond measure,
Gaily live we while we may.

———

Life is a summer's day
When as it were for aye
  We sport and play.

Anon the night comes on,
The ploughman's work is done,
  And day is gone.

We read in this one page
Both Youth, Manhood, and Age
  That hoary Sage.

The morning is our prime,
That laughs to scorn old Time,
  And knows no crime.

The noon comes on apace,
And then with swel'tring face
  We run our race.

When eve comes stealing o'er
We ponder at our door
  On days of yore.

The patient kine, they say,
At dawn do frisk and play,
    And well they may.

By noon their sports abate,
For then, as bards relate,
    They vegetate.

When eventide hath come,
And grey flies cease their hum,
    And now are dumb,

They leave the tender bud,
That's cooling to the blood,
    And chew the cud.

———

Let's make the most of morn,
Ere grey flies wind their horn,
    And it is gone.

———

"Long life and success to you."
                    UBIQUE.

I love a careless streamlet,
That takes a mad-cap leap,
And like a sparkling beamlet
Goes dashing down the steep.

———

Like torrents of the mountain
We've coursed along the lea,
From many a crystal fountain
Toward the far-distant sea.

And now we've gained life's valley,
And through the lowlands roam,
No longer may'st thou dally,
No longer spout and foam.

May pleasant meads await thee,
Where thou may'st freely roll
Towards that bright heavenly sea,
Thy resting place and goal.

And when thou reach'st life's down-hill,
So gentle be thy stream,
As would not turn a grist-mill
Without the aid of steam.

———

Pens to mend, and hands to guide.
Oh who would a schoolmaster be?

———

Each summer sound
Is a summer round.

Friendship

I think awhile of Love, and while I think,
    Love is to me a world,
    Sole meat and sweetest drink,
    And close connecting link
      Tween heaven and earth.

I only know it is, not how or why,
    My greatest happiness;
    However hard I try,
    Not if I were to die,
      Can I explain.

I fain would ask my friend how it can be,
    But when the time arrives,
    Then Love is more lovely
    Than anything to me,
      And so I'm dumb.

For if the truth were known, Love cannot speak,
    But only thinks and does;
    Though surely out 'twill leak
    Without the help of Greek,
      Or any tongue.

A man may love the truth and practise it,
    Beauty he may admire,
    And goodness not omit,
    As much as may befit
      To reverence.

But only when these three together meet,
    As they always incline,
    And make one soul the seat,
    And favorite retreat
      Of loveliness;

When under kindred shape, like loves and hates
 And a kindred nature,
 Proclaim us to be mates,
 Exposed to equal fates
  Eternally;

And each may other help, and service do,
 Drawing Love's bands more tight,
 Service he ne'er shall rue
 While one and one make two,
  And two are one;

In such case only doth man fully prove
 Fully as man can do,
 What power there is in Love
 His inmost soul to move
  Resistlessly.

———

Two sturdy oaks I mean, which side by side,
 Withstand the winter's storm,
 And spite of wind and tide,
 Grow up the meadow's pride,
  For both are strong

Above they barely touch, but undermined
 Down to their deepest source,
 Admiring you shall find
 Their roots are intertwined
  Insep'rably.

When breathless noon hath paused on hill and vale,
And now no more the woodman plies his axe,
Nor mower whets his scythe,
Somewhat it is, sole sojourner on earth,
To hear the veery on her oaken perch
Ringing her modest trill—
Sole sound of all the din that makes a world,
And I sole ear.
Fondly to nestle me in that sweet melody,
And own a kindred soul, speaking to me
From out the depths of universal being.
O'er birch and hazle, through the sultry air,
Comes that faint sound this way,
On Zephyr borne, straight to my ear.
No longer time or place, nor faintest trace
Of earth, the landscape's shimmer is my only space,
Sole remnant of a world.
Anon that throat has done, and familiar sounds
Swell strangely on the breeze, the low of cattle,
And the novel cries of sturdy swains
That plod the neighboring vale—
And I walk once more confounded a denizen of earth.

The Bluebirds

In the midst of the poplar that stands by our door,
We planted a bluebird box,
And we hoped before the summer was o'er
A transient pair to coax.

One warm summer's day the bluebirds came
And lighted on our tree,
But at first the wand'rers were not so tame
But they were afraid of me.

They seemed to come from the distant south,
Just over the Walden wood,
And they skimmed it along with open mouth
Close by where the bellows stood.

Warbling they swept round the distant cliff,
And they warbled it over the lea,
And over the blacksmith's shop in a jiff
Did they come warbling to me.

They came and sat on the box's top
Without looking into the hole,
And only from this side to that did they hop,
As 'twere a common well-pole.

Methinks I had never seen them before,
Nor indeed had they seen me,
Till I chanced to stand by our back door,
And they came to the poplar tree.

In course of time they built their nest
And reared a happy brood,
And every morn they piped their best
As they flew away to the wood.

Thus wore the summer hours away
To the bluebirds and to me,
And every hour was a summer's day,
So pleasantly lived we.

They were a world within themselves,
And I a world in me,
Up in the tree—the little elves—
With their callow family.

One morn the wind blowed cold and strong,
And the leaves when whirling away;
The birds prepared for their journey long
That raw and gusty day.

Boreas came blust'ring down from the north,
And ruffled their azure smocks,
So they launched them forth, though somewhat loth,
By way of the old Cliff rocks.

Meanwhile the earth jogged steadily on
In her mantle of purest white,
And anon another spring was born
When winter was vanished quite.

And I wandered forth o'er the steamy earth,
And gazed at the mellow sky,
But never before from the hour of my birth
Had I wandered so thoughtfully.

For never before was the earth so still,
And never so mild was the sky,
The river, the fields, the woods, and the hill,
Seemed to heave an audible sigh.

I felt that the heavens were all around,
And the earth was all below,
As when in the ears there rushes a sound
Which thrills you from top to toe.

I dreamed that I was an waking thought—
A something I hardly knew—
Not a solid piece, nor an empty nought,
But a drop of morning dew.

'Twas the world and I at a game of bo-peep,
As a man would dodge his shadow,
An idea becalmed in eternity's deep—
'Tween Lima and Segraddo.

Anon a faintly warbled note
From out the azure deep,
Into my ears did gently float
As is the approach of sleep.

It thrilled but startled not my soul;
Across my mind strange mem'ries gleamed,
As often distant scenes unroll
When we have lately dreamed

The bluebird had come from the distant South
To his box in the poplar tree,
And he opened wide his slender mouth,
On purpose to sing to me.

May Morning

The school boy loitered on his way to school,
Scorning to live so rare a day by rule.
So mild the air a pleasure 'twas to breathe,
For what seems heaven above was earth beneath.

Soured neighbors chatted by the garden pale,
Nor quarrelled who should drive the needed nail—
The most unsocial made new friends that day,
As when the sun shines husbandmen make hay

How long I slept I know not, but at last
I felt my consciousness returning fast,
For Zephyr rustled past with leafy tread,
And heedlessly with one heel grazed my head.

My eyelids opened on a field of blue,
For close above a nodding violet grew,
A part of heaven it seemed, which one could scent,
Its blue commingling with the firmament.

Walden

—True, our converse a stranger is to speech,
Only the practised ear can catch the surging words,
That break and die upon thy pebbled lips.
Thy flow of thought is noiseless as the lapse of thy own
  waters,
Wafted as is the morning mist up from thy surface,
So that the passive Soul doth breathe it in,
And is infected with the truth thou wouldst express.

E'en the remotest stars have come in troops
And stooped low to catch the benediction
Of thy countenance. Oft as the day came round,
Impartial has the sun exhibited himself
Before thy narrow skylight—nor has the moon
For cycles failed to roll this way
As oft as elsewhither, and tell thee of the night.
No cloud so rare but hitherward it stalked,
And in thy face looked doubly beautiful.
O! tell me what the winds have writ within these thousand
  years,
On the blue vault that spans thy flood—
Or sun transferred and delicately reprinted
For thy own private reading. Somewhat
Within these latter days I've read,
But surely there was much that would have thrilled the Soul,
Which human eye saw not
I would give much to read that first bright page,
Wet from a virgin press, when Eurus—Boreas—
And the host of airy quill-drivers
First dipped their pens in mist.

———

Truth—Goodness—Beauty—those celestial thrins,
Continually are born; e'en now the Universe,
With thousand throats—and eke with greener smiles,
Its joy confesses at their recent birth.

———

Strange that so many fickle gods, as fickle as the weather,
Throughout Dame Natures provinces should always pull
    together.

———

In the busy streets, domains of trade,
Man is a surly porter, or a vain and hectoring bully,
Who can claim no nearer kindredship with me
Than brotherhood by law.

———

I knew a man by sight,
    A blameless wight,
Who, for a year or more,
Had daily passed my door,
Yet converse none had had with him.

I met him in a lane,
    Him and his cane,
About three miles from home,
Where I had chanced to roam,
And volumes stared at him, and he at me.

In a more distant place
    I glimpsed his face,
And bowed instinctively;
    Starting he bowed to me,
Bowed simultaneously, and passed along.

Next, in a foreign land
  I grasped his hand,
And had a social chat,
About this thing and that,
As I had known him well a thousand years.

Late in a wilderness
  I shared his mess,
For he had hardships seen,
And I a wanderer been;
He was my bosom friend, and I was his.

And as, methinks, shall all,
  Both great and small,
That ever lived on earth,
Early or late their birth,
Stranger and foe, one day each other know.

Cliffs

The loudest sound that burdens here the breeze
Is the wood's whisper; 'tis when we choose to list
Audible sound, and when we list not,
It is calm profound. Tongues were provided
But to vex the ear with superficial thoughts.
When deeper thoughts upswell, the jarring discord
Of harsh speech is hushed, and senses seem
As little as may be to share the extacy.

My Boots

Anon with gaping fearlessness they quaff
The dewy nectar with a natural thirst,
Or wet their leathern lungs where cranberries lurk,
With sweeter wine than Chian, Lesbian, or Falernian far.
Theirs was the inward lustre that bespeaks

An open sole—unknowing to exclude
The cheerful day—a worthier glory far
Than that which gilds the outmost rind with darkness
  visible—
Virtues that fast abide through lapse of years,
Rather rubbed in than off.

Noon

What time the bittern, solitary bird,
Hides now her head amid the whispering fern,
And not a paddock vexes all the shore—
Nor feather ruffles the incumbent air,
Save where the wagtail interrupts the noon.

Fair Haven

When Winter fringes every bough
  With his fantastic wreath,
And puts the seal of silence now
  Upon the leaves beneath;

When every stream in its pent-house
  Goes gurgling on its way,
And in his gallery the mouse
  Nibbleth the meadow hay;

Methinks the summer still is nigh,
  And lurketh underneath,
As that same meadow mouse doth lie
  Snug in the last year's heath.

And if perchance the chicadee
  Lisp a faint note anon,
The snow in summer's canopy,
  Which she herself put on.

Fair blossoms deck the cheerful trees,
   And dazzling fruits depend,
The north wind sighs a summer breeze,
   The nipping frosts to fend,

Bringing glad tidings unto me,
   The while I stand all ear,
Of a serene eternity,
   Which need not winter fear.

Out on the silent pond straightway
   The restless ice doth crack,
And pond sprites merry gambols play
   Amid the deafening rack.

Eager I hasten to the vale,
   As if I heard brave news,
How nature held high festival,
   Which it were hard to lose.

I gambol with my neighbor ice,
   And sympathizing quake,
As each new crack darts in a trice
   Across the gladsome lake.

One with the cricket in the ground,
   And faggot on the hearth,
Resounds the rare domestic sound
   Along the forest path.

The Thaw

—

I saw the civil sun drying earth's tears—
Her tears of joy that only faster flowed,

—

Fain would I stretch me by the highway side,
To thaw and trickle with the melting snow,
That mingled soul and body with the tide,
I too may through the pores of nature flow.

—

But I alas nor tinkle can nor fume,
One jot to forward the great work of Time,
'Tis mine to hearken while these ply the loom,
So shall my silence with their music chime.

—

Last night as I lay gazing with shut eyes
        Into the golden land of dreams,
    I thought I gazed adown a quiet reach
        Of land and water prospect,
            Whose low beach
Was peopled with the now subsiding hum
Of happy industry—whose work is done.

And as I turned me on my pillow o'er,
I heard the lapse of waves upon the shore,
Distinct as it had been at broad noonday,
An I were wandering at Rockaway.

Love

We two that planets erst had been
Are now a double star,
And in the heavens may be seen,
Where that we fixed are.

Yet whirled with subtle power along,
Into new space we enter,
And evermore with spheral song
Revolve about one centre.

———

The deeds of king and meanest hedger,
Stand side by side in heaven's ledger.

———

'T will soon appear if we but look
At evening into earth's day book,
Which way the great account doth stand
Between the heavens and the land.

The Evening Wind

The eastern mail comes lumbering in
With outmost waves of Europe's din;
The western sighs adown the slope,
Or mid the rustling leaves doth grope,
Laden with news from Californ',
Whateer transpired hath since morn,
How wags The world by brier and brake,
From hence to Athabasca lake.

The Peal of the Bells

When the world grows old by the chimney side,
Then forth to the youngling rocks I glide—
Where over the water, and over the land,
The bells are booming on either hand.

Now up they go ding, then down again dong,
And awhile they swing to the same old song,
And the metal goes round 't a single bound,
A-lulling the fields with its measured sound—
Till the tired tongue falls with a lengthened boom,
As solemn and loud as the crack of doom.
Then changed is their measure to tone upon tone,
And seldom it is that one sound comes alone,
For they ring out their peals in a mingled throng,
And the breezes waft the loud ding-dong along.

When the echo has reached me in this lone vale,
I am straightway a hero in coat of mail,
I tug at my belt and I march on my post,
And feel myself more than a match for a host.

I am on the alert for some wonderful Thing,
Which somewhere's a taking place,
'Tis perchance the salute which our planet doth ring
When it meeteth another in space.

The Shrike

Hark—hark—from out the thickest fog
Warbles with might and main
The fearless shrike, as all agog
To find in fog his gain.

His steady sail he never furls
At any time o' year,
And perched now on winter's curls,
He whistles in his ear.

Sympathy

Lately alas I knew a gentle boy,
Whose features all were cast in Virtue's mould,
As one she had designed for Beauty's toy,
But after manned him for her own stronghold.

On every side he open was as day,
That you might see no lack of strength within,
For walls and ports do only serve alway
For a pretence to feebleness and sin.

Say not that Caesar was victorious,
With toil and strife who stormed the House of Fame
In other sense this youth was glorious,
Himself a kingdom wheresoe'er he came.

No strength went out to get him victory,
When all was income of its own accord;
For where he went none other was to see,
But all were parcel of their noble lord.

He forayed like the subtle haze of summer,
That stilly shows fresh landscapes to our eyes,
And revolutions works without a murmur,
Or rustling of a leaf beneath the skies.

So was I taken unawares by this,
I quite forgot my homage to confess;
Yet now am forced to know, though hard it is,
I might have loved him, had I loved him less.

Each moment, as we nearer drew to each,
A stern respect withheld us farther yet,
So that we seemed beyond each other's reach,
And less acquainted than when first we met.

We two were one while we did sympathize
So could we not the simplest bargain drive;
And what avails it now that we are wise,
If absence doth this doubleness contrive?

Eternity may not the chance repeat,
But I must tread my single way alone,
In sad remembrance that we once did meet,
And know that bliss irrevocably gone.

The spheres henceforth my elegy shall sing,
For elegy has other subject none;
Each strain of music in my ears shall ring
Knell of departure from that other one.

Make haste and celebrate my tragedy;
With fitting strain resound ye woods and fields;
Sorrow is dearer in such case to me
Than all the joys other occasion yields.

Is't then too late the damage to repair?
Distance, forsooth, from my weak grasp hath reft
The empty husk, and clutched the useless tare,
But in my hands the wheat and kernel left.

If I but love that virtue which he is,
Though it be scented in the morning air,
Still shall we be truest acquaintances,
Nor mortals know a sympathy more rare.

The "Book of Gems"

—With cunning plates the polished leaves were decked,
Each one a window to the poet's world,
So rich a prospect that you might suspect
In that small space all paradise unfurled.
It was a right delightful road to go,
    marching through pastures of such fair herbage,
O'er hill and dale it lead, and to and fro,
From bard to bard, making an easy stage.

Where ever and anon I slaked my thirst
Like a tired traveller at some poet's well,
Which from the teeming ground did bubbling burst,
And tinkling thence adown the page it fell.
Still through the leaves its music you might hear,
Till other springs fell faintly on the ear.

The Assabet

Up this pleasant stream let's row
For the livelong summer's day,
Sprinkling foam where'er we go
In wreaths as white as driven snow—
Ply the oars, away! away!

Now we glide along the shore,
Chucking lilies as we go,
While the yellow-sanded floor
Doggedly resists the oar,
Like some turtle dull and slow.

Now we stem the middle tide
Ploughing through the deepest soil,
Ridges pile on either side,
While we through the furrow glide,
Reaping bubbles for our toil.

Dew before and drought behind,
Onward all doth seem to fly;
Nought contents the eager mind,
Only rapids now are kind,
Forward are the earth and sky.

Sudden music strikes the ear,
Leaking out from yonder bank,
Fit such voyagers to cheer—
Sure there must be naiads here,
Who have kindly played this prank.

There I know the cunning pack
Where yon self-sufficient rill
All its telltale hath kept back,
Through the meadows held its clack,
And now babbleth its fill.

Silent flows the parent stream,
And if rocks do lie below
Smothers with her waves the din,
As it were a youthful sin,
Just as still and just as slow.

But this gleeful little rill,
Purling round its storied pebble,
Tinkles to the self same tune
From December until June,
Nor doth any drought enfeeble.

See the sun behind the willows,
Rising through the golden haze,
How he gleams along the billows—
Their white crests the easy pillows
Of his dew besprinkled rays.

Forward press we to the dawning,
For Aurora leads the way,
Sultry noon and twilight scorning,
In each dew drop of the morning
Lies the promise of a day.

Rivers from the sun do flow,
Springing with the dewy morn,
Voyageurs 'gainst time do row,
Idle noon nor sunset know,
Even even with the dawn.

Since that first away! away!
Many a lengthy league we've rowed,
Still the sparrow on the spray,
Hastes to usher in the day
With her simple stanza'd ode.

The Breeze's Invitation

Come let's roam the breezy pastures,
Where the freest zephyrs blow,
Batten on the oak tree's rustle,
And the pleasant insect bustle,
Dripping with the streamlet's flow.

What if I no wings do wear,
Thro' this solid seeming air
I can skim like any swallow
Who so dareth let her follow,
And we'll be a jovial pair.

Like two careless swifts let's sail,
Zephyrus shall think for me—
Over hill and over dale,
Riding on the easy gale,
We will scan the earth and sea.

Yonder see that willow tree
Winnowing the buxom air,
You a gnat and I a bee,
With our merry minstrelsy
We will make a concert there.

One green leaf shall be our screen,
Till the sun doth go to bed,
I the king and you the queen
Of that peaceful little green,
Without any subject's aid.

To our music Time will linger,
And earth open wide her ear,
Nor shall any need to tarry
To immortal verse to marry
Such sweet music as he'll hear.

Stanzas

Nature doth have her dawn each day,
But mine are far between;
Content, I cry, for sooth to say,
Mine brightest are, I ween.

For when my sun doth deign to rise,
Though it be her noontide,
Her fairest field in shadow lies,
Nor can my light abide.

Sometimes I bask me in her day,
Conversing with my mate;
But if we interchange one ray,
Forthwith her heats abate.

Through his discourse I climb and see,
As from some eastern hill,
A brighter morrow rise to me
Than lieth in her skill.

As 't were two summer days in one,
Two Sundays come together,
Our rays united make one Sun,
With fairest summer weather.

Loves Farewell

Light hearted, careless, shall I take my way,
When I to thee this being have resigned,
Well knowing where upon a future day,
With usurer's craft, more than myself to find.

Each more melodious note I hear
Brings this reproach to me,
That I alone afford the ear,
Who would the music be.

The Fisher's Son

I know the world where land and water meet,
By yonder hill abutting on the main,
One while I hear the waves incessant beat,
Then turning round survey the land again.

Within a humble cot that looks to sea
Daily I breathe this curious warm life,
Beneath a friendly haven's sheltering lea
My noiseless day with myst'ry still is rife.

'Tis here, they say, my simple life began,
And easy credit to the tale I lend,
For well I know 'tis here I am a man,
But who will simply tell me of the end?

These eyes fresh opened spied the far off Sea,
Which like a silent godfather did stand,
Nor uttered one explaining word to me,
But introduced straight godmother Land.

And yonder still stretches that silent main,
With many glancing ships besprinkled o'er,
And earnest still I gaze and gaze again
Upon the self same waves and friendly shore.

Till like a watery humor on the eye
It still appears whichever way I turn,
Its silent waste and mute oerarching sky
With close shut eyes I clearly still discern.

And yet with lingering doubt I haste each morn
To see if Ocean still my gaze will greet,
And with each day once more to life am born,
And tread the earth once more with tott'ring feet.

—

My years are like a stroll upon the beach,
As near the ocean's edge as I can go;
My tardy steps its waves sometimes o'erreach,
Sometimes I stay to let them overflow.

Infinite work my hands find there to do,
Gathering the relics which the waves up cast;
Each tempest scours the deep for something new,
And every time the strangest is the last.

My sole employment 'tis and scrupulous care,
To place my gains beyond the reach of tides,
Each smoother pebble and each shell more rare
Which Ocean kindly to my hand confides.

I have but few companions on the shore,
They scorn the strand who sail upon the sea,
Yet oft I think the ocean they've sailed oer
Is deeper known upon the strand to me.

My neighbors sometimes come with lumb'ring carts,
As if they wished my pleasant toil to share,
But straight they go again to distant marts
For only weeds and ballast are their care.

—

'Tis by some strange coincidence if I
Make common cause with Ocean when he storms
Who can so well support a separate sky,
And people it with multitude of forms.

Oft in the stillness of the night I hear
Some restless bird presage the coming din,
And distant murmurs faintly strike my ear
From some bold bluff projecting far within.

My stillest depths straightway do inly heave
More genially than rests the summer's calm,
The howling winds through my soul's cordage grieve,
Till every shelf and ledge gives the alarm.

Oft at some ruling star my tide has swelled,
The sea can scarcely brag more wrecks than I,
Ere other influence my waves has quelled
The staunchest bark that floats is high and dry.

Friendship

"Friends, Romans, Countrymen, and Lovers."

Let such pure hate still underprop
Our love, that we may be
Each other's conscience,
And have our sympathy
Mainly from thence.

We'll one another treat like gods,
And all the faith we have
In virtue and in truth, bestow
On either, and suspicion leave
To gods below.

Two solitary stars—
Unmeasured systems far
Between us roll,
But by our conscious light we are
Determined to one pole.

What need confound the sphere—
God can afford to wait,
For him no hour's too late
That witnesseth one duty's end,
Or to another doth beginning lend.

Love will subserve no use,
More than the tints of flowers,
Only the independent guest
Frequents its bowers,
Inherits its bequest.

No speech though kind has it,
But kinder silence doles
Unto its mates,
By night consoles,
By day congratulates.

What saith the tongue to tongue?
What heareth ear of ear?
By the decrees of fate
From year to year,
Does it communicate.

Pathless the gulf of feeling yawns—
No trivial bridge of words,
Or arch of boldest span,
Can leap the moat that girds
The sincere man.

No show of bolts and bars
Can keep the foeman out,
Or 'scape his secret mine
Who entered with the doubt
That drew the line.

No warder at the gate
Can let the friendly in,
But like the sun o'er all
He will the castle win,
And shine along the wall.

There's nothing in the world I know
That can escape from love,
For every depth it goes below,
And every height above.

It waits as waits the sky,
Until the clouds go by,
Yet shines serenely on
With an eternal day,
Alike when they are gone,
And when they stay.

Implacable is Love,—
Foes may be bought or teased
From their hostile intent,
But he goes unappeased
Who is on kindness bent.

The Freshet

——A stir is on the Worc'ter hills,
And Nobscott too the valley fills—
Where scarce you'd fill an acorn cup
In summer when the sun was up,
No more you'll find a cup at all,
But in its place a waterfall.

Oh that the moon were in conjunction
To the dry land's extremest unction,
Till every dyke and pier were flooded,
And all the land with islands studded,
For once to teach all human kind,
Both those that plough and those that grind,
There is no fixture in the land,
But all unstable is as sand.

———

———

The river swelleth more and more,
Like some sweet influence stealing o'er
The passive town; and for awhile
Each tussock makes a tiny isle,
Where, on some friendly Ararat,
Resteth the weary water rat.

No ripple shows Musketaquid,
Her very current e'en is hid,
As deepest souls do calmest rest
When thoughts are swelling in the breast;
And she that in the summer's drought
Doth make a rippling and a rout,
Sleeps from Nawshawtuct to the cliff,
Unruffled by a single skiff;
So like a deep and placid mind
Whose currents underneath it wind—
For by a thousand distant hills
The louder roar a thousand rills,
And many a spring which now is dumb,
And many a stream with smothered hum,
Doth faster well and swifter glide
Though buried deep beneath the tide.

Our village shows a rural Venice,
Its broad lagunes where yonder fen is,
Far lovelier than the Bay of Naples
Yon placid cove amid the maples,
And in my neighbor's field of corn
I recognise the Golden Horn.

Here Nature taught from year to year,
When only red men came to hear,
Methinks 'twas in this school of art
Venice and Naples learned their part,
But still their mistress, to my mind,
Her young disciples leaves behind.

The Poet's Delay

In vain I see the morning rise,
In vain observe the western blaze,
Who idly look to other skies,
Expecting life by other ways.

Amidst such boundless wealth without,
I only still am poor within,
The birds have sung their summer out,
But still my spring does not begin.

Shall I then wait the autumn wind,
Compelled to seek a milder day,
And leave no curious nest behind,
No woods still echoing to my lay?

The Summer Rain

My books I'd fain cast off, I cannot read,
'Twixt every page my thoughts go stray at large
Down in the meadow, where is richer feed,
And will not mind to hit their proper targe.

Plutarch was good, and so was Homer too,
Our Shakspeare's life was rich to live again,
What Plutarch read that was not good nor true,
Nor Shakspeare's books, unless his books were men.

Here while I lie beneath this walnut bough,
What care I for the Greeks, or for Troy town,
If juster battles are enacted now
Between the ants upon this hummock's crown.

Bid Homer wait till I the issue learn,
If red or black the gods will favor most,
Or yonder Ajax will the phalanx turn,
Struggling to heave some rock against the host.

Tell Shakspeare to attend some leisure hour,
For now I've business with this drop of dew,
And see you not, the clouds prepare a shower,—
I'll meet him shortly when the sky is blue.

This bed of herdsgrass and wild oats was spread
Last year with nicer skill than monarchs use,
A clover tuft is pillow for my head,
And violets quite overtop my shoes.

And now the cordial clouds have shut all in,
And gently swells the wind to say all's well,
The scattered drops are falling fast and thin,
Some in the pond, some in the lily bell.

Drip, drip the trees for all the country round,
And richness rare distils from every bough,
The wind alone it is makes every sound,
Shaking down crystals on the leaves below.

For shame the sun will never show himself,
Who could not with his beams e'er melt me so,
My dripping locks—they would become an elf
Who in a beaded coat does gaily go.

Guido's Aurora

The God of day rolls his car up the slopes,
Reining his prancing steeds with steady hand,
The moon's pale orb through western shadows gropes,
While morning sheds its light o'er sea and land.

Castles and cities by the sounding main
Resound with all the busy din of life,
The fisherman unfurls his sails again
And the recruited warrior bides the strife.

The early breeze ruffles the poplar leaves,
The curling waves reflect the washed light,
The slumbering sea with the day's impulse heaves,
While o'er the western hills retires the drowsy night.

The sea birds dip their bills in ocean's foam,
Far circling out over the frothy waves—

I've heard my neighbor's pump at night,
Long after Lyra sunk her light,
As if it were a natural sound,
And proper utterance of the ground—
Perchance some bittern in a fen—
Or else the squeak of a meadow hen.

Who sleeps by day and walks by night,
Will meet no spirit but some sprite.

When with pale cheek and sunken eye I sang
Unto the slumbering world at midnights hour,
How it no more resounded with war's clang,
And virtue was decayed in Peace's bower;

How in these days no hero was abroad,
But puny men, afraid of war's alarms,
Stood forth to fight the battles of their Lord,
Who scarce could stand beneath a hero's arms;

A faint, reproachful, reassuring strain,
From some harp's strings touched by unskilful hands
Brought back the days of chivalry again,
And the surrounding fields made holy lands.

A bustling camp and an embattled host
Extending far on either hand I saw,
For I alone had slumbered at my post,
Dreaming of peace when all around was war.

I arose before light
To work with all my might,
With my arms braced for toil
Which no obstacle could foil,
For it robbed me of my rest
Like an anvil on my breast.

But as a brittle cup
I've held the hammer up,
And no sound from my forge
Has been heard in the gorge.
I look forward into night,
And seem to get some light;
E're long the forge will ring
With its ding-dong-ding,
For the iron will be hot
And my wages will be got.

I'm guided in the darkest night
By flashes of auroral light,
Which over dart thy eastern home
And teach me not in vain to roam.
Thy steady light on t'other side
Pales the sunset, makes day abide,
And after sunrise stays the dawn,
Forerunner of a brighter morn.

There is no being here to me
But staying here to be
When others laugh I am not glad,
When others cry I am not sad,
But be they grieved or be they merry
I'm supernumerary.
I am a miser without blame

Am conscience stricken without shame.
An idler am I without leisure,
A busy body without pleasure.
I did not think so bright a day
Would issue in so dark a night.
I did not think such sober play
Would leave me in so sad a plight,
And I should be most sorely spent
Where first I was most innocent.
I thought by loving all beside
To prove to you my love was wide,
And by the rites I soared above
To show you my peculiar love.

———

    Friends—
They cannot help,
They cannot hurt,
Nor in indifference rest,
But when for a host's service girt,
They are a mutual guest.

They are a single power
Plenipotentiary,
No minister of state,
Anxious and wary
Decides their fate.

Where interest's self is
There is no go-between,
But where another reaps,
They do but glean
In scanty heaps.

They have learned well to hate,
And never grant reprieve,
Nor e'er succumb to love,
But sternly grieve,
And look above.

—

If faults arise, my friend will send for me
As some great god,
Who will the matter try,
Holding the scales, even or odd,
Under the sky—

Who will award strict justice
All the while,
Confounding mine and thine,
And share his smile,
When they 'gainst me incline.

—

When in some cove I lie,
A placid lake at rest,
Scanning the distant hills,
A murmur from the west,
And gleam of thousand rills
Which gently swell my breast,
Announce the friendly thought,
And in one wave sun-lit
I'm softly brought
Seaward with it.

—

Who hears the parson
Will not hear the bell,
But if he deafly pass on
He will hear of hell.

I' faith the people go to church
To leave the devil in the lurch,
But since they've carpeted the pews
To squat with hymn book he doth use.

Sic Vita

I am a parcel of vain strivings tied
     By a chance bond together,
   Dangling this way and that, their links
      Were made so loose and wide,
         Methinks,
       For milder weather.

A bunch of violets without their roots,
     And sorrel intermixed,
   Encircled by a wisp of straw
      Once coiled about their shoots,
        The law
       By which I'm fixed.

A nosegay which Time clutched from out
     Those fair Elysian fields,
   With weeds and broken stems, in haste,
      Doth make the rabble rout
        That waste
       The day he yields.

And here I bloom for a short hour unseen,
     Drinking my juices up,
   Which have no root in the land
      To keep my branches green,

But stand
In a bare cup.

Some tender buds were left upon my stem
In mimicry of life,
But ah! the children will not know
Till time has withered them,
The woe
With which they're rife.

But now I see I was not plucked for nought,
And after in life's vase
Of glass set while I might survive,
But by a kind hand brought
Alive
To a strange place.

That stock thus thinned will soon redeem its hours,
And by another year
Such as God knows, with freer air,
More fruits and fairer flowers
Will bear,
While I droop here.

———

Wait not till I invite thee, but observe
I'm glad to see thee when thou com'st.

Friendship

Now we are partners in such legal trade,
We'll look to the beginnings, not the ends,
Nor to pay day—knowing true wealth is made
For current stock and not for dividends.

On the Sun Coming Out in the Afternoon

Methinks all things have travelled since you shined,
But only Time, and clouds, Time's team, have moved;
Again foul weather shall not change my mind,
But In the shade I will believe what in the sun I loved.

———

They who prepare my evening meal below
Carelessly hit the kettle as they go
With tongs or shovel,
And ringing round and round,
Out of this hovel
It makes an eastern temple by the sound.

At first I thought a cow-bell right at hand
Mid birches sounded o'er the open land,
Where I plucked flowers
Many years ago,
Spending midsummer hours
With such secure delight they hardly seemed to flow.

———

My ground is high,
But 'tis not dry,
What you call dew
Comes filtering through;
Though in the sky,
It still is nigh;
Its soil is blue
And virgin too.

———

If from your price ye will not swerve,
Why then Ill think the gods reserve
A greater bargain there above,
Out of their sup'rabundant love,
Have meantime better for me cared,
And so will get my stock prepared,
Plows of new pattern, hoes the same,
Designed a different soil to tame,
And sow my seed broadcast in air,
Certain to reap my harvest there.

————

Death cannot come too soon
Where it can come at all,
But always is too late
Unless the fates it call.

The Mountains in the Horizon

With frontier strength ye stand your ground—
With grand content ye circle round—
Tumultuous silence for all sound,
Ye springing nursery of rills,
Monadnock and the Peterborough hills—
Staid argument that never stirs,
Outcircling the philosophers.
While we enjoy a lingering ray,
Ye still oertop the western day,
Reposing yonder on God's croft
Like solid stacks of hay.
The iris of the sky,
Ye run
Round the horizon of its eye
Whose pupil is the sun.

Upon a fresh and airy day,
When our globe ploughs its way
In salter seas of light,
Right opposite the bight
Of some elysian bay,
Ye are its dorsal fin,
Tossing th'etherial spray
With breezy din.
From on Fair Haven's pier,
For many a year.
I've seen ye westward bound,
Without a sound,
Like some vast fleet
Sailing through rain and sleet,
Through winters cold and summer's heat.
Ships of the line each one
That westward run,
Always before the gale,
Under a press of sail,
Convoying clouds
Which cluster in your shrouds—
With your slant masts 'tis sixes and sevens
But that ye rake the heavens,
So near the edge ye go,
Under the roof so low;
With weight of metal all untold,
I seem to feel ye in my firm seat here,
Immeasurable depth of hold,
And breadth of beam, and length of running gear.
The vessels on the sea
Are relative to ye,
Sailing by sympathy.
Late enterprises of mankind
Some near income to find.
Flitting from shore to shore,
Their voyages soon are oer,
But ye hold on upon your high emprise,
Until ye find a shore
Amid the skies.

Crossing the pliant flood
By swifter period,
They with the noontide weigh,
And glide before its ray
To some retired bay,
Their haunt—
Whence under tropic sun,
They ceaseless run,
Bearing gum Senegal and Tragicant.
For such small ends
Time gladly spends
Itself into eternity,
For this was ocean meant,
For this the sun was sent,
And moon was lent,
And 'tis the winds' employment.
Time waits but till the field is tilled,
With such small deeds
His lap is filled
As that with seeds.

Man's little acts are grand
Beheld from land to land,
There as they lie in time
Within their native clime
For which the world did wait,
They are so great.
    No doubt that in the port from whence ye hail
    Your masters did not fail
    To register your wealth,
    For ye sail not by stealth,
    Skulking close in to land,
    With cargo contraband,
    But they who sent a venture out by ye
    Have set the sun to see
    Their honesty.

Especial I remember thee,
Wachusett, who like me
Standest alone without society.

My life is like a western sky
Unto an eastern eye
Of calm repose,
Each moment tinted variously
As the wind blows.
Now streaming like the northern light,
Each yet more north, more high, more bright,
Subsiding on the shores of night,
Like yonder field of grain
It alway doth remain
Firm at its root,
Bending through all its length
With graceful strength,
Only the shadows glide
From side to side,
But still the deep grain doth abide.
  Anon it sighs along
  Like the breath of a song,
  Or the wind on the sedge,
  Or a tempest on the ledge,
  First swells then dies away
  Like a harp strain,
  Only a string doth stay
  To invite the wind again,—
  But thou art far and blue and still,
  Mocking my infirm will,
  Thou steadfast hill.
  Upholding heaven, holding down earth,
  Thy pastime from thy birth,
  Not steadied by the one nor leaning on the other,
  May I approve myself thy worthy brother.

  Thy far blue eye,
  A remnant of the sky,
  See through the clearing or the gorge,
  Or from the windows of the forge
  Doth leaven all it passes by.
  Thou art our rostrum in the west,
  Some ancient victory's bequest,

With nature's trophies fringed,
And natural colors tinged,
Not with the Tyrian dye,
But with the azure of the sky
Fronting an amphitheater of glory
Greater than Greek or Roman story—
Their old nobility westering with the sun,
Here to be done, perchance, or else begun.

Nothing is true
But stands 'tween me and you,
Thou western pioneer
Who know'st not shame nor fear,
By venturous spirit driven
Under the eaves of heaven,
And canst expand thee there?
And breath enough of air?
The sun doth go behind thee not before,
Briefly to mend his store,
Even beyond the west
With thy small stock thou migratest
Into unclouded tracts,
Without a pilgrims axe,
Upon a loftier way
Than our low western rout,
Cleaving thy road on high
With thy well tempered brow,
And mak'st thyself a clearing in the sky.

⁓

The needles of the pine,
All to the west incline.

The Echo of the Sabbath Bell—

heard in the Woods

Dong—sounds the brass in the east—
As if for a civic feast,
But I like that sound the best
Out of the fluttering west.

The steeple rings a knell,
But the fairies' silvery bell
Is the voice of that gentle folk—
Or else the horizon that spoke.

Its metal is not of brass,
But air and water and glass,
And under a cloud it is swung,
And by the wind is rung,
With a slim silver tongue

When the steeple tolls the noon
It soundeth not so soon,
Yet it rings an earlier hour,
And the sun has not reached its tower.

———

Low in the eastern sky
Is set thy glancing eye;
And though its gracious light
Ne'er riseth to my sight,
Yet every star that climbs
Above the gnarled limbs
  Of yonder hill,
Conveys thy gentle will.

Believe I knew thy thought,
And that the zephyrs brought
Thy kindest wishes through,
As mine they bear to you,

That some attentive cloud
Did pause amid the crowd
    Over my head,
While gentle things were said.

Believe the thrushes sung,
And that the flower-bells rung,
That herbs exhaled their scent,
And beasts knew what was meant,
The trees a welcome waved,
And lakes their margins laved,
    When thy free mind
To my retreat did wind.

It was a summer eve,
The air did gently heave
While yet a low-hung cloud
Thy eastern skies did shroud;
The lightning's silent gleam,
Startling my drowsy dream,
    Seemed like the flash
Under thy dark eyelash.

Still will I strive to be
As if thou wert with me;
Whatever path I take,
It shall be for thy sake,
Of gentle slope and wide,
As thou wert by my side,
    Without a root
To trip thy gentle foot.

I'll walk with gentle pace,
And choose the smoothest place,
And careful dip the oar,
And shun the winding shore,
And gently steer my boat
Where water-lilies float,
    And cardinal flowers
Stand in their sylvan bowers.

My life has been the poem I would have writ,
But I could not both live and utter it.

To the Mountains

And when the sun puts out his lamp
We'll sleep serene within the camp,
Trusting to his invet'rate skill
Who leads the stars oer yonder hill,
Whose discipline doth never cease
To watch the slumberings of peace,
And from the virtuous hold afar
The melancholy din of war.—
For ye our sentries still outlie,
The earth your pallet and your screen the sky.

From steadfastness I will not swerve
Remembering my sweet reserve.

With all your kindness shown from year to year
Ye do but civil demons still appear,
Still to my mind
Ye are inhuman and unkind,
And bear an untamed aspect to my sight
After the "civil-suited" night
As if ye had lain out
Like to the Indian scout
Who lingers in the purlieus of the towns
With unexplored grace and savage frowns.

Greater is the depth of sadness
Than is any height of gladness.

Where I have been
There was none seen.

Better wait
Than be too late.

Independence
My life more civil is and free
Than any civil polity.

Ye princes keep your realms
And circumscribed power,
Not wide as are my dreams,
Nor rich as is this hour.

What can ye give which I have not?
What can ye take which I have got?
Can ye defend the dangerless?
Can ye inherit nakedness?

To all true wants times ear is deaf,
Penurious states lend no relief
Out of their pelf—
But a free soul—thank God—
Can help itself.

Be sure your fate
Doth keep apart its state—
Not linked with any band—
Even the nobles of the land

In tented fields with cloth of gold—
No place doth hold
But is more chivalrous than they are.
And sigheth for a nobler war.
A finer strain its trumpet sings—
A brighter gleam its armor flings.

The life that I aspire to live
No man proposeth me—
No trade upon the street
Wears its emblazonry.

Cock-crowing

Upon my bed at early dawn
I hear the cocks proclaim the day,
Though the moon shines serenely on,
As if her queenly course they could not stay—

—

Nor pull her down with their faint din
From riding at that lofty height,
Who in her shining knows no sin,
As if unconscious of a nobler light.

—

Far in the east their larum rings,
As if a watchful host there thronged,
Where now its early clarion sings,
So bravely is their martial note prolonged.

—

One on more distant perch, more clear,
But fainter brags him still,
But ah! he promises, I fear,
More than his master's household will fulfill.

—

The stars withhold their shining not
Or singly or in scattered crowds,
But seem like Parthian arrows shot
By yielding night 'mid the advancing clouds.

—

Some wakeful steer exalts his trump
Afar oer the sonorous ground,
And with a sounding eastern pomp
It grandly marcheth the horizon round.

—

Invades each recess of the wood,
Awakes each slumbering bird,
Till every fowl leads forth her brood,
Which on her nest the tuneful summons heard.

—

Methinks that Time has reached his prime,
Eternity is in the flower,
I hear their faint confused chime
Now ushering in the sacred hour.

—

Over the hill top I have run
For fear to be too late,
I've left behind the luggard sun,
Travelling at such a rate,
To be in at creation,
To be up with fate.

—

And has time got so forward then?
From what perennial fount of joy,
Do ye inspire the hearts of men,
And teach them how the day-light to employ?

—

From your abundance pray impart
Who dost so freely spill,
Some bravery unto my heart,
Or let me taste of thy perennial rill.

———

There is such health and length of years
In the elixir of that note,
That God himself more young appears,
And a more youthful world through space doth float.

The tidy night with woolen feet,
I'm sure has lately passed this way,
And with her trim despatch so neat,
She has arranged the furniture of the day.

———

In yon thin sheet of mist spread oer
The lowland trees of leaves bereft,
Which round her head at eve she wore,
Methinks I see the housewife's duster left.

———

The fragrant mist exhales the scent
Of aromatic herbs, so you
Would say she blest whereer she went,
And through the fields had sprinkled perfumed dew.

Inspiration

Whate'er we leave to God, God does,
   And blesses us;
The work we choose should be our own,
   God lets alone.

———

If with light head erect I sing,
Though all the muses lend their force,
From my poor love of anything,
The verse is weak and shallow as its source.

—

But if with bended neck I grope,
Listening behind me for my wit,
With faith superior to hope,
More anxious to keep back than forward it,

—

Making my soul accomplice there
Unto the flame my heart hath lit,
Then will the verse forever wear,
Time cannot bend the line which God hath writ.

—

Always the general show of things
Floats in review before my mind,
And such true love and reverence brings,
That sometimes I forget that I am blind.

—

But soon there comes unsought, unseen,
Some clear divine electuary,
And I, who had but sensual been,
Grow sensible, and as God is am wary.

I hearing get who had but ears,
And sight who had but eyes before,
I moments live who lived but years,
And truth discern who knew but learning's lore.

—

I hear beyond the range of sound,
I see beyond the verge of sight,
New earths—new skies—new seas—around,
And in my noon the sun doth pale his light.

—

A clear and ancient harmony
Peirces my soul through all its din,
As through its utmost melody,
Further behind than they, further within.

—

More swift its bolt than lightning is,
Its voice than thunder is more loud,
It doth expand my privacies
To all, and leave me single in the crowd.

—

It speaks with such authority,
With so serene and lofty tone,
That idle Time runs gadding by,
And leaves me with Eternity alone.

—

Then chiefly is my natal hour,
And only then my prime of life,
Of manhood's strength it is the flower,
'T is peace's end and wars beginning strife.

—

'T hath come in summer's broadest noon,
By a grey wall or some chance place,
Unseasoned time, insulted June,
And vexed the day with its presuming face.

—

Such fragrance round my sleep it makes,
More rich than are Arabian drugs,
That my soul scents its life, and wakes
The body up—from 'neath its perfumed rugs.

—

—

Such is the Muse—the heavenly maid,
The star that guides our mortal course,
Which shows where life's true kernel's laid,
Its wheat's fine flower, and its undying force.

———

Who with one breath attunes the spheres,
And also my poor human heart,
With one impulse propels the years
Around, and gives my throbbing pulse its start.

———

I will not doubt forever more,
Nor falter from an iron faith,
For if the system be turned oer,
God takes not back the word which once he saith.

———

I will believe the love untold,
Which not my worth nor want hath bought,
Which wood me young and woos me old,
And call the stars to witness now my thought.

———

My memory I'll educate
To know the one historic truth,
Remembering to the latest date
The only true, and sole immortal youth.

———

Be but thy inspiration given,
No matter through what dangers sought,
I'll fathom hell or climb to heaven,
And yet esteem that cheap which love has bought.

Fame cannot tempt the bard
    Who's famous with his God,
    Nor laurel him reward,
    Who hath his maker's nod.

The Soul's Season

Thank God who seasons thus the year,
And sometimes kindly slants his rays,
For in his winter he's most near,
And plainest seen upon the shortest days.

———

Who gently tempers now his heats,
And then his harsher cold, lest we
Should surfeit on the Summer's sweets,
Or pine upon the Winter's crudity.

———

Grown tired of this rank summer's wealth,
Its raw and superficial show,
I fain would hie away by stealth
Where no roads meet, but still 't doth trivial grow.

———

Methinks by dalliance it hath caught
The shallow habits of the town,
Itself infected most, which ought
With sterner face upon our tameness frown.

———

A sober mind will walk alone
Apart from nature if need be,
And only its own seasons own,
For nature having its humanity.

———

Sometimes a late Autumnal thought
Has crossed my mind in green July,
And to its early freshness brought
Late ripened fruits and an autumnal sky.

A dry but golden thought which gleamed
Across the greenness of my mind,
And prematurely wise it seemed,
Too ripe 'mid summer's youthful bowers to find.

—

So have I seen one yellow leaf
Amid the glossy leaves of June,
Which pensive hung, though not with grief,
Like some fair flower, it had changed so soon.

—

I scent my med'cine from afar,
Where the rude simpler of the year,
October leads the rustling war,
And strews his honors on the summer's bier.

The Fall of the Leaf

Grown tired of this rank summer's wealth,
    Its raw and superficial show,
I fain would hie away by stealth
    Where no roads meet, but still 't doth trivial grow.

A sober mind will walk alone,
    Apart from nature if need be,
And only its own seasons own,
    For nature having its humanity.

Sometimes a late autumnal thought
    Has crossed my mind in green July,
And to its early freshness brought
    Late ripend fruits and an autumnal sky.

A dry but golden thought which gleamed
    Athwart the greenness of my mind,
And prematurely wise it seemed,
    Too ripe mid summer's youthful bowers to find.

So have I seen one yellow leaf
    Amid the glossy leaves of June,
Which pensive hung, though not with grief,
    Like some fair flower, it had changed so soon.

I scent my med'cine from afar,
  Where the rude simpler of the year
October leads the rustling war,
  And strews his honors on the summer's bier.

The evening of the year draws on,
  The fields a later aspect wear,
Since summer's garishness is gone
  Some grains of night tincture the noontide air.

Behold the shadows of the trees
  Now circle wider 'bout their stem,
Like sentries which by slow degrees
  Perform their rounds, gently protecting them.

And as the season doth decline
  The sun affords a scantier light,
Behind each needle of the pine
  There lurks a small auxiliar of the night.

After each shrub and straggling fence
  That marks the meadow's pensive green,
And shows the meadow's opulence,
  Evening's insidious foot at noon is seen.

Wave upon wave a mellower air
  Flows over all the region,
As if there were some tincture there
  Of ripeness caught from the long summer's sun.

I hear the cricket's slumbrous lay
  Around, beneath me, and on high,
It rocks the night, it lulls the day,
  And everywhere 'tis nature's lullaby.

But most he chirps beneath the sod,
  Where he hath made his winter's bed,
His creak grown fainter, but more broad,
  A film of autumn o'er the summer spread.

Upon my bed at early dawn
   I hear the cocks proclaim the day,
Though the moon shines serenely on
   As if her queenly course they could not stay;

Nor pull her down with their faint din
   From riding at that lofty height,
Who in her shining knows no sin,
   But is unconscious of a nobler light.

The stars withhold their shining not
   Or singly or in scattered crowds,
But seem like Parthian arrows shot
   By yielding night 'mid the advancing clouds.

And has time got so forward then?
   From what perennial fount of joy
Do ye inspire the hearts of men,
   And teach them how the daylight to employ?

From your abundance pray impart,
   Who dost so freely spill,
Some bravery unto my heart,
   Or let me taste of thy perennial rill.

Small birds in fleets migrating by
   Now beat across some meadow's bay,
And as they tack and veer on high,
   With faint and hurried click beguile the way.

The moon is ripe fruit in the sky
   Which overhangs her harvest now,
The sun doth break his stem well nigh
   From summer's height he has declined so low.

The greedy earth doth pluck his fruit,
   And cast it in night's lap,
The stars more brightly glisten, mute
   Though their tears be, to see their lords mishap.

The harvest rattles in the wind,
   Ripe apples overhang the hay,
The cereal flavor of my mind
   Natheless, tells me I am as ripe as they.

I hearing get who had but ears,
   And sight who had but eyes before,
I moments live who lived but years,
   And truth discern who knew but learning's lore.

Far in the woods these golden days
   Some leaf obeys its maker's call,
And through their hollow aisles it plays
   With delicate touch the prelude of the fall.

Gently withdrawing from its stem
   It lightly lays itself along,
Where the same hand hath pillowed them
   Resigned to sleep upon the old year's throng.

The loneliest birch is brown and sere,
   The farthest pool is strewn with leaves,
Which float upon their watery bier,
   Where is no eye that sees, no heart that grieves.

I marked when first the wind grew rude
   Each leaf curled like a living thing,
As if with the ripe air it would
   Secure some faint memorial of the spring.

Then for its sake it turned a boat
   And dared new elements to brave,
A painted palace which did float
   A summer's hoarded wealth to save.

Oh could I catch these sounds remote,
   Could I preserve to human ear,
The strains which on the breezes float,
   And sing the requiem of the dying year.

I stood beside an oaken copse
    When the first gale of autumn sighed,
It gently waved the birch tree tops
    Then rustled the oak leaves and died

But not the strains which it awoke,
    For in my inmost sense I hear
The melody of which it spoke
    Still faintly rising on my inward ear.

A ripple on the river fell,
    A shadow o'er the landscape passed,
And still the whispering ferns could tell
    Whither the stranger travelled so fast.

How stand the cottages of men
    In these so fair October days,
Along the wood along the fen
    I see them looming through the mellow haze.

Immersed in Nature there they lie
    Against some cliff or chestnuts shade
Scarce obvious to the travellers eye
    Who thoughtful traverses the forest glade.

The harvest lies about the door
    The chestnut drops its burs around
As if they were the stock that bore
    The yellow crops that strew the ground.

The lily loves the river's tide
    The meadow's are the daisy's haunt
The aspens on the mountain side
    Here child of nature grows the human plant.

The jay screams through the chestnut wood
    The crisped and yellow leaves around
Are hue and texture of my mood,
    And these rough burs my heirlooms on the ground.

The thread bare trees so poor and thin
    They are no wealthier than I,
But with as brave a core within
    They rear their boughs to the October sky.

Poor knights they are which bravely wait
    The charge of winter's cavalry,
Keeping a simple Roman state
    Discumbered of their Persian luxury.

Thank God who seasons thus the year
    And sometimes kindly slants his rays,
For in his winter he's most near
    And plainest seen upon the shortest days.

Who gently tempers now his heats
    And then his harsher cold, lest we
Should surfeit on the summer's sweets,
    Or pine upon the winter's crudity.

Delay

No generous action can delay
Or thwart our higher, steadier aims,
But if sincere and true are they,
It will arouse our sight and nerve our frames.

Inspiration

If thou wilt but stand by my ear,
When through the field thy anthem's rung,
When that is done I will not fear
But the same power will abet my tongue.

———

Ive searched my faculties around
To learn why life to me was lent
I will attend his faintest sound
And then declare to man what God hath meant

———

Who equallest the coward's haste
And still inspires the faintest heart
Whose lofty fame is not disgraced
Though it assume the lowest part

The Vireo

Upon the lofty elm tree sprays
The vireo rings the changes sweet,
During the trivial summer days,
Striving to lift our thoughts above the street.

———

The coward ever sings no song,
He listens to no chime,
He has no heart, he has no tongue,
To build the lofty rhyme.

———

Only the slave knows of the slave,
Only the free the free,
For what ye principally have,
That only can ye see.

———

Great God, I ask thee for no meaner pelf
Than that I may not disappoint myself,
That in my action I may soar as high,
As I can now discern with this clear eye.

And next in value, which thy kindness lends,
That I may greatly disappoint my friends,
Howe'er they think or hope that it may be,
They may not dream how thou'st distinguished me.

That my weak hand may equal my firm faith,
And my life practice more than my tongue saith;
That my low conduct may not show,
Nor my relenting lines,
That I thy purpose did not know,
Or overrated thy designs.

The Inward Morning

Packed in my mind lie all the clothes
    Which outward nature wears,
And in its fashion's hourly change
    It all things else repairs.

In vain I look for change abroad,
    And can no difference find,
Till some new ray of peace uncalled
    Illumes my inmost mind.

What is it gilds the trees and clouds,
    And paints the heavens so gay,
But yonder fast abiding light
    With its unchanging ray?

Lo, when the sun streams through the wood
    Upon a winter's morn,
Wher'er his silent beams intrude
    The murky night is gone.

How could the patient pine have known
    The morning breeze would come,
Or humble flowers anticipate
    The insect's noonday hum?

Till the new light with morning cheer
    From far streamed through the aisles,
And nimbly told the forest trees
    For many stretching miles.

I've heard within my inmost soul
    Such cheerful morning news,
In the horizon of my mind
    Have seen such orient hues,

As in the twilight of the dawn,
    When the first birds awake,
Are heard within some silent wood,
    Where they the small twigs break,

Or in the eastern skies are seen,
    Before the sun appears,
The harbingers of summer heats
    Which from afar he bears.

Within the circuit of this plodding life
There enter moments of an azure hue,
Untarnished fair as is the violet
Or anemone, when the spring strews them
By some meandering rivulet, which make
The best philosophy untrue that aims
But to console man for his grievances.
I have remembered when the winter came,
High in my chamber in the frosty nights,
When in the still light of the cheerful moon,
On every twig and rail and jutting spout,
The icy spears were adding to their length
Against the arrows of the coming sun,
How in the shimmering noon of summer past
Some unrecorded beam slanted across
The upland pastures where the Johnswort grew;
Or heard, amid the verdure of my mind,
The bee's long smothered hum, on the blue flag
Loitering amidst the mead; or busy rill,
Which now through all its course stands still and dumb
Its own memorial,— purling at its play
Along the slopes, and through the meadows next,
Until its youthful sound was hushed at last
In the staid current of the lowland stream;
Or seen the furrows shine but late upturned,
And where the fieldfare followed in the rear,
When all the fields around lay bound and hoar
Beneath a thick integument of snow.
So by God's cheap economy made rich
To go upon my winter's task again.

To Edith

Thou little bud of being, Edith named,
With whom I've made acquaintance on this earth,
Who knowest me without impediment,
As flowers know the winds that stir their leaves,

And rid'st upon my shoulders as the sphere,
Turning on me thy sage reserved eye,
Behind whose broad & charitable gaze
Floats the still true & universal soul
With the pure azure of the general day,
Not yet a peopled & a vulgar town,
Rather a pure untarnished country ground;
For thou art whole, not yet begun to die,
While men look on me with their shrivelled rays
Streaming through some small chink of the broad sky;
Pure youthful soul, thou hast begun to be,
To cumulate thy sin & piety.

Delay in Friendship

The blossoms on the tree
Swell not too fast for me.
God does not want quick work but sure
Not to be tempted by so cheap a lure.

Owing to slow steps I shall be never
By my friend out run,
More than the tide can land from ocean sever,
Or earth distance the sun.

The friend is patient, he can stay
Some centuries yet,
Though then I may not get
So on my way
As fit to be his mate.

Wilt thou not wait for me my friend,
Or give a longer lease?
Why think I can wait for myself,
If so I please.

Now as ye take one step away
Thinking to leave me here—
The heavens will still beyond ye lay,
And though ye are far they will be near.

Ye will be pilgrims on the road
Whither my heart has single gone,
And never looks back from its abode
On ye thus left forlorn.

Love equals swift and slow
And high & low—
Racer and lame—
The hunter and his game.

———

Ah, 'tis in vain the peaceful din
    That wakes the ignoble town,
Not thus did braver spirits win
    A patriot's renown.

There is one field beside this stream,
    Wherein no foot does fall,
But yet it beareth in my dream
    A richer crop than all.

Let me believe a dream so dear,
    Some heart beat high that day,
Above the petty Province here,
    And Britain far away;

Some hero of the ancient mould,
    Some arm of knightly worth,
Of strength unbought, and faith unsold,
    Honored this spot of earth;

Who sought the prize his heart described,
    And did not ask release,
Whose free-born valor was not bribed
    By prospect of a peace.

The men who stood on yonder height
    That day are long since gone;
Not the same hand directs the fight
    And monumental stone.

Ye were the Grecian cities then,
    The Romes of modern birth,
Where the New England husbandmen
    Have shown a Roman worth.

In vain I search a foreign land
    To find our Bunker Hill,
And Lexington and Concord stand
    By no Laconian rill.

———

Between the traveller and the setting sun,
Upon some drifting sand heap of the shore,
A hound stands o'er the carcass of a man.

———

Have ye no work for a man to do—
No earnest work that will expand the frame,
And give a soundness to the muscles too?
How ye do waste your time!
Pray make it worth the while to live,
Or worth the while to die.
Show us great actions piled on high,
Tasking our utmost strength touching the sky,

As if we lived in a mountainous country.
   Hell were not quite so hard to bear
  If one were honored with its hottest place.
And did ye fear ye should spoil Hell
By making it sublime?

———

I sailed up a river with a pleasant wind,
New lands, new people, and new thoughts to find;
Many fair reaches and headlands appeared,
And many dangers were there to be feared;
But when I remember where I have been,
And the fair landscapes that I have seen,
THOU seemest the only permanent shore,
The cape never rounded, nor wandered o'er.

———

I was made erect and lone
And within me is the bone
Still my vision will be clear
Still my life will not be drear
To the center all is near
Where I sit there is my throne
If age choose to sit apart
If age choose give me the start
Take the sap and leave the heart

———

I'm not alone
If I stand by myself,
But more than one,
And not in my own pelf.

I'm understood
If my intent is good,
For who obeys
The truth finds his own praise.

Our Country

It is a noble country where we dwell,
Fit for a stalwart race to summer in;
From Madawaska to Red River raft,
From Florid keys to the Missouri forks,
See what unwearied (and) copious streams
Come tumbling to the east and southern shore,
To find a man stand on their lowland banks:
Behold the innumerous rivers and the licks
Where he may drink to quench his summer's thirst,
And the broad corn and rice fields yonder, where
His hands may gather for his winter's store.

See the fair reaches of the northern lakes
To cool his summer with their inland breeze,
And the long slumbering Appalachian range
Offering its slopes to his unwearied knees!
See what a long-lipped sea doth clip the shores,
And noble strands where navies may find port;
See Boston, Baltimore, and New York stand
Fair in the sunshine on the eastern sea,
And yonder too the fair green prairie.

See the red race with sullen step retreat,
Emptying its graves, striking the wigwam tent,
And where the rude camps of its brethern stand,
Dotting the distant green, their herds around;

In serried ranks, and with a distant clang,
Their fowl fly o'er, bound to the northern lakes,
Whose plashing waves invite their webbéd feet.
Such the fair reach and prospect of the land,
The journeying summer creeps from south to north
With wearied feet, resting in many a vale;
Its length doth tire the seasons to o'ercome,
Its widening breadth doth make the sea-breeze pause
And spend its breath against the mountain's side:
Still serene Summer paints the southern fields,
While the stern Winter reigns on northern hills.

Look nearer,—know the lineaments of each face,—
Learn the far-travelled race, and find here met
The so long gathering congress of the world!
The Afric race brought here to curse its fate,
Erin to bless,—the patient German too,
Th' industrious Swiss, the fickle, sanguine Gaul,
And manly Saxon, leading all the rest.
All things invite this earth's inhabitants
To rear their lives to an unheard-of height,
And meet the expectation of the land;
To give at length the restless race of man
A pause in the long westering caravan.

———

Pray to what earth does this sweet cold belong,
Which asks no duties and no conscience?
The moon goes up by leaps her cheerful path
In some far summer stratum of the sky,
While stars with their cold shine bedot her way.
The fields gleam mildly back upon the sky,
And far and near upon the leafless shrubs
The snow dust still emits a silvery light.
Under the hedge, where drift banks are their screen,
The titmice now pursue their downy dreams,
As often in the sweltering summer nights

The bee doth drop asleep in the flower cup,
When evening overtakes him with his load.
By the brooksides, in the still genial night,
The more adventurous wanderer may hear
The crystals shoot and form, and winter slow
Increase his rule by gentlest summer means.

———

True kindness is a pure divine affinity,
Not founded upon human consanguinity.
It is a spirit, not a blood relation,
Superior to family and station.

———

Until at length the north winds blow,
And beating high mid ice and snow,
The sturdy goose brings up the rear,
Leaving behind the cold cold year.

———

Spes sibi quisque
Each one his own hope

Wait not till slaves pronounce the word
To set the captive free,
Be free yourselves, be not deferred,
And farewell slavery.

Ye are all slaves, ye have your price,
And gang but cries to gang.
Then rise, the highest of ye rise,
I hear your fetters clang.

Think not the tyrant sits afar
   In your own breasts ye have
The District of Columbia
   And power to free the Slave.

The warmest heart the north doth breed,
   Is still too cold and far,
The colored man's release must come
   From outcast Africa.

Make haste & set the captive free!—
   Are ye so free that cry?
The lowest depths of slavery
   Leave freedom for a sigh.

The Funeral Bell

One more is gone
Out of the busy throng
That tread these paths;
The church bell tolls,
Its sad knell rolls
To many hearths.

Flower bells toll not,
Their echoes roll not
Unto my ear;—
There still perchance,
That gentle spirit haunts
A fragrant bier.

Low lies the pall,
Lowly the mourners all
Their passage grope;—
No sable hue
Mars the serene blue
Of heaven's cope.

In distant dell
Faint sounds the funeral bell,
A heavenly chime;
Some poet there
Weaves the light burthened air
Into sweet rhyme.

———

Sometimes I hear the veery's clarion,
Or brazen trump of the impatient jay,
And in secluded woods the chicadee
Doles out her scanty notes, which sing the praise
Of heroes, and set forth the loveliness
Of virtue evermore.

———

Thou dusky spirit of the wood,
Bird of an ancient brood,
Flitting thy lonely way,
A meteor in the summer's day,
From wood to wood, from hill to hill,
Low over forest, field and rill,
What wouldst thou say?
Why shouldst thou haunt the day?
What makes thy melancholy float?
What bravery inspires thy throat,
And bears thee up above the clouds,
Over desponding human crowds,
Which far below
Lay thy haunts low?

Not unconcerned Wachusett rears his head
Above the fields so late from nature won
With patient brow unmoved as one who read
New annals in the history of man.

Nature

O nature I do not aspire
To be the highest in thy quire,
To be a meteor in the sky
Or comet that may range on high,
Only a zephyr that may blow
Among the reeds by the river low.
Give me thy most privy place
Where to run my airy race.
In some withdrawn unpublic mead
Let me sigh upon a reed,
Or in the woods with leafy din
Whisper the still evening in,
For I had rather be thy child
And pupil in the forest wild
Than be the king of men elsewhere
And most sovereign slave of care
To have one moment of thy dawn
Than share the city's year forlorn.
Some still work give me to do
Only be it near to you.

Godfrey of Boulogne

The moon hung low o'er Provence vales,
   'Twas night upon the sea,
Fair France was woo'd by Afric gales
   And paid in minstrelsy.
Along the Rhone then moves a band,
   Their banner in the breeze,
Of mail-clad men with iron hand,
   And steel on breast and knees.
The herdsman following his droves
   Far in the night alone,
Read faintly through the olive groves,—
   'Twas Godfrey of Boulogne

The mist still slumbered on the heights
   The glaciers lay in shade,
The stars withdrew with faded lights,
   The moon went down the glade.
Proud Jura saw the day from far,
   And showed it to the plain;
She heard the din of coming war,
   But told it not again.
The goatherd seated on the rocks,
   Dreaming of battles none
Was wakened by his startled flocks,—
   'Twas Godfrey of Boulogne.

Night hung upon the Danube's stream,
   Deep midnight on the vales,
Along the shore no beacons gleam,
   No sound is on the gales.
The Turkish lord has banished care
   The harem sleeps profound,
Save one fair Georgian sitting there
   Upon the Moslem ground.
The lightning flashed a transient gleam,
   A glancing banner shone,
A host swept swiftly down the stream,—
   'Twas Godfrey of Boulogne.

'Twas noon upon Byzantium,
 On street and tower and sea,
On Europe's edge a warlike hum
 Of gathered chivalry.
A troop went boldly through the throng,
 Of Ethiops, Arabs, Huns,
Jews Greeks and Turk, to right their wrong
 Their swords flashed thousand suns.
Their banner cleaved Byzantium's dust,
 And like the sun it shone,
their armor had acquired no rust,—
 'Twas Godfrey of Boulogne.

———

 The Rabbit leaps
 The mouse outcreeps
 The flag out-peeps
  Beside the brook.

 The ferret weeps
 The marmot sleeps
 The owlet keeps
  In his snug nook.

 The apples thaw
 The ravens caw
 The squirrels gnaw
  The frozen fruit;

 To their retreat
 We track the feet
 Of mice that eat
  The apples root.

 The willows droop
 The alders stoop
 The pheasants group
  Beneath the snow.

The catkins green
Cast o'er the scene
A summer sheen
  A genial glow.

The snow dust falls
The otter crawls
The partridge calls
  Far in the wood

The traveller dreams
The tree-ice gleams
The blue jay screams
  In angry mood.

———

I am the Autumnal sun,
With Autumn gales my race is run.
When will the hazle put forth its flowers,
And the grape ripen under my bowers?
When will the harvest and the hunter's moon
Turn my midnight into midnoon?
  I am all sere & yellow,
  And to my core mellow.
The mast is dropping within my woods
The winter is lurking within my moods
And the rustling of the withered leaf
Is the constant music of my grief,
  My gay colored grief,
  My autumnal relief.

———

Where'er thou sail'st who sailed with me,
Though now thou climbest loftier mounts
And fairer rivers dost ascend
Be thou my muse, my Brother.

I was born upon thy bank river
My blood flows in thy stream
And thou meanderest forever
At the bottom of my dream

Salmon Brook
Pennichook
Ye sweet waters of my brain
When shall I look
Or cast the hook
In thy waves again?

Silver eels
Wooden creels
These the baits that still allure
And dragon fly
That floated by
May they still endure?

The moon now rises to her absolute rule,
And the husbandman and hunter
Acknowledge her for their mistress.
Asters and golden reign in the fields
And the life everlasting withers not.
The fields are reaped and shorn of their pride
But an inward verdure still crowns them
The thistle scatters its down on the pool
And yellow leaves clothe the river—
And nought disturbs the serious life of men.

But behind the sheaves and under the sod
There lurks a ripe fruit which the reapers have not gathered
The true harvest of the year—the boreal fruit
Which it bears forever.
With fondness annually watering and maturing it.
But man never severs the stalk
Which bears this palatable fruit.

———

My friends, why should we live?
Life is an idle war a toilsome peace;
    To-day I would not give
One small consent for its securest ease.

    Shall we out-wear the year
In our pavilions on its dusty plain
    And yet no signal hear
To strike our tents and take the road again?

    Or else drag up the slope
The heavy ordnance of nature's train?
    Useless but in the hope,
Some far remote and heavenward hill to gain.

———

I mark the summer's swift decline
The springing sward its grave clothes weaves
Whose rustling woods the gales confine
The aged year turns on its couch of leaves.

Oh could I catch the sounds remote
Could I but tell to human ear—
The strains which on the breezes float
And sing the requiem of the dying year.

My love must be as free
　　As is the eagle's wing,
Hovering o'er land and sea
　　And everything.

I must not dim my eye
　　In thy saloon,
I must not leave my sky
　　And nightly moon.

Be not the fowler's net
　　Which stays my flight,
And craftily is set
　　T' allure the sight.

But be the favoring gale
　　That bears me on,
And still doth fill my sail
　　When thou art gone.

I cannot leave my sky
　　For thy caprice,
True love would soar as high
　　As heaven is.

The eagle would not brook
　　Her mate thus won,
Who trained his eye to look
　　Beneath the sun.

The Moon

Time wears her not; she doth his chariot guide;
   Mortality below her orb is placed.
                                   —RALEIGH.

The full-orbed moon with unchanged ray
   Mounts up the eastern sky,
Not doomed to these short nights for aye,
   But shining steadily.

She does not wane, but my fortune,
   Which her rays do not bless,
My wayward path declineth soon,
   But she shines not the less.

And if she faintly glimmers here,
   And paled is her light,
Yet always in her proper sphere
   She's mistress of the night.

Rumors From an Aeolian Harp

There is a vale which none hath seen,
Where foot of man has never been,
Such as here lives with toil and strife,
An anxious and a sinful life.

There every virtue has its birth,
Ere it descends upon the earth,
And thither every deed returns,
Which in the generous bosom burns.

There love is warm, and youth is young,
And poetry is yet unsung,
For Virtue still adventures there,
And freely breathes her native air.

And ever, if you hearken well,
You still may hear its vesper bell,
And tread of high-souled men go by,
Their thoughts conversing with the sky.

———

On shoulders whirled in some eccentric orbit
Just by old Paestum's temples and the perch
Where Time doth plume his wings.

———

Far oer The bow
Amid the drowsy noon
Souhegan creeping slow
    Appeareth soon.

Where gleaming fields of haze
Meet the voyageurs gaze,
And above the heated air
Seems to make a river there.

The pines stand up with pride
By the Souhegan's side,
And the hemlock and the larch
With their triumphal arch
Have accompanied its march
    To the sea.

No wind stirs its waves
But the spirits of the braves
    Hov'ring o'er
Whose antiquated graves
Its still water laves
    On the shore.

But with an Indian's stealthy tread
It goes sleeping in its bed
Without joy or grief
Or the rustle of a leaf
From the Lyndeboro' hills
To the merrimack mills

Without a ripple or a billow
Or the sigh of a willow
Which trails in its stream
The mid current of its dream.

Not a sound is floated o'er
save the mallet on shore
Which echoing on high
Seems a caulking the sky.

experienced river
Hast thou flown for ever?
Souhegan soundeth old
But the half is not told.

What names hast thou borne
In the ages far gone?
When the Xanthus and Meander
Commenced to wander—
Eer the brown bear hunted
On thy forest floor
Or nature had planted
The pines by thy shore.

With a louder din
Did thy current begin
When melted the snow
On the far mountain's brow
And the drops came together
In that rainy weather.

Methinks that by a strict behavior
I could elicit back the brightest star
That lurks behind a cloud.

———

I have rolled near some other spirits path
And with a pleased anxiety have felt
Its purer influence on my opaque mass
But always was I doomed to learn, alas!
I had scarce changed its sidireal time.

Fog

Thou drifting meadow of the air
Where bloom The dasied banks & violets
And in whose fenny labyrinths
The bittern booms, and curlew peeps
The heron wades and boding rain crow clucks;
    Low anchored cloud,
    Newfoundland air,
Fountain head and source of rivers,
Ocean branch that flowest to the sun,
Diluvian spirit, or Deucaleon shroud,
Dew cloth dream drapery
And napkin spread by fays—
Spirit of lakes and seas and rivers—
      Sea fowl that with the east wind
  Seeks't the shore— Groping thy way inland
By which ever name I please to call thee
  Bear only perfumes and the scent
  Of healing herbs to just men's fields.

———

How little curious is man
Who hath not searched his mystery a span
But dreams of mines of treasure
Which he neglects to measure
For three score years and ten
Walks to and fro amid his fellow men
Oer this firm tract of continental land
His fancy bearing no divining wand.
Our uninquiring corpses lie more low
Than our lifes curiosity doth go
Our most ambitious steps climb not so high
As in their hourly sport the sparrows fly.
And yonder cloud's blown farther in a day
Than our most vagrant feet may ever stray.
Surely, O Lord, he hath not greatly erred
Who hath so little from his birth place stirred.
He wanders through this low and shallow world
Scarcely his bolder thoughts and hopes unfurled
Through this low walled world which his huge sin
Hath hardly room to rest and harbor in.
Bearing his head just oer some fallow ground
Some cowslip'd meadows where the bitterns sound.
He wanders round until his end draws nigh
And then lays down his aged head to die.
And this is life—this is that famous strife.

His head doth coast a fathom from the land
Six feet from where his grovelling feet do stand.

To the Comet

My sincerity doth surpass
    The pretence of optic glass.

Say what are the highlands yonder
Which do keep the spheres asunder
The streams of light which centre in our sun
And those which from some other system run?

Distinguished stranger, system ranger,
Plenipotentiary to our sphere,
Dost thou know of any danger,
War or famine near?

Special envoy, foreign minister,
From the empire of the sky,
Dost thou threaten aught that's sinister
By thy course on high?

Runner of the firmament
On what errand wast thou sent,
Art thou some great general's scout
Come to spy our weakness out?
Sculling thy way without a sail,
Mid the stars and constellations,
The pioneer*er* of a tail
Through the stary nations.
    Thou celestial privateer
We entreat thee come not near.

Haze

Woof of the sun, ethereal gauze,
Woven of Nature's richest stuffs,
Visible heat, air-water, and dry sea,
Last conquest of the eye;
Toil of the day displayed, sun-dust,
Aerial surf upon the shores of earth,
Ethereal estuary, frith of light,
Breakers of air, billows of heat,
Fine summer spray on inland seas;
Bird of the sun, transparent-winged
Owlet of noon, soft-pinioned,
From heath or stubble rising without song;
Establish thy serenity o'er the fields.

Smoke

Light-winged smoke, Icarian bird,
Melting thy pinions in thy upward flight,
Lark without song, and messenger of dawn,
Circling above the hamlets as thy nest;
Or else, departing dream, and shadowy form
Of midnight vision, gathering up thy skirts;
By night star-veiling, and by day
Darkening the light and blotting out the sun;
Go thou my incense upward from this hearth,
And ask the Gods to pardon this clear flame.

To a Stray Fowl

Poor bird! destined to lead thy life
    Far in the adventurous west,
And here to be debarred to-night
    From thy accustomed nest;
Must thou fall back upon old instinct now—
Well nigh extinct under man's fickle care?
Did heaven bestow its quenchless inner light
So long ago, for thy small want to-night?
Why stand'st upon thy toes to crow so late?
The moon is deaf to thy low feathered fate;
Or dost thou think so to possess the night,
And people the drear dark with thy brave sprite?
And now with anxious eye thou look'st about,
While the relentless shade draws on its veil,
For some sure shelter from approaching dews,
And the insidious steps of nightly foes.
I fear imprisonment has dulled thy wit,
Or ingrained servitude extinguished it.
But no,—dim memory of the days of yore,
By Brahmapootra and the Jumna's shore,
Where thy proud race flew swiftly o'er the heath,
And sought its food the jungle's shade beneath,
Has taught thy wings to seek yon friendly trees,
As erst by Indus' bank and far Ganges.

The Departure

In this roadstead I have ridden
In this covert I have hidden
Friendly thoughts were cliffs to me
And I hid beneath their lea.

This true people took the stranger
And warm hearted housed the ranger
They received their roving guest,
And have fed him with the best

Whatsoe'er the land afforded
To the stranger's wish accorded,
Shook the olive, stripped the vine,
And expressed the strengthening wine.

And at night they did spread o'er him
What by day they spread before him,
That good-will which was repast
Was his covering at last.

The stranger moored him to their pier
Without anxiety or fear;
By day he walked the sloping land,
    By night the gentle heavens he scanned.

When first his bark stood inland
To the coast of this far Finland,
Sweet-watered brooks came tumbling to the shore
The weary mariner to restore.

And still he stayed from day to day
If he their kindness might repay
But more and more
The sullen waves came rolling to the shore.

And still the more the stranger waited
The less his argosy was freighted,
And still the more he stayed
The less his debt was paid.

So He unfurled his mast
To receive the fragrant blast,
And that same refreshing gale
Which had woo'd him to remain
   Again and again—
It was that filled his sail
   And drove him to the main.

All day the low hung clouds
   Dropt tears into the sea
And the wind amid the shrouds
   Sighed plaintively.

———

Brother where dost thou dwell?
   What sun shines for thee now?
Dost thou indeed farewell?
   As we wished here below.

What season didst thou find?
   'Twas winter here.
Are not the fates more kind
   Than they appear?

Is thy brow clear again
   As in thy youthful years?
And was that ugly pain
   The summit of thy fears?

Yet thou wast cheery still,
   They could not quench thy fire,
Thou dids't abide their will,
   And then retire.

Where chiefly shall I look
   To feel thy presence near?
Along the neighboring brook
   May I thy voice still hear?

Dost thou still haunt the brink
   Of yonder river's tide?
And may I ever think
   That thou art at my side?

What bird wilt thou employ
   To bring me word of thee?
For it would give them joy,
   'Twould give them liberty,
   To serve their former lord
   With wing and minstrelsy.

A sadder strain has mixed with their song,
   They've slowlier built their nests,
Since thou art gone
   Their lively labor rests.

Where is the finch—the thrush,
   I used to hear?
Ah! they could well abide
   The dying year.

Now they no more return,
   I hear them not;
They have remained to mourn,
   Or else forgot.

———

All things are current found
Oer the uneven ground.
   Spirits and elements
   Have their descents.

Night and day—year on year,
   High and low far and near,
   These are our own aspects
   These are our own regrets.

Ye gods of the shore
Who abide evermore,
I see your far headland
Stretching on either hand.

I hear the sweet evening sounds
From your undecaying grounds
Cheat me no more with time
Take me to your clime.

———

On fields oer which the reaper's hand has passed,
Lit by the harvest moon and autumn sun,
My thoughts like stubble floating in the wind
And of such fineness as October airs,
There after harvest could I glean my life
A richer harvest reaping without toil,
And weaving gorgeous fancies at my will
In subtler webs than finest summer haze.

Epitaph on an Engraver

By death's favor
Here lies the engraver
And now I think o't
Where lies he not?
If the archangel look but where he lies
He ne'er will get translated to the skies.

Epitaph on Pursy

Traveller, this is no prison,
He is not dead, but risen.
  Then is there need,
  To fill his grave,
  And truth to save,
  That we should read,—
  In Pursy's favor
  Here lies the engraver.

Ep on a Good Man

  Here lies—the world
  There rises one.

Epitaph

Here lies an honest man
    Rear Admiral Van.
Faith, then ye have
Two in one grave,
For by your favor
Here too lies the engraver.

Ep on the World

Here lies the body of this world,
Whose soul alas to hell is hurled.
This golden youth long since was past,
Its silver manhood went as fast,
And iron age drew on at last;
'Tis vain its character to tell,
The several fates which it befell,
What year it died, when 'twill arise,
We only know that here it lies.

The sluggish smoke curls up from some deep dell,
The stiffened air exploring in the dawn,
And making slow acquaintance with the day;
Delaying now upon its heavenward course,
In wreathed loiterings dallying with itself,
With as uncertain purpose and slow deed,
As its half-wakened master by the hearth,
Whose mind still slumbering and sluggish thoughts
Have not yet swept into the onward current
Of the new day;—and now it streams afar,
The while the chopper goes with step direct,
And mind intent to swing the early axe.

   First in the dusky dawn he sends abroad
His early scout, his emissary, smoke,
The earliest, latest pilgrim from the roof,
To feel the frosty air, inform the day;
And while he crouches still beside the hearth,
Nor musters courage to unbar the door,
It has gone down the glen with the light wind,
And o'er the plain unfurled its venturous wreath,
Draped the tree tops, loitered upon the hill,
And warmed the pinions of the early bird;
And now, perchance, high in the crispy air,
Has caught sight of the day o'er the earth's edge,
And greets its master's eye at his low door,
As some refulgent cloud in the upper sky.

On Ponkawtasset, since, we took our way,
Down this still stream to far Billericay,
A poet wise has settled, whose fine ray
Doth often shine on Concord's twilight day.

Like those first stars, whose silver beams on high,
Shining more brightly as the day goes by,
Most travellers cannot at first descry,
But eyes that wont to range the evening sky,

And know celestial lights, do plainly see,
And gladly hail them, numbering two or three;
For lore that's deep must deeply studied be,
As from deep wells men read star-poetry.

These stars are never paled, though out of sight,
But like the sun they shine forever bright;
Ay, *they* are suns, though earth must in its flight
Put out its eyes that it may see their light.

Who would neglect the least celestial sound,
Or faintest light that falls on earthly ground,
If he could know it one day would be found
That star in Cygnus whither we are bound,
And pale our sun with heavenly radiance round?

To a Marsh Hawk in Spring

There is health in thy gray wing
Health of nature's furnishing.
Say thou modern-winged antique,
Was thy mistress ever sick?
In each heaving of thy wing
Thou dost health and leisure bring,
Thou dost waive disease & pain
And resume new life again.

Great Friend

I walk in nature still alone
    And know no one
Discern no lineament nor feature
    Of any creature.

Though all the firmament
   Is oer me bent,
Yet still I miss the grace
   Of an intelligent and kindred face.

I still must seek the friend
Who does with nature blend,
Who is the person in her mask,
He is the man I ask.

Who is the expression of her meaning,
Who is the uprightness of her leaning,
Who is the grown child of her weaning

The center of this world,
The face of nature,
The site of human life,
Some sure foundation
And nucleus of a nation—
At least a private station.

We twain would walk together
Through every weather,
And see this aged nature,
Go with a bending stature.

The offer

I make ye an offer,
Ye gods hear the scoffer,
The scheme will not hurt you,
If ye will find goodness I will find virtue.
Though I am your creature,
And child of your nature,
I have pride still unbended,
And blood undescended,
Some free independence,
And my own descendents.

If ye will deal plainly,
I will strive mainly,
If ye will discover
Great plans to your lover,
And give him a sphere
Somewhat larger than here.

Morning

Thou unconverted saint
Early Christian without taint—
Heathen without reproach
Who dost upon the evil day encroach,
Who ever since thy birth
Hast trod the outskirts of the earth.
Strict anchorite who dost simply feast
On freshest dews—I'll be thy guest,
And daily bend my steps to east
While the late risen world goes west.

The Friend

The great friend
Dwells at the land's end,
There lives he
Next to the sea.
Fleets come and go,
Carrying commerce to and fro,
But still sits he on the sand
And maketh firm that headland.
Mariners steer them by his light
Safely in the darkest night,
He holds no visible communion
For his friendship is a union.
Many men dwell far inland,
But he alone sits on the strand,
Whether he ponders men or books
Ever still he seaward looks,

Feels the sea-breeze on his cheek,
At each word the landsmen speak;
From some distant port he hears
Of the ventures of past years
In the sullen ocean's roar
Of wrecks upon a distant shore;
In every companion's eye
A sailing vessel doth descry;
Marine news he ever reads
And the slightest glances heeds.

Near is India to him
Though his native shore is dim,
But the bark which long was due,
Never—never—heaves in view,
Which shall put an end to commerce
And bring back what it took from us,
(Which shall make Siberia free
Of the climes beyond the sea)
Fetch the Indies in its hold,
All their spices and their gold,
  And men sail the sea no more
  The sea itself become a shore,
  To a broader deeper sea,
  A profounder mystery.

Yet let us Thank the purblind race,
  Who still have thought it good
With lasting stone to mark the place
  Where braver men have stood.

In concord, town of quiet name
  And quiet fame as well,

Ye do command me to all virtue ever
And simple truth the law by which we live
Methinks that I can trust your clearer sense
And your immediate knowledge of the truth.
I would obey your influence—one with fate

———

Ive seen ye, sisters, on the mountain-side
When your green mantles fluttered in the wind
Ive seen your foot-prints on the lakes smooth shore
Lesser than man's, a more ethereal trace,
I have heard of ye as some far-famed race—
Daughters of gods whom I should one day meet—
Or mothers I might say of all our race.
I reverence your natures so like mine
Yct strangely different, like but still unlike
Thou only stranger that hast crossed my path
Accept my hospitality—let me hear
The message which thou bring'st
    Made different from me
  Perchance thou't made to be
   The creature of a different destiny.
I know not who ye are that meekly stand
Thus side by side with man in every land.
When did ye form alliance with our race
Ye children of the moon who in placid nights
Vaulted upon the hills and sought this earth.
Reveal that which I fear ye can not tell
Wherein ye are not I, wherein ye dwell
Where I can never come.
What boots it that I do regard ye so
Does it make suns to shine or crops to grow?
What boots that I never should forget
Thee, I have sisters sitting for me yet
And what are sisters
The robust man who can so stoutly strive
In this bleak world is hardly kept alive.
And who is it protects *ye* smooths *your* way

I am bound, I am bound, for a distant shore,
By a lonely isle, by a far Azore,
There it is, there it is, the treasure I seek,
On the barren sands of a desolate creek.

The Hero

What doth he ask?
Some worthy task.
Never to run
Till that be done,
that never done
Under the sun.
Here to begin
All things to win
By his endeavor
Forever and ever—
Happy and well
On this ground to dwell
This soil subdue
Plant and renew.
By might & main
Health & strength gain
So to give nerve
To his slenderness
Yet Some mighty pain
He would sustain.
So to preserve
His tenderness.
Not be deceived
Of suffring bereaved
Not lose his life
By living too well
Nor escape strife

In his lonely cell
And so find out Heaven
By not knowing Hell.
Strength like the rock
To withstand any shock—
Yet some Aaron's rod
Some smiting by god
Occasion to gain
To shed human tears
And to entertain
Still divine fears.
Not once for all, forever, blest,
Still to be cheered out of the west
Not from his heart to banish all sighs
Still be encouraged by the sun rise
Forever to love and to love and to love
Within him, around him—beneath him above
To love is to know, is to feel, is to be
At once 'tis his birth & his destiny
For earthly pleasures
Celestial pains
Heavenly losses
For earthly gains.
Must we still eat
The bread we have spurned
Must we rekindle
The faggots we've burned—
Must we go out
By the poor man's gate
Die by degrees
Not by new fate.
Is then no road
This way my friend
Is there no road
Without any end—
When I have slumbered
I have heard sounds

As travellers passing
Over my grounds—
'Twas a sweet music
Wafted them by
I could not tell
If far off or nigh.
Unless I dreamed it
This was of yore—
But I never told it
To mortal before—
Never remembered
But in my dreams
What to me waking
A miracle seems
If you will give of your pulse or your grain
We will rekindle those flames again
Here will we tarry it is without doubt
Till a miracle putteth that fire out.

At midnight's hour I raised my head
The owls were seeking for their bread
The foxes barked impatient still
At their wan fate they bear so ill—
I thought me of eternities delayed
And of commands but half obeyed—
The night wind rustled through the glade
As if a force of men there staid
The word was whispered through the ranks
And every hero seized his lance
The word was whispered through the ranks
    Advance.

I seek the Present Time,
No other clime,
Life in to-day,
Not to sail another way,
To Paris or to Rome,
Or farther still from home.
That man, whoe'er he is,
Lives but a moral death,
Whose life is not coeval
With his breath.
What are deeds done
Away from home?
What the best essay
On the Ruins of Rome?
The dusty highways,
What Scripture says,
This pleasant weather
And all signs together—
The river's meander,
All things, in short,
Forbid me to wander
In deed or in thought.
In cold or in drouth,
seek Not the sunny South,
But make the whole tour
Of the sunny Present Hour.
For here if thou fail,
Where canst thou prevail?
If you love not
Your own land most,
You'll find nothing lovely
Upon a distant coast.
If you love not
The latest sunset,
What is there in pictures
Or old gems set?

If no man should travel
Till he had the means,
There'd be little travelling

For kings or for Queens.
The means, what are they!
They are the wherewithal
Great expenses to pay;—
Life got, and some to spare,
Great works on hand,
And freedom from care.
Plenty of time well spent,
To use,—
Clothes paid for, and no rent
In your shoes;—
Something to eat,
And something to burn,
And, above all, no need to return;—
For they who come back,
,have they not failed,
Wherever they've ridden
Or steamed it, or sailed?
All your grass hayed,—
All your debts paid,—
All your wills made?
Then you might as well have stayed,
For are you not dead,
Only not buried?

The way unto "Today",
The rail road to "Here,"
They never'll grade that way,
Nor shorten it, I fear.
There are plenty of depots
All the world o'er,
But not a single station
At a man's door;
If we would get near
To the secret of things,
We shall not have to hear
When the engine bell rings.

Tell me ye wise ones if ye can
Whither and whence the race of man.
For I have seen his slender clan
Clinging to hoar hills with their feet
Threading the forest for their meat
Moss and lichens bark & grain
They racke together with might & main
And they digest them with anxiety & pain.
I meet them in their rags and unwashed hair
Instructed to eke out their scanty fare
Brave race—with a yet humbler prayer
Beggars they are aye on the largest scale
They beg their daily bread at heavens door
    And if their this years crop alone shoud fail
They neither bread nor begging would know more.
    They are the Titmans of their race
    And hug the vales with mincing pace
    Like Troglodites, and fight with cranes
    We walk 'mid great relations feet
    What they let fall alone we eat
    We are only able
    to catch the fragments from their table
        These elder brothers of our race
        By us unseen with larger pace
        Walk oer our heads, and live our lives
        embody our desires and dreams
        Anticipate our hoped for gleams
            We grub the earth for our food
            We know not what is good.
        Where does the fragrance of our orchards go
        Our vineyards whiie we toil below—
        A finer race and finer fed
        Feast and revel above our head.
        The tints and fragrance of the flowers & fruits
        Are but the crumbs from off their table
        While we consume the pulp and roots
        Some times we do assert our kin
        And stand a moment where once they have been
        We hear their sounds and see their sights

And we experience their delights—
But for the moment that we stand
Astonished on the Olympian land.
We do discern no traveller's face
No elder brother of our race.
To lead us to the monarch's court
And represent our case.
But straightway we must journey back
retracing slow the arduous track
Without the privelege to tell
Even, the sight we know so well

———

Behold these flowers—
let us be up with Time
not dreaming of 3000 years
ago. Erect ourselves and let
those columns lie—not stoop
to raise a foil against the
sky— Where is the *spirit*
of that time but in this
present day this present line
3000 years ago are not
agone—they are still lingering
here aye every one, Where
there is memory which com-
pelleth time the muse's mother
and the muses nine— There are
all ages—past and future
time unwearied memory that
does not forget the actions
of the past—that does
not forego—to stamp them
freshly—. That old mortality
industrious to retouch the mon-
uments of time, in the world's

cemetery through-out every clime/
And Memnon's mother sprightly greets us now
Wears still her youthful blushes on her brow
And Carnac's columns why stand they on the plain?
T'enjoy our opportunities they would fain remain

This is my Carnac whose unmeasured dome
Shelters the measuring art & measurer's home
Whose propylaeum is the system nigh
And sculptured facade the visible sky

———

My friends, my noble friends, know ye—
That in my waking hours I think of ye
—Ever in godlike band uncompromised & free

The Earth

Which seems so barren once gave birth
To heroes—who oerran her plains,
Who plowed her seas and reaped her grains

———

But now "no war nor battle's sound"
Invades this peaceful battleground
But waves of Concord murmuring by
flowing with gentle harmony.
Yet since we sailed, some things have failed
And many a dream gone down the stream
Here then an aged shepherd dwellt

Who to his flock his substance dealt
And ruled them with a vigorous crook
According to the sacred Book.
But he the pierless bridge passed o'er
And solitary left the shore
Anon a youthful pastor came
Whose crook was not unknown to fame
His lambs he viewed with gentle glance
Spread oer the country's wide expanse
And fed with "mosses from the manse"—
Yonder the rocky seat where late
With soothed and patient ear we sat
Beside our Hawthorne in the dale
And listened to his Twice told Tale.—

Such water do the gods distill
And pour down every hill
For their new England men.
A draught of this wild water bring
And I will never taste the spring
Of Helicon again.
But yesterday in dew it fell
This morn its streams began to swell
And with the sun it downward flowd
So fresh it hardly knew its road.

Die and be buried who will,
I mean to live my fill.
My nature grows ever more young
The primitive pines among.

I have seen some frozenfaced connecticut
Or Down east man in his crack coaster
With tort sail, with folded arms standing
Beside his galley with his dog & man
While his cock crowed aboard, scud thro the surf
By some fast anchored Staten island farm,
But just outside the vast and stirring line
Where the astonished Dutchman digs his clams
Or but half ploughs his cabbage garden plot
With unbroken steeds & ropy harness—
And some squat bantam whom the shore wind drownd
Feebly responded there for all reply,
While the triumphant Yankee's farm swept by.

———

Such near aspects had we
Of our life's scenery.

Travelling

If e'er our minds be ill at ease
It is in vain to cross the seas
Or when the fates do prove unkind
To leave our native land behind.
The ship becalmed at length stands still
The steed will rest beneath the hill.
But swiftly still our fortunes pace
To find us out in every place.

The Atlantides

The smothered streams of love, which flow
More bright than Phlegethon, more low,
Island us ever, like the sea,
In an Atlantic mystery.
Our fabled shores none ever reach,
No mariner has found our beach,
Scarcely our mirage now is seen,
And neighboring waves with floating green,
Yet still the oldest charts contain
Some dotted outline of our main;
In ancient times midsummer days
Unto the western islands' gaze,
To Teneriffe and the Azores,
Have shown our faint and cloud-like shores.

But sink not yet, ye desolate isles,
Anon your coast with commerce smiles,
And richer freights ye'll furnish far
Than Africa or Malabar.
Be fair, be fertile evermore,
Ye rumored but untrodden shore,
Princes and monarchs will contend
Who first unto your land shall send,
And pawn the jewels of the crown
To call your distant soil their own.

Conscience is instinct bred in the house,
Feeling and Thinking propagate the sin
By an unnatural breeding in and in.
I say, Turn it out doors,
Into the moors.
I love a life whose plot is simple,
And does not thicken with every pimple,
A soul so sound no sickly conscience binds it,

That makes the universe no worse than 't finds it.
I love an earnest soul,
Whose mighty joy and sorrow
Are not drowned in a bowl,
And brought to life to-morrow;
That lives one tragedy,
And not seventy;
A conscience worth keeping,
Laughing not weeping;
A conscience wise and steady,
And forever ready;
Not changing with events,
Dealing in compliments;
A conscience exercised about
Large things, where one *may* doubt.
I love a soul not all of wood,
Predestinated to be good,
But true to the backbone
Unto itself alone,
And false to none;
Born to its own affairs,
Its own joys and own cares;
By whom the work which God begun
Is finished, and not undone;
Taken up where he left off,
Whether to worship or to scoff;
If not good, why then evil,
If not good god, good devil.
Goodness! you hypocrite, come out of that,
Live your life, do your work, then take your hat.
I have no patience towards
Such conscientious cowards.
Give me simple laboring folk,
Who love their work,
Whose virtue is a song
To cheer God along.

That Phaeton of our day,
Who'd make another milky way,
And burn the world up with his ray;

By us an undisputed seer,—
Who'd drive his flaming car so near
Unto our shuddering mortal sphere,

Disgracing all our slender worth,
And scorching up the living earth,
To prove his heavenly birth.

The silver spokes, the golden tire,
Are glowing with unwonted fire,
And ever nigher roll and nigher;

The pins and axle melted are,
The silver radii fly afar,
Ah, he will spoil his Father's car!

Who let him have the steeds he cannot steer?
Henceforth the sun will not shine for a year;
And we shall Ethiops all appear.

———

Then spend an age in whetting thy desire,
Thou needs't not *hasten* if thou dost *stand fast*.

———

We see the *planet* fall,
And that is all.

We should not mind if on our ear there fell
Some less of cunning, more of oracle.

Men say they know many things
But lo! they have taken wings,
The arts & sciences.
And a thousand appliances—
The wind that blows
Is all that anybody knows.

Away! away! away! away!
   Ye have not kept your secret well,
I will abide that other day,
   Those other lands ye tell.

Has time no leisure left for these,
   The acts that ye rehearse?
Is not eternity a lease
   For better deeds than verse?

'T is sweet to hear of heroes dead,
   To know them still alive,
But sweeter if we earn their bread,
   And in us they survive.

Our life should feed the springs of fame
   With a perennial wave,
As ocean feeds the babbling founts
   Which find in it their grave.

Ye skies drop gently round my breast,
  And be my corselet blue,
Ye earth receive my lance in rest,
  My faithful charger you;

Ye stars my spear-heads in the sky,
  My arrow-tips ye are,—
I see the routed foemen fly,
  My bright spears fixed are.

Give me an angel for a foe,
  Fix now the place and time,
And straight to meet him I will go
  Above the starry chime.

And with our clashing bucklers' clang
  The heavenly spheres shall ring,
While bright the northern lights shall hang
  Beside our tourneying.

And if she lose her champion true,
  Tell Heaven not despair,
For I will be her champion new,
  Her fame I will repair.

———

    In the East fames are won,
    In the West deeds are done.

———

The good how can we trust?
Only the wise are just.
The good we use,
The wise we cannot choose.
These there are none above;
The good they know & love,
But are not known again
By those of lesser ken.—
They do not charm us with their eyes,
But they transfix with their advice.
No partial sympathy they feel,
With private woe or private weal,
But with the Universe joy & sigh,
Whose knowledge is their sympathy.

Greece

When life contracts into a vulgar span
And human nature tires to be a man,
I thank the gods for Greece
That permanent realm of peace,
For as the rising moon far in the night
Checquers the shade with her forerunning light,
So in my darkest hour my senses seem
To catch from her Acropolis a gleam,
Greece who am I that should remember thee?
Thy Marathon and thy Thermopylae
Is my life vulgar my fate mean
Which on such golden memories can lean?

Poverty

If I am poor it is that I am proud,
If God has made me naked and a boor
He did not think it fit his work to shroud.

The poor man comes from heaven direct to earth
As stars drop down the sky and tropic beams.
The rich receives in our gross air his birth,
As from low suns are slanted golden gleams.

Men are by birth equal in this that given
Themselves and their condition they are even.
The less of inward essence is to leaven
The more of outward circumstance is given.

Yon sun is naked bare of satellite
Unless our earths and moons that office hold,
Though his perpetual day feareth no night
And his perennial summer dreads no cold.

Where are his gilded rays but in our sky?
His solid disk doth float far from us still,
The orb which through the central way doth fly
Shall naked seem though proudly circumstanced.

Ill leave my mineral wealth hoarded in earth?
Buried in seas in mines and ocean caves
More safely kept than is the merchant's worth,
Which every storm committeth to the waves.

Man kind may delve but cannot my wealth spend,
If I no partial store appropriate
no armed ships into the Indies send
To rob me of my orient estate

The rich man's clothes keep out the genial sun
But scarce defend him from the piercing cold
If he did not his heavenly garment shun
He would not need to hide beneath a fold.

The respectable folks,
Where dwell they?
They whisper in the oaks,
And they sigh in the hay,
Summer and winter, night and day,
Out on the meadow, there dwell they.
They drink at the brooks and the pilgrim's cup,
And with the owl and the nighthawk sup;
They suck the breath of the morning wind,
And they make their own all the good they find.
They never die,
Nor snivel nor cry,
For they have a lease of immortality.
A sound estate forever they mend,
To every asker readily lend,
To the ocean wealth,
To the meadow health,
To Time his length,
To the rocks strength,
To the stars light
To the weary night,
To the busy day,
To the idle play,
And so their good cheer never ends,
For all are their debtors and all their friends.

Farewell

Whether we've far withdrawn
   Or come more near
Equally the outward form
   Doth no more appear.
Not thou by distance lost
No—for regret doth bind
Me faster to thee now
   Than neighborhood confined.

Where thy love followeth me
Is enough society.
Thy indelible mild eye
   Is my sky.
Whether by land or sea
   I wander to and fro,
Oft as I think of thee
   The heavens hang more low
The pure glance of thy eye
Doth purge the summer's sky,
And thy breath so rare
Doth refine the winter's air.
my feet would weary be
Ere they travelled from thee.
I discover by thy face
That we are of one race
Flowed in one vein our blood
Ere the sea found its flood
The worm may be divided
And each part become a whole,
But the nobler creature man
May not separate a span.

          ——

For though the eaves were rabitted,
   And the well sweeps were slanted,
Each house seemed not inhabited
   But haunted.

The pensive traveller held his way,
   Silent & melancholy,
For every man an ideot was,
   And every house a folly.

          ——

You Boston folks & Roxbury people
Will want Tom Hyde to mend your kettle

———

I will obey the strictest law of love
As if I dealt with cherubim above.
 I will accept no half gift from my friend
 By which he thinks for hate to make amend.
But every friendly thought
Will come to me unbought
 My friend may do whate'er he will
  And I shall love him
   If he doth it from love.
 But let him do whateer he will
 I think that I must hate him still
  If lower motives move.

 I love not all
  I love not one alway
But that I love is one & all
 And lasteth ever and aye.

 I will leave him I hate
  And cleave to him I love
I will forsake my earthly mate
  And seek my mate above.

Though my friends are dull and cold
I will be quick and warm.
Though their love groweth old
Mine shall be new born

Though they understand me not
 I shall be understood
Though by them I am forgot
 Not therefore by the good.

My friend can wound me
For to him I bare my breast—
But his wounds save me
From a foe's embrace
  But these are honorable scars
  And fit the wounded heart for Love's more glorious
      wars.

These wounds are not fatal though inflicted on the heart
For the heart's not less a vital than a mortal part.
    Unlike the inferior part
      The wounded heart
      Is not repaired with wood
      But by fresh currents from above
      Which fit it for a purer love
For all that's true & beautiful & good.

———

Why toll the bell today—
Its knell has died away—

———

  And once again
When I went a-maying—
& once or twice more I had seen thee before.
For there grow the May flower
  (*Epigaea repens*)
& the mt cranberry
  & the screech owl *strepens*

The Old Marlborough Road

Where they once dug for money,
But never found any;
Where sometimes Martial Miles
Singly files,
And Elijah Wood,
I fear for no good:
No other man,
Save Elisha Dugan,—
O man of wild habits,
Partridges and rabbits,
Who hast no cares
Only to set snares,
Who liv'st all alone,
Close to the bone,
And where life is sweetest
Constantly eatest.
When the spring stirs my blood
With the instinct to travel,
I can get enough gravel
On the Old Marlborough Road.
Nobody repairs it,
For nobody wears it;
It is a living way,
As the Christians say.
Not many there be
Who enter therein,
Only the guests of the
Irishman Quin.
What is it, what is it,
But a direction out there,
And the bare possibility
Of going somewhere?
Great guide-boards of stone,
But travellers none;
Cenotaphs of the towns
Named on their crowns.
It is worth going to see
Where you *might* be.

What king
Did the thing,
I am still wondering;
Set up how or when,
By what selectmen,
Gourgas or Lee,
Clark or Darby?
They're a great endeavor
To be something forever;
Blank tablets of stone,
Where a traveller might groan,
And in one sentence
Grave all that it known;
Which another might read,
In his extreme need.
I know one or two
Lines that would do,
Literature that might stand
All over the land,
Which a man could remember
Till next December,
And read again in the spring,
After the thawing.
If with fancy unfurled
You leave your abode,
You may go round the world
By the Old Marlborough Road.

Old meeting-house bell
I love thy music well
It peals through the air
Sweetly full & fair
As in the early times
When I listened to its chimes.

It is a real place,
Boston, I tell it to your face.
And no dream of mine
To ornament a line
I can not come nearer to God & Heaven
Than I live to Walden even.
It is a part of me which I have not prophaned
I live by the shore of me detained.
Laden with my dregs
I stand on my legs,
While all my pure wine
I to nature consign.
I am its stoney shore
And the breeze that passes o'er
In the hollow of my hand
Are its water and its sand;
Its deepest resort
Lies high in my thought,

Among the worst of men that ever lived
However we did seriously attend
A little space we let our thoughts ascend
Experienced our religion & confessed
'Twas good for us to be there—be anywhere
Then to a heap of apples we addressed
& cleared the topmost rider *sine* care
But our Icarian thoughts returned to ground
And we went on to heaven the long way round.

What's the rail-road to me?
I never go to see
Where it ends
It fills a few hollows
And makes banks for the swallows
It sets the sand a flowing
And blackberries a growing

.

Tall Ambrosia

Among the signs of autumn I perceive
The Roman wormwood (called by learned men
Ambrosia elatior, food for gods,—
For to impartial science the humblest weed
Is as immortal once as the proudest flower—)
Sprinkles its yellow dust over my shoes
As I cross the now neglected garden
—We trample under foot the food of gods
& spill their nectar in each drop of dew—
My honest shoes Fast friends that never stray
far from my couch thus powdered countryfied
Bearing many a mile the marks of their adventure
At the post-house disgrace the Gallic gloss
Of those well dressed ones who no morning dew
Nor Roman wormwood ever have been through
Who never walk but are *transported* rather—
For what old crime of theirs I do not gather

—————

'Tis very fit the ambrosia of the gods
Should be a weed on earth. As nectar is
The morning dew with which we wet our shoes
For the gods are simple folks and we should pine
                    upon their humble fare

I saw a delicate flower had grown up 2 feet high
Between the horse's paths & the wheel track
Which Dakin's & Maynards wagons had
Passed over many a time
An inch more to right or left had sealed its fate
Or an inch higher. And yet it lived & flourished
As much as if it had a thousand acres
Of untrodden space around it—and never
Knew the danger it incurred.
It did not borrow trouble nor invite an
Evil fate by apprehending it.
For though the distant market-wagon
Every other day—inevitably rolled
This way—it just as inevitably rolled
In those ruts—And the same
Charioteer who steered the flower
Upward—guided the horse & cart aside from it.
There were other flowers which you would say
Incurred less danger grew more out of the way
Which no cart rattled near, no walker daily passed.
But at length one rambling deviously
For no rut restrained plucked them
And then it appeared that they stood
Directly in his way though he had come
From farther than the market wagon—

To day I climbed a handsome rounded hill
Covered with hickory trees wishing to see
The country from its top—for low hills
show unexpected prospects—I looked
many miles over a woody low-land
Toward Marlborough Framingham & Sudbury
And as I sat amid the hickory trees

I am the little Irish boy
  That lives in the shanty
I am four years old today
  And shall soon be one and twenty
  I shall grow up
  And be a great man
  And shovel all day
  As hard as I can.

  Down in the deep cut
  Where the men lived
  Who made the Rail road.

for supper
  I have some potatoe
  And sometimes some bread
  And then if it's cold
    I go right to bed.

  I lie on some straw
  Under my fathers coat

  My mother does not cry
  And my father does not scold
  For I am a little Irish Boy
  And I'm four years old.

  Every day I go to school
  Along the Railroad
  It was so cold it made me cry
  The day that it snowed.

  And if my feet ache
  I do not mind the cold
  For I am a little Irish boy
  & I'm four years old.

In Adams fall
We sinned all.
In the new Adam's rise
We shall all reach the skies.

Life

My life is like a stately warrior horse,
That walks with fluent pace along the way,
And I the upright horseman that bestrides
His flexuous back, feeding my private thoughts.—
Alas, when will this rambling head and neck
Be welded to that firm and brawny breast?—
But still my steady steed goes proudly forth,
Mincing his stately steps along the road;
The sun may set, the silver moon may rise,
But my unresting steed holds on his way.
He is far gone ere this, you fain would say,
He is far going. Plants grow and rivers run;
You ne'er may look upon the ocean waves,
At morn or eventide, but you will see
Far in th' horizon with expanded sail,
Some solitary bark stand out to sea,
Far bound—well so my life sails far,
To double some far cape not yet explored.
A cloud ne'er standeth in the summer's sky,
The eagle sailing high, with outspread wings
Cleaving the silent air, resteth him not
A moment in his flight, the air is not his perch.
Nor doth my life fold its unwearied wings,
And hide its head within its downy breast,
But still it plows the shoreless seas of time,
Breasting the waves with an unsanded bow.

The moon moves up her smooth and sheeny path
Without impediment; and happily
The brook Glides by lulled by its tinkling;
Meteeors drop down the sky without chagrin
And rise again; but my cares never rest.
No charitable laws alas cut me
An easy orbit round the sun, but I
Must make my way through rocks and seas and earth
my steep and devious way Uncertain still.
My current never rounds into a lake
In whose fair heart the heavens come to bathe
Nor does my life drop freely but a rod
By its resistless course
As Meteors do.

I'm thankful that my life doth not deceive
Itself with a low loftiness, half height,
And think it soars when still it dip its way
Beneath the clouds on noiseless pinion
Like the crow or owl, but it doth know
The full extent of all its trivialness,
Compared with the splendid heights above.
    See how it waits to watch the mail come in
While 'hind its back *the sun goes out perchance.*
And yet their lumbering cart brings me no word
Not one scrawled leaf such as my neighbors get
To cheer them with the slight events forsooth
Faint ups and downs of their far distant friends—
And now tis passed. What next? See the long train
Of teams wreathed in dust, their atmosphere;
Shall I attend until the last is passed?
Else why these ears that hear the leader's bells
Or eyes that link me in procession.

But hark! the drowsy day has done its task,
Far in yon hazy field where stands a barn
Unanxious hens improve the sultry hour
And with contented voice now brag their deed—
A new laid egg—Now let the day decline—
They'll lay another by tomorrow's sun.

Manhood

I love to see the man, a long-lived child,
As yet uninjured by all worldly taint
As the fresh infant whose whole life is play.
'Tis a serene spectacle for a serene day;
But better still I love to contemplate
The mature soul of lesser innocence,
Who hath travelled far on life's dusty road
Far from the starting point of infancy
And proudly bears his small degen'racy
Blazon'd on his memorial standard high
Who from the sad experience of his fate
Since his bark struck on that unlucky rock
Has proudly steered his life with his own hands.
Though his face harbors less of innocence
Yet there do chiefly lurk within its depths
Furrowed by care, but yet all over spread
With the ripe bloom of a self-wrought content
Noble resolves which do reprove the gods
And it doth more assert man's eminence
Above the happy level of the brute
And more doth advertise me of the heights
To which no natural path doth ever lead
No natural light can ever light our steps,
—But the far-piercing ray that shines
From the recesses of a brave man's eye.

Music

Far from this atmosphere that music sounds
Bursting some azure chink in the dull clouds
Of sense that overarch my recent years
And steal his freshness from the noonday sun.
Ah, I have wandered many ways and lost
The boyant step, the whole responsive life
That stood with joy to hear what seemed then
Its echo, its own harmony borne back
Upon its ear. This tells of better space,
Far far beyond the hills the woods the clouds
That bound my low and plodding valley life,
Far from my sin, remote from my distrust,
When first my healthy morning life perchance
Trod lightly as on clouds, and not as yet
My weary and faint hearted noon had sunk
Upon the clod while the bright day went by.
    Lately, I feared my life was empty, now
I know though a frail tenement that it still
Is worth repair, if yet its hollowness
Doth entertain so fine a guest within, and through
Its empty aisles there still doth ring
Though but the echo of so high a strain;
It shall be swept again and cleansed from sin
To be a thoroughfare for celestial airs;
Perchance the God who is proprietor
Will pity take on his poor tenant here
And countenance his efforts to improve
His property and make it worthy to revert,
At some late day Unto himself again.

The Just Made Perfect

A stately music rises on my ear,
Borne on the breeze from some adjacent vale;
A host of knights, my own true ancestors,
Tread to the lofty strains and pass away
In long procession; to this music's sound
The Just move onward in deep serried ranks,
With looks serene of hope, and gleaming brows,
As if they were the temples of the Day.

Gilt by an unseen sun's resplendent ray
They firmly move, sure as the lapse of Time;
Departed worth, leaving these trivial fields
Where sedate valor finds no worthy aim,
And still is Fame the noblest cause of all.

Forward they press and with exalted eye,
As if their road, which seems a level plain,
Did still ascend, and were again subdued
'Neath their proud feet. Forward they move, and leave
The sun and moon and stars alone behind:
And now, by the still fainter strains, I know
They surely pass; and soon their quivering harp,
And faintly clashing cymbal, will have ceased
To feed my ear.

It is the steadiest motion eye hath seen,
A Godlike progress; e'en the hills and rocks
Do forward come, so to congratulate
Their feet; the rivers eddy backward, and
The waves recurl to accompany their march.

Onward they move, like to the life of man,
Which cannot rest, but goes without delay
Right to the gates of Death, not losing time
In its majestic tread to Eternity,
As if Man's blood, a river, flowed right on
Far as the eye could reach, to the Heart of hearts,
Nor eddied round about these complex limbs.

'Tis the slow march of life,—I feel the feet
Of tiny drops go pattering through *my* veins;
Their arteries flow with an Assyrian pace,
And empires rise and fall beneath their stride.

Still, as they move, flees the horizon wall;
The low-roofed sky o'erarches their true path;
For they have caught at last the pace of Heaven,
Their great Commander's true and timely tread.

Lo! how the sky before them is cast up
Into an archèd road, like to the gallery
Of the small mouse that bores the meadow's turf:
Chapels of ease swift open o'er the path,
And domes continuous span the lengthening way.

———

I do not fear my thoughts will die
For never yet it was so dry
as to scorch the azure of the sky.
It knows no withering & no drought
Though all eyes crop it ne'er gives out
My eyes my flocks are
Mountains my crops are
I do not fear my flocks will stray
For they were made to roam the day
For they can wander with the latest light
Yet be at home at night.

———

I'm contented you should stay
    For ever and aye
If you can take yourself away
    Any day.

———

Man Man is the Devil
The source of all evil.

———

You must not only aim aright,
But draw the bow with all your might.

———

He knows no change who knows the true,
    And on it keeps his eye,
Who always still the unseen doth view;
    Only the false & the apparent die.

Things change, but change not far
    From what they are not but to what they are,
Or rather 'tis our ignorance that dies;
    Forever lives the knowledge of the wise.

———

When the toads begin to ring,
Then thinner clothing bring
or Off your greatcoat fling

———

The chicadee
Hops near to me.

———

'Twas 30 years ago
In a rocky pasture field
Sprang an infant apple grove
low planted & concealed—
I sing the wild apple theme enough for me.
I love the racy fruit & I reverence the tree—
In that small family there was one that
loved the sun—which sent its root down deep/—
& took fast hold on life/—while the others
went to sleep
In 2 years time 't had thus
Reached the level of the rocks—
Admired the stretching world
Nor feared the wandering flocks—

But at this tender age
Its sufferings began—
There came a browsing ox
And cut it down a span.

Its heart did bleed all day
& When the birds were hushed—

———

Forever in my dream & in my morning thought
Eastward a mount ascends—
But when in the sunbeam its hard outline is sought—
It all dissolves & ends.
The woods that way are gates—the pastures too slope up
To an unearthly ground—
But when I ask my mates, to take the staff & cup,
It can no more be found—
Perchance I have no shoes fit for the lofty soil
Where my thoughts graze—

No properly spun clues—nor well strained mid day oil
    Or—must I mend my ways?
It is a promised land which I have not yet earned,
    I have not made beginning
With consecrated hand—I have not even learned
    To lay the underpinning.
The mountain sinks by day—as do my lofty thoughts,
    Because I'm not highminded.
If I could think alway above these hills & warts
    I should see it, though blinded.
It is a spiral path within the pilgrim's soul
    Leads to this mountain's brow
Commencing at his hearth he reaches to this goal
    He knows not when nor how.

———

    Except, returning, by the Marlboro,
    A way, methinks, might safely be allowed
    To pilgrims of the holiest character
    We marked, I say, the barberry's brilliant fruit,
    Which on our hill & pasture grows to waste
    Not the less sweet to see though sour to taste—
    And in a rocky lane through which we passed
    Not so much lengthwise as diagonally
    In our saint-terrering over hill & valley
    We plucked wild apples of the fairest hew
    Filling our pockets out with eagerness,
    Excellent whether to eat or look at,
    Or to throw at one another & the
    Squirrels in sport; & afterward tame ones
    In orchards heaped by a penurious hind,
    Who saw but heaps of dollars in his mind;
    Some what less tame to us for being stolen,
    Although our pockets were already swolen;
    And, one more proof, I saw at Willis Lake
    Where we had come our nature's thirst to slake
    The willow bed which ornaments its edge

Mixed with the cranberry—button bush & sedge
Touched by the frost send forth its scarlet flames,
Which far surpassed all oriental dyes
Reminding me of the wild wealth of the skies
And of the red man who once on this shore
Beheld it, ere *his* last summer was oer.
So we returned from Willis Pond & Hill,
I climb the last & drink the former still.

The Rosa Sanguinea

As often as a martyr dies,
This opes its petals to the skies;
And Nature by this trace alone
Informs us which way he is gone.

———

Any fool can make a rule
And every fool will mind it.

———

All things decay
& so must our sleigh

Chronology

1817   Born July 12, in Concord, Massachusetts, third of four children (Helen, b. 1812, John, b. 1815, and Sophia, b. 1819) of John and Cynthia (Dunbar) Thoreau, and christened October 12 as David Henry Thoreau. (Grandfather Jean Thoreau, a descendant of French Protestant refugees, came to Boston from the Isle of Jersey in 1773, served on Revolutionary War privateers, and became a prosperous merchant; after his death his estate was plundered by its executor. Maternal grandfather, the Rev. Asa Dunbar, resigned from the ministry in 1779 because of poor health and practiced law in Keene, New Hampshire. Maternal grandmother, Mary Jones, of a wealthy Loyalist family, helped her brothers escape to Canada during the Revolution.) Father farms, and manages store in Concord.

1818–21   Family moves to Chelmsford, a village ten miles north of Concord, where father opens grocery store. Thoreau enjoys sledding and suffers a series of accidents, including the loss of part of a toe while playing with an axe. In 1821, father closes failing grocery store and moves family to Boston, where he teaches school.

1822   Sees Walden Pond for the first time while visiting grandmother Mary Jones. (Later writes: "That woodland vision for a long time made the drapery of my dreams.")

1823–27   Family returns to Concord, where father takes over pencil-making business started by brother-in-law Charles Dunbar. Attends Phoebe Wheeler's private "infant school" and then the town-run Center School. Memorizes passages from the Bible, Shakespeare, Bunyan, and Samuel Johnson. Classmates call him "the Judge" because of his stern demeanor. Financial uncertainty causes mother to take in boarders and family to move twice within Concord. Begins lifelong exploration of surrounding countryside. Mother becomes active in town charity work.

1828   Thoreau and brother, John, enroll in Concord Academy, a private school founded in 1822 by prominent town citizens. Studies French, Latin, Greek, geography, history, and science.

1829   Attends lectures in natural history at newly founded Concord Lyceum.

1833   Family is able to send only one son to college, and Henry is considered the more scholarly; he enrolls in Harvard College after barely passing entrance examinations. John and Helen, now schoolteachers, and Thoreau's aunts help parents pay his expenses. Goes beyond the required curriculum by taking Italian, French, German, and Spanish and attending lectures on mineralogy, anatomy, and natural history. Remembered by a classmate as being "cold and unimpressionable," his academic performance is above average but not exceptional. Spends much time alone, reading and walking.

1835–36   Ralph Waldo Emerson moves to Concord. Thoreau takes a leave of absence for winter term to earn money by teaching in Canton, Massachusetts. Boards for six weeks with Orestes Brownson, Unitarian minister and New England intellectual, and studies German with him. (Later writes of these weeks: "They were an era in my life—the morning of a new Lebenstag. They are to me as a dream that is dreamt, but which returns from time to time in all its original freshness.") In May 1836, briefly leaves Harvard because of illness, possibly first attack of tuberculosis. Attends dedication of Concord Bridge Memorial in July and joins with choir in singing Emerson's "Concord Hymn." Lives for six weeks in hut on shore of Flint's Pond in Lincoln with Harvard friend Charles Stearns Wheeler. Visits New York City with father to sell pencils.

1837   Receives grant of $25 from Harvard Corporation after Emerson writes recommendation to President Quincy. Graduates nineteenth in his class of approximately fifty, taking part in commencement honors conference on "The Commercial Spirit of Modern Times." ("This curious world which we inhabit is more wonderful than convenient; more beautiful than it is useful; it is more to be admired and enjoyed than used.") Begins teaching at Center School, but resigns after flogging six students (including a family servant) against his own wishes at the direction of a superior. Becomes member of informal group of New England Transcendentalists, the "Hedge Club," including Brownson, Margaret Fuller, Frederic Henry Hedge, George Ripley, Jones Very, Elizabeth Peabody, Bronson Alcott, and Theodore Parker, who meet irregularly in Emerson's study. Begins his journal, ultimately to comprise nearly two million words, on October 22. Works on improving lead quality in pencils; learns from Scottish encyclopedia in Harvard Library to mix graphite with Bavarian clay, designs grinding mill to produce more finely powdered graphite. Changes name from David Henry to Henry David.

1838   Plans to go with brother to Kentucky in search of work; trip is postponed and then abandoned when John finds job in Roxbury. Goes to Maine in futile search for teaching job. June, opens small private school in parents' house, then takes over Concord Academy in September. Delivers first lecture to Concord Lyceum, "Society," on April 11, and is elected Lyceum secretary and curator in fall, serving two years.

1839   Increased enrollment (approximately 25 students) allows John to join Thoreau at the Concord Academy. John teaches "English branches"; Henry teaches Latin, Greek, French, and sciences. (One pupil reports later that John "was more human, loving" and Henry "rigid," but most remember both brothers with great affection: "It was a peculiar school, there was never a boy flogged or threatened, yet I never saw so absolutely military discipline. . . . Even the incorrigible were brought into line.") Innovative curriculum stresses reasoning over rote memorization and features field trips to workshops and countryside. In July Thoreau meets Ellen Sewall of Scituate, Massachusetts, 17-year-old sister of one of his students, and both he and John fall in love with her. August 31, Henry and John leave for two-week trip on the Concord and Merrimack rivers in their homemade boat, *Musketaquid*. Emerson helps found Transcendentalist quarterly *The Dial* and writes, "My Henry Thoreau will be a great poet for such a company & one of these days for all companies."

1840   Louisa May Alcott enrolls in Concord Academy, begin-
        ning her lifelong admiration for Thoreau. First issue of
        The Dial, edited by Margaret Fuller, appears in July, with
        Thoreau's poem "Sympathy" and essay "Aulus Persius
        Flaccus"; Thoreau eventually publishes 31 poems, essays,
        and translations in *The Dial*'s 16 issues. Ellen Sewall re-
        jects as suitors first John and then Henry. Thoreau
        teaches himself surveying, later an important source of in-
        come. Meets Ellery Channing, poet and nephew of Uni-
        tarian minister William Ellery Channing, who becomes
        intimate friend and (in 1873) first biographer.

1841   Declines invitation to join Brook Farm community ("I
        had rather keep bachelor's hall in hell than go board in
        heaven"). Closes Concord Academy on April 1 because of
        John's poor health and moves into Emerson household
        for two years as handyman and gardener. Borrows from
        Emerson's library to read further in Greek classics and
        English poetry, and begins reading Oriental literature.
        Transcribes edited version of first two volumes of journal
        into new notebooks. Composes longest poem of his ca-
        reer. Still seeking a way to support himself, nearly buys
        rundown farm, and dreams of going to live by Flint's
        Pond in Lincoln. ("My friends ask what I will do when I
        get there. Will it not be employment enough to watch
        the progress of the seasons?") The Flints, owners of the
        land, refuse permission to build cabin.

1842   January 1, John suffers razor cut, develops lockjaw, and
        dies on January 11 in Thoreau's arms. Soon afterward
        Thoreau is stricken for weeks with psychosomatic attack
        of the same paralytic symptoms, followed by months of
        depression. In summer meets Nathaniel Hawthorne, who
        becomes an intermittent literary sponsor after reading "A
        Natural History of Massachusetts" in the July 1842 *Dial*.
        Hawthorne describes him as "a young man with much of
        wild original nature still remaining in him. . . . He is as
        ugly as sin, long-nosed, queer-mouthed, and with un-
        couth and somewhat rustic, although courteous manners,
        corresponding very well with such an exterior. He was ed-
        ucated, I believe, at Cambridge, . . . but for two or
        three years back, he has repudiated all regular modes of
        getting a living, and seems inclined to lead a sort of In-
        dian life among civilized men—an Indian life, I mean, as

respects the absence of any systematic effort for a liveli-
hood." Sells Hawthorne *Musketaquid* for seven dollars
and teaches him to paddle. In the winter goes skating
with Emerson and Hawthorne; Hawthorne's wife,
Sophia, describes him "figuring dithyrambic dances and
Bacchic leaps on the ice—very remarkable, but very ugly,
methought."

1843 Lectures on "Sir Walter Raleigh" in February. Edits April
issue of *The Dial*, substituting for Emerson, and includes
in it "Dark Ages," a short essay on ancient history. In May
goes to Staten Island, New York, as tutor to children of
Emerson's brother William. Meets Horace Greeley, Henry
James, Sr., and the abolitionist William Tappan; hears so-
cial reformer Lucretia Mott at Quaker meeting and is fa-
vorably impressed. Enjoys walks along Staten Island shore
and frequents various New York libraries, reading Ossian
and Francis Quarles with particular interest, but writes of
New York City: "It is a thousand times meaner than I
could have imagined." Homesick, he returns to Concord
in December and moves back into family home. "Paradise
(To Be) Regained," criticizing technological utopianism,
published in *United States Magazine and Democratic Re-
view*, November.

1844 In series of lectures and discussions on reform at Boston's
Amory Hall, delivers "The Conservative and the Re-
former." Writes essay for *The Dial* praising Nathaniel P.
Rogers, abolitionist publisher who advocates the dissolu-
tion of antislavery societies on the grounds that they re-
strict the exercise of individual freedom. Devises a drilling
machine that allows lead to be inserted into pencils with-
out splitting the wood; develops different grades of lead
hardness. April 30, on camping trip with Edward Hoar,
accidentally sets fire to three hundred acres of Concord
woods, causing over $2,000 damage. Meets Isaac Thomas
Hecker, future founder of the Paulist Fathers, who pro-
poses that they make a pilgrimage to Rome "in the old
middleage fashion." Thoreau declines, and resists
Hecker's attempts to convert him to Roman Catholicism.
July, takes walking trip through Berkshires and Catskills
with Ellery Channing. August 1, rings First Parish Church
bell to summon town to annual fair of Concord Women's
Anti-Slavery Society (which his mother had helped

found); there Emerson delivers address on West Indian Emancipation, which Thoreau arranges to be published as a pamphlet. In fall, helps build new family house in the open southwestern "prairie" of Concord (the "Texas house").

1845   Spring, starts building cabin in Emerson's woodlot at Walden Pond, and moves in July 4. Works on manuscript about 1839 boat trip with John on Concord and Merrimack rivers, and on a lecture about Thomas Carlyle. Throughout his 26-month stay, remains in close contact with family and friends.

1846   Begins writing *Walden*. Delivers Carlyle lecture at Concord Lyceum in February. July, arrested and jailed for one night by Concord constable Sam Staples for not paying several years' poll tax in protest against role of the state in perpetuating slavery. (Emerson writes disapprovingly in his journal: "Don't run amuck against the world. As long as the state means you well, do not refuse your pistareen." Alcott, arrested in 1843 for failure to pay his town tax, praises Thoreau's "dignified non-compliance with the injunction of civil power.") Tax is paid that evening by anonymous person (probably aunt Maria Thoreau). The next morning Thoreau is thrown out of jail when he refuses to leave. For the remainder of his life, his aunt and others pay tax to avoid further confrontation. August 1, Anti-Slavery Society fair held at Walden. August 31 through early September, trip to Maine to climb Mount Katahdin with cousin George Thatcher of Bangor.

1847   Reads "A History of Myself," part of first draft of *Walden*, at Concord Lyceum in February. Collects zoological specimens for Louis Agassiz of Harvard. Leaves Walden on September 6, having finished his manuscript of *A Week on the Concord and Merrimack Rivers* and most or all of the first version of *Walden*. In October moves into Emerson house for ten months to help care for Lydia Emerson and the children while Waldo is in Europe. Responds to tenth anniversary questionnaire from his Harvard class: "I am a Schoolmaster—a private Tutor, a Surveyor—a Gardener, a Farmer—a Painter, I mean a House Painter, a Carpenter, a Mason, a Day-Laborer, a

Pencil-Maker, a Glass-paper Maker, a Writer, and some-times a Poetaster."

1848   January 26, delivers lecture to Concord Lyceum on "the relation of the individual to the State," published in 1849 as "Resistance to Civil Government" (posthumously re-titled "Civil Disobedience") in Elizabeth Peabody's *Aesthetic Papers*. Responding to appreciative letter, begins extensive correspondence with Worcester, Massachusetts, schoolteacher Harrison Blake. July–November, "Ktaadn, and the Maine Woods" serialized in John Sartain's *Union Magazine* and strongly promoted in the New York *Tribune* by Horace Greeley, now Thoreau's enthusiastic backer and literary agent. Begins more extensive lecturing in New England. Satirized by James Russell Lowell in "A Fable for Critics" (published October 31) as a mere shadow of Emerson. Extensively revises *A Week* and begins second version of *Walden*.

1849   *A Week on the Concord and Merrimack Rivers* published May 30 by James Munroe and Company of Boston after Thoreau agrees to pay the cost from his royalties. It receives mixed reviews and sells poorly. Continues to correct and revise text. (In 1853 Thoreau takes back 706 of the original 1,000 copies and stores them in the family attic, remarking, "I have now a library of nearly nine hundred volumes, over seven hundred of which I wrote myself.") June 14, sister Helen dies of tuberculosis. Autumn, family buys larger house nearer to center of Concord (the "Yellow House") out of growing profits from pencil business, which has begun to concentrate on supplying ground lead for electrotyping. Finds surveying a preferable way to support himself and establishes a reputation for extreme accuracy. Friendship with Emerson cools. Emerson writes in his journal: "Thoreau wants a little ambition in his mixture. . . . Instead of being the head of American engineers, he is captain of a huckleberry party." Thoreau is suspicious of the effect on Emerson of growing fame and acceptance, annoyed by charge that he is merely Emerson's follower, and offended that Emerson does not do more to promote *A Week*. October, first trip to Cape Cod, with Ellery Channing, going via Cohasset and Sandwich, returning by steamer from Provincetown.

1850   Increases reading on natural history and American Indi-
            ans, recording nearly 3,000 pages of notes and quotations
            in "Indian Books" between 1847 and 1861. Collects in his
            attic room in the Yellow House hundreds of arrowheads
            and other Indian artifacts, as well as hundreds of dried
            plant specimens. June, second trip to Cape Cod, alone, by
            steamer to Provincetown and back to Boston. July, sent
            by Emerson to Fire Island, New York, to search for body
            and manuscripts of Margaret Fuller Ossoli, who had died
            in a shipwreck with her husband and child and Horace
            Sumner, brother of Massachusetts senator Charles Sum-
            ner. The wreck is plundered before he arrives and he finds
            only a few insignificant items. Writes of an unidentifiable
            skeleton he saw: "It reigned over the shore. That dead
            body possessed the shore as no living one could. It
            showed a title to the sands which no living ruler could."
            September, trip to Montreal, Quebec City, and the north-
            ern bank of the St. Lawrence with Ellery Channing.

1851   Stops removing leaves from journal volumes for use in
            drafts of lectures and essays and begins to record detailed
            observations of natural phenomena that he uses later in
            essays and phrenological charts. Passage of Fugitive Slave
            Act enrages him; writes in journal: "I do not believe that
            the North will soon come to blows with the South on this
            question. It would be too bright a page to be written . . .
            at present." Becomes increasingly involved in Under-
            ground Railroad, which he has been assisting for several
            years, sheltering escaped slaves in the family house and
            aiding their flight to Canada.

1852   Excerpts from fourth version of *Walden* published in
            Union Magazine attract little attention, and Thoreau re-
            ceives no money when the magazine ceases publication.

1853   January–March, first three installments of "A Yankee in
            Canada," based on 1850 trip, appear in *Putnam's Monthly
            Magazine*. Publication stops when Thoreau objects to ed-
            itor George William Curtis removing passages Curtis con-
            siders "heresies." Declines invitation to join American
            Association for the Advancement of Science. September,
            second trip to Maine, with George Thatcher and Indian
            guide Joe Aitteon.

1854 Arrest in Boston of fugitive slave Anthony Burns incites Thoreau to write "Slavery in Massachusetts" and read it at Framingham, Massachusetts, rally organized by William Lloyd Garrison, July 4. It is printed in the *Anti-Slavery Standard*, *The Liberator*, and the New York *Tribune*. *Walden* published August 9 by Boston firm of Ticknor and Fields in an edition of 2,000, the result of over seven years of work and seven major revisions of the text. Although a few reviews are harsh (*Boston Atlas*: "There is not a page . . . giving one sign of liberality, charitableness, kind feeling, generosity, in a word—heart"; *Knickerbocker* reviews it with P. T. Barnum's autobiography under the title "Town and Rural Humbugs"), most are very enthusiastic. (The popular *Graham's Magazine* concludes: "Through all the audacities of his eccentric protests, a careful eye can easily discern the movement of a powerful and accomplished mind.") By the end of the year, 1,744 copies are sold, plus several hundred more before it goes out of print in 1859. (Some are shipped to England, where George Eliot favorably reviews it in 1856: ". . . we have a bit of pure American life . . . animated by that energetic, yet calm spirit of innovation, that practical as well as theoretic independence of formulae, which is peculiar to some of the finer American minds.") Encouraged by *Walden's* success, Thoreau urges Ticknor and Fields to reissue *A Week*, but they decline. Enjoys wider popularity as lecturer throughout the Northeast; introduces "Getting a Living," critique of American acquisitiveness (later published as "Life without Principle"). Begins to attract a circle of admirers, including English traveler and author Thomas Cholmondeley; Quaker Daniel Ricketson, later historian of New Bedford; and abolitionist, educator, and writer F. B. Sanborn.

1855 Develops weakness in legs that afflicts him intermittently for the next two years. "Cape Cod," drawn from visits to region, published in *Putnam's Monthly Magazine* June–August. Curtis cancels publication of further installments, probably fearing that Cape Cod residents will be offended by Thoreau's depictions. July, third trip to Cape Cod, accompanied by Ellery Channing, taking a schooner to Provincetown, spending two weeks at Highland Light, and returning by sailboat *Olata* from Provincetown to

Boston. In return for Thoreau's hospitality in Concord, Thomas Cholmondeley sends 44 volumes of Oriental philosophy, religion, and history, for which Thoreau makes a special bookcase from Concord River driftwood. Sends Cholmondeley *Walden*, Emerson's poems, and Whitman's *Leaves of Grass*.

1856   October, goes to Perth Amboy, New Jersey, to survey at Eagleswood, a former utopian community being converted into suburban estates. In early November visits with Bronson Alcott in New York. They hear Henry Ward Beecher preach at Plymouth Church in Brooklyn; Thoreau is unimpressed. The next day Thoreau and Alcott meet Walt Whitman. ("He is apparently the greatest democrat the world has seen," Thoreau later writes to Harrison Blake. "Kings and aristocracy go by the board at once, as they have long deserved to. A remarkably strong though coarse nature, of a sweet disposition, and much prized by his friends.") Whitman presents him with an inscribed copy of the 1856 *Leaves of Grass*. Thoreau is dismayed by its sensuality but calls it "a great primitive poem,—an alarum or trumpet note ringing through the American camp."

1857   Meets John Brown in early March when Brown visits F. B. Sanborn in Concord and takes noon meal at Thoreau's house. Hears Brown speak and makes small monetary contribution; writes that Brown "had the courage to face his country herself when she was in the wrong." June 12–22, makes his last visit to Cape Cod, alone. (Only trip not described in *Cape Cod*, published by Ticknor and Fields in 1865.) July 20–August 7, travels through Maine with Edward Hoar and Indian guide Joe Polis. Grows full beard.

1858   James Russell Lowell solicits account of 1857 Maine travels for *Atlantic Monthly*. Fearing that his portrayal of Polis is too candid, Thoreau submits instead "Chesuncook," drawn from 1853 trip, published June–August. When sentence praising a pine tree—"It is as immortal as I am, and perchance will go to as high a heaven"—is omitted from July installment against Thoreau's explicit instructions, writes to Lowell, "I do not ask anybody to adopt my opinions, but I do expect that when they ask for them in print, they will print them, or obtain my consent to their alteration or omission." Demands that Lowell print the omitted sentence in the August issue. Lowell does not, and delays paying Thoreau $198 owed to him. (Revised versions of "Ktaadn," "Chesuncook," and 1857 trip account, together with appendix, published as *The Maine Woods* by Ticknor and Fields in 1864.) Travels through the White Mountains and climbs Mount Washington, July 2–19.

1859   February 3, father dies, leaving Thoreau financially responsible for mother and sister. Begins writing "Wild Fruits" (unpublished until 2000). May 8, hears John Brown speak at Concord Town Hall. October, news of Brown's raid on Harpers Ferry reaches Concord. Thoreau delivers a defiant tribute, "A Plea for Captain John Brown," to large audiences in Concord, Boston, and Worcester, October 30 to November 3. Helps organize and speaks at memorial meeting in Concord on Brown's execution day, December 2. Aids fugitive member of Brown's band in escape to Canada.

1860   Reads Darwin's *Origin of Species* and defends it to Emerson against Louis Agassiz's attacks. Visited by William Dean Howells, who finds Thoreau "dreamy" and "orphic," and later describes the encounter as "a rout" of his hopes. Joins townspeople in protecting F. B. Sanborn against arrest by federal marshals trying to subpoena him to appear before Senate investigation of Harpers Ferry raid. Writes "The Last Days of John Brown." Begins expanding "The Succession of Forest Trees" into "The Dispersion of Seeds." December, catches a bad cold that quickly turns to bronchitis.

1861   Comments on Civil War in a letter to cousin George Thatcher: "If the people of the north thus come to see clearly that there can be no *Union* between freemen & slaveholders, & vote & act accordingly, I shall think that we have purchased that progress cheaply by this revolution. A nation of 20 millions of freemen will be far more respectable & powerful, than if 10 millions of slaves & slave holders were added to them." Seeking to improve his health, to observe Indians, and to compare flora and fauna of Concord with that of the Middle West, he goes to Minnesota in May with young friend Horace Mann, Jr.

They collect botanical specimens and take an excursion steamer to Lower Sioux Agency at Redwood, where Thoreau witnesses annual government payment to Indians and sees Chief Little Crow, who will lead the 1862 Sioux uprising. Observes and sympathizes with the Indians' discontent. Returns to Concord in early July, tired and no better. Resigned to an early death, makes last revisions in *A Week* (posthumous new edition is published by Ticknor and Fields in 1868). Arranges with sister for posthumous publication of *The Maine Woods*, *Cape Cod*, and other writings. "You know it's respectable to leave an estate to one's friends," he tells one of his many bedside visitors. Makes last visit to Walden Pond in September and final journal entry on November 3.

1862   Confined to his house, refuses opiates and continues to receive visitors. February–April, works to complete "Life without Principle," "Autumnal Tints," "Walking," and "Wild Apples" for publication in James T. Fields's *Atlantic Monthly*. April 12, sells attic stock of *A Week* to publisher James T. Fields, who reissues it two months later with new title page. Dies May 6 of tuberculosis, his last intelligible words "moose" and "Indian." Buried May 9, in New Burying Ground, Concord, later moved to nearby Sleepy Hollow Cemetery.

Note on the Texts

This volume contains a selection of 27 essays and 203 poems by Henry David Thoreau, arranged in the approximate order of their composition between 1836 and the time of Thoreau's death in 1862. Most of the essays were published during Thoreau's lifetime, but most of the poems existed only in manuscript at the time of his death.

Of the 27 essays included in this volume, the texts of 16 are taken from *Reform Papers* and *Early Essays and Miscellanies*, two volumes of the Princeton University Press edition of *The Writings of Henry D. Thoreau*. The texts of this edition have been prepared according to the standards established by—and they have received the official approval of—the Center for Editions of American Authors of the Modern Language Association of America. (See its Statement of Editorial Principles and Procedures, revised edition, 1972.) The texts printed in this volume of "The Service," "Paradise (To Be) Regained," "Herald of Freedom," "Wendell Phillips Before Concord Lyceum," "Slavery in Massachusetts," "Life Without Principle," "A Plea for Captain John Brown," "Martyrdom of John Brown," and "The Last Days of John Brown" are taken from *Reform Papers*, edited by Wendell Glick (Princeton: Princeton University Press, 1973), while the texts of "Aulus Persius Flaccus," "Sir Walter Raleigh," "Dark Ages," "Homer. Ossian. Chaucer.," "Thomas Carlyle and His Works," "Love," and "Chastity & Sensuality" are taken from *Early Essays and Miscellanies*, edited by Joseph J. Moldenhauer and Edwin Moser, with Alexander Kern (Princeton: Princeton University Press, 1975). The essays from *Reform Papers* and *Early Essays and Miscellanies* from *The Writings of Henry David Thoreau*, edited by Elizabeth Witherell, © 1972 Princeton University Press, are printed by permission of Princeton University Press. "Huckleberries," a section of a long manuscript on fruits that Thoreau worked on toward the end of his life, is taken from an edition prepared by Leo Stoller and published in 1970 by the Windhover Press and the New York Public Library. *Huckleberries,* © 1970 the New York Public Library, Astor, Lenox, and Tilden Foundations, is reprinted with permission. The texts of the ten remaining essays are taken from periodical or book publications published during Thoreau's lifetime or shortly after his death.

Thoreau wrote "Aulus Persius Flaccus" and "The Service" in 1840 and submitted both essays to *The Dial* for publication. "Aulus

Persius Flaccus" was edited by Ralph Waldo Emerson and printed in *The Dial* in July 1840. Thoreau incorporated the essay in the "Thursday" chapter of *A Week on the Concord and Merrimack Rivers* (1849), making a few changes of wording and cutting three sentences. The text in *Reform Papers* (1973), based on Thoreau's copy of the July 1840 *Dial* with his corrections, is printed here. "The Service" was rejected by Margaret Fuller, editor of *The Dial*, and was not printed during Thoreau's lifetime. The text in *Reform Papers*, based on manuscripts at the Pierpont Morgan Library, is the text printed here.

Thoreau composed "Natural History of Massachusetts" in spring 1842, after Emerson asked him to write an essay for *The Dial* about several scientific surveys of the state. It was published in *The Dial* in July 1842, and *The Dial* text is printed here. In the autumn of 1842 Thoreau wrote "A Walk to Wachusett," which was published in *The Boston Miscellany* in January 1843. *The Boston Miscellany* text is printed here.

"Sir Walter Raleigh," "Dark Ages," "A Winter Walk," "The Landlord," "Paradise (To Be) Regained," and "Homer. Ossian. Chaucer." were written in 1843. Thoreau gave a lecture on Raleigh at the Concord Lyceum on February 8, 1843, and he may have submitted "Sir Walter Raleigh" to *The Dial* later that year. Part of the essay was included in *A Week on the Concord and Merrimack Rivers*. The text in *Early Essays and Miscellanies* is based on a manuscript at the Huntington Library and is the text printed here. "Dark Ages" was published in *The Dial* in April 1843 and was later incorporated in the "Monday" chapter of *A Week on the Concord and Merrimack Rivers*; this volume prints the text from *Early Essays and Miscellanies*, which is based on Thoreau's copy of the magazine printing. "A Winter Walk" appeared in *The Dial* in October 1843, and *The Dial* text is printed here. "The Landlord" and "Paradise (To Be) Regained" were published in *The United States Magazine, and Democratic Review* in October 1843 and November 1843, respectively. The text printed here of "The Landlord" is taken from *The United States Magazine, and Democratic Review*. The text of "Paradise (To Be) Regained" in *Reform Papers* (1973) is based on the version published in *The United States Magazine, and Democratic Review*, and is the text printed here. "Homer. Ossian. Chaucer." was published in *The Dial* in January 1844 after a version of the essay was presented as a lecture entitled "Ancient Poets" at the Concord Lyceum on November 23, 1843. *Early Essays and Miscellanies* bases its text on the version published in *The Dial* and incorporates some of the corrections Thoreau made in his copy of the magazine printing. The *Early Essays and Miscellanies* text is printed here.

Thoreau wrote "Herald of Freedom" in the spring of 1844. It was first published in the April 1844 issue of *The Dial*, and then appeared in a slightly different version the following month in *Herald of Freedom*, the antislavery periodical edited by Nathaniel Rogers. After Rogers' death on October 16, 1846, Thoreau wrote several additional paragraphs about Rogers and his periodical. A revised version of the essay appeared in the posthumous collection *A Yankee in Canada, with Anti-Slavery and Reform Papers* (Boston: Ticknor & Fields, 1866). The text in *Reform Papers* (1973) is based on the version printed in *The Dial* and incorporates the four manuscript pages Thoreau wrote after Rogers' death, citing evidence that Thoreau planned to publish this expanded version of "Herald of Freedom." The *Reform Papers* text is printed here.

When Wendell Phillips was invited to speak against slavery at the Concord Lyceum in March 1845, three of the Lyceum's curators resigned in protest. Thoreau, Emerson, and Samuel Barrett replaced them, and Phillips delivered his speech on March 11. Thoreau sent a letter defending Phillips to *The Liberator*, where it was published on March 28, 1845. The letter was reprinted under the title "Wendell Phillips Before the Concord Lyceum" in *A Yankee in Canada, with Anti-Slavery and Reform Papers* (1866). The text in *Reform Papers* (1973), based on Thoreau's letter in *The Liberator*, is printed here.

"Thomas Carlyle and His Works," originally presented as a lecture at the Concord Lyceum on February 4, 1846, was first published in two installments of *Graham's American Monthly Magazine* (March and April 1847). A shorter version was published in *A Yankee in Canada, with Anti-Slavery and Reform Papers* (1866). This volume prints the text from *Early Essays and Miscellanies*, which is based on the version in *Graham's American Monthly Magazine.*

"Civil Disobedience" is derived from two lectures Thoreau delivered at the Concord Lyceum early in 1848. The lectures were given —at least in part—in response to his neighbors' curiosity about why he had chosen in July 1846 to spend a night in prison rather than pay his poll tax. In the spring of 1849 Thoreau was invited by Elizabeth Peabody to submit a written version to her periodical *Aesthetic Papers*, where the essay appeared under the title of "Resistance to Civil Government" on May 14, 1849. It was published posthumously under the title "Civil Disobedience" in *A Yankee in Canada, with Anti-Slavery and Reform Papers* (1866), in a version that differs from the *Aesthetic Papers* version in four significant readings, including the title. Because of a lack of holographic evidence, it cannot be known definitively if Thoreau was responsible for these revisions. However, two passages that appear in the version published in *A Yankee in*

Canada, with Anti-Slavery and Reform Papers have sources in commonplace books Thoreau kept and consulted for quotations as he worked on pieces from the 1840s until just before his death in 1862: lines from George Peele's "The Battle of Alcazar" and a sentence about Mencius's belief that the individual is the basis for the empire. It is unlikely that anyone but Thoreau would have made these changes; accepting them as authoritative acknowledges Thoreau's involvement in revising the essay and raises the strong possibility that he made the other two changes as well. The version of the essay that appears in *Reform Papers* (1973) as "Resistance to Civil Government" is based on the 1849 *Aestethic Papers* text and does not include these changes. The present volume prints the text of "Civil Disobedience" that appeared in *A Yankee in Canada, with Anti-Slavery and Reform Papers* (1866).

Thoreau delivered a lecture entitled "The Wild" to the Concord Lyceum on April 23, 1851. This lecture was revised and expanded into two lectures, "Walking" and "The Wild," that Thoreau delivered frequently during the 1850s, sometimes combined as a single lecture. Shortly before his death, he sold an essay titled "Walking" to the *Atlantic Monthly*, which published it in July 1862. The *Atlantic Monthly* text is printed here.

In September 1850 Thoreau and Ellery Channing traveled to Montreal, Quebec City, and the northern bank of the St. Lawrence. Soon after his return in October, Thoreau began writing about the trip. He worked on the essay during the winter of 1850 and throughout 1851, reading accounts of Canadian history and filling a notebook with quotations about Canada. He delivered two lectures adapted from his essay at the Concord Lyceum in 1852, the first on January 7, the second on March 17. Horace Greeley then suggested revisions that might be made in the manuscript, now titled "A Yankee in Canada." After two magazines rejected it, the essay was accepted by *Putnam's Monthly Magazine*. George William Curtis, Thoreau's friend and an editor at *Putnam's*, removed passages that he called "heresies," such as Thoreau's statement that "I am not sure but this Catholic religion would be an admirable one if the priests were quite omitted," from the three serial installments published in the magazine's January, February, and March numbers in 1853. The remaining installments in *Putnam's* were canceled after Thoreau objected to the editing and asked for the return of his manuscript. "A Yankee in Canada" was not published in full until the posthumous *A Yankee in Canada, with Anti-Slavery and Reform Papers* (1866), which is the text printed here.

"Love" and "Chastity & Sensuality" were enclosed in a letter to Thoreau's friend Harrison G. O. Blake in September 1852. Both essays were first published in the posthumous *Letters to Various Persons* (Boston: Ticknor & Fields, 1865), edited by Emerson. An incomplete draft of "Love" is in a manuscript now at the Huntington Library. *Early Essays and Miscellanies* bases its text of "Love" on this manuscript and on the version printed in *Letters to Various Persons*, and it is the source of the text printed here. A complete manuscript of "Chastity & Sensuality" is in the Huntington Library. The text in *Early Essays and Miscellanies* is based on this manuscript and is the text printed here.

"Slavery in Massachusetts" originated in a lecture given by Thoreau at Framingham, Massachusetts, on July 4, 1854. A longer version of the speech was published in the July 21, 1854, number of *The Liberator*, and versions also appeared in *The New-York Daily Tribune*, August 2, 1854, and in *The National Anti-Slavery Standard*, August 12, 1854. It was included in *A Yankee in Canada, with Anti-Slavery and Reform Papers* (1866). The text in *Reform Papers* (1973) is based on the version that was published in *The Liberator* and is the text printed here.

Thoreau gave a lecture entitled "Getting a Living" in New Bedford, Massachusetts, on December 26, 1854. He revised and delivered this lecture often between 1854 and 1860, using the titles "The Connection Between Man's Employment and His Higher Life," "What Shall It Profit?," and "Life Misspent." Shortly before his death, Thoreau sent a manuscript of the essay, prepared with the help of his sister Sophia and using the working title "The Higher Law," to the *Atlantic Monthly*. He gave the essay the title "Life without Principle," in a letter dated March 4, 1862, to James T. Field of the *Atlantic Monthly*. The essay appeared in the October 1863 number of the *Atlantic Monthly* and was reprinted in *A Yankee in Canada, with Anti-Slavery and Reform Papers* (1866). The text in *Reform Papers* (1973), based on the *Atlantic Monthly* version, is the text printed here.

"Autumnal Tints" was first delivered as a lecture in Worcester on February 22, 1859; Thoreau repeated the lecture on several occasions in 1859. It appeared posthumously in the *Atlantic Monthly* in November 1862, which is the source of the text printed here.

"A Plea for John Brown," "Martyrdom of John Brown," and "The Last Days of John Brown" were written in the aftermath of Brown's raid on Harpers Ferry in October 1859. "A Plea for John Brown" was given as a speech on October 18, 1859, and delivered several times in the weeks that followed. It was first published in

Echoes of Harper's Ferry (Boston: Thayer and Eldridge, 1860), a col-
lection of essays edited by James Redpath. The text in *Reform Papers*
(1973) is based on the version that appears in *Echoes of Harper's Ferry*
and is the text printed here. "Martyrdom of John Brown" was de-
livered as a speech at the Concord Town Hall on December 2, 1859,
the day of Brown's execution, and then published as a broadside. It
also appeared in *Echoes of Harper's Ferry*, under the title "Remarks at
Concord on the Day of the Execution of John Brown." The *Reform
Papers* text, based on the printer's copy of the December 1859 broad-
side, is printed here. "The Last Days of John Brown" was derived
from entries in Thoreau's journal, dating from November and De-
cember 1859, that he did not incorporate into his two speeches about
Brown. It was first published as an untitled piece in *The Liberator* on
July 27, 1860, and was printed under the title "The Last Days of
John Brown" in *A Yankee in Canada, with Anti-Slavery and Reform
Papers* (1866). The text in *Reform Papers* (1973) is based on *The Lib-
erator* version but uses the title from *A Yankee in Canada, with
Anti-Slavery and Reform Papers*, and it is the text printed here.

Thoreau delivered "The Succession of Forest Trees" as a lecture
to the Middlesex Agricultural Society at the Concord Town Hall on
September 20, 1860. The text of the lecture appeared in the *New
York Weekly Tribune* on October 6, 1860. It was also reprinted in the
Transactions of the Middlesex Agricultural Society and, in shortened
form, in a report of the Massachusetts Board of Agriculture pub-
lished in 1860. It was incorporated into a longer work on seed dis-
persion that Thoreau did not live to complete. This volume prints
the *New York Weekly Tribune* text.

"Wild Apples" was first given as a lecture at the Concord Lyceum
on February 8, 1860, although much of it is derived from journal en-
tries composed in the early 1850s. Thoreau revised the essay after de-
livering it as a lecture, and it was published for the first time in the
Atlantic Monthly in November 1862. It was also incorporated into
"Wild Fruits," a manuscript that Thoreau worked on during the last
years of his life and did not live to finish. This volume prints the *At-
lantic Monthly* text.

"Huckleberries" is also part of "Wild Fruits." The writings on
huckleberries exist in a more advanced form than the other essays
in "Wild Fruits," with the exception of "Wild Apples." The text
of "Huckleberries" printed here is taken from the edition prepared
by Leo Stoller in *Huckleberries*, published in 1970 by the Wind-
hover Press of the University of Iowa and the New York Public
Library, © 1970 the New York Public Library, Astor, Lenox, and
Tilden Foundations; reprinted with permission.

Thoreau wrote more than 200 poems, 85 of which were published in some form in his lifetime. Most of his poems were written between 1837 and 1845. Fifteen were published in *The Dial*, excluding translations and poems that appear in essays; one additional poem, "Great God, I ask thee for no meaner pelf," was included in Emerson's essay "Prayers," which appeared in *The Dial* in July 1842. The majority of Thoreau's published poems are interspersed throughout *A Week on the Concord and Merrimack Rivers*, and other poems appear in *Walden*, *The Maine Woods*, and in several of his essays. The poems Thoreau included in his essays and books were usually written before the prose works, and they are often longer in their manuscript versions, since he would excerpt lines from these manuscripts when incorporating his poetry into his essays and books. For example, "The Assabet," composed in 1839, contains lines that appear in revised form in three separate passages in *A Week on the Concord and Merrimack Rivers* as "Some tumultuous little rill," "Ply the oars! away! away!," and "Since that first 'away! away!'"

Drafts of many poems appear in the journal that Thoreau kept from 1837 until the end of his life, although he wrote few poems after 1847. In some instances Thoreau revised these drafts for separate publication in *The Dial*, or in his prose works, or for subsequent manuscript versions of the poem. In other cases the journal version of the poem is the only surviving version. Journal entries that are dated between October 1837 and September 1841 are usually taken from the five manuscript volumes that Thoreau used to copy entries from two volumes of an earlier journal, of which only a few leaves survive. When Thoreau copied these entries in the fall of 1841, he gave the transcribed entries their original dates. Drafts of poems also appear in the "Long Book," a manuscript volume that contains transcribed journal entries and original material, including a version of "Wendell Phillips at the Concord Lyceum" and a draft of a lecture on the Concord River delivered in March 1845. Thoreau began copying passages from earlier journals into the Long Book in fall 1844, gathering material for what would eventually become *A Week on the Concord and Merrimack Rivers*. Most of the entries in the Long Book are not dated; the latest entries were composed in 1846.

During the last ten years of his life, Thoreau virtually stopped writing poetry, and he never collected his poems. The first posthumous edition of his poetry, *Poems of Nature* (1895), edited by Henry S. Salt and Franklin B. Sanborn, contained unauthorized changes. The first critical edition, *Collected Poems of Henry Thoreau*, edited by Carl Bode, was published in 1943; a revised and expanded version, containing 16 additional poems and omitting two poems incorrectly attributed to Thoreau in the first edition, was published in 1964 by Johns Hopkins University Press.

Since *Collected Poems of Henry Thoreau* was published, a new edition of some of Thoreau's poems has appeared as a doctoral dissertation by Elizabeth Hall Witherell, "The Poetry of Henry David Thoreau: A Selected Critical Edition" (1979). The present volume uses the Witherell edition as the source for the 49 poems it contains, since Witherell had access to more manuscripts than Bode and was able to clarify the realtionship among versions of what might be considered the same poem. Five additional poems are printed from Witherell's article "Thoreau's Watershed Season as a Poet: The Hidden Fruits of the Summer and Fall of 1841," published in the 1990 volume of *Studies in the American Renaissance*, edited by Joel Myerson; this article is an expanded version of an appendix to the Witherell edition. The texts of 141 poems are printed from the 1964 revised edition of Carl Bode's *Collected Poems of Henry Thoreau.* (*Collected Poems* is the source of "Delay in Friendship," one of the poems in the Witherell edition.) In printing poems from *Collected Poems of Henry Thoreau*, this volume sometimes adopts the alternate titles listed in its table of contents but does not follow its practice of printing the first line of an untitled poem as its title; instead, the present volume prints the poem without a title. Nine poems are printed from manuscript sources.

Witherell's "The Poetry of Henry David Thoreau: A Selected Critical Edition" presents texts grouped together on the basis of shared content, such as a line or lines in common. For example, "The Inward Morning," published in the October 1842 *Dial* and included in *A Week on the Concord and Merrimack Rivers*, contains lines that appear in two manuscript poems in Thoreau's journal, "Packed in my mind lie all the clothes" and "What is it gilds the trees and clouds." The Witherell edition regards these four texts together as versions of a single poem. The present volume follows the Witherell edition's groupings of manuscript and printed sources, but it prints only one version of each poem. For poems included in the Witherell edition that were published during Thoreau's lifetime, this volume prints the published version with Thoreau's latest revisions, unless the published version was part of a larger prose work such as *A Week on the Concord and Merrimack Rivers, Walden,* or one of Thoreau's essays. For poems included in the Witherell edition that appear in Thoreau's prose works, this volume prints the version with Thoreau's latest revisions before the poem was made part of a prose work. In the case of poems included *A Week on the Concord and Merrimack Rivers* for which no earlier manuscript version is known to survive, this volume prints texts from the Witherell edition that are based on the proofsheets of *A Week* (now at the Huntington Library), which Thoreau continued to correct and revise after the book was published in 1849. When the only existing version of a poem appeared in a prose work other than *A Week*, this volume prints the text from the Witherell edition in which the text is based on the published prose work.

"Independence," "Cock-crowing," "Inspiration" ("Whate'er we leave to God, God does"), "The Soul's Season," and "The Fall of the Leaf" are part of a group of interrelated poems that Thoreau worked on during the summer and fall of 1841, of which nearly 20 versions survive, ranging in length from four to about 300 lines. Versions of these five poems survive as titled fair copies, written out in ink by Thoreau. The texts of "Independence," "Cock-crowing," "Inspiration," "The Soul's Season," and "The Fall of the Leaf" printed here are taken from Elizabeth Hall Witherell, "Thoreau's Watershed Season as a Poet: The Hidden Fruits of the Summer and Fall of 1841," published in *Studies in the American Renaissance 1990*, edited by Joel Myerson (Charlottesville: University Press of Virginia, 1991).

The texts printed here of two poems that were included in *Collected Poems of Henry Thoreau* are transcribed from manuscripts not available to Bode when he was preparing his edition. "In days of yore, 'tis said, the swimming alder," appeared in *Collected Poems* as "In times of yore, 'tis said, the swimming alder," based on a version that appeared in *The Life of Henry Thoreau* by Franklin B. Sanborn (Boston: Houghton Mifflin, 1917). The text printed here is taken from a manuscript at the University of Illinois. "The Rabbit leaps" appeared in *Collected Poems* as "A Winter and a Spring Scene," also based on a version published in *The Life of Henry Thoreau*. The text printed here is based on a manuscript at Southern Illinois University.

Seven poems included in this volume—"Pens to mend and hands to glide," "The coward ever sings no song," "Only the slave knows of the slave," "I have seen some frozenfaced connecticut," "You Boston folk & Roxbury people," "Why toll the bell today—," and "Except, returning, by the Marlboro"—are taken from manuscript sources listed below.

The following is a list, in the approximate order of composition, of the poems contained in this volume, indicating the source text and other relevant information. Abbreviations refer to the following:

CP   *Collected Poems of Henry Thoreau*, revised and expanded edition, edited by Carl Bode (Baltimore: Johns Hopkins University Press, 1964).

EHW   Elizabeth Hall Witherell, "The Poetry of Henry David Thoreau: A Selected Critical Edition." Doctoral dissertation, University of Wisconsin, 1979.

SAR   Elizabeth Hall Witherell, "Thoreau's Watershed Season as a Poet: The Hidden Fruits of the Summer and Fall of 1841," in Joel Myerson (ed.), *Studies in the American Renaissance 1990* (Charlottesville: University Press of Virginia, 1991), pp. 49–106.

A Week   *A Week on the Concord and Merrimack Rivers* (Boston: James Munroe and Company, 1849).

In days of yore, tis said, the swimming alder. Manuscript, University of Illinois Rare Book Room, in holograph copy of August 5, 1836, letter from Thoreau to Charles Wyatt Rice. Reprinted with permission.

Fair Haven ("When little hills like lambs did skip"). *CP.*

Voyagers Song. *CP.* A revised version of the second and the third stanzas appear in *A Week.*

Life is a summer's day. *CP.*

I love a careless streamlet. *CP.*

Pens to mend and hands to guide. Manuscript, New York Public Library, Berg Collection, in a letter from Thoreau to Henry Vose, October 13, 1837. Reprinted with permission of the New York Public Library, Berg Collection, Astor, Lenox, and Tilden Foundations.

Each summer sound. *CP.* Appears in journal, February 19, 1838, and is included in "Natural History of Massachusetts."

Friendship ("I think awhile of Love, and while I think"). *CP.* Appears in journal, April 8, 1838.

When breathless noon hath paused on hill and vale. *CP*, under the title "The Cliffs & Springs."

The Bluebirds. *CP.* Appears in journal, April 26, 1838.

May Morning. *CP.* Appears in journal, May 21, 1838.

Walden. *CP.* Appears in journal, June 3, 1838.

Truth—Goodness—Beauty—those celestial thrins. *CP.* Appears in journal, June 14, 1838.

Strange that so many fickle gods, as fickle as the weather. *CP.* Appears in journal, June 14, 1838.

In the busy streets, domains of trade. *CP.* Appears in journal, June 16, 1838.

I knew a man by sight. *CP.*

Cliffs. *CP.* Appears in journal, July 8, 1838.

My Boots. *CP.* Appears in journal, October 16, 1838.

Noon. *CP.* Appears in journal, October 16, 1838.

Fair Haven ("When Winter fringes every bough"). *CP.* Appears in journal, December 15, 1838. An untitled version of the poem was included in "A Winter Walk."

The Thaw. *EHW*, from journal, January 11, 1839, MA 1302:1. Reprinted with permission of the Pierpont Morgan Library, New York. Published in *Dial*, July 1842. A slightly revised version of the opening couplet appears in "The Natural History of Massachusetts." A version of lines 3–6 appears in Long Book.

Last night as I lay gazing with shut eyes. *EHW*, from journal, January 20, 1839, MA 1302:1, with pencil revisions made after December 1843. Reprinted with permission of the Pierpont Morgan Library, New York. A version of the last stanza appears in *A Week*.

Love. *CP*. Appears in journal, January 20, 1839.

The deeds of king and meanest hedger. *CP*. Appears in journal, February 3, 1839.

'Twill soon appear if we but look. *CP*. Appears in journal, February 3, 1839.

The Evening Wind. *EHW*, from journal, February 13, 1839, MA 1302:1. Reprinted with permission of the Pierpont Morgan Library, New York. A revised version of the poem is included in *A Week*.

The Peal of the Bells. *CP*. Appears in journal, February 10, 1839.

The Shrike. *EHW*, from journal, February 25, 1839, MA 1302:1. Reprinted with permission of the Pierpont Morgan Library, New York. The second stanza is included in "The Natural History of Massachusetts."

Sympathy. *EHW*, from journal, June 24, 1839, MA 1302:1. Reprinted with permission of the Pierpont Morgan Library, New York. The poem was published in the July 1840 *Dial*, set from a copy by Emerson that contained misreadings and unauthorized revisions. The poem was revised for inclusion in *A Week*.

The "Book of Gems." *CP*. Appears in journal, July 4, 1839.

The Assabet. *EHW*, from journal, July 18, 1839, MA 1302:1. Reprinted with permission of the Pierpont Morgan Library, New York. A later manuscript version contains two stanzas, the eleventh and the tenth, of "The Assabet." Lines originating in "The Assabet" appear in *A Week* in three places: a version of stanzas six and seven appear in "Sunday"; two stanzas beginning "Ply the oars! away! away!" and a version of the last stanza appears in "Tuesday."

The Breeze's Invitation. *CP*. Appears in journal, July 20, 1839.

Stanzas. *EHW*, from *Dial*, January 1841. A version of the poem appears in journal, July 24, 1839. It is included without a title in *A Week*.

Loves Farewell. *CP*. Appears under the title "Farewell" in journal, November 19, 1839.

Each more melodious note I hear. *CP*. Appears in journal, December 1839, and is included in "The Service."

The Fisher's Son. *EHW*, from manuscript, Abernathy Library, Middlebury College, on two single leaves of an early journal that Thoreau apparently saved because they were blank, though the poem is not part of that journal. The manuscript contains Thoreau's pencil revisions. Reprinted with permission. A version of the poem appears in Thoreau's journal, January 10, 1840; stanzas eight, ten, eleven, and twelve were revised and included in *A Week*.

Friendship ("Let such pure hate still underprop"). *EHW*, from Thoreau's corrected copy of the October 1841 *Dial*, where the poem was first published. Thoreau corrected two errors in his copy. The poem appeared without a title in *A Week*. A quatrain that was the final stanza of an early draft of the poem appears in Thoreau's journal, January 19, 1840.

The Freshet. *EHW*, from journal, February 24, 1840, MA 1302:2. Reprinted with permission of the Pierpont Morgan Library, New York. A revised version was included in "Natural History of Massachusetts." A version of the first stanza appears in Long Book.

The Poet's Delay. *EHW*, from *Dial*, October 1842. An untitled version, with two additional stanzas and the order of the first and second stanzas reversed, appears in Thoreau's journal between entries dated March 8, 1840, and March 16, 1840. The poem was reprinted in *A Week*.

The Summer Rain. *EHW*, from Thoreau's copy of the October 1842 *Dial*, where Thoreau changed "greater" to "juster" in the third stanza. A revised version of the poem was included in *A Week*.

Guido's Aurora. *CP*.

I've heard my neighbor's pump at night. *CP*, which erroneously prints "Who sleeps by day and walks by night" as its final couplet. This volume follows *CP*'s transcription of Thoreau's manuscript but prints "I've heard my neighbor's pump at night" and "Who sleeps by day and walks by night" as separate poems. Both poems appear on the flyleaf of the third volume of Thoreau's journal.

Who sleeps by day and walks by night. *CP*. It was included in *A Week*.

When with pale cheek and sunken eye I sang. *CP*. Appears in journal, August 12, 1840.

I arose before light. *CP*. Appears in journal, October 14, 1840.

I'm guided in the darkest night. *CP*. Appears in journal, November 7, 1840.

Friends—. *CP*. Published in *Dial*, December 28, 1841, and copied into journal, January 1841.

When in some cove I lie. *CP*. Appears in journal, January 1841.

Who hears the parson. *CP*. Appears in journal, January 10, 1841.

Sic Vita. *EHW*, from *Dial*, July 1841. The poem appears without a title in *A Week*, and in journal.

Wait not till I invite thee, but observe. *CP*. Appears in journal, April 7, 1841.

Friendship ("Now we are partners in such legal trade"). *CP*. Appears in journal, March 30, 1841.

On the Sun Coming Out in the Afternoon. *CP*. Appears in journal, April 1, 1841.

They who prepare my evening meal below. *CP*. Appears in journal, April 4, 1841.

My ground is high. *CP*. Appears in journal, April 7, 1841.

If from your price ye will not swerve. *CP*. Appears in journal, April 7, 1841.

Death cannot come too soon. *CP*. Appears in journal, April 18, 1841.

The Mountains in the Horizon. *EHW*, from manuscript, Am 1280.214.1 (2), Houghton Library, Harvard University. Reprinted with permission. Revised versions of the poem were included in "A Walk to Wachusett" and *A Week*.

The needles of the pine. *CP*. Appears in journal, May 9, 1841, and in "A Walk to Wachusett."

The Echo of the Sabbath Bell—. *EHW*, from journal, May 9, 1841, MA 1302:5. Reprinted with permission of the Pierpont Morgan Library, New York. A revised version, untitled, was included in *A Week*.

Low in the eastern sky. *CP*. First published under the title, "To the Maiden in the East," in *Dial*, October 1842. Thoreau omitted three stanzas when including the poem in *A Week*. The version in *CP* reflects these revisions.

My life has been the poem I would have writ. *CP*. Appears in journal, August 28, 1841, and in *A Week*.

To the Mountains. *CP*.

Greater is the depth of sadness. *CP*. Appears in journal, September 5, 1841.

Where I have been. *CP*. Appears in journal, September 7, 1841.

Better wait. *CP*. Appears in journal, September 30, 1841.

Independence. *SAR*. Manuscript dated July 30, 1841, now in the Yale Collection of American Literature, Beinecke Rare Book and Manuscript Library. A version titled "The Black Knight" was published in *The Dial*, October 1842.

Cock-crowing. *SAR*. Manuscript, Berg Collection, New York Public Library. Reprinted with permission of the New York Public Library, Berg Collection, Astor, Lenox, and Tilden Foundations.

Inspiration ("Whate'er we leave to God, God does"). *SAR*. Based on a photograph of an unlocated manuscript made from a negative by Herbert Cahoon, formerly Robert H. Taylor Curator of Autograph Manuscripts at the Pierpont Morgan Library, New York.

The Soul's Season. *SAR*. Manuscript, Robert H. Taylor Collection, Department of Rare Books and Special Collections, Princeton University Library. Reprinted with permission.

The Fall of the Leaf. *SAR*. Manuscript, Berg Collection, New York Public Library. Reprinted with permission of the New York Public Library, Berg Collection, Astor, Lenox, and Tilden Foundations.

Delay. *CP*.

Inspiration ("If thou wilt but stand by my ear"). *CP*.

Ive searched my faculties around. *CP*.

Who equallest the coward's haste. *CP*.

The Vireo. *CP*. The lines appear without a title in "Natural History of Massachusetts."

The coward ever sings no song. Manuscript, MS Am 1280 (137), Houghton Library, Harvard University. Reprinted with permission.

Only the slave knows of the slave. Manuscript, MS Am 1280 (137), Houghton Library, Harvard University. Reprinted with permission.

Great God, I ask thee for no meaner pelf. *CP*. The poem appeared under the heading "Metrical Prayer" in Emerson's essay "Prayers," which was published in *The Dial*, July 1842.

The Inward Morning. *EHW*, from *Dial*, October 1842. The poem was included in *A Week*. Early drafts appear in journal, November–December 1841.

Within the circuit of this plodding life. *EHW*, from manuscript, dated December 30, 1841, MS 1302:6. Reprinted with permission of the Pierpont Morgan Library, New York. A revised version appears in "Natural History of Massachusetts."

To Edith. *CP*.

Delay in Friendship. *CP*. Appears in *EHW*, which uses *CP* as its text. A version of the final stanza appears in *A Week*.

Ah, 'tis in vain the peaceful din. *CP*. Included in *A Week*.

Between the traveller and the setting sun. *CP*.

Have ye no work for a man to do—. *CP*.

I sailed up a river with a pleasant wind. *CP*. Included in *A Week*.

I was made erect and lone. *CP*.

I'm not alone. *CP*.

Our Country. *CP*.

Pray to what earth does this sweet cold belong. *CP*.

True kindness is a pure divine affinity. *CP*. Included in *A Week*.

Until at length the north winds blow. *CP*.

Wait not till slaves pronounce the word. *CP*.

The Funeral Bell. *CP*. The first eight lines appear in journal, July 18, 1842.

Sometimes I hear the veery's clarion. *CP*. The lines are included in "Natural History of Massachusetts." A prose version dated 1838 appears in Thoreau's journal.

Thou dusky spirit of the wood. *CP*. The lines are included in "Natural History of Massachusetts."

Not unconcerned Wachusett rears his head. *EHW*, from "A Walk to Wachusett," *Boston Miscellany*, January 1843.

Nature. *CP*.

Godfrey of Boulogne. *CP*. A draft appears in journal, 1842 (after August 23).

The Rabbit leaps. Manuscript, VFM 1091, Special Collections, Morris Library, Southern Illinois University, Carbondale. Drafts of the poem appear in journal, 1842 (after August 23).

I am the Autumnal sun. *EHW*, from Long Book, MA 1303. Reprinted with permission of the Pierpont Morgan Library, New York. Appears in *A Week*.

Where'er thou sail'st who sailed with me. *EHW*, from manuscript, from Long Book, 1842, MA 1303. Reprinted with permission of the Pierpont Morgan Library, New York. It was included in *A Week*.

I was born upon thy bank river. *CP*. Appears in Long Book, 1842.

Salmon Brook. *EHW*, from Long Book, September 1, 1842, MA 1303. Reprinted with permission of the Pierpont Morgan Library, New York. Appears in *A Week*.

The moon now rises to her absolute rule. *CP*. Appears in Long Book, September 1842.

My friends, why should we live? *CP*. Appears in Long Book, September 1842.

I mark the summer's swift decline. *CP*. Appears in Long Book, September 1842.

My love must be as free. *CP*. Published as "Free Love" in *Dial*, October 1842; included without a title in *A Week*.

The Moon. *CP*. Published in *The Dial*, October 1842.

Rumors From an Aeolian Harp. *CP*. Published in *The Dial*, October 1842, and revised for inclusion in *A Week*.

On shoulders whirled in some eccentric orbit. *CP*.

Far oer The bow. *EHW*, from Long Book, MA 1303. Reprinted with permission of the Pierpont Morgan Library, New York. Lines that appear in two places in *A Week*, "The waves slowly beat" and "Where gleaming fields of haze," have their origin in this poem.

Methinks that by a strict behavior. *CP*. Appears in Long Book.

I have rolled near some other spirits path. *CP*. Appears in Long Book.

Fog. *EHW*, from Long Book, MA 1303. Reprinted with permission of the Pierpont Morgan Library, New York. A draft appears in journal, 1843 (after January 16). A revised version of the poem beginning with the line "Low-anchored cloud" is included in *A Week*.

How little curious is man. *EHW*, from Long Book, with Thoreau's pencil revisions. Lines 9–10 were incorporated into *A Week*.

To the Comet. *CP*.

Haze. *CP*. Published in *Dial*, April 1843, then included, without a title, in *A Week*.

Smoke. *EHW*, from *Dial*, April 1843. Appeared without a title in *Walden*.

To a Stray Fowl. *EHW*, from *Dial*, April 1843. A slightly revised version of the poem was incorporated into an early draft of *Walden*.

The Departure. *CP*.

Brother where dost thou dwell? *CP*.

All things are current found. *EHW*, from Long Book, MA 1303, with Thoreau's ink revisions. Reprinted with permission of the Pierpont Morgan Library, New York. The poem was included in *A Week*.

On fields oer which the reaper's hand has passed. *CP*. Appears in Long Book.

Epitaph on an Engraver. *CP*. Versions appear in journal, October 22, 1843, in Long Book, and in *A Week*.

Epitaph on Pursy. *CP*. Appears in journal, October 22, 1843.

Ep on a Good Man. *CP*. Appears in journal, October 22, 1843, and in Long Book.

Epitaph. *EHW*, from Long Book, Collection of W. Stephen Thomas, Rochester, New York. A slightly revised version was included in *A Week*.

Ep on the World. *CP*. Appears in journal, October 22, 1843.

The sluggish smoke curls up from some deep dell. *CP*. Included in "A Winter Walk."

On Ponkawtasset, since, we took our way. *CP*. Included in *A Week*.

To a Marsh Hawk in Spring. *CP*. Appears in Long Book.

Great Friend. *CP*. Version appears in Long Book.

The offer. *EHW*, from manuscript, from Long Book, MA 1303. A slightly revised version of the poem appears in *A Week*. Reprinted with permission of the Pierpont Morgan Library, New York.

Morning. *EHW*, from manuscript, from Long Book. Reprinted by permission of the Huntington Library, San Marino, California, HM 13188. The six lines in *A Week* beginning "An early unconverted saint" were revised from this version of the poem.

The Friend. *EHW*, from Long Book. Reprinted by permission of the Huntington Library, San Marino, California, HM 13188. A revised version of the poem appears in *A Week*.

Yet let us Thank the purblind race. *CP*. Appears in Long Book.

Ye do command me to all virtue ever. *CP*. Appears in Long Book.

Ive seen ye, sisters, on the mountain-side. *CP*. Appears in Long Book.

I am bound, I am bound, for a distant shore. *EHW*, from proofsheets of *A Week*. A version appears in Long Book, 1845 (after March 11).

The Hero. *CP*. A version of this poem appears in a draft of *Walden*.

At midnight's hour I raised my head. *CP.*

I seek the Present Time. *CP.* A version of this poem appears in a draft of *Walden* but was not included in the published work.

Tell me ye wise ones if ye can. *EHW,* from journal. Lines 33 to 42 were revised and appear as an 8-line poem in *A Week.*

Behold these flowers—. *EHW,* from journal, August 6, 1845, MA 1302:8, with Thoreau's ink revisions. Reprinted with permission of the Pierpont Morgan Library, New York. The final stanza was revised and included in *A Week.*

My friends, my noble friends, know ye—. *CP.*

The Earth. *CP.*

But now "no war nor battle's sound". *EHW,* from journal (after July 24, 1846), Berg Collection, New York Public Library, with Thoreau's revisions made in pencil and ink. Reprinted with permission of the New York Public Library, Berg Collection, Astor, Lenox, and Tilden Foundations. It was revised for inclusion in *A Week.*

Such water do the gods distill. *EHW,* from journal (after July 24, 1846), Berg Collection, New York Public Library, with Thoreau's revisions. Reprinted with permission of the New York Public Library, Berg Collection, Astor, Lenox, and Tilden Foundations. It was revised for inclusion in *A Week.*

Die and be buried who will. *EHW,* from manuscript draft of "Ktaadn" that Thoreau wrote in late 1846 or 1847, now at the Brown University Library. Reprinted with permission. The quatrain appears in slightly altered form in *The Maine Woods.*

I have seen some frozenfaced connecticut. Manuscript, Robert H. Taylor Collection, Department of Rare Books and Special Collections, Princeton University Library. Reprinted with permission.

Such near aspects had we. *EHW,* from proofsheets of *A Week.* Reprinted by permission of the Huntington Library, San Marino, California, HM 13195.

Travelling ("If e'er our minds be ill at ease"). *EHW,* from manuscript, MA 920. Reprinted with permission of the Pierpont Morgan Library, New York. A longer version, beginning with the line "Though all the fates should prove unkind," was published in *A Week.*

The Atlantides. *CP.* Included in *A Week.*

Conscience is instinct bred in the house. *CP.* Included in *A Week.*

That Phaeton of our day. *CP.* Included in *A Week.*

Then spend an age in whetting thy desire. *CP.* Included in *A Week.*

We see the *planet* fall. *CP.* Included in *A Week.*

We should not mind if on our ear there fell. *CP.* Included in *A Week.*

Men say they know many things. *EHW,* from proofsheets of *Walden.* Reprinted by permission of The Huntington Library, San Marino, California, HM 924.

Away! away! away! *EHW,* from proofsheets of *A Week.*

In the East fames are won. *CP.* Appears in "Thomas Carlyle and His Works."

The good how can we trust? *EHW,* from manuscript, New York Public Library, included in a letter to Emerson dated December 29, 1847. Reprinted with permission of the New York Public Library, Berg Collection, Astor, Lenox, and Tilden Foundations. The poem appears in *A Week.*

Greece. *EHW*, from manuscript, MA 920. Reprinted with permission of the Pierpont Morgan Library, New York. A version of the last 4 lines were included in *A Week*.

Poverty. *EHW*, from manuscript, MA 920. Reprinted with permission of the Pierpont Morgan Library, New York. Versions of lines 8–9 and 24–27 appear in *A Week*.

The respectable folks. *EHW*, from proofsheets of *A Week*. Reprinted by permission of the Huntington Library, San Marino, California, HM 13182.

Farewell. *CP*.

For though the eaves were rabitted. *CP*. *CP*'s transcription of "caves" in the poem's first line is here emended to "eaves," based on a review of the manuscript. Appears in journal (after September 11, 1849).

You Boston folks & Roxbury people. Manuscript, the Huntington Library, San Marino, California, HM 13182. Reprinted with permission.

I will obey the strictest law of love. *CP*. A version appears in journal (after October 28, 1849).

Why toll the bell today—. Manuscript, the Huntington Library, San Marino, California, HM 13182. Reprinted with permission.

And once again. *CP*. Appears in journal, 1850 (after July 29).

The Old Marlborough Road. *CP*. Versions appear in journal, 1850 (after July 29), and in "Walking."

Old meeting-house bell. *CP*. Appears in journal, 1850.

It is a real place. *EHW*, from a draft of *Walden*. Reprinted by permission of the Huntington Library, San Marino, California, HM 924. The manuscript is incomplete. An incomplete draft of the poem appears in the journal, 1850 (between July 29, 1850, and August 31, 1850). A version of the poem, beginning with the line "It is no dream of mine," appears in *Walden*.

Among the worst of men that ever lived. *CP*. Appears in journal, August 1850.

What's the rail-road to me? *EHW*, from journal (between July 29, 1850, and August 31, 1850), MA 1302:9. Reprinted with permission of the Pierpont Morgan Library, New York. The poem was included in *Walden*.

Tall Ambrosia. *CP*. Appears in journal, August 31, 1850.

'Tis very fit the ambrosia of the gods. *CP*. *CP* prints two versions as a single poem, "Th'ambrosia of the Gods 's a weed on earth." The present volume prints the final five lines of *CP*'s "Th'ambrosia of the Gods 's a weed on earth," since this is the final version of the poem. The first version reads: "Th'ambrosia of the Gods 's a weed on earth / Their nectar is the morning dew which on / 'ly our shoes taste—For they are simple folks". Appears in journal, August 31, 1850.

I saw a delicate flower had grown up 2 feet high. *CP*. Appears in journal, September 9, 1850.

To day I climbed a handsome rounded hill. *CP*. Appears in journal, September 6, 1850.

I am the little Irish boy. *CP*. Appears in journal, November 28, 1850.

In Adams fall. *CP*. Appears in journal, February 12, 1851.

Life. *CP*.

The moon moves up her smooth and sheeny path. *CP*.

I'm thankful that my life does not deceive. *CP*.

Manhood. *CP*.

Music. *CP*.

The Just Made Perfect. *CP*.

I do not fear my thoughts will die. *CP*. Appears in journal, November 13, 1851.

I'm contented you should stay. *CP*.

Man man is the Devil. *CP*. Appears in journal, January 3, 1853.

You must not only aim aright. *CP*.

He knows no change who knows the true. *CP*.

When the toads begin to ring. *CP*. Appears in journal, April 26, 1854.

The chicadee. *CP*. Appears in journal, November 8, 1857.

'Twas 30 years ago. *EHW*, from journal, October 28, 1857, MA 1302:30. Reprinted with permission of the Pierpont Morgan Library, New York. A version of lines 11–18 was included in "Wild Apples."

Forever in my dream & in my morning thought. Appears in journal October 29, 1857. *CP*.

Except, returning, by the Marlboro. Manuscript, New York Public Library, with papers related to manuscript "The Dispersion of Seeds." Reprinted with permission of the New York Public Library, Berg Collection, Astor, Lenox, and Tilden Foundations.

The Rosa Sanguinea. *CP*.

Any fool can make a rule. *CP*. Appears in journal, February 3, 1860.

All things decay. *CP*. Appears in journal, March 25, 1860.

    This volume presents the texts of the original printings and manuscripts chosen for inclusion here, but it does not attempt to reproduce features of their layout or design, such as display capitalization of chapter openings. The texts are presented without change, except for the correction of typographical errors. Spelling, punctuation, and capitalization are often expressive features and are not altered, even when inconsistent or irregular. The following is a list of pages where a stanza break coincides with the foot of the page (except where such breaks are apparent from the regular stanzaic structure of the poem): 42, 226, 525, 533, 534, 545, 546, 553, 571, 588, 591, 594, 595, 600, 602, 620, 624, 636. The following is a list of typographical errors corrected, cited by page and line number: 24.25, skiful; 47.14, side, is by; 51.14, attis; 53.22, Massachussets; 98.36, phæbes; 108.37, fair-weather-and foul; 109.40, essentiais; 110.28, ascends; 130.18, even crystal; 161.4, "*he*; 222.40, slavery, but; 355.30, Where-/ever; 365.37, Message,; 414.6, dont; 429.30–31, as certained; 432.5, the of; 436.40, *leuco pus*; 438.40, dissemminating; 439.11, cheeck-pouches; 443.11, farmers; 468.15, Oinan; 473.8–9, sphagneous; 477.6, exhilirating; 481.2, testimomony; 483.19, Raslles; 500.27, salvages; 524.13, whereso'eer.

Notes

In the notes below, the reference numbers denote page and line of this volume (the line count includes chapter headings). No note is made for material included in standard desk-reference books such as Webster's *Collegiate*, *Biographical*, and *Geographical* dictionaries. Biblical quotations are keyed to the King James Version. Quotations from Shakespeare are keyed to *The Riverside Shakespeare*, ed. G. Blakemore Evans (Boston: Houghton Mifflin, 1974). For further biographical information than is contained in the Chronology, see William Ellery Channing II, *Thoreau, the Poet-Naturalist*, enlarged edition, edited by Franklin B. Sanborn (Boston: Charles E. Goodspeed, 1902); Edward Waldo Emerson, *Henry Thoreau as Remembered by a Young Friend* (Boston: Houghton Mifflin, 1917); Steven Fink, *Prophet in the Marketplace: Thoreau's Development as a Professional Writer* (Princeton: Princeton University Press, 1992); Walter Harding, *The Days of Henry Thoreau*, revised edition (Princeton: Princeton University Press, 1982); Richard Lebeaux, *Young Man Thoreau* (Amherst: University of Massachusetts Press, 1977); Richard Lebeaux, *Thoreau's Seasons* (Amherst: University of Massachusetts Press, 1984); Robert D. Richardson, Jr., *Henry Thoreau: A Life of the Mind* (Berkeley: University of California Press, 1986).

3.6–7 "Ipse . . . nostrum."] "I half pagan / Bring my verses to the shrine of the poets." (Thoreau's translation.)

3.32–33 *particeps criminis*] Party to the crime; an accomplice.

5.1–3 "Haud . . . voto."] "It is not easy for every one to take murmurs and low / Whispers out of the temples, and live with open vow." (Thoreau's translation.)

5.23–25 "Est aliquid . . . vivis?"] "Is there anything to which thou tendest, and against which thou directest thy bow? / Or dost thou pursue crows, at random, with pottery or clay, / Careless whither thy feet bear thee, and live *ex tempore*?" (Thoreau's translation.)

6.26–27 "Stat . . . agendo."] "Reason opposes, and whispers in the secret ear, / That it is not lawful to do that which one will spoil by doing." (Thoreau's translation.)

8.3–4 Spes . . . hope.] *Aeneid*, Book XI.

8.18–21 "bearing . . . wish."] Aeschylus, *The Seven Against Thebes*.

9.16 "Discretion . . . soul,"] John Donne, "To the Countesse of Bedford (Honour Is So Sublime Perfection)" (c. 1600), line 40.

9.24 colures] Two large circles that intersect at right angles at the poles.

11.8 "made Fortune sirname to Fortitude,"] Plutarch, *Morals*, IV.

11.11–12 *vir summae fortis*] Man of highest courage.

11.12–13 "carry Caesar and Caesar's fortune."] According to Plutarch, Caesar was a hidden passenger on a boat when a storm caused the captain to order the vessel turned around. Caesar revealed himself to the captain and convinced him to proceed through the storm, saying, "Go on, my friend, and fear nothing; you carry Caesar and his fortune in your boat."

11.17–18 "Tumble . . . yet."] Robert Herrick, "To Fortune," lines 1–2.

12.2–5 "things terrestrial . . . right hand."] Plutarch, *Morals*, II.

13.33–40 "Plato . . . agreement."] Plutarch, *Morals*, I.

15.4–5 "What's brave . . . Roman fashion."] *Antony and Cleopatra*, IV.xv.87.

15.9 cope] The firmament.

15.18 Idomeneus] Cretan king, son of Minos, who fights against the Trojans in the *Iliad*.

15.21 bay of Aulis] Harbor where the ships of the Greek fleet assembled before sailing to Troy.

16.15–20 —returns . . . Surrounds—] Milton, *Paradise Lost*, Book III, lines 41–46.

16.34–36 "Sit not down . . . unto God."] From Sir Thomas Browne, *A Letter to a Friend*, published posthumously in 1690.

17.10–12 before . . . close] Milton, *Paradise Lost*, Book II, lines 535–37.

18.30–31 Guido's Aurora] "Phoebus and the Hours, Preceded by Aurora," fresco (1613) by the Bolognese artist Guido Reni (1575–1642).

19.9 Godfrey and Gonzalo] Godfrey of Bouillon (c. 1060–1100), Duke of Lower Lorraine who participated in the First Crusade in 1096; Godfrey is the hero of Torquato Tasso's *Jerusalem Delivered* (1581). Hernandez Gonzalo de Cordoba (1453?–1515), Spanish general and subject of novel *Gonsalve de Cardoue* (1791) by Jean Pierre Claris de Florian.

20.18–19 Isaak Walton and White of Selborne] Isaak Walton (1593–1683), English author of *The Compleat Angler* (1653); Gilbert White (1720–1793), English naturalist and curate, author of *The Natural History of Selborne* (1851).

22.11 life-everlasting] American cudweed.

24.9–27　Anacreon's ode . . . like the gods."]　This poem and the poem at 25.20–26.3 are from the "Anacreontea," poems incorrectly attributed to Anacreon.

26.9　harrows]　Diagonal arrangements of migratory fowl in the air.

26.26　Nuttall]　Thomas Nuttall (1786–1859), American botanist and ornithologist, author of *A Manual of the Ornithology of the United States and Canada* (1832–34).

26.37–38　the Argonautic expedition]　In Greek legend, the ship *Argo* carried Jason on a mission to retrieve the Golden Fleece.

27.1　described by Goldsmith]　See "The Deserted Village" (1770), line 44: "The hollow-sounding bittern guards its nest."

31.15　Pilpay]　Also known as Bidpai, supposed author of a version of the Sanskrit collection of tales the *Panchatantra*.

32.26　Angler's Souvenir]　Popular English fisherman's guide (1835) by "P. Fisher Esq.," pseudonym of William Andrew Chatto (1799–1864).

32.28–29　"Can these . . . cloud?"]　Shakespeare, *Macbeth*, III.iv.109–10.

35.1　cucullo]　Also "cucuyo," the West Indian firefly.

37.18　"winter of *their* discontent"]　Cf. Shakespeare, *Richard III*, I.i.1.

40.33　Bigelow]　Jacob Bigelow (1786–1879), an American physician, botanist, and author of *Florula Bostoniensis* (1814) and *American Medical Botany* (1817–20).

44.16　Rasselas]　Hero of Samuel Johnson's *The History of Rasselas, Prince of Abissinia* (1759), whose home is the Happy Valley.

45.1　rifle]　A piece of wood used by mowers to sharpen their scythes.

46.16–17　We could get no further . . . Romæ]　The seventh line of Virgil's *Aeneid*.

46.28–32　"He shook . . . the flint."]　*Georgics*, Book 1.

46.38　the wars of . . . Lancaster]　King Philip's War (1675–76).

47.17　*gelidæ valles*]　Cold valleys.

47.20–21　"The sultry . . . was nigh,"]　William Collins, "Hassan; or the Camel-Driver," from *Persian Eclogues* (1742), lines 7–8.

47.23–25　our fellow-traveller . . . my way."]　Collins, "Hassan; or the Camel-Driver," lines 13–14.

50.24–30　"And he . . . stars."]　Wordsworth, *Peter Bell (1798)*, Part First, lines 34–40.

50.31   Helvellyn]   Mountain in the Lake District in England.

51.13–16   Et jam summa . . . high mountains.]   The final lines of Virgil's first eclogue.

54.32–33   the scene of Mrs. Rowlandson's capture]   On February 10, 1676, during King Philip's War, Mary Rowlandson (c. 1635–c. 1678) was captured during a Narrangansett raid on Lancaster and held prisoner for 82 days. She wrote of her captivity in *The Sovereignty & Goodness of God, Together with the Faithfulness of His Promises Displayed; Being a Narrative of the Captivity and Restauration of Mrs. Mary Rowlandson* (1682).

55.2–3   Paugus . . . Church, or Lovell]   Paugus was a war-chief of the Pequawkets killed in King Philip's War; Captain Benjamin Church (1639–1718) and John Lovewell (1691–1725) were prominent soldiers fighting for the Puritans in King Philip's War.

55.11–12   Robin Hood ballads]   Thoreau's source is *Robin Hood: A Collection of All the Ancient Poems, Songs, and Ballads,* compiled by Joseph Ritson (1795).

57.1   *Sir Walter Raleigh*]   Thoreau's source for most of his quotations by Raleigh is *The Works of Sir Walter Raleigh, Kt. now first collected: to which are prefixed the lives of the author by Oldys and Birch.* (8 vols., Oxford: The University Press, 1829).

57.9   the Bayard]   Pierre Terrail, Seigneur de Bayard (c. 1473–1524), French knight and soldier.

61.35–36   the incident of the cloak]   According to tradition, Raleigh spread his cloak in the mud for Queen Elizabeth I to walk over.

63.31   Roger Ashton]   Catholic martyr, executed in 1592.

64.18–19   his connexion . . . prince Henry]   At the request of Prince Henry, the eldest son of James I, Raleigh argued against a proposal to marry Henry and his sister Elizabeth to Spanish royalty. Raleigh wrote in the preface to his *History of the World* that the work was written "for the service of that inestimable Prince Henry."

66.21   watched]   Also "watchet," a shade of light blue.

69.26   Lord Mayor's day]   November 9, when the Lord Mayor and other city dignitaries march in procession to Westminster to receive the Crown's assent to the election.

70.19   Hic Iacet]   "Here lies," a phrase used in epitaphs.

70.24   Fuller]   Thomas Fuller (1608–1661), English clergyman and author.

76.22   Syracides]   Joshua ben Sira, author of the Apocryphal Book of Ecclesiasticus. Thoreau quotes Ecclesiasticus 43:16.

77.17   Dubartas']   French Protestant poet (1544–1590).

78.1–5   *Inde genus . . .* stony nature are.] Ovid, *Metamorphoses*, Book I.

85.33   Aubrey] John Aubrey (1626–1697), English author.

88.34–38   *"Largior . . .* stars.] *Aeneid*, Book VI.

89.30   Alwákidi's Arabian Chronicle] Chronicle of Moslem conquest of Syria; Thoreau's source for the quotation that follows is the first volume of Simon Ockley's *History of the Saracens* (1708–18).

97.10–11   "The foodless . . . inhabitants."] James Thomson, "Winter: A Poem" (1726), lines 233–34.

97.22   Plicipennes] Name given to the caddis fly by French entomologist Pierre Latreille (1762–1833).

100.18   Abu Musa] Arab alchemist and mystic (c. 721–c. 815).

103.33   "the mower whet his scythe,"] Milton, "L'Allegro" (1631), line 66.

104.5   *hortus siccus*] A dry garden; herbarium.

105.31–36   "The snow flakes . . . the waves."] Homer, *Iliad*, Book XII.

106.4–6   "Drooping . . . toil."] Thomson, "Winter," lines 228–30.

107.9–12   "The full . . . pole."] Thomson, "Winter," lines 738–41.

116.26   Hygeian] Hygeia, Greek goddess of health.

118.3   Hymettus and Hybla] Sites renowned in antiquity for their honey. Hymettus was a mountain in Attica, Hybla a Sicilian town.

118.8   Columella] Roman author (1st century A.D.) of treatise on agriculture, *De re rustica*.

129.7–8   "tie up . . . the wind,"] Sir Thomas Browne, *Christian Morals*, published posthumously in 1716.

129.13–14   George Fox's suit of leather] George Fox, the founder of the Society of Friends, was known for wearing a leather suit that he was supposed to have made himself.

134.32   The Divine . . . nature] From Euripides' *Orestes*, a translation of the Greek line at 134.31.

136.36   Veeshnoo Sarma] In the July 1842 issue of *The Dial*, Thoreau wrote an introduction to "Extracts from *The Heetopades of Veeshnoo-Sarma*," also known as *The Amicable Instructions of Veeshno Sarma*, translated by Charles Wilkins (1787). The *Heetopades* are instructive fables told by an aged Hindu priest to educate the sons of the king.

139.5–10   "As from the clouds . . . Zeus."] *Iliad*, Book XI.

139.14–24   "While it was dawn . . . rank to rank."] *Iliad*, Book XI.

139.28–140.2   "They, thinking . . . before Ilium."] *Iliad*, Book VIII.

140.5–10   "Went down . . . Olympus."]   *Iliad*, Book XV.

140.20–21   The statue of Memnon is cast down] A colossal statue near Thebes was believed to represent Memnon, a son of the goddess of dawn. According to legend, it made a musical sound when struck by rays of the morning sun, said to be Memnon's greeting to his mother. The statue was later destroyed in an earthquake.

142.1–4   "The wrathful . . . move."]   *Ca-Lodin*, III, 138–41.

142.13–14   "Mounds . . . years."]   *Timora*, VI, 391–92.

142.21–23   "His soul . . . bleak."]   *Ca-Lodin*, II, 134–36.

142.26–27   "The weak . . . bend it."]   *Fingal*, V, 280–81.

143.5–6   "I straightway . . . verse."]   *Oinamoru*, I, 182–83.

143.9–21   "Whence . . .times."]   *Ca-Lodin*, II, 137–49.

143.23–28   "Strangers . . . in song.'"]   *Carric*, 167–72.

144.1   "Thou . . . ships."]   *Ca-Lodin*, I, 125.

144.3–4   "With murmurs . . . moved."]   *Ca-Lodin*, II, 132–33.

144.6–8   "dragging . . . it dies."]   *Fingal*, III, 252–54.

144.10–11   "A thousand . . . Fingal."]   *Garon*, 176–77.

144.15–17   "Thy mother . . . her son."]   *Fingal*, VI, 292–94.

144.26–30   "He strode . . . lance."]   *Timora*, III, 343–47.

145.1–13   "'My eyes . . . Croma.'"]   *Croma*, 195–207.

145.16–17   "How beauteous . . . strength?"]   *Garon*, 176–77.

147.38–39   "right as divers . . . to Rome."] From the opening of Chaucer's *A Treatise on the Astrolabe* (c. 1391).

147.39   Testament of Love] Now attributed to Thomas Usk (d. 1388), a contemporary of Chaucer.

149.3   the Black Prince] Edward, Prince of Wales (1453–1471).

149.27–28   "For first . . . mouth astart."] From stanza 187 of "The Court of Life," a poem once attributed to Chaucer.

151.20–22   "if that God . . . semeliness."] Chaucer, *The Legend of Good Women* (c. 1385), lines 1039–41.

157.22   *Moses Norris's*] Democratic congressman (1799–1855) from New Hampshire.

157.36   'hinds' feet'] Cf. Habakkuk 3:19, Psalm 18:32–33, and II Samuel 22:34.

157.42   'on Fabyan's White Mountain horn.'] Fabyan is a town in the White Mountains of New Hampshire.

159.26   Webster's plea] Daniel Webster represented relatives of Phila-
delphia merchant Stephen Girard (1750–1831) who challenged provisions of
Girard's will that established a boarding school for white orphan boys.
Unsuccessfully arguing the case before the U.S. Supreme Court in 1844,
Webster criticized the will's provision excluding clergymen from the school.

159.29   the Comeouters] Abolitionist group that advocated "coming
out" of the church because of its toleration of slavery.

159.36   the conflict with Carolina Hayne] In January 1830, Webster op-
posed Senator Robert Young Hayne (1791–1831) in a series of debates where
the topics included slavery, tariffs, and federalism.

160.2   the President's] John Tyler's.

162.1   *Wendell . . . Lyceum*] When the abolitionist Wendell Phillips was
invited to speak on the subject of slavery at the Concord Lyceum in 1845, three
of the Lyceum's curators resigned in protest. Thoreau, Emerson, and Samuel
Barrett replaced them and Phillips delivered his speech on March 11. Thoreau's
letter defending Phillips was published in *The Liberator* on March 28.

164.26   Paynim] Pagan or non-Christian, especially Islamic.

164.30   the Red-cross knight] Hero of the first book (1590) of Edmund
Spenser's *The Faerie Queene*.

165.13   Edward Irving] Scottish clergyman (1792–1834), whose followers
founded the Catholic Apostolic Church.

167.32   moss-troopers] Bandits who made raids along the Scottish bor-
der in the 17th century.

169.38   Arethuse] Fountain of the Muses.

170.1   Hercynian forest] Wooded mountains of Thuringia and Bohemia.

172.30   "Lieferung."] Installment.

173.8–9   "sire, . . . revolution."] Reply of Duc de La Rochefoucauld-
Laincourt to Louis XVI's statement, "Why, it's only a revolt," upon hearing of
the storming of the Bastille.

174.30   "Sauerteig,"] One of Carlyle's ironic personae; others include
Dryasdust, Smelfungus, Plugson of Undershot, and Sir Jabesh Windbag.

176.1   Richter's] Jean Paul Friedrich Richter (1763–1825), German writer.

177.13   "Past and Present,"] 1843 book by Carlyle.

177.22   *Opera Omnia*] Complete works.

178.14   dandy pumps] Shoes worn by Victorian men for ballroom dancing.

185.34–35   The condition of England question] Phrase appearing in
Carlyle's 1839 pamphlet *Chartism*, which discusses the conflict between the
extremes of wealth and poverty resulting from the Industrial Revolution.

187.9–10   reminded of the "Brest Shipping,"]   See *The French Revolution*, II.5.iv.

188.2   Jötuns]   In the Norse Eddas, the oldest of all living creatures and the main foes of the gods.

188.27   *Oratoris est celare artem*]   "The speaker conceals his art," a variation of *Ars est celare artem*, "Art lies in concealing art" (Ovid, *Art of Love*).

189.30–31   "sacred . . . matter"]   From Carlyle's *Heroes, Hero-Worship, and the Heroic in History* (1840).

192.24   Serbonian bog]   Lake Serbonis in Lower Egypt. See Milton, *Paradise Lost*, Book II, line 592.

193.3   Lubberland]   An imaginary land of abundance for those who are lazy.

193.16   Baphometic Baptism]   The Templars were accused of worshipping Baphomet, an idol. See Carlyle, *Sartor Resartus* (1833–34), II.vii, "My Spiritual New-birth, or Baphometic Fire-baptism."

197.13   blown his ram's horn about Jericho]   Cf. Joshua 6:4–5.

197.16–17   those dibblers of beans on St. George's Hill]   On April 16, 1649, a group of twenty to thirty peasants, part of a movement known as "the Diggers," overtook St. George's Hill in Weybridge, Surrey. They established a squatter's colony there, planting parsnips, carrots, and beans to "lay the Foundation of making the Earth a Common Treasury for All, both Rich and Poor."

197.30–31   "Our chief . . . fortitude."]   Milton, "To the Lord General Cromwell" (1652), lines 1, 3.

204.39–40   powder-monkeys]   Boys employed on ships to carry gunpowder from the powder room to the guns.

205.14–17   "Not a drum . . . we buried."]   Charles Wolfe, "The Burial of Sir John Moore at Corunna" (1817).

205.36–37   "stop a hole to keep the wind away"]   Shakespeare, *Hamlet* V.i.214.

206.1–4   "I am . . . the world."]   Shakespeare, *King John* V.ii.79–82.

206.33–207.5   Paley . . . the other."]   William Paley, *The Principles of Moral and Political Philosophy*, 2 vols. (1806).

207.19–21   "A drab of state . . . the dirt."]   Cyril Tourneur, *The Revenger's Tragedie* (1607), Act V.

214.30–40   Christ . . . to know]   See Matthew 22:19–22.

215.19–23   Confucius said . . . of shame."]   Thoreau's translation from Jean-Pierre-Guillaume Pauthier, *Confucius et Mencius ou les quatres livres de philosophie moral et politique de la Chine* (Paris: Charpentier, 1841).

219.30   "My Prisons."]   Autobiography of Sylvio Pellico (1789–1854), translated into English in 1836.

221.15–20   "We must affect . . . or benefit."]   George Peele, *The Battle of Alcazar* (1594), II.ii.425–30.

225.30   Peter the Hermit]   Also called Peter of Amiens (c. 1050–1115), French monk and leader of the First Crusade, who made pilgrimages to reclaim Christ's tomb. He is the basis for a character in Tasso's *Jerusalem Delivered* (1581).

226.27   *Ambulator nascitur, non fit*]   "The walker is born, not made," adaptation of Latin motto *Poeta nascitur, non fit* ("The poet is born, not made").

226.36–227.4   "When he came . . . donne dere."]   Two stanzas from the final eight of Chaucer's "A Gest of Robyn Hode."

227.28–29   Bonaparte may talk . . . courage]   As recorded in his memoirs, *Mémorial de Ste-Hélène* (1823), dictated to Emmanuel de Las Cases, Napoleon said, " I have very rarely met with the two o'clock in the morning courage: I mean unprepared courage."

231.6   Varro]   Marcus Terentius Varro (116–27 B.C.), Roman author.

231.22   Menu]   Menu, or Manu, son of Brahma, the Hindu progenitor of and lawgiver to the human race, to whom is ascribed *Institutes of Hindu Law*, rules governing ritual and daily life, compiled 200 B.C.–A.D. 200.

232.39–40   Gourgas . . . Darby?]   F. R. Gourgas, William Lee, Daniel Clark, and Joseph Darby, Concord town officials during the 1840s.

235.31–32   "Than longen folk . . . strondes."]   Chaucer, the General Prologue to *The Canterbury Tales*, lines 9–10.

236.10–13   "And now the sun . . . pastures new."]   Milton, *Lycidas* (1637), lines 190–93.

236.17   Michaux]   François-André Michaux (1770–1855), French botanist and traveler; author of *The North American Sylva* (1819).

238.21   "Westward the star . . . its way."]   Cf. George Berkeley, "Verses on the Prospect of Planting Arts and Learning in America" (1752).

239.24   Romulus and Remus]   According to Roman legend, twin sons of Mars and Rhea Silvia who were cast into the Tiber to drown, but, protected by the gods, washed ashore and were suckled by a she-wolf. Romulus became the founder of Rome.

240.32   "How near to good is what is fair!"]   From the "Song of the Second Priest" in Jonson's masque *Love Freed from Ignorance and Folly* (1616).

247.15–16   stop . . . away]   See note 205.36–37.

247.17–19   Confucius . . . tanned."]   Cf. *Analects* 12.8.

249.20–21   letters . . . Cadmus invented]   In Greek mythology, Cadmus, founder of Thebes, invented the alphabet.

249.25–26   Society . . . Knowledge]   Organization founded in Boston in 1829.

250.27   Chaldean Oracles]   A prophetic poem written during Marcus Aurelius' rule (A.D. 196–217), attributed to Julianus of Chaldea.

250.36   Vishnu Purana]   Hindu sacred texts; Thoreau read H. H. Wilson's 1840 translation *The Vishnu Parána, a System of Hindu Mythology and Tradition*.

251.35   moss-trooper]   See note 167.32.

256.4   JOSSELYN'S RARETIES]   *New Englands Rarities Discovered* (1672) by the English scientific writer John Josselyn (fl. 1638–75).

258.4–5   "my cousin Westmoreland"]   Shakespeare, *Henry V*, IV.iii.18–19.

261.4–5   the Acton Blues]   Militia of Acton, Massachusetts.

265.9–10   "Truth never . . . upon him."]   Thomas Middleton and William Rowley, *A Fair Quarrel* (1617), III.i.196–97.

268.28   Kalm]   Pehr Kalm (1716–1779), Swedish scientist, came to America in 1748 and stayed three years; an account of his journey was translated into English and published as *Travels into North America* (1770–71).

268.34   Hontan]   French officer and traveler Louis Armand De Lom D'Arce, Baron de La Hontan (1666–1715) was in Canada intermittently from 1683 to 1693, and published an account of his travels in *Voyages du Baron de La Hontan dans l'Amérique Septentrionale* (1705).

269.9   the spot where . . . 1775]   Major General Richard Montgomery (b. 1736) was killed at the Siege of Quebec, December 31, 1775.

269.35   in his relation]   Accounts of the missionaries in New France to their Superior General in Quebec were published annually in Paris as *Relations de ce qui s'est passé en la Nouvelle France* (1632–73).

270.4–5   Froissart's Chronicles]   The history of Europe from 1325 to 1400 by Jean Froissart (1333?–c. 1405).

270.8   Castle William]   A large round fort on Governor's Island in New York Harbor, completed in 1811.

270.30   bungtown coppers]   Valueless coins.

271.31–32   those lines . . . Verona]   Cf. Roman poet Claudian (A.D. 370–405), *Carmina minores*, 20: "Of an old man of Verona who never left his home."

272.37   bladder-campion] Common name of *Silene inflata*, named for its inflated calyx.

273.23–25   Olaf Trygesson the Northman . . . his bride] Olaf Tryggvesson (c. 964–1000), king of Norway, married Gyda, princess of Dublin, and lived in England and Ireland for several years.

274.14   sawing logs pit-fashion] Using a long two-handed saw, two men, one at the bottom of a pit and the other on a raised platform, saw logs placed over the pit.

274.21–23   Warburton, remarked . . . men] In *Hochelaga; or, England in the New World* (1846), by George Draught Warburton.

274.39   Charlevoix] Pierre François Xavier de Charlevoix (1682–1761), French Jesuit missionary and author of *Histoire et Description Générale de la Nouvelle France* (1744).

275.25   Oak Hall] A large Boston clothing store.

278.28   *Pouvez-vous . . . nuit?*] Can you give us a bed for the night?

278.34–35   *Y a-t-il . . . ici?*] Is there an inn here?

278.35   *auberge*] Inn, hostel.

279.16   literal signification] "To God."

280.30–31   Roberval's pilot . . . 1542] The account of Jean Alphonse de Xanctoigne (né Jean de Fonteneau), who guided Jean François de Roberval's fleet up the St. Lawrence River, was published in *Voyages de découverte au Canada, entre les années 1534 et 1542.*

282.2   Bouchette's] Joseph Bouchette (1774–1841), Canadian geographer.

283.18   *censitaires*] According to feudal custom, freemen who have obtained legal immunity from servitude by paying "quit-rent."

285.15   *pour la vierge*] For the virgin.

285.15   *Iniri*] (*Iesus Nazarenus Rex Iudaeorum*) Jesus of Nazareth, King of the Jews.

286.4   *"Ici git"*] "Here lies."

286.5   *"Priez pour lui."*] "Pray for him."

286.6   Père la Chaise] Père-Lachaise, a cemetery in Paris.

286.18–19   *appris . . . dans les États-Unis*] Learned to speak French in the United States.

286.28   Sir Francis Head] English traveler and author (1793–1845) who served as lieutenant of Upper Canada from 1835 to 1837.

287.4   according to Richardson] Sir John Richardson, *Fauna boreali-americana; or The Zoology of the Northern Parts of British America* (1829–37).

287.5   Rupert's Land] The Hudson Bay Territory, incorporated into Canada in 1870.

290.11   Potherie] Claude-Charles le Roy Bacqueville de la Potherie (1663–1736), *Histoire de l'Amérique septentrionale* (1722).

293.4   *Friponne*] A female swindler.

293.40   *Trois quatres lieue*] Three-quarter league, or about 7½ miles.

297.21   *en roture*] Obliged to a lord for land.

302.4   dasher] Dashboard.

305.9–11   those seven . . . the latter] In Greek mythology, seven princes attempted to install Oedipus' son Polynices as King of Thebes, which was ruled by Polynices' brother Eteocles. Each prince attacked a different gate of the city.

307.22–23 the siege of Jerusalem, and St. Jean d'Acre] Jerusalem was sacked in A.D. 70. St. Jean d'Acre, now known as Akko, Israel, was battled over during the First and Third Crusades.

308.35–40 Silliman states . . . cold."] In *Remarks Made on a Short Tour between Hartford and Quebec, in the Autumn of 1819* (1824), by the American chemist, geologist, and physicist Benjamin Silliman (1779–1864).

309.40   wash-leather] A soft kind of sheepskin leather dressed to imitate chamois leather.

310.18   his essay on the Northmen] *Journal of a Residence in Norway during the years 1834, 1835, & 1836* (1837).

311.27–28 play the game of the Kilkenny cats] Destroy each other. The phrase is derived from a popular limerick; Kilkenny is a city in Ireland.

315.26   fabulous . . . Frislant] Legendary islands that appeared on early maps of the North Atlantic. On his 1542 voyage to the New World, Roberval, enraged at his niece's affair with one of his officers, banished the couple and a nurse to an island off the coast of Newfoundland. The officer, the nurse, and the child of the couple died there; Marguerite was rescued two years and five months after her banishment. She told her story, in which she claimed to be attacked by demons, to André Trevet, whose *The Peculiarities of Antarctic France, Also Called America* (1558) reported accounts of fantastic beasts on the Isle of Demons. Frisland, an imaginary island bearing characteristics of Iceland and the Faroe Islands, was first described by the Venetian traveler Niccolò Zeno after his 1380 voyage to the North Sea.

316.24–25 Boucher says in 1664] In *Histoire véritable et naturelle des moeurs et productions du pays de la Nouvelle France, vulgairement dite la Canada*.

318.27   Grey writes] In Hugh Gray, *Letters from Canada, Written During a Residence There in the Years 1806, 1807, 1808* (1809).

320.3   Jesuit Relations] See note 269.35.

321.30   Moore's verses] "Canadian Boat Song," ballad by the Irish poet Thomas Moore (1779–1852), who traveled to North America in 1804.

321.36   Donnacona] Iroquois chief who met Cartier during the explorer's second New World expedition in 1535; Cartier kidnapped him and brought him to France, where he died.

323.11   Hearne or McKenzie] Samuel Hearne (1745–1792), English explorer; Sir Alexander Mackenzie (1764–1820), Scottish explorer.

326.30   Trenck mining in the ground] Baron Friedrick von der Trenck (1726–1794) was imprisoned in 1754 for ten years by Frederick the Great, and made several attempts to escape by digging his way out.

333.6   destiny of Nebraska] In January 1854 Senator Stephen A. Douglas of Illinois introduced legislation for organizing Kansas and Nebraska as federal territories that repealed the prohibition against slavery in federal territory north of 36°30' and allowed the question of whether slavery would be permitted in the new territories to be decided by their elected legislatures. The Kansas-Nebraska Act was passed by the Senate, 37–14, on March 4 and by the House of Representatives, 113–100, on May 22, then signed into law by President Franklin Pierce on May 30, 1854.

333.16–17   Our Buttricks . . . Hosmers] In the fighting at the North Bridge in Concord on April 19, 1775, John Buttrick gave the initial order to the Massachusetts militia to open fire after British shots killed Isaac Davis and Abner Hosmer.

333.25   Fugitive Slave Law] In 1793 Congress adopted a fugitive slave law allowing slaveholders to use the federal courts to regain possession of runaway slaves. As part of the "Compromise of 1850" Congress passed a new fugitive slave law that gave jurisdiction over fugitive slave cases to federal commissioners appointed by the courts, authorized federal marshals to summon all citizens to assist in enforcing the law, and established criminal penalties for harboring fugitives. Both the 1793 and 1850 laws denied persons accused of being runaway slaves the right to seek a writ of habeas corpus, to be tried by a jury, or to testify on their own behalf.

333.27–28   compromise compact of 1820] In March 1820 Congress voted to admit Missouri as a slave state while prohibiting slavery in the remainder of the Louisiana Purchase north of latitude 36°30' N. The prohibition was repealed by the Kansas-Nebraska Act in 1854.

333.36–334.1   Again it happens . . . SLAVE.] Anthony Burns (1834–1862), a fugitive from Virginia, was arrested in Boston on May 24, 1854. On May 26 a federal deputy marshal was fatally shot when a crowd led by the Rev. Thomas Wentworth Higginson stormed the courthouse in an unsuccessful attempt to rescue Burns. With the approval of President Franklin Pierce, several companies of soldiers and marines were sent to guard the courthouse against further assault. On June 2 Burns was taken on board a federal revenue cutter as 1,500 militiamen stood guard. Higginson, Theodore Parker, Wendell Phillips, and five other men were charged for their role in the May 26 riot, but the indictments were dismissed in 1855 on a technicality.

334.2   Mr. Loring's decision]   U.S. Commissioner Edward G. Loring presided over Burns's case and ruled that he be sent back to slavery.

334.12   Governor]   Emory Washburn (1800–1877), governor in 1854, a Whig.

334.28   Governor of Massachusetts]   George Sewall Boutwell (1818–1905), governor in 1851.

334.26   Simm's tragedy]   Thomas Sims, a fugitive slave from Georgia, was arrested in Boston on April 3, 1851, and kept in the courthouse under heavy guard until April 12, when he was escorted to the harbor by 300 armed deputies and militiamen and placed on a ship bound for Savannah, Georgia. Efforts to buy his freedom were unsuccessful, and Sims was sold at auction.

336.16–18   Three years ago . . . into slavery]   See note 334.26.

337.1   the events of the 12th of April, 1851]   See note 334.26.

340.19–20   the dog that returns to his vomit]   See Proverbs 26:11, II Peter 2:22.

340.39   Mitchell's *Citizen*]   John Mitchell (1815–1875), an Irish nationalist, was convicted of treason in 1848 and sentenced to 14 years transportation. In 1853 he escaped from Van Diemen's Land (Tasmania) and went to New York, where he began publishing *The Citizen*, a proslavery newspaper, in January 1854.

343.11–12   tintamar]   Uproar, clamor.

346.32–33   Missouri Compromise]   See note 333.27–28.

346.33–34   *Nymphæa Douglassii*]   Senator Stephen A. Douglas, a Democrat from Illinois, was the author of the Kansas-Nebraska Act and had played a major role in winning passage through Congress of the measures regarding slavery known as the "Compromise of 1850."

346.37–38   Boston Mayor]   Jerome V. C. Smith (1800–1879), mayor of Boston from 1854 to 1855.

352.12–13   I shall never . . . pottage.]   See Genesis 27:1–41.

355.6–7   Howitt's account . . . gold-diggings]   William Howitt, *Land, Labour, and Gold; or, Two Years in Victoria* (1855).

355.27–28   Ballarat . . . Sulky Gully]   Gold-diggings mentioned in *Land, Labour, and Gold*.

356.9–10   cradles . . . toms]   Equipment for digging gold.

357.3   "Burker's Guide."]   Refers to the murderer William Burke (1792–1829), who (with William Hare) sold corpses of his victims to Edinburgh medical schools. Burke and Hare also robbed graves for the same purpose.

357.32–33   Dr. Kane . . . Sir John Franklin]   Elisha Kent Kane (1820–1857), American explorer who traveled to the Arctic to search for Sir John Franklin (1786–1847), an English explorer who perished in an earlier expedition.

357.38   D.D.s]   Doctors of Divinity.

359.1   Kossuth]   Lajos Kossuth (1802–1894), Hungarian patriot and revolutionary who in 1851–52 toured the United States seeking support for the Hungarian revolt against Austria. His visit was widely publicized in American newspapers.

364.7–8   "the first true gentleman that ever breathed."]   Thomas Dekker and Thomas Middleton, *The Honest Whore* (1604), Part One, Act I, Scene 12.

365.5–10   Lieutenant Herndon . . . country]   In William L. Herndon and Lardner Gibbon, *Exploration of the Valley of the Amazon, Made Under the Direction of the Navy Department* (1853–54).

379.12   *Lycopodium lucidulum*]   Shining clubmoss.

379.17–18   it was like . . . new spring]   See Numbers 20:10–11.

380.17   Charon's boat]   A boat-shaped leaf (*cymbifolius*), named for the ferry that crossed the river Styx.

382.11   Mount Auburn]   Cemetery in Cambridge and Watertown, Massachusetts.

382.18   Greenwood Cemetery]   In Brooklyn, New York.

384.32   Chobdars]   Attendants.

385.30   egg-pop]   Eggnog.

386.8   Ivy *never sear*]   Cf. Milton, "Lycidas," line 2.

387.11–14   "Wrought . . . beauty grew."]   Ralph Waldo Emerson, "The Problem," lines 21–24.

389.3–5   as Dionysius . . . Oriental Plane-tree]   According to John Claudius Loudon, *Arboretum et Fruticetum Britannicum* (1844).

394.8–9   *Juncaceæ* and *Gramineæ*]   Rushes and grasses.

394.19   Brocken spectre]   An optical phenomenon seen at high altitudes in which a shadow, ringed with a halo, appears on a cloud.

396.1 *Captain John Brown*] On October 16, 1859, John Brown (1800–1859) led a raid on a federal arsenal at Harpers Ferry, Virginia (now West Virginia), with intent to use its weapons in a slave insurrection. Brown and 21 of his followers occupied the arsenal until forced out by troops commanded by Colonel Robert E. Lee. Ten of Brown's followers were killed in the fighting, and Brown was wounded and captured. Tried and convicted of treason, Brown was hanged on December 2, 1859. (Brown had previously held the rank of captain with the Pottawatomie Rifles, an antislavery militia in Kansas.)

396.35 the troubles in Kansas] Armed conflict broke out in Kansas in 1856 between proslavery and antislavery settlers. About 200 people were killed before federal troops suppressed the fighting in the fall of 1856.

397.27 Stark] John Stark (1728–1822), Revolutionary War officer who fought at Bunker Hill in June 1775 and commanded the forces that defeated the British at Bennington, Vermont, in August 1777.

398.28 Buford ruffians] Jefferson Buford of Alabama organized the emigration of about 300 men from the South to Kansas in 1856.

399.24–25 talking to Buncombe] Giving a long-winded and politically expedient speech, a phrase allegedly derived from an address by North Carolina congressman Felix Walker (1753–1828), whose district included Buncombe County.

400.27 Mr. Vallandigham] Clement Larid Vallandigham (1820–1871), Democratic Ohio congressman who met with Brown after his capture and claimed that Brown had acted as part of a national abolitionist conspiracy.

401.39–40 Governor of Virginia] Henry A. Wise (1807–1876), governor of Virginia from 1856 to 1860, who signed Brown's death warrant.

402.30–33 The momentary charge . . . poet laureate] Tennyson, in "The Charge of the Light Brigade" (1854).

403.2 that feat of Putnam] A legend about Revolutionary War soldier Israel Putnam claimed that he killed a she-wolf that had been terrorizing flocks of sheep in Pomfret, Connecticut.

403.5 Tract Society] The American Tract Society, benevolent society and publisher whose evangelical pamphlets were often aimed at eradicating social ills such as gambling and alcoholism.

404.36 Wilson's last speech] Henry Wilson (1812–1875) was an antislavery U.S. senator from Massachusetts.

407.3–4 Walker . . . South] Robert J. Walker (1801–1869), senator from Mississippi, 1835–45, secretary of the treasury, 1845–49, was governor of Kansas Territory from April 1857 to December 1857. Walker resigned in protest when the Buchanan administration refused to submit the proslavery constitution drafted at Lecompton to a fair referendum.

408.2–3   Fugitive Slave Law]   See note 333.25.

408.17   Read . . . Mason and others]   Shortly after his capture, Brown was visited by Virginia senator James Murray Mason, Virginia governor Henry Wise, Ohio congressman Clement Vallandigham, and a correspondent for the *New York World*, among others. Brown's remarks during this interview were widely circulated in Northern newspapers.

408.21   Gessler]   Austrian bailiff who, according to legend, ordered William Tell to shoot an apple off his own son's head as punishment for defying Gessler's authority.

409.29   Colonel Washington]   Lewis W. Washington, a colonel on the staff of Virginia governor Henry Wise, who was among the hostages taken during Brown's raid.

409.38–39   Almost . . . respect!]   Cf. Chief Justice Roger B. Taney's opinion in *Dred Scott* v. *Sandford* (1857), which stated that blacks "had no rights which . . . white man was bound to respect."

410.13   the Plug Uglies]   Ardent proslavery advocates in the struggle for Kansas (see note 396.35).

411.11   coffle]   A train of slaves fastened together.

411.29   Vigilant Committee]   An organization dedicated to aiding fugitive slaves.

411.30   Cadi]   In the Middle East and Asia Minor, a civil judge, usually of a town or village.

413.33–34   cleared the temple]   Cf. Matthew 21:12–13, Jesus and the moneychangers.

415.4–5   "Unless above . . . is man!"]   Samuel Daniel, "To the Lady Margaret, Countess of Cumberland" (c. 1600), lines 95–96.

418.17–24   "When the sword . . . successful crimes."]   Marvell, "Tom May's Death" (ca. 1650).

418.24   suff'ring]   Marvell's poem reads "wretched".

418.27–30   "All heads . . . in the dust."]   Adapted from James Shirley, "Contention of Ajax and Ulysses" (1659).

420.30   Agricola]   Roman general who was the subject of a biography by his son-in-law, Tacitus (in A.D. 98).

422.7   Winkelried]   Legendary Swiss patriot said to have won the battle of Sempach for his countrymen in 1386.

426.21   death of Irving]   Washington Irving died on November 28, 1859.

426.36   pebbles in your mouth or not]   According to Plutarch, Demosthenes overcame a stammer and his difficulty in articulating words by speaking with pebbles in his mouth.

427.29–34   'He nothing common . . . upon a bed.'] Marvell, "An Horatian Ode Upon Cromwell's Return to Ireland" (1650), lines 57–64.

435.19   Loudon] John Claudius Loudon (1783–1843), Scottish horticultural writer, author of *Arboretum et Fruticetum Britannicum* (1844), *An Encyclopedia of Agriculture* (1844), and *Encyclopedia of plants* (1855).

438.28–32   the experience of Kane . . . becoming Esquimaux] See note 357.32–33.

438.36   Dukes of Athol] James, Duke of Athol and his son John were Scottish planters, with estates at Dunkeld and Athol; Duke John added 14 million larch trees to the Athol estate.

439.36   nuciferous] Bearing nuts.

441.1   Dr. Carpenter] William Carpenter, author of *Vegetable Physiology, and Systematic Botany* (1858).

441.11   Dr. Chas. T. Jackson] State geologist of Maine and brother-in-law of Ralph Waldo Emerson; he published yearly reports (1838, 1839) on the geology of Maine and Massachusetts.

443.11   Signor Blitz] Antonio Blitz (1810–1877), German-born magician and ventriloquist.

444.8–10   that unknown primitive people . . . Swiss lakes] The first systematic excavation of prehistoric settlements on Lake Zurich was initiated by Swiss archaeologist Ferdinand Keller in 1854, followed by excavations at other Swiss lakes.

444.16   Niebuhr] German philologist and historian Barthold Georg Niebuhr (1776–1831), author of a 3-volume history of early Rome (1835).

444.35–36   "As the apple-tree . . . sons."] Song of Solomon 2:3.

444.36–445.1   "Stay me . . . apples."] Song of Solomon 2:5.

445.5–6   Ulysses saw . . . fruit"] *Odyssey*, Book VII.

445.11   Prose Edda] Collection of Old Norse myths compiled and written by Snorri Sturluson.

447.28   Pomona] Roman goddess of fruits.

448.17–20   Iduna's apples . . . wrinkled and gray] In Norse mythology, Loki, the god of destruction, and the giant Thjazi kidnap Iduna, the goddess who watches over the apples that preserve eternal youth. The gods age rapidly and the state of the world declines until Thjazi is destroyed by fire. The gods summon up the last of their strength and force Loki to bring back Iduna's tree, whose apples restore their youth.

450.10–14   "Wassaile . . . wassailing."] Robert Herrick, "Another (Ceremonie for Christmas)."

450.15–17   to sing of cider . . . better than English Phillips]   The English poet John Phillips (1676–1709) was the author of "Cyder, in Two Books" (1708).

452.24   Michaux]   See note 236.17.

456.3   Van Mons and Knight]   The horticulturists and botanists Jean-Baptiste Van Mons (1765–1842) and Thomas Andrew Knight (1759–1824).

457.7–8   "highest plot . . . Bergamot."]   Andrew Marvell, "An Horatian Ode upon Cromwell's Return from Ireland" (1650), lines 31–32.

458.11–12   "Fruits and Fruit-Trees of America,"]   1845 book by Andrew J. Downing.

459.3   Evelyn says]   In *Sylva, or a Discourse on Forest-Trees* (1679), by John Evelyn.

459.19–21   Tityrus . . . chestnuts]   See Virgil's *Eclogues*, I, lines 80–81.

460.19   *Prunes sibarelles*]   Whistling plums.

463.12–13   *Cholera morbifera . . . dilectissima*]   "Cholera Moribus and dysentery, esteemed by young boys."

463.13   the Apple which Atalanta stopped to pick up]   In Greek mythology, Atalanta agreed to marry the suitor who could defeat her in a race. During a race with Milanion, she stopped to pick up three golden apples that he had dropped, causing her to lose the race and become his wife.

463.18   *Pedestrium Solatium*]   Solitary walker.

463.21–26   As Bodæus exclaims . . . *wild apples.*"]   From the commentary on Theophrastus by Johannes Bodaeus, published in 1644.

464.15–16   (as Curzon . . . mouldy cellar)]   Robert Curzon, 14th Baron Zouche (1810–1872) conducted a tour from 1834 to 1837 collecting ecclesiastical manuscripts. In an Egyptian monastery, he found a cellar filled with rotting manuscripts being used as lids for storage containers. He published an account of the trip in *The Monasteries of the Levant* (1849).

464.29   Topsell's Gesner]   *The Historie of Four-Footed Beasts and Serpents and Insects*, Edward Topsell's 1607 translation of zoological writings by the Swiss naturalist Konrad von Gesner (1516–1565).

467.3–26   "The word of the Lord . . . sons of men."]   Joel 1:1–12.

468.2–5   *Agrestem . . .* things.]   Virgil, *Eclogues*, Book VI, lines 8–9.

468.14–15   the horse Columbus—or Mr. Blank]   In 1860, Columbus was considered to be the fastest horse alive. "Mr. Blank" was John C. Heenan (1833–1873), a professional boxer known as "the Benecia boy."

468.23–24   Mr. Seward or Caleb Cushing]   Senators from, respectively, New York and Massachusetts.

470.8–9   French chemist] Joseph Louis Gay-Lussac (1778–1850).

472.3   *Gaylussacia resinosa var. erythrocarpa*] Red huckleberry.

473.9–10   *Andromeda polifolia* and *Kalmia glauca*] Bog rosemary and Pale laurel.

474.32   George B. Emerson] Naturalist and educator (1797–1881), author of *A Report on the Trees and Shrubs Growing Naturally in the Forests of Massachusetts* (1846).

475.9   Lawson in 1709] In *A New Voyage to Carolina* by John Lawson (d. 1711), surveyor-general of North Carolina.

476.3   Loudon] See note 435.19.

476.35   Coleman in his "Woodland, Heaths, and Hedges,"] *Our Woodlands, Heaths, and Hedges: A Popular Description of Trees, Shrubs, Wild Fruits, etc.* (1859) by the English naturalist William Stephen Coleman (1829–1904).

477.25   Dr. Manassah Cutler] Clergyman and botanist (1743–1823) who published an account of American plants in the first volume of *Memoirs of the American Academy of Arts and Sciences* (1785).

479.18   Crantz says] In David Crantz, *The History of Greenland* (1767).

481.36–37   Gabriel Sagard . . . 1624] In *Le grand voyage du pays des Hurons* (1632).

482.23–24   Mr. Oldham's death in 1636] John Oldham (c. 1600–1636) was killed by Pequot Indians while on a trading expedition to Block Island.

483.2   in the life of Captain Church] Thomas Church's *Entertaining Passages Relating to Philip's War* (1716), based on the notes of his father, Captain Benjamin Church.

483.13   La Hontan in 1689] See note 268.34.

483.19   Father Rasles] Father Sébastien Rasles (also spelled Rale, Rasle, and Ralle), 1652–1724, was a missionary to the Abnaki people from 1694 until his death in an English raid on the village. His *Dictionary of the Abnaki Language in North America*, stolen in the raid, was published in 1833.

484.8   *Jacea* or *Saratula*] *Centauria Jacea* is also known as brown knapweed. *Serratula* is sawwort.

484.11   Kalm] See note 268.28.

484.29   *Pinus Banksiana*] Jack pine, also called scrub pine or Hudson bay pine.

485.38–39   Tourneforte . . . *Mount Ida*] Joseph Tournefort (1656–1708), French botanist, a founder of modern systematic botany, and author of

Éléments de botanique (1694). Mount Ida was a sacred place for Cybele, the mother of gods.

491.24   mantua-maker]   The maker of a loose gown.

493.1–2   *Sic transit gloria ruris*]   "So the glory of the countryside passes away," adaptation of Latin motto *Sic transit gloria mundis* ("So the glory of the world passes away").

495.12–13   not that . . . Rome more]   Cf. Shakespeare, *Julius Caesar,* III.ii.21–22.

501.6   Darien Grounds]   The eastern coast of Panama.

505.10   wise men 3 of Gotham]   The magi. See Matthew 2:1–12.

516.32   thrins]   Triplets.

521.26   wandering at Rockaway]   Thoreau visited Rockaway Beach, in present-day New York City, while living on Staten Island, May–December 1843.

532.10   "Friends, Romans, Countrymen, and Lovers."]   Cf. Shakespeare, *Julius Caesar,* III.ii.73.

537.17   *Guido's Aurora*]   See note 18.30–31.

555.3   Parthian arrows]   Parthian cavalry would shoot volleys of arrows at their enemies while retreating.

577.18–19   Spes . . . hope]   See note 8.3–4.

581.1   *Godfrey of Boulogne*]   See note 19.9.

584.23   golden]   Goldenrod.

587.2–4   Time . . . RALEIGH.]   From "Prais'd be Diana's fair and harmless light" (1593).

587.17   *Aeolian Harp*]   A stringed instrument which produces musical sounds when struck by the wind.

588.7   Paestum's temples]   Paestum, a coastal town in southern Italy, had Roman temples dedicated to Neptune and Ceres dating from the sixth and fifth centuries B.C.

589.12–14   the mallet . . . caulking the sky]   A caulking mallet is used to strike an iron that drives loose rope fiber into the seams of a ship to prevent leaks.

590.20   Deucaleon shroud]   In Greek myth, Deucalion, son of Prometheus and Clymene, survived a flood sent by Zeus. In order to renew the human race, Deucalion and his wife Pyrrha were told to shroud their faces and cast the bones of Clymene behind them. They threw stones instead, which were transformed into men and women.

593.32   Brahmapootra and the Jumna's shore]   The Brahmaputra and the Jumna are tributaries of the Ganges.

606.6   Aaron's rod]   See Numbers 20:10–11.

610.16   Titmans]   Dwarfs; in the vernacular of New England, the smallest pig in a litter.

612.2   Memnon's mother]   See note 140.20–21.

612.4   Carnac's columns]   A complex of menhirs, single stones stood on end, in Carnac, Brittany, France.

613.13–14   Hawthorne . . . Twice told Tale.]   Nathaniel Hawthorne's collection of stories *Twice-told Tales* was first published in 1837.

613.20–21   the spring of Helicon]   Hippocrene, a spring on Mount Helicon in Boeotia, legendary for giving inspiration to those who drink from it.

614.3   tort]   Twisted.

615.1   *The Atlantides*]   Daughters of Atlas and Hesperis, also called Hesperides.

615.3   Phlegethon]   In Greek mythology, a river of fire in the underworld.

620.1–14   The good . . . sympathy]   A draft of this poem written in late 1847 reads:

> If Love fails in strife with love
> Then it boldly looks above
> And appeals to higher Love.
>
> My Friend, my Friend,
> I ask not Love but Hate without end.
> Erect me, restore me, hearten me then
> With some dear severity fatal to men.
> Sear my humanity,
> Cure my insanity,
> O wrack me, grind me, crush without end,
> And I will pronounce thee my dearest friend.
>
> With a tough tenderness
> Strengthen my slenderness,
> Waste me with care,
> Send me despair,
> Give me my deserts,
> Confound me with hurts.
> Be so kind as be just,
> Let me taste of the worst.

Sweet Friend—sweet Friend,
Let pity have end,
I pray Thee let mercy cease,
Let me have my release;
Smile not again;
Give me a glance that will wither my frame;
With poisoned darts pierce me through & through,
Only be true.

O my Friend—my Friend,
Let me feel once condemned.
Then I will not doubt,
Then I'll find the out,
Then our love will be sure,
Then our love will endure,
Then I shall believe that thou knowest me well,
And I shall not have a confession to tell.

Give me some token
That our first love is broken—
Then Love born of Love,
Love pure from above,
Will forge a true chain
To bind us again.

Love not me at all
But love all.
Know that I love not thee,
But thy destiny.
Canst thou range earth sea & air,
And so meet me everywhere?
Through all events I will pursue thee
Through all persons I will woo thee.
    Who loves me alone
    Is not flesh of my flesh, bone of my bone.
    Canst thou be kind
    To the north wind?
Dost thou affect sun, moon, & star,
And all creatures near & far?
Dost thou love the morning air,
And the creator every where?
Dost thou *love* God?
Is he thy mate—?
Hast thou feeling for the sod—
And sympathy with Death & Fate?
    Treat tenderly these powers,—
    Lend them some flowers,

Give them some loving tears
To soothe their sorrow,
And all thy worthless years
To gild their morrow.

Cant thou love with thy mind
And reason with thy heart?
Cant thou be kind,
And from thy darling part?

The good—how can we trust?
Only the wise are just.
Conform, Conform, with awe,
Think not thou mak'st the law
We're indiscriminately kind like clods,
But justice is the kindness of the Gods.
    The good we use,
    The wise we cannot choose.
    These there are none above.
    The good they know & love,
    But are not known again
    By those of lesser ken.—

They do not charm us with their eyes,
But they transfix with their advice.
No partial sympathy they feel
With private woe or private weal,
But with the universe joy & sigh
Whose knowledge is their sympathy.

624.2   Tom Hyde] See *Walden*, "Conclusion": "Say what you have to say, not what you ought. Any truth is better than make-believe. Tom Hyde, the tinker, standing on the gallows, was asked if he had any thing to say. 'Tell the tailors,' said he, 'to remember to make a knot in their thread before they take the first stitch.' His companion's prayer is forgotten."

627.6–7   Gourgas . . . Darby?] See note 232.39–40.

628.27   *sine*] Latin, "without."

630.4   Dakin's & Maynards] Neighbors of Thoreau.

640.9   warts] From "warth," a flat meadow, especially one close to a stream.

640.24   saint-terrering] See "Walking," 225.12–29.

Index of Titles and First Lines

Library of Congress Cataloging-in-Publication Data

Thoreau, Henry David, 1817–1862.
   [Selections. 2001]
   Collected essays and poems / Henry David Thoreau.
      p. cm. — (The Library of America ; 124)
   Includes bibliographical references and index.
   ISBN 1–883011–95–7 (alk. paper)
   I. Title. II. Series.
PS3042   2001
818'.309—dc21   00–046234

THE LIBRARY OF AMERICA SERIES

The Library of America helps to preserve our nation's literary heritage by publishing, and keeping permanently in print, authoritative editions of America's best and most significant writing. An independent nonprofit organization, it was founded in 1979 with seed money from the National Endowment for the Humanities and the Ford Foundation.

This book is set in 10 point Linotron Galliard,
a face designed for photocomposition by Matthew Carter
and based on the sixteenth-century face Granjon. The paper is
acid-free Ecusta Nyalite and meets the requirements for permanence
of the American National Standards Institute. The binding
material is Brillianta, a woven rayon cloth made by
Van Heek-Scholco Textielfabrieken, Holland.
The composition is by The Clarinda
Company. Printing and binding by
R.R.Donnelley & Sons Company.
Designed by Bruce Campbell.